GEORGE JUNKIN, D.D., LL.D.

Geo. Junkin.

THE REVEREND

GEORGE JUNKIN, D.D., LL.D.

A

HISTORICAL BIOGRAPHY.

BY

D. X. JUNKIN, D.D.

"Not slothful in business; fervent in spirit; serving the Lord."

PHILADELPHIA:
J. B. LIPPINCOTT & CO.
1871.

PREFACE.

"NO man liveth to himself, and no man dieth to himself." However humble, in point of endowments, education, resources, or social position, each member of the human family stands so related to others and to the whole, that his life and death must affect others for weal or woe. Each individual makes the world different from what it would have been without him; and it is a process, by no means useless or uninteresting, to trace the relations of the individual to society, and the influence which he imparts to or receives from it. It is by this process that the philosophy of life, individual and social, is to be ascertained, and its lessons made available.

The spirit of inspiration recognizes these great truths, not only in the Scripture cited above, but in many others, and in the fact that the Holy Book is largely occupied with biographical sketches of the godly and the wicked that have lived of old; the one class being designed for *examples*, the other, for *warnings*, to those who should live after. Inspired biography, it is true, is the only infallible record of the kind; and it is in reference to it, doubtless, that the apostolic exhortation is given, "Be ye followers (imitators) of them who, through faith and patience, inherit the promises." But inasmuch as the ordinary grace of God produces similar results in the formation of character, in whatever age or nation its subject may live, the record of children of God who have been illustrious for natural endowments, great attainments, or valuable services may be greatly useful, even when penned by uninspired agency. The life of a Payson may prove as beneficial as that of a Paul, saving the fallibility of the record; for, apart from his inspiration, Paul was a mere man, and the grace of God which made him what he was, was the same that wrought in Payson, and the God of grace is entitled to a revenue of glory from every generation of men. It is well to mark the progress of the Saviour's work as illustrated in each successive age, and in every land; and the very peculiarities of each become instructive, and impart a freshness to the lessons derived from the examples of the holy.

There is one characteristic of inspired biography which we in vain expect in any merely human writing, —that is, its uncompromising faithfulness. It

> "Nothing extenuates, nor sets down aught in malice."

Unlike all human narratives, it records, with severe accuracy, the faults, as well as the virtues, of its favorite characters. Its portraits are sternly truthful; it knows no flattery; its characters are truthfully human. From an American biography of our beloved and revered Washington, no one can gather that he had any faults or frailties; but when the character of the prince of the patriarchs, or of the Washington of Israel, is portrayed, their faults and frailties are faithfully recorded. The sacred biographies are no fancy sketches, but are drawn unerringly from life. Were there no other proof of the inspiration of the Scriptures, this characteristic alone would mark the Bible as divine, and prove that its writers must have been constrained by the spirit of truth faithfully to record facts, which stain the reputation of their favorite personages, and which pride and patriotism would tempt them to suppress.

To such perfection of faithfulness the writer of the following biography does not lay claim,—he is conscious of a love and veneration for its subject that might swerve to partiality a sterner nature than his own,—but it has been his aim, and his prayer, and his steadfast effort to be faithful to truth in the array of facts; and to let the facts, rather than epithets, portray the life of the man and the minister whose story he here places on record. Conscious that the task is dictated by fraternal love, such as rarely glows in human hearts, and by a reverence almost filial, which the close familiarity of fifty years has never abated, he has striven to guard against the errors into which such feelings might betray him; and he fears that he has sometimes become frigid, in his effort to avoid fervor. But if he has erred in this direction, the peculiarity of his theme seemed to demand it.

It was the lot of the subject of this memoir to live through times of great public agitation, both in church and state. He sustained peculiar relations to the educational interests of both; and in the doctrinal discussions and ecclesiastical movements of his era he bore a prominent part. It is too early yet for the verdict of posterity and of history to be calmly and dispassionately rendered, in regard to these great events in which he was an actor; and this fact has embarrassed his biographer, for it has kept him constantly on his guard, lest any statement should receive a partisan tinge. Against this he has watched and prayed; and he ventures to hope that the truthfulness and fairness of his record will not be questioned by impartial minds.

The biographer found it impossible to do justice to the immediate subject of his memoir, without putting on record more of the general history of the times in which he lived than usually pertains to the narrative of an individual life. Dr. Junkin was so involved in some of the most important movements of the period in which he lived, that to attempt to isolate his individual history from them would destroy at once the completeness and the fairness of the narrative.

The reader will, therefore, find upon the following pages much of the history of the Presbyterian Church in the United States for the last forty years, with links of connection joining it with her preceding history. This includes the history of opinion in regard to doctrine, order, and missionary organization, and effort.

It is always a delicate task to write the history of opinion, and especially of controversy. The difficulty is increased when persons have been involved and parties arrayed. If a writer has no opinions of his own, he is wholly unfit for the undertaking; if he has, he will be suspected of partiality to his own side. The author of this book does not pretend *so* to have performed such a difficult task as to place him beyond such a suspicion. But of one thing he is conscious, that he has *aimed* at impartiality and fairness of statement, and that he has endeavored to make CHARITY his amanuensis, especially when historic faithfulness required the record of facts which piety might deplore.

Dr. Junkin had preserved files of his life-long correspondence, arranged according to date. From these, and from documentary sources, the narrative has been chiefly drawn. Among his papers was found, after his decease, the commencement of a record of his personal reminiscences, which was begun soon after his exodus from Virginia, at the beginning of the civil war; but the hurry and excitement of the events of that fearful struggle called him into activities that prevented the prosecution of the record beyond the period of his early manhood. It was evidently designed only for the private reading of his children and immediate friends, not for more public use; and whilst it has been of great service in ascertaining the incidents of his early life, it is not in a shape to be used except in occasional quotations. This use has been made of it, and, it is hoped, with advantage to the narrative. Where quotations have been made, reference is made thereto by the letters "Rem."

The following is the introduction to these notes, from memory, which we insert by way of showing their object:

"REMINISCENCES.

"At the earnest and oft-repeated request of my dear brother, D. X. Junkin, I have, at last, and perhaps too late for completion, undertaken to put down a few personal recollections; the perusal of which may afford pleasing and mournful interest to my surviving friends. An autobiography, begun at the age of seventy-one, must necessarily be defective; especially, as in this case, where no diary has been kept. All I propose is a record of such events as have left an impression upon my memory; with such occasional remarks as may be useful to my children and my children's children.

"That the record may be blessed to their spiritual benefit, is my sincere prayer and ardent hope.

"GEO. JUNKIN.

"PRICE STREET, GERMANTOWN.
"Aug. 27, 1861."

The work has been prepared under the pressure of a severe bodily affliction, and amid the many toils, and cares, and interruptions incident to a large pastoral charge and other public duties. And it is commended to the candor and forbearance of the public, with the hope and the prayer that it may be the humble instrument of good.

LIFE

OF

DR. GEORGE JUNKIN.

CHAPTER I.

Descent—Parentage—Family—Incidents and Traditions in Family History —Immigration—American Home—Nativity.

"OF my family I know but little," said the subject of this memoir, in the notes mentioned on the preceding page. "Heraldry has not blazoned its name. Edmonson's book contains it not." But, if not written in books of earthly heraldry, the names of many of his ancestors are recorded in a more ancient and enduring volume,—"the Lamb's book of life." His lineage was of that stalwart, godly, and heroic race, the Puritans (Covenanters) of Scotland; the men and the women who braved persecution for Christ's crown and covenant; and, despite the curses of the Charleses and the claymores of Claverhouse, witnessed so long and so steadfastly for God and his truth.

When the second George was upon the British throne; when Pennsylvania was a nascent province only fifty-six years old; when the Susquehanna flowed through an almost unbroken wilderness, there crossed that river, at Harris's Ferry, now Harrisburg, two youthful Scotch-Irish immigants—Joseph Junkin and Elizabeth, his wife. They had been married a short time before, probably at the place where Oxford, Chester County, now stands, having the year before arrived from their native country, landing most probably at New Castle, Delaware. A previous immigration of Junkins had halted and acquired lands, upon a part of which the town of Oxford now stands. They were uncles and cousins of Joseph, who probably remained with them for a few months; but soon plunged into the wilderness of what is now Cumberland County, Pennsylvania.

This Joseph Junkin came from Antrim County, Ireland. His father and mother had immigrated to that country from Scotland during the persecution under the Stuarts. They were Covenanters of the straitest type, and left their country for conscience' sake. This migration occurred some time before the revolution of 1688. The Junkin family had resided near Inverness, and the name is probably of Danish origin, and they were, most likely, of the number of those adventurers from Denmark which, at an early period, took possession of parts of the coast of North Britain.

The paternal grandmother of Dr. Junkin was Elizabeth Wallace, also of Scottish parentage; her mother having come from Scotland previous to the siege of Londonderry; for she was in that city, and, with her family, endured the horrors of that siege, successful resistance to which gave William of Orange that vantage which established him upon the British throne,—the champion of the Protestant religion and the liberties of the world. "She heard the booming of many a cannon of the allies of the Stuarts; and she saw from the walls of glorious old Derry the smoke of the most important gun ever fired,—the lee-gun of the Mountjoy, whose rebound righted the ship, broke the boom, relieved the starving city and garrison, forced the allies to raise the siege and fall back upon the Boyne, where the arms of William and of liberty triumphed, and completed the glorious revolution of 1688."*

---

* Reminiscences.

In the estimation of military and political philosophers, Derry was the key of that great conflict.

There is a tradition, derived from this grandmother, differing somewhat from that mentioned by Charlotte Elizabeth, and more probable than hers. During the siege, and when starvation was nigh accomplishing what French artillery had failed to do,—when roasted rats had become a luxury,—empty barrels were carried in the night to the public square (or, rather, the ellipse) of the town, and so placed that they could be seen from the enemy's lines, and upon their upturned bottoms a little meal or lime was spread; and, in the morning, motions made as if meal was being distributed to the people, thus producing the impression that abundant provisions had been thrown in.

Joseph Junkin, Sr., and Elizabeth Wallace were married after arriving in America, and located, as already stated, in what is now Cumberland County, where he "took up" five hundred acres of land, including the site of the present town of Kingston. He might have secured fifty times that quantity, for, as his grandson states, "When he built his stone house (the second dwelling he erected), he might have secured fifty thousand acres of land, which is now (1861) valued at one hundred to one hundred and fifty dollars per acre. The only expense or limit of obtaining land was the office-fees and the cost of surveying. He had the funds requisite; yet, instead of securing so large a domain, he invested his 'Spanish milled dollars' in a stone house, which stands there to this day, a monument of his folly or his wisdom." This fact he mentions in his Reminiscences, as proof of the wonderful changes that have taken place in the last one hundred and thirty years.

Upon this domain the immigrant built a house, in which Joseph Junkin, the father of the subject of this memoir, was born, A.D. 1750. "I remember this house distinctly. It stood over a spring, directly north of the stone tavern which now (1861) stands one-third of a mile east of Kingston. It was built of hewn logs, covered with shingles. In the division of the estate this (east) portion fell to my uncle Benjamin, the west moiety to my father. He improved his share about A.D. 1775, building a stone dwelling and other suitable erections, near to a beautiful spring that gushed from the hill-side, and still flows on. In that dwelling I was born."*

But the progress of these improvements, as probably also the marriage of his father and mother, was delayed by the course of public events. The father, previous to his marriage, performed three campaigns of military service in the War of the American Revolution, having volunteered to aid in the struggle for his country's independence. In 1776 and '77 he served against the British, and in 1778 against the Indians and British on the Upper Juniata frontier. He assisted in the erection of a fort near to the site of Hollidaysburg. In 1776 he served chiefly in New Jersey. In 1777 he commanded a company of Cumberland volunteers in the battle of Brandywine. In a letter to his son George, while the latter was laboring as a missionary in Philadelphia, in 1819, we find an allusion to this, which exhibits the spirit of the sire, whilst it throws light upon the minuter details of our Revolutionary struggle.

"The battle of Brandywine was fought on the 11th of September, 1777, at which I commanded a company. Our army was forced to retreat. Great confusion followed, both among the troops and in the surrounding country. The dead found an asylum, but there was none for the wounded. On the 16th a skirmish with the enemy occurred near the White Horse Tavern, in Chester County, in which I received a musket-ball through my right arm, which shattered the bone. I could find no place to retire to for cure or subsistence. The army was in motion; I could not go

---

* Reminiscences.

with them. A horse was procured for me by Captain Fisher; a rope was my bridle; my knapsack, stuffed with hay, was my saddle; and thus equipped, and wrapped in my bloody garments, I arrived at home, a distance of ninety miles, in three days. I then took boarding in Carlisle, put myself under the care of Dr. Samuel A. McCoskry,* and paid all the expenses attendant upon my cure, besides which I lost a full year of the prime of my life. I once was urged to place myself upon the pension list, under the law of Pennsylvania, passed the 10th of March, 1787, but, being in good circumstances, declined it."

The details of his escape from the British lines, within which, after he fell, he was left; the noble conduct of William Smith and his wife, elderly people, and Whig Quakers of Chester County, in concealing the wounded soldier from British dragoons, sheltering him, feeding him, dressing his wounds, and sending him on his way; his mock capture by some American horsemen clad in British scarlet; and the almost overpowering reaction of feeling upon discovering the rough jest and finding himself with his own regiment, cannot be here detailed. After marching him as a prisoner some half a mile, and just as he was about to make a desperate effort to escape, they pointed him down a side road, saying, "Just beyond that woods you will find your regiment encamped."

The narrative formed some of the most striking incidents of a prize story, written some years ago by his granddaughter, and was one of those real episodes in military history that constitute its romance. And these events in the life of the father are alluded to here, only to show that the patriotism of the son, so conspicuous during the late civil conflict, was not only a *principle*, but an *inheritance*.

"My mother," says the memorandum already quoted, "as I have it from the book, was born on a farm, adjoin-

* Father of Bishop McCoskry, of Michigan.

ing what is now Waynesboro', Franklin County, Pennsylvania. Her father, John Cochran, emigrated from the north of Ireland, although also of Scotch descent, and located, about 1750, upon that outskirt of civilization next to the Indians. His wife, a Baird, came over single, and they married soon after. The Cochrans were very strict Covenanters. I remember seeing my grandfather Cochran but once; quaint in his attire, and walking with a staff. My father often spoke of him as a man of exemplary piety. As an example of his religious habit, he said that, in harvest-time, he always had family worship before daylight, singing, reading, and prayer, when the family and all hands must be present. Then a lunch, with a little *whisky*, was partaken of, always preceded by invocation of the divine blessing, then to work awhile before breakfast. Another instance of the strictness of these old Covenanters was related to me by one who had lived in the Cochran family. In walking on Sabbath to worship, over a ridge that abounded in whortleberries, the young folks dared not gather any, as it was considered a breach of the Sabbath. We smile at this, and it may be one extreme, but it contrasts, to our disadvantage, with the other extreme that marks this age of Sabbath desecration.

"From my mother I have often heard the following tale of her preservation from a dreadful death. When she was about seven or eight years old (1767–8), she was one day kept home from school (with another girl, a little older than she, who was there going to school) to take care of the smaller children, whilst the adults of the family, assisted by neighbors, joined in the 'flax pulling.' That day a party of Indians came upon the school, and murdered the master, and either killed or carried into captivity all the pupils except one. That one was named Archie Little, and he reported the sad catastrophe. The master was first knocked down, with the tomahawk, then the children, including Little, who was the largest boy in the school. He fell under the blow and was scalped, as all the rest were. But he recovered, kept still, and heard the Indians driving the hatchet into the skulls of such as showed any signs of life, whilst, by lying quiet as if dead, he escaped a second blow, and lived to tell the sad tale."*

---

* Rem.

Thus was the mother of George Junkin providentially preserved, in childhood, to be the mother of a large family, two of whom became ministers, and four others ruling elders, in the church of Christ. The writer of this volume once related the above incident to that eminent jurist and polished gentleman, the late Hon. George Chambers, of Chambersburg, when he replied, "The other little girl, thus providentially preserved, was *my mother.*"

Joseph Junkin, the second, and Eleanor Cochran were united in marriage, by the Rev. Alexander Dobbin, D.D., May 24th, 1779. The issue of this marriage were fourteen children, of whom GEORGE was the sixth child, and the fourth son. They were, except David, the youngest, born in the stone house, erected about 1775, and which still stands a short distance north of Kingston, and, from the slope of the ridge, overlooks that valley of teeming fruitfulness and almost peerless beauty. There, on the 1st day of November, A.D. 1790, the subject of this memoir was born.

CHAPTER II.

Birthplace Influences—Family History—Refugees—Frontiersmen—Indian Depredations—Quaker Policy—"The Paxton Boys."

WITH our American prejudices against aristocracy, and our disregard of ancestry, we are in danger of underestimating many of the most important influences that affect the formation of character. This is unphilosophical. If history and biography are of any value at all, it is for the lessons they impart. But if the events which form their staple are effects without causes, or if the record ignores the causes that produced the results, it is valueless as a guide in future progress. If the Scripture guarantee, "train up a child in the way he should go, and when he is old he will not depart from it," is reliable, then is it important to trace the phenomena of individual character and conduct to the surroundings of childhood, and to the training which he received, just as we trace other effects to their causes. And, without a process of this kind, the true philosophy of history can never be unfolded.

Dr. Junkin himself was accustomed to attribute much of what he was, and what he was enabled to do for God and his generation, to early home influences, and especially to a mother's love, piety, and faithfulness, whilst he ascribed all, ultimately, to God. With this thought in view, a few additional lines concerning his parentage, family, and the surroundings of his birthplace will not be deemed unnecessary.

We have seen that his ancestry, both paternal and maternal, were *Puritan;* for the Covenanters were genuine Puritans, and the limitation of this term to the early settlers of New England is an unauthorized restriction. His ancestors had passed through the purifying process of persecution, so well adapted to beget loyalty to principle. Taught in the stern school of revolution, in the fatherland, the Scotch-Irish immigrants brought to the forests of the American frontier a character peculiarly adapted to such a field of exertion. And the field itself was well adapted to develop all the better elements of that character. In regard to men, self-reliant, independent, liberty-loving; yet in regard to God, self-renouncing, dependent, conscientious, and reverential; there was in the combination the choicest elements of energy and success. The great dogma of Calvinism, that *means* have efficacy *because* God hath decreed it, formed the very chain in the web of their creed. The war-cry of the hero of Marston Moor, "Trust in the Lord, and depend on your pikes," was by them applied alike to the arts of peace and to the martial defence of their frontier homes, and it begat energy in both. The Bible, the Confession of Faith, and the catechisms, formed the staple of their reading and their thought, the Psalms of David and Asaph their song. With these, and the voice of family prayer, their cabins were vocal. The itinerant missionary from Scotland or Ulster preached to them, in familiar dialect, the gospel of God's grace; first in private dwellings, or in the "tent" beneath the forest's shades, beside some gushing spring, and afterwards in the rude log structures, which answered the double purpose of schoolhouse and sanctuary.

Coming, as most of them did, from the rural districts of the "old country," they sought the frontier, where lands were to be had for the "taking up," with small fees for records and surveying. And hence it came to pass that the Scotch-Irish, with sometimes a small admixture of Germans, became the frontiersmen of many of the colonies, especially of Pennsylvania and Virginia. There they made homes for themselves, with the axe and the mattock, which they often were compelled to defend, against a savage foe, with their rifles. Their entire surroundings called for great exertion, indomitable courage, and unfailing patience. The struggle was for bread, for education, and for religion; and it taxed all their powers, and, by taxing, developed them. To create a civilization in the forest, distant from all facilities of improvement, might well have made a strong race out of a feeble one. But, when men of godly principles and high resolve, men descended from a hardy and energetic ancestry, were placed in circumstances so favorable to the development of the nobler attributes of humanity, we need not wonder that a high style of manhood resulted, and a desirable condition of society.

It is true, there were countervailing tendencies. The very energy and fondness for adventure, which such a state of things fostered, tended to unsettle some minds, make them restless in their homes, and lead them to seek, in the remoter frontier, that occupation and excitement which were not found in the older settlements. It was, accordingly, not a rare occurrence for some, after having subdued the forest and made improvements, to "sell out" to later comers, and plunge farther into the wilderness in search of new homes and new adventure.

This accounts for the fact, that, in the early settlements of the middle colonies, the Scotch-Irish Presbyterians formed the bulk of the frontiersmen who subdued the forest and battled with the savage.

And, in Pennsylvania, they did the latter with very little aid from the government. They fought the battles with their own strong arms, their own rifles, ammunition, and provisions. The colonial government of Pennsylvania was, for a long time, under the control of "the people called Quakers," that sect having a large and steady majority in the colonial assembly. Their peace principles, which were part of their religious creed, forbade them either to bear arms themselves, or to aid and abet war of any kind, and they would not vote war subsidies. The policy inaugurated by Penn, of not only buying the land from the Indians, but of buying them off from hostilities by *presents*, was maintained, until the latter became injurious and defeated its own end. The Indians became more and more exorbitant in their demands, and would commit atrocious barbarities upon the frontier inhabitants, not only for purposes of vengeance and plunder, but also with the expectation that the government would buy a peace with still more liberal presents.

So far was this system carried, that the frontiersmen began to look upon these gratuities of the colonial government as *bribes* to the savages to commit more murders and depredations. Hence arose a state of exasperated feeling among the frontier settlements against both the government and the savages, which resulted in some unhappy outbreaks. It was this exasperation that prompted "the Paxton Boys" to the unjustifiable slaughter of the Conestoga Indians, in the Lancaster Jail, in 1763, and to march to Philadelphia, to the great consternation of the inhabitants of that peace-loving city. This unlawful enterprise was rashly undertaken by some young hot-headed and irresponsible frontiersmen, in what is now Dauphin County, with a few from what are now York and Cumberland, but was resisted by the older and more considerate inhabitants. The perpetrators were mostly young men who had lost kindred or neighbors by the murderous incursions of the savages, and who had conceived that indiscriminate hatred against the Indians which was always too rife upon the border. They suspected the Conestoga Indians (perhaps unjustly) of giving information to the wild Indians where and when to strike. They were exasperated that a government which taxed them, and which they defended with their arms, would do nothing to protect their homes; and this indignant feeling broke out, and resulted in the unfortunate and excuseless massacre of people probably innocent.

Great efforts were made by those in the interests of the Quaker legislature to impute to the whole Presbyterian population of the frontier the blame of this atrocious act; but the letter of the Rev. John Elder, pastor of Paxton and Derry, to Governor John Penn, and the governor's answer to him, completely prove the injustice of such a charge.*

The exciting incidents above mentioned took place when Joseph Junkin (father of the Doctor) was in his thirteenth year; and although neither he nor any of his family were participants, they form part of the history of the community in which he was reared, and amid which his childhood was passed. Often did the family leave their dwelling at evening, and pass the night in the cornfield or the "flax-patch," for fear of assault by the savage foe. When in his sixth year (1755), during the French and Indian War, his parents escaped, with their family, from savage barbarities, and fled to Chester County, where they abode for a season with their relatives. The first night after their flight they found refuge in a "block-house," on Paxton Creek, near to the place where Harrisburg now stands. That same night, a Mr. Graham, with his family, took refuge in the same wooden fortress. He was the father of the Rev. William Graham, a minister of the gospel and the founder of Washington College, Lexington, Va., of which college the son (George) of his fellow-refugee afterwards became president. From that college that son himself became a refugee, when the civil war began in 1861.

In 1778 the Upper Susquehanna was overrun by the

---

* See Archives of Pa., vol. iv. pp. 148, 153.

Indians in British pay, and the Wyoming massacre occurred. The settlers fled for refuge to the older settlements. A family named Montgomery found refuge in the house of Dr. Junkin's father. "He was the father," says Dr. J., "of my lamented friend and helper in good works, the late noble-hearted General Daniel Montgomery, of Danville, Pa., with whom, in after-years, I took sweet counsel. This incident I had from the general himself in the first years of our acquaintance."

He records in his Reminiscences several incidents of the early life of his parents, as connected with the first years of the War of Independence. But, although they illustrate the condition and history of those times, they are not necessarily connected with the object of this volume, and are therefore not introduced.

It is scarcely necessary to say that "Tories," as the adherents of the king were called, were rarely found among the Scotch-Irish Presbyterians. They were proverbial for their zeal in the cause of Independence. The father of Dr. Junkin has left on record some incidents of which he was personally cognizant just before he marched to New Jersey in 1776. One occurred at Carlisle previous to the Declaration of Independence, but after the subject had been proposed in Congress. A large number of the inhabitants of Cumberland Valley had congregated at Carlisle to confer about public affairs. They were assembled in the public square, and it was proposed to have an expression of public sentiment upon the subject. An eminent lawyer of the place, Mr. ———, made a lengthy address, setting forth the folly and the madness of the attempt to become independent of Great Britain. He portrayed the vast wealth and military power of Great Britain in contrast with the poverty, weakness, and want of military resources of the colonies. He urged them to seek nothing beyond a reasonable redress of grievances, and assured them that an attempt at independence would result only in disaster and ruin to the colonies. When he had closed, another lawyer, a Mr. Wm. Lyon, made a short address, and proposed that all who favored independence should move to the north side of the square, and those who opposed it, to the south. The great mass of the people, our father with them, promptly moved to the north side; a few, three or four, moved neither way; but *none went to the south side.*

Shortly after this there was a battalion drill in the vicinity of Silver's Spring, at which nearly all the people of the lower valley, that were not in the army, were present. Whilst the parade was in progress, and the men were engaged in putting green branches in their hats as a token that they were willing to volunteer, a courier rode along, bringing the tidings that independence had been declared three days before at Philadelphia, and carrying a hand-bill announcing the declaration. It was read to the multitude, and there ratified unanimously and with acclamation, and a large company of volunteers organized on the spot. Such was the spirit of old Cumberland at that trying time.

The facilities for education in a frontier settlement were, of course, meagre; and yet the Presbyterians, whatever else they lacked, would provide schools. Of course their school-houses, like their dwellings, were at first but rude cabins, such as we have seen the mother attended; but the teachers were often persons of mature education; and if the books and other appliances were few and simple, the drill was often more thorough than it now is. The parents, who had been taught in the schools of the mother country, were also effective teachers; and around the blazing fires of home, in the long winter evenings, imparted to their children the learning they had acquired in their youth. With such meagre advantages, Dr. Junkin's parents acquired an education such as is even yet deemed respectable. The father, by diligence in study out of the hours of labor, made himself a very accurate English scholar. He was fond of exact science, made considerable progress in mathematics and natural philosophy, wrote with vigor and grammatical correctness, and was an accurate practical land surveyor. He was a man of unusual natural force and perspicuity of mind; reasoned with strength, and wrote in a style plain, but accurate and vigorous, and was rather fond of discussion. Accustomed to think, and fond of conversation, he could not but impress upon his children habits of thought, especially upon the one (George) who, more, perhaps, than any other, inherited the father's massive mental structure.

Both parents had been thoroughly instructed in the doctrines of the Bible and of the Westminster Symbols, and both, from early life, were professors of religion. The father grasped the doctrines with a clearness and a vigor that made him a formidable disputant; and the type of his religion, whilst it lacked not tenderness and humility, was more marked by intellectual force than by devotional fervor. The mother's, on the other hand, whilst also intelligent, was characterized by unusual fervor of devotion and practical Christian earnestness. Equally firm in the faith with her husband, she excelled him in earnest and conscientious efforts to apply its principles in everyday duties. She was, indeed, a woman of eminent godliness. She taught her children to do everything in reference to God and upon religious principle; and she trained them not only in the preceptive, but in the practical also.

In every community in which she resided she was remarkable as a successful peace-maker, and earned the beatitude attached to that character. Her system was quiet, but effective. If she knew of alienation and strife between neighbors or church-members, especially if females, she would seek interviews with them separately. She would converse with one of the hostile parties about the other, aiming with skill and tact to elicit *some favorable* expression concerning the absent. This she would repeat to the other, keeping to herself any unkind thing that might have been said. This would bring out some kind expression in turn, which she would take occasion to repeat, thus gradually "slaying the enmity." And when, by this process, she had prepared the way, she would contrive an interview, often at her own tea-table, where the reconciliation would be perfected.

Such, in a religious point of view, were the parents of George Junkin. Of Covenanter stock, they early became members of that (the Reformed Presbyterian) church; and when, in 1782, that church united with the "Associate Presbyterian Synod," forming the "Associate Reformed Church of North America," they joined in the union, and for many years the father was a prominent ruling elder in that body. Referred to the influence of such a parentage, in connection with later surroundings, it is not difficult to account for the peculiarities of Dr. Junkin's religious character, strength and clearness of intellectual perceptions, fervor of devotion, and earnest practicalness. He himself often spoke of his maternal training and pious influence with deeply grateful and reverential feelings.

"My father and mother had fourteen children: Elizabeth, Eleanor, Joseph, who died young, John, Joseph, George, William, who died in childhood, Mary and Agnes, twins, Benjamin, one unnamed, who died in infancy, William Findley, Matthew Oliver, and David. All were born in the same old stone mansion, already described, except the last named, who was born at Hope Mills, in Mercer County. Eleven of them attained adult life, married, and all raised families, except the oldest daughter, Elizabeth, who, with her first child, died shortly after its birth."*

Elizabeth was the wife of the Hon. John Findley, of Mercer County; Eleanor, the wife of the Hon. Walter

---

* Rem.

Oliver, for many years a member of the State legislature; Mary, the wife of the Rev. George Buchanan, pastor for nearly fifty years of the A. R. Church of Steubenville, Ohio; and Agnes was the wife of the Rev. James Galloway, first pastor of Mercer, and she afterwards married Hugh Bingham, Esq., father of the Hon. John A. Bingham.

Of the immediate family of Joseph Junkin, Senior, including sons-in-law and grandsons, *fifteen* were ministers of the gospel and *twenty-one* ruling elders in the church,—in all *thirty-six* office-bearers in Presbyterian churches. Of these, ten ministers and ten elders still live. The others have fallen asleep.

CHAPTER III.

"Widow Junkin's Tent"—Early Missionaries of Cumberland Valley—Churches—Baptism—A. R. Church formed—Early Religious Instruction—Confidence in God's Covenant—Schools and Teachers—Romance—Recollections of Early Preachers.

JOSEPH JUNKIN, the grandfather of the Doctor, died in 1777, before the marriage of Joseph, the second, but his wife Elizabeth survived until 1796. The first place of holding public worship in the vicinity was upon her estate in the woods. "It was known from my earliest memory," says Dr. J. in his Reminiscences, "as 'Widow Junkin's tent,' and stood three hundred yards from the dwelling first erected by my grandfather. About the dawn of my memory that 'tent' was removed one mile west, to James Bell's place. In 'Bell's tent' I have often heard Dr. Black, Dr. Culbertson and others of the old Covenanters, preach. That tent (a simple stand or dais, with a shelter for the minister, and a board on which to lay the Bible) stood, braced up against a large black-oak tree, more than forty-five years. When I passed the place last May (1861) it was gone; and the Bells, Junkins, and all the worshippers are gone."

The Dr. Culbertson, or, rather, Cuthbertson, above mentioned, was a Scotsman of eminent piety and devotedness. He landed at New Castle, Delaware, in 1744, and immediately began a series of missionary journeys and toils that extended until near the close of the century (1799).

"I often have heard my parents speak of Doctor Clark, a Covenanter minister, who traversed the middle and southern colonies as a missionary. He was a man of great talents, learning, piety, and zeal. His labors were signally blessed in many places.

"Mr. Culbertson joined in the Union of 1782, and was pastor of the A. R. Church of Big Spring, Newville. The Rev. Dr. Alexander Dobbin, of Adams County, adhered to the same body, and ministered at Marsh Creek, where he conducted a grammar-school, at which many eminent men were trained. He also served a congregation on Antietam Creek, near where my mother was born. It was at one of the sacramental services which he administered there that my parents dedicated me to God in the ordinance of baptism, which Dr. Dobbin administered."*

Of his early religious instructions, and of his first schools and teachers, we gather the following from his Reminiscences:

"I have no recollection as to the first religious instructions I received and the early influence of family worship. But from my mother's teachings of those younger than myself, which do come within the scope of my memory, I *infer* what she had done for me, beyond the range of memory. This ought to be the case with all family training. It was careful, constant, kind, though firm, and it was *Christian*. Blessed is that family that is so trained. It cannot be that it should fail to rear a godly seed. There stands the covenant promise, 'I will be a God to thee and to thy seed after thee.' It cannot fail, for God is faithful."

And this high estimate of the value of godly training in the family, and the faithfulness of God's covenant, drawn as it was from his own experience, from observation, and from the Holy Word, grew upon him through all his life, and was often expressed in his preaching and his writings. He was in the habit of teaching that parental faithfulness and care, with devout prayer, could (instrumentally) transmit to offspring the *piety* pledged in the covenant of grace, and the *heavenly inheritance* connected with it, with greater

* Rem.

certainty than the worldly estate which they might design to bequeath to them.

"I cannot date precisely my first school days. They must have been in my sixth or seventh year. The school-house to which my older brothers went was two and a half miles from our home, but, before I commenced, my father had succeeded in having one built within one and a half miles east of us, on the summit of the ridge. It was a hewn log structure, and very respectable and comfortable. The windows were made by cutting out about ten feet of a log on each side, and inserting a low, narrow sash to fill the opening. The desks were attached firmly to the wall, so that the faces of the pupils were towards this long, low window when writing, and the smaller children seated in the central parts of the room. I doubt whether much improvement has yet been made upon this simple and convenient arrangement. The site of our school-house was extremely pleasant. A beautiful open grove of forest trees in the rear, and a magnificent view southward over the valley, terminated only by the peaks of the 'Blue Ridge.' In the intermediate space lay the broad rolling plain of the Cumberland Valley, then called 'The Barrens,' because destitute of timber, but now esteemed soil of great fertility. There I received all my 'schooling' until I entered the preparatory department of Jefferson College in 1809.

"My first schoolmaster was William Jamieson, a lame man, who walked with a crutch and staff; and many a time I have run races with him, in going home from or coming to school. He often outran me, hopping on his three legs. It was then the custom for the teacher to board round among the pupils, and, though often disagreeable to him, it had its advantages. If he was an agreeable person (and if not he ought not to be in the office), he learned the habits of the homes, could hint useful things to the parents, become familiar with all, and it tended to permanency. We were very ambitious to get 'Master Jamieson' home with us, and he often had difficulty in deciding between our claims. He was a beautiful penman, a pretty good teacher, was truly benevolent, and therefore greatly beloved. He had great administrative ability; knew how to obey Solomon in the use of the rod, though erring rather on the side of lenity. He was jocose without descending to familiarity. He continued our teacher for many years.

"My next schoolmaster was an Irishman named Henderson, a good mathematician. Then a Yankee—Augustus Searl—somewhat of a classic, teaching Latin to one or two of the boys. He occasionally got drunk, and then he always closed the school with prayer—never when sober. Next to him came James Smith, a Scot, who taught two years. He was a man of ability.

"My next teacher was Andrew Caruthers, whose story was connected with one of the tragedies of the valley. He was born in our neighborhood, and had learned the trade of a carpenter. During one of his visits to his family, the food of the household was mixed with arsenic, by a young woman who lived in the family, named Sarah Clark. Her object was to destroy one of the daughters, who, she thought, stood between her and the affections of J. D., whom she herself loved. She succeeded in murdering part of the family, and was afterwards executed for the crime at Carlisle. Andrew Caruthers was rendered decrepit by the poison, and, no longer able to work, began study and entered Dickinson College. During his college course he left college and taught, to obtain means, and thus became my teacher. He afterwards became eminent as a lawyer and a judge, and was distinguished as a law instructor. His hands were so distorted by the poison that he could not make pens in his school, and he devolved this work chiefly upon me, and he paid me richly by special attentions. It was he who put it into my father's mind to give me a college education. My last schoolmaster was James Smith, of Carlisle. Diligent and faithful, but not very efficient."*

Thus did his mind, in old age, recall with minuteness and affection the names and the peculiarities of his early teachers, and, with a detail that we need not here copy, he proceeds to describe the things taught, the modes of teaching, the few school-books used, the systems of reward,

---

* Rem.

the "trapping," and other modes of exciting emulation in the learners, together with incidents that would not interest the general reader, but all of which illustrate the early rise in his mind of that which proved the business, we might say the passion, of his life—*education*—the development and culture of the mind. "The Bible was the chief reading book. The Catechism was universally taught; usually one question was required of every pupil each morning, and a general recitation of it the last hour of the week."

He describes, also, the games of the playground, by which amusement was sought and physical development promoted; and they are much the same as those prevailing among our youth of the present day. The discipline of the school, with rod, rule, rebuke, report at home, and occasionally the fool's-cap, or the fool's-corner, are recalled, as well as some scenes in which the boys showed themselves to be the fathers of the men.

"About 1798, political excitement ran high in the country, and was rife in the school. Between Federalists and anti-Federalists, in the school, the strife was very virulent. Fists, sticks, and snowballs sometimes were employed to enforce arguments. The Aikens and Walkers (of which family Hon. Robert J. Walker was one) were violent Federals, whilst the Loudons and Junkins were anti-Federals. The fights would break out at the close of school, and Master Jamieson was often not able to quell them. On one of these occasions I had the only fisticuff battle of my life, in my eighth year. The big boys, afraid to engage themselves, managed to urge on Bill Aiken, a full cousin of Robert J. Walker, and myself to do battle. It was not of long continuance. I got my antagonist down, and banged anti-federalism (republicanism, as it began to be called) into him *ad posteriorem,* until he cried 'Enough.' Then the Republican boys made the welkin ring with shouts of victory, and the parties drew off to nurse their wrath and meet another day. I have lost sight of my friend and antagonist, Aiken; if alive, he is now seventy-two years old."*

"In the summer of 1799, my father lived on a farm which he owned, two miles east of Newville, having removed to it for the purpose of making improvements, having meanwhile leased the homestead at Kingston. My memory is crowded with incidents of that summer, pleasant to recall, but not worthy of special record. . . . . That summer I went to school to William McKean, in a log schoolhouse, near to one Myers' house, a tenant of Mr. Leiper's. Joseph Ritner was then Myers' hired boy, and one of Leiper's girls became his wife. I saw them, many years afterwards, in Harrisburg, when he (Ritner) was governor of Pennsylvania. . . . My parents belonged to the A. R. Church at Newville, of which, at that time, the Rev. James McConnel, a 'United Irishman,' was pastor. He had some imagination, considerable flow of language, much self-possession, and was orthodox, but bigoted. These opinions of him are the result of subsequent knowledge, not of my observations at the time. My only recollections of him, as he then was, are that he was tedious and confused. He never won my attention, or made me in the least the wiser. But oh! his 'fourth places,' and 'fifth places,' and his '*last* places,' of which last he had often many in the same discourse,—I remember what weariness they produced.

"And yet, towards the last of that summer, my mind was very much exercised in regard to heaven and hell, and all that relates to eternity. But I cannot connect any of my mental exercises with the pastor's sermons. He was assisted at a sacramental service, on one occasion, by the Rev. James Walker, also an Irishman. His text and sermon I remember, 'Put on the whole armor of God, etc.' It was not the instrument of my awakening, but aided me in my serious impressions. His appearance I can distinctly recall. He was of grave and solemn demeanor, whilst the pastor was too jovial to accomplish much good."†

It was during this summer, and the next winter, that the

* Rem. † Rem.

mental process which he thinks resulted in his spiritual change was experienced. He records this with that simplicity which was an element of his character, and with that microscopic detail which might be expected of one accustomed to a careful observing of the connection between cause and effect. In his child-experience was realized the fact, that God often causes "the wrath of man to praise him." It not unfrequently happens that the Lord employs some outbreak of natural depravity, as the means of showing to his chosen ones the plague of their own hearts, with a view to convincing them of sin. It was so with him, as he naively tells:

"When at school one day I became greatly distressed by a trifling loss (a pocket brass inkstand of my brother John's), and, whilst weeping for this cause, my memory recalled and placed at the bar of conscience a wicked act I had long before committed against my sister Elizabeth, who now lived far away, in Mercer County, having married and emigrated thither. The act was done before her marriage; when, on one occasion, she restrained me in some trifle, I became furious, and threw in her face some bread I was eating at the time. Months had elapsed; but this unkind treatment of my dear, and now distant, sister seemed to plant a dagger in my heart, and this sorrow absorbed the other, and made me feel very remorseful. A sense of sin was awakened in my heart that continued to grow deeper from time to time. Shortly after this, one night, there was a tremendous storm of thunder, lightning, and rain. The teeming of the rain upon the roof, the flash of the lightning, and the roar of heaven's dread artillery, brought the ideas of death and eternity vividly before me. My cruel treatment of my absent sister, and other sins, came rushing upon my heart. I lay long awake, fearing, trembling, weeping, and praying. I have never felt such deep and painful emotions of the kind as that night. My conscience seconded all these, and made me taste the bitterness of sin.

"Late in November, my uncle, William Findley (who for twenty-two consecutive years represented the Westmoreland district in Congress, and who won the sobriquet of 'the Chronicler of Congress'), came to my father's, on his way to Philadelphia, where that body then sat. His conversation, and especially his singing and prayers, were comfortable to me. Later still, and after we had returned to the old homestead below Carlisle, my sister, Elizabeth Findley, returned from the West to spend the winter and encounter the first perils of maternity under her mother's care. One day, after the birth of her child, Dr. McCoskry, as he was leaving the house after a professional call, said, very sorrowfully, 'It is all over with her; she is already in the agonies of death.' Oh, how this riveted the convictions of the last few months! I went out to the pond, behind the spring-house, and lay down on my face upon the clean slate gravel, and wept, and prayed, and prayed and wept, as I had never done before. And now, (1861), at the distance of sixty-two years, I am not certain but that this was the time of my spiritual birth." (This was in his tenth year.) "I made no profession of religion for twelve years afterwards; but from that day my conscience has never been beaten down, but has controlled my conduct. It has never, except momentarily, failed to secure obedience, and to keep me in a prayerful frame. I never used profane language in my life, but, from the time just specified, have felt a peculiar shrinking from it, and, indeed, from all sinful outbreakings. Much of this is due to education under my mother's training and prayers, all *efficiently* to the grace of God. *I never heard a profane oath from one of her children,* nor from any of the name. . . . . . . Now these things are not mentioned by way of boasting, but as an expression of gratitude to God, for giving me such parents, and especially *such a mother*, and for blessing her prayers and efforts in educating my conscience, and bringing down the Holy Spirit to sanctify my heart and restrain my naturally quick and violent temper. When I look back upon the temptations to profanity by men and boys all around me, I cannot account for the escape of myself and brothers except on this ground. God interposed, and, by home restraints, saved us."*

---

* Rem.

CHAPTER IV.

Causes of Removal to the West—Emigration—Incidents of Journey—Hope Mills—Three Years at that Place—Their Influence upon his Future—Ministers at Mercer—Rev. Samuel Tait—Rev. Campbell.

"NOTHING occurs to my memory worthy of note until 1804. That year, for the first, I made 'a hand' at the sickle in my father's harvesting. The sickle, in those days, was the chief instrument for cutting grain. The fields were laid out in 'lands' of eight feet wide, and two hands took 'a land,' and must always clean up the right hand furrow; hence my partner, by doing a little more than his share, made a hand of me.

"Whisky was always used in harvest, yet I never saw a man drunk on my father's farm. He was a moderate drinker at harvest for more than seventy years, and yet never was intoxicated, so far as I ever saw or heard of. Fixed principle only saved him.

"The summer and autumn of 1804 were marked by sickness (fever and ague) prevailing all through the Cumberland Valley. Our entire family, twelve, were taken. I the last one taken down. It was probably this, together with the wish of getting land for all his children, that led my father to meditate a removal to the west end of the State. Wayne's victory over the Indians, in the battle of the Maumee, and the subsequent treaty with them (1798), had opened to settlement the large district that lies between the Ohio and the lake, and the Alleghany and the Ohio line, a district of great beauty, and possessing many resources of wealth. To the county of Mercer, in that region, my brother-in-law, John Findley, had migrated (from Westmoreland), in 1799, and my father made purchase of large tracts of land in and after 1800. In the fall of 1805, my two older brothers, John and Joseph, were detailed and sent to improve the Hope farm, two and a half miles south of the town of Mercer. This was before he sold the homestead in Cumberland. Next year he sold it, and, on the 15th of April, 1806, set out with his family for Mercer County.

"It was a tedious, and sometimes perilous, journey, for the road over the Alleghany Mountains was of the most primitive and impracticable kind. A week brought us to Mr. Findley's, in Westmoreland. The present town of Latrobe occupies part of his estate. There we remained over Sabbath and Monday. At Pittsburg we had to lighten our wagons by leaving part of their loads, for the road to Mercer was new, through deep forests, and over steep hills. At the ferry-house, opposite Pittsburg, at what is now the foot of Federal Street, Alleghany, my father found an old Scotch-Irishman, named Wm. Robinson, who used to thrash rye for my father in Cumberland. He owned the ferry and the farm, on which the central parts of Alleghany City now stand, and urged my father to buy it, offering all, from the second bank to the foot of the great hill, for four thousand dollars. Nor was my father ignorant of the prospective value of the property. I heard him remark, 'There will one day be the great city, and Pittsburg will be a small town of stores and shops.' He had money on hand to make the purchase, but Mr. Findley dissuaded him. Had he made that purchase it might have ruined his children, for he would have become very rich.

"Our progress was so slow that the next Sabbath was spent at the house of a Mr. Sample, a Cumberland family that lived at the mouth of Girty's Run, and we only arrived at Hope farm on the 1st of May. Here, for a season, we lived in a somewhat spacious 'cabin,' until the large mansion-house, still standing, was erected. It was a dense cabin population; for, besides our own large family, we had many men employed in building dam, mills, mansion-house, and other improvements. Our master millwright was Joseph Smith, Esq., father of the Rev. Dr. Joseph T. Smith, of Baltimore. Early in the autumn we entered the large house, and left the cabin to the horses.

"Nothing specially worthy of record occurred during the ensuing three years that I remained at home before going to college. I worked at all kinds of labor—carpentry, cabinet-making, farming, sawing lumber, grinding grain, and wool-carding. Just before going to college, I

4

made a neat cherry cradle for my brother David, then a baby. . . . The first summer of our sojourn, I killed seventeen rattlesnakes."*

Further details of the formation of the new home at "Hope Mills," and of the trials incident thereto, are given in his notes; but, whilst interesting to his family and intimate friends, they would not prove so much so to the general reader. The foregoing has been transcribed because it throws light upon the development of those remarkable powers, physical, moral, and intellectual, which made Dr. Junkin the man he was. The sketches which he has given of his youth, graphic, simple, and unaffected as they are, enable us to account for the remarkable constitution of his manhood, especially for that "*mens sana in corpore sano*" which enabled him to do such a life-work as we hope to record. His triune constitution, "body, soul, and spirit," was finely, proportionately, and vigorously developed by the surroundings and employments of his earlier life. His bodily frame, although below medium height, was massive, firmly knit, and wondrously muscular. Energy and endurance pervaded every joint, nerve, and fibre. Quickness of mechanical perception, and an intuitive promptness to apply the mechanical powers, gave efficacy to his physical exertions. An early fondness for inquiring after the *reasons* of things was fostered both by paternal example and by his daily employments. The very meagreness of his opportunities and appliances of education but stimulated a mind like his to higher exertion, whilst the entire process of development went on amid domestic, social, and church influences, all tending to produce a consecration of all his powers to the higher and holier spheres of human duty and exertion.

During these three years the new homestead at Hope

---

* Rem.

Mills was founded, the farm opened, a flouring-mill, the largest in the country, and with the first set of French burr millstones north of the Ohio, erected, carding-machines, a fulling and cloth-dressing mill established, the first in the county, and other improvements made. In all this the youth of sixteen to nineteen bore a full share, and, next to the oldest brother, was probably the most efficient. Meantime, his efforts at self-improvement were not relaxed, nor "the great concern" neglected.

"During these years," continue the Reminiscences, "the Rev. Samuel Tait was the Presbyterian minister in Mercer and vicinity, the first that was settled there, having come in 1800. I seldom heard him, as our family was connected with the Associate Reformed body. He was zealous, warm-hearted, often wept whilst preaching, had little education, and less logic, but was earnest and useful. His preaching failed to make the gospel plan clearly understood, and his reproofs often had a hardening influence. The Associate (seceders), the Reformed Presbyterians (Covenanters), and the A. R. Church had frequent supplies, and Mr. T. sometimes made hard allusions to them; but I now think his ministrations were more useful than theirs, which were too dryly doctrinal, and inclined to Antinomianism."

George Junkin had now passed his eighteenth year, and, if his cherished wish to obtain a liberal education was ever to be gratified, steps looking thereto must soon be taken. The father, who had once, upon Mr. Caruther's suggestion, formed the purpose of sending him to college, seems to have somewhat faltered in regard to the purpose. But the mother, who, like Hannah, had given him in her heart and her prayers to the Lord, continued steadfast in her wish to have him educated. She prevailed, and arrangements were made accordingly.

CHAPTER V.

Enters College—Dr. Wylie—Governor Hendricks—Dr. McMillan—Dr. Ramsey—Mode of Study—Franklin Society—As a Student—Correspondence with Home Circle—Its Character and Influence—The Father's Letters—Predestination.

"IN May, 1809, father and mother and I set out in the family carriage for Canonsburg, they to make some purchases in Pittsburg, and I to enter the grammar-school of Jefferson College. Arriving at Canonsburg in the middle of vacation, they concluded to make a visit to my cousin, Gen. Thomas Patterson's family, and leave me there until college should open. Mrs. Patterson was the oldest daughter (Elizabeth) of Hon. Wm. Findley, previously mentioned, whose wife was my mother's sister. Gen. Patterson was a man of some mark in Washington County, member of Congress and general of militia. He was the first to introduce the merino sheep into that (now) great wool-growing county. There I remained two weeks, and then went to Canonsburg.

"At Jefferson I boarded for a time with Mrs. Canon, the widow of the proprietor of the town, in her family dwelling. Afterwards with a Mr. Daily, with whom also boarded the late President Andrew B. Wylie, and the late Governor Hendricks, of Indiana, both then in the junior class. Mr. Wylie was my tutor in Latin. I usually attended the ministrations of the Rev. John McMillan, afterward Dr. McMillan, in the old stone church of Chartiers, one mile south of the town; sometimes at Dr. Ramsay's (seceder), half a mile west of the village. Dr. McMillan was a man of a good deal of strength of mind, but did not study much. His preaching was warm and hortatory, his reproofs blunt, and often injurious, by reason of their harshness. Yet had he been the instrument of great good among the pioneers of that region, not only in preaching the gospel, but also in bringing out young men, and training them for the ministry. His log-cabin academy and theological school was really the nucleus of Jefferson College, and the parent of much of the education of the West.

"Mr. (afterwards Dr.) Ramsey was a student and a reasoner, and a man of great Christian amiability. His enunciation was slow, his attitudes ungainly, and he rubbed his chin so incessantly with his hand that his whole delivery was tedious and unattractive. Yet his discourses were clear and instructive to one willing to wait on his tardiness. I often thought that if these two men could be combined in one it would be a decided advantage to all parties.

"Upon entering college, or rather its grammar-school, Ross's Latin Grammar was put into my hand, and no other study assigned. We were required to commit certain parts to memory, and recite by rote. Mr. Wylie never took a book in hand, having the whole in memory. No explanation was given until we had committed the book, and gone twice over it. The third time we parsed the examples under the Syntax rules, and committed most of the notes. Then we took to reading *Corderii Colloquia*, and other primary books. I doubt whether this plan be not better than our present methods. It requires *faith* in the teacher, and creates memory. After all my experience, I think it best to study language *first*, and afterwards the *philosophy* of language. For two sessions we studied Latin, then began the Greek."*

During the time of his connection with college, events occurred that form part of his own and the history of his times, which doubtless had their influence upon his forming character, but which he has not mentioned. He soon developed a talent for writing and discussion, which made him somewhat distinguished among his fellows. He was a member of the "Franklin Literary Society" of the college, and was twice, as the old archives of the society show, chosen "contestor," and won honors for the society in its annual "contests" with the rival organization, the "Philo Literary Society."

His contemporaries in college spoke of him as a grave

---

* Rem.

and rather reserved youth, intent upon study, and full and accurate in his recitations. His powers of generalization and analysis, and his logical acumen, were early developed, and made him of mark as a reasoner; and it was conceded that he was the best debater in the college. The institution was then in its formative state, and the regular college classes were small. The senior class, with which he graduated, consisted of but five members; but this had the advantage of calling for frequent individual recitations, and consequent thorough training.

Whilst in college, correspondence with his family was kept up. It is to be regretted that very few of his letters home are preserved; but the tone of the letters from home to him (for we find many if not all of them on his files) is indicative of not only the deep affection with which he was regarded in the home circle, but also of the unwonted respect and confidence with which brothers and sisters looked upon him. They all betray great solicitude for his spiritual and intellectual progress, and they seem to have shown more reverence to him than in America is usually accorded even to the oldest son, although he was the fourth. The father's letters to him are fraught with paternal solicitude and wise counsel, and they sometimes betray a measure of respect for the judgment and the opinions of the son, which, from such a father, was highly complimentary to the maturity of the youth's understanding. It is to be regretted that the son's replies are lost; but the father's letters disclose the fact that they discussed, in their correspondence, some of the gravest subjects in religion, morals, and civil government. This was, no doubt, one of the means of developing, in the young student, that capacity for thorough discussion which was characteristic of his maturer years. This was, in part, the training that qualified him for becoming such a master of the great principles of morals and of constitutional law, and for rendering such valuable service in the two great controversies in which he bore a prominent part,—the struggle for church reform in 1834–38, and the struggle for national unity of 1861–65. His quenchless love for the Union, and his veneration for the Constitution of his country, and his ability to defend both, were fostered by the conversation and the correspondence of a father, who had bled, and toiled, and sacrificed for the establishment of both. He was early qualified to be the author of such a book as the "Political Fallacies."

This correspondence cannot be largely quoted; an extract or two will suffice to show its general tone. In a letter, dated Mercer, June 17th, 1809, a note merely of fifteen lines, we read:

> "MY SON,—I received your letter, and was glad to learn that you are well,—we at home are all well. . . . . . You, I hope, will pay all due attention to your morals, your health, and your college studies, and make use of all opportunities to get your mind stored with useful ideas. If there is any book here which you would wish to have, mention it in your next letter, and perhaps I can send it. I think Buchanan's Syntax would be of use to you, but you can ask your instructors. I send by Mr. Johnson the money you require. I much approve of your plan of keeping a particular account of all your outlayings, and be careful of your money. Shun bad company, do not get too soon intimate with any person, try all you can to keep both tables of the Law, viz., your duty to God and to man.
>
> "I remain your affectionate father,
>
> "JOSEPH JUNKIN."

Another, dated a year and a half later, contains a succinct argument in support of the position that the doctrine of predestination does not destroy mental *freedom* or *responsibility*, nor supersede the use of means. So much only is inserted as will give a specimen of the father's mode of thought, which the son inherited and improved.

"January 29, 1811.

"My Son,—If you receive this letter you will have it in your power to read it or not read it, to burn it or not burn it, to show it to a fellow-student or not to show it. These, and many other things relative to it, you will feel yourself at liberty to do or not to do; and whichever of them you *shall* do is exactly what was predetermined to be done. Here, I think, is freedom of will, and here is predestination,—both existing without much contradiction.

"That it is perfectly agreeable to the nature of things as divinely constituted that the destination of each should be unalterably fixed or predetermined, and that it is impossible it should be otherwise, seems to me an undeniable truth. A person must either die, or live forever, and only one of these can possibly take place, for it is self-evident that he cannot both die and continue to live here forever. And if he dies he must die at some one time, in some one place, and in some one manner, for he cannot die at two different times, and in two different places and ways; therefore it follows that whichever of the two events, death or life, with the one time, place, and manner thereof, is the only one possible, and must have been fixed.

"Moreover, all the thoughts, words, and actions of mankind, all the movements, both of the animate and inanimate creation, must necessarily go on in a certain manner, because it is impossible to reverse the actual state of things, or cause it *not to be*. A man's mother is his mother, and he is her son, and this relation is unalterably so.

"On the other hand, suppose them to be *alterable*, and nothing but absurdity follows. The time of a man's birth or death might not be the set time; the manner of it might not be the appointed manner; and the vast movements of creation and providence would be worse than a game of hazard.

"Suppose a man should assert that his destination was not unalterably fixed, but that by Christ's death he was placed in such a state of salvability as that he could save himself, and that he now had it in his power to go either to heaven or hell, as he pleased. Now, by the foregoing reasoning, that same man will be either saved or not saved, for he cannot be both saved and damned; and, even if he has the power of choice, I would say his destiny was fixed;

because whatever may be the event was the very thing predestined; and all the *steps* and *means* used to bring about the event were also fixed, and none else could take place. On the whole, I cannot see that even the admission of the above Arminian sentiment, in its full force, will shake the doctrine of predestination, or involve the Calvinist in greater difficulties than the Arminian. . . . .

"A very dreadful calamity lately occurred at the Falls of Niagara. Four men were crossing the stream on a boat loaded with salt. They were, by the force of the current and a storm, forced into the tremendous rapids; the steering oar was thrown off, and one of the men, leaping upon it, struggled for the shore, and was saved. The boat, with the other three, was driven over the falls, and seen no more. Now will any man say that, if this fourth man had sat still in the boat, he would not have gone over with the rest, or that he would have been saved without using any means or exertion to save himself? I presume not. So the means must be used, in spiritual things also, or the end cannot be attained; and both the *means* and the *end* are alike predetermined, and in such a manner as to leave the agent *so far free* as to make him responsible, and the object of blame, if duty be neglected.

"Had the man sat still in the boat, and reasoned thus, 'My doom is fixed: if born to be drowned I cannot escape, and if not, I may: I will make no exertion;' or, after reaching the oar, had he, under a similar abuse of the doctrine, ceased to make exertion, he would have been lost. But he found himself in possession of *means* of escape (not very promising, either); he used the means with all his might, and was saved. Had he neglected exertion, he had failed in duty. But, believing that the oar and his own efforts were the *predestined means* of deliverance, *he used means*. . . . . . I have not brought forward Scripture in this letter, though there is abundance which would apply; but this you can find in your Bible. . . .

"Your affectionate father,

"JOSEPH JUNKIN."

CHAPTER VI.

War—Patriotism—Mercer Blues—Professes Religion—Rev. James Galloway—Closet in a Thicket—Religious Experience—Family Changes—Alleghany City in 1812—Sad Tidings from Home—Returns Home—Perils by the Way—The Mother's Death—Graduation.

WHILST Mr. Junkin was still in college, the troubles between the United States and Great Britain reached their crisis, and resulted in the war between these powers, begun in 1812, and public affairs were discussed in the correspondence between the home circle and the student. The letters all indicate strong indignation against the wrongs of America, and against the insults offered to our flag. There was organized at Mercer a large company of volunteer soldiers, of which the older brother, John Junkin, was captain, and the brother-in-law, Walter Oliver, and the second brother, Joseph Junkin, were subalterns. They tendered their services to aid General Harrison in his Northwestern campaign, in 1812-13. Previous to their marching, and during one of his visits home, the student was invited to deliver an address before this body of soldiers. The writer has heard survivors of that gallant band speak of that address with warm admiration; and it is manifest that the youth of 1812 exhibited in his oration the same spirit of devotion to country, which, half a century afterwards, the old man of threescore and twelve displayed in the "Political Fallacies," and in many an address, and in many an effort to preserve the American Union.

That company, the "Mercer Blues" as they were called, was a remarkable body of citizen soldiers. They numbered some eighty rifles; and so large a proportion of them were pious young men, that, in every tent except two, family worship was maintained by the mess during the campaign, and in those two the captain often officiated. Nor did their devotion diminish the perfection of their military discipline and efficiency. Their drill was as perfect as that of regulars, and General Harrison often complimented them for their gallantry and soldierly bearing.

But during these college years another important step in his moral and religious history was taken. The evidence of the great change, which, as we have seen, he thought had occurred in his tenth year, became more satisfactory; his perception of the plan of salvation became clearer; and, having embraced the promises of the covenant of grace, he made public profession of his faith in Christ.

"During these four and a half (college) years, I was greatly exercised on the subject of my soul's welfare. Sometimes I thought that if two Sabbaths could come together I would get through my difficulties. Often, under Dr. McMillan's preaching, my feelings became intense. No one ever said a word to me privately. I felt the burden of sin, but was long in obtaining a clear view of the method of deliverance. I still incline to the belief that the mustard-seed was planted and became a living thing in 1799; but its growth was slow,—ah, how slow! But, nevertheless, I was regular in prayer, and always attentive to public and social worship; yet in this last I was sometimes wearied and impatient at the long prayers of some of Dr. M.'s elders; doubtless my want of heart in the matter formed an element in my weariness.

"In 1811, when at home, I first became acquainted with the Rev. James Galloway, who had some time before been ordained and installed over the Associate Reformed Church of Mercer, of which my father was a ruling elder. He was not a very profound scholar, but was naturally shrewd, logical, eloquent, and earnest. He was a graduate of Jefferson, and of Dr. Mason's Seminary. His preaching gave me the first clear views of the atonement and justification, and led me to enjoy comfort in believing, and to profess Christ. My father had told me, before I had heard Mr. Galloway, that I would hear 'something entirely different' from the preaching I had been accustomed to hear. And so I found it. The way of deliverance from sin by the blood of Christ,—of justification by his righteousness,—of sanctification by his Spirit, all became plain. My doubts and fears passed away, and I came to enjoy a good hope. I found more comfort in secret devotion. I used to walk out in the morning, for secret prayer and meditation. I selected a retired spot, on the bank of the Neshannock Creek, in the midst of a thicket of elder-bushes, as my closet; and there I wrestled often with the Angel of the covenant. When in Mercer County last, ten years ago (1851), I went down and looked at the place. That year I formally united with the church, came to the holy sacrament of the Supper, and have enjoyed a general calm and steady hope ever since. It was in the courthouse, in Mercer, where the congregation then worshipped, that I first sealed the covenant. Often, indeed, up to the present time, have I had fights with Satan and 'the lust of the flesh, the lust of the eyes, and the pride of life;' but through grace I have been kept for these fifty years, and God will keep me to the end."*

During the summer of 1811, he spent most of the time at Hope Mills, and all his vacations were spent there, except the spring vacation of 1813, which was passed at Canonsburg. Whilst at home, his young pastor, Mr. Galloway, was his room-mate, and he not only heard him often from the pulpit, but was much in his private society; and doubtless this intercourse was blessed, as a means of producing the result above described.

In the March (12) of 1812, Mr. Galloway was married to the sister (Agnes) of Mr. Junkin, by the Rev. George Buchanan, pastor of the Associate Reformed Church, of Steubenville; and on the 6th of the following June, Mr. Buchanan was married, by Mr. Galloway, to another sister, Mary. These sisters were twins, and bore so close a resemblance to each other, that even their own children

* Rem.

sometimes failed to distinguish them. They were women of remarkable intelligence and decided Christian character.

Other events in the family history of an exciting, and some of them of a sad character, were now to follow in rapid succession. We have mentioned that the adult "boys" of the family had volunteered in the military service of their country. They marched to the frontier just before the student returned to college, in the autumn of 1812. On his way to Canonsburg *via* Pittsburg, to make some arrangements, he passed their encampment.

"I found them, with other troops, encamped near to the base of 'Hog-back,' now Alleghany City. The plain on which that part of the city now stands was overgrown with thick bushes eight or ten feet high. They had cut off the bushes from a space upon the spot where the Western Penitentiary now stands, and there they had pitched their tents; and thence they marched to reinforce General Harrison, at Fort Meigs. They had volunteered for six months, but remained more than seven, until Harrison said he was safe without them. They (the Mercer Blues) found their own clothing, uniform, and all their own rifles, tomahawks, and knives, and their own Bibles and Psalm-books. From Canonsburg I proceeded to Steubenville, Ohio, to visit my sister (Mrs. Buchanan) and family.

"There I heard of General Hull's surrender of the fort and army at Detroit, and witnessed the departure of Colonel Andrew's regiment for the Northwest, General Ben Tappan at its head. Brother Buchanan and I had accompanied the troops a few miles, and when we returned to town, we found a neighbor of the family at Hope Mills, who had ridden express, to bear to us the sad tidings that our mother had fallen, broke her spinal column, and would probably die. My sister set out with him forthwith, direct for Mercer. I mounted and rode for Pittsburg, to call on an eminent physician there. I rode thirty-six miles that night,—tried to force my horse into the swollen current of Chartiers's Creek, but he refused to enter. God would not permit me to drown myself and horse. I was compelled to wait for daylight. Next day rode to Pittsburg, and thence home, sixty-five miles in all,—the longest horseback ride I ever made in one day. My dear mother suffered greatly. She said from the first she must die. She had often said, when the conversation had turned upon the approaching conflict with Britain, that she had seen one war, and she hoped she might not see another. Her wishes were gratified, though not precisely as she meant. She spoke calmly, almost triumphantly, of her approaching death, admonished us all to prepare, and remarked that none of us would be any great charge except David (the youngest). I told her not to be uneasy, that I would see that he should be taken care of. She said, 'The Lord will take care of you all if you only trust in Him.' I asked her if she felt that He had done so for her. She replied, 'Oh, yes, I trust He has.' The family was standing around the bed as the last moment drew on; and after speech failed, she turned her eyes upon those on the right, then upon those on the left, looking each deliberately in the face, as if to look farewell, until she came to father, and on him she gazed to the last. . . . . Oh, how my heart did bleed! and, oh, how earnestly I did pray the Lord to receive her to Himself! This prayer was, I have not a doubt, answered to the full, for she had for scores of years labored to glorify Him before the world, in a lovely and consistent Christian life."*

It is with a full and grateful heart, that the writer of these pages records that the pledge given to his dying mother, by this beloved brother, fifty-eight years ago, was faithfully and lovingly redeemed. He *did* care for his baby-brother, with all a brother's tenderness, with all a father's solicitude; cared for him then,—cared for him through the educational period; and the more than paternal affection and fellowship of half a century have attested the strength and warmth of that love, which was enjoined by a dying mother's latest breath, and cherished, most likely, by her unseen angel-ministrations.

---

* Rem.

In September, 1813, he passed his final examinations, and was admitted to the first degree in the arts, and shortly afterwards proceeded to Philadelphia, and thence to New York, to begin the study of theology under the great Dr. Mason. But as his journey thither was in strong contrast, as to time and mode, with journeys made between the same points now, we give his own account of it. This, with some retrospective matters, will be given in the next chapter.

CHAPTER VII.

Repairs to the Theological Seminary—Sets out—Last Interview with his Elder Brother—Correspondence between the Soldier and the Student—Journey to Philadelphia—Visit to Cumberland—The School—Disappointment—Philadelphia—First Interviews with Life-long Companions.

"IN October, 1813, I left home for New York, to study theology with Dr. Mason. My father gave me a horse and an outfit, and some money. At Pittsburg I met my eldest brother, John, homeward bound from Washington City. We stayed together that night at a hotel, and next morning we parted, never more to meet on earth. He had been appointed to a captaincy in the regular army of the U. S., at the instance, as we always supposed, of General Harrison. My brother proceeded to Erie, and acted there as aid to General Tanehill. Afterwards was ordered on recruiting service to Mercer. Some of his men were taken sick in barracks, and in attending them he contracted a camp fever, and died April 27, 1814. He was a man of piety and prayer, of superior talents, great administrative ability, and very much of a favorite with the army and the public. His wife had died whilst he was absent in the Northwestern army, leaving an only daughter, now the wife of Hon. Wm. M. Francis, of Lawrence Co."*

The two brothers, whose last earthly interview is recorded above, were both remarkable men; and their characters, as formed under the influence of parental piety and prayer, give great encouragement to parents to be faithful, whilst they attest the truth of a covenant-keeping God.

Captain John Junkin was the only one of the seven brothers who was not either a minister or an elder in the

* Rem.

church, and he was, perhaps, the most devout of the seven who attained man's estate; but, as above mentioned, he died young. He had already excited high expectations in the public mind of his future usefulness and eminence. The people of his district had, in his absence, nominated him for a seat in the State legislature, but he declined it, on account of his military engagements. A few extracts from letters that passed between the student brother in college, and the soldier brother on the tented field, will show something of the spirit by which they were animated, whilst they will shed light upon the history of the period. The student thus writes:

"HOME, October 21, 1812.

"DEAR BROTHER,—Not that I can convey any important news, nor that I can communicate any instruction, but with the hope of administering some consolation and Christian exhortation, I take this opportunity of addressing you.

"Since receiving news from you, Martha [the soldier's wife] is quite cheerful, and appears quite resigned to the dispensation of Providence that separates you, and you may be sure that if you write often you will relieve the anxiety of all your friends. To-morrow I intend starting for Canonsburg, and if you will direct your letters to that place I will receive them, but the uncertainty of your location will render it difficult for my letters to reach you. But let not this prevent you from writing to me.

"You doubtless know that Christian duties are apt to be shamefully neglected in all armies, and from your Bible you have learned, that when the Israelites neglected their Creator He punished them; but when their armies went forth trusting in and calling upon their God, He granted their requests, and made them to triumph over their enemies. This will ever be the case; and I confidently expect (and this forms part of my daily prayer), that those men who daily called upon the Lord while abiding in quiet, peaceful homes, will not now, when called into danger, neglect this important duty. You know that military duty is apt to become irksome, on account of the men having so little to do. What employment, then, could engage the attention of the Christian soldier better than reading and meditating upon that volume of inspiration which is worthy the study of the wisest? In this you will find abundant employment for your leisure moments. When I picture to myself a band of soldiers, sitting in the howling wilderness, surrounded by the savage foe, singing the praises of their God, I say to myself, Surely the Lord will go forth with their hosts, and my mind is filled with the highest hopes for your success. . . . . I must conclude, commending you to the care of Him who has ever preserved you, and assuring you that your welfare and success are near my heart. Remember me to 'the Mercer Blues' in terms of the highest respect.

"Your friend and brother,

"GEO. JUNKIN."

The soldier brother writes to the student as follows:

"NORTHWESTERN ARMY, NEAR MANSFIELD, OHIO,
"November 30, 1812.

"DEAR BROTHER,—I am happy to inform you that I am well, and that all my company are fit for duty except two. . . I expect both will soon be well. A melancholy accident happened yesterday morning before daylight. A violent storm of wind blew down a tree upon our line of tents (Capt. Dawson's company), which killed one, and severely wounded five others. . . . You can imagine what a distressing scene this was to us; but it might have been more so. He who ruleth all things hath his design in every event that takes place. Let man, poor mortal man, who cannot see one moment before him, be always ready to meet his fate, whether prosperous or adverse. Our battalion marched from here to-day as a guard to the artillery (thirty-one pieces) for Upper Sandusky. A body of troops lie at Lower Sandusky, a body at Huron, and the Kentuckians and Virginians move on to meet us at Upper Sandusky. General Tupper, with five hundred men, gave the Indians a severe brush at the rapids of Maumee, without the loss of a man in battle. He lost four killed and one wounded afterwards by a fire from a cornfield. I do not think we will see any Indian enemy this side of Detroit River; but if we should, and have to meet them in battle, I trust I shall be enabled to discharge my duty, both as a soldier and a Christian, putting my trust where it may be safely placed. Our cause is a just one, and I have engaged in it, believing it to be so; and I will go forward with a full persuasion of assistance and protection from Him who is the Lord of armies, and who ruleth them as He sees proper. Do not forget to write to me often, and forgive my negligence, for I have little time to spare, and a very inconvenient way of writing. But believe me, sir, your most affectionate brother,

"JOHN JUNKIN."

The answer to the above, alluded to in the following, is not preserved. The soldier brother writes:

"HEADQUARTERS, MIAMI RAPIDS,
"February 12, 1813.*

"DEAR BROTHER,—I received yours of the 26th ult., and intended answering it from Upper Sandusky, but was ordered off suddenly, and had not time; and now you can have but barely an acknowledgment. We arrived here yesterday. Our force I do not precisely know—perhaps five thousand. More will soon join us. Winchester's misfortune, at the river Raisin, you will have heard of perhaps more correctly than I could state it. Harrison pursued a body of Indians, two nights since, about twenty-five miles. They headed for Malden, and he returned to camp. Our army is well supplied. . . . . Desertion is not now frequent. The *cowards*, I think, are now all drained from among us, and the men now present in the army will do more than if they that have deserted had remained with us.

"What the intended movements of the army are, none but General Harrison knows; and it is right it should be so. What the results of the movements may be, God only knows. He who ruleth the armies of men, and giveth the battle to whom He pleaseth, can save by many or by few. That we may all be enabled to place our trust in the King of kings is the prayer of your

"Most affectionate brother,
"JOHN JUNKIN."

---

* Two days after the date of this letter, the young wife of the writer of it died, at his home at the Hope Mills.

This much of the correspondence between these brothers will suffice to show the spirit of the young men, as Christians and as patriots; and we digress no further. The student brother always retained a deep affection for the soldier. They met no more in this life after the parting above described. The one returned to his military duties upon our threatened frontier, the other proceeded to New York to prosecute his theological studies. We give, in his own words, his reminiscences of that journey:

"Next day, after leaving Pittsburg, as I was ascending Turtle Creek Hill, eastward, I met some wagons hauling goods from Philadelphia. They had doubled teams *going down hill*, and yet were 'stalled' in the mud, with seven horses in a team. One of them shouted, as I passed, 'Glorious work for ten dollars a hundred!' Thus, in October, 1813, men complained that ten dollars was too little compensation for hauling one hundred and twelve pounds of goods from Philadelphia to Pittsburg. Lo, the change! Now it can be done for one-twentieth of that sum. On Sideling Hill, near Mercersburg, I fell in with the Rev. John Jamieson, once pastor at Newville, and we rode together nearly to that town. He was the grandfather of the Rev. Jesse M. Jamieson, our missionary to India."

He then gives details of his visits in Cumberland County, which, although interesting to the family and their circle of acquaintances, would not interest the general reader. He visited his native mansion, walked over the grounds and through the apartments, and called upon many friends of his boyhood:

"I hitched my horse in front of the old schoolhouse, and went in, and tried whether Master Jamieson would know me. But he did not. When I told him who I was, he seemed much moved, and very glad to see me. There were no scholars that I knew, though others of the same old families filled the benches. Seven years had made more changes in the schoolhouse than elsewhere in the neighborhood. I went down to D—— W——'s, but ——* was not there. She was at Dr. Smith's, in Princeton, New Jersey.

"Next day I went through Harrisburg. The bridge over the Susquehanna at that place was partly built, but we crossed in a scow. At Lancaster I sold (by auctioneer in the street) my horse, saddle, and bridle, and next day set out by stage for Philadelphia. Arrived there, I proceeded to deliver a letter of introduction from Mr. Galloway to the Rev. Dr. Gray, by whom and his family I was very kindly received. I was there introduced to Mr. John Knox† and his brother Samuel. The former, like myself, was on his way to Dr. Mason's seminary, at New York; the latter had come to take back the horse which he had ridden, for at that time there was no public conveyance from Gettysburg, near to which, in Adams County, the Knox family lived.

"Next day, a young lady came in from the marble house, just round the corner (Tenth and Market) from Dr. Gray's. Her father was a ruling elder in the (Scots') church of which Dr. Gray was pastor, and the families were in close intimacy; and there, in that back parlor, I for the first time met one who was destined to bless me in a life of peace and joy known to few married pairs. Thanks be to God for his wondrous goodness.

"Mr. Knox and I remained two or three days in Philadelphia, both probably having some attractions. I was a *novus homo*, and had many sights to see in the city; and the acquaintances we had made were pleasant. By this delay we lost Dr. Mason's introductory lecture. For two years there was before my eyes a vivid image of her whom I had met at Dr. Gray's. Then I heard in New York that the Rev. Charles G. McLean had married one of the Misses M. 'Which of them?' I inquired. 'The handsomest,' was the reply. This threw a damper over my

---

* Mrs. W. had been the widow of Dr. Witherspoon, and was now the wife of Mr. W——, and her daughter is alluded to in the text; the object of a boy affection. She was afterwards the wife of Dr. Woods, of Lewistown.

† Here began an acquaintance and friendship that was life-long. See Appendix A.

spirits,—I dared no further inquiry. More than a year passed after this before I ascertained that Mr. McLean had married the third Miss M., whom I had not seen when in Philadelphia, she having been with her sick father at their country-seat, near Valley Forge. So the youngest was still left."

CHAPTER VIII.

Journey to New York—State of Travel in 1813—Crossing the Hudson—The Slidells—First Meeting with Dr. Mason—Sketch of that Great Man—His Mode of Teaching—Commentators—Dr. Mason as a Preacher—His Wonderful Labors—The First Prayer-Meeting—The First Sabbath-School in N. Y.—Mr. J. the First Superintendent—Mr. J. Teaches—Elder Garrett Hyer—Pupils—Mrs. Bethune—Mrs. Graham—Dr. G. W. Bethune—Seminary Friendships—Eminent Contemporaries—Correspondence—Return to Hope Mills—Thirty Pieces of Silver.

"BUT, to return to historical order. Brother Knox and I started for New York by the 'swift sure line' of stages. We left Philadelphia at daylight, crossed the Delaware at New Hope, and lodged the first night at Somerville, and reached Paulus Hook a little before sunset the next day. I have lived to pass from city to city in a little more than three hours. We crossed the Hudson in a 'shallop,' shaped a good deal like a clam-shell. Cross ledges were nailed to the bottom at either end, to prevent horses from slipping as they entered or went out. A similar contrivance gave them sure footing upon the inclined plane, formed of planks, that constituted the landing on either side; and this plane was far under water, as to its lower portion, at high tide. The shallop had a mast and sails, as well as oars. It would sail only when there was a full load, and, as the stage did not go over, we had to wait a considerable while, until a sufficient number of carts and horses came to justify the voyage. Such was travel between the two great cities fifty years ago.

"My emotions were very vivid when Brother Knox, who had been to the seminary before, pointed out, from the top of Bergen Hill, the various steeples of the city, and, among them, that of Dr. Mason's church, in Murray Street, where I expected to be a worshipper for four years. . . . . I remained with Brother Knox that night at his boarding-house in Walker Street, and the next morning went to see my friend McElroy,* at his boarding-place in Lispenard Street, and with him went to Dr. Mason's, and was introduced to that great man, great preacher, and great teacher, together with many of his students. . . . . I went to boarding with a Mrs. Watson, in Liberty Street, near Greenwich. There were eight inmates of the family, . . . all now dead, unless it be H. Dodge, who has since been U. S. Senator from Wisconsin, and myself. How transient and vain is human life! . . . . There was no gas in New York then, and the first candles I bought were short six-dips, bought from John Slidell, a tallow-chandler in Broadway, whose shop, a one story, or story and a half, frame, stood opposite the lower part of Trinity Churchyard. This tallow-chandler was a respectable man, and, in my judgment, far superior to his son John, of secession notoriety, who was the boy in the shop who served me with short sixes.

"Prof. James M. Matthews was instructor in Hebrew and church history in our seminary. He was at the same time pastor of Gardner Street—the South Dutch—Church. He was not very popular with the students in either department, and, indeed, it would have been difficult for even a man of abilities superior to his to have made any impression alongside of the great Mason. . . . . Of Dr. Mason the highest respect, veneration, and love pervaded all his students. His person was commanding, tall, erect, large, and dignified; his presence and manner graceful, kind, courteous. At first one felt awe-struck in his presence, but, after a few moments' conversation, felt perfectly at ease, and embosomed in friendship and confidence. He had a wonderful capacity to *draw out* a young man, and make him think for himself. Indeed, he often said, 'You must educate yourselves. I can do but little for you, and that little is just to guide you in the work of self-education.'

"Dr. Mason's method of instruction was the conversational lecture. He held that a system of read lectures was never efficient; this he called the pumping system. . . . To aid the student in thinking, he submitted a series of questions upon every subject studied. He carried on three

---

* Dr. Joseph McElroy, another life-long friend.

courses,—Old Testament difficulties, New Testament difficulties, and Systematic Theology, the Confession of Faith being the text-book. On the other subjects the original Hebrew and Greek were the only text-books, but reference was made to authors for aid. He everywhere interrogated his students, stating difficulties and asking their solution. He was never satisfied with a statement of what the reference books said, but 'What do *you* think and say on this subject? What does the *Bible* say? How do *you* understand its teaching?' Human authority in divine things he always and utterly ignored. He rather discouraged reading, and especially commentators. 'First of all,' he would say, 'go to the originals; study, labor, compare; and when you have worked out your matter yourself, then you may consult commentators to advantage; but do not go to them in the first instance, or you will sacrifice the independence of your own minds, and take for commandments the doctrines of men.'

"As a preacher, my estimate of him may be inferred from the fact that during the first three sessions he never delivered a discourse in New York that I did not hear. The fourth I missed some, because, having been licensed to preach, I was often called to preach myself, and so could not hear him. His power in the pulpit as an expounder and enforcer of Bible truth was unique, and bid defiance to all comparison. I never heard any other preacher in whom I could find the elements of a comparison. The grand subject of our Saviour's divinity, anything that tended to enhance our estimate of the glory of the Son of God, instantly aroused him, and called forth all the energies of this intellectual giant. No man, in the range of my knowledge, could ever roar like this lion, or soar like this eagle. Oh, how often I have wished that I could live always in New York and be under his ministry!

"He never used notes in the pulpit until near his end, and was much opposed to the practice. Reading is not preaching, and no man can throw his soul into his utterances who is tied down to paper. But there is no man so strong but that he may be overburdened and broken down. He was Provost of Columbia College, pastor of a new and large church, and professor in the seminary. He had about sixteen sermons, lectures, and recitations per week. He had no salary as professor of the seminary, and that from the congregation was inadequate to support his family, *therefore* he undertook the college labor, and was thus crushed down in the middle of his days! The church, by imposing upon one man the work of three, broke him down by his fiftieth year, thus losing twenty years' service of this great champion of truth."*

Whilst in attendance at the theological seminary, that earnest spirit of Christian enterprise that marked the whole career of Dr. Junkin began to develop itself. He was one of the organizers of the first public social prayer-meetings held in the Associate Reformed Church; and he opened with prayer the meeting called to organize the first Sabbath-school, and of that school he was the first superintendent. Of these facts the following mention is made in the Reminiscences:

"The great *desideratum* of that day, in the Associate Reformed Churches, was the social prayer-meeting. There were two or three small private meetings, of perhaps eight to fifteen persons, kept up in private parlors. One of these, which I generally attended, was held at the house of Elder Rich. These were useful, but there was no prayer-meeting of a public character, to which all were invited, until 1815. Brother Robert McCartee (afterwards Dr. McCartee) and I busied ourselves in regard to this matter. We went to the pastors, Drs. Mason, Clarke, and McLeod, and, obtaining their consent, commenced a meeting which never stopped. We got the ministers to come, generally, and make addresses, and the laymen to lead in prayer. It was opened in the schoolroom of the old Scotch Church in Pine Street, now Dr. McElroy's in Fourteenth Street. Of the early and active promoters of the prayer-meetings, was ruling elder Garrett Hyer, a wholesale grocer and an active co-laborer with Dr. Mason in the Murray Street Church. At the close of my first session, in the spring of 1814, this gentleman invited me to make one of his family, and oversee the studies of his children, and see

---

* Rem.

that they got their lessons well for the schools which they attended. Besides this, I taught arithmetic one hour a day in a female seminary, conducted by Miss McLeod. There were only two boys in the school, by special favor, Alexander Slidell, brother of John, and Alexander Rogers, grandson of Dr. Rodgers, pastor of the First Presbyterian Church. The former had his name changed, by the addition of McKenzie; he became an officer in the U. S. navy, and was the same who hung, at the yard-arm, young Spencer and another youth for attempted mutiny, and whose own neck was afterwards broken by his horse falling in the streets of Sing Sing.

"In February or March, 1815, Dr. Mason gave notice from the pulpit, one Sabbath morning, inviting the people, gentlemen particularly, to remain after the congregation was dismissed, to take into consideration the formation of a Sabbath-school. Alderman McCartee, an elder, asked me to open the meeting with prayer, which I did. Arrangements were made and a school organized by the next Sabbath. I was made superintendent, and remained so till I left the city. Mrs. Bethune had held a school in her parlor the Sabbath before. But ours was the first public organization of a Sabbath-school. Others, however, were formed the same day. Mrs. Bethune had received papers from Mr. Bogue, of England, giving accounts of their operation in that country.

"This eminently godly woman is too well known to need mention from me. The daughter of that eminent saint, Isabella Graham, and wife of that man of God, Divie Bethune, she was the mother of that very popular and impressive preacher, George W. Bethune, D.D. By way, as I supposed, of aiding me, and of getting George trained to regular habits of study, she sent him to me, for instruction in history, etc., one hour a day.

"In 1815, the ladies of Mr. Hyer's family and myself spent some two months of the hot term at the seashore, near Shrewsbury River. Mr. Hyer and the boys came down generally on Saturday, and we enjoyed salt-water and sea-air, with rough country fare, with a zest. This rustication was of great advantage to my health."

During these years of seminary life, Mr. Junkin had

formed friendships with a pretty large circle of his fellow-students, many of whom have been eminent lights of the church and the world in their generation. These friendships were fostered by close and genial Christian intimacy in term-time, and by correspondence during vacations, and after some of his friends who were further advanced in their studies had left the seminary and entered upon active ministerial life. Many of these friendships proved life-long, and of a warmth and permanency rarely witnessed in this world of selfishness. It has often and truthfully been remarked, that Dr. Mason's students retained for each other a very ardent and lasting regard, which years, distance, and the cares of life and of official duty seemed powerless to abate. And they were no ordinary men. A remarkable proportion of them became eminent in the sacred profession, occupied the high places of the field, and were noted for ability, efficiency, and usefulness in their Master's service. Such were Drs. Knox, McElroy, Phillips, DeWitt, of Harrisburg, Duncan, McClelland, Duffield, Campbell, C. G. McLean, Presley, of Pittsburg, Steel, Galloway, MacDill, Van Vechten, and many others.

The writer has had opportunities of noting this characteristic of Dr. Mason's pupils, a phenomenon in social and even in Christian life as unusual as it is pleasing. He has heard others commenting upon it, and cannot but think that it is attributable, in great measure, to the impress left upon them by that great master in Israel. Rarely has there been such a combination of transcendent intellect, large and loving heart, gentle magnanimity, profound erudition, childlike humility, commanding physique, courtly yet conciliatory manners, and impressive presence, as met in Dr. Mason. Rarely has there arisen a great teacher who could so impress *himself* upon his pupils; and rarely has one been found, the *tout ensemble* of whose character and presence so tended to wither, in those who approached him, the baser elements of manhood. Meanness quailed before him, and he seemed to possess an almost magnetic power of attracting others to the emulation of his own high habitude. Loving Christ with intense fervor, and loving his students for Christ's sake, they seemed to breathe, whilst with him, an atmosphere of love, that ever after drew them to one another. In the eloquent language of his worthy grandson:

"Dr. Mason's moral qualities were commensurate with his towering mental endowments. His standard of excellence was a lofty one. That which was low and mean and grovelling he could not abide. It was spurned from his presence. Yet was he tender as the most loving woman, and ready to condescend to those of low estate, and help them to rise. His students were his friends and his brethren. They were gathered to his heart in the most sincere regard and love, and whatever he had, or could command, was freely devoted to their use and enjoyment. It was not, then, wonderful, that in this seminary were formed friendships of the tenderest and most enduring character, and that from it went forth, to the service of the church, men fully equipped to do duty most effectively, and in the sublime spirit of true Christian devotion. It is not wonderful, that, to their latest hours, they loved each other with a mighty love, and kindled always into a fervent glow in the memories of the years they had spent under the instruction of their almost idolized preceptor!"*

Dr. Junkin, with that systematic order which marked his life and was an element of his success, had preserved, in regular files, most, if not all, of his correspondence; and the letters from his fellow-students, extending through a period of fifty-five years, contain abundant proof of the facts just commented upon. The writer was strongly tempted to make copious extracts from these and other letters, not only to illustrate the above interesting fact,

* Dr. J. H. Mason Knox's discourse, commemorative of Dr. Junkin.

but because they afford very interesting indices of the *spirit* of the periods at which they were written, contain many facts not elsewhere recorded, and evolve, in no small measure, the inner life that gave shape to much of the ecclesiastical history of the period in which these distinguished men were actors. He is restrained only by the considerations that these letters were not written for the public eye,—that most of their authors have gone to their reward, and their consent cannot be obtained,—and because their insertion would swell this volume beyond the allotted limits.

Circumstances occurred which induced Mr. Junkin to defer attendance upon the fourth year's studies in the seminary course until after his licensure, and some time was spent in actual labor in the field. These circumstances he details in his Reminiscences, as follows:

"Early in June, we received information [he was then at the seashore] that Dr. Mason was about to make a voyage to Europe, and would be absent a year. I did not care to spend a session at the seminary without his presence and instructions. I concluded, under advice of my Presbytery, to take license to preach, and await Dr. M.'s return. The rule of the Associate Reformed Church made it obligatory upon all their students to study four years at the seminary before licensure. I accepted the proffer of license, upon the express condition, that I should be permitted to spend the fourth session at the seminary after Dr. Mason should return, as the studies of the fourth year were chiefly under his instruction. Dr. M. heard of my proposed license, and wrote to me a most earnest letter, remonstrating against my course, closing with this remark: 'Never sacrifice great general principles to mere temporary expedients.'

"The Presbytery [of Monongahela] having assigned me subjects for trial, I went West with a view to meet Presbytery. My friend McElroy, the two Lees, and myself, procured a two-horse conveyance, and set out to go *via* Easton, Allentown, Reading, Harrisburg, and Carlisle, direct to Pittsburg. We were rather a jovial party, and the journey, though long, was a pleasant one. After spending a Sabbath in Cumberland County, we reached Pittsburg in safety. The chief embarrassment in travelling, at that period, was the want of money that would pass. Specie was hid away. There was nothing to be had but paper rags, mostly of local circulation. My kind friend Mrs. Hyer, anticipating this difficulty, had quietly stored away, for my use, all the silver pieces she could obtain; so that I had enough to bear me through: all, too, in small pieces. After arriving at Mercer I had some left, and gave thirty pieces of silver to the Mercer Bible Society, remarking, in a public meeting, 'Here are thirty pieces of silver, the same *number* at which a great personage was valued. I give it to promote His glorious cause.' "

CHAPTER IX.

Licensed to Preach—Refused at first by the Presbytery on account of his Liberal Views on Catholic Communion—First Sermon—Worship in the Woods—Casuistic Illustrations—Itinerates—The Fallen Minister and the Temperance Resolve—Called to Newville—Declines it—Synod—First Sermon in Philadelphia—Proceeds as an Itinerant—Visits Northern New York—Final Parting with Galloway—Last Session at the Seminary—Invited to Newburg—Declines—Pearl Street—Wall Street—Dr. Phillips—Leaves New York for Philadelphia—Enters upon Missionary Work—Silas E. Weir—Mrs. Duncan's Vow and Church—Philadelphia in 1817—Ordination—High Sense of Duty—Matrimonial Engagement.

"IN September, with all my trials ready, I went to meet the Presbytery, at Noblestown, Alleghany County, Pa. My exercises were all sustained; but whilst under examination, the Rev. Mungo Dick asked my opinion in regard to intercommunion with other branches of the church,—a subject which, at that time, was exciting great commotion. I stated that my opinions coincided with those of Dr. Mason, who had published a book upon the subject, viz., that all true believers were one in Christ, and might, when occasion offered, hold fellowship at the Lord's table, etc. I was then asked to promise not to preach this doctrine. To this I objected, alleging that there was, in the book directing the mode of license, no such promise authorized or required. I said I did not design to preach it among their churches at that exciting time; but I would not consent to bind myself indefinitely. The Presbytery then refused to license me to preach the gospel. I then asked for a dismission, to place myself under the care of the Presbytery of Big Spring, east of the mountains. They hesitated at this request; and, after some time, they revoked the refusal, licensed me, and gave me appointments to preach in their vacant churches."*

---

* Rem.

It thus appears that, even before he was licensed to preach, Mr. Junkin had taken a firm stand against the restrictive policy in regard to Christian communion, and, whilst willing to submit to his brethren so far as to promise not to agitate this subject among their churches, was firm in adhering to principle, even at the risk of great inconvenience in the disconcerting of his plans.

"The first of the vacancies which I was appointed to supply was Butler, Pa. The appointment was made near sundown on 16th of September, 1816, the day on which I was licensed. Butler was forty-six miles distant,—no notice had been given,—but I reached the place on Saturday P.M., and the next day I preached twice in the court-house of that place. This was my first service as a preacher of the Word. Next Sabbath, September 24, I preached at White-Oak Spring, six miles from Butler, where a tent or *rostrum* was erected, in the wild woods. This was the first time worship was held upon that spot. Afterwards it became the seat of a flourishing church. . . . . The details of my preaching may be found in the memoranda I have always kept. . . . . By these my children can ascertain, if they wish, where I was and what I preached from, any Sabbath since I was licensed, except a very few instances.

"Shortly after the meeting at which I was licensed, the Presbytery met in Pittsburg, to ordain and install, over the first A. R. Church of that city, my dear friend McElroy. During the ordination service, the two ministers who had chiefly opposed my licensure—one from Ireland and another from North Britain—were spending their time at the tavern where they had left their horses. These men were too holy to participate in the ordination of a man who felt himself not too holy to commune with evangelical Christians out of his own denomination; but they were not too holy to drink gin and speak censoriously of the Presbytery and of the man whom they were ordaining. How marvellous the modifications of the human conscience! To sing a hymn or a psalm not of the approved version, or to go to the table of the Lord in another church than your own, is a grievous sin; but to drink gin is no sin, if it be done in connection with ardent zeal for the orthodox faith!

"The next Sabbath (Oct. 1) I spent at Mercer, near to the home of my father. It was sacramental occasion, and I preached four times. . . . . On the last Sabbath of the year I preached in a cabin, some thirty miles west of Cadiz, Ohio. The cabin was about eighteen feet by eighteen, and served for kitchen, parlor, and bedroom, and, on this occasion, for church. It was filled with people to hear the Word, and many, though it was winter, stood outside. . . . . Upon this spot, then nearly a wilderness, there now stands a town, with a college, three churches, and a thrifty population. Next day I reached Pittsburg, and on the following (New Year's) dined with my friend McElroy, upon whom I had waited at his marriage a few weeks before. . . . From Pittsburg I went to Newville, Cumberland Co.; spent a Sabbath at a preaching station down the Juniata, below Bedford, and passed through Black-Log and Ambrose Valleys, and over Black-Log Mountain by an almost impassable bridle-path, and arrived at Newville, where I was asked to preach, with a view to the pastorate. There I preached two Sabbaths. Between them I went to Carlisle, and preached of a Wednesday evening for Brother Duffield.* In his study, at Dr. Armstrong's, he informed me of the fall of the Rev. ——, one of our ministers of brilliant abilities, under the fell power of alcohol. Then and there, before I rose from my seat, I secretly decided a question which the frequent presentation of intoxicating drinks, as a token of hospitality, had forced upon me; and I resolved 'that, God helping me, I would never again drink any ardent spirits, unless indispensable as a medicine.' I never was drunk in my life, never approximated that state, although my father, like others, had always kept it about the house, and it had been used constantly in harvest and under any peculiar exposure. But I had seen so much of its tendency, and had been so often importuned to drink, that I saw my only safety was in total abstinence.

"My visit to Newville resulted in a call, which I was constrained to decline, from considerations frankly and fully expressed to the representatives of the church."†‡

---

* Dr. George Duffield, late of Detroit. † Rem.

‡ One was insufficient support, the other that too much whiskey was used among the people.

In the spring of 1817 Mr. Junkin was at Philadelphia at the meeting of Synod, where he and his friend McElroy were the guests of Mrs. Engles, mother of the Rev. Dr. Wm. M. Engles and his equally learned and excellent brother, Joseph P. Engles. During the sessions of Synod, he preached his first sermon in Philadelphia, from the text, I. John v. 20, "This is the true God." There he renewed his acquaintance with the Miller family, into which he afterwards married. Dr. Mason had, meanwhile, returned from his European tour, and was present at the Synod, and, in the presence of that body, gave a graphic and amusing account of the state of religion in Europe, and especially in France, where most of his time had been spent. After the Synod adjourned, Mr. J. went to New York, accompanied by his brother-in-law, the Rev. James Galloway, travelling on horseback. Mr. Galloway's health was failing, and his tour was made in hope of restoring it.

"The General Synod of the A. R. Church had control of all licentiates and unsettled ministers, and distributed their labors among the Presbyteries according to their several needs. Each Presbytery appointed them to supply particular vacancies whilst within its bounds. I was sent into the bounds of the Presbyteries of New York and Saratoga. Whilst in New York, I preached my first sermon in Dr. Mason's church, and then proceeded to labor until Fall in the bounds of the above-named Presbyteries. My first point, after leaving the city, was Newburg, a vacancy. We crossed at Hoboken, and travelled on horseback up the west side of the river. . . .

"At Newburg we joined Mr. Allen D. Campbell (afterwards Rev. Dr. Campbell, of Pittsburg). After a few days we separated, they, Galloway and Campbell, crossing the North River. I gazed after them as long as they could be discerned, believing, in regard to my dear Galloway, that it was my last sight of him on earth. And so it proved. After preaching two Sabbaths at Newburg, I passed up through Albany and Troy to Cambridge, my next station. Troy was then an insignificant village. I visited Salem, where then resided that eminently godly man, Dr. Proudfit. I never was in a family where religion seemed so much the business of the household. Three times a day they held family worship. His son John, then a boy, was afterwards Dr. Proudfit, Professor in Rutgers College.

"From Salem I went to White Hall,—the Skeensborough of the Revolutionary period,—a small village at the head of Lake Champlain. There I saw the hulks of McDonough's fleet, made of pine timber, and fast decaying. Hence I proceeded to Florida, one of my stations. Thence I visited Union College, at Schenectady. Thence to Caledonia, where I preached two Sabbaths. The congregation here were all Scotch. They showed me great kindness, and made a very pressing request that I should permit them to make out a call for me. But I persisted in my purpose of returning to the seminary. At Caledonia my nice strawberry-roan horse died, and I took stage to Newburg, and thence to New York by a sloop from Kingston.

"I had been written to by the Session of the Second A. R. Church, Pearl Street near Broadway, New York, to come and supply them, but felt bound to fulfil my appointments at Caledonia. Before I returned to the city and had an opportunity of preaching to them, my beloved classmate Phillips* had preached for them, and was called to be their pastor. He labored among them for a few years, and was then called to the pastorate of the First Presbyterian Church, of which he is still (1862) pastor. Their house of worship then stood in Wall Street, between Nassau and Broadway. They subsequently built the house now in Fifth Avenue, and the old stone First Church was taken to Jersey City, stone by stone, and re-erected there, precisely as it stood in Wall Street.

"During the session of 1817–18, I preached again at Newburg, N. Y., and was urged to permit them to make a call for me; but, having visited Philadelphia during the holidays, my attention was drawn to the Margaret Duncan Church, in Thirteenth Street, just erected, and to the proposal to attempt building up a congregation there. I therefore declined acceding to the proposal from Newburg.

---

* Dr. W. W. Phillips.

I spent the winter in New York, at the seminary, occasionally preaching the gospel.*

"In March, 1818, I left New York, and proceeded to Philadelphia. Dr. Mason had just returned from a visit to that city, and informed me that Mrs. Duncan's church edifice, Thirteenth Street, was completed and was a vacancy, and he encouraged me to make an effort to gather a congregation in it. He said the building was too small to contain a congregation large enough to support a minister, but that, if the effort should be successful, the edifice could be enlarged, and that provision would be made for my support as an evangelist. As I was departing from his house, he accompanied me to the door, and gave me a parting blessing, 'Let not your heart be troubled, neither let it be afraid.'

"At Philadelphia, I became an inmate of the family of Mr. Silas E. Weir; and here I remained, at free quarters, until July, when the family left the city, a generous contribution to the missionary effort. And for thirty-six years his house was my home, when in the city. Mr. Weir was a Scotch-Irishman, and a noble specimen of the high-minded and generous Christian gentleman. Besides this, I received from the Philadelphia Missionary Society a small stipend of fifty dollars per month.

"The church edifice stood in Thirteenth Street, half a square north of Market, and was a small but substantial brick structure. It was built in pursuance of the will of Mrs. Margaret Duncan, grandmother of the late Rev. Dr. John M. Duncan, of Baltimore, who had made a vow, during the perils of a storm at sea, that, if spared, she would build a house unto the Lord.†

---

* Rem.

† The Rev. John Chambers, whose ministry was also begun in this house, gives, in an appendix to the sermon preached upon the fortieth anniversary of his pastorate, the following account of this matter:

"The vessel in which Mrs. Duncan came a passenger from Ireland, her native land, was overtaken by a violent storm, which lasted for several days, until the captain and crew gave up in despair, and so announced to the ship's company. Mrs. Duncan, being pre-eminently a woman of God, went, in the midst of the howling tempest and wild wailings of the passengers and crew, in faith to the God of the winds and waves, and invoked his gracious interposition and protection. At the same time, while bowed be-

"My preaching stations were, in the morning of each Lord's day in the Camden Academy, N. J., in Moyamensing in the afternoon, in the Thirteenth Street Church at night, and in a schoolhouse on Front above Arch, Wednesday evenings.

"There were but four or five small houses on Thirteenth near Market Street, four two-story bricks in Market, and a few wooden houses between Thirteenth and 'Centre *Square*,' as it was called, although it was inclosed at that period in one large circular paled fence, with gates for foot-passengers in the centre of Market and Broad Streets. There was a small house for water-works in the centre of the circle, and a vault for oil-barrels on the west side of it. West of this there were not more than six or seven houses, of inferior structure, in Market Street. All the space west of Broad Street, north and south, was unoccupied waste, except a few frame buildings near Paul Beck's shot-tower, on Arch Street about three blocks from the Schuylkill, occupied by the employees about the tower. There was also a little hamlet of small houses about Sixteenth and Walnut, occupied by persons employed about the brick-yards in that locality.

"Such was my missionary field in Philadelphia. Here I labored for six months. But the enterprise was premature. There was but a sparse population and few buildings, and the experiment was but partially successful. Although there was a nucleus for a congregation gathered at Thirteenth Street, it was not such as to encourage an organization, previous to the time I left the field."*

Mr. Junkin was ordained as an Evangelist, *sine titulo*, on the 29th day of June of this year (1818), by the Associate Reformed Presbytery of Philadelphia. The Presbytery felt authorized to take this step in consideration of the

---

fore the God of the Covenant, Mrs. Duncan entered into covenant with God, that, if he would abate the storm and carry the ship's company safe to land, she would cause to be erected a house of worship to his honor and glory. God heard her prayer, the ship was brought safe to land, with her crew and passengers, and Mrs. Duncan fulfilled her vow by the erection of the church on Thirteenth above Market Street."

* Rem.

facts that he had been "a probationer" two years; had proved very acceptable to the congregations; had been proffered several calls to the pastoral office, and that his missionary work required it. The ordination solemnity took place in the A. R. Church, Gettysburg, Pa., in the very place where, forty-five years afterwards, he was found assiduously laboring among the wounded and the dying, during the weeks that succeeded the terrible battle of July 3, 1863. The Rev. John Mason Duncan, of Baltimore, preached the sermon, and the Rev. Dr. Ebenezer Dickey gave the charge.

Mr. Junkin, a year later, became, by his marriage, the brother-in-law of Dr. Dickey, and also of Dr. McLean, the pastor of the church in which he was ordained. The candidate had observed the day preceding his ordination as a day of prayer, with strict fasting. He evidently was impressed with a very high and solemn estimate of the importance and sacredness of the ministerial office, and entered upon the full work of that office with fear and diffidence, and yet with earnest determination to be faithful to his ordination vows. Speaking in his Reminiscences of the occasion of his ordination, he says: "It was a solemn scene. Paul's charge to Timothy lay heavy on my soul." Of the binding obligation of his ordination vows, in all their details, he ever retained a delicate and solemn conviction. He entered the ministry as a life-work; and looked upon ordination vows, not as transient promises, to be kept or not as personal convenience or popularity might suggest, but as engagements made, under the most solemn sanctions to God and to his church, to be literally and faithfully interpreted, and to be of life-long obligation. If those Christians of his generation, who have spoken censoriously of his zeal for God's precious truth, could have looked in upon the chamber of the young licentiate during that day of fasting and prayer at Gettysburg;

could they have witnessed his earnest wrestling with God for grace to be faithful to the vows he was about to assume; and could they have understood, as he did, the promise "to be zealous and faithful in maintaining the truths of the gospel and the peace and purity of the church, whatever persecution or opposition may arise unto you on that account;" they might have been able to make a more just estimate of his life-long and unflinching loyalty to truth. He believed that ordination vows are made to God; that they are registered in heaven; that they bind the conscience, and that in their plain and obvious sense; and that to violate them is a crime partaking of the nature of both *sacrilege* and *perjury.*

After his ordination he returned to Philadelphia and resumed his missionary labor. In the following August he was absent from the city, supplying Mr. Duncan's church in Baltimore for two Sabbaths, and Gettysburg, Bedford, and McConnellsburg, one Sabbath each. He had been importuned by Mr. Duncan and his people, in March and April, to accept of a more protracted engagement in Baltimore, on account of the illness of that distinguished minister. And the correspondence, still on file, is illustrative of Mr. Junkin's scrupulous adherence to the *minutiæ* of what he deemed right. He resisted the importunity to leave, even for a time, his missionary field in Philadelphia, although to have yielded promised pecuniary and other advantages. A brief extract from one of the letters will explain this matter, and show that the young licentiate was as firm in adhering to what he supposed to be his obligations as was the mature man of later life:

"I hope you will not think us too importunate or pressing. If you knew the state of our city, in point of evangelic preaching; the manner in which our people are scattered on the Sabbath, when I am laid by, without a substitute to take my place, and contrast our situation with that of those to whom you minister as a missionary, I know I should find no difficulty to induce you to reconsider the decision you have formed. It is true 'an engagement is sacred, and ought not to be violated, even in appearance, without a reason paramount to the obligation' or sufficient to justify a departure from it. But can you not promise a future compliance? Can you not get somebody to step for the present into your shoes? or can you not arrange the various duties in such a manner as to divide them among a number of ministers? I wish you would explore every avenue, try every expedient, and admit every allowance."

But the young licentiate considered his "engagement so sacred" with his missionary field, that he resisted this importunity, and, with the exception of the two Sabbaths above mentioned, declined laboring in Baltimore.

The Miller family were on a visit to Gettysburg at the time he preached there in August, and on his return journey to Philadelphia Mr. Junkin escorted them to Oxford, Chester County, the seat of the Rev. Dr. Dickey. Meanwhile his intimacy with that family, and especially with the younger daughter, was maturing; and the consummation, which he so earnestly desired, was "engaged" to be made before he left Oxford. "I returned to Philadelphia with feelings of gratitude to God and love to *her*, which human language was not intended to express."* He resumed with diligence his missionary work in Philadelphia, and prosecuted it for some time. But when he more fully compared views in regard to the future, with the lady who was the chosen companion of his life, he found her judgment adverse to remaining in the city: she alleging that "she was unsuited to be the wife of a city pastor!" An estimate of her qualifications which perhaps no human being, besides herself, who knew her, would make. None who

* Rem.

knew her would have hesitated to pronounce her eminently fitted to such a position. But she was as modest of her abilities as she was eminent in every virtue and accomplishment. Yet such was her judgment; and partly influenced by this, and partly by the discouragements connected with the enterprise in which he was engaged in Philadelphia, he began to look elsewhere for a permanent field of labor.

CHAPTER X.

Visit to Milton—Penuel Church—Resumes Work in Philadelphia—Visits his Western Home—Call to Mercer—Frank Response to People of Milton—Marriage—Settlement at Milton.

THERE was a small congregation of the Associate Reformed Church in the vicinity of Milton, Northumberland County, Pennsylvania, and several families attached to that church, living in and near that large and thriving borough, who had as yet no church organization. Having been invited to visit the place, he complied, and preached there for the first time on Sabbath, October 4, 1818.

The church edifice in which the organized congregation worshipped, was more than three miles from the town of Milton, and stood in a fine old pine forest, near to where the village of McEwensville now stands,—about the eighth of a mile south of it. It was a structure of hewn logs, about forty feet square, and, at the time of Mr. Junkin's advent, it was only roofed and floored, with windows and doors, but no gallery or pews. Subsequently it was furnished with pulpit, pews, and a gallery around three sides of the building, which last was reached by a flight of stairs constructed outside the walls of the building. These improvements were made shortly after his settlement, and as the result of his activity. Further on in his ministry it was finished outside with white stucco and pebbles, and neatly plastered within. This building was a place of worship for some years after Dr. Junkin left the field, but was ultimately abandoned, removed, the beautiful grove cut down, and now the plowshare is driven over its site. Though so far from the village of Milton, the families that lived in the village adhering to the A. R. Church, worshipped in this edifice, and hence the congregation was known as the congregation of Milton. But after Mr. Junkin was settled among them, he officiated part of the time in Milton, and, after an edifice was erected in the borough, the church near McEwensville was called, probably at Mr. J.'s suggestion, PENIEL, or more usually PENUEL (see Gen. xxxii. 30–31), and the village church was called SHILOH.

On the 4th day of October, 1818, being Sabbath, he preached twice in the Peniel church, in the morning from Acts xvi. 31, and in the afternoon from John iii. 36. On the Tuesday evening following, he preached his first sermon in the borough of Milton, from Isai. xxxiii. 14, last clause of the verse. On the afternoon of the 7th, he preached in White Deer Valley, on the west side of the Susquehanna, to a congregation that subsequently became a very interesting portion of his pastoral charge. On the 9th, he preached at Milton (Peniel), preparatory to the Lord's Supper; and on the 11th, in the same place, when he administered the Lord's Supper, preaching the same evening in the village. He then returned to Philadelphia, and continued his missionary work. From his preaching register, we ascertain that his stations for holding worship and preaching the Word, were numerous and widely extended. The church in Thirteenth Street was his centre of operations. But, besides this, he had stations in Camden, Schuylkill Front, Moyamensing, and the Philadelphia Almshouse, and occasionally at the corner of Eleventh and Filbert Streets. These labors he continued until the 22d of November, when he left the city and made a visit to his friends in Western Pennsylvania and Ohio, journeying *via* Baltimore, where he preached on the 27th of November,

Chambersburg, and McConnellsburg, at each of which places he officiated on his way westward.

Previous to his departure from Philadelphia on this journey, he had been informed that a call would be made by the people of Peniel and Milton for his pastoral services; and, having decided to accept of this call, he determined, before entering upon his pastoral duties, to make a general visit to his kindred.

It was during this year that a call to the Associate Reformed Churches of Mercer and Shenango, in Mercer County, Pa., was urgently pressed upon him. Early in the spring of 1818 this movement was made, as we gather from his correspondence; but in a letter dated July 19th of that year, and addressed to his brother-in-law, the Hon. John Findley, of Mercer, he assigns reasons why he declined acceding to the wishes of those congregations. Indeed, before the death of the first pastor of that charge, his brother-in-law, the Rev. James Galloway, but after that death became inevitable, Mr. Findley, who was a ruling elder, had written to him upon the subject, and was very importunate. Mr. Junkin's answers to these various letters are lost, but from the replies to them we learn, that the proverb that a "prophet is not without honor save in his own country and among his own kindred," was a dominant consideration with him in declining to enter that field. Another consideration was, that the Presbytery of Monongahela, by which he was licensed, and under the care of which the Mercer charge was, held views on the subject of catholic communion which Mr. Junkin could not adopt. They held to close communion, he repudiated that restriction.

As an illustration of the earnestness with which his labors were sought by the people of Mercer, and as a rather curious specimen of logic and Scripture interpretation, a few extracts from one of the letters (from Mr. Findley) are given:

"I shall now endeavor to convince you that your objections are not sufficient; nay, that your basing your determination upon that text, 'a prophet is not without honor,' etc., is setting it in direct opposition to the conduct of our Saviour himself and that of his Apostles. He and they did preach the gospel among their own kindred. He continued to labor and preach the gospel in his own city until the inhabitants rejected him, cast him out, and sought to destroy him; and it was in reference to this he quoted this proverb. He spent his whole ministerial labors among his kindred according to the flesh; and so did they, until he sent them, by providential indications, to present it to the Gentiles also. . . . . Many of our ministers are settled in the congregation in which they were raised,—Dr. Mason, Mr. Lind, Mr. Henderson, and others; and who are more respected by their flocks, and who are more useful in their generation? . . . . We have had preaching only once since Mr. G.'s death. Mr. F. administered the Lord's Supper. If we remain in this state, what ruin and desolation must result! My four sons are growing up without the benefit of the preached gospel,—your brothers, your brother's children, and many others, are in like condition; and if you were here, many of these young plants might be brought into the vineyard, and some raised up under your ministry to preach the glad tidings of salvation to others. . . . . Pardon me if I am moved to tears in view of our situation."

This letter was dated September 20, 1818.

After he had determined to leave Philadelphia, and after the people of Milton had expressed a desire to obtain his services, he wrote to an elder of that church a frank and explicit statement of the conditions upon which he would be willing to accede to their wishes. After stating that, so far as providential indications showed, he felt it his duty to enter that field, this letter proceeds:

"And that there be no misunderstanding, let me tell you that I must live by the gospel. I intend to spend *all* my time and talents in your service, and to obey the divine command, 'Give thyself wholly unto these things;'

and, therefore, I expect you (I mean the people whose call I shall accept) to hear and obey the command, 'muzzle not the ox that treadeth out the corn;' 'the laborer is worthy of his hire.' . . . . It is to be understood that I am to preach half the time in the village and half the time in the church (the Pines); I cannot think of being *officially* connected with more than two places, though I have not such strong objections to a preaching excursion occasionally into the neighboring country. . . . . You have my mind,—you have it plainly. Do as your sense of duty shall dictate. But this remember, that, although you have not a certainty, yet it comes as near to a certainty as human affairs will permit, of obtaining a man to break the bread of life to your hungry souls, if you meet his wishes by ministering to him in carnal things; and, oh! as you value your souls, and the souls of your children, remember, if God has given you the opportunity and the means, and you neglect both, you shall answer for it at the great day of the Redeemer's appearing. Accordingly, I expect you to proceed immediately to business; and if you find yourselves strong enough,—that is, *willing* enough, to feed and clothe this body (and God knows I want nothing more than a support), appear at Presbytery by a commissioner, and petition for the moderation of a call. But in the mean time let me know your purposes. I am in trim for action, and must act promptly. Importunate and reiterated cries from the congregation where my aged father and all my kindred are, wring tears from these eyes and blood from this heart; but a 'prophet hath no honor in his own country.' I cannot and will not go, if a door is opened with you." . . . .

In pursuance of the suggestions made in this letter, a call was made out by the people of Milton. The Presbytery of Philadelphia (A. R.) appointed the Rev. C. G. McLean to moderate it, and it was done on the 15th of March, 1819. In the extracts made from this letter we see indices of that frankness, explicitness, and honesty which were always characteristic of the man, whilst we have proof that the little flock, that lay scattered in and around

Milton, was in an inchoate condition, needing direction in the forms of procedure, and needing a forming hand to shape them into an energetic church organization.

After writing the foregoing letter, dated November 2d, 1818, Mr. Junkin made the journey to the West, alluded to above. In the progress of the journey, he preached the gospel in many places, and with much frequency. Besides the places already named, he preached seven times in Mercer County, once in Steubenville, Ohio, four times in Pittsburg, and three times on his return journey. Where-ever he was expected to preach, whether on the Sabbath or other days of the week, crowds came to hear him. The writer of this was a small boy at the time, but he retains a distinct recollection of the wide-spread and deep impression made by his sermons during this visit, and he has heard the old people speaking of it many years afterwards.

He spent most part of the month of December in Mercer County, Pennsylvania, and at the beginning of the year 1819 went to Steubenville to visit his sister Mary, the wife of the Rev. George Buchanan. In this visit he was accompanied by his venerable father, who came with him to Pittsburg, where he preached in his friend McElroy's pulpit on the 8th, 9th, 10th, and 11th of January. From Pittsburg he went to Franklin County, thence back to McConnellsburg, and thence across the country. In the progress of this journey he mentions having lodged at the house of the Rev. Mr. ——, "one of our ministers who followed stilling whiskey." He preached three Sabbaths, the last of January and the first two of February, 1819, at the Milton charge, one sermon in the Presbyterian congregation of Warrior Run, and then returned to Philadelphia. He does not appear to have entered upon labor in his former missionary field, having, as is supposed, terminated his connection with it the preceding November, although he preached often in Camden.

In March, 1819, we find him again on the Susquehanna, preaching in the Milton charge, and various other places in the region. But he returned to Philadelphia early in May.

On the 1st of June, 1819, he was married to Miss Julia Rush Miller, daughter of John and Margaret Miller, of Philadelphia. The marriage was solemnized by his venerated Professor, Dr. Mason.

Mr. Miller and his wife were natives of Scotland,—she Margaret Irvin,—and both descended from families of highly respectable social position. Mr. Miller had died previous to the marriage of his daughter. He had been a ruling elder in the Scots' Presbyterian Church, and a man of wealth, enterprise, and enlarged benevolence and public spirit. On terms of close intimacy with the celebrated Dr. Rush, he co-operated with that eminent philanthropist in many of the public charities of the city, and was distinguished for his courageous and self-denying labors with the sick and distressed during the visits of that terrible scourge—the yellow fever. Remaining in the city whilst others fled, he contributed by his means and his personal attentions to alleviate the distress and horrors of those awful calamities. He was prominent in the establishment of the almshouse, the hospital, and other charitable institutions of the city, and was recognized as one of its benefactors.

The next day after their marriage, they set out upon a visit to her relatives in Oxford and Gettysburg. From Gettysburg he went to Washington City, where he preached on the 26th of June. Returning to Gettysburg, they proceeded thence to Milton, where he entered upon the duties of his pastorate.

Their "own hired house" was not thoroughly completed

when they entered it; and for Mrs. Junkin, accustomed, as she had been, to the spacious apartments and the various appliances of human comfort, for which Philadelphia has always been remarkable, the change must have been great; but she conformed to it with that lovely Christian cheerfulness which formed an ornament of her character.

CHAPTER XI.

Pastorate at Milton—State of the Churches—Pastors Hood, Bryson, Patterson, Smith, and Grier—Installation—Sabbath-School, Tract, Bible, and Temperance Labors—Barriers—General Montgomery—Union of A. R. Church with General Assembly—Joins the Presbytery of Northumberland—Shiloh.

IN order to appreciate the results of Mr. Junkin's labors and influence during the eleven years of his pastorate at Milton, it is necessary to have an adequate knowledge of the state of religion and of the churches at the time of his advent to the Susquehanna region. Whilst there were some faithful and earnest men in the Presbyterian churches of that region, there was a deplorable amount of formalism pervading the masses. Mr. Junkin's charge was the only one within seventy miles of Milton that was connected with the Associate Reformed Church. And although there were isolated families and some small clusters of people, scattered through the surrounding counties that preferred that organization, they were not of sufficient numbers to be organized into churches, and they usually worshipped with the Presbyterian congregations. This state of things called for frequent excursions to preach in the regions beyond his immediate pastoral charge. That charge covered the same territory with the Presbyterian congregations of Milton and Warrior Run; the former under the pastoral care of the Rev. Thomas Hood, the latter under that of the venerable Rev. John Bryson, even then almost an octogenarian. The lovely and beloved Rev. John B. Patterson was pastor of the united churches of Derry and Mahoning (Danville), the Rev. William R. Smith over those of Sunbury and Northumberland, and the venerable

Rev. John Grier, of Pine Creek. Mr. Junkin found his own particular charge in a cold and formal state. Orthodox, and affected with a hereditary zeal for the peculiarities of their denomination, especially for "the Psalms of David in metre," there existed between them and the other branch of the Presbyterian family a mutual prejudice that restrained them from co-operation. Family worship was kept up in some families, but in many it was neglected. Discipline had rarely been exercised, and the standard of Christian morality was low, and that of piety and active efforts for souls still lower. And this description was equally true of most of the congregations in that region in connection with the General Assembly. Indeed, discipline in nearly all the churches was sadly relaxed, and the lines between the church and the world but dimly drawn. Whiskey drinking was almost universal. A funeral even could not be conducted without the circulation of the bottle and the tumbler. Elders of the church deemed it not inconsistent with their Christian profession or their official position, to engage in the manufacture and sale of whiskey. The sacraments of the church were approached by many whose profession of piety was not attested by the commonest indices of conversion. The masses were at ease in Zion. The sacrament of baptism was claimed for children, neither of whose parents was a communicant in the church, and a morbid public sentiment sanctioned the claim, and compelled the ministers, either to baptize promiscuously, or to encounter opposition of a serious character. At the time of his entrance upon this field, there was no church organization in Milton Borough, and no house of worship belonging to the people whom he served. When he officiated in the village, he preached in a large schoolhouse in the winter season, and in the summer in a hewn log-house, that had been built north of the town for an Episcopal church. It had been floored and fitted up with deep, old-fashioned pews, but had never been ceiled, and, at the time he occupied it, the roof was decayed, so that, except in pleasant weather, it was not a secure shelter. His chief station, and where most of the church members lived, was at "The Pines," the place already described as Peniel, in Turbot Township, three miles north of the Borough.

Such was his first permanent field of labor. His taking a station in the Borough of Milton excited at first some little jealousy and opposition from a part of the Presbyterian congregation, who enjoyed the ministrations of the Rev. Mr. Hood every alternate Sabbath. But this feeling soon abated after the people became better acquainted with Mr. Junkin, and learned to appreciate his catholic spirit, and the earnestness and ability of his labors in the cause of Christ. And as the Presbyterian congregation had but half of their pastor's time, and he lived several miles in the country, with the river, then unbridged, between his residence and the village, much of the pastoral work, such as visiting the sick, soon fell to Mr. J., and many of the people attended upon his preaching, which never interfered, in point of time, with that of Mr. Hood. And, indeed, there soon arose a delightful state of fellowship between the members of the two congregations, and no collision or misunderstanding ever occurred between the pastors.

On the 17th of October, 1819, he was installed pastor by the A. R. Presbytery of Philadelphia; Dr. C. G. McLean, Dr. McCartee, Dr. Duncan, and the Rev. Messrs. Lind and Gibson being present and taking part in the solemnities of the occasion. But before his formal installation, he had entered upon the duties of his pastorate with that zeal and energy which was never relaxed until the hand of death was laid upon him, nearly half a century afterwards.

Having taken part, when a student, in the organization of the first Sabbath-schools established in New York, he was not long in inaugurating them in his new field of labor. And such was his thorough comprehension of the principles and methods upon which these schools should be conducted, and such was his skill in introducing *system*, and adapting means to the end, that the schools in his charge were *models*, and, indeed, such good models, that fifty years' experience has made little advance upon the system inaugurated by him at Milton.

He also introduced the Bible-class, then a new mode of pastoral usefulness, and in it he shortly trained a corps of very efficient Sabbath-school teachers. He was methodical in all his labors. He early announced to his people, that he desired his mornings to be uninterrupted, that they might be devoted to study. He requested to be exempt from calls until after twelve o'clock; after that hour he was accessible. But in case of sickness he was ready to respond to calls at any hour of the day or night.

"I had not much aid from the eldership of the church. I never heard but one of them offer prayer in family or in public. Piety was a dull flame with all except that one (Mr. Russell), and he resided beyond the Susquehanna. Indeed, this was the case at first with nearly all the church members except a few women. And there was very little active piety, either in town or country. There was no prayer-meeting in any congregation in the vicinity except in Milton. There we began a little meeting in private houses, at which a few males and a score of females attended. William Housel, a watchmaker, and a member of Mr. Hood's charge, was the chief auxiliary. In White Deer Valley the prospect was more cheering. That was the most fruitful part of my field, for, although I was never pastor of the congregation in that valley, I labored a portion of the time in it, and with much comfort and success."*

* Rem.

Mr. Junkin never received an adequate support from the people to whom he ministered. They had promised him in his call a competency, but he rarely realized more than half of what was promised. The people seemed to take it for granted that, having means independent of them, they need not make exertion to maintain their pastor.

The fact, that he and his charge were so isolated and far removed from other churches and pastors of his denomination, very greatly restricted his usefulness; and the other fact, that the Associate Reformed Church confined their people to the use of the "Psalms of David in metre," as versified by Sir Francis Rouse, was another hindrance. When he consented, in the fourth year of his ministry, to supply the congregation of White Deer, he was constrained to stipulate that they should use these Psalms exclusively. They had been accustomed to use the collection of Psalms and Hymns generally used in the Presbyterian churches, but, for the sake of obtaining his services, they consented to the change. But notwithstanding these hindrances, his usefulness steadily increased, and the range of his influence was extended. His services were sought and were rendered in many places beside those in which he statedly ministered. In Lewisburg, Hartleton, New Berlin, and Mifflinburg, in Union County, and in Muncy, in Lycoming County, he often preached, laying foundations upon which, in some cases, thriving churches were afterwards built. In the last-named place he for a long time maintained a Wednesday lecture, or preaching service.

Mr. Junkin early threw himself, his energies and means, into those co-operative efforts in which evangelical Christians have united,—the Bible, the Tract, the Sabbath-school, and the Temperance enterprises. In all these he soon became the recognized leader in the region that lies around the Forks of the Susquehanna. At the time of Mr. Junkin's advent to Milton, that eminent Christian and philanthropist, General Daniel Montgomery, of Danville, was living, and in the height of his usefulness. He was soon attracted to the young "seceder," as the denomination of Mr. Junkin was sometimes called; and recognizing and appreciating his talents, learning, energy, and zeal, he was forward in giving to him that position in the religious enterprises of the region for which those qualifications adapted him. A friendship soon sprung up between these eminent men, which grew with years, and only terminated with the General's life. It was on General Montgomery's motion, that Mr. Junkin's first address before the Susquehanna Bible Society was published; and this address did much to stimulate and encourage the friends of the Bible cause, whilst it drew attention to its author as a man of ability and Christian enterprise.*

The Susquehanna Bible Society, auxiliary to the Pennsylvania Bible Society, was, during Mr. Junkin's residence in Milton, the most efficient society in the Commonwealth, out of Philadelphia. It pledged and it effected the thorough supply of four large counties with the Holy Scriptures, and sent a handsome surplus to the parent society. It was established upon the federative principle,—a general society, with auxiliaries, called Bible Associations, in townships and smaller districts. So energetic was Mr. J. in inaugurating this plan, that he personally organized no less than thirty-two of these associations in a few months. The S. B. S. held anniversary meetings in the larger towns, —Milton, Danville, Northumberland, Sunbury, and Wil-

* A lady, who was present at the delivery of this address, has informed the writer that, during its delivery, the venerable Rev. J. B. Patterson, who was in the pulpit with Mr. Junkin, was so affected that he rose to his feet, apparently unconscious of what he was doing, and took a position where he could see the speaker's face, and leaned towards him in an attitude of intense attention and delight; and that the whole assembly spontaneously leaned forward as if spell-bound by the speaker's power.

liamsport, to which the associations sent deputations; and these anniversaries were occasions of great religious and social interest, and contributed very efficiently to spread valuable thought and intelligence, and to rouse and sustain a Christian zeal and enterprise, that had never previously existed in that region. He not only infused his own spirit and zeal into others, and brought them up to work for the cause, but he was himself a hard worker. He travelled and toiled much, and at his own charges, in advancing the cause. He was not one of those whose zeal and industry in Christ's cause were all expended in an oration upon the boards of an anniversary; he labored personally, and contributed liberally, to urge forward every enterprise that seemed to him scriptural and right.

At the sessions of the General Assembly and of the General Synod of the Associate Reformed Church, held in Philadelphia in May, 1822, a union was consummated between the two bodies. The proposal for this union was made by the General Assembly a year previous. These were favorably received by the Synod then in session in the same city. Committees of conference were appointed. A basis of union was agreed upon; and at the time mentioned, both bodies adopted the basis, and the Synod met with the Assembly, and enjoyed a delightful season of fraternal fellowship. By the terms of the basis of union, it was left optional with the Presbyteries of the Associate Reformed Church, either to retain their organization and attach themselves to the most convenient Synod under the General Assembly, or to dissolve and their several members and churches unite with the Presbyteries within whose bounds they might be located. "In the former case, they shall have as full powers and privileges as any other Presbyteries in the united body." Some of the Presbyteries retained their organization, as the Second Presbytery of New York. Others pursued the latter alternative, and became amalgamated with the Presbyteries most convenient to the ministers and churches severally. The Presbytery to which Mr. Junkin belonged, the A. R. Presbytery of Philadelphia, appears to have retained a separate existence for a short time; but in the years 1824–5, they perfected their arrangements for a dissolution, and united with the Presbyteries most convenient. This Presbytery extended over a large territory, including in its limits Philadelphia, Baltimore, Washington, D.C., Carlisle, Hagerstown, and McConnellsburg. Some of the ministers and churches fell into the bounds of the Presbytery of Philadelphia, others into that of Baltimore, others to Carlisle, others to New Castle, and Mr. Junkin and his congregations into the Presbytery of Northumberland. This change of Church and Presbyterial connection greatly enlarged his sphere of influence and of usefulness. He was located near the geographical centre of the Presbytery, in its then largest town, and among its most enterprising people.

He was received by the Presbytery of Northumberland with a large and cordial welcome. He was already known to them as an able and earnest worker. In the intercourse incident to the meeting of the Bible Society and other co-operative efforts, they had learned his worth as a warm-hearted and energetic champion of every good cause; and they soon, as by common consent, seemed to recognize him as their leader in every good work. On his part, he at once identified himself with the interests of the whole Presbytery and of the whole denomination with which his lot was now cast; and he entered into their work as if he never had been an alien, and with all the ardor of his earnest nature.

About a year after his arrival at Milton, he purchased half an acre of ground in a pleasant and convenient location, and, with the aid of the citizens, built a small and comfortable place of worship. This he named *Shiloh*, and here he officiated almost every Sabbath, preaching in the evenings of those Sabbaths on the mornings of which he had labored in the country portions of his charge. Mr. Hood rarely preached more than in the daylight of the Sabbath, so that the evening service in Shiloh, and the alternate Sabbath-morning service, did not interfere with the ministrations in the other Presbyterian church. At that time the Presbyterian congregation occupied a building of rather imposing appearance, which they had built in connection with two German congregations, the Lutheran and the German Reformed. Of course they were entitled to use it but one-half of the time, which excluded them every alternate Sabbath.

In "Shiloh" Mr. Junkin gathered a considerable congregation, and there he preached for eleven years those precious doctrines of grace, of which, in later life, he became the defender, both through the press and in the church courts. Besides a sermon each day, he usually had a series of expository lectures in progress, in which he expounded book after book of the Scriptures. These were attended upon by large numbers of interested and intelligent people; and it might be truly said of him, more than of most ministers, in the language of McCheyne, that he "made the people understand the Bible." In these expository discourses he began to array material, which, later in life, and with more mature study, he embodied in works which he prepared for the press. In Shiloh his lectures upon the Epistle to the Hebrews were first delivered, as also his application of the lessons of the Mosaic ritual to the elucidation of New-Testament truth, and some of his lectures on the prophecies.

After his union with the Presbytery of Northumberland, he continued to use, as a general thing, in his own churches, the old version of the Psalms. This he did, not because he had conscientious scruples against using other sacred songs, but because many of his people, especially the more aged, preferred the Psalmody to which they had so long been accustomed. But in the prayer-meetings, Sabbath-schools, and when officiating in churches where other hymnology had been introduced, he was glad to use the Psalms and Hymns of Watts and others.

CHAPTER XII.

Pastorate at Milton, continued—A Reformer—Labors in the Temperance Reform—Rum at Funerals—His Protest—Presbyterial Action—Opposition—His Steadfastness—Beecher's Lectures—Chambers's Medicine—Early Educational Labors—Milton Academy—Dr. Kirkpatrick—Widespread Usefulness of that School—Its Distinguished Pupils.

THE subject of this memoir soon found himself surrounded by a band of warm-hearted, Christian people, ready to co-operate with him in the work of the Lord. But it was not to be expected that this work could make marked progress without encountering opposition. Nor was it to be expected that a man of such decided convictions and pronounced character could take the lead in works of reformation without becoming, to some extent, the target at which the shafts of the enemy would be especially aimed. It has been already stated, that a condition of things, somewhat analogous to the *moderatism* of the Church of Scotland, pervaded the congregations in the region of his labors. In his own charge, and in many others, there was a large amount of practical antinomianism. Worldly conformity marked the conduct of most professors of religion; many vices abounded in the community, such as intemperance, gambling, Sabbath-desecration, and profanity; and all these arrayed themselves against the efforts made for the revival of spiritual piety. Even church members, in many cases, resented and resisted the inroads attempted to be made upon the cold formalism that palsied the churches. But regardless of all opposition, from whatever quarter it came, Mr. Junkin steadily persisted in efforts at the much-needed reform. He poured forth from the pulpit faithful, earnest, and affectionate remonstrances and entreaties. He rallied the friends of religion and good order, and led them on in assaults upon prevailing evils, whilst he held forth the gospel as the grand remedy for all the ills of society.

The temperance reformation had not yet assumed the aspect and the vantage which it gained a few years later. He took ground in advance of any general movement that had as yet been made. We have seen, that before he left the Theological Seminary he had privately taken, substantially, the Nazarite's vow, so far as intoxicating drink is concerned. He had refused the first call made for his pastoral services, chiefly because whiskey-drinking was so prevalent in the congregation. And, when settled in a pastoral charge, he early commenced an earnest crusade against intemperance, a crusade that ended only with his life.

Before any temperance society was thought of in his region, he practised and preached total abstinence. His first public demonstration against the bottle was a refusal to attend any funeral where strong drink was exhibited. On one occasion he attended the funeral of a neighbor not of his flock, but when the bottle made its appearance he withdrew, and, although followed by a brother minister and urged to return, he persisted in withdrawing, and thus protesting against a custom that he deemed to be alike dishonoring to the dead and injurious to the living. Soon after becoming a member of the Presbytery of Northumberland, he presented a set of resolutions upon this subject, and secured the adoption of them. One of these resolutions was, that the members of the Presbytery would not attend or officiate at any funeral at which spirituous liquors should be offered to the guests. This was probably the first definite and effective action taken in this country by any ecclesiastical body against the monster vice of intemperance. For, although Synods and Assemblies had occasionally uttered warnings against the sin of intemperance, and borne testimony against it, no *means* of practical efficiency had been suggested for arresting the progress of the destroyer. The discipline of the church, it is true, had sometimes been brought to bear upon the crime of drunkenness, but this always came too late as a remedy, for the fatal disease is contracted, and the dangerous habit formed, before the individual becomes, by overt transgression, the subject of church censure. There was need of some more effective protest against, not the sin merely, but the *cause* of the sin, which lay in the use of intoxicating beverages. This protest Mr. Junkin made in the form already mentioned, and he persisted in the protest, in connection with his brethren of the Presbytery, until the custom of exhibiting liquor at funerals was entirely broken up, not only in Presbyterian families, but very generally throughout the community.

Nor was he contented with this measure of opposition to intemperance and its cause. In private and in public, orally and with his pen, he continued to "reprove, rebuke, and exhort, with all long-suffering and doctrine." About the time he began the temperance work at Milton, the able and celebrated Dr. Lyman Beecher had begun it in Boston and New England. That eminent man delivered a series of "Lectures on Intemperance," which were published in a small volume, and which were marked by the vigor of thought and pungency of appeal that were peculiar to their author. These lectures Mr. Junkin procured and endeavored to circulate. But finding the people slow to buy and read them, he made appointments of public meetings, and read these lectures to them, with occasional remarks of his own. Great numbers attended these readings, and these were the first "temperance meetings" held in the Susquehanna region. The fact that a man of Mr. Junkin's acknowledged ability would read the lectures of another, is proof, that it was the *cause* he had at heart, and not the winning of personal *éclat*.

So uncompromising was his hostility to intemperance, and so deep his sympathy and concern for the inebriate, that he seized upon every auxiliary of reform. About that time, a certain Dr. Chambers had invented, as he professed, a remedy for intemperance, of a medicinal kind. "Chambers's Remedy for Intemperance" was, for a time, much in vogue, and, in some cases, did appear to effect reform, by producing in the patient disgust for liquor. But its efficacy appeared to depend upon the law of association, and, by producing intense *nausea*, associated that nausea with the liquor in which the medicine was infused. Mr. Junkin heard of this remedy, procured a quantity of it, and, sometimes with the consent of the victim, sometimes without his knowledge, but with the consent of his family, attempted to exorcise the demon. In many cases there was temporary deliverance from the destroying appetite; in a few cases, permanent rescue. But, after a short-lived popularity, the remedy, like many other *nostrums*, proved a failure. Many of the scenes connected with the exhibition of "Chambers's Remedy" were ludicrous in the extreme, especially when the patients, or the victims, did not know that they had drunk anything but their favorite beverage in its purity. The physical commotion produced was indeed alarming, and was well calculated to frighten and disgust the unfortunate into abstinence.

It may excite surprise that such a remedy for intemperance should gain such extensive popularity, and that men so judicious as Dr. Junkin, and many others of his brethren in the ministry, should lend themselves to its distribution. But if it be remembered, that drunkenness is a disease of the stomach and nervous system, as well as a sin, we need not wonder that earnest philanthropists would seize upon any physical remedy (coming from a respectable medical source, and commended, as it was, by great names) that might promise to eradicate a habit so ruinous to soul, body, and estate.

Mr. Junkin's family physician was a gentleman of fine talents, good education, and of eminent skill in his profession. He was, withal, a man of generous impulses, kind heart, and fine social qualities. But he was likely to fall before this destroyer, who had slain so many strong men. This physician and his family attended upon Mr. Junkin's ministrations; and a close intimacy subsisted between the families. The pastor's regard for the gifted yet tempted physician was intensified by the assiduous care and skill which the latter bestowed upon him during the only very serious illness of his life, previous to his last. With God's blessing, the pastor's life was spared, and, after his recovery, he showed his gratitude by writing to the physician a series of letters, eight in number, couched in the most earnest, pungent, and affectionate terms, remonstrating and reasoning with him upon the subject of his dangerous and sinful habit. We may again recur to this correspondence, and only mention it here as illustrative of the indefatigable zeal and unshrinking faithfulness with which Mr. J. sought to snatch souls as brands from that terrible burning.

Before dismissing the subject of his labors, at Milton and elsewhere, in the temperance reformation, it may as well be stated that, after he became an editor, the columns of the periodical which he issued contained from time to time strong articles in advocacy of that reform. He assailed the evil in all its phases. He was among the first, if not the first, to attack the manufacture and traffic of intoxicating drinks. He assailed the social habits of the people, that required the bottle and the glass to be put to the neighbor's mouth. He bore down upon the custom, then and still too prevalent, of using liquor as the agent of bribery at elections. Of course these assaults upon the enemy drew their fire, which came, not in the form of argument, for of this they had none, but in the shape of discontinuances of his paper, abusive letters, both anonymous and with names, coarse attacks in the secular papers, petty personal annoyances, and, in a few cases, discontinuance of social comities. A prominent politician and military gentleman, who afterwards figured in the Mexican War, and was brought home from it dead, took intense umbrage at an article headed "WHISKEY BRIBERY," and sent a curt and cross note discontinuing the paper, and assigning as a reason the article in question. This led to a sharp correspondence, in which the reverend editor boldly maintained his ground, and in which the soldier proved that the pen was possibly less puissant with him than the sword. All these things, whilst they perhaps occasioned the champion of temperance pecuniary loss, and some personal annoyance, nevertheless aroused the public mind to inquiry and consideration, spread true principles, and prepared the way for the triumph of that cause in which he was a suffering laborer.

Gambling, horse-racing, Sabbath-breaking, profanity, and all those vices that feed upon the master vice of intemperance, received a due proportion of the reformer's attention, both from press, pulpit, and rostrum; and, as a matter of course, the practicers and abettors of these vices, when not convinced and converted from the errors of their ways, were roused to fierce opposition. This opposition did not always vent itself in mere curses, but resorted to various petty annoyances and private injuries. On one occasion the gamblers sent an unsuspecting negro man to Mr. Junkin's house, during his absence, to ask for a pack of cards; and this was a moderate specimen of the means resorted to by the sons of Belial. "But none of these things moved him." When his friends would sometimes tremble for his safety, and express anxiety for the results of his bold assaults upon prevailing sins, he would calmly smile at their fears, bid them have patience and trust in God; and, in regard to the misrepresentations to which the gainsayers often resorted, would quietly quote the Proverb (xii. 19), "the lying tongue is but for a moment." Indeed, throughout his whole life, this and similar Scripture assurances seemed to be his shield against the voice of slander; and such was his *implicit confidence* in such portions of the Holy Word, that he never was as much moved or vexed by misrepresentation as most other men are.

But whilst his labors in his own charge, and in the cause of the Bible, the Sabbath, the Sabbath-school, the Tract Society, and the Temperance reform, were various, ample, and indefatigable, other Christian and philanthropic enterprises received at the same time a large share of his attention and his toil. Although he had as yet no children of his own of suitable age to educate, he early inaugurated measures to improve the facilities for education in the community in which he lived. He found the schools in a very backward and imperfect condition, and soon began to agitate for their improvement. By conversation, by pulpit instruction, and by occasional appeals through the press, he succeeded in awakening an interest in the subject, and in forming a joint-stock company, for the purpose of establishing an English, Mathematical, and Classical Academy. He was himself a liberal subscriber, and the movement resulted in the founding of the celebrated "Milton Academy," which, under the principalship of that renowned teacher, the late Rev. David Kirkpatrick, D.D., was a very popular and effective school.

Mr. Kirkpatrick, a native of the North of Ireland, a student of Belfast Collegiate Institution, and a graduate of the University of Glasgow, was employed for a short time teaching a classical school in Oxford, Chester County, Pa., under the auspices of the Rev. Dr. Dickey, the brother-in-law of Mr. Junkin. There the last-named made the acquaintance of the young Scotch-Irishman, and induced him to come to Milton and become the Principal of the incipient academy. Pending the erection of the academy building, which was located upon an eminence, beautiful for situation, east of the village, temporary accommodations for the school were hired; and the institution opened under very favorable prospects. It soon rose into distinction, and not only retained that portion of the youth of the town who formerly were sent abroad for instruction, but attracted students from distant parts of the Commonwealth, and from other States. Perhaps no institution of the kind, with such a meagre expenditure of funds in its establishment, ever accomplished a larger measure of educational benefit. This was chiefly owing to the efficiency and skill of the Principal and his assistants; but the influence of the subject of this memoir was constantly exerted, not only in founding it, but in sustaining its discipline and thoroughness of drill, in extending its fame, and in bringing students to its classes. His frequent visits to the school, and his unflagging interest in its welfare, did much to sustain and encourage the Principal, and to encourage the pupils. The Principal of the school and the pastor of the church became close friends,—a friendship that terminated only with their lives. They died in the same year.

It is impossible to measure, by any human standard of calculation, the influences for good which Mr. Junkin set in operation when he succeeded in inaugurating the Milton Academy. Streams, for many years, continued to issue from that fountain, that refreshed the country and distant parts of the world, whilst they made glad the city of our God. Not only was it a religious and educational advantage to the community in which it was located, but also to distant communities in our own country, to distant continents and islands of the sea. Asia, Africa, Europe, America, and the Pacific Islands have felt, and still feel, the influence of that unpretending institution.

The first missionary to Arkansas; one of the first missionaries of the Presbyterian Church to Africa; a missionary to the Sandwich Islands, the man who more than any other shaped the educational and governmental systems of those islands—many ministers of the gospel of eminence, many eminent lawyers and statesmen, many eminent physicians, and—what is not the least important in regard to wide-spread usefulness—many eminent teachers, were educated at that academy, and mostly under the ministerial influence of Mr. Junkin.

That academy gave two Governors to Pennsylvania, Pollock and Curtin, the latter of whom is now Ambassador at the Court of Russia. It gave a Professor of Natural Philosophy to the University of Georgia, a President to the College of South Carolina, Charles F. McCay, LL.D., and a Professor of Belles-Lettres to Lafayette College. It gave to the State and the country such men as Judge Comly and Judge Naudain, with Senators and Congressmen who adorned their station; and it gave to the church such men as J. W. Moore, Matthew Laird, the first missionary to Western Africa, Dr. Richard Armstrong, missionary to the Sandwich Islands, and Minister of Public Instruction for that kingdom, and who did perhaps more for its civilization than any other; Dr. John M. Dickey, a useful pastor, and the chief founder of Lincoln University; Dr. S. S. Sheddan, of New Jersey; Rev. J. Mason Galloway, late of Clearfield; Dr. George Marshall, an eminent pastor and educator, of Western Pennsylvania; the late Rev. Robt. Bryson; the Rev. P. B. Marr, a preacher of great ability; Rev. Daniel M. Barber; Rev. Daniel Gaston, late of Philadelphia; Dr. James C. Hepburn, the devoted and efficient missionary, first to China and now in Japan. These, and many others, did this institution give to the church and country, whose names have adorned the rolls of the church, and whose influence for good has been wide-spread and effective. The writer of this memoir, too, owes more to the Milton Academy than to any other institution for any attainments in solid learning that he has been enabled to make. Had Mr. Junkin accomplished nothing in the department of education but the founding of this Academy, he had not lived in vain!

CHAPTER XIII.

Inadequate Maintenance—Purchase of a Farm, and Removal to it—Socinian Controversy—Discussion of Baptism—The Religious Farmer—Pastoral Labors—Sickness—Matthew Laird—A Vow—How his Mind was drawn to the Subject of Manual Labor Education—Manner—Helpmeet—The Covenant—Prophecy—Rev. J. W. Moore's Letter—The Storm.

ABOUT the time of Mr. Junkin's entrance upon his pastorate at Milton, the question whether religion could be supported upon the voluntary principle was fast approaching a negative solution in most parts of America. A few, but far from all, of the city pastors received a stipend barely adequate to support their families, but the great majority of pastors, in town and country, received much less than a competence, and were generally constrained to resort to other methods of eking out a support. Things are assuming a better condition of late years; but, for a long time, the voluntary system of church support threatened to be a failure.

The people of his charge had promised Mr. J. in their call what would have been at that day sufficient to support a family upon an economical scale; but, not from inability, but heedlessness, little more than half of it was ever paid. In view of this, he purchased a small piece of woodland (sixty acres), two miles from the town of Milton, on the road to his country church, Penuel. To his already arduous labors he then added the cares of superintending the clearing of a farm, the erection of a house and barn, and, subsequently, the management of the farm. Whatever he did, he did with energy, and upon everything he undertook he sought to throw the best lights of science. The experience of his earlier life was now of practical benefit, and he sought to apply to agriculture the science which he had acquired, and also to gather from agricultural books and periodicals the experience of others. He thus became one of the earliest scientific farmers in the fertile and lovely valley of the Susquehanna; and it cannot be doubted, that the light which he threw upon the subject by his conversation, publications, and example, tended greatly to improve the practical farming of that whole region.

This farm enterprise, taken in connection with events already mentioned, and others now to be introduced, led him to add to his other labors the toils and cares of editorship. In his Bible, tract, Sunday-school, and temperance labors, he felt the want of a convenient medium of communication with the religious public, and a vehicle of religious intelligence. Religious newspapers were not at that day so numerous as now, and all that were published issued from the cities of Philadelphia, Boston, and New York, then much more distant, in point of time, from the interior than they now are. Now a notice of a religious assembly can be sent to one of the cities, printed in a religious paper, and widely circulated, in almost any part of the country, in a few days. Then it required weeks to do it, and as but few copies of these city papers circulated, they formed a very insufficient medium of communication with people living in the remote rural districts. This religious want of his vicinage, and a similar want in the means of agricultural information, made him hope that a local periodical might be of great benefit to all these interests.

Other considerations, now to be mentioned, led his mind in the same direction. There lived and preached at that time, in the town of Northumberland, a Unitarian clergyman, the Rev. Mr. K——, a native of England. He came to Milton, also, at stated times, and officiated for such as would go to hear him. He was a gentleman of high culture, and reputed a mature scholar. He was not content with assailing the doctrine of our Lord's Supreme Divinity and the doctrine of the Trinity from the pulpit, but resorted to the press in default of obtaining large audiences to address orally. He published one or more essays in *The Miltonian*, a secular paper, issued in Milton. Mr. Junkin felt it to be his duty to reply to them, and he was thus drawn into a protracted controversy upon these topics. His replies were published in *The State's Advocate*, the other local weekly.

The manuscript of his part in this controversy is still preserved, and furnishes proof of the great ability and learning which he displayed in defence of our Lord's Supreme Divinity. Many competent judges, educated men, pronounced it the ablest argument which they had ever read upon the subject. It was generally conceded that the learned Socinian was vanquished. The writer of these pages is not a sufficiently impartial judge, but must make the record that he has never met with any discussion of these great themes quite so satisfactory and convincing.

About the time this discussion was closing, Mr. Junkin had, as a matter of Christian courtesy, loaned to a Baptist minister the use of his (Shiloh) church in Milton, to be occupied on the days in which Mr. J. officiated in the country. There were a few Baptist families in Milton and vicinity, but they had no place of worship. The Rev. Eugenio Kinkaid, afterwards the Rev. Dr. Kinkaid, a distinguished missionary of the Baptist Church in the Burman Empire, was the person who obtained the use of Shiloh Church, and, as the number of Baptists was very small, his congregation was largely composed of those who waited upon Mr. Junkin's ministry. Under these circumstances, it might have been presumed that Mr. K. would be content to preach the doctrines of our common Christianity, without introducing the points in controversy between his sect and the Presbyterians. But such did not appear to be his sense of duty. He assailed the doctrines of the Presbyterians on the subject of Baptism from a Presbyterian pulpit and before an audience chiefly Presbyterian. After this had been done several times, Mr. Junkin replied, and this opened up another discussion. And as he had thus been providentially drawn into a position in which he must either prove unfaithful to duty or stand forth as a defender of the faith, the necessity of having a paper under his own control, through whose columns he might advocate the principles that he was set to defend, was more strongly pressed upon his mind.

The following, found among his papers of that period, discloses the motives that prompted him to this undertaking, whilst it gives us an insight of the inner life of the man, and informs us of his method of entering upon any important enterprise or duty:

"Dec. 18th, 1827, half-past 11 o'clock.

"I have long and anxiously deliberated with myself and my friends on the subject of publishing the *Religious Farmer*. The want of an adequate subscription presents a serious objection. When I confer with flesh and blood, my dearest and best friends, on the subject, I am thrown into great perplexities as to the success of the measure; but when I seek advice from Him who is the wonderful Counsellor, my fears generally vanish away. I have just spent half an hour in converse with God about this matter. I bowed my knees, full of perplexity and doubts. I have, in a most solemn manner, sought direction; have examined my own heart afresh as to the leading motives; appealed to the heart-searching God to judge and let me know whether to thrust myself into public view, and to gain public applause, is a motive at all, and to what extent. And I now feel that if it is at all a motive in the corruption of this heart, it is one of very minor influence. I have asked again, that if a desire of worldly gain has any weight, He would let me see it. And here I fear the deceitfulness of my own heart; and yet the prospect of gain is so small, and of loss so certain, that I conclude that the desire for gain can have very little influence. I have appealed time after time, both now and on former occasions, to the All-seeing Eye to judge whether the prime moving cause of the inclination of my heart to this work is not a sincere desire to advance the welfare of Zion and the glory of her King. I have thought this to be the case, and have often prayed, with all the ardor and importunity of which my soul is capable, that, if it be not so, a thousand barriers may be thrown in the way of the commencement of this work. . . . And now I rise from the interview with God with scarcely a doubt as to the practicability and great usefulness of the undertaking. Because it does appear to me that if God did not intend good to his church from it, He would influence my mind against it. I think I feel *now*, more than I ever did, disposed to spend myself and all I possess or control in the service of Jesus Christ. And, if I am not mistaken in this thought, surely my Master will not frown upon this effort to do good. I know success depends upon Him. He only can enable me to conduct the paper in his fear. To Him I look for guidance. I think I have faith in Him, and, therefore, I lay myself to this work in the strength of the Lord my God; and in his name do I lift up this banner, feeling in my heart a delightful assurance that when displayed, the Lord will rally many friends around it."

Accordingly, he commenced, on the 1st of January, 1828, the publication of "THE RELIGIOUS FARMER," which was published once in two weeks. It was a royal octavo of sixteen pages, printed with two columns on each page. It was continued to the 1st of January, 1830, until a short time before he was called to preside over the institution at Germantown. The motto at the head of this little publication was truly descriptive of the character and life of its editor: "Not slothful in business; fervent in spirit; serving the Lord." The circulation was chiefly confined to the region of Pennsylvania of which Milton was the centre, and, whilst it was not a pecuniary success, it was instrumental in great good. It was devoted, as its title indicates, to the interests of religion and agriculture; but contained much other valuable matter bearing upon all the interests of religion, education, literature, and industrial economy. It widely extended his influence and usefulness, enabling him to speak at hundreds of firesides beyond the limits of his immediate pastoral charge. In its columns he waged a fearless war upon intemperance and other vices, and against error and immorality in all their forms, whilst, by disseminating intelligence concerning the benevolent operations of the day, he brought up the churches more effectively to the work. It may as well be here stated, that when, in 1830, he ceased the publication of this paper, he transferred the subscription-list, without compensation, to the only religious paper then printed in Philadelphia. The *Philadelphian* was, at that time, under the editorial control of Dr. Ezra Styles Ely, and to it Mr. Junkin transferred the subscription-list of the *Farmer*, little apprehending that, in less than three years, the paper, whose circulation he thus helped to extend, would become a virulent opponent of that reform in the church in which, in God's providence, he was destined to bear so conspicuous a part.

It might be supposed that a man upon whom rested the cares of a pastoral charge, of an editorial chair, and of the various Christian enterprises in which he bore so prominent a part, would have little time to devote to the details of any of them, or that, having so many things on his hands, some must needs be neglected. But it was not so. Every thing he undertook was well and thoroughly done. Not an item in the long schedule of his employments was neglected. His pulpit, his Bible-classes, his Sabbath-schools, his paper, his farm, all were carried on efficiently. He not only devised the system of Bible Society, Tract, and Sabbath-school efforts, but he was the chief actuary in working the system. The Bibles, tracts, and Sabbath-school books, for the supply of four large counties, were all sent to him, and, under his superintendence, distributed. The Bible, Tract, and Sabbath-school Depositories were kept at Milton under his eye. He obtained the gratuitous services of a highly intelligent and energetic young lady, one of his spiritual children, and the daughter of a leading merchant of the place, to manage the Sabbath-school Depository, keeping it at her father's house. But the Bibles, tracts, and so forth were distributed from his own house.

Nor were the minutiæ of pastoral duty neglected:

"It was my regular custom to visit every family contributing to the support of the congregations I served, once a year, and this I did in company with an elder. I announced on Sabbath the families I expected to visit on a given day, and in the order of successive calls, so that each could know about what time to expect us. Other visits, very many, I paid, especially in cases of sickness. The great difficulty always was, in drawing out the personal views and feelings of those with whom we conversed. It is amazing how reluctant people are to talk about religion, —the practical and personal phases of it. Mere doctrinal matters were more easily managed. I used the Shorter Catechism always, but of course never, at a single visit, got over the whole of it."*

When he undertook the publication of a paper, it became necessary that he should remove to town, and he accordingly purchased a house and lot in the borough of Milton, which he enlarged, and fitted up into a neat and comfortable mansion, and, when completed, removed his household to it. But incidents, interesting in themselves, and connected with his future history, occurred whilst residing upon his Turbot farm, which ought now to be related, and we go back in the narrative to bring up omissions:

"Whilst building my barn, I was attacked with a violent bilious fever, then extensively prevalent. It was the only

---

* Rem.

time in my life that I was dangerously sick. At times it seemed likely to prove fatal. My soul, during this illness, experienced great tenderness of religious affection, especially when my dear and precious wife and I talked of the possibility of our soon being separated. Never until this trying hour did I know the full value of a true-hearted, pious wife. Nor did I lack any possible kindness from neighbors. But, above all, from Mrs. W. and Mrs. P. (mother of Governor Pollock). Such kindness and most solicitous attention can never be exceeded, and never can my heart forget or cease to be grateful to them and to my God for their ministrations of love. No hour, day or night, during the time of my peril, but the eyes of one of these precious women were upon me.*

"It was during this sickness that Matthew Laird came under my interested attention. William Thomas, a pious Baptist, who attended my ministry, was doing the work on my barn, being a carpenter. I asked him to conduct family worship in the apartment at the foot of the stairs, the upper terminus of which was near my chamber-door, so that I could hear pretty well. On one occasion he put the service upon his apprentice, Matthew Laird. The young man's prayer went to my heart; it was fervent and tender. When my wife came up to my chamber I said to her, 'If God spares my life, that young man shall enter the ministry.' It pleased the Lord to spare my life, and I fulfilled my vow. Laird went as a missionary to Africa, and thence early ascended to the heavenly glory along with his devoted wife.

---

* Since the above was written, ex-Governor Pollock has related to the author the following incident connected with this illness, which he (the Governor) had from his mother. She was watching by the sick-bed of Mr. Junkin at the time the physician had almost abandoned hope of his recovery. The patient had lain for some hours in a stupor, when he suddenly awoke and repeated the 17th and 18th verses of the 118th Psalm, in the version of Sir Francis Rouse:

"I shall not die but live, and shall the works of God discover,
The Lord hath me chastised sore, but not to death given over."

And the utterance seemed prophetic; for, from that moment, he grew steadily, but slowly, better.

"That prayer of Matthew Laird is, in a certain sense, the *start-point* of Lafayette College, as it was the first link in the chain of divine providences that led me into the department of education. I received him into my family (the pious carpenter having generously relinquished the last year of his apprenticeship), and aided him in the expenses of his education, until, as mentioned, I saw him depart to a foreign field. This turned my mind more fully to the subject of Christian education for the ministry, and from that day to this it has been my chief life-work. Soon afterwards I was led to take Daniel Gaston out of a coach-maker's shop in Milton, and start him upon a similar career. He has long been a most useful minister of the gospel, and is now a pastor in Philadelphia.* In removing to Milton, one object had in view was to arrange for aiding such young men. In constructing my barn in town, I made space for a carpenter-shop, so as to afford employment and exercise to them when not engaged in study. In following up this idea, my mind was attracted to the Manual Labor Academy of Pennsylvania, located at Germantown, and the idea of combining with study the health-preserving labor of the hands, and so contribute to the expenses of education, got possession of my mind, and the development of that idea resulted in Lafayette College, as I shall show should I live to write the history of that noble institution."†

We copy the following allusion to the case of Mr. Laird from the annual report of the Board of Education for 1847, written by the pen of the sainted Dr. Cortlandt Van Rensselaer, who was a classmate of Mr. Laird in the Princeton Seminary:

WHAT A PASTOR DID FOR AFRICA.

"On the banks of the Susquehanna was once settled a Presbyterian pastor (yet alive) whom God afflicted with sickness. In the midst of languor and disease it was sweet for him to look to Christ, and to form high and solemn resolves to live more unreservedly to his glory if life were

---

* Mr. Gaston died before Dr. J.

† Rem.

spared. His meditations were one day interrupted by the hymns of praise which a young carpenter mingled with his daily work. And the sick man heard them. His pious and enterprising soul soon suggested the question, 'Why may not this young carpenter glorify the son of Joseph in the ministry of salvation?' He immediately determined that if the youth were of a suitable character, and had a love of souls, he would educate him, in the hope that the Spirit of Christ would count him worthy of the sacred calling. The pastor insisted upon his wife inviting the young man to lead in family prayers, which he did with unusual unction. Inquiries justified the favorable impression received. The pastor recovers. The carpenter lays aside his plane and his saw. He enters an academy, and then a college. He determines, by the grace of God, to devote himself to the ministry, and to be a missionary to the heathen. He enters Princeton Seminary. The peculiar savor of his piety is yet held in sacred remembrance there. He sails for Africa, and enters her vast fields waving with the harvest. In the midst of his labors the noon-day sun smote down the reaper; but doubtless he was carried home rejoicing, 'bringing his sheaves with him.' From the mansions of glory he testifies to the precious influences of a pastor's care."

The allusion was doubtless written from memory by Dr. Van Rensselaer, and whilst the statement does not embrace all the details, it is substantially correct.

After preparing for college at the Milton Academy, Mr. Laird repaired to Jefferson College, where he graduated; then to Princeton Seminary, where he completed the full course of study; and thence, after some delay in needful preparation, he sailed for Africa in company with the Rev. John Cloud. It pleased a wise Providence, that these devoted men should soon be cut down by the fever of that torrid clime, falling early martyrs to their missionary zeal. The writer of these pages knew them both intimately, and loved them dearly. "They were lovely and pleasant in their lives, and in death they were not divided."

The name of James C. Hepburn has been mentioned among the valuable men trained in part at the school of Dr. Kirkpatrick. He was brought up under the pastoral care of Dr. Junkin, and in a communication from Japan to the religious journals of this country, published a few years ago, bore testimony to the faithfulness, affection, and skill of his pastor in guiding him in the path of life, and ascribed to him much of that influence which turned his attention to the missionary work, and fitted him for the labors which he has been able to perform. Dr. Hepburn studied medicine after having graduated at Nassau Hall, and has spent most of his life in China and Japan as a missionary. Ill health compelled him to return for a season to this country. But, after practicing his profession for a few years in New York City, he again went upon missionary ground, and has done a great work for Christ and for civilization in the empire of Japan, having prepared a dictionary of that difficult language, and translated into it some portions of the Word of God. There he is still at work; and until the results of the labors of that modest, godly, scholarly, and accomplished man can be measured, the extent of the influences for good, begun by Mr. Junkin's instrumentality at Milton, can never be ascertained. In the spring of 1828 Mr. Junkin removed his family to his new residence in Milton, in which he continued to reside until called to the "Pennsylvania Manual Labor Institution," in 1830.

Whilst it is true that Mr. Laird was the first person, not of their own family connection, that Mr. and Mrs. Junkin received into their family, with a view to aid in his preparation for the gospel ministry, and whilst his case was the means of leading them more largely into the education enterprise, yet it is due alike to truth and to gratitude to record the fact, that the young carpenter was the fourth that they had thus received. For Mrs. Junkin's nephew, that eminent minister and philanthropist Dr. John M. Dickey, was, for a time, an inmate of their house, whilst pursuing his studies with Mr. Kirkpatrick; and the son of Mr. Galloway, Mr. Junkin's brother-in-law and pastor, was for years an inmate, and afterwards became an eminent and useful minister; and the writer of this narrative was similarly favored, and owes more to them, for any measure of good he has been able to accomplish, than to any other human beings.

Mrs. Junkin, the woman who, in her girlhood, shrunk from the responsibilities of a pastor's wife with self-distrust, proved, through all these years of toil and sacrifice, an helpmeet for him indeed. With quiet, unostentatious, and cheerful alacrity she seconded all his efforts for good. Possessing a sound and judicious mind, a heart of constant and unfailing kindness, and a mature and accomplished education, she not only made his home cheerful and happy, and the scene of refined hospitality, but in many points she made up for his lack of service. The multiplied cares and labors that rested upon him, naturally made him somewhat abstracted in his manner, and sometimes, when absorbed in thought or in business, he would appear cold and unsocial, although really of a warm, genial, and hospitable temperament. This lack of social manner was most admirably supplemented by her cordial habitude and social tact. And she would do it in such a way as to appear a part of her husband, and make the visitor feel as if it came from him, rather than to present herself as a contrast to his unconscious reserve. She was, too, a wise and safe counsellor, and to her, on all important occasions, the strong man turned, with as much confidence in the soundness of her judgment as in the affection of her heart.

But the impression must not be left that Dr. J. was ever *repulsive* in his manner. It was the calmness of abstraction, and discerning people soon got to understand it.

For when recalled to a sense of what was passing, no man was more genial in social intercourse, and, by all that knew him best, he was as much beloved as admired.

Before terminating our account of his pastorate and other diversified labors at Milton, a few incidents ought to be mentioned that shed light upon the inner life of his religious character and labors. His house was the centre of a religious circle of humble but earnest people, who, amid all the worldliness that surrounded them, maintained a close walk with God, and seemed to keep the incense burning upon the social altar when religion languished all around. The little prayer-meeting, mentioned in his Reminiscences, often met at his house, and was mostly marked by fervor in the devotional exercises. The judgment-day only can disclose the influence of that cluster of praying people. Some of the precious names are found appended to the following covenant, a copy of which, in the handwriting of the lamented Laird, has been transmitted to the writer, since he began these pages, by the fifth signer, and the only survivor of the eight whose names are affixed :

"*At the House of the Rev. Geo. Junkin, Thursday Evening, January 1st,* 1829.

"WE the subscribers, deeply impressed with a sense of our own sins and shortcomings during the past year, and desirous of feeling pungent sorrow for our lukewarmness in the service of our gracious Redeemer, and believing that a mutual *pledge* of increased attention to the duties of prayer, of self-denial, of diligence in the study of the Holy Scriptures, of all that provocation to love and good works, which the Bible recommends, might be a means of securing such attention, and of advancing our own souls in the practical knowledge of the divine life, do *hereby express our desire* and *intention* of *heart,* to love God and his people more purely and fervently during *this* year than we have done in the last, to serve Him and them better, to live more abstracted from the *anxious* cares of this life, more loose from the world, more steadily prepared for our transit to the heavenly state, more deeply and sensibly alive to the spiritual wants of our friends and neighbors, the church, and mankind at large, more actively at war with sin, less conformed to the world, and more transformed in the renewing of our minds; in short, we desire to feel as Paul felt when he said, 'To me to live is Christ, and to die is gain.' And if God, in his long-suffering, should spare our lives and open in his holy providence the door, it is our wish and desire to meet in this room, on the next New-Year's evening, to thank Him for his mercies, to confess our sins before Him and invoke his benediction. Or, if God shall see proper to send for any of us, the survivors will praise Him for any bright hopes He may have caused to play around the grave's devouring mouth, and to ask Him to bless the visitation of his rod. And now may the Lord our Redeemer display the might of his holy arm, in powerfully arresting and turning the attention of the people of this town and its vicinity to the great concerns of the eternal world.

"GEO. JUNKIN,
"MATTHEW LAIRD,
"WM. L. HOUSEL,
"JULIA R. JUNKIN,
"MARY MOORE,
"JOHN BODINE,
"SAMUEL MORRISON,
"DANIEL GASTON."

This is here inserted as an index of the spirit that pervaded the heart of its writer, the pastor, and the hearts of the seven who joined with him in the covenant. It was an odd coincidence that the copy reached the writer, by mail, just half a century after it was signed, having been sent in response to a notice in the *Presbyterian*, asking for material for this biography.

The lady who sent it, Mrs. Parke, of Pottsgrove, is the sister of the Rev. J. Wilson Moore, the first missionary to Arkansas Territory, before mentioned as a student of Milton Academy. When he heard of the death of Dr. Junkin, he sent to the *Central Presbyterian* a communication in regard to him, parts of which are here inserted, as containing the estimate of one who was reared, in a measure, under his influence at Milton, and because it will throw light upon that part of his life now being recorded. Half a century had not erased the impression made upon the mind of the writer, and, forty years after having last heard his voice in the pulpit, he was able thus to write:

REMINISCENCES OF A PIONEER.

"No faithful minister of the gospel has any proper conception of the effects of his own labors. He may often in the hours of his despondency imagine that he has labored in vain and spent his strength for nought; and ask the question, Who hath believed our report? But his words are remembered by others when they are forgotten by himself, and will influence the life and actions of many when his tongue lies silent in the grave.

"It was my happy lot in my younger days to sit under the instructions of the Rev. George Junkin in the early years of his ministry,—and though fifty years have glided away since the time I first heard him preach, and more than forty since I last heard his voice in the pulpit, I know not that a single day of all this period has passed in which some of the words he uttered have not risen in my remembrance; or that a single Sabbath has passed when I have not found myself influenced by the instructions I received from his lips.

"He had a mind of peculiar construction. His thoughts were profound and penetrating. His manner of elucidating and presenting divine truth was different from that of all men to whom I have ever listened. It was the testimony of most persons, that their memories could retain more of his discourses than of any other minister. His voice was peculiarly adapted to impress his thoughts. The Rev. Richard Armstrong, long a faithful and successful missionary in the Sandwich Isles, related to me that while a thoughtless boy he once heard Mr. Junkin repeat the words, 'And they *crucified* Him,' in such tones, that for a whole week they seemed to be sounding in his ears.

"He took unusual pains in showing the connection of

his text with the context, in defining the meaning of the words, and in pointing out the different shades of meaning in the original,—and often, when preaching from the Old Testament, in comparing it with the Septuagint. This, to some, seemed unnecessary, but he was at that time, though unconsciously to himself, preparing the minds of a number of his younger hearers, not only to think, but to labor with success in the vineyard of their Divine Master.

"When he had thus prepared the field before him, his presentation of doctrinal truth was overwhelming. He dwelt more than most ministers I have heard on the sovereignty of God, and the peculiar doctrines of grace. He dwelt much upon the electing love of God. This excited great opposition in the minds of those who were inclined to Arminian sentiments. I once saw him publicly and rudely assailed, as being guilty of inconsistency, when he had, at a funeral, held out in glowing terms the freeness of salvation to all who were willing to receive it as offered in the gospel. The objector told him that the doctrine he preached in the pulpit, viz., Calvinism, was the most dangerous in the world. He replied by simply requesting him to compare the lives of his congregation with the lives of those who preached a different doctrine.

"The conclusion of his discourses was of the most animating and moving character. I once heard a clergyman of great learning and judgment say, that he coveted nothing more than to be able to 'sum up' his discourses as did Mr. Junkin. 'For my own part,' said he, 'I expend my strength and feelings before I come to the close,—but Mr. J. reserves his to the last charge.' This is a most important point in the delivery of sermons. Many, after preaching good discourses, close by some scattering and pointless remarks, which leave the minds of their hearers unimpressed. Jonathan Edwards is said to have labored more in the preparation of his 'application,' than on any other part of his discourses. A convincing application is like having the last speech in a great debate. Of the celebrated Dr. Ryland it is said, that it was customary for the good old ladies of his congregation, at the close of his discourses, to whisper to each other through their tears,—'Well, of all Mr. Ryland's sermons, *this* was the best.'

"Mr. Junkin was connected with the Associate Reformed

Church when I first knew him, but he shortly after became a member of the Northumberland Presbytery. Like most other men of superior talents and decided character, he had bitter enemies and warm friends. He never counted the cost in reproving sin. His enemies hated him with a cordial hatred, and his friends would have laid down their lives for his sake. But what may seem strange, there were some of his brethren in the ministry who always treated him with marked coolness. But this surprise will vanish when we call to mind, that even among the disciples there was a strife, as to which of them should be the greatest. Men do not become angels on earth. It is not uncommon, however deplorable, for good men to envy others of superior talents. I never could perceive any evidence of unhallowed ambition on the part of Mr. Junkin.

"Every one who has entered the ministry from proper motives will agree that the hour of his ordination to the sacred office was to him the most solemn and impressive of his life. In view of it he has often doubted. He has toiled and wept and prayed, perhaps for years. The hour has now come when he is about to receive his commission as an ambassador from the King of kings. He feels his own weakness and nothingness, and asks, Who is sufficient for these things? My thoughts now run far back to that solemn hour. I almost realize myself standing before a large and silent assembly, congregated in an old edifice, on the East Branch of the lovely Susquehanna,—a river not unknown to song,—for the place where I stood was not far below the village of Wyoming, which Campbell has rendered immortal by the story of its Gertrude. Before me rose the grave aspect of Mr. Junkin to deliver to me the charge.

"There were times when his vivid and poetic imagination carried him beyond his ordinary performances. This was one of those times. After alluding to the distance and unknown character of the region to which I was about to be ordained as an evangelist, he represented me as about to enter one of the dens of the Prince of Darkness, where I must contend with him alone. Then, suddenly passing from the scenes of time, he painted the coming of the Son of man; the myriads of all ages ascending from the land and from the sea to meet Him in the air; the separation of the righteous from the wicked; the joyful meeting of faithful ministers with those whom they have instrumentally saved and prepared for that day. He then graphically and awfully represented Apollyon, the great destroyer, as dragged before the tribunal of the Judge to hear his final doom. 'And *you*,' said he, 'must be able in that day to point to many a scar inflicted on his front by your right hand.' The imagery I cannot pretend to describe, but the impression will leave me, if ever, only in my dying hour. It followed me in my long journey. It has animated me a thousand times in my trials, when I have imagined myself engaged almost personally and literally in the figurative conflict described in a period long past.

"How blessed is the memory of the righteous! What a reward of grace awaits some persons! How glorious must be their entrance upon it!

"I was anxious to know something of the last hours of Dr. Junkin. His gifted daughter writes me that his last words were, 'Saviour,' 'Heaven.' How suggestive of the laborious past, and the blissful future!

"Let me die the death of the righteous, and let my last end be like his!

> "As swells abroad the last trump's sound,
> Let me be found where he is found;
> As sinks beneath my foot the land,
> Let me but stand where he doth stand!"
>
> *Central Presbyterian.*

* * * * * * *

The enemies, who the above writer says hated him with a cordial hatred, could not have been numerous, and consisted of those whose sins he pungently reproved, and, it may be, of a few whom he had worsted in argument, or whose "liquor traffic" was interfered with by his temperance efforts. None, who intimately knew the man, could cordially hate him, for the purity of his motives and of his life disarmed hatred.

A characteristic of Mr. Junkin's piety that imparted a peculiar cast to his ministry, was the implicitness of his belief "of the whole word of God," and the confidence with which he seemed to expect the fulfilment of every promise and every prophecy. He "received the kingdom of God as a little child," with uncaviling faith; and never seemed to doubt what was recorded of God's past working, nor what was predicted of His future operations. He took broad and comprehensive views of Christ's mediatorial kingdom, and considered all things else subservient to its interests. Hence he studied history, and noted contemporary providences, in the light of the Scriptures, and especially of prophecy. And whilst admitting that the interpretation of prophecy, antecedent to its fulfilment, was difficult, and to be attempted with modesty, yet he believed that "the testimony of Jesus is the spirit of prophecy," and that it was a duty to study the prophetic writings as well as other portions of the Scriptures. Accordingly, he kept his eye steadily upon the development of God's providential scheme in the progress of contemporary history, and failed not to compare history in its unfoldings with history prescript in the prophecies. He accordingly bestowed more attention upon the subject of prophecy, throughout his entire ministry, than is usual among ministers of the gospel.

The struggle of Greece with the Ottoman power, which resulted in the independence of the former, occasioned the first public effort of this kind. The decisive battle of Navarino, in which the fleets of England and France almost annihilated that of the Turk, aroused his mind to the consideration of those prophecies that, as he supposed, related to "the false Prophet," and to the downfall of the Ottoman Empire. He published a series of essays upon this subject in 1828–9, and the subsequent history of that power has gone far to confirm the correctness of his interpretations.

Many incidents in the history of Mr. Junkin's ministrations at Milton might be recorded illustrative of his zeal, fervor, fearlessness, and power in the pulpit; but it would swell this narrative beyond convenient dimensions. One incident is so vividly impressed upon the writer's memory, and on the memory of many still living, that it comes up with the freshness of a present reality. It was a sultry Sabbath afternoon. The little Shiloh Church was full of hearers. Mr. Junkin was in the pulpit. His theme was the judgment to come. Suddenly there swept down from the northwest a dark, portentous cloud, which came rapidly careering upon the wings of the wind. In a few minutes it burst upon the town with the violence of a tornado. So loud was the thunder and the howling of the storm that the crash of a huge walnut-tree that was blown against the church-building was scarcely perceived. The voice of the speaker was soon lost in the voice of the storm. He paused, but remained erect in the pulpit, calm and composed, and apparently engaged in silent prayer. Consternation sat upon every countenance in the assembly. Suddenly some of the windows gave way, and the storm burst in; and the part of the audience that occupied the north side of the house rushed—seemed almost to be swept—to the other side. The crush of the edifice seemed inevitable; but it withstood the pressure, and the storm swept past; and as its wail died in the distance, there was a solemn silence in the church, that might be felt. With a calm, steady, solemn voice, and an impressiveness of manner corresponding with the scene, the preacher exclaimed, "If such be the tones of his voice, and such the mere lifting of his finger,—if we thus quail before the mere whisper of his wrath, oh! what shall be its tones when the Archangel's trump shall peal! What the exhibition of his power when his arm is bared for final vengeance! What our terror, if we abide the storms of his righteous and eternal indignation! Oh! fly for refuge to the Ark of Salvation!"

The effect was such, for the moment at least, as is rarely produced upon an audience; and with a prayer and the benediction he dismissed them.

CHAPTER XIV.

At Milton—Mr. Kirkpatrick—Reformation of 1828—Mr. Barber's Mission and Request—Action of the Presbytery—Resolutions concerning Church Discipline and Sacraments—Wide-spread Effect—Letters on Temperance—Remedies—In the General Assembly—Elected Principal of M. L. Academy.

ALLUSION has been made in a previous chapter to the state of the churches in the region of the Susquehannas. This state of things was deplored by Mr. Junkin, and by most of his brethren of the Presbytery, as well as by many godly laymen. All desired a revival and a reformation of existing abuses; but previous to Mr. J.'s union with the Presbytery there was no one who seemed willing to breast the storm of popular opposition with which, it was apprehended, the needed reforms would be met. Nor was it to be expected that he would at once assume a position which more properly belonged to the older members of the body. A newcomer would of course encounter more odium than one who had long held a place in the Sanhedrim of the district. Whilst, therefore, he was prompt to make efforts against intemperance, Sabbath-breaking, and profanity, Mr. J. waited a little while for some providential opportunity of assailing other evils that were more fully within the church. But he lost no time in preparing the way for such assault. He conversed often with his brethren upon these topics, discussed them in his own pulpit, and wherever else opportunity offered; and in this way prepared the minds of others to co-operate in needed changes. Nor was it very long until, in God's providence, an occasion was offered that called out the action he desired. This occasion shall be presently mentioned.

It ought to have been mentioned that Mr. Junkin's intimate friend and coadjutor in the educational work, the Rev. David Kirkpatrick, had come also into the Presbytery of Northumberland. One of the last acts of the Presbytery of Philadelphia (A. R.) was to ordain Mr. Kirkpatrick, who was a licentiate before leaving Ireland, to the work of the ministry as an evangelist. This ordination took place in Shiloh Church, Milton, and Mr. K. continued, as long as he resided in Milton, to supply the church of Mifflinburg, and occasionally others, with the ministration of the Word and ordinances. Mr. K. was in constant intercourse with Mr. Junkin; and they often took counsel together about the interests of Zion. The eminent Teacher fully coincided with the Pastor in his views of church discipline, but was not blessed with that firmness of nerve that fitted him for leadership. He was always a faithful auxiliary.

The occasion which opened the way for the needed reform in regard to the matter of the sacraments was as follows: Mr. Daniel Barber, a licentiate of the Presbytery, an earnest and warm preacher of the gospel, had been laboring in a missionary field upon the head-waters of the Susquehanna, West Branch. The woodsmen and lumbermen of that wild region had rarely heard the gospel; no churches were organized, and the few that in their former homes had been members of the church, had mostly lost sight of their Christian obligations, and differed in little from the people of the world. But Mr. Barber's preaching produced a strong impression. Many were awakened to a sense of their spiritual need. Conversions took place. Some who had been members of the church were aroused to the remembrance of their former vows, and a very general wish was expressed to have the Lord's Supper administered, and to have the children baptized. Mr. Barber labored under the auspices of the Northumberland Missionary Society, but made his reports to the Presbytery under whose direction this society was conducted. He laid the above facts before the Presbytery, and, in view of them, he was ordained as an evangelist. He then asked for instructions. He informed the Presbytery, that when he should return to Sinnemahoning, with the full powers of a Minister of the gospel, the importunities for ordinances, which had beset him when a licentiate, would be renewed, and he wished to know whether he ought to baptize all the children that were offered, or only those, one or both of whose parents professed faith in Jesus, and became members of the church. This request for instructions was made just after the ordination solemnity closed, Nov. 21, 1827, and just as the Presbytery was about adjourning. As there was no time to discuss matters of such grave importance, the subject was referred to a committee, of which Mr. Junkin was made chairman, and the Presbytery adjourned to the eleventh day of January, 1828, to hear and act upon the report.

Thus called by an unexpected providence to the very work which he had been so long pondering, Mr. Junkin aimed to do it faithfully and thoroughly. He was aware, that the attempt to promulgate and reduce to practice in the churches the principles which he believed to be accordant with God's word and the standards of the church, would occasion great commotion, and encounter much opposition. He knew that the laxity in the practice of the churches had superinduced loose conceptions of the sacredness and of the obligations of the Sacraments. He knew that the practice of administering baptism privately had almost caused it to be no longer esteemed a public ordinance of the Lord's house, and that to restrict it to the children of parents, one or both of whom were in full communion with the church, would be resisted by all, or nearly all, who had taken advantage of the loose practice, and possibly by many of his brethren who had yielded to this popular demand. And he knew that the chief *odium populi* would fall upon his own head. But where principle and what he believed to be necessary for the welfare of the church were involved, he never faltered. He, in connection with the committee, prepared an elaborate report, well argued out, from the Scriptures and the standards, and not only meeting the points raised by Mr. Barber's request for instruction, but others necessarily and logically connected with them.

Meanwhile the idea had gone forth that this Committee would propose some radical reforms. And when the day for the meeting of the Presbytery came, although it proved inclement, the church in which they met (Penuel) was crowded to its utmost capacity. The Presbytery, too, was full. The report was presented. It was ably and prayerfully discussed for the space of two full days. On the second day, the Presbytery, and a large assembly of the people, continued seven hours, without recess and without commotion.

> "Before the vote was taken upon each resolution, and after argument upon it had ceased, the Moderator called upon some member to address the throne of grace for divine direction in the special vote about to be taken. This gave a peculiar solemnity to the scene, and, as all thought, brought the blessing of God upon the deliberations. On no other ground can we account for such perfect unanimity upon subjects upon which there had previously prevailed considerable diversity in practice."—*Religious Farmer.*

The writer, then a schoolboy, was present at this meeting, and well remembers the profound stillness and solemnity that pervaded it. He remembers that Mr. Kirkpatrick, in a speech of deep seriousness, asked the Presbytery to consider the momentous results of adopting such a paper.

He said it would strike deep, sweep wide, and revolutionize the practice of the churches. His heart and conscience went with the measure, yet he could not but apprehend serious commotions in the congregations. "It will cause," said he, "a breaking up like the breaking up of the Susquehanna in the spring freshet."

The resolutions adopted by the Presbytery at that time were seven in number, and each was sustained in the report by a succinct argument drawn from Scripture, the Standards, and the reason of the case. The first asserted that in the judgment of the Presbytery, according to the Word of God and the Standards of the Presbyterian Church, no parents have a right to present their children in baptism but those who (one or both) make a credible profession of faith in Christ, and obedience to Him, and evidence the same by obeying his dying command. The second declared the opinion that Baptism was a public sealing ordinance, and not, on ordinary occasions, to be privately administered. The third, expressed chiefly in the energetic language of Dr. Mason, declared "That an adult, in order to his right reception into the Christian church, must be acquainted with the leading doctrines of grace, must be able to 'give a reason of the hope that is within him,' must make an open and unequivocal avowal of the Redeemer's name, and must be reasonably vigilant in the habitual discharge of his religious and moral duty." The fourth asserted that the "Form of Government" and the Bible make it the duty and exclusive right of the Church Session to examine and admit persons to sealing Ordinances. The fifth asserted that the moral turpitude of faithless baptismal vows, and of unhallowed approach to the Lord's table, lay, in part, at the door of every member of a Session that admitted improper persons to these ordinances, being cognizant of the facts. The sixth claimed that Sessions ought to inquire of heads of families directly, whether family worship was observed or not, and not to admit habitual neglecters of it to sealing ordinances. And the seventh asserted "That a sound judgment, familiar acquaintance with Scripture doctrines, piety, and prayer, with capacity to rule, are indispensable qualifications for the office of ruling elder; and, where these cannot be found, that people are not ready to be organized into a congregation."

As was expected, this paper occasioned great commotion throughout the churches, not only within the bounds of the Presbytery, but beyond them. It was noticed and commented upon in the religious journals of the day, and occasioned much discussion of the subjects involved in different parts of the church. Some favored and some gainsaid the action of the Presbytery of Northumberland, yet few objections were made to the truth and righteousness of it, objection being chiefly raised against its expediency and the practicability of enforcing it. But such was the intrinsic reasonableness of the measures, and so conclusive were the argumentative parts of the paper, that there was far less objection to it within the bounds of the Presbytery than had been apprehended. It led thousands to think of the true nature and uses of church ordinances and of church discipline, and the members of Presbytery found much less difficulty in applying the principles assumed than they expected. It did good. It elevated the standard of church membership; it did much to restore the ordinance of baptism to its normal position and uses; it erected many a family altar where none had been before, and restored others that had fallen down; it roused the minds of the people to consider the solemn responsibilities involved in church membership; it struck an effective blow at worldly conformity and formalism; it strengthened the hands of Pastors and Sessions, in denying ordinances to the unworthy; it thus drew a broader line of demarcation between the church and the world, made the church purer, and thus more efficient for good, and produced many incidental benefits.

Whilst Mr. Junkin was the author of this paper, and bore a chief part in securing its adoption and promulgation from every pulpit in the Presbytery, having also, at the request of the Presbytery, published it in his periodical, it is due to truth to state, that nearly all the members of Presbytery stood up to the work with brave hearts and strong hands. The venerable Patterson, and Painter, and Smith, and Barber, and Kirkpatrick, and indeed all, acquiesced, and most were forward in the movement.

Although this ecclesiastical action occurred in the quiet domain of a rural Presbytery, and was done comparatively in a corner, yet was its influence wide-spread, and it is here recorded because it was one of the most important events of Mr. Junkin's labors in that region, and because it proves that from first to last he was found ready to toil and sacrifice his personal popularity and ease for what he believed to make for the purity, peace, and prosperity of Christ's blood-bought church. Sound doctrine, faithful discipline, and earnest Christian effort always found in him a zealous and unflinching advocate.

Allusion has been made to Mr. J.'s early temperance labors, and also to eight letters written after his recovery from the only serious illness of his life, to the gifted and noble physician whose attentions were the means, under God, of his recovery, but who was in danger from the convivial habits of the times. For obvious reasons, the name is suppressed; nor is it proposed to print these letters, although they might be productive of much good, being adapted to all similar cases, with the exception of a few personal allusions. But it is proposed to give a single extract, with a view of showing that the writer of these letters was then, as he generally has been, ahead of his times in regard to great and important principles and measures of reform. After reasoning most earnestly and logically with his friend, with a view to bring him to a sense of the danger of his course; after bringing arguments from the acknowledged principles of medical science, from the Bible, from history, from his friend's social and professional position and interests, from the sacred circle of domestic endearments, from the claims of honor, religion, and humanity, from Heaven, Earth, and Hell, he, in the sixth and seventh letters, suggests *remedies* for the terrible evil against which he sought to guard the gifted and accomplished victim; and these remedies, suggested in the infancy of the temperance movement, are such as the experience and the advance of half a century have not yet outstripped. They were,—

"1. Every morning go into a private room, read a chapter in the Bible, and bow your knees to the Father of Mercies, and ask Him to break off your fetters and set you free. This is the most important direction I have to give; . . . . for I cannot think a mere human resolve will ever effect the desired change. Look at the history of your own experience. How often have you resolved to avoid the peril, and in what have your resolves issued? In disappointment. And why? Because they were based upon human strength, not on divine power! As well might King Canute say to the ocean's swelling tide, 'Hitherto, and no farther.' So long as you depend upon your own firmness of purpose, you will fail. So long as you seek not divine aid, you flatter your own pride, and assume that you do not need God's guidance and help. . . . . Be entreated, then, as you value the interests dearest to your heart, to make experiment of this simple remedy. It will cost you about twenty minutes *per diem;* and it may save you twenty years of time, twenty thousand dollars in money, and secure you twenty millions of ages of heavenly joys in eternity.

"2. Cultivate the endearments of the domestic hearth. No man ever became intemperate in company of a wife and children whom he loved. God has given *you* a very high degree of those kindly feelings which are such lovely elements in the character of the husband and father. Despise not these gifts. Yield to the charm that is in the word *home.*" This is pressed at some more length.

"3. Study general science. If in a slack time of business you are at a loss for employment and amusement, and the dulness of idleness becomes wearisome, you are tempted to seek a cure in *company.* This is wrong; and to prevent this, let some branch of general science be always before your mind. . . . . Thus pleasant and profitable employment will prevent the *tedium* that leads to evil company.

"4. Abstain from visiting public houses altogether." This he reasons out at some length.

"5. Shun the society of such men as love to *sit* in the tavern. Company—*bad* company—is the curse of life. Shall a man who has an intelligent wife and sweet babes at home,—shall such a man be at a loss for company? . . . . 'But, somehow, you have got entangled with certain men, and it is difficult to get away.' I know it. I know that they have even dragged you into the bar by main force. But, stop! let us not blame them altogether. Had the house been on fire, and had they then attempted to drag you into the flames, would they have succeeded? I have no doubt that you would have beaten the whole of them to the ground. You *can,* if you *will,* fight your way out from among these men.

"6. My sixth direction is, Court the society of serious people. It is impossible to avoid being influenced by the company we keep. All the reasoning under the fifth rule applies here; and therefore I pass to another.

"7. Frequent places of public and social worship. Here I think you are too often wanting to yourself; and here a physician lies under peculiar temptation. It is often his *duty* to labor in his profession on the Sabbath. This *work of mercy,* if he be not greatly on his guard, will diminish in his mind a *sense of obligation* to obey the Fourth Commandment: and he who forms a *habit* of thinking lightly of *any part* of God's revealed will, is very liable to be led on to similar thoughts about other parts. The question is, therefore, of immense importance,—How shall a physician preserve upon his mind a due reverential regard for the Sabbath-day? I answer,—

"1st. Let him, when called upon, satisfy himself that the case is one of real necessity, and not one of those that have been put off for three or four days, in order to save time, by sending for the doctor and taking medicine on the Sabbath.

"2d. Let him either never *charge* for the labors of the Sabbath, or, if he charge the rich, let him give the fee to the poor or to some object of Christian charity. Then will it be indeed a work of mercy. This was Dr. Rush's practice; and it is easy to see how it will aid in judging of the *necessity* of each case. The contrary custom presents to the mind of the physician a moneyed temptation to labor on the Lord's day, without the call of necessity and mercy. If people know you *will* not come on the Sabbath unless it be a case of urgent necessity, they will send for you *before* or wait till after that holy day is over. Dr. Rush made it a rule to attend at least once every Sabbath at a place of worship.

"8. TOTAL ABSTINENCE FROM EVERYTHING INTOXICATING. I have long been of opinion, and so have *you*, and so have all reflecting men, that for a man of intemperate habits to break off *by degrees*, using it *moderately*, is an impossibility. The laws of matter and of mind must be changed before this can be. I had been of the opinion that total abstinence from *ardent spirits* might suffice; but *I now doubt it.* I fear the constitution that has been *accustomed* to artificial stimulants will foster the appetite, by the use of any of the milder stimulants. Even fermented drinks will keep alive the terrible thirst when once awakened; and that fell appetite can only die of starvation. It will live so long as any food for it is supplied. Here, then, are the remedies which I prescribe. They commend themselves to your reason. There is no quackery; they are infallible," etc.

These extracts, particularly the last, show that Mr. Junkin was years ahead of his times in the philosophy, the theory, and the practical measures of the temperance reformation. For, ten years after the date of the last of these letters, the writer of these passages was pronounced an extremist, for advocating abstinence from wines and the milder drinks.

The reader may be curious to know whether these letters accomplished the object for which they were written. It is not *known* that they did. The fact of their having been written remained, so far as the writer is informed, a secret between their author and his wife, on the one side, and the recipient on the other. Although a member of Dr. Junkin's family at the time most of them were written, the biographer knew nothing of them until he found the copies among his deceased brother's papers. The eminent physician to whom they were addressed did not seem, at the time, to have fully yielded to their reasonings and remonstrances; but we are happy to add that a few years later he resumed his manhood, and, by God's grace, it is believed, became an exemplary man and a member of the Presbyterian Church. Whether the good seed sown by the faithful pastor, and watered with his tears and prayers, had any direct influence in working the happy change, is known only to God and to the physician himself.

Thus in the humble sphere of the village and rural Pastor and Editor, did the subject of this memoir employ his time and talents for a little more than eleven years, maturing his powers for a wider range and a higher sphere of usefulness in the years to follow. His reputation as a scholar, a thinker, a preacher, a debater, and a writer, had extended far beyond the region of his immediate labors. Many precious seasons of encouragement in his work had brightened these years of toil and trial. Confidence in the purity of his motives, the correctness of his principles, the integrity of his life, the faithfulness and courage of his efforts, and the general wisdom of his measures, had slowly but steadily grown upon the public mind. Admiration for his talents, and love to his person, were in thousands strong, in many enthusiastic. And whilst some, even of his best friends, thought that a less rigid and a more compromising line of policy might have accomplished as much good and at less sacrifice on his part, yet all conceded that he had not passed, indeed, that he had not yet reached the zenith of his popularity and usefulness, when, in God's providence, he was summoned to another field of labor. All conceded, that at the time he departed from Milton, he was more admired, trusted, and loved than at any previous period of his sojourn there. For that departure Providence was now preparing the way.

Mr. Junkin had, not long after his union with the Presbytery of Northumberland, been sent by that Presbytery as a commissioner to the General Assembly of 1826. "In this body I felt so timid, that I fairly quivered when the Clerk, in reading the roll, came near to my name. I could scarcely speak enough to say 'Here!' "* Strange, that nerves that never trembled when maintaining the right in opposition to exasperated sons of Belial, should "quiver" when surrounded by the venerable and distinguished ministers of the church in a solemn assembly.

"At this time the semi-Pelagian controversy was about rising in the Presbyterian Church. The American Education Society, through its Presbyterian branch, was liberally aiding our candidates. Rev. Wm. T. Hamilton, as its agent, visited Milton, and I got a scholarship subscribed in my church. With some zeal I entered into the plan, not then understanding, in all its complications, the whole bearing of the scheme."†

This shows his readiness to co-operate in every undertaking that appeared to make for the advancement of the cause of Christ. He afterwards became convinced that this society, in connection with the Home Missionary Society, with which he also had co-operated, being external to the Presbyterian Church, yet working within it, exerted influences unfavorable to its purity and peace. He thought that the system pursued by the Education Society at that

* Rem. † Rem.

time of taking vouchers of indebtedness from its beneficiaries, to be paid after they entered the ministry, tended to *enthral* the young men, and gave this Society a power over them which destroyed their independence, and bound them, not so much by ties of gratitude as by pecuniary obligations, to the Society to which these notes were payable, and, in this way, gave to the officers of the Society an undue control over the ministers of the church who had been aided by them. But, at this date, the questions pertaining to voluntary associations for such purposes, as distinguished from ecclesiastical organization, had not risen into prominence, and Mr. J. was active in co-operation with both these Societies, as also with the American Board of Foreign Missions. The Milton Missionary Society, which he was instrumental in organizing, was auxiliary to the latter, and, as the Presbyterian Church at that time had no general missionary organization, he did what he could through the American Board.

In 1829 he was again commissioned to the General Assembly, and the next year also. This second appointment was made by his brethren both as a token of their confidence, and to facilitate his attendance upon the ordination of his nephew, the (now) Rev. Dr. John M. Dickey, who was ordained pastor of the church of New Castle, Delaware. In both these last-mentioned Assemblies he saw indices of the rising controversy, in which he was afterwards involved. There had appeared in the first General Assembly of which he was a member, some of the difficulties growing out of "The Plan of Union" of 1801. A Mr. Bissell, from the Presbytery of Rochester, who was not a ruling elder, but only a "committeeman," appeared as a commissioner, and, after some opposition, was admitted as a member of the Assembly. Against this action forty-two members protested. A similar case had occurred in 1820, and continued to recur until the crisis of 1837 was brought on.

"It was whilst sitting in the Assembly of 1830 that Brother Robert Steel, pastor of Abington, came to me and told me of the vacancy that had just occurred, by the resignation of Professor Monteith, in the presidency of the 'Manual Labor Academy of Pennsylvania' at Germantown, and called my attention to it as a field of very promising labor. Mr. Steel took me out to visit the Academy. The whole enterprise was so nearly what I had previously conceived as a mode of education, that, upon my friend's urgency, I consented to become a candidate, convinced that I might be more useful in bringing into the ministry men of the right stamp, and thus do more than I could in my pastoral position. There was, too, in the vicinity of the Academy, a fine church, and a small nucleus of a congregation, offering a pretty good field of labor. The election took place, and in due time I was informed of my having been appointed. Even then, parties had been so far arrayed in Philadelphia, that some members of the Board objected to me as too 'Old School;' but these objections were overruled."*

He, after prayerful and careful consideration of the subject, became convinced that the indications of God's providence pointed him to the field of Education as the one for his future toils, and, with him, such a conviction was the immediate precursor of action.

---

* Rem.

CHAPTER XV.

Mutual Regrets of Parting—Farewell Sermons—Removal to Germantown—Entrance upon Duty—State of the Institution—Revived Efficiency—Practical Difficulties of Location—Contemplated Removal.

THE tidings that Mr. Junkin had been invited to another field of labor spread rapidly through his congregations, and throughout the district in which he had been so long prominent and so much beloved, and it was received with unfeigned sorrow. To a man of his deep and sensitive emotional nature, the thought of such a change awakened the tenderest feelings. He could not, without great pain to his natural sensibilities, tear away from so many dear friends. But with him, though a man of strong feeling, conscience and judgment always held control. He made prompt preparations for the removal. He delivered farewell discourses in each of his congregations, and in several of the places where he had preached with frequency. In the Valley he delivered his last discourse on July 28th, and at Penuel and Shiloh, August 8th, 1830. These were attended by crowds of people, and Bochim was the proper name for each occasion, for there were weepings such as had never before been known on a like occasion in that country. Rev. iii. 11 and II. Tim. i. 13 were the subjects of his sermons: "Hold that fast which thou hast, that no man take thy crown." "Hold fast the form of sound words, which thou hast heard of me," etc. And those who heard them said that he had surpassed himself in strength and tenderness.

He proceeded immediately to Germantown, and entered upon public duty there; for on the next Sabbath after his farewell at Milton we find him occupying the pulpit at the former place.

The institution over which he was now called to preside had been inaugurated, a few years before, by some philanthropic gentlemen of the Presbyterian Church, in and around Philadelphia, with a view to facilitate the education of young men for the Christian ministry. Three principal objects were aimed at in its plan. First, to preserve the health of students, and promote bodily development, by regular exercise at manual labor; secondly, to enable young men in moderate circumstances to defray a part of the expenses of their education, by laboring a portion of each day; and thus, thirdly, to encourage a greater number to seek a thorough education, especially with a view to increasing the ranks of the Gospel ministry.

Mr. Junkin, as we have seen, had already attempted the system, upon a small scale, at his home in Milton, and his heart was already in the scheme. He was also peculiarly qualified for the station, not merely by the force of his talents and the maturity of his scholarship and aptness to teach, but also by his power of systematic organizing, and by a wonderful, almost instinctive, skill in mechanics and agriculture. Of these last he had practical knowledge, unusual in an educated man. He entered upon his educational career with energy and enthusiasm. The institution, which had been for some time in a languishing condition, began to revive. Students flocked to it, until no more could be received for want of accommodations. Many young men from the region of the Susquehanna followed him to Germantown, attracted by their love to his person and confidence in his ability. But the institution was without funds. A debt rested upon the real estate that had been purchased for its accommodation, and Mr. Junkin soon found, that unless he advanced funds out of his private fortune to purchase materials for the farm and the workshops, as well as some needed appliances of education, the enterprise would not succeed. The novelty of the undertaking had somewhat worn off, under the administration of his predecessors. A measure of apathy had invaded the Board of Trustees, with the exception of a few of the Ministers; and Mr. J. soon discovered, that the entire responsibility of carrying forward the undertaking was devolved upon himself. He had to employ professors, and meet all pecuniary claims, upon his own responsibility, with little co-operation from those who had, with apparent zeal for the cause, called him from his pastorate to these toils and responsibilities. But he was not a man to become soon discouraged. His heart and hands were both in the work, and it went forward. In the twenty months of his administration the school continued to flourish, and many young men, who have since made their mark in the learned professions, and in the councils of States and the nation, obtained part of their education in this school. It assumed, indeed, very much the character of a College, with its literary societies, and other stimulants and aids to improvement. That eminent scholar, philosopher, and educator Charles F. McCay, afterwards LL.D., and Professor of Natural Philosophy in the University of Georgia, and President of the College of South Carolina, was his very efficient coadjutor in the instruction. Mr. J.'s brother, the writer of these pages, was for a time teacher in languages, and others, with these, gave efficiency to the instruction.

But a year's experiment convinced the Principal, that Germantown was not a proper location for the Academy. The staples of subsistence were as costly as in the City, whilst the material for the workshops had to be purchased at city prices, brought out over a turnpike at great cost of transportation, under heavy tolls, and then the manufactures returned at similar cost to the City, to compete in the market with the products of city workmen, subject to none of these charges. Boxes and trunks, in which to pack goods for shipment, were the articles principally manufactured in the shops of the school, and the students could not, with such odds against them, compete with the city workmen. But, as they were paid a stipulated price per hour for their labor, the losses fell upon the institution, *i.e.* upon the Principal.

These difficulties were laid before the Board of Trustees, who readily appreciated them; and it was resolved to remove the Academy to a more favorable location. A site on the banks of the Delaware, above the City, where the advantage of water transportation could be obtained, was selected, and steps began to be taken for the removal. But of course the property at Germantown must be sold, the new premises purchased, and buildings erected. These measures required time. Meanwhile the institution went vigorously on. But events were providentially evolving that gave a different direction to the future of Mr. Junkin, and of the Academy. These must be now narrated.

In a future chapter it will be necessary to detail the gradual rise of that controversy which resulted, in 1838, in the disruption of the Presbyterian Church. Symptoms of that great struggle began to show themselves in 1820, before Dr. Junkin became a member of the body. In 1831 the parties, which had long been forming under influences hereafter to be described, stood out in distinct array. The lines had been partially drawn the preceding year; but in 1831 it was made a question in the election of Moderator, the choice falling upon Dr. Beman, of Troy, a man identified with the intenser type of the new Theology, and with the movements of the Voluntary Societies, who proposed to conduct the educational and missionary work of the church. And although no very decided step was taken by the majority of that year, it being quite small, its decisions and protests called out no little feeling; and nearly everybody took sides. It was not to be expected, that a minister of Mr. Junkin's decided character and pronounced Presbyterianism could remain neutral. He of course sided with the "Old School;" and events soon occurred in his own Presbytery (Philadelphia,—for he had become a member of it in the fall of 1830), which not only precluded the possibility of his remaining neutral, but also, in connection with other providences, led him to make that change in the field of his labors which resulted in the founding of Lafayette College.

In the Board of Trustees of the Academy were some men of New England origin, who naturally sympathized with the "New School" party in the church. Added to these were some who sympathized with Mr. Barnes in his troubles with the Presbytery and Synod of Philadelphia and in the General Assembly. That gentleman had preached and published at Morristown, N. J., where he was pastor of the First Presbyterian Church of the place, a sermon entitled "The Way of Salvation." Shortly after this, and chiefly upon the merits of this sermon, Mr. Barnes was called to the pastorate of the First Presbyterian Church of Philadelphia. When the call was presented to the Presbytery of Philadelphia, and leave asked by the congregation to prosecute it, opposition was made to granting leave on account of the errors in doctrine alleged to be contained in that discourse, and on account of the fact, that Mr. Barnes had never preached before the congregation that called him. The church which had called Mr. Barnes was large and influential with the Presbytery, and a majority voted to grant leave to prosecute the call.

Shortly after this a meeting of the Presbytery *pro re nata* was called for the purpose of receiving Mr. Barnes, and, if the way should be clear, taking steps for his installation. At this meeting, after reading the minutes of the previous meeting relating to his case, it was moved that he be received; and, after some discussion, Dr. Ely moved that this motion be postponed "in order that before deciding it any member of the Presbytery, who may deem it necessary, may ask of Mr. Barnes such explanations of his doctrinal views as may be deemed necessary." This motion was lost (18 to 20), and Mr. Barnes was received as a member of Presbytery. Charges were then formally tabled against Mr. Barnes, by the Rev. Brogun Hoff, for unsoundness in the faith, as a bar to his installation; but the Moderator, who sympathized with the majority, decided that they were out of order, on the grounds that they would be new business at a *pro re nata* meeting. The minority contended that it was pertinent to the business for which the Presbytery was called, and belonged to the question of the way being clear. Dr. Ely appealed from this decision, but the majority sustained the decision, and installed Mr. Barnes on the 25th of June following. These events took place in April, 1830, before Mr. Junkin became a member of the Presbytery. The minority, with the venerable Dr. Ashbel Green at their head, complained of these proceedings to the Synod of Philadelphia. The Synod, which met at Lancaster in the following October (1830), sustained the complaint, and adopted two resolutions explanatory of their decision, and mandatory to the Presbytery,—1st, That the Presbytery gave just ground of complaint in not allowing the examination of Mr. Barnes in view of his published sermon; and 2d, Enjoining the Presbytery "to hear and decide on the objections to the orthodoxy of the sermon of Mr. Barnes, and to take such order on the whole subject as is required by a regard to the purity of the church and its acknowledged doctrine and order." (Minutes of Synod, p. 13; also Baird's Digest, p. 650.)

Up to this point, Mr. Junkin had taken no active part in this unhappy controversy; and although he no doubt felt that the judgment of the Synod was a righteous one, he had remained quiet, unwilling needlessly to jeopard the interests of the institution over which he presided, by taking unnecessary part in a matter upon which the Trustees of it were divided in opinion. But events soon forced him, either to prove recreant to his convictions of right and of fair dealing, or to stand in defence of them.

The Presbytery of Philadelphia, at the close of the Synod, was called together by the Moderator, and rather hastily adjourned to meet in Philadelphia, at a time so soon (twenty-five hours) after the rising of the Synod as to make it almost physically impossible for all the members to get to the meeting, unless they could have obtained seats in the coaches that first left Lancaster. This the "Old School" members did not succeed in doing, as did their shrewder brethren, and of course were delayed in getting to the meeting. Mr. Junkin, having his own conveyance, got to the meeting in season, still not suspecting that the majority would seriously contemplate taking up the case of Mr. Barnes, in the absence, under such circumstances, of so many of the members. And when the effort was made, his love of fair dealing compelled him to resist it. He warned and besought his brethren not to do a thing which even honorable men of the world would condemn. He and a few others continued their resistance until the delayed brethren arrived.

Among other illustrations which he employed upon the occasion, was that such a procedure would prove, like a bucket of live coals thoughtlessly placed near combustible material, the cause of a conflagration which they all might deplore. Baffled by the man's firmness, there was some feeling aroused in the Presbytery against him; and a distinguished elder of the Presbytery, who was a member of the Board of Trustees of the Academy, said, with some bitterness, "Mr. Junkin's bucket of coals may make his present place too hot for him." From that time forth it became manifest, that he could not expect such co-operation of the entire Board as assured ultimate success. Still, as there was no overt opposition, he continued to toil on, and the institution retained its prosperity, although at heavy cost to its Principal.

During the time of his residence at Germantown, Mr. Junkin preached the gospel almost every Sabbath, either in that place, in Philadelphia, or elsewhere. He maintained a Bible-class in the Institution, and a weekly prayer-meeting; and was ever ready to lend a helping hand in any evangelical effort. Here, as in his former charge, his Bible-classes were schools of rich instruction, and many of his pupils, who afterwards entered the ministry, have said that they had derived from his Bible-class instructions a large proportion of their theological knowledge. In Germantown, as in his previous fields of labor, he won many hearts, and his departure was a matter of sincere and general regret. Part of the time of his sojourn in Germantown, the venerable and lovely Dr. Wm. Neill was the stated supply of the church, and the intercourse between him and Mr. Junkin was of the most fraternal kind.

CHAPTER XVI.

Elected President of Lafayette College—Visits Easton—A College on Paper that ignored God—Presidency accepted—Removal of Pennsylvania M. L. Academy as to its entire Personnel to Easton—Incidents—Manual Labor System—Its Advantages and Difficulties—His Wonderful Labors—His Theory of Education—Progress.

DURING the winter of 1832, the attention of Mr. Junkin was called to Lafayette College, Easton, Pa., as a better field for his labors in the cause of education than the one he was then occupying. His friend and former fellow-student, the Rev. Robert Steel (the late Dr. Steel, of Abington), was the instrument, in this instance also, of his removal. When on a visit to Easton, Mr. Steel's attention was directed to the nascent College at that place, and through him Mr. Junkin was approached with a tender of the presidency.

The College as yet only existed on paper. A charter had been obtained in 1826 from the Legislature, granting to a Board of Trustees ample franchises for a college, in which military instruction and discipline were to be combined with the usual college *curriculum;* and repeated efforts had been made to organize and set it in operation. But one element of its constitution, as proposed by the leading persons in the enterprise, proved fatal to their earlier efforts,—they avowed the intention of founding a college in which religion should have no place, and in which no Minister of the Gospel of any sect should hold office. The God whom they proposed to ignore thwarted all their efforts, and no endowment was obtained, no lands or buildings procured, and no professors or students.

In process of time some of the very men who proposed to found a college without God and religion, professed conversion, and became the friends of Christ; and then they turned to a Minister of Jesus to help them to carry out their oft-defeated enterprise. Mr. Junkin was elected President, visited the place, and consented to accept upon certain conditions. These conditions were, that the charter should be so modified as to substitute *manual labor* instead of military drill, with such other changes as would adapt it to the ends of a manual labor college. These modifications of the charter were promptly obtained from the Legislature, then in session, through the energetic efforts of the President of the Board, the Hon. James Madison Porter.

A farm of some seventy acres, with spacious mansion and other buildings, was leased for the temporary accommodation of the institution. This farm lay on the south bank of the Lehigh, adjoining Easton, near to the site now occupied by the railroad station. Early in April, 1832, Mr. Junkin, having previously resigned the presidency of the Pennsylvania Manual Labor Academy, removed to Easton and commenced the college enterprise. The professors and nearly all the students of the Academy joined in this migration. Prof. McCay had been appointed to the Chair of Mathematics and Natural Philosophy in the College; and James I. Kuhn, Esq., was soon after appointed to the Chair of Ancient Languages.

But every material appliance of a college had to be created. Temporary recitation-rooms and shops were erected, and in a short time affairs assumed the state of order and energy, which the eye and the hand of Mr. Junkin always evoked. There were no funds for the endowment of the College, and the Board of Trustees, having no property, had, as a Board, no credit. The President was therefore under the necessity of assuming, as in his former field, all pecuniary responsibility, and to depend upon the income of the institution for indemnity. Some subscriptions were made by citizens of Easton; but no funds, at all adequate even to the beginning of such an enterprise, had been provided.

But the President had strong faith in God and in the value and importance of the enterprise, and he went forward. Students came in encouraging numbers; the literary societies that had existed in the Academy at Germantown resumed and continued their functions, and all the arrangements for giving thorough instruction were increased.

So soon as the institution was placed in working order, so that his presence was not imperatively necessary, Mr. Junkin entered upon the arduous and self-denying duty of collecting funds for erecting a college edifice, and for providing other necessary appliances of education. In prosecuting this part of the work, he travelled extensively and toiled arduously, in visiting churches and individuals. He preached and made addresses frequently, wrote series after series of articles for the press, explanatory of the undertaking in which he was engaged, and performed an amount of labor that seemed impossible for the powers of one man to accomplish. Over the signature "Fellenberg," he published a series of essays on education, and the connection of study with physical culture, by means of manual labor. These were marked by great vigor of thought and style, and were extensively read. He was very sanguine in the hope, that "the health-preserving labor of the hands would defray the expenses of education;" and at this period, the system was much in vogue and was growing in popularity. His writings and addresses contributed largely to increase the public confidence in the system; and not only those students whose slender means made it necessary, but even the sons of the wealthy, resorted to this and similar institutions, in order to avoid that prostration of the physical frame that is too often the price of a course of college study.

Nor did Dr. Junkin EVER lose confidence in the system which he had so eloquently advocated, and which he sacrificed so much to inaugurate. He continued always to believe that it is the normal mode of educating human beings ; and, whilst he was not blind to the intrinsic, as well as the adventitious difficulties of the system, he never faltered in the belief that those difficulties could be largely forestalled, under proper organization and with adequate means, and that the valuable results would amply repay the hindrances to be removed. The intrinsic obstacles lay in the difficulty of giving employment to all the students, and at the same time securing regularity in study and recitations,—in the difficulty of passing from some kinds of labor to study or the class-room, of securing proper alternations of study and labor, and of awarding just compensation for labor, so that the lazy and unskilled might not be rewarded as much as the skilful and industrious.

The adventitious difficulties lay in the prejudices of society, the foolish ideas that labor is degrading, that to ply a mechanic or agricultural art is unworthy the gentleman, and that the student ought not to be robust and vigorous, but pale and effeminate. Prejudices against interference with the business of workmen in the regular trade also embarrass an institution of the kind. Tradespeople look with jealousy upon any efforts at production on the part of persons whose main business is not to produce. The same objections that are raised against the products of penitentiary labor are started against the products of a manual labor school or college, and it is difficult, on this account, to find fair and ready market for them.

To insure the success of this system over all these difficulties and against all these prejudices, would have required at least as large an endowment as is deemed requisite to establish a college upon the old system, and would have demanded the earnest co-operation of a Board of Trust, a Faculty with their *hearts* in the work, and a fair measure of public confidence in the system. But for a single individual, with but a limited private fortune, without any endowment either to support professors or to provide appliances of education and workshops, tools and a stock of material for the manual labor department, it was an undertaking requiring strong faith and indomitable energy,—an undertaking, the success of which could hardly be expected upon any basis of ordinary calculation. But Mr. Junkin's whole soul was intent upon the work of education, and especially upon the work of raising up well-educated and efficient Ministers of the Gospel. His idea of education was, that it consisted in *drawing out* all the powers of the human being, physical, mental, and spiritual, developing these powers by appropriate exercise, and training them to appropriate ends. He held that, in order to normal education, the entire human trinity—body, soul, and spirit—must be consentaneously and proportionately developed; and that if either of the parts of the man—physical, mental, or moral—be cultured to the neglect of the others, it will result in a monstrous development, and not in a perfect man. "*Mens sana in corpore sano*," was what he aimed to produce in the case of every student placed under his care; and perhaps no educator of his period bestowed so much care and effort to secure that result. And, as he believed that *useful* employment—exercise with a valuable *aim* and with palpable and useful *results*—is best adapted to physical development in connection with mental and moral culture, his confidence in the manual labor system was never shaken. So long as his first connection with Lafayette College lasted, he maintained that system in the face of difficulties that would have appalled any other man.

And had he possessed the means of giving the system a fair and full trial, it is the opinion of many that he would have demonstrated its value and practicability to the entire satisfaction of the public. As it was, *it never failed in his hands*. But its success in his hands was at great cost of money and toil. It was impossible to obtain a corps of teachers who sympathized in the system, or who had confidence in it. So far from this, his professors, whilst men of ability and scholarly attainment and skill as instructors, had been educated under the old system, and thought that a college must be just the copy of their several *Almæ Matres*. They thought that the hands that held books ought not to hold tools, that it was more dignified to exert the muscles in hitting a ball than in driving a nail, in pitching a quoit than in pushing a plane or a handsaw, in wielding a bat than in handling the hoe. And with these prejudices in the minds even of their instructors, it was a much more difficult task than it would otherwise have been for the President to preserve among the students a proper sentiment in regard to the useful system of gymnastics that he sought to introduce. And when to this we add the indifference or incredulity of the public, and the natural indolence of youth, it is a matter of wonder that the system was as successful as it was.

When Mr. Junkin was translated to the Miami University, the manual labor system gradually fell into disuse in Lafayette College; and, upon his being recalled to the presidency of the latter, four years afterward, he found it so far lost sight of that it was only restored as a voluntary system,—*i.e.* only those students worked who desired to do it.

No mind, unacquainted with the detail of facts, can form any adequate conception of the amount of care, vexation, wearing responsibility, mental exertion, and bodily toil involved in establishing a college, even upon the ordinary plan. All these are vastly augmented and intensified in the case of a manual labor college, in which, to the toils and cares of ordinary administration, are added the solicitude and labors of extensive workshops, farming and gardening operations, the laying in of material, the superintendence of labor, the keeping separate accounts of the labor of each student, the sale of proceeds, the purchase of subsistence for so large a body of pupils, the control of boarding establishments, and many other cares; all of which devolved upon the President. For, although he appointed business agents, he had to plan for the whole, superintend the whole, and was personally and pecuniarily responsible for all. Yet did Mr. Junkin endure it all, and not only did his share of the teaching, after the higher college classes were organized, but managed the whole complicated enterprise, at home and abroad.

CHAPTER XVII.

The Pennsylvania Manual Labor Academy the Nucleus of Lafayette—Progress of the Latter Institution—Labors in the Cause of General Education—Influence upon the Legislature—Governor Wolf—Thaddeus Stevens—Dr. J. one of the Founders of the Pennsylvania System—Established the First Normal School—College Site bought—Edifice begun—Completed—Example—Mrs. Junkin.

THE fact that, with the exception of two or three who were ready to enter the higher classes in college, all the students of the institution at Germantown followed or accompanied him to Easton, attests the confidence which they and their parents reposed in Dr. Junkin as an educator. Indeed, the school at Germantown, in almost its entire personnel, became the nucleus of Lafayette College. Professor McCay continued in the Department of Mathematics and Philosophy, and Professor Kuhn, soon after, entered upon the duties of the Chair of Languages. Accessions to the ranks of the students came in numbers beyond the capacity of the buildings to receive them. And it ought to be recorded to the honor of the noble band of youth that followed Mr. Junkin to this new scene of his toils, that they zealously co-operated with him in the necessary efforts to get the institution under way in the new locality, and cheerfully submitted to the inconvenience and discomfort occasioned by their straitened quarters and by the lack of adaptation of the buildings to the purposes of a college. With their own hands they erected temporary buildings to accommodate the increasing numbers of students, until more permanent edifices could be erected.

The lands, being more extensive than those at Germantown, offered more scope for agricultural labor by the students. But workshops were provided, and facilities for mechanical labor were offered, whilst the regular routine of studies was effectively kept up. By the Presbyterian portion of the population of Easton and the region of which it is the centre, and by a goodly number of the other citizens, the College was warmly welcomed. But by others it was looked upon with coldness, and by some with aversion, and for a time it had to struggle against adverse influences. In the end, however, it won its way to the confidence of the community, and became one of its cherished institutions.

The Board of Trustees was, at the time of Dr. Junkin's advent, and for a considerable time after (for it is a close corporation), composed of a great variety of men, of diverse positions in life, and of various religious predilections, a few of whom knew something of colleges, but the great majority had no knowledge of the necessities and workings of such institutions. Of course, from a body thus constituted, the President could not expect that hearty and intelligent co-operation which would have been afforded by men more familiar with the processes of higher education. But there were a few earnest sympathizers in the enterprise, both in and out of the Board, who deserve the gratitude of the friends of the College. Still, the burden rested upon the President; and if the detail of his toils, trials, and sacrifices in the founding of Lafayette College should be here recorded, it would amaze the reader, and he would wonder how any one man could endure the amount of labor, bodily and mental, which he actually performed; and, much more, that it could be borne in connection with such heavy anxieties as must have continually pressed upon his mind and heart. He set the students an example not only of diligence in study, but of alacrity in manual labor. He very often put to his hand, in the quarry, in the workshop, or on the farm, and in the various parts of the work of erecting buildings, fences, and the nameless other details of preparing college accommodations and grounds. The students would work but a few hours at a time; the writer has known the President to toil whole days at a time. accomplishing much more work in a given period than the most expert laborers are wont to do. "Whatsoever his hand found to do, he did it with his might," and his energetic example was felt throughout the whole institution.

Nor were his labors confined to the institution itself. He travelled extensively in efforts to collect funds, to awaken public interest in the enterprise, and to induce the Legislature of the Commonwealth to appropriate pecuniary aid. He made many visits to the State Capital, and by public addresses, by personal interviews, by letters, and by memorials he labored to awaken an interest not only in the particular institution which he represented, but in the cause of general education.

Perhaps no citizen of the Commonwealth contributed more, by personal labor and influence, towards the inauguration of the Public School System of Pennsylvania, than did Dr. Junkin. In his frequent public addresses, in different parts of the State, and in his numerous publications, he urged upon the citizens and upon the Legislature the necessity of ampler facilities for the universal education of the people. He tried to arouse the natives of the State to a sense of shame, by pointing to the fact, that, for want of proper systems of education, a large proportion of the Judges and other prominent public functionaries of the State were natives of other States. He urged his broad and liberal views of the subject upon the committees of education of the Legislature. And some of the ablest reports of these committees were framed chiefly by him, during the years 1833 to 1837.

At the time Dr. Junkin was urging this great interest upon the State Legislature, the Hon. George Wolf was Governor of the Commonwealth. He was a citizen of Easton at the time of his election, and a Trustee of Lafayette College, and it was the glory of his administration, that the entire weight of his official position was thrown in favor of a general system of education. With him Dr. Junkin had frequent conferences upon the subject, and to his urgency may, in some degree, be attributed the zeal and explicitness with which that excellent chief magistrate urged the subject of general education in his messages to the General Assembly of the State. For this he was censured by many of his own party, the scheme of general education by State aid being as yet far from popular. It was in reply to some of these animadversions, that the late Hon. Thaddeus Stevens, then a representative from Adams County and a political opponent of the Governor, delivered one of his most eloquent speeches in advocacy of education, and in defence of the Governor's course in regard to it. In this speech Mr. Stevens uttered the memorable words, "I love the man whose banner streams in light!"

Dr. Junkin may justly be classed among the founders of the Public School System of Pennsylvania. He was not a man of one idea. His conceptions of the great theme of human education were too broad to permit him to confine his efforts to the one enterprise with which he stood connected, and accordingly, wherever he went, in his agency for the College, he discoursed on education in all its interests and bearings. He unfolded the philosophy of education in a style adapted to the masses. He showed the connection between the college or university and all schools of inferior grade, and inculcated the idea that all should be parts of one grand system, so connected together as to be co-operative and mutually auxiliary to each other and the whole. Having gathered information in regard to the most improved modes of education, both in Europe and in other sections of our own country, he was probably in advance of any other native Pennsylvanian in the maturity of his opinions upon the subject. So far as is known to the writer, he was the first to insist that the business of teaching should be raised to the dignity and the immunities of a Profession. He was the first to advocate the establishment of normal schools for the training of teachers, and, as we shall see, he established, at his own cost, the first normal school in the Commonwealth. In his applications to the Legislature for aid, he was subjected to frequent disappointments and delays. His brother-in-law, Hon. Walter Oliver, the representative from Mercer County, exerted all his influence to further the interests of Lafayette and other colleges. Mr. Stevens, also, was forward and earnest in the good work, and others lent a helping hand. Several times a Bill to aid Lafayette and other colleges came to a third reading by hopeful majorities, and then was defeated. These failures were not attributable to the opposition of the members who voted "nay" to the cause of education, so much as to dread of their constituents, for in most of the counties the people were prejudiced against aiding colleges by State bounty.

Still Dr. Junkin persevered, amidst all discouragements, until finally a law was passed appropriating to Lafayette and Pennsylvania Colleges a few thousand dollars. But previous to this, encouraged by the sums which the President had collected from churches and individuals, the Trustees ventured, in the winter of 1833, to purchase the land upon which the College now stands, and, in the following spring, to commence the erection of a college edifice. The building was planned by the President; and early in March, 1833, in the presence of some of the Trustees, the students, and a few of the citizens, he, with his own hands, broke ground and removed the first spadefuls of earth from the site of the foundation. On the 4th day of July following, attended by a civic and military procession, assisted by the Hon. James M. Porter, President of the Board of Trustees, he laid the corner-stone; and the building progressed slowly yet steadily towards completion, so that upon the last of March, 1834, it was occupied by the Faculty and students.

It may as well be here recorded, that a little more than thirty-four years after laying the corner-stone of the main building, he, by invitation, laid the corner-stone of the eastern extension of the edifice, at a time when the enterprise which he had begun in faith, more than thirty-five years before, had attained to eminent success, and Lafayette College had taken rank with the best endowed and the best manned and appointed Universities of the continent.

He was formally inaugurated President of the College on the 1st of May, 1834, with appropriate formalities. On this occasion prayer was offered by the Rev. Isaac N. Candee, then of Belvidere, N. J. (now Dr. Candee, of Illinois). The Hon. James M. Porter, President of the Board, made an address to the President and Professor Kuhn who was installed at the same time, performed the inaugural ceremony, and read the laws of the institution. A beautiful ode, adapted to the occasion, from the gifted pen of Mrs. J. L. Gray, was sung. Dr. Junkin delivered his inaugural address on the topic, "The true idea of education, and especially its religious element;" and the concluding prayer was offered by Rev. Mr. Macklin. Professor Kuhn is now, 1871, an eminent lawyer in Pittsburg.

Whilst the building was in progress, the exercises of the College, mental and manual, continued upon the rented premises already mentioned. Some of the labor upon the new site was performed by details of students, in working-hours. But on account of the distance, and the fact that most of the work was done by contract, this labor was limited chiefly to the excavation of the site and the levelling of the grounds. The writer has often seen the President of the College, at the head of a band of noble youth, who were not ashamed of honest toil, quarrying and removing rocks, and walling in and levelling off the grounds of the new College; and the amazing strength and mechanical skill of the President made him a worthy example to his more youthful co-laborers. It may be thought that it was beneath the dignity of the chief of a literary institution thus to toil with his hands, and that he might have consigned to hired laborers such work as he thus performed. But if it be remembered, that his great aim was to found an institution, in which "the health-preserving labor of the hands should defray the expenses of education," the propriety of his *example* will be confessed. He wished to banish from the minds of his pupils the shallow and un-American idea, that labor is dishonorable; and he aimed to demonstrate before their eyes, that manual labor and earnest and effective study were not incompatible. And this he did. For at the very time he was thus toiling with his hands, he imparted instructions, of which his pupils speak with gratitude and admiration to this day; and it was during this period of toil that "Fellenberg" and his valuable work on Justification were written, whilst other labors, presently to be mentioned, were accomplished.

It would be impossible for any one, not familiar with the details, to form an adequate estimate of the amount of labor, mental and bodily, which, during these years, Dr. Junkin performed. Before the work upon the college edifice was half completed, the funds began to fail; and the progress of the work depended upon his success in collecting money. This called for an extensive and laborious correspondence, for frequent journeys, for much toil in speaking and canvassing, and for frequent appeals through the newspapers; whilst the consciousness of the heavy personal responsibilities which he incurred, and his solicitude for his family and for the students, when away from them, rested with crushing anxiety upon him. Yet amid it all he was *calm*, *cheerful*, *persistent;* and when others trembled for him, and despaired of the enterprise, his confidence seemed never to falter! If the reader asks for the great secret of this, he has his answer in a single fact,—DR. JUNKIN WAS A MAN OF STRONG FAITH IN CHRIST AND OF MUCH PRAYER!

He never entered upon any important undertaking without solemn self-examination and earnest prayer to God for direction. More than any man whom the writer has ever known, his constant inquiry was, "Lord, what wilt thou have me to do?" And he aimed maturely to consider every question of duty, begged of the Lord to help him to scrutinize his own motives; and when fairly satisfied that he ought to enter upon a given enterprise, he dismissed doubt and hesitancy, and threw all his heart and all his powers into the undertaking. More than once did the writer of these lines join with others in the endeavor to persuade Dr. Junkin to abandon the college enterprise, to which there appeared so many hindrances and discouragements, and in which he seemed likely to sacrifice his entire substance. He would listen calmly and attentively to these reasonings, seem to take them into consideration, and after we had supposed the subject to be dismissed from his mind, he would recur to it, and give his reasons for the conviction that he ought to persevere in his efforts to establish a college. On one occasion, this conviction was expressed in the words, "Destroy it not, for a blessing is in it!"

In this conviction his faith never faltered. And even when away from "lovely Lafayette," as he was fond to call it, toiling in other fields, and when the prospects of the

College were darkest, he held on to the hope—the *belief*, rather—that the College would surmount her difficulties, and, by God's good hand, rise above the opposition of enemies and the apathy and folly of false friends, and prove a great blessing to the church, the country, and the world. "I cannot be persuaded," wrote he to his brother, "that an institution begun—as I believe it was—in faith, and founded in so many prayers and tears, and in which the Lord led me, as I think, to expend so much toil and substance, is to prove a failure. Lovely Lafayette will yet flourish!" Even when the property of the College was advertised to be sold by the sheriff, after his resignation of the presidency, he never lost confidence in its ultimate success; and, as the writer believes, never ceased to pray for its success. How much of that success was resultant from his faith, his prayers, and his singular, paternal love for the College, is only known to Him who hears the prayers and bottles the tears of his devoted servants.

There was another mind and another heart engaged in praying, toiling, and sacrificing for the establishment of Lafayette College, of which it were wrong not to make mention in connection with the name of its founder. All such enterprises have a secret and unobserved as well as a public history. And whilst the influence and the work of woman in promoting them may not appear in "reports" and "catalogues," nor in the journals of the day, they are often not only very great but sometimes essential to success. In all his plans, toils and trials in founding the College, Dr. Junkin was cheered, consoled, encouraged, and aided by the lovely and accomplished woman who called him husband. Indeed, it was mainly her means that enabled him to assume the pecuniary responsibilities of the position, and to suffer the losses incurred. Of gentle and unassuming yet attractive manners; of unusually sound judgment; patient, hopeful and cheerful under trials and discouragements; in full sympathy with her husband's aims, and zealous in promoting them; and, withal, a woman of strong faith in God, and of devout, prayerful habits,—she was indeed a helpmeet for a man engaged in such an arduous work. Her letters to him, during his frequent absences from home collecting funds for the College, disclose the amount of care, and even of business, that sometimes devolved upon her. Over their large family she presided with judicious efficiency in his absence; and not only so, but the business agents of the institution, and even the Professors, often resorted to her for counsel when difficulties arose. In her letters, which are models at once of wifely affection and considerateness, and of clearness and fulness of business detail, she kept him posted in regard to the condition of the home and the College. And whilst they sometimes betray the yearning of her heart for his presence, and regret at the necessity of separation, yet no murmur escapes that might sadden his heart or discourage him in his work; but, on the contrary, they were well adapted to cheer and sustain him. Accustomed in her girlhood to the ease and the elegant comforts of a wealthy home, she conformed to the cares and sacrifices incident to her position with a Christian cheerfulness worthy of all praise and of imitation.

A few extracts from these letters may disclose at once the perplexities and cares incident to such an enterprise as her husband was prosecuting, and the spirit with which both he and she encountered them:

"MOUNT LAFAYETTE, May 8th, 1835.

"MY DEAR HUSBAND,—You have by this time, I hope, reached Pittsburg in safety, and perhaps are engaged just now in writing to tell me so. I feel a good deal anxious to hear from you, especially to know if you are better in health. . . . We are getting along as well as we can without *you*, but miss you very much. Several new students have come, but few of the old ones have yet arrived. Mr. Kuhn (Professor of Languages) says about eighty are now here. The letters which come, requesting information, I give to him to answer. . . . The steaming apparatus (for culinary and laundry purposes) does not answer very well. It requires great heat to make it boil, and Mr. G. (the business superintendent) thinks there is too large a body of water, and too little surface on top, to generate steam enough. I believe he is trying his best to make it work."

"May 18th.

". . . College affairs move on very well. The students have been very orderly. . . . They have got the steam fixtures to work finely, and the cook is in good spirits, and is sorry I had told you it did not do well, fearing it would vex you. Mr. Godown (steward) told me to tell you that he is trying to divide the money in hand as well as he can, to meet demands on the college expenses. . . . He went to Mr. Porter to try and get some of the State money, but he told him it could not be had till Mr. McKeen returned. . . . I endeavor to keep my mind easy, and rest all my burdens upon the Lord. But ah! I find my faith weak; unbelieving fears will intrude and disturb my peace. I feel very sensibly the want of that dear bosom on which I can lean and pour out all my joys and sorrows; but I know it is wrong to trust to any earthly support. 'Oh for a closer walk with God,' a more implicit confidence in that *Friend* who sticketh closer than a brother!"

The above were written to him whilst in attendance upon the Pittsburg Convention and the General Assembly, of which he was that year a member. After the Assembly adjourned, he returned home, but soon resumed his toils in visiting different sections to collect funds for the college. The following extracts are from letters addressed to him whilst thus engaged:

"MOUNT LAFAYETTE, Nov. 14th, 1835.

"MY DEAR HUSBAND,— . . . You appear to be in pretty good heart about the college. I do sincerely pray that the Lord may prosper you, and that your labor may not be in vain. You have spent many anxious hours about it, and endured much fatigue; but if you can by it promote the Redeemer's kingdom, I know you will feel amply rewarded. From the way things went in Synod, I should think the present a favorable time for your application. We have not heard whether Mr. B. submits to his sentence. . . . . As far as I know, things go on very smoothly in the college. The students are generally much pleased with the change in the faculty. . . . There is a very respectable body of students here now. They conduct themselves with a great deal of propriety. They are nearly all anxious to work, and Mr. G. says he finds much difficulty in getting sufficient work for those who want to work in the shops. . . . S., M., J., Jos., and E. have walked over to Uncle D.'s to-day; G., E., and W. are playing up by the shops; little J. is asleep in the cradle beside me; we have all enjoyed good health since you left us. Oh that we were duly thankful! Do not preach too much, especially at night. *When will* you be home? We do indeed miss you *very much.* I believe all try to do as well as they can; but still the head is wanting, and you will probably find, on your return, that many things have not been attended to as you wished. . . . Good-by, my dear husband. May the Lord bless and prosper you, and restore you to us *soon* in health and peace.

"Your affectionate

"JULIA."

"MOUNT LAFAYETTE, Dec. 21st, 1835.

"MY DEAR HUSBAND,—I have had some doubts whether it is worth while to write to you, thinking that you will perhaps be home in a few days. 1st. Because, in a letter received from Mr. Breckenridge, since you left us, he says this is not a good time for you to go to Baltimore; and—2d. If it was not a good time to beg there when he wrote, it will certainly be worse now, as the sufferers by the dreadful fire in N. Y. will require all the funds the charitable have to spare. We have not heard any of the particulars yet, but expect we will by this evening's mail. The *Observer* has not come, and probably was not printed. A short notice in the last Philadelphia paper mentioned that seven entire blocks were destroyed, in one of which was the Middle Dutch Church. Dr. Knox of course must be burned out. It is an awful dispensation! How quickly can He who rules the raging elements send them to lay low the pride of man! Many who were rolling in affluence when you were in N. Y., will find a sad change now. . . I am kept pretty busy, as, in addition to my other cares, I have undertaken to teach E—— and Wm. I found if I did not do it they would run wild altogether, for Mr. K. has not time to attend to them."

Similar extracts might be multiplied, many of them going even more into the detail of the perplexing cares that, in his absence, devolved upon her, and upon the agents he had left in charge of the various departments of the institution, but all exhibiting the same spirit of devotion to a work which she considered to be promotive of her Redeemer's kingdom. But it seems not desirable to present more than will enable the reader to form an estimate of the toils and trials to which this noble Christian woman, in common with her husband, submitted, for Christ's sake, in laying the foundations of a seat of learning that has proved, and is likely still further to prove, a great blessing to the church, the country, and the world. Only one more extract from these letters shall be made, showing that a suggestion of hers led to the adoption of a different plan of operations, which enabled the President to bestow more attention upon the home interests of the College:

"The evening we received your letter from Baltimore we had *some* expectation of seeing yourself, and you may know it was a *damper* to hear that you were about starting to go through the New Castle Presbytery. I really fear you will have your labor for your pains. If you were getting any funds worth the while, I would submit more contentedly to your absence from home, which I do feel very much; but I try to bear it as well as I can, knowing that I have still many mercies of which I am unworthy. It is certainly a disadvantage to the college for you to be so much away, not to speak of your own family; and I think an agent might be procured who would be as *good a beggar* as *you*. What think you of Benjamin Tyler?* There is a possibility, perhaps a probability, that he would accept. He is a warm friend to you and to the college; he says there is no institution in the land in which he feels so much interest; he is a great advocate of manual labor, has a good address, and is personally acquainted with the management of affairs in the institution. He is at present at Princeton, and I think if you would write to him, and urge him a little, he would undertake it."

This suggestion was adopted. Mr. Tyler consented, and after Dr. Junkin had labored a few months longer in the work of collecting, he devolved it cheerfully upon Mr. Tyler. After he had served for a time with varying success, he accepted a pastoral charge, and retired from the agency. Another was appointed, but his efforts accomplished but little, and the time drew on when Dr. Junkin was to be separated for a season from the institution, and its struggles were to be continued under the administration of other men.

It was deemed best to give in a consecutive statement an account of Dr. Junkin's direct labors in founding Lafayette College, so as to convey some faint conception of their nature and amount. But during these years of toil in this enterprise, other and very important events in his history occurred, and other labors, arduous and self-denying, yet not so directly connected with the College, were performed. To record these it will be necessary to go back to the period of his advent to Easton, and bring up the narrative of these contemporaneous events and labors. This will be done in the chapters next ensuing.

---

* A former student of Lafayette, just then licensed; afterwards a minister at Deerfield, N. J.

CHAPTER XVIII.

Dr. Junkin as a Peace-Maker—Dr. Elliott's Testimony—Joins the Presbytery of Newton—Labors in the Gospel—Sermon on Transmission of Piety from Parent to Child—New Village—Degree of D.D. Conferred—Success as President, and its Causes—Heart-Sympathy—Death in the Household.

FOR a time after his removal to Easton, Dr. Junkin continued to be a member of the Presbytery of Philadelphia, and was its Moderator for a season. About the time of his removal the difficulties in the old Second Church of that city, which eventually resulted in the division of it and the formation of the Central Church, were at their height. The Presbytery itself was much divided in opinion, most of the members sympathizing with the one party or the other so strongly as to lose their influence with the opposite party. Mr. Junkin was almost the only member in whose impartiality both parties retained such confidence as pointed him out as a mediator, and he was appealed to to act in this capacity, and made several journeys to the city, and was at much toil and pains to effect an adjustment of these troubles. And, what is very unusual in the history of mere human mediators, he retained the affection and confidence of all concerned after the troubles were ended. This incident is mentioned as illustrative of a trait in Dr. Junkin's character, which was a marked and prominent one, but in which he has by some been supposed to be deficient,—capability to be a wise and impartial peace-maker. The unflinching firmness which he always exhibited in defence of what he deemed important truth, has left the impression upon many minds that he was a man of war rather than a man of peace. But those who knew him best did not so estimate his character. They knew him to be gentle as a woman, and as guileless as Nathanael. And his life was gemmed all along with those quiet and wisely-performed acts of charity which win the beatitude of the peace-maker. One of his distinguished contemporaries, the venerable Dr. David Elliott, in a letter to the writer, says:

"Of his disposition to remove offences, and to promote harmony among brethren, I have had some evidence. In a case of offence, in which the party offended was about to seek redress for the supposed injury, Dr. Junkin, having come to the knowledge of it, and fearing that the offended party might be too much excited to manage the matter successfully, volunteered to mediate in the case. This was accepted, and he conducted the matter with so much candor and good temper that the offence, which arose from a misapprehension of facts, was removed, and the parties were ever afterwards good friends. Of this fact I had personal knowledge, and I mention it as illustrative of the doctor's disposition, and also to show how easily supposed offences may be removed by the kind offices of a Christian friend, and the exercise of Christian temper by the parties."

Dr. Junkin became a member of the Presbytery of Newton, which at that time embraced the churches of Easton and vicinity, in April, 1833. He had been Moderator of the Synod of Philadelphia for the year 1831–32, and had opened its sessions at Lewistown, October 25, 1832, with a sermon upon II. Tim. i. 13. His change of Presbyterial relation brought him to be a member of the Synod of New Jersey, in connection with which he continued so long as he was President of Lafayette College.

His intellectual power, great experience and skill as a Presbyter, and his devout and earnest zeal for everything that promised to promote the good of the church and the glory of her Head, were soon recognized by his brethren in his new relations, and they early and cordially accorded him that influence in their counsels for which such endowments fitted him. Both pastors and the people of the congregations sought and welcomed his labors; and, although he was so devoted to the great work of education, he loved to preach the gospel, and, in fact, his pulpit labors were quite as abundant as those of any of the pastors. He early inaugurated regular Sabbath services in Brainerd Hall, the principal assembly-room of the college; and he regularly, when at home, conducted a Bible-class composed of the students. Not content with these arduous labors, he often preached for the pastors of Easton and of the surrounding country; whilst in his frequent absences upon collecting tours, he never spent a silent Sabbath. His register of preaching shows that he always preached once, and oftener twice and thrice, upon the Lord's day, and, very often, during the week.

On the 6th of September, 1833, he preached in Hackettstown, New Jersey, a sermon founded upon Gen. xviii. 19. It was a time of special spiritual interest, and he was assisting the Rev. Dr. Joseph Campbell in a series of meetings, during which he preached four discourses. The discourse mentioned was the last of the four, and made such an impression that the pastor and people obtained a copy of it, which was published. It was a remarkable sermon, in which the preacher took high ground in regard to God's faithfulness to his covenant and to his covenant people, and in regard to the efficacy of parental training. He aimed to prove, that where heads of families are faithful in a Scriptural way in "commanding their household after them," the members of the household "shall keep the way of the Lord," and that the Lord will invariably "fulfil all that he hath spoken." He maintained, that with the stipulations of the well-ordered covenant before them, parents can, by God's grace, more surely transmit their piety to their offspring than their worldly estate; that, under God, the transmission from parent to child of the incorruptible inheritance may be more certainly effected than that of worldly goods.

In maintaining this doctrine he fully acknowledged God's sovereignty in dispensing grace, and man's utter dependence upon that grace, but insisted that a faithful God had bound himself by promise that, when the means are faithfully used by believing parents, the blessing will follow with as unvarying certainty as effect follows cause in any department of the divine administration. He held that cause and effect are as indissolubly connected in the field of grace as in the field of nature; that, by a divine constitution, the family is made the agency for raising up not a natural seed only, but also a holy seed; and that where the conditions and means thereunto are faithfully provided, the grace of God stands pledged to secure the blessed result. And he was of opinion that, in cases where that result was not realized, the failure was in man, not in a covenant-keeping God. He urged that no other view of this subject can furnish adequate encouragement to parental faithfulness. Whatever may be thought of the doctrine, by those who hold loose opinions in regard to the covenant of grace, it received remarkable illustration in the households of his father and himself. He was one of fourteen children, all of whom, except four who died in infancy, maintained a reputable profession of godliness; and all of his own children, nine in number, excepting one who died in early infancy, were hopefully pious.

In January, 1834, Dr. J., at the request of some of the inhabitants, commenced preaching in a house of worship near New Village, N. J., about six miles from the College. He gave a series of lectures upon the Epistle to the Hebrews, which attracted large congregations, and accomplished much good.

In the autumn of 1833, Jefferson College, Pennsylvania, conferred upon Mr. Junkin the honorary degree of Doctor in Divinity. At that period these distinctions did not come in periodical showers, as they have since; and as the recipient in this case was not in a position to confer any favor upon the institution that thus honored him, it may be fairly assumed to have been a disinterested tribute to his merit.

As President of the College, Dr. Junkin was the father and pastor of the students. He often visited them in their rooms, conversed with them about their spiritual interests, and prayed with and for them. When any of them were sick, he showed a father's solicitude and care. And in the few cases of death that occurred during his presidency, all the deep feelings of his warm heart were stirred.

This deep affection for his pupils was one of the secrets of Dr. J.'s great power in governing young men in college. And it was all the more powerful in its influence by the fact that it was undemonstrative. His pupils found out that Dr. Junkin had *heart*, as well as head,—not from his professions of affection for them, for he never made any, but from the occasional and irrepressible outgushings of tenderness in his intercourse with them, and in the discharge of his duties as head of the College. HEART is an indispensable element of qualification of a college president, especially among American youth. But it must be genuine, natural, unaffected heart. If they discover that the *semblance* of affection is *put on*, and that it is perfunctory and conventional, they will be chilled and disgusted, whilst genuine affection flashing forth unbidden, even from beneath a stern and undemonstrative exterior, wins its way directly to their hearts.

We have mentioned that the new college edifice was occupied on the 1st of April, 1834. But a fortnight previous to this, viz., on the 15th of March, a severe domestic infliction was added to the other pressing cares of the President. Death for the first time invaded his household.

A little baby-boy, of peculiar beauty and promise, was suddenly snatched from the fond parental embrace. The event awoke a measure of intense sympathy in the community, quite unusual in case of the death of one so young; and this fact won for the kind people of Easton a deeper place in the hearts of the stricken parents. But whilst they deeply mourned the loss of their beloved (Heb., David), every one was impressed with the singularly triumphing faith with which they followed him to glory. Never has the writer witnessed, in the afflicted, a faith so realizing and assured.

This sorrow seems to have been designed to fit Dr. Junkin for toils and trials soon thereafter to be encountered. The mellowing effect of it was noticeable in his piety. The salvation of infants was ever after a more frequent theme of his conversation and of his preaching, and it led him to broader and deeper discoveries of the work of Christ as the great Shepherd who redeems the flock and "feeds it, and gathereth the lambs with his arm, and carrieth them in his bosom."

Thus have we brought our sketch of the life of Dr. Junkin down to the period at which he became identified with the great doctrinal and ecclesiastical struggle which resulted in the division of the Presbyterian Church. Some incidents of a later date have been anticipated, because they grouped readily with other incidents that illustrated the character and disposition of the man, and because they were not of a character demanding chronological mention. We now come to the very delicate and difficult task of narrating the part he bore in the ecclesiastical history of his times.

CHAPTER XIX.

History of Opinion Important—Delicacy of the Writer's Task—History of the Disruption of 1838—Plan of Union—Its Objects and Results—New England Men and Measures—Opposition to Workings of the Plan of Union begun in 1820—Continued till 1831—Party Lines drawn—The Church always a Missionary Society—Rise of the Board of Missions—Education Efforts—American Education and Home Missionary Societies—Programme of Innovation—Proofs—Results in both Schools.

THE history of men would be incomplete without the history of opinion. The facts which they believe and the opinions which they maintain give character to men, shape their conduct, and impart vivacity to their history. Indeed, a history that would ignore the principles of men, would be no history at all, for principles impart impulse to the actions of men. Who could write a life of Paul the Apostle in which the doctrine of justification by faith and its cognate opinions should be ignored? Who would read a life of Luther, or Calvin, or Zwingle in which no statement is made of the great principles of the Protestant Reformation? Who would deem a biography of Hampden, or Sidney, or Washington complete and satisfactory which made no mention of their opinions and of the principles of regulated liberty and the rights of man? Such narrative would be utterly destitute of life and interest, and would, indeed, lack the essential element of *truth*, for no incident, in the history of a man or of society, can be truthfully stated unless the causes from which it resulted are also given. Men act under the influence of opinion, and from motives furnished by their real belief; and without a knowledge of these, the events of history would be like boulders on the strand, dead facts, without connection, without ascertained causes, and without practical value. Opinion, thought, principles, furnish the most vital and enduring staple of history. Men are born, live, die and pass away; generation succeeds generation, as wave follows wave on the bosom of the deep; but principles, if right and true, endure. Opinions survive the men who maintained them. The martyr dies, but his principles live and furnish the animating impulse of other struggles and the soul of other histories. Truth is eternal as its source. As the blood-circulation to the bodily life of man, so is opinion to the vitality of history.

And yet the history of opinion is difficult to write, especially whilst the conflict of opinion still goes on, or whilst the smoke and débris of the battle have scarcely disappeared from the field of strife. Men are so apt to misapprehend the opinions of opponents, to use terminology in such diverse senses, and to so understand an opponent as to intensify his error, that more than usual caution, candor and charity are demanded of those who write the narrative of controversy.

These remarks apply to all classes of opinion, whether relating to physics or metaphysics, to political or social philosophy, or to morals. And they apply with especial force to the field of theological investigation.

There are seasons, too, in which it is especially difficult so to write the history of systems of opinion as to make it satisfactory, even if fairly and truly written. There are times in which men are impatient of allusions to a recent past, the history of which may involve matters not pleasant to remember, and the reminiscences of which, they may fear, will jeopard the programme of the immediate future.

Considerations of this kind have pressed, with a weight almost appalling, upon the mind of the writer of these pages. He had begun the work before the recent union between the two branches of the Presbyterian Church was certain of being accomplished; and since its happy and wonderful consummation, he has, at times, been ready to abandon the task, in view of the peculiar delicacy and difficulty of writing that history of opinion, without which, a biography of Dr. Junkin would be not only incomplete, but unfair and injurious to its beloved subject. The fear has arisen that such a narrative might seem like the opening of wounds so recently and so happily healed; and that, in recording truth, the writer might appear to wound sweet charity. But he has been encouraged to persevere in his work by such considerations as the following:

1. God is in history, and, when truly written, it is a record of His providence.

2. The history of the Presbyterian Church, for the last forty years, is as important as that of any other period. It cannot be ignored or left out: *somebody* will write it.

3. Some *have* undertaken to write it, and that at a period much earlier than the present. Books of biography and history *have* been written, and that, too, before the dust of recent conflicts had been swept away by the zephyrs of returning peace. And it is here confessed, that in these books, on both sides, there is found a measure of candor and fairness scarcely to be expected from writers occupying a party stand-point; and

4. The present writer hopes, by God's grace, to exercise at least an equal degree of candor and kindness, and, whilst faithful to the truth of history, and to the memory of the departed, to do no violence to the law of charity. Nor does he despair of so performing his task as to contribute to the more perfect healing of old wounds, and the closer union, in the truth, of that great church to which he has given his warmest affections, and in whose unity he rejoices. His task has been rendered less embarrassing by the fact, conceded on all hands, that the chief causes

of the division had disappeared before the reunion, and are now entirely eliminated. To give a compact and fair history of the various causes that led to the disruption shall now be attempted.

The opening of the nineteenth century found our country rapidly extending her population westward, and the evangelical churches making efforts to establish the institutions of religion among the sparse populations of the new settlements. Many of those settlements were composed partly of the Calvinistic denominations,—Presbyterians and Congregationalists. Agreeing in the main in regard to doctrine and worship, these denominations of Christians differed only in the matter of church government and discipline; the former maintaining a representative republican form of government, the latter a pure democracy, in which all the members of the church vote in cases of discipline. Western New York, and the "Western Reserve" in Ohio, were being rapidly settled with people of both denominations; and it sometimes happened that neither were separately able to support Christian ordinances, whilst, by uniting, they might do it. The Western (or Connecticut) Reserve, in the northeastern portion of Ohio, was chiefly settled by people from Connecticut, with an admixture from other States, some of whom were Presbyterians.

The state of things here described led to the adoption, by the General Assembly and by the Association of Connecticut, of an arrangement which has become celebrated in our church history as "The Plan of Union."

The proposal that led to this measure came from the General Association of Connecticut, and was laid before the Assembly of 1801 by a committee appointed by the Association. The object avowed in this communication was, "to prevent alienation, to promote harmony, and to establish, as far as possible, a uniform system of church government between those inhabitants of the new settlements who are attached to the Presbyterian form of church government, and those who are attached to the Congregational form."

The proposal was referred to a committee, which reported a Plan, which was adopted by both the bodies. It contained four sections. The first enjoined upon the missionaries "to promote mutual forbearance and a spirit of accommodation, between those inhabitants of the new settlements" who adhered severally to one or the other form of government. The second provided, that "if any church in the new settlements, of the Congregational order, shall settle a minister of the Presbyterian order, that church may, if they choose, conduct their discipline according to Congregational principles, settling their difficulties among themselves, or by a council mutually agreed upon for that purpose. But if any difficulty shall exist between the minister and the church, or any member of it, it shall be referred to the Presbytery to which the minister shall belong, provided both parties agree to it, otherwise by a council, one-half Congregationalists and the other Presbyterians, mutually agreed upon by the parties." The third made precisely similar provisions, *mutatis mutandis*, in case a Presbyterian church settled a Congregational minister. The fourth provided, "that if any congregation consist partly of those who hold the Congregational form of discipline, and partly of those who hold the Presbyterian form, we recommend to both parties that this be no obstruction to uniting in one church and settling a minister, and that, in this case, the church choose a standing committee from the communicants of said church, whose business it shall be to call to account every member of the church who shall conduct himself inconsistently with the laws of Christianity, and to give judgment on such conduct. That if the person condemned shall be a Presbyterian, he shall have liberty to appeal to the Presbytery; if he be a Congregationalist, he shall have liberty to appeal to the body of the male communicants of the church. In the former case, the determination of the Presbytery shall be final, unless the church shall consent to a further appeal to the Synod or the General Assembly; and, in the latter case, if the party condemned shall wish for a trial by a mutual council, the case shall be referred to such a council. And provided the said standing committee of any church shall depute one of themselves to attend the Presbytery, he may have the same right to sit and act in the Presbytery as a ruling elder of the Presbyterian Church." This plan was adopted next year (1802) by the Association of Connecticut. It led to the adoption of plans of fraternal intercourse by the Presbytery and Synod of Albany, and the Congregational bodies occupying the same or adjacent territory; and endured much longer, and was extended much more widely, than seems to have been contemplated by the stipulating bodies on either side.

Whilst there is no doubt that the purest and noblest Christian impulses led to the adoption of this famous Plan of Union, and whilst no doubt great benefits did arise out of it in the new settlements, it is also true that it was extended far beyond the conception of its framers, used for purposes never contemplated by them, and that it brought into existence a large number of churches of hybrid constitution and growth, which, in the end, marred the peace of both denominations, and prevented the edification of these churches themselves.

Other incidental evils, by no means confined to "the new settlements," grew out of this abnormal system, and rapidly extended over the whole Church, doing injury to both denominations. It arrested the progress of strict Congregationalism almost entirely; and it produced a fungous growth upon the Presbyterian body inconsistent with its health and efficiency. It cannot be denied that pure Congregationalism was the greater loser by this scheme; whilst the gain of the Presbyterian Church was an abnormal and unhealthy one.

As early as 1820, the attention of the General Assembly was drawn to the abnormal working of this system by the claim of a Mr. Lathrop, a Congregationalist and a Committeeman, to sit as a Commissioner in the General Assembly. His right was resisted, but conceded. (See Minutes, pp. 721, 722, 724.) Again, in the first General Assembly in which Mr. Junkin sat (1826), a similar case occurred, and forty-two members protested. (Minutes, 1826, pp. 8, 23, 28.) Again, in 1831, in the case of Clement Tuttle, a committeeman from Grand River Presbytery. He was admitted, and a protest against it entered. But at the same session a resolution was passed to the effect, that the appointment of committeemen as commissioners to the Assembly was "inexpedient and of questionable constitutionality, and therefore ought not in future to be made." (Minutes, pp. 158, 185, 190.) Against this act of the Assembly those members, who about this time began to be called the "New School," protested. (192.)

Next year the same Presbytery sent up two "committeemen" as commissioners. Their case was referred to the committee on elections, who reported that these commissions had been withdrawn. (Minutes, 1832, pp. 314, 315.)

Concomitant with the governmental difficulties arising out of the "Plan of Union," were others of a more serious character, affecting the doctrinal purity of the churches. New England had a surplus of preachers, as well as of other educated men, who naturally sought employment in other States, particularly in the West. The system of Congregationalism was not so effective in securing careful examination of candidates for the holy office as was the system of Presbytery. For many years the theology of New England, once thoroughly Calvinistic, had in certain quarters, and in certain schools, been undergoing a gradual, almost imperceptible, but still real change in the direction of greater laxity of opinion. The Socinian or Unitarian element had crept in; and although it was learnedly and ably resisted by many of the best New England minds, it had made alarming progress. Harvard College, founded by the zeal, the prayers and the gifts of godly and orthodox worshippers of the Son of God, had passed under the control of those who denied his supreme Divinity. Many Congregational churches, once orthodox, had gone over to the Unitarians. Others had become divided, some of the members adhering to the orthodox views, and others embracing the Christ-dishonoring error. And in the progress of the doctrinal conflict, even those who adhered to orthodoxy were led, in some cases, by stress of circumstances, and by what they supposed to be the justifiable necessities of controversy, to *modify*, in many points, the stern old dogmas of the Calvinistic creed of their fathers, and present new views of theology, which they hoped might be more defensible as against the specious and popular thrusts of the Socinians. This was one cause of the rise of what has been known as the "New Theology."

Other modifications of the doctrines of Christianity, as laid down in the Westminster standards, the Saybrook Platform and other evangelical formularies, arose from the fondness for speculation, and especially from a desire to get clear of certain objections which had always been raised against the Calvinistic system. These dogmas of the New Theology will be noted further on. This much of their history is here given, for the purpose of enabling the reader to understand the time and the mode of the rise of that theological controversy, in the progress of which the subject of this narrative bore a conspicuous part.

The Plan of Union, as we have seen, opened the way for

the free ingress of New England preachers into the Presbyterian Church. And whilst many of them were sound and excellent men, not a few were more or less imbued with the speculations of the New Theology. Men of this stamp found their way, not only into the mixed churches in the new settlements, but also into important pastoral charges in the older Presbyteries, in which the Plan of Union was never intended, by its framers, to operate. That "Plan of Union" did much to make the people and the Presbyteries feel that the two systems were identical; that Congregational and Presbyterian ministers were so nearly the same, that the transit from one body to the other scarcely involved any change of opinion, and demanded no examination of the men *in transitu*. The consequence was, that scrutiny of doctrinal views was relaxed, and ministers and licentiates passed from one body to the other without suspicion and without challenge, clean papers only being demanded. This state of things might seem very accordant with fraternal confidence and charity, and very fair and equal in its operations. But when it is remembered that the transits were nearly all in *one direction*, viz., from New England and the Congregational Associations into the bounds and the Presbyteries of the Presbyterian Church, it will be seen that the rule worked only one way, and soon threw into the latter Church a large, shrewd, and enterprising body of men who were Presbyterian not from *conviction* but for *convenience*. There were few new churches organized in New England; and as their Colleges and Seminaries teemed with young men who wanted places and could not find them upon Congregational ground, it was a very nice arrangement by which the surplus could flow into the Presbyterian congregations. Whilst the "Plan of Union" opened the way for this process, other agencies were called into exercise for vigorously helping forward the process. The American Education

Society and the American Home Missionary Society, both under control of Congregational men, constituted efficient agencies for this purpose; the one providing the men, the other sending them forth and sustaining them. Through such a door, and by such agencies, were many men, who were brought up with Congregational prepossessions and in the New Theology, thrown broadcast over the Presbyterian Church, many of them into positions of influence. The greater number, it is true, were to be found in the State of New York, Northern Ohio, and the West; but sporadic cases of such element were found in other localities, even in the distant South.

The fruits of an ecclesiastical system so lax and unguarded, soon began to appear. Diverse opinions, both in doctrine and order, arose, and became more and more strongly marked, and, from 1820 onward to 1837, these conflicts of opinion increased in earnestness until they resulted in disruption.

It would be impossible to write a just and complete biography of Dr. George Junkin without exhibiting the part he bore in the events which resulted in the division of the church; and it will be impossible to exhibit this without going into a pretty full detail of the doctrinal and ecclesiastical conflicts that marked the period. Perhaps no man in the ranks of the "Old School" was the object of more bitter resentment, nor the subject of intenser animadversion, than was he, and none of them made such sacrifices of private interests, personal feeling, bodily and intellectual toil, and public consideration. No man, unless it was Dr. Robert J. Breckenridge, was for a time more obnoxious to the "New School," and to that portion of the public that sympathized with them. This was in part owing to the following facts: 1st. Dr. Junkin encountered the odium that is apt to attach to a public prosecutor, especially when the accused is a favorite with a large party. 2d. He was the instrument of bringing the doctrinal questions at issue to a judicial decision, and of demonstrating that these questions affected fundamentals in the faith of the church. 3d. Whenever great questions of doctrine or constitutional principles were discussed, he was among the prominent and effective debaters. 4th. He took less pains than most men do to "set himself right" with the public. His habitual forgetfulness of self when he thought truth and right were at stake, prevented any questions about the *popularity* of his course from arising in his mind. He was one of the men who would rather be *right* than be *popular;* and, aiming to do right in the fear of God, he was not given to make calculations in regard to the effect it might have on his private interests or his personal popularity. He had faith in God and in the future, and was perhaps too indifferent to the transient censures of heated partisans, and the currents of popular opinion. Hence he was often misunderstood and misrepresented in regard to his motives and conduct, especially by those who did not personally know him.

The CAUSES of the disruption of 1838 may all be comprehended under four classes, affiliated, however, in their operation, viz., 1. Alleged error in doctrine; 2. Alleged departure from Presbyterian order; 3. What were technically called "New Measures;" and 4. Diversity of opinion in regard to the modes of conducting the aggressive work of the church; one party claiming that it is the right and the duty of the church to conduct Missions in her own name, and through her own organization; the other party insisting that it may be done through the agency of Voluntary Societies. The first class of causes will be treated further on; the second class we have noticed as growing out of "the Plan of Union;" the third, the "New Measures," were certain methods of conducting revival efforts, which had been introduced by zealous ministers and laymen, and which had been carried to such extremes by Mr. Finney, Mr. Burchard, and others, as to awaken resistance to them, on the part of those who dreaded excitement and extravagances. Dr. Nettleton and others in New England raised the first opposition to these "New Measures;" but both the measures themselves, and opposition to them, were soon transferred to the Presbyterian churches. Many sound men (doctrinally) favored them to some extent, under the conviction that they promoted conversions and a lively type of piety. As a general thing, they were opposed by the "Old School" and favored by the "New;" and there can be no doubt that many sound men were led to sympathize with the New School more than they otherwise would have done, under the impression that there was more earnest Christian activity and less "dead orthodoxy" with the latter. Still it is true that many of the Old School used the "inquiry meeting," and sometimes the "anxious seats." But, as the subject of our memoir was never involved in any of the discussions connected with this matter, and as it was not before the church courts, we dismiss it. The fourth cause needs fuller mention.

From her earliest history in this land, the Presbyterian Church has been practically an education and a missionary organization. The Mother Presbytery (Philadelphia) passed a missionary order at the very first meeting, the records of which are preserved (1707). Indeed, one of the avowed objects of the formation of the Presbytery was to operate it as a missionary society. This is stated in a letter, written in 1709, to Sir Edmund Harrison. [See letter in Records of Presbyterian Church, page 16.] And all down through the history of the church, the idea was practically recognized, that the church was a missionary society *per se*, and that evangelizing work was her mission. Into the very woof of her constitution and history this idea was woven, and the attempt to eliminate it, and to deprive the church of direct control over her own work, did more to arouse the "Old School," and consolidate their strength, than even the alleged ingress of doctrinal error.

From the earliest years of her history in this land, at the close of the sixteenth and the beginning of the seventeenth century, her ministers and her Presbyteries gave attention to educating at home, or procuring from abroad, ministers to supply the increasing destitutions, so that the cause of education and of home missions was coeval with the founding of our denomination. The proposal to take this work out of the hands of the church herself and to consign it to the agency of Voluntary Societies, not amenable to the church courts, and beyond the control of her spiritual authorities, seemed like surrendering the Keys of the Kingdom, and it startled those who clung to the ancient usages of the church, and did more to unite them in opposition to the alleged innovations than any other one cause. And as this proposal seemed to be a part of an extended programme by which, as they feared, errors in doctrine and changes in ecclesiastical government were being widely and rapidly propagated, a firm resistance to that scheme was aroused.

On the other hand, the authors and advocates of this scheme, deeming, no doubt, that the best interests of religion would be promoted by the proposed innovations, pressed them with ardor, vigor, and adroitness.

That the church courts always claimed to be missionary organizations is fully avouched by the records. The first Presbytery, as we have seen, assumed and acted upon the claim. The Synod did the same. And when the General Assembly was organized, the right and the duty of the church courts to prosecute and control evangelical work was distinctly asserted in the XVIII. chapter of the Form of Government. That chapter gives to each Presbytery the right to supervise missions within its own bounds; requires of every missionary coming within its bounds to "be ready to produce his credentials to the Presbytery through which he may pass;" and declares that "the General Assembly may, of their own knowledge, send missions to any part to plant churches, or to supply vacancies," etc. And it was a conceded doctrine, that the Assembly had supreme control over the whole subject of missions; for, so early as 1791, when, on account of their distance and the peculiar condition of the currency in the Southern States, the Synod of the Carolinas wished to collect and disburse their own missionary funds, they applied to the General Assembly, and *permission* was formally granted. It was "Resolved that the Synod of the Carolinas be allowed to manage the matter of sending missionaries to destitute places, . . . *provided* that the Synod shall send annually to the General Assembly a particular account of their proceedings on the above subject, and a regular statement of the money that may be collected and disbursed." [Minutes of 1791, p. 38.]

With such provision in the written constitution of the church, and with such a history before them, it is not matter of surprise that the "Old School" should be unwilling, that the great principle of ecclesiastical responsibility and control should be either ignored or denied. It was under the operation of ecclesiastical control and organization that the little germ, planted by Makemie, Simpson, Riddel, and their companions, had grown to be a luxuriant vine, overshadowing the land; and they were unwilling to relinquish a system under which such blessed results had been realized. The Mother Presbytery, four years after her organization, assumed the control of the education of a candidate for the ministry, David Evans. [See Records.] In 1717 a "Fund for pious uses" was formed. In 1771 a systematic plan for educating candidates was adopted by the General Synod; and the work of training and sending forth ministers to evangelize the rapidly growing population was carried steadily on.

Nor was the Foreign Missionary work neglected. In 1751, in view of "the exigencies of the great affair of propagating the gospel among the heathen," a standing order was issued that a collection be made in each of the churches, once a year, for that object. The Rev. John Brainerd was supported as a missionary among the Indians of New Jersey by this fund, until his death in 1781.

After the organization of the General Assembly, that body for a long time transacted missionary business whilst in session. But, on account of the long intervals between its sessions, and the growing importance of the missionary work, it was deemed expedient to appoint a standing Committee on Missions, to collect and arrange information for the Assembly. This was done in 1802. This Committee was appointed from year to year; its powers were gradually increased, until, in 1816, its name was changed to "The Board of Missions," and the whole business of missions committed to it, subject to the direction and control of the Assembly, to which it was required annually to report.

As early as 1805, the attention of the Assembly was engaged in efforts to increase facilities for the education of young men for the ministry. The Presbyteries were earnestly urged to increase their zeal in this work, and to report their transactions to the Assembly annually. These movements, whilst they increased the educational efforts, did not produce results adequate to the necessities of the church and country.

In 1815, a voluntary association, called the American Educational Society, was organized at Boston, which made vigorous exertions to unite all the evangelical denominations of the country in a grand educational movement under its auspices. And at one time there seemed a likelihood that this society would grasp all the funds, and control the entire work of educating men for the ministry. Good men in all the evangelical churches, who were not posted in regard to the progress of the New Theology, were ready to hail this movement as the harbinger of glorious things for Zion. Even the subject of this memoir joined heart and hand in furthering the interests of this society, in the region in which his first pastorate was exercised. But leading minds in the Presbyterian Church, who lived nearer to the centres of information and better understood the tendency of things, were alarmed at the idea of a society whose centre of operations lay beyond the boundaries of the church, and over which the church had no control, being permitted to have the training of her future ministry. They saw danger in consigning this very important part of the work of the church to irresponsible hands. And they were especially alarmed at the palpable fact, that most of the men who controlled the management of this society were identified with a type of theology different, in many important points, from that embodied in the standards of the church.

And as this Education Society was chiefly under Congregational control, and as the Home Missionary Society was located in New York, and was also largely under the same sort of control, they apprehended that the one Society would train preachers of a particular type of Theology, and with loose views of church order, and the other Society, standing as it were at the *door of entrance* to the Presbyterian Church, would scatter them broadcast through the church, to the imperilling of her doctrine and order. And the Old School believed that this process had already been carried on, and that, unless arrested, it would revolutionize the church, and give permanent ascendency to the New Theology, and to the control of the Voluntary associations. This result they were honest in deploring as disastrous, for they sincerely believed that the cause of true religion, at home and abroad, would be injured by the propagation of the new views.

We are not disposed to attribute to the great body of the New School party in the church a deliberate purpose to effect the revolution, which the other party dreaded. Nor do we suppose, that even a majority of them suspected that such a revolution was designed by their leaders. Indeed, it is probable that, if the scheme was laid for the purpose, as the Old School alleged, the plan was known only to the few shrewd and energetic minds who had somehow been placed at the head of the movement, and of the organizations by which it was to be carried out. And it is now matter of history, that many of these belonged to the Congregational element in the church, and actually withdrew from the New School body, after the division took place, and returned to a more congenial ecclesiastical connection.

The writer of these pages was a pastor in the city of Washington at the time the New School General Assembly met in that city in 1852. And he well remembers, that the chief portion of the time of the Assembly was occupied in an ardent discussion of some of the very questions which had originally divided them from the Old School in 1830–1837,—the questions of ecclesiastical *control* of education and missions *versus* the control of voluntary societies. He distinctly remembers, that the late venerable Dr. George Duffield approached him, as he sat listening to the discussions, and whispered, "You see, Dr. Junkin, that we are here discussing among ourselves the very questions over which we battled with you fifteen years ago." They discussed them ably. The original pronounced Presbyterians were generally found advocating ecclesiastical control; and these views gradually gained ground, until our New School brethren fully adopted them, and reduced them to practice in the organization of church Boards or Committees. The element that was adverse to this reform had been gradually sloughing off from the body; and continued to do so until it became, previous to the late reunion, quite a thoroughly homogeneous Presbyterian body.

And with this foreign element, it cannot be doubted, there was carried out of that branch of the church much of that fondness for a novel terminology in Theology, which had awakened the apprehensions of the Old School, and which led to the agitations which resulted in disruption.

If this statement be historically true,—and we think no man thoroughly posted will deny it,—it proves two things: First, That there DID EXIST serious and grave causes, doctrinal and ecclesiastical, for the troubles of 1830–1837, causes which earnest and honest men of the Old School views could not conscientiously ignore; and Second, That these causes have been, in the progress of events, almost, if not wholly, removed; so that the Reunion was almost as inevitable a result of the course of things, as the Disruption was at the time it occurred.

CHAPTER XX.

History of Doctrinal Opinion—English Presbyterianism always Defective—Man of Straw—Congregatio-Presbyterianism of New England—Effect upon Doctrinal Opinion—New Terminology and its Probable Causes—American Presbyterianism of Scottish Origin—The "Adopting Act"—Ingress of New Theology—Hopkinsianism—Semi-Pelagianism—Taylorism—State of Parties.

IT will not be necessary to the completeness of this memoir, to give a full history of the doctrinal opinions involved in the controversy in which Dr. Junkin bore a part. It is in itself a very interesting one, running back into the seventeenth century; for the pedigree of opinion is as distinctly traceable as are the genealogies of men. Views of doctrine in one generation are influenced by those held in a preceding one; and he has but shallow conceptions of the philosophy of thought who ignores this connection. In the troublous times succeeding the great Civil Revolution in England the church was tossed upon the billows of civil commotion, and was in a state distracted and unsettled. Although the Westminster Assembly had adopted the Confession of Faith and the Presbyterian form of government, and the Long Parliament had given it a modified sanction, yet there was never a general acceptance of either in England. In some cases, those of the clergy who were Presbyterian in sentiment, organized into Presbyteries; but such organization never became general. The Protector, being an Independent, threw all the weight of his influence against Presbyterianism; and, upon the restoration of the Stuarts, the Presbyterians were objects of violent persecution, so that the people usually called Presbyterians never were fully such in the sense in which that term is now understood. There never was a general organization of the people thus denominated; nor did any considerable number of them so adhere to the Westminster Symbols, as to be entitled to be called Presbyterians in the sense in which the Church of Scotland, or the American Church, is called Presbyterian. There was no such organization among them as could hold any minister responsible for departures from the Standards of Westminster. They had really no church authority, except such as might be voluntarily yielded. Persecuted whenever they assumed publicity, and many of them subjected to the licentious influences of the reign of the second Charles, they had, by the time the Act of Toleration under William of Orange gave them respite from persecution, lost almost everything distinctive of Presbyterianism but the name. As a people they really had never fully understood the Presbyterian system, and had never been trained to a stalwart maintenance of its principles. The pressure of political circumstances, and the attraction of fellowship in common dangers and persecutions, had drawn them and the Independents together; and the result was, in many cases, an amalgamation of the two systems, constituting modern Congregationalism. Of course, in a state of things so little favorable to the exercise of church authority, little restraint could be laid upon error in doctrine, and little or no discipline exercised for departures from the orthodox faith.

From this statement, which cannot be truthfully gainsaid, two positions are deducible,—1st. That the indiscriminate charges made by writers of English history against the Presbyterians, are made against a man of straw,—a body that never had either organized existence or organized political power; that such allegations apply to persons who were in no sense true Presbyterians; and therefore, whether true or false, as to fact, are slanders upon Presbyterians; and 2d. That it was to be expected that colonists, coming from such a state of things in the Old World, would be likely to transfer it to the New. Accordingly we find that, although a majority of the colonists of New England were Independents, there was an admixture of that sort of Presbyterianism that existed in England. In reply to inquiries made by the Lords of Trade and Plantations concerning the colonists, and their condition and prospects, the authorities of the colony of Connecticut stated (in 1680) that "some are strict Congregational men, others more large Congregational men, and some moderate Presbyterians."* And what was true of Connecticut was true also of Massachusetts, and to some extent of all New England. No wonder that, with such elements of religious society, the effort to combine them should result in various compromises, ranging from the civico-ecclesiastical platform of Cambridge to the semi-Presbyterian one of Saybrook. Doubtless the sparseness of population, and the difficulty of maintaining ordinances in a new country, were motives for sacrificing extreme views of church order, and originating the peculiar Congregatio-Presbyterianism of New England. And the union of the two, thus effected in the colonies, was imitated in the mother-country; and, under the influence of the Rev. Increase Mather, a union of Presbyterians, Baptists, and Independents was formed in London, and in other parts of the kingdom, in 1690, under articles entitled "Heads of Agreement."†

Of course, in such an amalgam distinctive Presbyterianism would be neutralized; and pronounced adherence to accurate doctrinal statement would be relinquished. A zeal for union that could bring together such elements, would make large demands for the surrender of doctrinal opinions; whilst, in the discussions necessary to effect such

---

* Hinman's Antiquities of Connecticut, p. 141.

† Bogue and Bennet, vol. i. p. 381; and Magnalia Americana, vol. ii. p. 233.

a union, a fondness for speculation would be fostered, and skill therein acquired. Such a habitude theological would be favorable to the truth in well-balanced minds that were truly led by the Holy Spirit. But in minds less logical, and of less decided piety, the spirit of speculation was apt to conduct to results hurtful to sound doctrine and practical piety.

The reader, if he choose to examine, may find in Mather's Magnalia Americana (vol. i. p. 266 *et al.*) proof that a number of the very questions that agitated the church in 1830–1837 were discussed in the days of Increase Mather and Richard Baxter; some of the orthodox New England divines deploring and protesting against Baxter's denial of the doctrine of Adam's and Christ's covenant Headship and representative character. And whilst, in later days, a new theological nomenclature has been adopted by the abettors of what has been termed the New Theology, yet most of the dogmas thereof can be found in the earlier disquisitions to which reference has been made. There is little doubt that, in many cases, the adoption of new terms and new modes of statement was prompted by the amiable wish to render the doctrines of the Gospel less objectionable to the natural man, and less assailable by cavilers. Whilst in others, it is to be feared, dislike to the sterner and less palatable truths prompted the effort to assail them. The desire to make "the offence of the Cross to cease," by softening or denying such of its doctrines as rouse the hostility of the carnal heart, led, in many cases, good men to abet the New Theology; whilst less commendable motives may have prompted others.

The Presbyterian Church in the United States was founded, and, in its earlier years, replenished, by men who had been trained in Scotland and in Ireland, under the Westminster Standards, in their stricter interpretation. At an early period (1729) the Mother Synod passed the

Adopting Act, by which those Standards, with the exception of the chapters relating to the power of the civil magistrate in ecclesiastical matters, were fully received as the Confession of Faith, Form of Government, Book of Discipline, and Directory for Worship of the Church in America; and that Act, together with the circumstances of its adoption, makes it perfectly plain that the Calvinism of Westminster, and no modification of it, was the theology of our Church. And whilst the Calvinism of New England was generally as thorough as that of Westminster, yet departures therefrom were to be found in many individual cases; and the loose ecclesiastical system, which we have described, did not possess power to check or eliminate it. At an early period, some of the new views in theology began to be introduced into the bounds of the Presbyterian Church, by the processes already described.

The first importation that excited apprehension was Hopkinsianism, so called from the Rev. Samuel Hopkins, D.D., of Newport, R. I., who, in 1793, had published his "System of Doctrines." From that time forward other "New Views in Theology," of various shades, arose in New England. The great Unitarian heresy, and the semi-Pelagianism that led to it, had agitated and torn the churches of New England; and even among divines who resisted that heresy, opinions, which many believed to be subversive of the Augustinian faith, were promulgated. Finally arose the school of New Haven, with Dr. Taylor as its leader; and the conflict of opinion waxed warmer, both in New England itself, and in the Presbyterian Church.

It will not be necessary here to give in detail the opinions that furnished the staple of these controversies. They will be sufficiently brought out in the history of the great trial, which resulted in defining with precision the doctrinal positions occupied by the two Schools, into which the church was unhappily divided, and in which final trial

Dr. Junkin was the prosecutor. We shall begin that history in the next chapter; but, before closing this, will repeat what we have said in another form, that we are far from supposing that a majority of our New School brethren had adopted the alleged errors; nor indeed that any very large number had adopted the more dangerous and offensive features of the "New Divinity." The Old School held that that Divinity ought not to be taught by ministers in the Presbyterian Church, and that ministers who held it ought not to come into, or to be tolerated in, the church. Many of the New School, who did not receive the New Divinity, were willing to tolerate those who did; whilst others were slow to be convinced that these doctrines were held by those accused of them, and others still, could not deem them so dangerous as to demand discipline.

CHAPTER XXI.

Things necessary to the Vindication of the Prosecutor of Mr. Barnes—The First Trial of Mr. Barnes, and Events antecedent to the Second—History of his Case—Referred to the General Assembly—Complaints of Minority—Progress of the Conflict about Home Missions—Assembly of 1831—How constituted—Its Acts—Opinion of a New England Delegate—Right to be heard denied—Mr. McCalla—Mr. Breckenridge.

IT has already been said that no clergyman in the ranks of the Old School, was the object of intenser animadversion, on the part of opponents, than was Dr. Junkin; and none of them made such sacrifices of private interests, personal feeling, bodily and intellectual toil, and public consideration.

In order, then, to vindicate the purity of his motives and the unselfishness of his aims, it will not suffice to make mere assertions and express opinions, without adducing the proofs furnished by the facts of the history of that period. Into these, therefore, we must go with a particularity which we would gladly otherwise avoid. And yet, the truth of history requires that they be placed on record.

The first troubles that arose in the church, in connection with the translation of the Rev. Albert Barnes from Morristown to Philadelphia, and the first trial of that minister, have been briefly mentioned in a previous chapter. With that trial Dr. Junkin had very little to do,—nothing, indeed, except what has been related. A more detailed account will be necessary, in order fairly to understand the necessity for, and the importance of, the second trial of that distinguished pastor and writer, in which Dr. Junkin was the prosecutor.

When the First Presbyterian Church, Philadelphia, extended a call to Mr. Barnes, the congregation had never heard him preach, and in the call the usual formulary "from our past experience of your ministrations among us" was omitted. The call was confessedly based upon the favorable report of a committee which had gone to Morristown to hear him, and upon the merits of the published sermon, or "The Way of Salvation," already mentioned.* This sermon, as some of the members of Presbytery alleged, contained errors in doctrine, which they deemed fundamental. Mr. Gillett admits that it "contained expressions which some of his (Mr. Barnes') friends regretted."†

When the call was presented to the Presbytery, and leave was asked to prosecute it, objections were made upon these grounds, and because but fifty out of two hundred and twenty votes had been given for Mr. Barnes.* Yet leave was granted by a small majority. At a *pro re nata* meeting subsequently held (June 18), for the purpose of receiving Mr. Barnes, and, if the way should be clear, installing him as pastor, opposition was made to his reception on the grounds of doctrinal errors avowed in the above-mentioned sermon. Dr. Ely moved that the motion to receive should be postponed, in order to give to any member of Presbytery an opportunity of asking Mr. Barnes for an explanation of his doctrinal views. This motion was negatived (20 to 18), and Mr. Barnes was received as a member. The Rev. Mr. Hoff then presented charges of holding erroneous doctrines against Mr. Barnes in bar of his installation. The Moderator pronounced them out of order. Dr. Ely appealed from this decision, but the majority sustained the ruling of the Moderator, and Mr. Barnes was installed.

---

* Min. Syn. Phila., 1831, p. 5.

† Hist. Presbyterian Church, vol. ii. p. 460.

Against this action of the Presbytery, the venerable Dr. Ashbel Green, and twelve others, complained to the Synod of Philadelphia; and the decision of the Synod, made in October, 1831, has been recorded in a previous chapter. The Synod censured the Presbytery, and directed them to take up and issue the case of Mr. Barnes, and adjudicate it fairly. Mention has been also made of the effort of the majority of Presbytery to press the case through in the absence of most of the Old School members, at a meeting held some twenty-five hours after the adjournment of Synod. That effort was followed by a series of acts which, whether justly or not, the Old School deemed dilatory, evasive, and calculated to defeat the ends of discipline. In these discussions, the Old School members claimed that Presbytery had a right to decide upon the orthodoxy of Mr. Barnes' sermon, apart from formal judicial process. The New School members insisted that a judicial process against the author was necessary before this could be rightfully done. Three days were consumed in the discussions; and, as the opposers of the New Theology were now in the majority in the Presbytery, they were about to proceed to examine the sermon, with a view to judge of its conformity or non-conformity to the Bible and the Standards, when the minority entered a protest, declaring the proposed course unconstitutional, and saying that, if persisted in, "the undersigned must withdraw from all participation in such proceedings, and complain to the next General Assembly." Notwithstanding this threat to withdraw, the signers of the protest continued to exercise freely the right to speak and vote on all questions of order, and to embarrass the proceedings. And they asked and obtained from Presbytery the right to dissent, protest, and complain against the acts of Presbytery, a thing which, without permission, such recusants could not lawfully have done.

When the examination of the sermon was beginning, Mr.

Barnes asked whether he had a right to appeal to the Assembly, and thus arrest proceedings. Being answered that such appeal would not be orderly, he presented a paper, acknowledging the authorship of the sermon, and offering himself for trial. This offer the Presbytery declined to receive, for reasons stated in their minutes. Mr. Barnes then asked leave of absence. He said he felt confident that he could so explain his sermon as to satisfy the Presbytery that it was in harmony with the Confession of Faith; but, after consultation with his friends, he had determined not to do it *then*. Dr. Green most earnestly besought him, after leave of absence had been voted, to remain, and give the explanations which he said he was able to do, and thus promote the peace of the church. This he did not do.

The Presbytery then proceeded to examine the sermon, and, after a careful discussion and analysis of it, a paper, presented by Dr. Green, was read by paragraphs, amended, and adopted. In this paper it was affirmed that the sermon contained dangerous doctrinal errors, especially upon the points of original sin, the atonement, and justification.

It was then moved "That Dr. Green, Mr. McCalla, and Mr. Latta be a committee to wait on Mr. Barnes to communicate to him the result of the deliberations of Presbytery in the examination of his sermon, and to converse with him freely and affectionately on the points excepted to in that sermon, in the hope and expectation that the interview will result in removing or diminishing the difficulties that have arisen in his case, and that they report the next meeting of Presbytery."

The minority opposed this motion as involving a direct insult to Mr. Barnes. It was, however, adopted, and the minority gave notice of complaint against this action to the General Assembly. At an early period after their appointment, the committee sought an interview with Mr. Barnes at his study. He received them in a courteous manner, but refused to hold any converse with them as a committee, expressing, however, a willingness to converse with them as individuals in a private capacity; and, when they were about departing, he handed to them a paper, in which he assigned, as reasons for his refusal, the alleged unconstitutionality of the proceedings of Presbytery, and his unwillingness to recognize their binding force.

In April, 1831, the committee reported these facts to the Presbytery, with Mr. Barnes' written answer. After some deliberation, the Presbytery referred the whole case to the General Assembly. This reference may be found *in extenso* in the minutes of the Presbytery, and, by those who have not access to them, in the Assembly's Digest, pp. 654–55. Besides asking the Assembly to decide the case of Mr. Barnes, this reference respectfully asked the General Assembly to decide four other questions relating to the rights and duties of Presbyterians, under the constitution of the church, viz.:

1. The question whether, when a minister presented clean papers from another Presbytery, the Presbytery to which he applied was bound to receive him without examination, or whether they had a right to examine him?

2. Whether it is competent for a Presbytery to take up, examine, and pronounce upon the doctrines of any printed publication, and declare them to be dangerous and erroneous or otherwise, without instituting formal trial of its author, in case he be a member of their body?

3. Do the doctrinal standards of the Presbyterian Church embrace the Larger and Shorter Catechisms; or is the Confession of Faith *alone* obligatory?

Along with this reference by the majority (O. S.) of the Presbytery, there went up to the Assembly sundry complaints from the minority, against the action of the Presbytery. It was alleged by the Old School, that these complaints were designed to prevent the decision of the doctrinal and ordinal questions, contained in the reference, by the whole undivided Assembly. They (the complainants) had made the effort to convert the Presbytery of Philadelphia into a party, and thus exclude their commissioners from a vote. And this use was made of the complaints in the Assembly of 1831.

In that General Assembly the New School had a small majority, and elected Dr. Beman Moderator, who, of course, had the shaping of the judicial and other committees. All the papers, the reference, and the complaints appear to have been referred to the judicial committee, which reported the complaint of the minority of the Presbytery of Philadelphia. The whole proceedings of the Presbytery in the case were read; and also the sermon of Mr. Barnes; the parties submitted the case without argument; and it was resolved to refer the whole case to a select committee. Drs. Miller, Matthews, Lansing, Fisk, Spring, and McDowell, Mr. Bacon (delegate from the Association of Connecticut), Mr. Ross, Mr. Elisha White, with Elders Jessup and Napier, were appointed this committee.

It is worthy of record, because it throws light upon the *animus* of the men now unhappily arrayed into parties, in the Presbytery of Philadelphia, that, in their complaint to the Assembly, the minority (N. S.) acknowledge that they were wrong in sustaining the decision of their Moderator, by which the charges preferred by Mr. Hoff and others against Mr. Barnes, at the time of his reception, and before his installation, were pronounced out of order and refused. Their language is,—"This decision, the undersigned, of whom the Moderator referred to is one, *now* judge to have been incorrect, because that special meeting was called, not only to *receive* Mr. Barnes, but to transact *any business* relative to his installation. These charges should have been constitutionally disposed of, either by declaring them irrelevant or by taking the requisite steps for trying Mr. Barnes on the same."* The Old School alleged at the time, that this confession of error, by which they, the then minority, had been deprived of their rights, was part of a change in the general plan now adopted for the evasion of an explicit decision of the doctrinal question. At first, the friends of Mr. Barnes resisted the condemnation of the *book*,—then they rejected charges against the *man;* but when the *book* was likely to come under the judgment of the General Assembly, they called for a trial of the *man* instead, and as this demand was inconsistent with their former action, they were now ready to acknowledge that action to be wrong. This item of record makes it manifest, that the call for a trial of Mr. Barnes, on charges made against the *man*, first came from himself and his *friends;* and that when, some years afterwards, and after he had published his Notes on the Romans, Dr. Junkin came forward and tabled charges against the author, he did but respond to the call originated and reiterated by the very men who raised a clamor against him for doing the precise thing which they had demanded.

The committee of the Assembly, to which the case of Mr. Barnes was referred, made a report, originally written by Dr. Miller, but greatly modified and emasculated by the majority of the committee, which was evidently meant as a compromise. This report was adopted, and as it was the first official act of the Supreme Judicatory of the church, that seemed to look towards a toleration in the church of the New Theology, it is put on record in these pages. It is as follows:

"That after bestowing on the case the most deliberate and serious consideration, the committee are of opinion, that it is neither necessary nor for edification, to go into discussion of all the various and minute details which are

---

* Minutes of General Assembly of 1831, p. 176 *et al.*

comprehended in the documents relating to the case. For the purpose, however, of bringing the matter in controversy, as far as possible, to a regular and satisfactory issue, they would recommend to the Assembly the adoption of the following resolutions:

"1. *Resolved,* That the General Assembly, while it appreciates the conscientious zeal for the purity of the church, by which the Presbytery of Philadelphia is believed to have been actuated, in its proceedings in the case of Mr. Barnes; and while it judges that the sermon of Mr. Barnes, entitled 'The Way of Salvation,' contains a number of unguarded and objectionable passages; yet it is of opinion that, especially after the explanations given by him of those passages, the Presbytery ought to have suffered the whole to pass without further notice.

"2. *Resolved,* That, in the judgment of this Assembly, the Presbytery of Philadelphia ought to suspend all further proceedings in the case of Mr. Barnes.

"3. *Resolved,* That it will be expedient, as soon as the regular steps can be taken, to divide the Presbytery in such a way as will be best calculated to promote the peace of the ministers and churches belonging to the Presbytery.

"With respect to the abstract points proposed to the Assembly for their decision, in the reference of the Presbytery, the committee are of the opinion that, if they be answered, they had better be discussed and decided *in thesi,* separate from the case of Mr. Barnes." [Min. 1831, pp. 176–180.]

This action of the Assembly gave great dissatisfaction to the Old School men in the church; and, taken in connection with other acts of the same Assembly, and with utterances of the leaders of the other party, afforded proof, as they thought, of a fixed purpose to thwart discipline, to protect error, and to delay a decision of the great doctrinal questions at issue, until the party abetting these measures could become so strong as to revolutionize the church. It may be that their apprehensions exceeded the measure of the danger; and there can be little doubt that many good men, who voted with the New School, did so with the hope of promoting peace, and because they were not convinced that the errors and innovations complained of were really so serious and so wide-spread. But in the light of events that have since transpired, there can be no reasonable doubt, that the leaders of the New School party seriously contemplated effecting that which the Old School deemed revolutionary. In saying this, their motives are not impugned, for it is to be presumed that they deemed what they aimed at to be desirable and right.

It is now manifest, that great preparation had been made by the friends of innovation for securing a majority in the Assembly of 1831. The gentleman who became the Moderator of that body had made an extensive tour in the South during the preceding winter, and, whilst care for his health may have been the prominent object thereof, yet the fact that he stated to Dr. Spring that he had known, three months before, that, if a member, he would be chosen Moderator, and that he had lost eight votes by absence of members from Virginia, was pretty clear proof that there had been some preconcert.

During the progress of the troubles connected with the case of Mr. Barnes,—1830, and the winter of 1831,—the conflict between the Boards of the church and the Voluntary societies which sought to supersede them in their work, was waxing warmer. The party which sustained Mr. Barnes was nearly identical with that which favored the Voluntary societies. Dr. Absalom Peters, a Welshman by birth, and a Congregationalist by conviction, a man of great ability, tact, and adroitness, was the Secretary of the Home Missionary Society. This gentleman had been endeavoring to effect a sort of union between the Assembly's Board and the Society of which he was the chief actuary. The Presbytery of Cincinnati had, doubtless through his suggestion and influence, addressed a communication to the Board of Missions upon the subject of this union. To this the Board replied, assigning reasons for declining the union, and showing its inexpediency. This letter of the Board furnished the pretext for six letters from Dr. Peters, headed "A Plea for Union in the West;" in which, with much adroitness and plausibility, he assailed the Board of Missions, charged it with inefficiency and a disposition to distract the efforts of the church, by refusing to co-operate with the Home Missionary Society, and strongly hinted that the Board did not "provide things honest in the sight of all men." In his sixth letter, he issued what was well understood to be a rallying call to those that agreed with him, to come in force to the next General Assembly. He said that he had endeavored "to persuade the contending parties"—*i.e.* the Board and the Home Missionary Society —"to become one," and declared that upon that result "my heart is fixed." And he farther says, "What measures ought now to be adopted I do not feel prepared even to suggest. So far as the Western States are concerned, I trust our brethren, on the ground, will be *prepared to express their wishes to the next General Assembly.*" These letters were published in the Cincinnati *Journal*, in December, 1830, and January, 1831, and soon afterward copied into the New York *Evangelist*. They were well adapted to shake the confidence of the churches in the integrity of the Assembly's Board, to promote its union with, or its absorption by, the Home Missionary Society, and, at the same time, to summon all the dependents and friends of that Society to come to the Assembly in force.

The Board replied to this "Plea for Union," in a pamphlet published on the 2d of March, 1831. Dr. Peters rejoined in April, in a forty-eight-page pamphlet.

Whilst the Home Missionary Society was thus rallying its friends, the friends of Mr. Barnes, and others who favored the New England divinity, were also active, and a considerable body of ministers and elders, who occupied a middle ground between the parties, men in the main sound in the faith, but who were willing to go almost any length for the sake of peace, also sought to be represented in the Assembly, in order to repress agitation and promote peace. Under such influences the Commissioners to the Assembly of 1831 were chosen.

Meanwhile, the discussions of the questions of doctrine and order, that were involved in the controversy, went on, and waxed warm—sometimes acrimonious. Mr. Barnes was installed in June, 1830, and shortly afterward a pamphlet, entitled "A Sketch of the Debate and Proceedings of the Presbytery of Philadelphia, in regard to the Installation of the Rev. Albert Barnes," was published in New York. This pamphlet was well adapted to intensify the spirit of party, by its provoking unfairness to the Old School men, and its adroit appeals to the zeal and passions of the New. It held up Mr. Barnes' opponents in the most offensive light, and strove to arouse public odium against them by partisan glosses of the facts.

Some three months after its publication, this pamphlet was answered and reviewed by the Rev. Wm. L. McCalla, in a pamphlet in which he gave a history of the proceedings in Mr. Barnes' case. Meanwhile, the religious newspapers contained many articles upon the agitating questions. All the weekly papers, at this time, were in the interest of the New School, or of the (so-called) "peace men." The *Philadelphian*, then edited by the Rev. Dr. E. S. Ely, had a pretty large circulation in Pennsylvania and the West. Dr. Ely at first seemed disposed to make his paper an impartial medium, but in a short time he became ardently enlisted in the New School cause, and threw the influence of his paper so fully upon that side, that it was deemed necessary to establish another paper in the interests of orthodoxy. This was the origin of the *Presbyterian*, which was commenced in 1831. Dr. Ely had published, in the *Philadelphian*, a history of the Barnes troubles, such as the Old School considered unfair and one-sided, and this led the clerk of the Presbytery, Mr. (afterwards Dr.) Engles, to publish in pamphlet form, "A True and Complete Narrative" of all the proceedings in that case.

The religious press of New England also took part in these agitating discussions. The organ of the New Haven theology, the *Christian Spectator*, interfered, and its number for June, 1831, was issued a month or more ahead of time, in order, as was supposed, to exert influence upon the approaching Assembly, in favor of Mr. Barnes and the Voluntary societies. With a forecast and a candor far transcending his ecclesiastical delicacy, the *Spectator* warns "those who seem bent on driving Mr. Barnes from the Presbytery of Philadelphia, that they are taking upon themselves a responsibility of no ordinary character, since the principle on which they act, if carried into full operation, must create a total disruption of the Presbyterian Church in the United States, and a consequent sacrifice, to an immense extent, of some of the dearest interests of the Redeemer's kingdom, both at home and abroad. We state the subject thus strongly, because every one, we suppose, understands that the case of Mr. Barnes is *not that of an individual.* The real question at issue is, whether *New England Calvinism* shall any longer be *tolerated* in the Presbyterian Church of this country." Thus did the organ of New Haven predict the disruption seven years before it occurred, and avowed that a refusal to tolerate the New Theology would inevitably lead to disruption. The only alternative was, *tolerate the new divinity* or submit to *disruption.*

The Old School party in the church, if disposed to make exertions to shape this important Assembly to their purposes, labored under great disadvantages, especially for want of the use of a religious press in their interest. The *Presbyterian* was yet in its infancy, all the other weeklies were either in the interest of the New School or of the middle men, and the *Biblical Repository*, though thoroughly sound in its theology, was slow to be convinced that there was any great necessity for the measures of resistance to innovation which the Old School had inaugurated. Besides this, it cannot be denied that the Old School men, relying upon the supposed goodness of their cause, were less skilful and energetic in using means to promote it.

Such were the circumstances and influences under which the General Assembly of 1831, whose proceedings we have in part recorded, was constituted. It proved the largest that had ever convened, and in its acts were more fully developed, than ever before, the elements of that great struggle, which, seven years later, resulted in the division of the Presbyterian Church. From its opening to its dissolution, the array of party was distinctly visible. The New School were in the ascendant, the result of influences indicated above. For Moderator they selected a man fully committed, by his sermons, and by his published work on the Atonement, to the New Theology, and also, by his education and associations, to the "new measures" employed to promote revivals, and to the hybrid form of government which had grown out of the "Plan of Union."

Not only did the decision in Mr. Barnes' case indicate that "the revolution was not to go back," but, at the very opening of the Assembly, Mr. Clement Tuttle, a "Committeeman," commissioned by the Presbytery of Grand River, was, by a vote of the majority, admitted to a seat as a member of the Assembly; and although towards the close, when the majority had changed by the departure of some members, it was declared irregular to appoint persons as commissioners who had never been ordained Ruling Elders, there was a disposition shown by the New

School to perpetuate the anomaly of receiving Committee-men.

But the policy of the New School party in this Assembly which excited the most alarm, was the effort boldly made to have the Board of Missions absorbed by the Home Missionary Society. The Annual Report of the Board brought the subject before the Assembly, and, besides this, there were several overtures from the West. The Report of the Board was this year more than usually encouraging; and, in view of their past success, and of pledges of large sums of money from "friends of the present Board of Missions," they declared it their purpose to "supply, in the course of five years, every vacant Presbyterian congregation and destitute district that may be disposed to receive aid from this Board, with a faithful minister of the gospel; and they do hereby pledge themselves to extend prompt and efficient aid to all feeble congregations throughout the Valley (of the Mississippi) which shall apply to them for assistance," etc.

The Home Missionary Society had been striving to get exclusive possession of the great Valley of the Mississippi, and this indication of a purpose on the part of the Assembly's Board to cultivate that field with energy, aroused the opposition of the majority of the Assembly, who favored the schemes of the Home Missionary Society. The usual vote to approve of the report was refused; it was proposed to strike out that part of the report which contained the pledge of aid to the feeble churches of the Valley; but this was forborne, and, with certain animadversions upon the report made by the committee to which it had been referred, it was "returned to the Board for its disposal."

The Memorials on Missions in the West had been referred to a committee, which reported Dr. Peters' plan for a union with the Home Missionary Society. A substitute was proposed, referring the subject to a conference of the Western Synods, with a view to have them agree upon a plan, and report it to the Assembly. "Pending the decision, the movements hostile to the Board reached a crisis. A motion had been made by Dr. Richards, that a committee should be raised to nominate a Board of Missions. Dr. William Wylie moved a postponement of this, to make room for a motion to reappoint the old Board. In the progress of the discussion, the Rev. E. N. Kirk* stated that he came to the Assembly for the purpose of accomplishing two objects,—the vindication of Mr. Barnes, and the dismissal of Mr. Russell from the service of the Board on account of his course in the case of Mr. Barnes. He intimated that these were the objects of his party, and that candor required their avowal. The means on which the party relied for the latter purpose was the election of a new Board, which was expected to amalgamate with the A. H. Missionary Society."†

Dr. Richards' motion was carried by a majority of twenty-two, and a committee, composed wholly of those hostile to the Assembly's Board, was appointed, with Dr. Hillyer, a member of the Board of Directors of the Home Missionary Society, as its chairman. This committee soon reported, nominating a list in which the enemies of the Board greatly preponderated. Many Old School men were on the list, but they were in remote parts of the church; whilst in the Synods immediately adjacent to Philadelphia, the place of the meetings of the Board, there were two to one of New School men. Dr. Green and a few of the old members were retained, but so few as to be powerless in a vote.

The plan was for the new Board to be constituted and to meet during the sessions of the Assembly, and the Old School feared that the design was to enter at once into such relations with the Home Missionary Society as would bind

---

* Shortly afterwards pastor of a Congregational church in Boston.

† Baird's Hist. N. School, pp. 377–78.

the church to act through it. The Assembly was thrown into an intense ferment by the Report of the Nominating Committee. The purpose was so transparent as no longer to be disguised. Many claimed the floor at once; the Moderator could not preserve order; and, to give time for the storm to lull, a short recess was taken.

After the recess the Assembly engaged in prayer for divine direction. Various plans of compromise were proposed, and finally a committee, composed of Rev. F. A. Ross, Dr. Peters, and Colonel Jessup on the one side, and Dr. Green, Dr. Spring, and Mr. R. J. Breckenridge on the other, was appointed. This committee very soon reported a proposition to refer the existing difficulties, growing out of the separate action of the Assembly's Board and the A. H. M. Society, to a conference of the seven Western Synods, with permission for all the Synods and Presbyteries of the Valley of the Mississippi to take part in the conference if they desired it, and recommending that the present Board of Missions be reappointed.*

An effort was made to strike out the clause of this report that admitted to the conference, if they should desire it, all the Synods and Presbyteries of the Valley; but the motion was lost, and the report adopted.

It will not be necessary to follow the conflict, in regard to this great question of missions, through all its subsequent stages. The object in placing on record so much as we have written, is to show that a great necessity existed for definitive action, both as regards doctrine and order; that the peace of the church could never be restored without such action; and that, in coming forward, with a view to secure a final decision of the great doctrinal issues, upon which all the others hung, Dr. Junkin undertook a work for his church, for his generation, and for posterity, the diffi-

* Minutes General Assembly, 1831, pp. 183, 184, 188, 189.

culties of which were only exceeded by its vast importance.

It may be satisfactory, however, to the readers of this book, who may not have access to other histories of that period, to state, in brief, the results of the action of the General Assembly, above detailed. The immediate result of the adoption of the report of the committee of compromise was, to save the Board of Missions from that destruction which at one time seemed so imminent, and to save the church from being handed over, with her hands tied, to the American Home Missionary Society.

Another valuable result was the gaining of time for the church to exercise a "sober second thought," and for the recuperative energy, inherent in Presbyterianism, to be called out. Every week's delay was a loss to the abettors of innovation. Every week shed more light before the people, and the office-bearers of the church, in regard to the real character of the issues of the conflict; and just so fast and so far as these became known, the mass of sound Presbyterians were roused to a sense of the church's danger.

This process of enlightenment was greatly aided by a publication made by the Rev. Mr. Bacon, the delegate to the Assembly from the Association of Connecticut. Mr. Bacon, though not really a member of the Assembly, had been put upon the committee that shaped the deliverance in the case of Mr. Barnes, and after he went home he wrote the article in question, in which he taunted the Assembly with having abandoned the principles of the Presbyterian form of government, in deciding the Barnes case, and with having adopted Congregational modes of acting in that case. After stating the course which he supposed a Presbyterian body would have pursued, he proceeds:

"But this course was not adopted. There was a reluctance, in a part of the Assembly, against a regular trial and decision in the case. . . . Not even the venerable editor of the *Christian Advocate* will charge the venerable professor, on whose repeated motion the Assembly at last consented to waive a regular trial, with being engaged in any conspiracy against the purity of the Presbyterian Church. Yet the fact was, that Dr. Miller did earnestly deprecate the evils which would follow a regular trial and decision, and on that ground persuaded the parties to forego their constitutional rights, and to submit their case, without trial, in the expectation that the Assembly would endeavor to find some ground on which the parties might be at peace. I was disappointed in this, and yet I rejoiced in it. As a curious observer, I was disappointed, because I expected to see the practical operation of your system of judicatories and appeals, in a case in which, if it has any superiority over our system of friendly arbitrations, that superiority would be manifest. . . . I came to the General Assembly disposed to learn what are the actual advantages of that towering system of ecclesiastical courts which constitutes the glory of Presbyterianism, and of that power to terminate all controversies which is supposed to reside in the supreme judicature.

"Of course, I could not but be at once astonished and gratified, to see that unconscious homage which was rendered to Congregational principles, when Presbyterians of the highest form, pure from every infection and tincture of independency, untouched with any suspicion of leaning towards New England, strenuously deprecated the regular action of the Presbyterian system, in a case which, of all cases, was obviously best fitted to demonstrate its excellence. I was astonished. . . . I could not but ask within myself, What is this lauded system of power and jurisdiction worth, these judicatures, court rising above court in regular gradation, what are they worth, if you are afraid to try your system in the hour of need? Yet, when I heard those brethren arguing in favor of referring the matter to a select committee, which should endeavor to mediate between the parties, and to propose some terms of peace and mutual oblivion; in other words, to act as a Congregational ecclesiastical council would act, I was convinced they were in the right. . . . And I supposed that the general conviction was that it was best to go to work, on that occasion, in something like the Congregational way, rather than in the Presbyterian."*

We have quoted just enough of this remarkable paper to show that, in the judgment of a Congregationalist whose heart was with the New School, and who had helped to effect the result reached by the majority of the Assembly, that action was a gross violation of the constitution and principles of the Presbyterian Church. The paper itself aided to convince the people of our church that this was so.

But it would be unfair to the minority of that Assembly to leave the impression that they did not resist, with all their power, this triumph of error, and this prostration of Presbyterian order. There were, in that Assembly, men firm and faithful, who raised their voices and their votes against every act of this huge burlesque on discipline. The Rev. Wm. L. McCalla, who was not in the house when the other members of the committee to defend the action of Presbytery waived their right to be heard, presented a paper asking for his right to perform the duty intrusted to him by his Presbytery. In this earnest paper he set forth that one side (in the Barnes case) had been heard, and the other not. "The complaint," said he, "is a protracted and highly argumentative document. As the Presbytery never saw it, they will expect their commissioners to answer it for them. My colleagues could not, and would not, waive my right. When my momentary absence, at the time, can be shown to be so disorderly as to deprive me of my commission, then, and then only, let my Presbytery be cut off from a hearing. . . . Let the complainants be cheered with the smiles of popular favor, and let me appear under the lowering frown of an

* Christian Advocate, 1832, p. 20.

overwhelming *majority*. Only allow me the constitutional right of speaking for Christ and his people, and I am satisfied. If refused, I shall call heaven and earth to witness that we are denied a hearing which we earnestly solicit, and to which we are entitled by the laws of God and man." But the majority refused him a hearing.

Another honest and vigorous voice was raised against these proceedings. A young lawyer from Kentucky, who had been in the Legislature of that State, and who was beginning to be known as a man of great intellect and indomitable courage, sat as a Ruling Elder in that Assembly. He, with a tone of solemn expostulation, and in words which none but himself could so effectively employ, pointed out the enormity of the conduct of all who acquiesced in the compromise. Both parties, he alleged, had acted against their avowed conscientious convictions, as expressed in their speeches. The friends of Mr. Barnes had voted to condemn as "unguarded and objectionable" that which they had previously fully endorsed; and his opponents had voted those to be only "incautious expressions" which they had declared to be dangerous errors; and they also voted to censure the Presbytery for what they believed to have been a proper course of action. "We have agreed," said he, "to bury the truth; and before two years God will correct us for it."* This young lawyer, some two years afterward, became a minister of the gospel, and has inscribed the name of Robert J. Breckenridge in an honorable and high place in the history of his church and of his generation.

---

* Baird's Hist., p. 371.

CHAPTER XXII.

Conflicting Views about Foreign Missions—Low State of Missionary Spirit—Dr. J. H. Rice's Memorial—Baltimore Action—Action of Assembly of 1831—Formation of Western Foreign Missionary Society—Position of the American Board—Dr. Alexander and Mr. Baird's Opinions—Home Missionary Contest—Cincinnati Convention—History of Doctrinal Conflict resumed—Action of Assembly of 1831 in Barnes' Case—"Elective Affinity" Presbytery recommended—Resistance of Synods of Philadelphia, Pittsburg, and Cincinnati—Rule of Examination—Reference to Assembly—Protests and Replies—Assembly erects an Elective Affinity Presbytery—Synod Nullifies—Duffield's Trial—Beecher's Trial.

IN addition to the causes, already mentioned, producing diversity of sentiment in the Presbyterian Church, and tending towards disruption, there arose about this time the question of the mode of conducting Foreign Missions. We have shown, in a former chapter, that the Presbyterian Church in America considered herself a missionary society, and that from her earliest organization she acted in that capacity. The General Synod, in 1752 and 1756, had voted funds to aid the Rev. David Brainerd in his mission among the Indians; and, as we have mentioned, collections were taken up at a later period for the use of his brother John in his Indian mission in New Jersey, and this was continued until his death, in 1781. In 1766, Messrs. Beatty and Duffield were appointed to make a missionary tour of exploration among the Western Indians; and they made a report of their tour to the Synod of 1767, detailing their journey as far as the Muskingum, and its results. But no missions were actually established until the beginning of the present century, when the commission of the Synod of Virginia sent out six missionaries to perform transient labor, two to Detroit, two to the Senecas, and two to the Muskingum. The Synod of Pittsburg, the daughter and successor of the Synod of Virginia, continued to make some efforts for the evangelizing of the Indians, and among others established a mission on the Maumee. About 1805, Mr. Blackburn planted mission-schools among the Cherokees in the South; and the Synod of the Carolinas had established one among the Catawbas.

In 1816, the General Assembly appointed a committee to correspond with similar committees of the Associate Reformed and the Dutch Reformed Churches, with a view to uniting all three bodies into a Missionary Society. This resulted next year in the formation of "The United Foreign Missionary Society," which was the organ of the three Presbyterian bodies which joined in its establishment, until 1826, when, after certain negotiations, it was united with the American Board, with the consent of the Synods and of the General Assembly, and by them this Board was recommended to the confidence and patronage of the churches.* The churches of our body continued to give to the American Board the money they collected for Foreign Missions; but it was becoming manifest, from every year's experience, that the church was not aroused to her duty in this great work, and probably never would be, unless other means of developing the missionary spirit should be found.

Men of broad evangelical views and of warm hearts, in different parts of the church, seem to have had their minds turned, without apparent concert, to the backward state of Foreign Missions in the church, and deplored it. Many lamented the fact that the church had been diverted from her original position as a Missionary Society to become a mere auxiliary of the American Board. Whilst they rejoiced in

---

* Baird's Digest, and Minutes of the Assembly.

the wisdom and prudence with which that Society managed its affairs, they saw that it was not in a position to develop the missionary energy of the Presbyterian Church. It may be, too, that this conviction was increased by the growing distrust in regard to some New England men, in connection with doctrinal troubles. But before the strife between the "Schools," Old and New, had reached any crisis looking to division, this feeling had grown strong.

In 1830, the subject of Foreign Missions was discussed in the ministers' meeting in Baltimore; and in October of that year the Rev. John Breckenridge, of lovely memory, offered a paper, which was adopted by the Presbytery of Baltimore, deploring the low state of the Foreign Missionary spirit in our church, recognizing the necessity of increased effort to meet the claims of the heathen world, and ending with

"*Resolved*, That we will make the attempt, as a body, from this time to support at least one missionary in the Foreign field."*

A few days after this action, as Mr. Baird informs us, as Dr. John H. Rice was passing through Baltimore, he was waited upon, at Dr. Nevins', by a committee of the Presbytery, and the great question was canvassed. Dr. Rice was asked to prepare a paper which might arouse the church to her duty. He promised "to think of it;" and fulfilled the promise by dictating from his death-bed an overture to the General Assembly, which was presented in the following May. That great and good man, in this memorial, did not seem to contemplate an entire separation of the Assembly from the American Board, but a "co-ordinate Presbyterian branch, sufficiently connected with the Assembly to satisfy scrupulous Presbyterians, yet

* Balt. Magazine, 1838, p. 221.

in union with the original Board." "The overture was presented, and a committee was appointed to confer with the American Board." It was considered by some as unwisely constituted,*—that is, if the object of Dr. Rice's overture was to be attained. The truth is, that it was made a party question by the majority of the Assembly. The committee was elected by ballot, and Drs. McDowell, Richards, and McAuley were chosen, all of whom were opposed, at that time, to any change in the relations of the church to the American Board. Drs. Alexander, John Breckenridge, and E. P. Swift were the defeated candidates. By this action of the majority of the Assembly, the cause of Foreign Missions was placed in the same category with that of Home Missions and Education,—the subject of ecclesiastical contention. The Old School saw, or thought they saw, a disposition on the part of the New to withhold the church, in her corporate ecclesiastical capacity, from all three of the fields of her legitimate labor,—Education, Home Missions, and Foreign Missions. They thought they discerned a fixed purpose to bind the Presbyterian Church to the three great voluntary societies, the American Education and Home Missionary Societies, and the American Board of Foreign Missions. From this they recoiled. And the words uttered in Dr. Nevin's study at the interview with Dr. Rice, became from 1831 onward the rallying-cry to the church,—"The Presbyterian Church a Missionary society!"†

Inasmuch as the vote in the General Assembly of 1831 indicated a disposition, on the part of the majority, to prevent the formation of an ecclesiastical organization for Foreign Missions, and a determination that the church should continue to act through the American Board, the

---

* Gillett, vol. ii. p. 454.

† Foote's Sketches of Virginia, vol. ii. p. 497.

friends of church action took prompt measures for ecclesiastical action. The Synod of Pittsburg resolved itself into "The Western Foreign Missionary Society" in that same Fall (1831), under a constitution which made provision for the co-operation of other Synods and Presbyteries, thus looking to its extension to the whole church, and its ultimate adoption by the General Assembly. In this movement such men as Drs. E. P. Swift, Thomas D. Baird, A. D. Campbell, W. C. Anderson, and the venerable Elisha McCurdy were active. The Hon. Harmar Denny was the first President; Rev. Thos. D. Baird, Vice-President; Dr. Swift, Corresponding Secretary; and Mr. McCurdy, Treasurer. Before the meeting of the Assembly of 1832, funds had been raised, Africa chosen as its first field of operations, and it was ready to enter upon its work. When the Assembly of 1832 convened, Dr. McAuley, from the committee to confer with the American Board, presented a report, signed by the conferees, which, in an elaborate argument, endeavored to prove that, on account of the national character of that Board, it was best for the churches that had hitherto operated through it to continue to do so; and proposed, that in order to bring the Presbyterian churches more fully up to the work, "the prudential committee of the American Board should take prompt and efficient measures, by agencies and other ways, to bring the subject of Foreign Missions before the individual members and congregations of the Presbyterian body; and that the General Assembly and subordinate judicatories of that church give their distinct and efficient sanction and aid to the measures that shall be adopted for this purpose."

At the meeting of the American Board, at which this report was considered, Dr. Miller, who was present as a member, offered the following minute as further expressive of its views, viz.:

"While this Board accept and approve of the foregoing report as expressing their firm opinion on the subject referred to the Committee of Conference,—*Resolved,* That if the General Assembly of the Presbyterian Church, or any of its subordinate judicatories, shall eventually think proper to form any association for conducting Foreign Missions separately from the American Board, this Board will regard such association with fraternal feelings, and without the least disposition to interfere with its organization or proceedings."

"This amendment," says Dr. Miller, "was very unceremoniously negatived, only two members of the Board rising in its favor."* Thus a fixed purpose was exhibited by the Board itself to hold the Presbyterian Church as its auxiliary, and not only to do for that church its Foreign Missionary work, but even to educate its congregations in their evangelical duties, "by agencies and otherwise," under the control of its "Prudential Committee." Resolutions to this effect were proposed as part of the report, and the attempt was made thus to forestall ecclesiastical action.

Dr. Baird resisted these resolutions, and informed the Assembly of the organization and activity of the Western Missionary Society; and warned them that the resolutions would "do the American Board more hurt than good." In opposition to them, Dr. A. Alexander said, "These resolutions will so commit the Assembly that we cannot with propriety, at any time or for any reason organize a Board of Foreign Missions. It also contains a virtual censure of the society already formed at Pittsburg. . . . I am in favor of the American Board. I am a member of it, and have confidence in it. . . . But I am not willing that the Assembly should thus bind themselves and their successors forever from acting by themselves. Suppose the charter-members, who all reside in Massachusetts,

* Baird's History, p. 458.

should hereafter fall into great errors in regard to the manner of conducting missions, or into fundamental errors in doctrine. I have no suspicion of the kind. But we have no security that such a thing will never take place. And is this supreme judicatory of the Presbyterian Church to be so committed that it cannot withdraw the control of its Foreign Missions from such a Board?"*

The resolutions were rejected. The Assembly refused to express any opinion upon the principles contained in the report; they recommended the American Board to the affection and patronage of the churches, but took no notice of the Western Foreign Missionary Society, except a brief allusion to its formation in the narrative of the state of religion, as indicative of a deeper interest in the subject of Foreign Missions.

The conflict in regard to the subject of Home Missions was transferred temporarily to Cincinnati by the action of the Assembly of 1831, referring that subject to the Synods and Presbyteries in the Valley of the Mississippi. Efforts were promptly made by the friends of the Home Missionary Society to call a Convention at Cincinnati, with the purpose of so defining its objects as to favor their plans, and to constitute the Society so that it would be rather a mass-meeting than a representative body. They proposed, in a circular, "to leave it to every Presbytery to send as many delegates as they choose, or may find convenient; allowing, also, any intelligent members of the Presbyterian churches to attend and aid in the deliberations, if they observe the same order as will be expected of delegates appointed by Presbyteries."†

This plan would have put it in the power of the New School men in and around Cincinnati to control the Convention. But the Presbytery of West Lexington was called

---

* Baird's History, pp. 459, 460.

† Ibid., vol. ii. p. 381.

together soon after the publication of this circular, and proposed a more equitable plan, asking all the Presbyteries to send delegates in the ratio of their representation in the Assembly. Several other Presbyteries approved this plan, and the Convention was organized upon it.

In this Convention appeared such men as Dr. Blythe, Dr. T. D. Baird, Dr. Steel, and R. J. Breckenridge, Esq. The first-named was President. It was in session a week. Its deliberations did much to inaugurate a more wholesome and conservative sentiment in regard to the duty of the church on the subject of Missions; and the final minute embodied a statement of the facts and views that were elicited during the discussions of the Convention, and the wishes of the several Presbyteries represented, as the basis of, and the reason for, the *Resolution,* "That, under these circumstances, they deem it inexpedient to propose any change in the General Assembly's mode of conducting Missions; as they fully approve of that now in successful operation; and that the purity, peace, and prosperity of the Presbyterian Church materially depend on the active and efficient aid which the Sessions and the Presbyteries under its care may afford the Assembly's Board." The minute was adopted by 54 to 15. A resolution was then offered commendatory of the work which the Home Missionary Society was doing within our church, but the resolution was indefinitely postponed by a strong vote.*

Having brought the history of the missionary phases of the great struggle to the point and period at which the tide was turned in favor of ecclesiastical organization, it will be necessary to go back and bring up the narrative of that part of the conflict which related to doctrine and discipline.

The Assembly of 1831, in the minute adopted in the case of Mr. Barnes, had not only failed to sustain an effort

* Minutes of Convention, as quoted by S. J. Baird, vol. ii. p. 386.

to arrest doctrinal error, which they acknowledged to have been prompted by "conscientious zeal for the purity of the church," but they gave judgment that all further efforts of the kind in Mr. Barnes' case ought to be suspended by the Presbytery of Philadelphia. Not only so, but they suggested the expediency of dividing that Presbytery in such a way as to separate those that were willing to tolerate the alleged errors from those who thought that such errors in doctrine ought not to be allowed in the Presbyterian Church. A memorial was presented to that Assembly, asking them to carry out this recommendation, and divide that Presbytery at once, and to erect the members who sustained Mr. Barnes into a second Presbytery. This was opposed on the ground of want of constitutional power in the Assembly to do it. Mr. R. J. Breckenridge made a powerful argument against it. The previous question being called and negatived, the whole matter was indefinitely postponed, under the operation of the rule.*

The Synod of Philadelphia met in Baltimore on the 27th of October, 1831. Dr. Junkin was chosen Moderator, and, of course, took no active part in its discussions or proceedings. In pursuance of the recommendation of the General Assembly, two propositions for the division of the Presbytery of Philadelphia were brought before the Synod, one from the majority (O. S.), asking for a geographical division by the line of Market Street; the other from the minority, asking that certain members named should be erected into a second Presbytery. Some of these members lived north and some south of Market Street. They also asked that certain churches on both sides of said line be attached to the new Presbytery. The request for a territorial division had been adopted by Presbytery in full session, on the 19th of October preceding; the other came

---

* Baird's Hist., p. 392.

up by memorial from eleven ministers, including Mr. Barnes. A motion to grant the request of the Presbytery for a geographical division was made, and discussed at length, the New School members opposing, and insisting upon eclectic division. At length Dr. Engles moved the following paper, which was adopted, viz.:

"*Whereas*, The Presbytery of Philadelphia, at their last stated meeting, resolved, in compliance with the decision of the General Assembly, to recommend a division of said Presbytery by a geographical line; and *whereas*, the minority of said Presbytery, dissatisfied with the aforesaid arrangement, have petitioned to divide the Presbytery upon other principles; and *whereas*, it appears to this Synod that it will best subserve the purity and peace of that section of the church embraced by said Presbytery, that they should remain in their present undivided state until the members of it can harmonize in a geographical division; it is therefore

"*Resolved*, That whilst this Synod respectfully regard the recommendation of the last General Assembly, yet believing that it has originated in a misapprehension of the real state of the church in this section of the country, they consider it, in every point of view, inexpedient to divide the said Presbytery, and do therefore dismiss both the recommendation of the Presbytery and the prayer of the petitioners."

After the adoption of this minute, Dr. Ely and others declared their intention of complaining to the next General Assembly, and asking *it* for a division of the Presbytery of Philadelphia.*

Before the Synod, at this meeting, also came a complaint, from the minority of the Presbytery of Philadelphia, against the action of said Presbytery in adopting the following standing rule, viz.:

"That every minister or licentiate coming to this Presbytery by certificate from another Presbytery or other

* Minutes of Synod, pp. 5, 6, 7, 9.

ecclesiastical body, shall submit to an examination before he be received."

The Synod took up and considered the complaint; the complainants and the Presbytery were fully heard; the roll was called and members expressed their opinion, and then it was resolved to refer the whole subject to the next General Assembly.*

Dr. Skinner and others gave notice of protest, and of their intention to complain to the next General Assembly. Just as the Synod was about to adjourn, this protest was presented, signed by twenty-two ministers and elders. The protestants assigned three reasons for their protest:

"1. Because the matter thereby referred to the Assembly would have been regularly brought before that body, and in a manner more likely to insure a definitive issue, by *appeal* or *complaint;* while in that case the complainants to the Synod would not have had to meet the disadvantage of having the Synod, who virtually gave judgment in a resolution of last year, among their judges in the Assembly. 2. Because the Book of Discipline requires, that after the roll has been called the final vote shall be taken. (Sec. iii. Art. IX.) 3. Because the Book of Discipline (Sec. ii. Art. III.), which speaks of references, while it concedes the right of reference '*for* ultimate *trial* and decision,' does not seem to contemplate a right of referring simply for *decision* after trial has been gone through."

As there was no time to prepare an answer to the protest before Synod adjourned, Messrs. Engles and Junkin, the Moderator, were appointed a committee to answer it, and publish the answer with the Minutes. They prepared an answer, which bears evidence of having been written by Mr. Junkin; and as it, together with the protest itself, throws light upon the *spirit* of those unhappy times, and

* Minutes of Synod, pp. 6, 7, 8.

the *modes* of conducting the controversy, we condense its answers to the several points of the protest:

"The protestants, in this case, have, in the opinion of your committee, no just grounds of protest, as they have not been in any sense aggrieved. Their first reason for protest is divided into two parts: 1st. The allegation that the matter in question would have been more likely to come to a definitive issue had it gone up by appeal, than by reference. This reason would be good if the matter had originated in the Synod; but as it originated in a Presbytery, and was brought to Synod by complaint, the Assembly will be under the same obligations to issue it as if it had gone directly, by complaint, from the Presbytery to the Assembly. 2d. They prefer it going up by complaint, because that would deprive the Synod of a vote in the Assembly on this constitutional question. In the opinion of your committee, a question like this, involving general principles, ought to be settled by the representatives of the whole church; and as the Synod of Philadelphia represent a large section of the church, whose rights and privileges they are bound to defend, they must regard the attempt of the protestants, to debar their votes in such a decision, as altogether improper and unreasonable. For, suppose two-thirds of the Synods in our body stood in the same condition as the Synod of Philadelphia, then, according to the doctrine of the protestants in this case, a single individual in each Synod might, by complaining, throw the settlement of this constitutional question into the hands of the remaining *one-third.* Would this be right? The protestants shrink from the idea of the Synod being 'among their judges in the Assembly.' But these protestants were not under trial in the Presbytery or Synod, nor are they to be under trial in the Assembly, there to be judged. We had thought that the Presbytery of Philadelphia had been arraigned by their brethren at the bar of the Synod for adopting a standing rule—that the Presbytery, and not their accusers, were the party up for trial. The matter to be tried before the Assembly is the standing rule of Presbytery, to examine persons before receiving them, not the brethren who oppose that rule. The second reason of protest is, that the Book prescribes that, after the roll has been called, the final vote shall be taken. This is true; and the *final vote was taken* when the Synod resolved to refer the matter to the Assembly. The Synod deviated neither from the letter nor the spirit of the Book. The third reason of protest is a mere conjecture. The article of the Book of Discipline, upon which it is founded, not only proves the right of the Synod to refer, but the propriety of such reference in this very case.

"Your committee further remark, that some of the protestants in this case have violated a rule in the Book of Discipline, Chap. viii., Sec. viii. Some of them were parties complainant, had no right to vote, and that rule says, 'None can join in a protest against a decision in any judicatory, excepting those who had a right to vote in said decision.'"*

The above extracts exhibit proof that party feeling ran high on both sides, and that on one there was a disposition, in the settlement of a simple question of constitutional right,—the right of examination,—to give it the character of a trial, so as to exclude the commissioners of the largest Synod from a vote in deciding that question.

Dr. Ely and others brought before the Assembly of 1832 a complaint against the Synod of Philadelphia for not dividing the Presbytery of that name, in accordance with the request of himself and his friends. They also presented a petition to the Assembly, asking that body to divide the Presbytery. The one paper complained of the Synod for not erecting a new Presbytery, to be composed of twenty-three specified ministers and certain specified churches. The other paper asked for the erection of a Presbytery of thirteen enumerated ministers and as many churches, differing from the list presented to the Synod in their petition to it.

The complaint was taken up in the Assembly, and, after a full hearing and a long discussion, the complaint was

---

* Minutes of Synod, pp. 13, 14.

sustained. No censure was passed upon the Synod. This result (the sustaining of the complaint) is attributable to several causes. First, the votes of all the commissioners from the large Synod of Philadelphia were ruled out. Second, some members of the Assembly voted to sustain from sympathy with the theological views, for the sheltering of which the new organization was designed. Third, some so voted from the hope that, by separating the contending parties, peace might be restored; whilst others considered the recommendation of the last Assembly as a compromise measure, which this Assembly was bound to carry out.

Mr. Robert J. Breckenridge moved, that as the judicial case was closed by sustaining the complaint, and as the petition now before the Assembly was a different one from that rejected by the Synod in the act complained of, the Commissioners of the Presbyteries of that Synod of Philadelphia be admitted to vote on the petition, as they have a right to do. This motion was rejected; and as often as renewed was rejected.* The result of all was, that the Assembly created a new Presbytery, to be called the Second Presbytery of Philadelphia, composed of fourteen ministers and as many churches. The motion was—

"*Resolved*, That the complaint be sustained and the prayer of the petitioners be granted."†

And yet, in reality, the thing granted by the Assembly was not that which the petitioners complained against the Synod for not granting. The Presbytery thus erected within the bounds of the Synod of Philadelphia came to be called "The Assembly's Presbytery," and "The Elective Affinity Presbytery;" the latter designation having, it is said, been suggested by a remark of Dr. Skinner, one of its members, during the discussion.

* Baird's Hist., p. 394.

† Minutes Assembly, 1832, pp. 320, 321.

When the Synod met, in Lewistown, in October of that year, quite a sharp and protracted contest was occasioned by the presentation of a paper, claiming to be for the purpose of completing the roll, excepting to the act of the General Assembly in constituting the Second Presbytery of Philadelphia (but recognizing that Presbytery as a constituent portion of the Synod); asserting that the act of the Assembly was an infringement of the constitutional rights of the Synod; and proposing to appoint a committee to prepare a memorial to the General Assembly, praying them to review the proceeding complained of, at their next session.*

The object of presenting this paper, previous to the completion of the roll, appears to have been to avoid the recognition of the constitutionality of the act of the Assembly, by admitting the Second Presbytery without protest. The introduction of the paper at that juncture was objected to as out of order. The Moderator (Mr. Junkin) pronounced it in order; an appeal was taken, and the decision of the Moderator was sustained. The first resolution in the paper, proposing to recognize the Second Presbytery of Philadelphia "as a constituent member of this Synod," was lost, yeas 29, nays 44, and the rest of the paper was postponed for the present, and a Moderator was elected.

A motion was made to enter the names of Dr. Ely, Rev. James Patterson, Rev. Albert Barnes, and Elder Henry Neill upon the roll. An amendment was offered in the words "as members of the Presbytery of Philadelphia." This was postponed to consider a resolution offered by Mr. Winchester, to admit these brethren as members of the Presbytery of Philadelphia. This was amended by the words "if they desire it;" and in that shape passed. They did not desire it, as might have been expected; and

---

* Minutes of Synod, p. 4.

in a respectful note, in reply to the resolution of Synod, they declined the condition of their enrollment, and claimed their right to sit as members of the Second Presbytery, under the authority of the General Assembly.*

At an early moment after the Synod convened, communications from the Synods of Pittsburg and Cincinnati had been presented, read, and referred to a committee. These communications contained the action of the said Synods, remonstrating against the act of Assembly creating the "Elective Affinity Presbytery." The committee to which they were referred, reported a series of resolutions proposing to join with the other two Synods in remonstrating to the next General Assembly against the formation of the Elective Affinity Presbytery, to appoint a committee to draught a remonstrance, and other measures.

The first two proposals were adopted, a committee appointed to draught a memorial, and the other measures postponed. A memorial was accordingly prepared (Dr. Engles, chairman) representing to the General Assembly the views of the Synod, setting forth the constitutional and other reasons why the Synod could not recognize a Presbytery that had, as they alleged, been erected in violation of the constitution of the church, disclosing what the Synod supposed to be the unjustifiable considerations prompting the New School ministers at Philadelphia to seek this erection, and beseeching the Assembly, in the most respectful and earnest terms, to reconsider and annul the act.

A protest against the proceedings of the Synod, in this business, was presented by fourteen members, and admitted to record. Mr. Junkin and Mr. Engles were appointed to prepare an answer. The former wrote the answer, which, with the protest, is in the Minutes, and is

---

* Minutes of Synod, p. 7.

a specimen of the author's skill in detecting and exposing the weak points of false reasoning.*

Complaints to the General Assembly were also announced; and thus the conflict went on. Different opinions may be entertained by dispassionate minds in regard to the wisdom, constitutionality, and expediency of the acts of the Synod in regard to this matter. To some it appeared like nullification, and resistance to superior authority. To others it seemed like justifiable opposition to a revolutionary movement. Those who entertained high notions of the supremacy and unlimited power of the General Assembly condemned the act, as savoring of contumacy. Those who contended that the powers of the General Assembly are specific and limited by a written constitution, and who urged that the ecclesiastical rights of God's people are only safe when the limitations of the constitution are respected, vindicated the doings cf Synod, as justifiable measures for preventing the prostration of that instrument, and resisting the usurpation, by the Assembly, of power which the constitution conferred exclusively upon the Synod. The weak point of the Synod's position, some thought, was in the oft-asserted principle, that even an unconstitutional law is binding, and ought to be submitted to, until it is pronounced unconstitutional by the competent tribunal; and many were of opinion that it would have been better for the Synod to have acquiesced in acts which they deemed unconstitutional, until they could have obtained redress, by a reversal of the objectionable acts. But others, looking upon the acts of the Assembly as unconstitutional and revolutionary, held that the Synod did well, acting upon the maxim *obsta principiis*, to assert their constitutional rights, and to "give consent by subjection, no, not for an hour," to a usurpation of their own prerogative by the Supe-

* Minutes of Synod, pp. 10, 11, 12, 13, and 18–22.

rior Court. Those who took this view of the subject alleged that, as there is no court above the Assembly to pronounce upon the constitutionality of its legislative or administrative acts, if those acts are palpably unconstitutional, resistance becomes a duty. The case was unprecedented, and good men on both sides may have erred.

Before this same Synod came the case of the Rev. George Duffield, upon his complaint against the Presbytery of Carlisle. The judicial committee reported it as in order, and recommended that it be taken up. But it appearing that neither the complaint nor the reasons for it had been given to the Presbytery or its Moderator within the prescribed ten days, it was, on motion of Mr. Junkin, resolved, that no complaint was regularly before the Synod. But, the Presbytery and Mr. Duffield having signified their willingness to proceed, the Synod took up the case. After reading the papers and hearing the parties, a motion, made by Mr. Junkin and seconded by Mr. Steel, was adopted, in the words following, viz.:

"*Whereas,* The principal complaint of Mr. Duffield against the proceedings of the Presbytery of Carlisle, and that on which the other two rest, and from which they spring, is 'that without the preferring of charges, citation, and other steps of judicial process, the Presbytery have, in fact, condemned him as heretical;' and

"*Whereas,* The Synod are distinctly informed that the Presbytery intend, as soon as practicable, to commence and issue such process: therefore,

"*Resolved,* That further progress in the present complaint is unnecessary, if not improper, until the Presbytery shall have brought the contemplated trial of Mr. Duffield to an issue, which they are hereby enjoined to do as soon as possible."*

This paper was offered at the close of Mr. Duffield's argument on his complaint, and before the defence of the

---

* Minutes, pp. 13, 14.

Presbytery was heard; but, on request, it was withdrawn until after the Presbytery was heard, and then adopted.

Mr. Duffield had written a book entitled "Duffield on Regeneration," containing, as the Presbytery alleged, very serious errors, kindred to some pertaining to the "New Divinity;" and, as in the case of Mr. Barnes, the Presbytery tried the *book* instead of the *man*. This, it would seem, Mr. Junkin did not esteem the right process of discipline, and hence he interposed with this paper. The facts are here recorded not only as part of the history of the great disruption, but in order to show that before Mr. Barnes' book on the Romans was published, and before Mr. Junkin could have anticipated that he would ever assume the unenviable position of a prosecutor, he was on record in favor of regular discipline, by trying not a book, but its author.

It may be proper to add here, in regard to Mr. Duffield's case, that his trial before his Presbytery began on the 11th of April the next year (1833). The charges were ten in number. The Presbytery found them all sustained except two; and then entered a minute stating that "As Mr. Duffield alleges that Presbytery has misinterpreted some of his expressions, and says, in fact, that he does hold all the doctrines of the Standards, and that he wishes to live in amity with his brethren, . . . therefore,

"*Resolved*, That Presbytery, at present, do not censure him, any further than to warn him to guard against such speculations as may impugn the doctrines of our church, and that he study to maintain the unity of the Spirit in the bond of peace."

Against this very gentle decision, Mr. Duffield gave notice of appeal to the General Assembly, but he never prosecuted it. When the case came before the Synod of Philadelphia for review, in October, 1833, the consideration of it was postponed on account of Mr. Duffield's absence from illness. Next year it was taken up, and the Synod censured the leniency of the Presbytery.* Thus ended the case of Mr. Duffield, adding another to the many proofs already furnished, in the history of this period, that error was spreading, and that, as yet, it had not been reached by effective discipline. All this was producing its effect upon the mind of the subject of this memoir; and whilst these things were calculated to discourage any ordinary mind from making any further attempts to arrest the progress of the New Theology, they but confirmed his in the conviction that it was somebody's duty to make a more effective effort.

Meanwhile the struggle went on in the public journals and in the various church courts; other combatants were entering the lists from without the church; and thus the necessity of conservative efforts became more and more apparent.

Arthur Tappan, Esq., had liberally endowed a Professorship in Lane Seminary, near Cincinnati, and, in 1832, nominated the Rev. Dr. Lyman Beecher, of Boston, to the Chair of Theology. Mr. Gillett says:

"The condition of the endowment was not unacceptable to the prominent men in the Western field. His accession to their ranks was hailed with gratulation, and Dr. Nelson, of Danville, and Dr. Wilson, of Cincinnati, as well as the Princeton Professors, were consulted in the matter, and gave expression of their satisfaction with the arrangement. Dr. Beecher accepted of the appointment, and removed to Cincinnati in September, 1832. *On his way* he transferred his ecclesiastical relations to the *Third Presbytery of New York*, and by that body was dismissed to the Presbytery of Cincinnati. It was a step well calculated to excite distrust; and he had been only a short time at his post when his doctrinal views began to excite suspicion. He was not a man to conceal his sentiments, and

* Baird's History, p. 467, and Min. of Synod of 1834, pp. 17, 18.

courted rather than shunned investigation. Dr. Wilson became his prosecutor."*

This trial of Dr. Beecher did not take place till 1835, and was almost synchronous with that of Mr. Barnes; and it is here alluded to, in order to show that there was a growing apprehension throughout the church that the doctrines of her Standards were being undermined, and the means of propagating error increased. Mr. Gillett justly says, that the mode of Dr. Beecher's translation from the Congregational Church to the Presbyterian was "well calculated to excite distrust." It was asked, Why did he not go directly to the Presbytery of Cincinnati, in the bounds of which he expected to labor? Why apply (in writing, too, and not by personal application) to the Third Presbytery of New York, which at that time was considered by the Old School as peculiarly zealous for the innovations in doctrine and order? And as this thing was done *on his way West*, it seemed entirely unnecessary, upon the hypothesis that he was what a Professor of Theology in a Presbyterian Seminary ought to be. He was credibly reported to have said to a distinguished Professor of a college in that region, "I have been chosen, and come to make the West what New England is, and I can do it. I have pledge of co-operation of eminent men; and you must help me."

No wonder, then, that under these circumstances his advent excited apprehension. When admitted to the Presbytery of Cincinnati, on certificate from the Third Presbytery of New York, the venerable Dr. J. L. Wilson offered a protest, which was refused a place on the record. Thereupon a motion was made to appoint a committee to inquire into the rumors charging Dr. Beecher with doctrinal error. This motion was rejected. A similar one, made in April, 1833, was indefinitely postponed. Other causes of

* Gillett's History, vol. ii. pp. 462, 463.

delay intervened; until at length, in November, 1834, Dr. Wilson tabled charges against Dr. Beecher for unsoundness in certain doctrines, for slandering the church of God by attributing these errors to her as her received doctrines, and for dissimulation in professing to adopt the Confession of Faith, when he did not really believe it. The Presbytery, the majority of which were New School, postponed the trial, first from November to April, and then to June, 1835.

"The trial," says Mr. Gillett, "continued for several days with unabated interest. But the vindication of Dr. Beecher was so complete that, by a vote of nearly two to one, it was resolved that the charges be not sustained. Dr. Wilson appealed to the Synod. Here the case was gone over anew, and again he was defeated. From the decision of the Synod he appealed to the Assembly of 1836; but, on learning of the facts in regard to another case, which was to come before that body, in which the same principles were involved, he asked and obtained leave to withdraw his appeal."*

Mr. Gillett appears not to have had access to the Minutes of the Synod, nor to have been informed of the process of trial before that body, or he would not have so curtly recorded as a fact that Dr. Wilson "was again defeated." The historical verity is, that Dr. Beecher made such statements and explanations as went far to satisfy the majority of Synod, and even Dr. Wilson himself, that he was not so far astray as had been feared. And yet, so far from being "defeated," Dr. Wilson's appeal was sustained, because there was no reason to censure him; and "Because,

---

* Gillett's History, vol. ii. p. 465. In a note at the bottom of that page, signed "F.," it is stated, "The real fact was, some rogue on the boat on the Ohio River stole the Doctor's coat, money, and papers in the case of Dr. Beecher; and he was glad of any excuse for dropping the matter." Who "F." is, or whence his information, I do not know; but I have means of knowing that the insinuation does injustice to Dr. Wilson.

although the charges of hypocrisy and slander are not proved; and although Synod see nothing in his views, *as explained by himself*, to justify any suspicion of unsoundness in the faith; yet, on the subject of the depraved nature of man, and total depravity, and the work of the Holy Spirit in effectual calling, and the subject of ability, they are of opinion that Dr. Beecher has indulged in a disposition to philosophize, instead of exhibiting in simplicity and plainness, the doctrines taught in the Scriptures; and has employed terms, and phrases, and modes of illustration, calculated to convey ideas inconsistent with the word of God and our Confession of Faith; and that he ought to be, and hereby is admonished to be, more guarded in future."

Dr. Beecher acquiesced in this decision; and the Synod advised him to publish "as early as possible, in pamphlet form, a concise statement of the argument and design of his sermon on native ability, and of his views of total depravity, original sin, and regeneration, agreeably to his declarations and explanations made before Synod." This Dr. Beecher did, in a pamphlet as large as a small volume, and which was received as substantially sound.

Now, the only aim of Dr. Wilson was to preserve the purity of the church in regard to doctrine; and when the Synod declared that they had just grounds of apprehension in regard to Dr. Beecher, and "admonished" the latter, and Dr. Beecher accepted the admonition, promised to do better, and actually did publish a correction of his "terms, and phrases, and modes of illustration, calculated to convey ideas inconsistent with the word of God and our Confession of Faith," it seems to us that, so far from being "defeated," Dr. Wilson substantially gained his cause. The real cause of his withdrawal of the appeal, Mr. Gillett truly states in his text, viz., the fact that the case of Mr. Barnes involved the same principles.

The history of this case, in all its stages, clearly proves

that, whilst the great majority of the ministers and elders were sound in the faith, there was a marked reluctance to administer discipline upon individuals, and a disposition to accept of any explanations that would, in the judgment of charity, relieve them from censure. So far from exhibiting a spirit of severity and persecution, the courts leaned to the opposite extreme, and exercised great lenity. All this but postponed a crisis which the tendency of things rendered inevitable.

CHAPTER XXIII.

Assembly of 1833—Beman's Secret Circular—Philadelphia Difficulties—Committee of Compromise—Refusal to hear the Synod—Compromise all on One Side—Action of Synod of Philadelphia of 1833—Second Presbytery nullifies—Assembly of 1834 erects an Elective Affinity Synod, named Wilmington—Protests and Answers—Western Memorial, its Origin and Objects—Its Treatment by the Assembly—Action in regard to it—Protest against said Action—Meeting of Old School Men—Act and Testimony—Its History and Contents—Its Reception by Different Parties, and Opposition to it—Position of Princeton—Gillett's Characteristies of it—Its Defenders—Dr. A. Alexander's Views—Results.

IN the Synod of Philadelphia of 1832, Mr. Junkin had been appointed chairman of a committee to defend the Synod in the following General Assembly, against the appeal of the Rev. George Duffield. Messrs. Kennedy, Potts, J. Williamson, and McCalla were members of the committee. He was also a member of the committee, of which Mr. McCalla was head, to defend the decision of the Synod in the case of the Second (Affinity) Presbytery of Philadelphia. Mr. Duffield's appeal was never prosecuted, and the General Assembly of 1833 managed to exclude the Synod from a hearing in the latter case, and did not even consult the committee privately; although, as we shall see, the action of the Assembly was professedly based, in part, upon an alleged consultation with thirty-one members of the Synod at an interview sought by the Assembly's committee.*

As the combat deepened, *numbers* became of importance to both parties in the General Assembly, and, no doubt, both, to some extent, used means for obtaining a majority

* Baird's History, p. 397; Min. Assembly, 1833.

of their friends. On the New School side a printed circular letter was quietly issued, and sent to parties supposed to be worthy of confidence, over the signature of Dr. N. S. S. Beman. This contained, among other things, the following requests:

"Will you look well to the Commissioners who attend the next General Assembly? Observe the following particulars: 1. Be sure to elect your full number, both lay and clerical. 2. Let them be peace and union men, men who will take correct ground in relation to those movements which are intended to excite jealousies and divisions in the Presbyterian Church. 3. Be sure and have all the commissioners attend. 4. Insist on their being present in Philadelphia at least a day before the Assembly opens. 5. Request them to attend and report their names at the lecture-room of Dr. Skinner's church, in Arch Street, on Wednesday, the 15th of May, at half-past seven o'clock. Affectionately yours,

"N. S. S. BEMAN."*

When, two years later, the Old School publicly called a Convention of their friends, before the meeting of the Assembly of Pittsburg, the measure was denounced as unpresbyterial and unjustifiable; and yet the proposed meeting in Dr. Skinner's church was but the prototype of the Convention. Thus rallied, the Assembly of 1833 was composed of commissioners, a majority of whom were in favor of further compromise measures. That majority was not entirely made up of New School men, but of them and of those called at the time "Middle men" and "Peace men."

The latter were sound in the faith, but disposed, as long and as far as possible, to avoid a resort to measures of reform which might be considered extreme.

The General Assembly appointed a "Committee of

---

* Presbyterian, 1833, pp. 63, 70.

Compromise," with instructions "to endeavor to effect a compromise, if practicable, between the parties concerned" in the Philadelphia cases. To this Committee the papers and parties were referred. But, instead of hearing the parties, or allowing them to be heard before the Assembly, this Committee called a meeting of such members of the Synod of Philadelphia as were in the city, a majority of whom happened to be of the New School. They did not give the Committee of Synod an audience, nor, so far as is known, consult their wishes. They voted that it was best to suppress all papers, and leave matters as they then were. They reported that they had had an interview with several members of the Second Presbytery of Philadelphia, and subsequently with thirty-one members of the Synod of Philadelphia, assembled at the request of the Committee ; that, after a free conference with both parties, ... the Committee are enabled to recommend to the Assembly the following resolution, viz. :

"*Resolved*, That the complainants in these cases have leave to withdraw their complaints, and that the consideration of all other papers relating to the Second Presbytery be indefinitely postponed."

Thus, by an indirection, and without hearing the complaints against the Synod of Philadelphia, or the Synod's Committee in defence of her acts, the Assembly, in effect, sustained the complaints, disregarded the expressed wishes of that Synod and the Synods of Pittsburg and Cincinnati, and perpetuated the Elective Affinity Presbytery. The Committee appointed to defend the action of Synod sent in at once a remonstrance against the course pursued, and claimed their right to be heard. Efforts were made to induce them to withdraw this paper, but the Committee of the Synod refused to do it, and it was consigned to a convenient grave in the Committee of Bills and Overtures.

At the meeting of the Synod of Philadelphia in the ensuing October, held in Columbia, Mr. McCalla, as Chairman of the Committee to defend the Synod against the complaints in the case of the Second Presbytery, made report of the result in the General Assembly. Mr. Gilbert moved the recognition, by the Synod, of the Second Presbytery, and the rescinding of all former acts of the Synod inconsistent therewith. Mr. Engles moved a substitute, which recited, in a preamble, the history of the case; and then, in a series of resolutions, which, first reprobating the acts of the General Assembly in erecting and continuing the Presbytery as unconstitutional, and tending to prostrate discipline, recognized the Presbytery (Second) as a constituent element of Synod, united it to the First Presbytery, and then divided the Presbytery thus united, into two, by a line extending through Market Street.* This was proposed to be done by the unquestioned constitutional right of a Synod to unite and divide Presbyteries. Dr. Green proposed another paper, embodying substantially the same principles, yet proposing to treat the Elective Affinity Presbytery as a nullity, and refusing to admit its members as members of Synod unless they would consider and treat the so-called Presbytery as a nullity. After considerable discussion, the Synod refused to postpone Mr. Engles' paper, and, after an amendment, running the line up the Schuylkill from the west end of Market Street, it was adopted.†

The Second Presbytery nullified this action of the Synod, and continued its meetings and business. Appeal and complaint against the action of Synod were carried up, and the war about Elective Affinity courts went on.

The Assembly of 1834, constituted much as its immediate predecessor had been, as regards parties, sustained the complaints against the Synod; and not only reversed the

* Min. Synod, pp. 6, 7.

† Ibid., pp. 7, 11.

act of Synod by which the two Philadelphia Presbyteries were united, but pronounced it to be void, whilst they at the same time recognized *that part* of the *same* action by which the (Old) Presbytery had been divided to be valid, and continued that division.* By this action, the Assembly not only, as the Old School alleged, usurped the prerogative of the Synod, but, after creating a Presbytery against the will of the Synod, and forcing it into the Synod, at the same time made it independent of the Synod, in contravention of the powers explicitly guaranteed to Synods by the constitution.

But, not contented with this action, the General Assembly proceeded to insure the life of the Elective Affinity Presbytery, against the power of the Synod of Philadelphia, by erecting a new Synod for its protection.

The Synod had very recently erected the Presbytery of Wilmington out of that of New Castle, and there was a small Presbytery, named Lewes, in the State of Delaware. Majorities in both these Presbyteries sympathized with the Second Presbytery of Philadelphia (Assembly's), and out of these three the Synod of Delaware was erected.† Thus was there not only a Presbytery without fixed geographical limits, but a Synod also, presenting the anomalous condition of an *imperium in imperio.* It was in the course of the discussions upon the subject of the Elective Affinity Presbytery, that the venerable and excellent Rev. James Patterson, with a frankness which his more wary brethren scarcely relished at the time, argued that there was a necessity for such a Presbytery for the convenience of licensing, ordaining, and admitting to the ministry men who could not so fully adopt the Confession as the old Presbytery and the old Synod required them to do.

Against the acts of the Assembly, based upon the "elect-

---

* Min. Assembly, 1834, p. 17. † Ibid., p. 37.

ive affinity principle," and usurping the powers of Synod, the voting minority solemnly protested. The Commissioners of the Synod, having been excluded from a vote, could not join in this protest. The protestants assigned as reasons for their opposition: 1. The unconstitutionality of the acts, being in contravention of powers exclusively belonging to Synods. 2. That the elective affinity principle of constituting church courts was subversive of all discipline. The majority replied to their arguments by asserting: 1. The supreme power of the Assembly to do such acts, under the clause giving that body power to "decide in all controversies respecting doctrine and discipline, and to issue all appeals and references brought before them from the inferior judicatories." 2. From precedents in which, in extraordinary occasions, the Assembly had exercised the right of organizing Presbyteries. [These were beyond the bounds of any Synod, or where the territory comprised in the new Presbytery belonged to two Synods.] 3. That the Assembly was the only judge of constitutional law. 4. They cited the precedents in the city of New York, where geographical boundaries had not been regarded in the construction of Presbyteries.*

The proceedings of the General Assembly, resulting in the erection of an elective affinity Synod, to protect, as the Old School alleged, the elective affinity Presbytery, aroused the intensest feeling of alarm among the friends of strict constitutional construction. They thought they saw, in these measures, a deliberate purpose to prostrate the discipline of the church, and open the doors for the influx of error in doctrine and order. They beheld the Supreme Judicatory of the Church discouraging efforts to resist the spread of error, and opening, as they

---

* Min. Assembly, pp. 657, 658.

verily believed, doors of entrance for ministers hostile to our system.

With Presbyteries pledged to admit intrants with clean papers, without examination, with a Synod to sanction the acts of these Presbyteries, and with the right of other Presbyteries to examine intrants and refuse admission, if they had regular credentials, denied; they deemed the facilities for flooding the church with unsound teaching wellnigh complete. They felt that a crisis had come, demanding extraordinary efforts to avert these dangers.*

Another part of the proceedings of this Assembly which tended to arouse the conservative elements of the church to vigorous action, was their treatment of an overture which has usually been designated as "The Western Memorial." The acts of the Assemblies of 1832 and 1833 had forced upon many of the most sound and godly men in the church a conviction that a revolution was in progress, which, if not arrested, would change the entire system of doctrine and order which she had so long and so firmly maintained. Conferences were held by ministers and elders, accompanied by much prayer, and a spirit of earnest, solemn resistance to the innovations was awakened. In one of these the "Western Memorial" originated. The first meeting was held at the house of Elder John Montfort, in Monroe Township, Butler County, Ohio. There were eleven ministers and ten ruling elders present. The Rev. Francis Montfort was Moderator, and the Revs. Sayers Gazlay and John L. Belville, clerks. Much time was spent in earnest prayer for Divine direction. Letters from Drs. Green, Wilson, and others were read. The evils which they deplored

* They honestly thought that the Presbytery (Assembly's) and the Synod of Delaware were erected to shield the errors attributed to Mr. Barnes, and to facilitate the influx of teachers of the New Theology. This design could not be attributed to all who voted for these measures, although to most it probably might.

were made subjects of conversation, and a Committee appointed to embody the thoughts and suggestions expressed by the members in a memorial to the General Assembly. The paper was submitted to the Conference during the next sessions of the Synod of Cincinnati.*

The memorial was a long and very able paper, too long to transfer to these pages. It can be found at length in the Assembly's Digest.† It set forth, in grave, dignified, and decisive, but respectful, terms, the evils by which the memorialists believed the church to be distracted and endangered; and enumerated certain acts of previous General Assemblies, which tended, as the memorialists thought, to perpetuate and increase these evils.

"These evils," they say, "have greatly disturbed the peace of our Zion, paralyzed its strength, and exposed it to reproach. And notwithstanding the efforts which have been made to arrest their progress, nothing satisfactory has been accomplished. . . . . Plainly as the path is marked out in our excellent constitution, it is with grief that we feel constrained to say that for some years past a policy of an evasive character has distinguished many of the proceedings of the General Assemblies, as also a number of inferior judicatories, wherein they have, apparently at least, sought to avoid a prompt discharge of their constitutional duties, and have substituted a course of procedure unknown and repugnant to the prescribed order of our form of government. Although this has been applauded as a policy wisely calculated to prevent evils and preserve peace, yet we are compelled to view it in a different light; and as indicating that there is a widely spread principle of evil operating in the Presbyterian Church, to the general change of its form of government and the character of its creed. We feel alarmed at the evidences which press upon us of the prevalence of unsoundness in doctrine and laxity in discipline; and we view it as an aggravating consideration, that the General Assembly, the constitutional guardian

---

* Baird's Hist., pp. 406–408.

† Digest, 659–668.

of the church's purity, even when a knowledge of such evils has been brought before it in an orderly manner, has, within a few years past, either directly or indirectly, refused to apply the constitutional remedy."

They then proceed to enumerate certain evils, and the sources of these evils. The Plan of Union of 1801; the custom of permitting candidates or intrants to adopt the Standards with a reservation of the right to put their own construction upon them; the ordination of men *sine titulo*, by Presbyteries in the East, to be sent to labor in the bounds of other Presbyteries. This last they allege to have been done in many cases for the purpose of introducing into our ministry men of inferior attainments or of unsound creed, and they specify cases where six, eight, and ten young men, just licensed, had been so ordained, and who, after being "suddenly, nominally, and geographically converted into Presbyterian ministers," had been thus sent forth. A fourth grievance was the operation of voluntary and irresponsible missionary associations within our church. They remonstrate against the erection of elective affinity courts; and, in the last place, they testify against nine enumerated errors in doctrine which they allege to be taught in the writings of Beman, Duffield, Barnes, and Beecher. They close their memorial with an earnest plea for redress of these grievances in a constitutional way.

As the innovating party, aided by the "middle men," had a controlling majority in this Assembly, this paper was treated in a way accordant with the wishes of that majority. When reported by the Committee of Bills and Overtures, it was put upon the docket without being read. There it remained until the ninth day of the session. Then it was referred to a special committee. That committee reported after three days; and as this report indicates the *animus* of the majority, and contains a demand for and a vindication of this course subsequently pursued by Dr. Junkin, it is here inserted.

After the usual formulary of a report, and the statement that the memorial had been adopted by about nine Presbyteries and signed by eighteen ministers and ninety-nine elders, they recommend the adoption of the following Resolutions:

"1. That this Assembly cannot sanction the censure contained in the memorial, against the proceedings and measures of former General Assemblies.

"2. That it is deemed inexpedient and undesirable to abrogate or interfere with the Plan of Union . . . adopted in 1801.

"3. That the previous action of the present Assembly on the subject of ordaining men, is deemed sufficient.

"4. That the duty of licensing and ordaining men to the office of the gospel ministry, and of guarding that office against the intrusion of men who are unqualified to discharge its solemn and responsible duties, or who are unsound in the faith, is committed to the Presbyteries. And should any already in that office be known to be fundamentally erroneous in doctrine, it is not only the privilege, but the *duty*, of Presbyteries constitutionally to arraign and depose them.

"5. That this Assembly bears solemn testimony against publishing to the world ministers in good and regular standing, as heretical or dangerous, without having been constitutionally tried and condemned, thereby greatly hindering their usefulness as ministers of Jesus Christ. Our excellent constitution makes ample provision for redressing all such grievances; and this Assembly enjoins, in all cases, a faithful compliance, in meekness and brotherly love, with its requisitions; having at all times a sound regard to the purity, peace, and prosperity of the church.

"6. That this Assembly have no authority to establish any exclusive mode of conducting missions; but while this matter is left to the discretion of individuals and inferior judicatories, we would recommend and solicit their willing and efficient co-operation with the Assembly's Board.

"7. That a due regard to the order of the church and the bonds of brotherhood require, in the opinion of this Assembly, that ministers, dismissed in good standing by sister Presbyteries, should be received by the Presbyteries which they are dismissed to join upon the credit of their constitutional testimonials, unless they shall have forfeited their good standing subsequently to their dismissal.

"8. That, in the opinion of this Assembly, to take up, and try, and condemn any printed publications as heretical and dangerous, is equivalent to condemning the author as heretical; that to condemn heresy in the abstract cannot be understood as the purpose of such trial; that the results of such trial are to bear upon and seriously affect the standing of the author; and that the fair mode of procedure is, if the author be alive and known to be of our communion, *to institute process against him*, and give him a fair and constitutional trial.

"9. That, in receiving and adopting the formularies of our church, every person ought to be supposed, without evidence to the contrary, to receive and adopt them according to the obvious, known, and established meaning of the terms, as the confession of his faith; and that if objections be made, the Presbytery, unless he withdraw such objections, should not license, ordain, or admit him.

"10. That, in the judgment of this Assembly, it is expedient that Presbyteries and Synods, in the spirit of charity and forbearance, adjust and settle, as far as practicable, all their matters of grievance and disquietude without bringing them before the General Assembly and the world; as, in many cases, this tends to aggravate and continue them, and to spread them over the whole church, to the great grief of its members, and injury of the cause of religion." (Minutes, 1834, pp. 25, 26.)

Against this action an earnest protest was entered by Dr. Ashbel Green, and thirty-five others. The reasons for protest were:

1. On account of the manner in which the memorial had been treated, in bringing it before the Assembly. The delay. The committing it to a committee hostile to its objects, who brought in a report opposed to nearly all the

memorialists asked, and that without allowing the memorial to be read and to speak for itself.

2. On account of the claim of infallibility for the General Assembly, and the censure inflicted upon the memorialists, in the first resolution of the report, for having called in question the wisdom of certain decisions of former Assemblies.

3. They protest against the proposal, in the second resolution, to render the Plan of Union permanent, together with all the evils that have grown out of that plan. The plan itself they pronounce unconstitutional.

4. They protest against the fifth resolution, as interfering with the liberty of speech, the liberty of the press, and with Christian duty. It would shut the mouths of God's ministers and people as witnesses for the truth, and estop all remonstrance and protest against error.

5. They protest against the seventh resolution, as denying the right of Presbyteries to examine and judge of the qualifications of their own members, or of those seeking to become members, and as opening doors for the unrestrained entrance of error and errorists. They claim the right of examination, as a right inherent in every Presbytery, and protest against this attempt, by the General Assembly, to sweep that right away, and thus subvert all Presbyterial order and government.

6. They protest against the eighth resolution, because it does the very thing which the Assembly censures the memorialists for doing, reflecting upon former General Assemblies for examining and condemning a heretical book before the author was tried. This had been done by the Assembly of 1810, in the case of Rev. W. C. Davis; and by that of 1798, in case of Mr. Balch. This eighth resolution, they alleged, tended to destroy the mission of the church as a testifying body, and to give license to the propagation of error if published in books. They alluded

to some other points to which they objected, and closed their protest with the following earnest plea:

"We do, therefore, by the offering of this protest, most solemnly and earnestly beseech the Assembly to pause; to consider the probable consequences of their action on this memorial, and yet to retrace their steps; lest the adherents to the Standards of our church, in their plain and obvious meaning, should find themselves constrained, however reluctantly, to resort to first principles, and make their final appeal to the great Head of the Church." (Minutes, 1834, p. 33.)

The acts of this Assembly in regard to all the great issues that troubled the church, especially those in regard to elective affinity courts, and to the Western memorial, did more to awaken the church to a sense of her danger than all that had occurred before. The conservative men saw, or thought they saw, in the acts of this Assembly full proof of what they had long feared did exist,—a determination to effect radical changes, both in the doctrinal creed and the ecclesiastical order of their beloved church. They saw every effort to obtain a condemnation of doctrines which they believed to be fundamentally erroneous, defeated. They saw men and opinions, their fathers would have promptly visited with censure, not only tolerated, but peculiarly honored, in the church. They saw the doors flung wide open for the influx of error, by the denial of the right to examine intrants, and by an order from the supreme court of the church to receive men upon the mere basis of credentials. They saw Presbyteries and a Synod organized for the very purpose, as they verily believed, of sheltering error, and giving credentials to men who were not sound in the faith. They saw a powerful and wealthy Society, which acknowledged no responsibility to the church courts, standing at her very gates, ready to send throughout the entire length and breadth of the church the men to whom these "liberal" Presbyteries would give credentials. And they saw that, by virtue of the hold which that Society had upon these men, who were supported by its bounty, the shrewd and talented Actuaries of that Society could rally to the General Assembly, and to many of the inferior judicatories, these zealous dependents, to vote the wishes of these denizen leaders. Many excellent brethren were slow to be convinced that men, bearing the Christian name, would do such things, and claim to do them in the name of the Lord. But when, by the action of this Assembly of 1834, the system of innovation was rendered so complete, and the plan so fully developed and put in working order, even the "middle men" were constrained to confess that things wore an alarming aspect.

During the sessions of the Assembly, a meeting of ministers and elders was held, on the 26th of May, for the purpose of deliberating on the best method of meeting this alarming crisis. The Rev. William Wylie presided, and Rev. D. R. Preston acted as clerk. After earnest prayer, and a free interchange of views, two committees were appointed; one to prepare a protest against the act of the Assembly in the matter of elective affinity courts, the other to draft an Act and Testimony to the churches on the present crisis. Of the former committee, Rev. Isaac V. Brown, of N. J., was Chairman, and of the latter, Dr. R. J. Breckenridge.

The first committee prepared the protest noticed above; the other prepared the Act and Testimony, a paper that has become historic in our church, having, perhaps, more than any other belonging to the great struggle, won the loyal adherence of its friends, and provoked the bitter criticism and opposition of its foes. It was understood to have proceeded from the pen of that master of vigorous thought and intense and lucid English, Dr. Robert J. Breckenridge. He consulted Dr. Charles Hodge in reference to the doctrinal statements it contained; and it was understood that, with one exception, the errors enumerated were defined by that eminent Theologian. The paper was reported to a meeting of the conference, held on the 28th of May. It was then referred to a new committee, who made some slight modifications, which were approved, when it was adopted and signed. Thirty-seven ministers and twenty-seven elders originally signed this document, but, as it made provision for receiving signatures throughout the church, it was ultimately signed by three hundred and seventy-four ministers, seventeen hundred and eighty-nine elders, and fourteen licentiates. It was also adopted by five Synods and thirty Presbyteries. Dr. Junkin's name appears the last on the list of ministers of its original signers, as printed in the Assembly's Digest.*

This remarkable paper can be seen at length in the Assembly's Digest, and we can place on record here but a brief syllabus.

After a grave and sedate, but affecting, introduction, appealing to the people and office-bearers of the church, the paper sets forth the dangers that threaten her, and the utter failure of the measures heretofore employed to avert those dangers; complains that the supreme judicatory had connived at and countenanced alarming errors; and then exclaims:

"Whither, then, can we look for relief but first to Him who is Head over all things, to the church, which is his body, and then to you, as constituting a part of that body, and as instruments in his hand to deliver the church from the oppression which she sorely feels?

"We love the Presbyterian Church, and look back, with sacred joy, to her instrumentality in promoting every good and every noble cause among men. . . . We delight to dwell on the things which our God hath wrought by her;

---

* Digest, p. 677.

and, by his grace enabling us, we are resolved that our children shall not have occasion to weep over an unfaithfulness which permitted us to stand idly by and behold the ruin of this glorious structure."

The paper and its signers then proceed to bear testimony—

1. Against the right of interpreting the Standards of the church in a sense different from that which had been always received, and according to every man's will.

2. Against the unchristian subterfuge to which many had recourse, of avowing adherence to the Standards *as a system*, and yet denying doctrines that are essential to it.

3. Against the conduct of those in our communion who hold, and preach, and publish Armenian and Pelagian heresies, pretending that they are consistent with our creed.

4. Against the conduct of those who, professing to adopt our doctrine and order, so preach and publish as to bring both into disrepute.

5. Against the following, as part of the errors which are held and taught by many in our church:

1. Errors in regard to our relation to Adam. 2. On the subject of native depravity. 3. On the subject of Imputation. 4. Ability. 5. Regeneration. 6. Divine influence in the work of grace; and 7. Errors on the Atonement, viz., the denial of the true and proper vicarious nature of Christ's sufferings.

The paper then sets forth, that the propagation of these errors in doctrine had broken up the peace and unity of the church, arrayed its members and ministers into parties, and increased the causes of mutual alienation. It recapitulates the efforts made for reform, and the manner of their defeat, and gives a list of grievances, including those inflicted by the last Assembly. It then points out the departures from, and the innovations upon, church order, of which they complain, and against which they bear testimony; and finally recommends a series of measures for redress of grievances, and the restoration of the church to her former condition of peace and prosperity in the truth. Of these there were eight, the last being the recommendation of a Convention to be held, on the second Thursday of May, 1835, in the city of Pittsburg, "to deliberate and consult on the present state of our church, and to adopt such measures as may be best suited to restore her prostrate standards." The paper closes with the following impressive words:

"And now, Brethren, our whole heart is laid open to you and to the world. If the majority of our church are against us, they will, we suppose, in the end, either see the infatuation of their course, and retrace their steps, or they will at last attempt to cut us off. If the former, we shall bless the God of Jacob; if the latter, we are ready, for the sake of Christ, and in support of the testimony now made, not only to be cut off, but, if need be, to die also. If, on the other hand, the body be yet in the main sound, as we would fondly hope, we have here, frankly, openly, and candidly, laid before our erring brethren the course we are, by the grace of God, irrevocably determined to pursue. It is our steadfast aim to reform the church, or to testify against its errors and defections, until testimony will be no longer heard. And we commit the issue into the hands of Him who is over all, God blessed forever. Amen."

There was a solemn earnestness in the tone of this paper, and in the men who signed it, that sent home to all hearts the conviction that they meant *work*, *prayer*, and *counsel*. It startled all parties in the church. A committee was appointed to publish and circulate it, and it soon began to produce various effects upon the Presbyterian public, such as might have been expected from the state of parties in the church. By the New School it was hailed with utterances of derision and displeasure, not without symptoms of dread of its probable results. By those who had stood for the order and doctrine of the church, amid accumulated discouragements, it was received as a harbinger of good. And it was the means of deciding many sound and good people, who clung to the hope that matters were not so bad as some imagined. Many of the "middle men" were at last convinced that serious dangers threatened the church, and that prompt efforts to avert them ought to be inaugurated. But others of that party were much excited in an opposite direction, and waged, upon the Act and Testimony and its friends, a war that certainly was not expected from men whose soundness in the faith, and love to our Zion, were so unquestioned. The *Biblical Repertory*, the learned and able Quarterly that was the exponent of the Theology and Polity of Princeton, bore down upon it with such heavy assaults as its gifted writers knew so well how to make.

A feeling of deep regret pervaded the Old School men who favored the Act and Testimony, produced by the very decided manner in which the *Repertory* spoke in reprobation of that document. The Presbytery of Newton, in the Synod of New Jersey, adopted the following minute in reference thereto:

"In view of the peculiar situation of our church, and of the importance of combined and systematic effort to rescue her from the dangers incident to this crisis,

"*Resolved*, That a committee be appointed to confer, by letter or otherwise, with the Professors of the Theological Seminary at Princeton, in order to give and receive such information, concerning the Act and Testimony, as may at once disabuse us of the odium thrown upon us and the other signers of that instrument, in a publication which it is said emanated from that Seminary, and also may operate in uniting their sentiments and ours, so as to produce, if possible, a concert of action."

Dr. Junkin, Mr. Gray, and Mr. Campbell were appointed this committee.

In pursuance of this appointment, a letter, dated Feb. 28th, 1835, was addressed by this committee to the Rev.

Drs. Alexander, Miller, and Hodge. It was a long letter, couched in very deferential terms, and characterized by a fraternal spirit. Neither of the brethren composing the committee had suggested the measure, for, in the first sentence of the letter, they say, "Dear brethren, *without any original movement of our own* upon the subject, we were appointed, by the Presbytery of Newton, and directed to correspond with you, and endeavor to remove a misconception, which is likely to prevent that harmonious action which our common principles seemed to guarantee and require. Having been early, and warm, and constant friends of that measure, we feel distressed that a very slight misunderstanding of the 'Act and Testimony' should not only prevent your harmonious and efficient co-operation with that instrument and its friends, but has caused you to throw a preponderating influence against it, and thus to aid in defeating a measure which we had fondly hoped would have wrought deliverance in Israel." The letter then proceeds to explain the designs of the signers, and to point out wherein Princeton had misapprehended the true meaning and object of that paper, and of the convention it proposed. It reminded them that one of themselves had, in 1831, attended a conference, similar to that proposed in the Act and Testimony, and there was nothing to be dreaded in a consultation of wise and good men. And it met, with facts and arguments, the objections against that document which had appeared in the *Repertory*.

We allude to this unfortunate diversity of opinion between prominent men in the Old School ranks, in regard to the best method of averting the dangers that threatened the church, not for the purpose of animadverting upon the facts, nor of blaming either side. The facts are recorded as part of the history of the period necessary to be known, in order to a just estimate of the difficulties which the friends of reform had to encounter. And it would be but just to add, that the position assumed, for a time, by Princeton and the orthodox middle men, can be accounted for upon principles not only entirely compatible with their thorough soundness and loyalty to the church, but such as might have been expected to influence men situated as they were. Professors in Colleges and Seminaries, who go rarely abroad among the churches, who spend much time in their studies, who have little experience of the sterner details of pastoral life, and who are more familiar with the *theory* of government and discipline than with its practical working, can hardly be expected to realize, as other ministers do, the evils which errors in doctrine and discipline produce in the congregations. Besides this, their position in public institutions, in which all parties in the church may claim an interest, seems to suggest the propriety of their doing what they can, and all they can, as peace-makers. Nor is it to be expected that the recluse in his study will always have the nerve that befits the soldier in the field. There was a wide contrast between Luther and Melanchthon. Each was well fitted for his mission, and in praising the one we do not condemn the other.

It is also to be considered, that it is not to be expected that men can always agree in judgment, in regard to the measures that it would be best to use in a great crisis like that to which the church was brought. The orthodox men, who condemned the Act and Testimony, no doubt sincerely thought it to be a rash and unwise measure. If they were wrong, it was an error of judgment, for which they are not to be blamed. Some of them no doubt sincerely distrusted the practical wisdom and tact of the Old School leaders who were most prominent. A writer in the *Princeton Review* expresses this distrust in pretty strong terms:

"We have no doubt that sound Old School principles would have fared better in the General Assembly—nay, they would have invariably triumphed—if they had been managed with even tolerable discretion."*

Now, this may have been so to some extent; but when it was proposed to add the wisdom of the serpent to the harmlessness of the dove, and to exercise "tolerable discretion" in the management of the future, the censure was perhaps ill-timed.

It seems to the writer to be no more than justice to the *Princeton Review* to give, in its own language, the reasons assigned for making such decided opposition to the "Act and Testimony." In the October number, 1834, we read as follows:

"The point now before us is, however, the true nature of its recommendations. We say they are extra-constitutional and revolutionary, and should be opposed by all those who do not believe that the crisis demands the dissolution of the church. If such a crisis be made out, or assumed, then all the rest is a mere question of the ways and means.

"We do not believe that any such crisis exists. That there has been much disorder of various kinds within our bounds, that there has been a good deal of erroneous doctrine preached and published, and that many judicatories have been criminally remiss, in matters of discipline, we do not doubt. These are evils, with regard to which the churches should be instructed and warned, and every constitutional means employed for their correction. But what we maintain is, that there has been no such corruption of doctrine or remissness in discipline as to justify the division of the church; and consequently, all measures having that design and tendency are wrong, and ought to be avoided."

We believe the writer of this, and his associates of the *Review*, lived to be fully convinced that the crisis was much more serious than they at that time thought it to be.

The Act and Testimony men had, during the year from

---

* Princeton Review, 1835, p. 65.

May, 1834, to May, 1835, to encounter a double fire,—the New School full in front; the middle men enfilading their flanks. Drs. Breckenridge, Engles, J. V. Brown, Baird, J. L. Wilson,* Junkin, and others defended the measure so successfully that it gained strength throughout the church every day. In justice to this document and its friends, it ought to be said, that it nowhere proposes to make signing it a TEST of orthodoxy. This was an inference of its opponents, wholly unsupported by the text of the paper, or by anything in the history of its origin or promulgation. Its signers simply claimed the right to testify against specific errors in doctrine and order, to recommend certain measures for effecting reform, and to ask all their brethren, who were willing, to co-operate with them in these measures. And if, in the progress of the struggle that ensued, some of its friends used it, to any extent, as a *test*, it was not until after both it and they had been severely assailed. This is history.

The efforts of the friends of reform were not confined to newspaper articles. They defended the Act and Testimony and the Convention, and other reform measures proposed, with vigorous pens; but they made more private efforts also to conciliate the orthodox who opposed these measures, by letters and by personal interviews. It is now known that, whilst he was prudently reticent, Dr. Archibald Alexander was by this time convinced that great dangers threatened the church, and that extraordinary

* Dr. Wilson, of Cincinnati, published a pamphlet reply to the Articles of the *Princeton Review*, with the title "The Moderates and the Ultra Partisans,"—this title having been suggested by a remark in the *Review*. In this pamphlet was the pertinent inquiry, "Why have not the Moderates done their duty, and showed the Old School how this thing can be done? Why have they not brought up *fairly* before the Assembly some of the 'few dozen' heretics of their acquaintance unconnected with 'peculiar, personal, local, or exciting circumstances,' so that the Assembly might have given one 'calm and dispassionate' decision?"

measures for averting them were needed. As early as 1831 he wrote to a former pupil: "My mind is full of gloomy apprehensions respecting the affairs of our church, since the meeting of the last General Assembly. I cannot foresee whither we shall be driven. I had never suspected that the new men and the new measures would *so soon prevail* in the supreme judicatory of our church . . . The burden and heat of the day will soon come upon the young men, who will have great need to be strong, to preserve the ark of the Lord from falling into the hands of the Philistines. Quit yourselves like men."* In a letter to Dr. Plumer, he writes: "Stand up bravely for the religion of your fathers, which is also ours by deliberate choice as well as inheritance." After the Assembly of 1834, he says: "If it is now found that our differences are so wide that we cannot live in peace, let us peaceably agree to separate into two distinct denominations." (*Ib.*) The Doctor never signed the Act and Testimony; but it is not known that by any public act or expression he opposed or disapproved it. His surroundings were such that he forbore to do anything that might wound the sensibilities of his colleagues.

---

* Life of Dr. Alexander, p. 475.

CHAPTER XXIV.

Pittsburg Convention—Mr. Gillett's Account—Observed a Day of Fasting and Prayer—Organization—Business Committee—Committee to Draught a Memorial, Dr. Junkin Chairman—Memorial reported—Its Adoption and Contents—" Cameronian Eloquence" misrepresented—Assembly of 1835—Old School in the Majority—Dr. Phillips Moderator—Memorial presented, referred, reported, referred to a Special Committee—Its Chief Points adopted by the Assembly—Synod of Delaware dissolved—Mr. Barnes' Notes on Romans.

"THE Act and Testimony Convention," says Mr. Gillett in his History, "met, according to appointment, at Pittsburg, previous to the meeting of the Assembly, in May, 1835. Forty-one Presbyteries and thirteen minorities of Presbyteries were represented. By this body a list of grievances was drawn up, to be presented to the Assembly, with an earnest demand for redress. These grievances were for the most part familiar,—the points presented by the Philadelphia Presbytery to the Assembly and re-echoed in the memorial. The closing paragraphs were in a style of petition not often employed in addressing a deliberative assembly. They were rather in the tone of Cameronian eloquence.

"'We pledge ourselves,' say the memorialists, 'in the face of high heaven, that the real Presbyterian Church will not shrink from the conflict; and though our earthen pitchers may be broken, our lights shall shine, and "the sword of the Lord and of Gideon" shall turn the eye of a gazing world to that point of the field where victory perches on the Banner of Truth.'

"The Assembly, thanks to the alarm of the Memorialists, contained a majority who sympathized with them. The grievances were taken up, and the action of the Assembly substantially reversed the proceedings of the Assembly of the preceding year."*

Thus curtly does the N. S. historian dispose of this Convention. Perhaps a little "Cameronian eloquence" was needed to stir the hearts of Presbyterians in a somewhat latitudinarian age. And as the subject of this memoir was the author of the memorial at which the historian thus sneers, it seems necessary to give a more extended account of the paper, and of the Convention that adopted it.

The Convention met in Pittsburg, May 14th, 1835, in the Second Presbyterian Church. The venerable Dr. Ashbel Green was chosen President, Rev. J. Witherspoon, Vice-President, and the Rev. Messrs. James Culbertson and A. G. Fairchild, Clerks; after organization, Dr. Blythe, by appointment, preached before the Convention.

Drs. Blythe, Magraw, Montgomery, and Phillips, with Elders Robert Wray, M.D., James Lenox, and Archibald George, were appointed a Committee to prepare and report business. The Convention observed the second day of the sessions (May 18th) as a day of fasting, humiliation, and prayer, in regard to the state of the church; and the whole day was thus devoted. Dr. Wilson preached in the morning, and Dr. Junkin at night.† Next day the Rev. Messrs. George Junkin, John Witherspoon, J. L. Wilson, Stuart, and Steel, and Elders Boyd, Owen, McPherson, Ferguson, and George, were appointed to prepare a respectful memorial, to be addressed to the Assembly, signed by the members as individuals, and by such other ministers and elders as might choose to unite with them.‡

The business committee presented, during the sessions, various subjects, which were discussed and referred to the committee on the memorial, sometimes with suggestions:

* Gillett, vol. ii. p. 491.

† Brown's Vindication, p. 190.

‡ Baird's Hist., p. 433.

so that this committee shaped the ultimate action of the body. They made their report on Tuesday afternoon, its author having had to spend nearly a whole night in its preparation; for he was present in the sessions of the Convention, and took part in its deliberations.* It was unanimously adopted on Wednesday afternoon, after full discussion. This was only the evening previous to the meeting of the Assembly, and there was not much time for obtaining signatures; but it was signed by seventy-two ministers and thirty-six elders.

This Memorial was couched in solemn, earnest, and respectful terms, and in a style of vigorous explicitness. It set forth eight grievances as matters of complaint, for which redress was sought. 1. The denial of the right of examining intrants. 2. The denial of the right of condemning and bearing testimony against printed heresy. 3. The erection of elective affinity church courts. 4. The existence and operation, within the church, of Missionary Societies, which are under no control of the church, and wholly irresponsible for their doings. 5. The education of young men for the ministry of our church by Societies not responsible to the church, and not friendly to her distinctive doctrine and order. 6. The evils growing out of the Plan of Union. 7. The correspondence, by delegates, with Congregational Associations of New England, which gives to them an influence in the councils of our church which cannot be exerted by us in theirs. 8. The failure of the General Assembly, in late years, to bear testimony against errors admitted to exist. "There is nothing worth contending for but *Truth;* and, if we are not greatly mistaken,

* The original draught of the memorial is still preserved; and in a note on the manuscript, signed by Dr. Junkin, he says, "The following was written, except a part of sixth or seventh items, between the hours of 8½ o'clock, Monday night, May 18th, and 3 o'clock on the morning of the 19th,—six hours and a half,—in my cousin's house, in Alleghany."

great and fearful inroads have been made on the doctrinal standards of our church, and that, too, not in matters of minor consequence, but in the very fundamental principles of the Gospel. One alarming feature of the errors, against which we would earnestly entreat this General Assembly to lift up a strong testimony, we beg leave to present. It is their systematic arrangement. Did a solitary individual, here and there, in cases few and far between, hold to a single insulated position that is false, and maintain it even with pertinacity, it would not afford ground of serious alarm. But the case is far otherwise. The errors abroad in the church are fundamental, vital, and systematic. The maintenance of one involves the whole, and must lead a logical mind to embrace the system. Now, the system appears to your memorialists to lead directly towards Socinianism. This language may seem harsh and severe. Alas! dear brethren, it is the harshness of love, and the severity of truth. It is not pleasant for us to entertain such an opinion; but the evidence rushes upon us from the pulpit and the press, and we cannot resist the conviction. . . . . Another alarming feature is the boldness with which the very existence of these errors is denied. To this General Assembly it would not be information, were we to state that the same system of error has been characterized by the same wily policy in every age of its appearance in the church,—first to deny its own existence, and when that was no longer practicable, to assume a mask, and clothe itself with zeal as a cloak. This strong feature of the modern, singularly identifies it with the ancient heresy."

A list of errors, corresponding with those enumerated in the Act and Testimony, is then given; and the document proceeds with the following appeal:

"Now, reverend Fathers and Brethren, we humbly conceive that this is another gospel; entirely and essentially different from that laid down in the Bible and our Confession of Faith. And we do most solemnly and sorrowfully believe that, unless the Spirit of the Lord raise up a standard against it, it will be followed in our church, as it has been elsewhere, by the entire system of Pelagianism, and ultimately of Socinianism. If the Atonement is not essentially vicarious and penal, why demand a *Divine* Redeemer? If an *exhibition* is all that is required, why not hold up Stephen, or Peter, or Paul, or John Huss, or John Rogers? This tendency towards Socinianism, we think, is plainly manifested in the denial of the eternal filiation of the Son of God. Again, if the Spirit's work is merely a moral suasion, why a Divine and Almighty Spirit? Must not the mind which denies the necessity of an omnipotent influence be strongly tempted to disbelieve the existence of an Omnipotent Agent?

"In pressing our petition for redress of all the grievances we have enumerated, and such others in regard to measures as the wisdom of this Assembly may select, we entreat you to turn your eyes upon the aspect of the world. Lo! what an inviting field for benevolent enterprise! And is there a body of believers in the whole church militant invested with so many of the qualifications to enter it, and gather the rich harvest of glory to our Divine Redeemer, as the Presbyterian Church? The position of our country points us out, the position of our church points us out, the position of the world points us out; the voice of unborn and unsanctified millions calls us to the conflict; the Lord of Hosts Himself has gone down into the plain before us, and chides our long delay. Now, we ask, brethren, what causes this delay? Why, when the armies of the living God begin to consolidate, and Himself gives the watchword—TRUTH and VICTORY,—oh! why this delay? Ah! there is division in the camp! 'There be some that trouble us.' *Innovation* distracts our counsels, alienates our affections, turns the sword of brother in upon brother; and the Master's work remains undone.

"Do you ask, How shall the evil be remedied? We reply, Let this Assembly come up to the work of reform. Let them establish the ancient landmarks of truth; let them unfurl the banner of the constitution. Let all who cannot fight under this, grasp the standard that suits their own views; put on their own approved armor;

descend into the plain, and stand or fall to their own Master."

Then follows the passage characterized by Mr. Gillett as "Cameronian eloquence"; and it will not increase the confidence of the public in the fairness of that historian to call attention to the fact, that he quotes it *so out of its connection*, as to leave the impression upon his readers that the words "We pledge ourselves, in the face of high heaven, that the real Presbyterian Church will not shrink from the conflict," etc., relates to the *ecclesiastical* conflict then in progress; whereas, it relates, as every reader can see for himself, to the missionary conflict with the powers of darkness which the church is waging, and which was the theme of the immediate preceding context.

The Memorial then concludes:

"Venerable Fathers and Brethren, we are done. With you, and God, and Christ, and his Spirit, we leave our cause. That He may direct all your counsels in this behalf to His own glory and the Church's good, is the sincere prayer of your humble memorialists."

Each of the points of grievance mentioned in this document was set forth with an array of facts, and compact and forceful argument, so that the very reading of the paper in the Assembly brought lucidly before that body just what its signers desired. The document itself is recorded in substance both in the Minutes of the Assembly and in Baird's Digest.

The General Assembly of 1835 met the next day after the Convention had concluded its labors. The Presbyteries, it appeared, had been aroused to the dangers that beset the church, and to action adapted to avert them. A majority of Old School men controlled its decisions. The Rev. W. W. Phillips, D.D., of New York, a signer of the Act and Testimony, was elected Moderator, by a majority of thirty-four, over the Rev. Mr. Leach, of Virginia, proof that up to this time Slavery had not entered in as an element in this controversy.*

The Memorial was presented to the Assembly early in its sessions, and referred to the Committee of Bills and Overtures. That committee, with little delay, reported it to the house, recommending that the several subjects which it embraces be referred to appropriate committees. Dr. Hill,

---

* A little episode in the history of the organization of this Assembly will illustrate Dr. Junkin's tact and forecast as an ecclesiastical parliamentarian. At such a crisis, when it was supposed that parties were possibly nearly balanced, it was important to each that it should control the organization of the house, and have the Moderator and the Committee of Elections of its own friends. Dr. Ely knew this, and sought to give the New School this advantage. Dr. Lindsley, the Moderator of the last year, was absent, but had, by letter, requested the Rev. Dr. Wm. A. McDowell to preside, and preach the opening sermon. He was present, but, being unwell, asked Dr. Miller to preach, intending himself to preside. After the opening religious services were over, and before Dr. McDowell could reach the chair, Dr. Ely rose and stated that he (as Stated Clerk) was the standing organ of the Presbyterian Church during the intervals of the General Assembly; and that as Dr. Beman was the only previous Moderator who was present, and a member of the present Assembly, he, according to the Constitution, was entitled to preside. Professing to quote from the Form of Government, he said, "the last Moderator present, *being a member of the house*," was entitled to preside. He made a motion that Dr. Beman should take the chair. This motion Dr. Ely put, and it was carried; but one "No" being heard, and that in the clear, shrill voice of Dr. Junkin. He saw what might be the effect of permitting that adroit party leader, Dr. Beman, to appoint the Committee of Elections, who were to decide on doubtful commissions.

So soon as Dr. Beman took the chair a recess was taken until afternoon. As the members passed out, many asked Dr. Junkin why he voted "No." He gave his reasons; said that Dr. Ely's citation of the Constitution was erroneous, and that several precedents of a contrary kind were on record. Dr. David Elliott proposed to get the minutes during recess, and examine. It was done, and found as Dr. Junkin had stated.

After recess, a motion was made to reconsider the vote calling Dr. Beman to the chair. A warm discussion ensued, in which Drs. Miller, Blythe, Junkin, and others took one side, and Dr. Ely, Judge Darling, and others the other; and it was carried to put Dr. McDowell in the chair. Dr. Ely's words were shown to be an interpolation.—*Statement of Dr. Elliott to the author, and Judge Ewing, in "The Presbyterian."*

of Va., and Dr. Wm. Wisner resisted this, on the ground that the Moderator was a memorialist, and might shape the committees to suit the petitioners. The latter thought, that while the Assembly was considering the memorial one not a memorialist should occupy the chair, and all that were memorialists should withdraw. It seemed to have been forgotten that, when the other party had the majority, every Old School measure was put into the hands of committees hostile to it. And the idea of excluding from a deliberative body, with judicial and administrative powers, all persons who had expressed opinions upon questions that were to come before the body, was quite a novel method of securing fair play. The Memorial, however, with other kindred papers, was referred to a committee, the chairman of which, Dr. Miller, of Princeton, was far from being a signer of the Act and Testimony, or of the Memorial, and of which Drs. Elliott, Hoge, and McElhenny, with Elders Stone, Street, and Banks, were the other members.

After several days' consideration, this committee reported a paper, in which, after an introduction stating that they had given the subjects committed to them that calm, impartial, and solemn consideration which their importance demanded, they say:

"In approaching these weighty subjects, the committee deemed it to be an obvious duty to exclude from their view all those principles which result from the wishes and plans of different parties in the church, and to take for their guide simply the Word of God, which we consider the only infallible rule of faith and practice, and those public formularies, by which we have solemnly agreed and stipulated with each other to be governed in all our proceedings. The moment we depart from these, we are not only exposed to all the evils of discord, but also run the risk of destroying those bonds of union by which we have been so long bound together as an ecclesiastical body."

The disastrous results of such a departure are then set

forth in clear and solemn terms, and then they recommend, for the adoption of the Assembly, eight extended resolutions, covering the points upon which the memorialists had asked them to make deliverances. These resolutions granted nearly all the memorialists sought; the only exception being in regard to the Voluntary Societies, which they deemed it unwise, at present, authoritatively to exclude. The resolution on this subject, however, declared it to be "the first and binding duty of the Presbyterian Church to sustain her own Boards; and that Voluntary Associations, operating within the church, ought to feel bound to neither educate nor send forth in her churches men who hold sentiments contrary to her Standards."

This was in their fifth resolution. The first asserted the inherent right of a Presbytery to examine intrants; the second, the right of any judicatory to take up, examine, condemn, and bear testimony against any heretical publications; the third condemned, as unconstitutional, the erection of judicatories upon the principle of elective affinity, *i.e.* with no geographical limits; therefore, in the fourth it was resolved, that "at and after the meeting of the Presbytery of Philadelphia, in October next, the Synod of Delaware shall be dissolved, and the Presbyteries composing it shall then and thereafter be annexed to the Synod of Philadelphia," and directed that Synod to take such order in regard to the division of Presbyteries, "as may be deemed expedient and constitutional;" the sixth declared it no longer desirable to form churches on the "Plan of Union," and requested the General Association of Connecticut to consent to the annulling of that Plan, from and after the next meeting of the Association; the seventh declined to terminate the plan of correspondence with the Associations of the Congregational churches of New England, since delegates under it were now divested of the voting power; and the eighth condemned the errors specified in the memorial, which the Assembly said they feared were too widely diffused through the church.*

The shape of the resolution dissolving the Synod of Delaware was modified in the progress of the discussion. Dr. Elliott had moved the dissolution of that Synod and of the Assembly's Presbytery; and it was evident that the motion was about to pass, when Dr. Ely brought in a compromise proposition, in which the words "at and after the next meeting of the Synod of Philadelphia" were inserted. Dr. Miller moved a briefer paper, but still including these words. Dr. Ely accepted it, and it was unanimously passed.

Thus ended, for the time, this great struggle. The innovating party were, of course, much dissatisfied, but by no means relinquished hope of ultimate success. They forthwith set about preparing for another General Assembly, and, as we shall see, took advantage of the phraseology which Dr. Ely had suggested, as above mentioned, to embarrass the process of discipline.

Meanwhile it became manifest, that the brethren who had adopted, in whole or in part, the New Theology, felt encouraged, by the protection extended to it, to wax bolder in its dissemination. Early in 1835, and before the meeting of the Assembly of that year, the Rev. Albert Barnes published his work on the Epistle to the Romans. In this book he reproduced, in a form more pronounced than in his Sermon, the same errors to which a portion of his Presbytery had objected when he first came to Philadelphia. This led to a formal prosecution and trial, in which Dr. Junkin bore an important part, and the history of which will occupy the next chapter.

---

* Minutes, 1835, p. 27.

CHAPTER XXV.

History of Barnes' Second Trial—Dr. Junkin prefers Charges—His *Animus*—Letter to Mr. Barnes—Mr. B.'s Reply—Dr. Steel's Agency—Difficulties started by Presbytery—Apparent Reluctanoe—Term Heresy—Refusal of Presbytery to go on with the Trial—Reconsideration—The Trial—The Decision—Questions about Appeal—Appeal to Synod—Dr. Boardman and Two Elders.

"IN February, 1835, I was in Philadelphia on business, and, whilst there, had my attention called to the new work of the Rev. Albert Barnes, on the Epistle to the Romans. This arrest of attention was by an unknown correspondent of the PRESBYTERIAN, over the signature of VERITAS, who presented a number of extracts from the work, accompanied by very judicious remarks, pointing out the errors of the notes, and their opposition to the standards of the Presbyterian Church. The new book was the subject of frequent conversation, and, among other places, at the table of my friend, the Rev. John Chambers, who stepped to his study and brought the book. I read a few pages, and was induced to procure a copy, to examine at my leisure. This examination resulted in the conviction, right or wrong, that, as no other person appeared disposed to do it, it would be proper for me to comply with the order of the General Assembly, and endeavor to procure an ultimate decision on these controverted subjects.

"After this determination, the next question was as to the manner; and here, too, it appeared to me the Assembly was correct; the only proper way was to bring charges against the Author. Before I could arrive at these conclusions it was early in March, and it appeared exceedingly desirable to have the whole matter embraced within as short a space of time as practicable, so as to give occasion to the least possible amount of agitation with its evils.

Hence the plan, proposed in my letter below, of making the case what, in civil matters, is called an amicable suit."*

The writer of these pages was in habits of almost daily intercourse with Dr. Junkin, at that time, and he knows that the conviction, that it was his duty to undertake this unpleasant and self-denying work, was the result of much prayer, self-examination, and reflection. It was no rash or ambitious resolve. As the writer one day entered Dr. J.'s study, the latter said, in a tone of subdued sadness, "I think it will be my duty to prefer charges against Mr. Barnes; the troubles of our church will never end until the doctrinal questions are definitely settled." This was perhaps the first utterance to human ears of a purpose which he seemed reluctantly to have formed. In the introduction to his book called "THE VINDICATION," he proceeds to narrate the steps he took in pursuance of his determination. He wrote to the Rev. Robert Steel to ascertain when Mr. Barnes' Presbytery was next to meet. Mr. Steel informed him that their next stated meeting was to have been late in April, but that a special meeting was called on the 20th of March, for the purpose of changing the time of the stated meeting to an earlier date. And Mr. Steel advised him to send forward his papers, to be presented at that meeting, if it should be resolved into a stated meeting. Dr. J.'s object was to have the case matured for the next General Assembly. Agreeably to this arrangement, Dr. Junkin wrote to Mr. Barnes as follows:

"LAFAYETTE COLLEGE, March 16th, 1835.

"REVEREND AND DEAR SIR,—In your Notes on the Epistle to the Romans, there are doctrines set forth, which, in my humble opinion, are contrary to the Standards of the Presbyterian Church and to the Word of God. It also appears to me, and has long so appeared, that these,

---

* Introduction to Dr. J.'s Vindication, p. iii.

and certain affiliated doctrines, have been the chief causes of the unhappy distractions over which we mourn.

"A third opinion, operating to the production of this communication, is, that peace and union in evangelical effort cannot take place so long as these important doctrinal points remain unsettled; and that, therefore, all the friends of such union and peace ought to desire their final adjustment by the proper judicatories of the church. It is certainly true that many have wished to see them brought up, fairly and legally, before the proper tribunals, unconnected with questions of merely ecclesiastical policy, and without any admixture of personal or congregational feelings. Regret has often been expressed by many, and by myself among others, that the Presbytery of Philadelphia had not, at the outset, instituted process against yourself, instead of the course which they pursued. I am sure, however, they did what they thought for the best. It is much easier to find fault, after a measure has been put in operation, than to foresee its defects and prevent them.

"Now, dear Brother, your recent publication has reopened the door, and, unworthy as I am, and incompetent to the solemn duty, yet duty I feel it to be to enter it, and, by an open, fair, candid, and Christian prosecution of the case, to bring out a formal and legal decision of your Presbytery on the points alluded to. I therefore intend, *Deo volente*, to prefer charges against you, founded solely upon your Notes on Romans, and referring to no other evidence for their support than what shall be deduced from that book.

"In prosecuting these charges, I hope I shall be enabled to act with gravity, solemnity, brotherly affection, and all the respect due to a Court of Christ. The object is *Peace* through union in the TRUTH; and I hope the God of truth and peace will direct us to a happy issue. Most conscientiously do I believe that you have fallen into dangerous error. I feel that *your* doctrine shakes the foundation of my personal hopes for eternity. If *it* be true, then I cannot 'read my title clear to mansions in the skies.' Around the discussion of a subject so solemn, I cannot doubt, the Son of God will throw a hallowed influence which will call up feelings very different from those that too often agitate ecclesiastical bodies, where principles of minor consequence acquire exciting power from adventitious circumstances.

"May I now ask of you the favor to transmit to Mr. Henry McKeen's, No. 142 Market Street, a note with responses to the following queries, viz.: 1. Will you admit the Notes on Romans, bearing your name, to be your own production, and save me the trouble of proving it? 2. Will you waive the constitutional right of ten days, etc. (Book, pp. 396–402), and so let the case come up and pass through the Presbytery, with as little delay as possible, provided I furnish you with a copy of the charges, at least that number of days beforehand? To these postulates I can see no reasonable objection on your part, and I presume there will be none. A friend of mine will receive your reply, and dispose of it agreeably to arrangements already made, and will also inform me of the time and place of the Presbytery's meeting.

"Your brother in the Lord,

"GEO. JUNKIN."

To this letter was returned the following answer:

"PHILADELPHIA, March 18th, 1835.

"REV. SIR,—Your letter of the 16th inst. came to hand to-day. In regard to the 'postulates' which you have submitted to my attention in your letter, I remark that the Notes on the Romans *are* my production, and that I trust I shall never so far forget myself as to put any one to the 'trouble of proving it.' On those Notes I have bestowed many an anxious, a prayerful, and a pleasant hour. They are the result of much deliberate attention; and of all the research which my circumstances and my time permitted. I commenced and continued them with the humble hope of extending my usefulness beyond the immediate sphere of my labors in the pulpit; nor have I any reason to doubt that, in this, I was under the governance and direction of that sacred Teacher by whom the Scriptures were inspired. If others *would* make a better book on the important Epistle in question, I should heartily rejoice in their doing it. I have never been so vain as to think that in the exposition of a book like the Epistle to the Romans—so intrinsically difficult, so profound, so often the subject of commentary and controversy—*my* work was infallible; or that there might not be room for much honest difference of opinion and exposition. Nor am I conscious of any such stubborn attachment to my own views, there expressed, as to be unwilling to be convinced of their error if they are incorrect, or to retract them if I am *convinced* of their error. Whether the act of *charging* a minister with heresy, of *arraigning* him for a high *crime*, without a friendly note, without a Christian interview, without any attempt to *convince* of erroneous interpretation, be the Scripture mode, or most likely to secure the desired end, belongs to others, not to me, to determine. I would just say that I have not so learned Matthew xviii. 15–17. I have no reason to *dread* a trial or its results. I mourn only that *your* time and mine, and that perhaps of some hundreds of others, should be taken from the direct work of saving men, and wasted in irritating strifes and contentions. On others, however, not on myself, will be the responsibility.

"In regard to the 'postulate' in your letter, that I 'would waive the constitutional right of ten days,' etc., I have only to say that if any man feel it his duty to arraign me before my Presbytery, I presume it would be best in the end, and most satisfactory to all parties concerned, that the principles and rules of the Book of Discipline be formally adhered to, and that it is not my purpose to make any further concessions.

"As I have no acquaintance with the gentleman whom you refer to in Market Street; as he has given me no occasion to address a letter to him; and as it is evidently not necessary that *our* correspondence on the subject should be conducted, like that of duellists, through the intervention of '*a friend*,' I thought it best not to address him, unless he shall make it proper, but to answer yourself without delay. I am yours, etc.

"ALBERT BARNES.

"Rev. G. JUNKIN, D.D."

On the 18th of March, Dr. Junkin forwarded, through Rev. Mr. Steel, to the Presbytery, the following letter:

"TO THE REV. MODERATOR AND SECOND PRESBYTERY OF PHILADELPHIA.

"BRETHREN,—To you belongs the solemn and responsible duty 'of condemning erroneous opinions, which injure the purity and peace of the church, of removing and judging ministers, of watching over the personal and professional conduct of all your members.'

"Now, one of your members has, as appears to me, published, in a recent work, certain erroneous opinions, of a dangerous tendency to the peace and purity of the church, and to the souls of its members. In that publication he has observed, 'He who holds an opinion on the subject of religion will not be ashamed to avow it.' As, therefore, he appears willing to let his opinions be known, and to abide their consequences, and as to me they appear dangerous, (in the absence of a more suitable advocate of the opposite truths) I ask of your reverend body the privilege of preferring CHARGES against the Rev. Albert Barnes.

"As I have stated in a letter to that brother, 'the object is *Peace*, through UNION in the TRUTH,' etc." [Here he quotes from his letter to Mr. Barnes, above cited, and then proceeds:] "Hence this measure. It is designed to secure a legal decision, and put an end to distractions consequent upon present fluctuations. I do, therefore, pray and beseech the Presbytery to take order in the premises, and to facilitate the issue with the least possible delay. I have no witnesses to cite but Brother Barnes himself; and shall be confined to his testimony contained in his Notes on Romans. These are referred to in part in connection with the charges, and other portions will be read on the trial for further proof and illustration.

"Your brother in the Lord,

"GEO. JUNKIN."

We have shown, in chapter xxiii., that the General Assembly of 1834, under the lead, in part, of the very men who were most prominent and influential in this Second Presbytery of Philadelphia, had declared that it was improper to take up, try, and condemn printed publications; and that "the fair mode of procedure is, if the author be alive, and known to be of our communion, to institute process against *him*, and give him a fair and constitutional trial." But when it was proposed to these brethren to carry out this "mode of procedure," they betrayed a strong reluctance to do it. Both on the part of the Presbytery and of the accused, needless delay and embarrassment were interposed. Although Mr. Barnes' letter to Dr. Junkin (inserted above) was dated on Wednesday the 18th March, it was not mailed until Saturday the 21st, so that it could not reach Easton until Monday evening the 23d,—the day the Presbytery was to meet,—rendering it impossible for Dr. Junkin to have been informed of the meeting. The *pro re nata* meeting was held on the 20th, and the 23d appointed as a stated meeting. In regard to this he asks, "Why did Mr. Barnes hold his answer to me from Wednesday until Saturday, so that it could not reach me until Monday? Why not send it, as I requested, to 142 Market Street? Did he suspect that if he should do so, it might enable Brother Steel, or some one else, to meet the Presbytery, and present the charges? Why did the Presbytery on Friday change their stated meeting until Monday? Did they wish to avoid receiving the charges of which they had received intimation? These queries are important, as they seem to evidence a disposition to shun a trial. 'Charity thinketh no evil:' she, however, 'rejoiceth in the truth.' "*

On Monday the 23d, the Second Presbytery met, and Mr. Steel presented Dr. Junkin's letter to the Presbytery above cited, and also the charges, of which Mr. Barnes *then* took a copy. This letter produced some sensation, and drew forth from members some unkind and unjust insinuations,—such as, There was secret collusion; there must have been a caucus, and the proposed Prosecutor was

---

* Vindication, p. vii.

but the *tool* of that caucus; Dr. Junkin could not prosecute before that Presbytery, for he had signed the Act and Testimony, which denied the legality of the court; Why was he not present in person? etc. etc. Dr. Steel assured them "that the suspicion of a conspiracy was as groundless as it was unkind;* that when last in the city, Dr. Junkin had not read Mr. Barnes' book; that the only preconcert was the arrangement with him (Dr. Steel) for the presentation of the papers in the necessary absence of Dr. Junkin;

---

* In noticing the commencement of the trial, *The Presbyterian* of the following week explicitly disavows for its Editor, and other persons named in connection with the idea of a caucus, any knowledge of Dr. Junkin's intention, until his letter was delivered to the Second Presbytery. The Editor spoke as follows:

"The (Assembly's) Second Presbytery met on Tuesday, June 30th, in the First Church, to try Mr. Barnes on the charges preferred against him by Dr. Junkin. The result of this trial may be easily anticipated. On this subject we feel obliged to notice a most unwarrantable and incendiary movement, executed by one or more of that party, who have so pathetically deprecated 'unhallowed excitement.' On Monday morning the following notice was placarded on the watch-boxes in the most public parts of the city:

"'NOTICE!

"'Dr. A. Green, Dr. Cuyler, Mr. Engles, and Mr. Winchester

vs.

"'The Rev. Albert Barnes!

"'The above case of religious PERSECUTION will be tried in the church on Washington Square, on Tuesday morning, the 30th inst. The prosecution to be conducted by Dr. Junkin, in behalf of the prosecutors.'

"The design of the above is obvious. It is to intimidate the orthodox, and to influence public opinion against them. An orderly trial cannot be conducted, in the very method suggested by our opponents, without subjecting prosecutors to all the consequences which might result from an appeal to the prejudices and passions of men not immediately interested. As far as the four individuals named are concerned, who are thus placarded as 'prosecutors,' the public should be apprised that they were *entirely ignorant* of Dr. Junkin's intention to prosecute Mr. Barnes until it was made public by his own letter to the Presbytery."

The writer of this memoir is of opinion, that it would be unjust to attribute the above-quoted placard to Mr. Barnes, or any of his more judicious friends. No doubt they would have disapproved of it. It was probably the work of some inconsiderate and heated young man.

that the reason of that absence is obvious,—you had fixed the time of your meeting so that he could not *possibly* know of the meeting; but let a time be set for the trial, and he will attend," etc.

The result was the adoption of the following Resolutions, which the Stated Clerk was directed to send to Dr. Junkin, viz.:

"*Resolved,* That this Presbytery cannot regard any *Letter* from an absent person as sufficient to constitute the commencement of a process against a gospel minister.

"*Resolved,* That the said letter be preserved on the files of this judicatory."

In the introductory minute the letter was described as "a letter received from the Rev. Robert Steel, purporting to have been addressed by the Rev. Dr. Junkin to this Presbytery." The letter was in his own handwriting, and signed with his own signature, well known to most of the members. Instead of fixing a day of meeting for this business, as Mr. Steel requested, the Presbytery adjourned to meet at the call of the Moderator. Thus they could be called together from time to time, on short notice, without publicity, so as to transact their ordinary business, and yet Dr. Junkin have no knowledge of the time and place of meeting.

Believing that he saw in these facts evidence of a reluctance to enter upon a trial,—indeed, to evade one, and prevent the decision of the doctrinal question,—Dr. Junkin determined to prevent the thwarting of his purpose by taking up a complaint to the General Assembly, which "brings the whole proceedings" up to the superior judicatory. He accordingly addressed to the Moderator of the Presbytery a notice of complaint, with reasons therefor.

His reasons for complaint were,—1. That the reason of the Presbytery for not commencing process had no foundation in the Constitution of the church; for the Book says that "charges must be reduced to writing" (p. 401); 2. Because the Presbytery had given him no notice of any future meeting, at which he might be personally present; 3. Because, although they had retained and filed the charges, they had virtually refused to permit Mr. Barnes to be tried on them; 4. Because such refusal is a violation of the Constitution, which makes it the duty of the Presbytery "to condemn erroneous opinions" (p. 359), and which implies, that when "some person or persons undertake to make out the charges" and "reduce them to writing," the duty of the Presbytery is to afford a fair, open, and candid trial; 5. Because said refusal is directly in opposition to the order of the last General Assembly (1834, Min. p. 26); and 6. Because the Presbytery was bound by the Book (chap. v. 8) forthwith to cite the pastor (Mr. Barnes) and myself to appear (which seems to imply their absence), and be heard at the next meeting.

Appended to this complaint was a semi-official note to the Moderator, Mr. Grant, in which, among other things, Dr. Junkin said:

"Brother Grant, may I not hope that the Presbytery will throw no obstacle in the way? Brother Barnes says: 'I have no reason to *dread* a trial or its result.' Now, my dear Brother, will not the true time-saving expedient here be, to come right up to the point? Will not putting off, and standing upon doubtful points of order, be the very way to make a protracted and a perplexing business of it? . . . Should you call a meeting about the 7th of April, I will have all the charges, and the testimony adduced in their support, written out, and lay a copy on your table, so that your Clerk will have no trouble in writing it, and you no delay. Brother Barnes surely needs no time to prepare; the whole testimony is already in his mind. He says, 'On these Notes I have bestowed many an anxious, a prayerful, and a pleasant hour.' He assuredly has not to labor, as I have, in arriving at their meaning. He has not his opinion to form. He has counted the cost. He believes the doctrines he has taught to be truth. If he and the Presbytery, after the proposed examination, shall still be of that opinion, I am sure they will say so. I may misunderstand his language. Let its true meaning appear. . . . . Should a meeting be appointed for the trial, as above requested, you will let me know. Or should it be thought necessary to have me present, before the charges will be admitted to lie, let me know. Only remember, our public examinations in College are on Monday, Tuesday, and Wednesday of next week. For my presence, I must confess, I see no color of reason; if obliged to go, I shall *feel* that I am put to trouble and expense without necessity and without law; yet I will go any time after Thursday next.

"Now, may I not hope that Mr. Grant's influence will go to meet my sense of duty? Allow me to add that, when I began this note, it was designed to be private. It may be viewed as semi-official.

"Very respectfully, your brother in the Lord,

"GEO. JUNKIN."

The Presbytery finally opened the way for a trial, and he therefore did not prosecute his Complaint.

On the 30th of March he received the following:

"PHILADELPHIA, March 28, 1835.

"DEAR BROTHER,—I have been desired officially to inform you that the Second Presbytery of Philadelphia will meet by adjournment, at the call of the Moderator, on Thursday, the 2d day of April, 1835, at nine o'clock A.M., in the Lecture-room of the First Presbyterian Church, on Washington Square. This being an adjourned meeting, Presbytery is competent to transact any business that may come before them.

"Attest, THOMAS EUSTACE, *Stated Clerk.*"

On the opposite page was the following private note:

"DEAR BROTHER,—You will see by the above that your wish has been promptly complied with. I believe there is no desire to shrink from an investigation on the part of Mr. Barnes or the Presbytery. Yours truly,

"THOMAS EUSTACE."

It is noteworthy, that although Dr. Junkin had told the Moderator that he would be engaged in the closing exercises of his College Session up to Thursday, the 2d of April, and said that any time *after Thursday* he could attend if need be, yet the Presbytery was called to meet at nine o'clock A.M. of that very day; and, in order to reach the City in season, he must needs travel the greater part of the preceding night. All these facts seemed to indicate a disposition to avoid the trial, and would lead impartial minds to infer that, but for the notice of Complaint, a hearing would not have been afforded; and that in the *very prompt* call of the Presbytery even, there was an effort to avoid an issue.

After completing his labors in the College examinations, on Wednesday, the 1st of April, Dr. Junkin set out, and, by travelling in the night (fifty-six miles), reached Philadelphia about nine o'clock on the morning of the 2d, and entered the Lecture-Room at fifteen minutes after the hour appointed for the meeting of the Presbytery. At that moment the Clerk was reading the complaint of Dr. J., although the minutes of the last meeting had not, as is usual, been read. After the reading was over, Dr. Junkin and some others were invited to sit as corresponding members. The Presbytery attended to different items of business, at every hiatus in which Dr. J. looked for an introduction of his own. But no allusion was made to it. He waited till Afternoon, yet no sign. Finally, about five o'clock P.M., he invited the Presbytery's attention to it himself. He stated that as he had tabled charges, and had received official notice that the Presbytery was to meet to-day, and as the ten days' stay was up, he hoped the trial would now proceed.

Dr. Ely said there had been no authoritative notice issued; if the clerk had sent such a paper, it was from not knowing his duty. Dr. J. then read the letter of the Clerk, but was assured that it was not designed as a citation, as the Presbytery had no charges before them, and was asked whether he had now any charges to table. He replied that he had not *now* any charges to table; they were already tabled, and had been *taken possession* of by the Court, and ordered, by a formal recorded Resolution, "to be preserved on the files of the Judicatory," and it was a strange procedure *now* to ask him for a paper that they themselves had put on file ten days ago.

It was then resolved to ask Dr. Junkin whether he *now* preferred these charges, and designed to sustain them. He replied that some ten days since he had presented them, and had now come prepared to prove their truth and relevancy.

Objection was made to the charges at this juncture, suggested by Mr. Duffield, then sitting as a corresponding member, because the term *Heresy* was not in them. But Dr. Ely made some judicious remarks, which seemed to satisfy the Court that the charges were sufficiently specific. Dr. Junkin explained his reasons for the omission of that term. He said the use of the term *heresy* was apt to excite terrific apparitions in the minds of some. In former times *heretics* had been burned, and people still associate the name heretic with the dungeon, the rack, the gibbet, and the stake. It was therefore calculated to excite unjust odium, both against an accused person and his accuser. He said he was resolved from the first to avoid all language that was calculated to excite improper feelings. Besides, the word heresy had no well-defined idea attached to it. It is difficult to define it; and no two would, perhaps, agree in a definition. For these and other reasons which he gave, he had avoided that odious and indefinite term.

Presbytery then directed Dr. Junkin to be admonished of the consequences of failure to prove charges against a gospel minister; which was done by the Moderator. It was then voted to put a copy of the charges into the hands of Mr. Barnes. He stated that he had, by permission of the Clerk, taken a copy when the paper was first presented (March 23). He was then asked whether he was ready for trial. In reply, he made a short address, in which he presented some difficulties. 1. That the rule (Matt. xviii. 15, 16), "If thy brother trespass against thee," etc., had not been complied with. 2. He found Dr. Junkin's name appended to a document which he held in his hand, called The Act and Testimony, and he could not see how he could consistently prosecute before a court whose constitutional organization he therein calls in question. 3. The case was one of most fearful solemnity, and ought not to be gone through with hastily, but with great deliberation. 4. His health had been in such a state as to compel him to omit some of his ordinary duties, and he could not be prepared in less than ten days, nor even then. 5. At the end of ten days Dr. Ely would be absent, as also Brothers Patterson and Grant and Dashiel, and in the absence of these influential members he would not wish the trial to proceed. He could see no reason for haste, declined immediate action, and hoped the trial would be postponed till June.

In reply to these remarks, the Prosecutor said—1. That the rule in Matt. xviii. 15, 16, had no reference to such a case as this whatever; it relates to private personal injuries only. Now, there was no private personal offence between the parties, no wounded feeling, no fault; it was a *public* concern, that *could not possibly* be hushed up by private explanation. 2. That his signature to the Act and Testimony had nothing to do with the case. He was willing to prosecute before this court—that was a sufficient recognition of its *jurisdiction*, but said nothing about the regularity of its *organization*. A foreigner, who prosecutes before a Court of the United States, only concedes its jurisdiction, expressing no opinion about its original organization. 3. The importance of the matter was a reason why there should be no unnecessary delay. The object was, *Peace through Union in the Truth*, and delay would only keep the community longer in a state of agitation; had he not hoped the case would have been issued before the General Assembly, he would not have brought the matter up at this time. He deprecated a whole year of paper war, which must follow if the case is not now tried.

Mr. Bradford, Ruling Elder, also argued strongly for immediate action, but in vain. The trial was postponed until the 30th of June, at nine o'clock A.M.*

It is not just to ascribe to men motives which they would perhaps disavow; and the writer has no disposition to do so. All he can do is to state facts, and let impartial readers put their own construction upon them. It is a fact, that, at the time, other reasons for the postponement of this trial were very generally supposed to have influenced the Presbytery. One reason attributed at the time, was the unwillingness to permit the case to reach the next General Assembly, which the Presbytery feared might prove not to be of the same complexion as the last. Another object was to delay a decision until the fate of the Synod of Delaware, and of the Elective Affinity principle, could be known.

Mr. Barnes having, in the course of his remarks, read from the Minutes of the General Assembly of 1824, p. 219, and assumed an observation there made about the definiteness of charges to be a rule, and having intimated his purpose to insist upon that, the Prosecutor transmitted to him a full series of references to the pages of his book, that would be quoted on the trial, and of the parts of the Standards violated by them. Thus the indictment con-

---

* Vindication, pp. x.-xiv.; also Minutes of the Presbytery.

tained not only the offences charged, but the proof and the law also. The letter containing this list was dated April 11th.

Such is the history of this case, up to the time the day of trial was fixed, by which it appears that Mr. Barnes had a copy of the charges and references to the proofs three months and eight days before the trial, and that the errors alleged against him were pointed out, the law indicated, and the proof presented, eighty days before trial. These facts show the laborious pains taken by the Prosecutor to give to Mr. Barnes every opportunity for making good his defence.

A short time previous to the day appointed for the trial, the Prosecutor learned that it was probable no trial would take place, and that, as the General Assembly had prospectively dissolved the Synod of Delaware, and inaugurated other reforms sought by the signers of the Act and Testimony, the objection to the charges on account of the omission of the word HERESY was to be revived, and the case dismissed on the grounds of informality. There was thus a likelihood that Mr. Barnes would be placed in the position of one standing ready for trial, and the Presbytery ready to try him, but, because of the Prosecutor's failure to charge heresy or any specific crime, the case was to be estopped. The wonder was circulated that a man of Dr. Junkin's acuteness of mind would make such a blunder, and it was charitably ascribed to inadvertence.

Of all this the Prosecutor was apprised before the day of trial came, and was not surprised when the facts proved the accuracy of this information. The effort was made. The details of discussion need not be recorded. It will be enough to say that the objection was again raised by Mr. Barnes and his friends, that the charges lacked preciseness, that no crime was charged, etc. The Rev. James Patterson was especially earnest in urging that it was hard to try a man for nothing,—that no specific charge of heresy was made. But "that if Brother Barnes was willing to go on at *such great disadvantage*, he would throw no obstacle in the way." This unfortunate remark placed Mr. Barnes in the dilemma of either consenting to go on, or of refusing to be tried upon the charges as presented. He did neither, but said this was a question for his brethren to decide, and he threw its decision upon them. If they deemed it fair and just that he should be tried without any specific charge of *crime* or *heresy*, he was ready. This was understood; and Mr. Patterson moved to permit the Prosecutor to take back his charges and amend them, or the Presbytery would not go on with the trial. The motion was passed, and Dr. Junkin was asked to comply. This he declined to do, knowing that then it would be a new Bill, and Mr. Barnes would be entitled to his ten days' delay again. He, at the same time, again stated his objections to using the term, adding that, in his view, the things charged amounted to heresy.

Thus the case was about to be arrested, agreeably to his previous information. The Presbytery were proceeding to other business, and Dr. Junkin rolled up his papers to take leave of the court. Before going out, however, he wrote upon a slip of paper the query, "After charges are received, admitted to lie, and a day appointed for trial, is it competent for the court to compel the Prosecutor to change his Bill of charges, and to dismiss the case if he refuse?" He handed this to Dr. Ely; who wrote, "I think not," and handed it back. It was passed to Mr. (now Dr.) Boardman, who nodded assent; then to Mr. Thomas Bradford, an elder and an eminent lawyer. He also assented, and, after a few minutes, arose and invited the Presbytery to consider the position in which they had placed themselves and Mr. Barnes by the resolution passed. Mr. Bradford recapitulated the facts: "Some three months ago, Dr. Junkin tabled these charges; the churches know it; the world knows it. He has come to attend to the prosecution and proof of the charges. He is just about to depart, after having been refused an opportunity to substantiate them. Has he shrunk from the trial? No; he desires to go on—yet there is no trial. Why? On whom rests the blame of failure? The public will ask this question. It must be answered. Who prevented the trial? Not Dr. Junkin. He stands ready to prove, as he says, the charges *he* has made. The public will think that either the Presbytery, or Brother Barnes, or both, arrested the trial. Did the latter, it will be asked, demand a trial, and the Presbytery refuse? Where does this place the Presbytery? Or why did Mr. Barnes not insist on a trial? Ought any man to consent to lie under such charges? If I were in Mr. Barnes' place, I would demand a trial, and if there is none, I would dread the impression on the public mind." Dr. Ely presented the same views, and the result was a reconsideration, and a resolution to go on with the trial. Such are the historic facts; no comment is added.

After the arguments of the parties had been fully heard, and the roll called, a Committee was appointed to prepare a minute, expressive of the judgment of the Court, and a recess taken till three o'clock P.M. A few minutes before that hour, Dr. Junkin met the Moderator of the Presbytery near the church, and inquired of him to which Synod his Appeal should be carried, or, in other words, whether the Synod of Delaware would ever meet again. He replied that it never would, because the time to which it stood adjourned was later than that to which the Synod of Philadelphia stood adjourned, and the Synod of Delaware was to be dissolved "at and after" that date. Dr. Junkin also inquired whether it would not be better to take the Appeal directly to the Assembly. The Moderator promptly said that it would be better, and promised to favor that view of the case in the Presbytery.

In the afternoon session, Dr. Junkin proposed to the Presbytery to take his Appeal direct to the General Assembly. To which Mr. Barnes objected, stating his desire that the business should take the regular constitutional steps. Dr. Junkin then asked to be informed whether the Appeal would go to the Synod of Delaware—would that body ever meet again? To this inquiry a number of voices responded, No! it cannot meet, it will be dissolved before the day to which it stands adjourned. "Then," said he, "the Appeal must be to the Synod of Philadelphia." To this there was no official, formal assent by act of the body; but a real, well-understood, and generally expressed acquiescence. So his Appeal was taken to the Synod of Philadelphia.

The decision of the Presbytery, as was expected by all, was in acquittal of Mr. Barnes. They judged him "not to be guilty of teaching or holding any heresy or erroneous doctrine, contrary to the Word of God and our Standards."

The minute adopted assigns ten lengthy reasons for this judgment; in which reasons they reargue the case for the accused, and endeavor to reconcile the language he employs in his Notes on Romans with the Standards of the church and with their views of the Scripture.

After stating these reasons, the minute concludes as follows:

"The Presbytery therefore judge, that the charges have not been maintained, and ought to be dismissed, and do acquit Mr. Barnes of having taught, in his Notes on the Romans, any dangerous errors or heresies, contrary to the Word of God and our Standards. And they do moreover judge, that the Christian spirit manifested by the Prosecutor during the progress of the trial, renders it inexpedient to inflict any censure on him; and the Presbytery would express the hope, that the result of all will be to promote the peace of the church and further the gospel of Christ."*

The sessions of the Presbytery, during this trial, were held in the Lecture-room of Mr. Barnes' church, where he usually met his people. Many of them were present, and by unmistakable signs expressed their sympathy for him, and their disapprobation of the prosecution. The congregation was at that time one of the most influential in the denomination; and it is not difficult to conceive that, in such a place and circumstances, it required a high degree of moral courage to conduct this prosecution of an admired and caressed Pastor. It was a sacrifice of self, on the altar of truth, which compelled the admiration even of those who were opposed to the Prosecutor; and the Court, whilst it acquitted the accused, unanimously bore testimony to the Christian spirit and bearing of Dr. Junkin.

The minute of acquittal, though passed by a large majority, was not unanimously passed. One minister in that Presbytery, and two elders, voted in the negative. There was, in that Presbytery, a young man, who had a short time before these events succeeded the Rev. Dr. McAuley in the pastorate of the Tenth Presbyterian Church, Philadelphia. That church had been set off with others into the Second (Assembly's) Presbytery, and by this circumstance, not by "Elective Affinity," had its young pastor become a member of the Presbytery that tried Mr. Barnes. A scholar mature beyond his years, with a mind clear, discriminating, dispassionate, and honest, with a heart instinct with the love of truth, and a conscience that shrunk from adopting a creed *pro forma*, whilst its essential truths were rejected, it could not be expected that he would consent to any act that he thought would compromise important truths

* Copy of Minute, attested by Thomas Eustace, Clerk.

of the Gospel. Nor did he. Whilst a judge, he listened with dignified and absorbed attention to the pleadings, and sought to secure fairness to both parties; he was deterred, probably by his youth in the ministry, from taking an active part, until the time came for giving his opinion on the case. Then, although *alone* among the ministerial members, he sought to do his duty. With that dignified manner and calm, impressive eloquence which have made him one of the ornaments of the American pulpit, he gave his opinion in an able argument of three hours, that the Notes on Romans did contain evidence that ought to sustain most of the charges, and those the most serious ones; and he voted accordingly. Dr. Junkin has often since those trying days expressed to the writer, how grateful he was to God, that HENRY A. BOARDMAN was a member of that Court. That minister still lives, the beloved Pastor of the same church which he has served for almost forty years.

Dr. Boardman was joined in desiring a judgment different from that which was given, by two venerable and eminent elders of the church, the late Thomas Bradford and John Stille, Esqs.

It was not expected, by either of the parties to the trial, that it would be terminated in the Presbytery. Indeed, the question of appeal was mooted before the trial began; and, accordingly, Dr. Junkin gave notice, within the constitutional period, of his intention to appeal to the Synod of Philadelphia against the decision of the Presbytery, with his reasons therefor. The first sentences of this Appeal will give the reader an idea of the spirit with which Dr. Junkin conducted this business. It begins as follows:

"LAFAYETTE COLLEGE, July 16, 1835.

"*To the Rev.* JOHN L. GRANT, *Moderator, and to the Reverend Second Presbytery of Philadelphia.*

"REV. AND DEAR BROTHER,—You are hereby officially informed, that I intend to appeal to the Synod of Philadelphia, at its next meeting, to be held in the borough of York, on the last Wednesday of October next, against your recent decision, in the case of the Rev. Albert Barnes. This appeal is from the 'definitive sentence.' Its general ground is 'a manifestation of prejudice in the case, and mistake,' and consequent 'injustice in the decision.'

"Allow me, before proceeding to specify the reasons which shut me up to the belief that the Court was prejudiced, and did err in judgment, to say that I impeach no motives,—I charge no *corrupt* prejudice,—no *intentional* mistake or error upon any man. Men do often err under the purest motives, and are often powerfully prejudiced, whilst perfectly unconscious of it. With this single remark I proceed to detail the reasons why I appeal on the above-named grounds."

He then gave ten reasons, which are too voluminous to transfer to these pages. The curious reader can find them *in extenso* in the volume called the Vindication, and also in the Appendix to the Minutes of the Synod of Philadelphia for 1835, pp. 43–47. In the same place, pp. 40–43, the decision of the Second Presbytery may be found. In brief, they were:—1. Insisting upon the use of the term heresy by the Prosecutor—refusing to proceed unless he would insert that term—using that term themselves, in their speeches—and trying to excite odium against the Prosecutor, by reference to "persecution" and "the inquisitorial toils," which one of the judges (Rev. John Smith) said the Prosecutor was employing. And they assumed heresy as the general charge. 2. Because the accused was not called upon to plead to each charge separately, nor to plead at all to the charge of teaching contrary to the Standards.* 3. Because the talents of the

* Mr. Barnes' special plea was as follows: "Until I am apprised whether these charges be of *crime*, *heresy*, or *schism*, I cannot answer in general whether I am guilty or not guilty. That some of the doctrines charged on me I hold, and some of them I do not hold; but that I neither have taught, nor do I teach, anything, according to my best judgment, contrary

accused, and the respectability of his congregation, were pleaded by some of the judges as a reason why he should not be condemned. "Never," said one of them, "let me be found condemning a man to whom God has given such mighty powers of mind, and a congregation so dignified and influential." 4. Because the Presbytery, in their decision, endorsed some of Mr. Barnes' errors, and made them their own, and therefore were biased in his favor. 5. Because Mr. Barnes admitted that on the fifth, sixth, and seventh charges he denied the doctrine of the Standards, and it is difficult to say whether the Presbytery do or not. Their sentence is equivocal. 6 and 7. Because of statements in their reasons which the Appellant affirms to be inaccurate. 8. Because one member of the court, at least, distinctly rejected the Standards of the church as a rule of judgment, and his speech was partly written. 9. Because the Presbytery took Mr. Barnes' present declarations as expository of the meaning of his language adduced by the Prosecutor in proof. They had no right to take the *present views* and *gloss* of a party at the bar as their correct meaning. This *gloss* could not accompany the book into all our families. 10. Because the decision of the Presbytery is not in accordance with the facts of the case as exhibited in the charges, the testimony, and the law. It is not a righteous decision.

The history of the trial of Mr. Barnes has been given, up to the time of the Appeal to the Synod, with some degree of minuteness, for two reasons: first, because it is an important part of our ecclesiastical history, in the field of opinion, and of ecclesiastical conflict. It was indeed the hinge upon which turned the events of the next third of a

---

to the Word of God; nor do I deny any truths taught in the Word of God, as it is alleged that I do in the indictment now before this Presbytery." See "Defence," and Report in *Presbyterian*, July 9, 1835.

century. And second, because the subject of this memoir was much misrepresented and maligned at the time, both as regards his motives and spirit, and as regards his conduct of the case; and it is due to an eminent man of God that the facts should be recorded for his vindication. Both the documentary facts and the testimony of Mr. Barnes and of the Presbytery attest that, in all this painful undertaking, Dr. Junkin bore himself with the meekness, the kindness, the "Christian spirit," and the calm, unquailing courage which become the champion of the truth.

CHAPTER XXVI.

Trial of Mr. Barnes by the Synod of Philadelphia—Dissolution of Synod of Delaware—Its Presbyteries refuse to submit their Records—Synod demands the Records and Documents of the Second Presbytery in the Barnes Case—Presbytery refuse—Synod censures them for Contumacy—Mr. Barnes refuses to be tried without the Records which his Presbytery withhold—Copies of the Papers in the Case presented and proved by Oath of Witnesses—Synod proceeds to issue the Appeal—Pleadings—Roll-Call—The Appeal of Dr. Junkin sustained—Mr. Barnes suspended—Submits—Appeals to the Assembly—Appeals to the Public in his "Defence"—"Persecution and Opposition" arise unto the Prosecutor—His Vindication.

WHEN the Synod of Philadelphia met at York, on the 28th of October, 1835, the roll, including the eight Presbyteries at that moment constituting the Synod, was called; and then the Moderator, Dr. Cuyler, read a certificate, signed by Dr. E. S. Ely as Stated Clerk of the General Assembly, attesting that "at and after the meeting of this Synod, in October next, the Synod of Delaware shall be dissolved, and the Presbyteries constituting the same shall be then and thereafter annexed to the Synod of Philadelphia, and that the latter Synod shall take such order," etc., reciting the directions of the Assembly. The Clerk then called the roll of the Presbyteries of Philadelphia (Second), Wilmington, and Lewes, and forty-six persons answered to their names, and were enrolled as members of Synod, and thus became, by their own act and consent, liable to its lawful authority.

On the afternoon of the second day of the sessions, the Judicial committee reported Dr. Junkin's Appeal as being in order, and recommended that it be taken up, and orderly issued. The next morning the Synod took up the case, and the Moderator inquired for the records and documents of the Presbytery appealed from. In response to this, Dr. Ely read a paper, which, he said, had been adopted by the Second Presbytery of Philadelphia at a meeting, held in York, the preceding day, and since the meeting of the Synod. It was as follows:

"*Whereas*, The General Assembly of our church dissolved the Synod of Delaware *at and after* the meeting of the Synod of Philadelphia, which occurred yesterday; *whereas*, The said Assembly passed no order for the transfer of the books, minutes, and unfinished proceedings of the Synod of Delaware and the Second Presbytery of Philadelphia, then belonging to the same, to any other Synod or judicatory; and *whereas*, It is utterly inconsistent with reason and the excellent Standards of our church that any Presbytery should be amenable to more than one Synod at the same time: therefore,

"*Resolved*, That the Presbytery will and hereby does decline to submit its books, records, and proceedings, prior to this date, to the review and control of the Synod of Philadelphia, until the General Assembly shall take some order upon this subject.

"A true extract from the minutes.

"GEO. DUFFIELD, *Clerk*."

The Moderator of Synod then asked Dr. Junkin whether he was prepared to prosecute his Appeal. Dr. Junkin answered in the affirmative. Mr. Barnes was also asked if he was prepared, and replied that he came there fully prepared, and, so far as he was personally concerned, was ready for the trial.

It was then, on motion, ordered that the Second Presbytery (Assembly's) be directed to lay their records, in the case of Mr. Barnes, on the table of the Synod; and that the Stated Clerk of the Synod forthwith put this order into the hands of the Moderator and Clerk of that Presbytery.

Dr. Junkin then read a paper, which he desired might

go upon the minutes of Synod. In this paper he stated, over his own signature, what has been recorded in the last chapter, that, at the close of the trial, he had proposed to appeal directly to the Assembly; that Mr. Barnes had objected; that he (Dr. Junkin) had then inquired what Synod he should appeal to; and had been promptly told, "To that of Philadelphia."

The Second Presbytery had leave to withdraw to consider the order of the Synod, and, in the afternoon, presented a paper, signed by the Clerk, refusing compliance with the order. Dr. Junkin presented a letter from the Stated Clerk of that Presbytery, which proved that the Presbytery expected the Appeal to be tried before this Synod. It is as follows:

"PHILADELPHIA, October 13, 1835.

"REV. GEORGE JUNKIN, D.D.

"DEAR BROTHER,—In accordance with the annexed resolution of the Presbytery, I have to request that you will cause to be deposited in my hands the written testimony, on your part, in the case of Mr. Barnes,—the charges I already have. As the meeting of Synod approaches, it is desirable to furnish it forthwith, that I may be enabled to send to Synod all the documents in the case.

"With best wishes, etc.,

"THOMAS EUSTACE.

"*Resolved*, That the written charges and testimony of Dr. Junkin, and the written defence of Mr. Barnes, be preserved on the files of this Presbytery.

"Attest, THOMAS EUSTACE,

"*Stated Clerk of the Presbytery of Philadelphia*."*

A paper was then presented to Synod, considered by paragraphs, and adopted, in which the foregoing facts were set forth as proof of contumacious conduct on the part of the Assembly's Presbytery, and of a design to deceive the Appellant, and prevent him from having any appeal from

---

* Minutes of Synod, pp. 10 to 13.

their decision; and upon these facts, and by the authority given in chapter vii. sec. iii. subsection 16, the Synod

"*Resolved*, That, in the judgment of this Synod, the conduct of the (Assembly's) Second Presbytery of Philadelphia, in all the premises, is *obstinate*, *vexatious*, *unjust*, *uncandid*, *contumacious*, and grossly *disorderly*. And in view of the facts, that the Presbytery had suppressed the records in the case of Mr. Barnes; and the Synod, after due effort, had failed to obtain the records in the case; that the original parties have declared their readiness for trial; that there is accessible an attested copy of the sentence appealed from, and of the original evidence used in the trial, in the court below; that the Appellee's case could not therefore be prejudiced by the conduct of his Presbytery; and that the cause of truth and the glory of God require the case to be issued; the Synod

"*Resolved*, To proceed to hear and dispose of the Appeal now pending."

A solemn prayer was then offered, and the trial was commenced. The Appeal was read. A copy of the original charges was presented, and proven by the oath of Mr. Steel, who, having previously read them, had handed them to the Presbytery. A letter from the Stated Clerk of the Presbytery, proving their reception, was read.* At this juncture Mr. Barnes arose and made some remarks, and concluded by presenting the following paper:

"When I was asked by the Moderator of the Synod this morning whether I was prepared for trial, I stated that before and since the trial before the Presbytery, I had made all the preparation which my time would permit, and that so far as I am personally concerned I was prepared for trial. I still say that, in the same sense, I am now ready. I did not, however, intend that I was ready to submit to an unconstitutional trial. In the present state of affairs I feel bound to inform the Synod that if an attested record of

---

* Minutes of Synod, pp. 14, 15.

the proceedings in my case cannot be produced, I must decline all further proceedings before the Synod in the case; my Presbytery having judged that it is their constitutional right to withhold the record. And the trial, if it proceed, whatever might be the issue, whether in my vindication or condemnation, must be an unconstitutional one. (Book of Dis., chap. iv.) Such a trial I hereby respectfully decline. I feel, however, desirous of a constitutional trial on the charges alleged against me, whenever the same can be legally had, before the proper tribunal."*

Such is the documentary history of this unprecedented proceeding. And in order that the reader may form a just estimate of the conduct of the actors in it, another fact or two ought to be noted. When Dr. Ely presented the minute of his Presbytery, refusing to submit their records, the Rev. Dr. John Breckenridge asked him, "If it was not he that drafted the minute of the Assembly in which the words 'at and after' were employed, thus leading that body to let the Synod of Delaware continue for a time, instead of instantly dissolving it, as was proposed? And whether it was compatible with honor and fair dealing for Dr. Ely to use that trap, of his own construction, to bar a fair trial?"

Dr. Ely replied, "that he did draft the minute; but as the Assembly did not order the Presbytery to put their records into the hands of this Synod, he was thankful a slip had been permitted in legislation; and thus 'in the providence of God' the way was opened for this action of his Presbytery."

Let it be remembered, in connection with this, that, as Mr. Eustace's letter above proves, the Presbytery had not so late as the 13th inst.—fifteen days before the meeting of Synod—thought of the course now pursued; and that it was resolved upon only after the Synod met; and, in view

---

* Minutes of Synod, pp. 15, 16.

of these facts, no mind can resist the conclusion that this expedient was resorted to at that late date for the purpose of avoiding a trial.

It is an old established maxim of the law, that "no party can take the benefit of his own wrong." Whether that maxim was violated, in the conduct of the Assembly's Presbytery, candid minds will judge. It ought to be stated that these things were done at a time when men were much excited with the spirit of their respective parties. The public mind was agitated. Good men were under the influence of the heat which a struggle for the supremacy is apt to produce. Sharp things were said on both sides; and if the one side was conscious of an honest purpose to vindicate the Standards and defend the truth, this fact did not always restrain them from those tones of censure that provoke retort, and which sometimes tempt zealous partisans to resort to expedients which their own judgment, in cooler times, would not approve. It should ever be remembered, too, in vindication of religion, that if her votaries sometimes betray a good deal of human frailty, it is the fault of nature, not of grace.

Although the Assembly's Presbytery withheld its records, and declined taking any part in the trial, some of its members participated in the incidental debate, and discussions sometimes waxed warm. It is the testimony of all parties, however, that Dr. Junkin maintained, throughout these trying scenes, entire self-possession, and calmly yet firmly did his duty as Prosecutor of his appeal.

The Synod proceeded with the trial, which occupied five days; after which the Appeal of Dr. Junkin was sustained, and the decision of the Presbytery reversed, by a vote of Ayes 142, Nays 16, Non Liquets 17, and Excused 1. A committee was appointed to prepare a minute expressive of the sense of the Synod in this case. This committee subsequently made a report, in which they recited the history of the case as it was issued before Synod, and proposed, for the adoption of the Synod, three resolutions; the substance of which was — 1. That in view of the proof, the Appeal be sustained, and the decision of the Presbytery *reversed*, as contrary to truth and righteousness; 2. That some of the errors charged and proved are *fundamental;* 3. "That the said Albert Barnes be, and he hereby is, suspended from the exercise of all the functions proper to the gospel ministry, until he shall retract the errors hereby condemned and give satisfactory evidence of repentance."

Dr. John Breckenridge moved as a substitute for the third resolution, one proposing, at this stage, to refer the case to the next General Assembly, in order to avoid even the *appearance of rashness or injustice.* This was negatived, and the whole paper was passed by 116 to 31.

Various opinions were expressed at the time, and various opinions would still be formed by different persons, in regard to the wisdom and expediency of the action of the Synod in trying the case under such circumstances. Perhaps it would have been wiser to have referred the case, under the motion of Dr. John Breckenridge; but, on account of the contumacy of the Court below, most of the Old School thought that the Synod did right in not permitting discipline to fail in their hands.

Although Mr. Barnes had not submitted to a trial in the Synod, and, therefore, was not technically entitled to an appeal (Book of Dis., chap. vii. sec. iii., subsec. ii.), yet he gave notice of appeal, and carried his case to the General Assembly. Meanwhile he submitted to the sentence of the Synod; and a great deal of sympathy was excited in his behalf by appeals to the public, oral and written. The press in the interest of the New Theology teemed with censures of the Synod, and expressions of sympathy with the suspended minister; and the accuser, although acquitted of any evil motive or unchristian spirit, both by the testimony of Mr. Barnes himself and of his Presbytery, was exposed to much odium, from those who leaned towards laxity of doctrine or discipline, or who were hostile to the truth as held by our church.

Soon after the close of the trial before the Second Presbytery, Dr. Junkin was applied to, by a Publisher, for a report of his charges, proofs, and arguments for publication. Mr. Barnes had consented to give his side, and expressed a wish (so the publisher said), that the Prosecutor should do so likewise. But Dr. Junkin refused to do so; and assigned as reasons for his refusal, that it never was designed that the case should stop short of the Assembly—that nothing should be done by either party to prejudice the courts above, by *ex-parte* statements, and the agitation of the public mind by premature publications; and that in order to the triumph of truth "the pivot, on which the balance of judgment turns, must be kept free from the rust of envy, or the rancid, dust-thickened oil of prejudice. This latter is best effected by cleansing, and a drop of the pure oil of charity." . . . "We, the *parties*, stand at the *judicial* bar; to that we have appealed; and I conceive that we have no right, *during the pending* of our own cause *there*, to litigate at another bar. We can have no *right* to a trial at two different tribunals, at the same time, and for the same thing."

Nevertheless, Mr. Barnes' "DEFENCE" was published, in a volume of considerable bulk, and widely disseminated. This fact Dr. Junkin mentions, in the preliminary note to his own argument, which he published some months after the appearance of Mr. Barnes' book, in a small volume of one hundred and sixty pages, called "THE VINDICATION." The fact that Mr. Barnes and his friends had gone before the public, is adduced in justification of the printing of the history of the case by Dr. Junkin, along with his argument. His words, in the preliminary note, are:

"Why publish your argument in the case of Mr. Barnes? I answer, Because new rights result from new wrongs. . . . Mr. Barnes has committed what I suppose to be a *wrong*, in refusing to appear before the bar of his own choice, and then preferring his plea before a tribunal unknown to our ecclesiastical constitution; and out of his wrong grows my right. He has arraigned me at the tribunal of the people; not, you will observe, of God's people only, but of the world at large. His 'DEFENCE' is made at a bar where no bill had been preferred against him, until after he there appeared. Not satisfied with the legitimate courts of Christ's house, he has actually spread before the world, in tens of thousands of copies, his entire written argument. Will not the reader justify me, in sending my argument for the truth after this '*defence*,' though it may lag far behind? Justice, wherever her throne be, is the same in her essential character and indispensable requisites. Whether in the popular bosom or on the supreme bench, she must have her balances and her facts. In the premature effort of my brother, she has had her scales thrown, indeed, into a very forbidding attitude; the one pressed to the ground, with its ponderous load, the other empty. This, however, will soon be rectified. Her hand is even now lowering to restore the empty scale to its just equipoise, and receive my argument. When this is fairly done, let her hand rise, and the Church of God, yea, the world itself, judge where abides eternal truth!"*

But, although his argument may have been put into the scale, and the hand of Justice raised, historic truth requires the fact to be noted, that, so far as the tribunal of the great public was concerned, Dr. Junkin stood before it at a great disadvantage. Not only did the "*Defence*" precede his "Vindication" several months, before that tribunal, but, on account of the fact that Mr. Barnes'

* Vindication, p. 3.

wealthy congregation, and other sympathizers, furnished funds for spreading his "Defence" broadcast over the land, thousands read the "Defence" who never saw the "Vindication." Dr. Junkin had no wealthy congregation, no organized ecclesiastical influence, to sustain him in his contest for what he verily believed to be God's truth. His own funds, which were not ample, were locked up in the College enterprise, which he was also sustaining single-handed; and if the Lord was not on his side, the contest was indeed unequal. It is true, no doubt, that he was upheld by the sympathies and the prayers of those who believed him to be sacrificing in the cause of truth; but even some of them had not the moral courage to face, with firmness, the cry of persecution and tide of obloquy which were raised against the man who, being the "President of a College" and "a member of another Presbytery," would begin a prosecution against the popular and cherished Pastor of so wealthy and influential a church. The "Defence," too, was of course written from a party standpoint, and at a moment of extreme irritation and excitement. It could not be expected to spare Dr. Junkin, but, on the contrary, to place him and his cause as much in the wrong as an *ex-parte* statement of the facts could effect; and it fell upon the public ear at a time when not only the New School portion of the church, but the undiscriminating and indifferent masses, were under the influence of that sympathy which always gathers around the condemned. The man who had been suspended from the ministry was in repute for talents, scholarship, and great literary industry. He was amiable, pious, and had pulpit powers which were solid and attractive. The opposition which he encountered, upon his first coming to Philadelphia, had not only aroused the friendly zeal of his immediate congregation, but had drawn to him a measure of public attention which many years in the quiet duties of a pastorate might not have won. His Notes on the Gospels and the Acts of the Apostles were, with the exception of a few passages, which indicated, without very explicitly stating, his peculiar views of theology, useful books, and their sale and circulation were doubtless increased by the very opposition which had been made to those views. So that, both as a Pastor and an Author, he was, probably, more widely known than, in so short a time, he would have become in other circumstances. There was so much of real good mixed with what his Old School brethren seriously deplored as evil, that the general public, unaccustomed to consider *systems* of doctrine, failed to see, or, at least, to acknowledge, anything but the good. And when such a man, and in such circumstances, was suspended from the Gospel ministry, his voice silenced, his pulpit left temporarily vacant, and his people bereft of the services of their Pastor, the public ear was startled by the tidings, the public heart was roused, and it was natural, and to be expected, that all of the Christian community, who did not receive the distinctive doctrines of grace as laid down in the Presbyterian standards, would throw their sympathies around the silenced minister. Of course this tendency would be also strong among the people of the world, and the popular tide would set against the Synod which had applied discipline, and the man who had produced the proof upon which it was done. The publication of Mr. Barnes' *ex-parte* defence would not, of course, assuage this excited sea; and, whilst the Old School and many of the discerning minds in other evangelical churches sustained the decision of the Synod, the popular tones that seemed the loudest, for a time at least, were those of disapproval.

There is a martyrdom almost as hard to endure as that of the stake. To a mind as sensitive and deep in its emotional nature as was Dr. Junkin's, yet not possessing his indomitable loyalty to principle, and his strong faith in God, the assaults made upon his course would have been appalling. It was in vain Mr. Barnes himself had closed his defence with a most explicit and emphatic testimony to the Christian spirit and the purity of motive which he believed had moved his Prosecutor;* in vain the Second Presbytery had officially recorded the same declaration; in vain all impartial persons, who witnessed the trials, expressed admiration of the calmness, the patience, the kindness, the solemnity, as well as the ability, with which he conducted them, before the Presbytery and Synod—he was in the attitude of a successful Prosecutor, and must, *therefore*, be a man to be spoken against. It is due to truth, and is illustrative of the Christian spirit of both Mr. Barnes and Dr. Junkin, to add, that, so far as known, there never was at any time any feeling of personal unkindness, much less of hostility, between them.

Dr. Junkin may have felt, doubtless did feel keenly, all this, but he never betrayed any impatience or resentment. And when his friends expressed, as they sometimes did, indignation at the misrepresentations of his motives, spirit, and conduct, he would rarely say more than to quote some passage from the Word of God, such as, "He that believeth shall not make haste," or, "The lying tongue is but for a moment."

The opposition of the unthinking world he could pity, without being discouraged by it; it was to be expected. The censure of the avowed adherents or protectors of the New Theology, he had anticipated, and was not surprised, nor much troubled, when it came. But when, as was sometimes the case, he was denounced by orthodox men under the influence of a morbid spirit of compromise, or because they had not the nerve to withstand the popular outcry, he

---

* See page 315.

seemed more grieved. No reader unacquainted with the details of this trying period of Dr. Junkin's history, can appreciate the sacrifices he made for the truth's sake, nor the amount of opposition he had to endure.

In a few instances, ministers, professing to be sound in the faith, took their sons from Lafayette College, and sent them elsewhere, because they would not be in any way identified with the Prosecutor of Mr. Barnes. Direct efforts were also made, sometimes by ministers, sometimes by laymen, to dissuade students from coming to the College, and to induce those already there to leave.

A case, which affected Dr. Junkin more, perhaps, than any other, because it was not only a personal thrust, but struck at his beloved College, may be stated as succinctly as in any other words, by copying an article from the *Presbyterian* of February 5th, 1836, signed "A Member of the Synod of New Jersey." We withhold the name of the eminent pastor alluded to; for whilst it is our duty, as a faithful biographer, to record the trials and sufferings of the subject of our memoir, we do not wish needlessly to put on record the conduct of others which we disapprove, in connection with their names. The best men have their weaknesses, and one of the most difficult things to do, in this land where public opinion is so puissant, is to withstand it, when it is wrong.

(From *The Presbyterian.*)

"MR. EDITOR,—It was with surprise, and grief for the writer, whose name I have respected and whose person I still love, that I read, in the *N. Y. Observer*, of January 30th, the following paragraph:

"'MESSRS. EDITORS,—I have understood that a recent paragraph in the "*Philadelphian*" animadverts with some severity upon me, for having given my name recommending the college under the care of the Rev. Dr. Junkin. I owe it to myself to state, that I did this very soon after my return from Europe, and before I had become acquainted with the course Dr. Junkin pursued in his prosecution of the Rev. Mr. Barnes. On reading the narrative of that trial, as published in the *N. Y. Observer*, I wrote to Dr. Junkin, requesting him to erase my name from the list of recommendations to his Seminary.

"'Yours, etc.

"'—— ——.'

"I say, *Mr. Editor*, I was surprised and grieved, upon reading a communication which, *in itself*, places the writer of it in so unenviable a light before a discerning public. Can it be that —— ——, D.D., *could* be induced to take such a step by any animadversions of the *Philadelphian !!* I, for one, would not have believed that that eminent minister of Christ could be driven in any direction by anything that could proceed from such a source, had he not confessed it in the above paragraph.

"But, with regard to the statement itself. He says he put his name to the recommendation of Lafayette College soon after his return from Europe, and before he had become acquainted with the course Dr. J. pursued in his prosecution of Mr. Barnes. Is it not to be regretted that Dr. —— should put his name to a paper characterized by such frankness and distinctness of avowal, as the one in question, without due consideration? Can he plead that he was ignorant of its contents? That he will not do. Was he ignorant of the fact that Dr. Junkin was the prosecutor of Mr. Barnes? This he does not pretend. He therefore confesses to *rashness*, and his plea for withdrawing his name is, *that he does not approve* of Dr. J.'s course in Mr. B.'s prosecution.

"Now, there are two or three things in this plea which I hope a candid public will consider: 1. The *evidence*, upon which Dr. —— made up his mind to make this effort to crush Dr. Junkin and Lafayette College, is, by his own confession, contained in the reports of the trial of Mr. B. in the *Observer*, PRIOR to the date of his card. Now, the readers of the *Observer* know that, for reasons best known to its Editors, that paper has never yet published a large part, and the most important part, of the evidence in the case, viz., Dr. Junkin's proofs and pleadings. These have *never yet been published.* And yet, upon this partial evidence, and before he had heard the whole narrative, Dr. —— condemns Dr. Junkin, and lends the weight of his name to blast him and the prospects of the infant but flourishing institution over which he presides!

"And Dr. —— does this with Mr. Barnes' own testimony before him, in which, at the close of his published 'Defence,' he declares as follows: 'I have only to add that I cherish no unkind feelings towards my prosecutor. I charge upon him no improper motives. I delight to add my humble testimony, in accordance with the *feelings of all who have heard the trial*, to his Christian spirit; and I rejoice to close by saying, that MY CONVICTION of the PIETY and CHRISTIAN TEMPER of my prosecutor HAS BEEN AUGMENTING throughout the entire prosecution.' Nor has Dr. —— read, in the *N. Y. Observer*, nor in any other print, any proof that a different spirit was manifested by the prosecutor before the Synod.

"2. But besides judging from partial evidence, and contrary to the testimony of Mr. Barnes, Dr. —— condemns Dr. Junkin unheard. He gave him no opportunity of explaining his course.

"3. This public censure upon Dr. Junkin's character and office, as the head of a literary institute, was unprovoked and uncalled for. The letter of recommendation was addressed to private individuals of wealth and benevolence. It was not a public document. But this renunciation and attack is made public, and circulated throughout the whole church.

"4. This plea shows to the whole church where Dr. —— stands. He, as a Presbyter, has *prejudged* a case pending before the supreme court of the whole church.

"If the public knew Dr. Junkin as well as does the writer of this communication; if they knew what sacrifices of personal comfort and property, what heart-sinking self-denial and hardships he has encountered for the sake of advancing the cause of truth and education; if they were aware of the fact, too, that he was at first induced to leave the retired and peaceful labors of the pastorate, and to enter the arduous field in which he is now toiling, by THE VERY MEN who now persecute him, and strive to thwart his aims and tear away his friends, I am persuaded that with one voice the course of the *Philadelphian* would be pronounced *cruel,* and that of Dr. —— unkind and unjust.

"A MEMBER OF THE SYNOD OF NEW JERSEY."

In addition to the uncontradicted testimony of Mr. Barnes, given at the close of his "Defence," and that of the Presbytery officially recorded in their judgment, others bore public testimony at the time to the Christian temper and gentlemanly propriety with which Dr. Junkin bore himself amid these exciting scenes. Says *The Presbyterian*:

"In reviewing the manner in which the prosecution was conducted, we are constrained to express our approbation of the Christian courtesy and unruffled temper displayed by Dr. Junkin; we believe this praise will be accorded to him by all parties. We pretend not to follow him in his argument, which was so well sustained by the Holy Scriptures and the formularies of the church, and occupied so many hours. But we hope he may be induced to prepare his notes for publication. On the part of the defendant the case was conducted with ingenuity and ability. . . . . We sincerely hope it will be published, . . . and we much mistake if, in the view of intelligent theological readers, it does not confirm, rather than refute, the charges."

The foregoing will sufficiently illustrate the points which the biographer desires to make plain: 1. That upon the supposition that discipline, for alleged departures from the written Standards of the church, is to be maintained at all, Dr. Junkin did, in this case, nothing more than was the *duty* of a man who had, at his ordination, solemnly promised "to be *zealous* and *faithful* in maintaining the truths of the gospel, and the *purity* and *peace* of the church, whatever persecution or opposition may arise unto you on that account." (See Form of Government, chap. xv.)

2. That the "persecution and opposition that arose unto him," especially so far as it came from his brethren, whose

consciences rested under the same vow, was unreasonable, undeserved, unjust, and unkind.

3. That that "persecution and opposition" had no just grounds in the *manner*, *motives*, or *spirit* with which he conducted the Barnes trial, but grew out of the spirit of party, or the timidity of good men, who sometimes are given up to fear popular clamor more than they should.

It must not be supposed that, amid the above-mentioned trials, Dr. Junkin was left alone, and uncheered by the sympathies of the friends of truth. If names of influence were arrayed against him and his cause, those of equal weight were among his friends. Such men as Ashbel Green, Joseph McElroy, W. W. Phillips, Robert J. Breckenridge, John Breckenridge, John M. Krebs, Wm. M. Engles, S. G. Winchester, Wm. L. McCalla, David Elliott, Elisha P. Swift, Joshua L. Wilson, James Hoge, David McKinney, Wm. Latta, and scores of others distinguished among the clergy; and James Lenox, John Stille, Archibald George, Ephraim Banks, James Kennedy, Thos. McKeen, Judge Ewing, and hundreds more of the Elders, proved themselves worthy of this trying crisis in their church's history.

CHAPTER XXVII.

Assembly of 1836—Its Characteristics—Old School in the Majority at the Start—New School afterwards—Large Body—The Barnes Trial—Appellant attentively heard—Contrary Treatment of Prosecutor—Incidents—Dr. Junkin's Pleadings—Difficulties of his Position—His Reasons for assuming it—Mr. Barnes' Objections answered—Mr. Barnes' Rule of Interpretation—Its Unsoundness—The Stranded Steamboat—Motives—Mr. Barnes' Appeal sustained—Causes of this Result—Protests and Answers—Startling Inconsistencies—Prospects of Peace—Why defeated—Dr. Beecher's Proposal and Assignation—Not met, and why—Breach of Contract with Western Foreign Missionary Society—Attempted Revolution of Board of Education—Conferences—Dr. Junkin returns to Easton.

THE General Assembly of 1836, as the preceding one had done, met in the city of Pittsburg. No doubt, both parties in the church had exerted themselves to secure a majority. The orthodox party, including those who adhered to the position assumed by Princeton, were in a small majority at the opening of the Assembly. The Rev. John Witherspoon, D.D., of South Carolina, who had been in the Act and Testimony Convention the year before, was chosen Moderator. It was a large Assembly, numbering over two hundred and fifty. Many of the most prominent ministers and elders of the church were in commission. Dr. Phillips opened with a sermon. The prominent New School leaders, including many who, after the division, went back to Congregationalism, were in attendance. Dr. Peters was there; Dr. Beecher was in attendance, though not in commission; Dr. Skinner, and others of the most learned and gifted of that party, were present. The great question, whether the New Theology, with its kindred discipline and measures, was to be tolerated in the Presbyterian Church, was expected to be solved. Two prominent and representative men of their party, Mr. Barnes and Dr. Beecher, were expected to be on trial before that Assembly, and commissioners poured in from all parts of the land. Men's minds were on the stretch, and it was expected that the struggle would be earnest in proportion to the great issues involved.

Mr. Barnes, having refused to submit to a trial before the court below, was not technically entitled to an appeal; but his appeal was entertained and taken up early in the session. The large edifice of the First Presbyterian Church was crowded to its utmost capacity by eager spectators.

Mr. Barnes, as the Appellant, was of course first heard in support of his reasons for appeal, and in defence of himself against the charges. His argument was long, able, and ingenious, and delivered with a calm modesty of manner, that made a very favorable impression. He was heard with profound and fixed attention. No noise or other evidence that any of his judges were inattentive could be heard. The galleries, too, were perfectly orderly, no movement being observed, except occasionally a quiet exchange of look or whisper of gratulation between the speaker's friends, when he made some good point in his argument, or some moving appeal *ad populum*.

But when Dr. Junkin arose to speak, the scene immediately assumed a different aspect. The New School weekly paper had been distributed in the pews occupied by members of the Assembly, before the sessions of that day began; and at the moment Dr. Junkin commenced his argument, a portion of the Assembly seemed to be simultaneously seized with an eager desire to become acquainted with the contents of that weekly. About a hundred of them were opened at the same time, and the voice of the speaker was, for awhile, quite drowned in the rustling of newspapers, whilst some of the *judges* appeared intent, not upon listening to him, but upon reading the news.

The writer of these pages was sitting in the body of the church, immediately behind a member of the court, whom he did not know. He was a handsome man, of perhaps thirty years, and seemed to be especially impatient at the prospect of listening to an argument upon what, at the time, he believed to be the wrong side. Nor was he able to fix his eye with interest upon the newspaper which he held in his hand. Leaning forward to one of the judges, who sat in the pew before him, he engaged him in conversation, in *sotto voce.* Meanwhile the gallery lost its quietude, and portions of its occupants became suddenly inspired with the spirit of conversation and of mirth; and for a time it appeared unlikely that the Defendant in appeal would be able to make himself heard. Indignant at this marked departure from the proprieties of a court of Christ, and at the evident unfairness of hearing one and not the other of the parties at its bar, the writer took the liberty—perhaps unwarrantable—of saying in a whisper to the gentleman, who was conversing with another member of the court, "Young man, permit a stranger to remind you that you are a judge in a court of Jesus Christ, sitting in a very solemn and important case." He seemed startled, and demanded, "What do you mean, sir?" Not wishing an altercation there, no answer was returned; and at that juncture a recess of ten minutes was moved, and there was a general retiring to the church-yard. Whilst there and conversing with a friend, the writer was approached by the judge to whom he had whispered, who said, "I demand what you meant, when you addressed me in the house?" "I meant just what I said, sir." "I demand an explanation, for I consider you have acted in an ungentlemanly way." The conversation with the friend was continued without noticing this last remark, but was somewhat harassed by demands from the young judge for an explanation. "I can have no further conversation with you, sir, until you recall the offensive term 'ungentlemanly,' which you have used." "Well, it was an improper term, and I recall it." "Then, I will hear you." "I wish to know what you meant, by your remark in the house?" "I meant this, sir: so long as the Appellant was presenting his case I noticed, with pleasure, that the court gave fixed and decorous attention to his plea, as was their duty. The moment Dr. Junkin rose to speak, his voice was drowned in a storm of rustling of newspapers, and a part of the court seemed to withdraw all attention from the speaker; and I noticed that you, sir, not only withdrew your own attention, but engaged another judge in conversation." "I have read Dr. Junkin's Vindication, sir, and did not think it necessary, on that account, to listen so closely to his argument." "You are not to presume that he will have nothing to say, in his present plea, except what is in that pamphlet; and I thought it unfair that you and others were refusing to hear him; and as I saw that, like myself, you are a young man, I took the liberty of giving the hint which I did." "My name is ——, I will thank you for yours; and if I have said or done anything improper, I am sorry, and ready to make amends." "My name is Junkin, I am brother to the Defendant in appeal in the case now before you; and if I have erred in addressing you as I did, I ask you to pardon me." He extended his hand, it received a brotherly grasp, and we parted, not to meet again until some years after the disruption, when he appeared in the Old School General Assembly, as a champion of the Old Theology, from a new Presbytery in one of the exscinded districts. There is reason for believing that this frank, noble, and gifted young man, then in sympathy with the New School, had, upon leaving the writer, after the above conversation, taken pains to converse with some of his brethren about the impropriety of their behavior at the time Dr. Junkin arose to speak; for whilst their attention was not always as undivided as was desirable, there was no repetition of the indecorum above described. Mr. —— was particularly attentive; and eight years afterward, when we happened to meet near Niagara, he told the writer that Dr. Junkin's argument had set him upon a re-examination of the distinctions between the Old and New Theology; and that it had resulted in the full conviction that the Old School Theology was not only that which is embodied in our standards, but the Theology taught in the Holy Scriptures. It may not be improper to add that this gentleman has proved one of our ablest ministers, and at the date of this writing still lives, an honored pastor of an important church.

The incident just narrated illustrates the spirit of those unhappy times, whilst it proves that many good and great minds were influenced by the force of circumstances, and by their local and social relations, to occupy ground which their cooler and more matured judgment did not approve. This may have been the case on both sides.

Dr. Junkin's array of the proofs, and his arguments upon them, was worthy of himself and of the great issues involved. It is not our purpose to transfer to these pages even a syllabus of that plea. It can be found, by those curious to see it, in its main points, at least, in his "Vindication," a book now nearly out of print. Justice to him seems to require that a part at least of his introduction and peroration be here inserted, as illustrative of the spirit with which he conducted this trial; and some specimens of his argument will be found in the Appendix to this volume.

He began with a graphic and impressive description of the solemn duties and tremendous responsibilities of the

Christian pastor, closing with, "In view of these exhausting labors, and consuming cares, and soul-burdening responsibilities, well may the man of God exclaim, 'Who is sufficient for these things?'" He then proceeds:

"To all this, Mr. Moderator, I know your heart most cordially responds. Deeply have you felt these responsibilities, and earnestly have your desires gone forth after that grace whereby only any man can be sustained under a sense of their magnitude. Why, then, you will say to me, why harass a Christian brother? Why increase the heavy burdens of a minister of God by such a prosecution as this? Has not this brother sufficient cares and labors already for any one man to sustain? Wherefore, then, add the spirit-chafing and patience-exhausting efforts necessary in defending himself against charges like these?

"These interrogatories are very natural and specious. And I am not wholly unapprised of the peculiar difficulties to which he is exposed who voluntarily steps forward to be a public prosecutor of a Christian brother, eminent for talents, and occupying a distinguished station in the Presbyterian Church. The simple fact creates, almost instinctively, a feeling of disgust towards the individual, and of indignation towards his conduct. Many will apply to such disturbers of the peace the language which John applies to Satan himself. Accordingly I have already been branded by not a few 'the accuser of the brethren,' and *motives* have been attributed to me which are not mine, either by original conception or by legal imputation. Hence, sir, it becomes necessary and just to premise a few remarks in reference to my present posture.

"I. Not all the duties of men and of ministers are pleasant. Doubtless to have embraced his brother Peter in all the warmth of fraternal feeling, would have been very gratifying to the heart of Paul, and most congenial to the spirit of love that animated all his conduct; and yet he 'withstood him to the face, because he was to be blamed.' And thus it often happens: the course most agreeable to our feelings is not the course of duty. Who that desires to preserve a conscience void of offence has never been constrained to meet duties, even of friendship and love, very trying to both?

"II. Among the duties of this kind is the very one in question; as in the case of Paul against Peter; and as contemplated in the constitution of our church (Dis., v. 5), where we are told that 'process against a gospel minister shall not be commenced, unless some person or persons undertake to make out the charge.' It is perfectly obvious that if a minister is ever to be prosecuted, some person or persons must do it. . . . It may, therefore, *sometimes* be the duty of *some person* to prosecute a Christian minister. Do you demand the reasons why I think this time is come, and this person is before you?

"III. This demand I shall meet, not, however, to justify my motives, but simply to exhibit reasons for my conduct. *Motives* unexpressed it is God's to judge. All impeachment of these I leave with Him. No man has a right to judge motives, only so far as they are exhibited in conduct. If by look, word, or action I should violate the law of love, then condemn me; but not upon the evidence of evil motives merely suspected and surmised. It is the purpose of my heart in all this business to be guided by that charity which thinketh no evil; and if I be found to err from this purpose, it will be through infirmity of nature, and not through unchristian wilfulness. On this point, Mr. Moderator, you will please to keep in mind that neither quickness of reply, nor elevation of voice, becoming disagreeably shrill as it rises, nor even vehemence of manner in action, are infallible evidences of bad temper in a speaker. By reason of these defects I have been frequently misunderstood in public discussion, and bad feeling has been imputed to me, where there was everything the reverse. . . As to warmth of manner, sometimes approaching to vehemence, you will bear with it. You love to see it in the pulpit, and why not even in a judicial assembly, when the occasion calls for it? If defect it be, it is one I am not very anxious to correct. My soul desires not alliance with him who can speak on the most serious and important subjects without emotion.

"IV. The great reason why I am before you in the odious character of a volunteer accuser is this, that *eternal truth is at stake.* Brother Barnes has, in these 'Notes on Romans,' impugned some of the leading doctrines of Christianity. To me it appears that he has uttered sentiments directly at variance with the Standards of our church and with the Bible; and these not of comparative insignificance, but of vital importance. There are doctrines set forth in this volume, as I suppose, *fundamentally* wrong. Nor am I alone in this opinion. That you may be convinced of this, and thereby disposed to give me a more patient hearing, let me present the opinions of the gentlemen who conduct the *Biblical Repertory.*" He then quotes from that Review, vol. ii. p. 92, and proceeds: "Other men, then, it seems, and men whose opinions are wont to be treated with respect, coincide with me in this opinion. . . . . Thus, you perceive, good reasons exist why *some person* should 'make out the charges,' and procure a sentence of condemnation of errors so fatal to the Christian system."

Mr. Barnes, in his Defence, had complained that the bringing of these charges against him had affected his fair fame, and was calculated to bring suspicion upon him.

"Suppose," said he, "that Dr. Junkin had arraigned me on a charge of adultery. Suppose that the fact was proclaimed abroad, and suspicions were excited, and counsel employed, and a jury empanelled, and the public mind agitated, and a strong bias should set against my character, and peace should flee from my family, and my public work should be closed. And *then* suppose that the public should be gravely told that all this was not designed to injure *me*, but to settle some mooted points about the crime in question, and in order to obtain a decision on the law. And would it be possible for the community to repress its indignation against conduct like this?"

To this *reductio ad odium* Dr. Junkin replied, that the case supposed by Mr. Barnes had no points of similarity to his own, but was totally different:

"1. The brother has never been arraigned for adultery; but all the world *knows* that for many years he has been, not *secretly suspected,* but *publicly accused,* of holding the errors here charged. For six years the religious press, and in some degree the secular press, have groaned under the weight of this controversy. This charge has been widely public and flagrant, long before my charges were written.

It is, therefore, idle, and worse than idle, to insinuate that I gave origin to these matters—have 'published them abroad'—have 'excited suspicions' to destroy ministerial character. No, sir, I never drew a pen, never published a line of the volumes that have been poured out upon the public within the last six years; and therefore I feel it to be unkind in Brother Barnes to attempt to represent me as an agitator, coming in after 'the agitations of that time had died somewhat away,' and opening afresh the bleeding wounds of a convalescent church. 'The agitations of these times had died somewhat away' *when* these charges were brought! Had they, indeed? What! in March, 1835? Why, Mr. Moderator, how had it been in the preceding Assembly? Were there no 'agitations' there? No! not a mountain-wave,—a sweeping tempest? Why, then, does my brother throw out so unkind an insinuation? Why does he seem to wish to have it understood that I intruded, like an evil angel, into the peaceful paradise of the Presbyterian Church, and threw it into agitation and angry strife? But (2) the hypothesis he presents proves the correctness of the remarks I made about the absurdity of abstract judicial process, whilst it differs from the present case in another most material point, viz., that a charge of adultery impeaches moral character; but a charge of teaching error does not; it exposes to civil penalties, the other does not. Let me press upon your notice the first as the chief point here. In preferring these charges I proclaimed nothing new. It was universally known that Brother Barnes was by many supposed to hold these opinions. Indeed, he himself stated it. 'Charges,' says he, 'similar to these had been alleged against me. Those accusations had been laid before the General Assembly.' Why, then, insinuate that the prosecutor has raised this storm? On the contrary, may we not ask, Who intruded this controversy into the Presbytery and the Synod of Philadelphia? Did this storm break upon the City of Brotherly Love *prior* to the introduction of Brother Barnes' WAY OF SALVATION?"

As the inquiry was often made at the time by those who were disposed to censure Dr. Junkin, "Why did he undertake this prosecution?" justice to his memory seems to require that we permit him to answer this question for himself. This he does, in the introduction to his speech before the Assembly, from which we have quoted above:

"There were special reasons inducing me to undertake this unpleasant service for the church: (1) I once belonged to the same Presbytery with Mr. Barnes; had lived in the midst of the agitations growing, as I always supposed, out of his peculiar opinions; had many opportunities of marking the origin and spread of this leaven at work in the mass, and had some little knowledge of the brethren in and around Philadelphia—their peculiar temperament and talents. (2) I do not now belong to that Synod. For more than two years I had ceased to mingle in the deliberations of any of its Presbyteries. Removed to a distance, not too great to prevent accurate observation of passing events, nor so small as to keep me in the whirl of excitement caused by the New Theology, I really thought I could look calmly on the scene, and rightly estimate the state of things. Therefore (3) I had observed one of the necessary practical results of the continuance of these controversies—the waning of Presbyterianism in that City. Grieved to witness this sad result, I was convinced that the cause must be removed, or the evil must increase. Convinced, as I still am, that the true answer to the church's complaint, 'Why is my pain perpetual, and my wound incurable, which refuseth to be healed?' (Jer. xv. 18) is found in the fact stated by the same prophet, 'They have healed the hurt of the daughter of my people slightly, saying Peace, peace, when there is no peace:' I could not avoid the opinion, that the man who would seize the probe, run it deep into the festering wound, and open up the hidden source of its irritation, though he must first expect the malediction of the patient, would nevertheless do her the highest service, and ultimately win her gratitude. (4) I had been thrown occasionally into the agitations of ecclesiastical strife, and though *naturally* of quick temperament, I thought, from past experience, that grace and prudence would carry me through this storm as well as others. (5) I had been a Pastor, and knew something of a Pastor's cares, and toils, and joys, and sorrows, and therefore felt that my sympathies stood ready to shield the brother from any severity which truth might drop from my tongue. (6) The republication of the doctrines of 'THE WAY OF SALVATION,' of which the General Assembly of 1831 had said it 'contains a number of unguarded and objectionable passages,' and their republication in a form more objectionable than before, shows that previous warnings have produced no good effect, and has opened the door and invited a prosecution, which stands entirely detached from the former collisions. (7) The charitable enterprises of the church have been long paralyzed by these agitations. Brethren have been *compelled* to resist innovation and to expend much force in this way, which might and would have been expended in the noble enterprises of the day, but for this necessity of defending their own firesides against the intrusions of a new theology.

"These are the leading reasons why this process is begun. But Brother Barnes has stated a variety of objections to the present prosecutor in *particular:* (1) 'He belongs to a different Presbytery from himself.' This I have shown to be a good reason for my undertaking it. (2) 'Brother B. was of good and fair standing in his Presbytery and church.' Answer—(*a*) That he stood fair with his people, IF he was known to teach dangerous doctrines, is a good reason why some person should make out the charges; for *if* his own people were dissatisfied with his doctrine, it would be evidence that they were not in danger of being drawn away from the Presbyterian Standards. (*b*) That his standing with his Presbytery was fair was to have been expected, because it was created expressly *for his protection*, all having been excluded from it who were likely to disturb him for his belief. If prosecuted at all, his prosecutor *must* come from another Presbytery. (3) Mr. Barnes objects, because he 'was pursuing the duties of a most arduous pastoral charge, requiring all his time and strength, and indeed exhausting the vigor of his life.' Oh, sir, if Mr. Barnes had met the requirement of this 'most arduous pastoral charge,' and devoted 'all his time and strength' sacredly to pastoral duties, you had never heard of this prosecution; for then these 'Notes' had never been written; and hundreds and thousands of Presbyterian youth, and hoary heads, also, had never been endangered by the alarming doctrines of this book. No, sir, this brother did not devote 'all his time, strength, and vigor' to pastoral labors. . . . He must needs write a book, containing the most 'objectionable' doctrines of his celebrated sermon, and thrust it forth among our Sunday-schools and Bible-classes, and churches and people, that thus he may teach tens of thousands sentiments subversive of our entire system of doctrines. Thus the fire that was smothered under by the slightly healing policy of the Assembly of 1831, is, by the breath of this peaceful brother, blown into a flame that sweeps across the continent. Then, from the meekness of his peaceful retreat, he looks forth upon this tempest of fire, and placidly complains that the uproar, produced by the efforts to extinguish it, has disturbed the quietness of his retreat. Oh that he had paused but a little for reflection, and considered the possibility that the refluent flame might sweep through the branches of his own olive-tree, and consume the oil of his own consolations! (4) 'These charges are substantially the same with those once before the Assembly.' So they are, and the Assembly condemned the sermon on 'The Way of Salvation' as 'containing a number of unguarded and objectionable passages' (Min., p. 180), but exculpated the writer on the ground of explanations given. And yet now, in this book of Notes, we have similar expressions, without an attempt to disguise by explanations. (5) 'To Dr. Junkin I had done no injury. . . . By bringing these charges he alleges, impliedly, that he has been injured, either *personally* or as *one of the Christian community*. If *not* injured, in one of these senses, there could have been no justifiable pretence for bringing them.' On the contrary, if the accused had injured me particularly, it would have been a constitutional bar against my prosecuting; for the Book says, 'Great caution ought to be exercised in receiving accusations from any person who is known to indulge a malignant spirit against the accused.' Now, injury received affords ground to suspect 'a malignant spirit,' and an interest in his conviction. (6) 'His opinions I have not attacked.' How he could make this statement it is difficult to surmise. My opinions are contained in the Confession of Faith and the Catechisms, and these are most unceremoniously attacked in this book. The very language of the Catechism is quoted in derision on page 117, thus, 'What idea is conveyed to men of common understanding by the expression "they sinned IN him"?' And so, as we shall see, on other pages. Has he not attacked my opinions? (7) I am President of a College, and therefore ought not to bring charges. 'Why should Dr. *Junkin* feel himself called to stand forth as the defender of orthodoxy and the accuser of his brethren? Why should the President of a literary institution feel himself called on to bring grave and solemn charges against a minister in another Presbytery?' In replying to this objection of Brother Barnes, it may be asked, why Presidents of Colleges, who have *charges* vastly more important to the church at large than any mere pastoral charge can be, should be deprived of any ministerial right? Why should men, who certainly *need* as much decision of character as any other class of citizens, be shut up to the degradation of everlasting fluctuation? . . . . Must Presidents of Colleges necessarily be men of indecision in all matters of doctrinal belief? . . . On the contrary, is it not entirely befitting those who are intrusted with the government of youth, and the training of their minds to habits of decided and independent action, to form for themselves, *cautiously* and *prudently*, and to express, on all proper occasions, explicitly, openly, and honestly, the moral and religious principles by which they themselves and their institutions are governed? Is there any class of men whose opinions the community has a deeper interest or a better right to know?

"Now, it may be proper to state that some friends did advise me, in regard to these agitations of the church, to keep quiet, and I confess the advice seemed plausible; and when the first *trial* of Mr. Barnes in the Presbytery of Philadelphia came on, I was providentially called to a distance from the scene, and was glad of it, and would still have been glad to escape the unhappiness of this position. But, then, every Minister has come under obligation to maintain the doctrines of our Standards against all opposition, wherever and whenever the God of providence shall present opportunity; and, therefore, though often tempted to stand afar off and witness the noble strife for truth, I still met my ordination vows. They forbade my shrinking. They told me of claims of conscience prior to those of any literary institution, and of more fearful import."

He next replied to the objection that the word *heresy* was not in the charges; but we have given the substance of this answer elsewhere, and need not repeat it.

Before entering upon the consideration of the charges, he alluded to the principle of interpretation adopted by Mr. Barnes, as expressed in the Preface to his book and in his defence:

"It was further my intention, in preparing these Notes, not to be influenced in the interpretation by a regard to any Creed or Confession of Faith whatever. I make this frank avowal because it is the deliberate and settled purpose of my mind, and because it is the principle by which I always expect to be governed."

Upon this, Dr. Junkin remarked:

"No man admires decision of character, independence of mind, freedom of thought and action more than I do. . . . . Accordingly, when about to expound a text or context, I *first* study the Scripture, usually in the original, and without consulting note or comment of others. *Afterwards* I examine authorities. This latter half of my rule is founded on the principle of my second remark, viz., that independence of mind does not consist in supercilious contempt of other men's opinions. Real humility appears to me entirely consistent with unflinching independence. To possess real decision, a man must possess clearness of perception and accuracy of discrimination; for truth is the foundation of this quality. It is the soul's perception of the truth that gives promptitude in counsel and firmness in purpose. If a man, without this perception, asserts his claim to decision of character, he mistakes self-sufficiency for independence of mind, and mere obstinacy for the highest intellectual attainment.

"3. I dissent from the rule laid down by Mr. Barnes, because every man is bound, by the highest authority, to interpret Scripture in consistency with Scripture, 'according to the analogy of faith,' Rom. xii. 6. No man is at liberty to take any given text and construe its terms according to their plain, natural meaning, *irrespective* of the drift and scope of the writer. . . . To do otherwise is to 'handle the word of God deceitfully.' . . . But Mr. Barnes rejects this obvious rule of interpretation, lest it should be applied to 'Systems of Theology,' and demand 'that we should interpret the Bible so as to accord with the system' contained in itself. The first thing to be done in interpreting any piece of writing is to read it all over, and ascertain its general drift, its grand leading substance, its system. This ascertained, we are to be guided by this in examining its details more minutely. And this the Presbyterian Church has done. This every minister of that church has solemnly declared, in the face of heaven and earth, that *he* has done in reference to the Bible. This declaration is made in his ordination vows. He has told the church that he has examined the Bible; that though he does not pretend to understand all of it in its minute parts, yet that he has arranged in his own mind its grand leading thoughts, its *system* of truth, and now he solemnly pledges himself to be guided by these in his subsequent researches. This pledge is just and reasonable, and no man can be a Presbyterian minister until after he has given such pledge. His ordination vow embraces the Confession, as containing the system of doctrines taught in the Holy Scriptures.

"Now, I contend that such pledge cannot be reconciled with the language of Mr. Barnes' rule above quoted. He professes to have given what he supposes, 'without *any* regard to any theological system, to be the meaning of the Apostle.' Whereas, neither he nor any other man has a right to interpret this particular section of Scripture *without any regard* to the theological system laid down in the Bible."*

The foregoing is deemed sufficient to enable the reader to judge of the reasons of Dr. Junkin for placing himself in the position of a Prosecutor, and also of the reasonableness of Mr. Barnes' objections to him as such. In

* Vindication, pp. 3-19.

the latter part of his exordium he shows that the author of the Notes had plainly violated his own rule of interpretation; but it is not deemed necessary to quote more extensively.

But little space can be spared for the conclusion of Dr. Junkin's address. After arraying the proof, with accompanying arguments, he proceeds:

"Such is the system of doctrine taught in these Notes. Now, Mr. Moderator, I do honestly, and in the fear of God, and in love to Brother Barnes, declare my belief that this leads, by a direct and short road, to downright, desolating, damning Socinianism. If this system is true, I'll be a Unitarian, or embrace the Deistical theory of the perfectibility of human nature, as the easiest mode of escape from all these perplexing theological controversies. To my mind, the advocates of this system, who are *gracious* men, appear like a boat and crew suspended from the lower extremity of Grand Island by a cable one mile and three-eighths in length. There they hang upon the tossing, foaming surface of the mighty river—just over Niagara's roaring cataract—and row all their might down-stream, and are only prevented from accomplishing the fearful plunge by the strength of the cable. That cable, sir, is the grace of God, but for which, that mistaken crew would make the disastrous descent into the horrible gulf of Socinianism! Now, cut this cable, and where are the crew? Put into this boat men who are not anchored to the throne of God by the very cords of grace which this system denies, and the moment they are let go,—where are they? Oh, let us do our duty in endeavors to dissuade our brethren from such mad experiments! If this system shall pervade our church, where will our children be?" etc. etc.

His closing paragraph was:

"Solemn indeed are the responsibilities that now rest upon this Assembly. This is to you an hour of no ordinary interest. Never, perhaps, has a body of ministers and elders met on this Continent to whose acts so much importance has been attached, and to whom so large a number of the friends and the enemies of truth and order are looking with intense anxiety. Never, perhaps, has so much ardent supplication ascended to the Throne of Divine mercy on behalf of any General Assembly. Let a knowledge of this fact encourage you to faithfulness in the solemn duties of your station. And let us all bear in mind that there is 'a great white throne,' before which we must each one, for his own personal and official conduct, give an account to Him, whose eyes are as a flaming fire, and who will rectify all our mistakes, and shall pronounce a judgment according to truth that shall stand forever! To you is now committed the final issue of this case on earth, and to Him in heaven!"

The result of the trial of Mr. Barnes before the General Assembly was that his appeal was sustained. The trial occupied about a week of the time of the Assembly; and the vote to sustain the appeal was carried by 134 to 96, six declining to vote,—and they of Old School sentiments, —and the large Synod of Philadelphia, of course, being excluded from the vote. It has been stated that, at the opening of the Assembly, the orthodox, including "middle men," had a small majority. This was changed, by the arrival of other commissioners from Illinois and Missouri, on the third day of the session, so that the New School had a decisive majority when the Synod of Philadelphia was excluded. The result was received with great delight by all the friends of innovation; and yet, when the process by which that result was reached is considered, there was not much ground for triumph on the part of the friends of Mr. Barnes and the New Theology. To explain this is due to the truth of history. It might be sufficient to say, that the majority in the Assembly was the legitimate offspring of the Plan of Union and of the Home Missionary Society. Dr. Peters, the chief actuary of that Society, was the New School candidate for Moderator, and probably failed of his election only because a steamboat, upon which many New School commissioners were embarked, had run upon a sand-bar, and did not arrive at Pittsburg until after the election. That gentleman, with others, had been, during the previous year, marshalling the forces that adhered to his views. For not only were the great questions of Theology to be settled, but those also of Domestic and Foreign Missions. It seemed evident that upon the complexion and decisions of this Assembly depended the questions, whether or not the New Theology was to be tolerated in the Presbyterian Church, and whether the church was to have the control of her own missionary operations, at home and abroad. The interests involved were vast; and the efforts of parties were proportionally energetic. The friends of innovation had this advantage of their opponents,—they were not restrained by strict constructions of the Constitution of the church; and if it were an object to gain numbers by dividing up Presbyteries so as to increase the count of commissioners, they did not hesitate to do it in the Synods in which they had the control. The strict construction principles of the Old School restrained them from this. Besides, the Missionary Presbyteries on the frontiers were often very small, and yet could send an equal number of commissioners to the Assembly with larger Presbyteries. And many of these Presbyteries were composed chiefly of missionaries of the American Home Missionary Society, of which Dr. Peters was the head.

Now, in saying what is true, that in rallying numbers the New School were more expert than their opponents,—and that they possessed greater facilities for making their forces effective,—and that they did it,—we impeach no motive, and charge no criminality. Whilst differing totally from them in their Theology and their Polity, we can readily conceive that men of their "liberal" way of thinking, and looking upon the interests of religion and the country from a less denominational stand-point, might "verily think that they ought to do many things contrary to" the old Theology and the stiffer Presbyterianism of the Old School. That they did this is now matter of history; and in order to account for their conduct, it is by no means necessary to ascribe to them unchristian or dishonorable motives.

That not a few of the leaders did intend to effect extensive changes in the Doctrinal testimonies of the church, and in her Ecclesiastical polity,—changes which the Old School deemed revolutionary,—was proven by competent witnesses, and put on record, not long after the dissolution of the Assembly of 1836. That they could form such a purpose does not imply that *they* did not think it right, expedient, and for the best interests of Christianity; for we have no right to judge that they were insincere in adopting their theological opinions; and when opinions are sincerely adopted, it is most natural to desire by all means to spread them. And it is, perhaps, impossible for an Old School mind, looking upon the history of this period from an Old School stand-point, and with his own rigid notions of church order, to form a judgment in regard thereto which would do simple and full justice to the actors in those scenes.

It was to be expected that a majority, secured most probably by the means above indicated, and composed of men holding the views we have described, would be loyal to their leaders and to the aims which inspired them. And they were. To quote the pregnant language of Dr. Peters, in regard to one of the questions before the Assembly, it might be said of every question,—"THAT IS TO BE DECIDED BY A MAJORITY OF VOTES."

In accounting for the result of the trial of Mr. Barnes, then, it is enough to know that the party which sympathized with him had a working majority; that some of the moderate men who were sound in doctrine, shrunk from the idea of silencing a minister; that six asked to be excused from voting, and that the commissioners of the large Synod of Philadelphia were excluded from voting. Besides this, it is evident that quite a number of the members, who were convinced that the proof of most of the charges was sufficient, voted to sustain the appeal with the full expectation, that if they would join in acquitting the *man*, a majority of the Court would afterwards condemn and bear testimony against the doctrines of the book.

Indeed, there is proof that, justly or not, this expectation was based upon supposed pledges of the New School; for immediately after the vote to reverse the decision of the Synod, and remove the suspension of Mr. Barnes, Dr. Samuel Miller offered a resolution, pronouncing the judgment of the Assembly to be, that "Mr. Barnes has published opinions materially at variance with the Confession of Faith and the Word of God, especially with regard to original sin, the relation of man to Adam, and justification by faith in the atoning sacrifice and righteousness of the Redeemer;" censuring the manner in which he had, in his book and speech, "controverted the language and doctrines of our public Standards;" and admonishing him to "review his work on the Romans, and to modify its objectionable language; and to be more careful in time to come to study the peace and purity of the church."*

There is no doubt that Dr. Miller and others had been led, probably by out-door conversations of members of the Court, to believe that if they would vote to sustain the appeal and remove the suspension of Mr. Barnes, the friends of that gentleman would consent to the adoption of such a resolution. But the simple-hearted and venerable Professor reckoned without his host. That question, too, was "decided by a majority of votes." And the wonder is that, after sustaining the appeal, there could be found one hun-

---

* Life of Dr. Miller, vol. ii. p. 237.

dred and nine votes to pass so severe a censure upon a book, the author of which they had just restored to the ministry! The vote stood 109 to 122; and it is a singular illustration of the forbearing spirit of Dr. Miller, and the moderate Old School men, towards *persons* accused of error, that they voted to acquit Mr. Barnes, and immediately after were anxious to say, in the resolution, that "the Assembly consider the manner in which Mr. Barnes has *controverted* the *language* and the *doctrine* of our public Standards as *very reprehensible*, and as *adapted* to *pervert* the *minds* of the rising generation from the *simplicity* and purity of the gospel plan. And although some of the most objectionable statements and expressions, which appeared in the earlier editions of the work in question, have been either removed or so far modified and explained as to render them more accordant with our public formularies, still the Assembly considers the work, even in its present amended form, as containing representations *which cannot be reconciled* with the *letter* or spirit of our public Standards; and would solemnly admonish Mr. Barnes," etc.*

Now, if the candid reader will consider that one hundred and nine members of the General Assembly gave the above written judgment in regard to the "amended edition" of Mr. Barnes' book; that Dr. Junkin's charges were based upon the first edition; that 145 to 16 voted to sustain Dr. Junkin's Appeal in the Synod; that 116 in the Synod voted for the sentence of suspension; that the majority in the General Assembly for sustaining Mr. Barnes' Appeal was only 38, 6 not voting, and the commissioners of eight Old School Presbyteries, in the Synod of Philadelphia (26), excluded, he will perceive that the verdict against Dr. Junkin was by no means a decisive one; indeed, that it was in his favor and against the accused; for—

---

* Life of Dr. Miller, vol. ii. p. 287, note.

1. Some of the votes for sustaining Mr. Barnes' Appeal would not have been given to that end, but for the hope that, whilst the *man* was to be acquitted, his doctrines were to be condemned. This is proved by Dr. Miller's resolution, and the vote it received.

2. In the process of the trials of Mr. Barnes, under Dr. Junkin's charges, two hundred and forty-seven of their peers voted that the charges were sustained (3 in the Second Presbytery, 145 in the Synod, and 109 in the Assembly), whilst only 134 of the Assembly, and say 20 of his own Presbytery,* making, in all, 154 of his peers, voted that they were not sustained. Acquitted technically by the peculiar operation of our system of Courts, the majority of all who voted on Mr. Barnes' case pronounced the charges proven. This is mentioned simply to show that Dr. Junkin was justifiable in bringing the charges, and that if he erred in judgment in believing that Mr. Barnes had taught the errors charged, he erred in common with a vast majority of the church.

Two Protests were recorded against the decision of the Assembly in the case of Mr. Barnes. One of these was signed by one hundred and one members, the other by sixteen. These sixteen state in their protest, that "they are of opinion that the Appeal of the Rev. A. Barnes should be sustained only in part, and that a modified decision should be made," which statement corroborates the view given in the last paragraph that Mr. Barnes' acquittal was technical. Had these sixteen voted to sustain, and the six who declined voting, voted with them, as they probably would have done, the result would have been different.

In their Protest the sixteen explicitly condemn the Second (Assembly's) Presbytery for withholding their records from the Synod of Philadelphia, and Mr. Barnes for refusing to

---

* The writer could not ascertain the exact vote in his Presbytery.

plead; and say that the act of the Synod, in trying Dr. Junkin's Appeal, was "questionable." They express the opinion that "the charges of Dr. Junkin were at least partially substantiated, and that on very important topics of the System of Doctrine contained in the Confession and the Word of God; and that therefore the Appeal could be sustained only in a modified sense, *if at all*, on this ground, without an implied approbation of his doctrinal views." 2. They express the opinion that the sentence of the Synod was perhaps unduly severe, in view of the alterations Mr. Barnes had made in his book; and 3. They aim to define their position in regard to this trial and its results, and conclude by saying, "nor will they conceal that they have painful apprehensions that these things will lead to increased dissension, and endanger the disruption of the holy bonds which hold us together as a church."*

Such was the profound conviction of these sixteen men, of whom Drs. Hoge and Miller and Judge Ewing were the first three on the list. It was the verdict of peace men, "middle men," in regard to the matters at issue; and if there were no other proof that Dr. Junkin had good grounds for his charges, this alone would be sufficient.

All except two of these sixteen signed the other Protest, which exhibited such names as W. W. Phillips, D.D., Joseph McElroy, D.D., James Hoge, D.D., Francis McFarland, D.D., Samuel Miller, D.D., William L. Breckenridge, James Lenox, and others worthy of such company. They protest against the action of the Assembly—

1. Because they believe the Standards of the church, in their plain and usually received meaning, to be the rule of judgment by which all doctrinal controversies are to be decided. And in the decision of the Assembly in the case of Mr. Barnes, there was a departure from that rule, a

* Minutes, 1836, p. 286.

refusal to bear testimony against errors, with an implied approbation of them, and a denial that ministers in our church are under obligations to conform to our doctrinal Standards.

2. Because the errors in question do not consist merely or chiefly in ambiguous expressions and illustrations, but in sentiments respecting the great and important doctrines of the Gospel which are utterly inconsistent with the Confession of Faith and the Word of God: "We sincerely and firmly believe that Mr. Barnes has denied, and that in a sneering manner, that Adam was the covenant head of the human race; that all mankind sinned in him as such, and were thus brought under the penalty of transgression; that Christ suffered the penalty of the law when he died for sin; and that the righteousness of Christ is imputed to us for justification," etc.

3. "Because this expression of approbation of his opinions was passed after, as we believe, it had been *clearly* and *sufficiently proved* to the Assembly that Mr. Barnes had denied these important truths, and had expressed opinions concerning original sin, the nature of faith, and the nature of justification, which cannot be reconciled with our Standards," etc.*

That readers of these pages may be able to judge for themselves whether the opinion of these protestants was founded in truth, or whether the action of the majority was so founded, a point or two will now be stated. The reply to the Protest asserts that "Mr. Barnes nowhere denies, much less sneers at, the idea that Adam was the covenant and federal head of his posterity. On the contrary, though he employs not these terms, he does, in other language, teach the same truths which are taught by the phraseology."

---

* Minutes, 1836, p. 283.

It should be noted that Dr. Junkin charged Mr. Barnes with denying that Adam was the federal head *and representative* of his natural posterity, and, as proof, he cited, among other passages from the book, the following, the comment upon Rom. v. 19:

"Nothing is said here of the doctrine of representation. It is not affirmed that Adam was the *representative* of his race, nor is that language used in regard to him in the Bible. (2) Nothing is said of a covenant with him. Nowhere in the Scriptures is the term *covenant* applied to any transaction with Adam. (3) All that is established here is the simple *fact* that Adam sinned, and that this made it certain that all his posterity would be sinners. Beyond this the language of the Apostle does not go, and all else that has been said of this is the result of mere philosophical speculation. . . . Various attempts have been made to explain this. The most common has been that Adam was the representative of his race; that he was a covenant head, and that his sin was *imputed* to his posterity, and that they were held liable to punishment for it as if they had committed it themselves. But to this there are great and insuperable objections: (1) There is not one word of it in the Bible. Neither the terms representative, covenant, nor impute are *ever* applied to the transaction in the sacred Scriptures. (2) It is a mere philosophical theory; an introduction of a speculation into theology, with an attempt to explain what the Bible has not explained."*

"The words *representative* and *federal head* are never applied to Adam in the Bible. The reason is that the word *representative* implies an idea which could not have existed in the case,—*the consent of those who are represented.* Besides, the Bible does not teach that they acted in him, or that he acted *for* them. No passage has ever yet been found that stated this doctrine."†

On Rom. v. 12, he says the Apostle "was inquiring into the cause why death was in the world; and it would not account *for that* to say that all sinned *in* Adam. . . .

---

* Notes on Romans, 1st edition, p. 128. † Ibid., p. 120.

The expression 'in whom all have sinned' conveys no intelligible idea. As men had no existence then, in any sense, they could not then sin. What idea is conveyed to men of common understanding by the expression 'they sinned in him'?"

With such statements before them, cited from Mr. Barnes' book, how could the majority of the Assembly solemnly vote, and put on record, that "Mr. B. nowhere denies, much less sneers at, the idea that Adam was the covenant and federal head of his posterity, . . . but *does*, in other language, *teach* the same truths which are taught by the phraseology"?

Not content with thus indorsing Mr. Barnes' orthodoxy, they solemnly declare, in the same reply, "that they do, cordially and *ex animo*, adopt the Confession of our church, on the points of doctrine in question, according to the obvious and most prevalent interpretation."* And in the same paragraph they express peculiar admiration for the Standards, and "deprecate any attempt to change the phraseology of our Standards, and disapprove of any language of light estimation of them."

How such declarations *could* be made in such a connection, and *why* they were made, it is difficult to surmise. If, as some supposed, the design was to lull the apprehensions of the Old School, and to reassure the "middle men," who gave evidence of alarm, it signally failed. For even the Peace men in the church perceived such irreconcilable inconsistency between the *acts* of the Assembly in acquitting Mr. Barnes, and the *professions* of the Assembly of loyalty to the Standards, that their confidence in those professions could not be won. From that time forth conviction was brought home to the minds of all who became acquainted with the circumstances, that the New Theology

---

* Minutes, 1836, p. 287.

was to be shielded and disseminated in our church, under specious protestations of love to her Standards, which are in direct antagonism to that Theology. The substantial ends of the prosecution were attained. It was not Dr. Junkin's aim at all to put Mr. Barnes out of the ministry, or keep him out, but to obtain authoritative censure of his errors, convince the church that they were errors, and prevent their spread as Presbyterian doctrine. He would have greatly rejoiced if, at any time during the progress of the trials, Mr. Barnes had been convinced that his language was opposed to the Standards, and had proposed a satisfactory modification of it. The vindication of truth was all the Prosecutor sought. Indeed, at one time, during the preliminary steps of the trial of the Appeal before the Assembly, there seemed to be a prospect of such an amicable adjustment. The explanations of Mr. Barnes were so full, his apparent retractions so satisfactory, and his professed acceptance of the Confession so hearty, upon the points of the charges, that Dr. Junkin was induced to say to the Assembly, "If the concessions which we heard yesterday can be put in a form that is satisfactory, I shall be willing to take a course that will save the time of the Assembly."

Had Mr. Barnes consented to put in writing statements which he had made on the floor, the trial might have been arrested, and possibly peace restored, and the unity of the church preserved. But Mr. Barnes declared, in answer to this proposal, that he meant not to retract anything, and never would.

There is good reason to believe that Mr. Barnes had at one time been counselled to consent to a conformation of the language of his book to the teaching of the Standards, and was well-nigh persuaded to do it; and that he was subsequently advised to resume his attitude of adherence to his published views.

An incident, illustrative of the probable influences that were gathered round the accused, occurred to the writer of these pages, then a young man in the second year of his ministry. This incident was detailed in a letter to Dr. G. W. Musgrave, in answer to one of inquiry from him, and published by him in the *Presbyterian* of 1837, p. 111. The writer had ridden out to Canonsburg, the seat of his Alma Mater, Jefferson College, and spent Sabbath, the 29th of May, at that place. Dr. Lyman Beecher was his fellow-guest of the venerable President Brown. On Monday morning, as the young preacher was leaving Canonsburg, he overtook Dr. Beecher, and as they were both mounted, they rode together towards Pittsburg.

The troubles of the church were soon introduced in the conversation by the Doctor. Both deplored them. Dr. B. seemed distressed at the prospect before our Zion. He inquired what terms Dr. Junkin would probably accept from Mr. Barnes as the basis of an amicable adjustment. He was assured, in reply, that all the Prosecutor sought was *Union in the Truth*, and that he and the Old School would be glad, so far as the writer knew, to accept of any terms that would preserve the inviolability of the Standards. "What terms of concession do you think, Mr. Junkin, would satisfy your brother?" "I am not authorized to speak for him, but it is my judgment and belief that, if Mr. Barnes will go as far in conforming his language and statements to the Confession of Faith as I understand *you* have done, in your recent publication of your views, my brother will be satisfied, and peace can be speedily reached." "Do you think so, Junkin?" said the Doctor, in his curt, emphatic way. "I think so. I have not read your book, nor has my brother, but from representations made of it to me, whilst it is not entirely such as we could wish it, we deem it substantially the truth; and if Mr. Barnes will do as much to satisfy his brethren as you have done, the war may end." "Barnes MUST do it—Barnes WILL do it!" After riding a short time in silence, the Doctor resumed, "Junkin, we must get to the City before the Assembly convenes,—you must see your brother and his friends,—I will see Barnes and his; we will have a meeting in the Lecture-room of Dr. Herron's church, and this trouble may be adjusted." The young preacher consented to the proposal—the horses were urged to a speed that was far from comfortable, the older man keeping ahead. Few words were exchanged till the riders reached the Monongahela bridge, when the Doctor drew rein, and waited for his travelling companion to come up, and then said, "Now we must be quick. You see your brother and his friends, and we will arrange a meeting as soon as possible." To this the writer assented, rode rapidly, and did what he could to arrange the proposed interview. But Dr. Beecher and Mr. Barnes did not approach him, or grant him an interview, and the reason for this has never been explained to this day. Some were uncharitable enough to say at the time, that the arrival of the delayed steamboat, with some thirty or more New School Commissioners, giving to that party a majority in the Assembly, had superseded the necessity of observing the arrangement, on Dr. Beecher's part. The foregoing dialogue is given for *substance:* the precise words may not be remembered, but it is substantially correct.

Other matters, of the gravest importance, came before the Assembly of 1836, and the manner in which they were disposed of hastened the crisis of disruption. Dr. Junkin was not a commissioner in this Assembly, and of course took no part in its deliberations on these subjects, but he was deeply interested for their proper termination.

A committee had been appointed, by the Assembly of 1835, to confer with the Synod of Pittsburg, in relation to a transfer of the control of the Western Foreign Missionary Society to the General Assembly, and to adjust terms of transfer. This Committee reported that they had performed the duty assigned them, that terms of transfer had been agreed upon, and were submitted, with their report, for the action of the Assembly. These terms can be seen in the Minutes, and in Baird's Digest, pp. 348, 349.

This report was referred to a Committee, of which Dr. Phillips was chairman. This Committee presented a lengthy report, tracing the history of the negotiation, showing that the General Assembly had originated the proposal for the transfer, and could not, without bad faith, recede; setting forth the duty of the church to engage more fully in Foreign Missions, detailing the advantages of accepting the generous terms of the Synod of Pittsburg, and closing with two resolutions, the first accepting of the transfer, and the second proposing to appoint a Board of Foreign Missions, the seat of whose operations should be in the city of New York.*

Dr. Thomas H. Skinner, a member of the Committee, dissented, and presented a counter report, as follows:

"*Whereas*, The American Board of Commissioners for Foreign Missions has been connected with the Presbyterian Church, from the year of its incorporation, by the very elements of its existence; *whereas*, at the present time, a majority of the whole Board are Presbyterians; and *whereas*, it is undesirable, in conducting the work of Foreign Missions, that there should be any collision at home or abroad; therefore,

"*Resolved*, That it is inexpedient that the Assembly should organize a separate Foreign Missionary Institution."†

"After protracted discussion, the previous question was moved, and the adoption of the report was rejected (106 to 110), and the Stated Clerk ordered to inform the Western

* Minutes, 1836, p. 253.

† Ibid., p. 257.

Foreign Missionary Society that the Assembly had not carried into effect the stipulations touching the receiving of that Society under their care."*

A Protest against this action was presented, signed by all of the minority still in the Assembly.

The Old School looked upon this result as part of a programme for subordinating the Presbyterian Church to the New England Boards, and to New England Theology. It produced, immediately, a startling impression throughout the church. It was well known, that the fact mentioned in Dr. Skinner's report, that a majority of the members of the American Board were Presbyterians, was fallacious. None but corporate members can vote,—it is a close corporation, filling its own vacancies; and whilst of its eighty-three members forty-four were, *at that juncture*, Presbyterians in name, they had been appointed members of the Board, not by the General Assembly, but by the Board itself, and of course were such as the local Board would prefer; and they were widely *scattered* from Maine to Mississippi, whilst the members who resided in and near Boston really controlled its operations.

It is worthy of notice, that the two Presbyteries of Wilmington and the (Assembly's) Second of Philadelphia, which had been dissolved for contumacy by the Synod to which they belonged, had nullified the order of Synod, continued their existence, and sent up commissioners to this Assembly, who were received, and that the Assembly restored the Presbyteries.

The Old School members of the Assembly held one or two meetings for consultation, in the Second Church, during these exciting sessions. These were held after open and public notice had been given on the floor of the Assembly.

---

* Minutes, 1836, pp. 278, 279.

At one of these meetings, a Committee, consisting of Drs. Phillips, McElroy, Potts, John Breckenridge, McFarland, W. A. McDowell, and Krebs, with Elders James Lenox, Hugh Auchincloss, and Henry Rankin, were appointed to correspond and consult with the orthodox brethren throughout the church, point out the dangers that were imminent, and, if it should be deemed expedient, call a Convention, preliminary to the next Assembly. Some, indeed, were for taking immediate steps towards a division, but the measure just mentioned was fixed upon as preferable.

In speaking of this, Mr. Gillett, the New School historian of the church, says:

> "The appeal of Mr. Barnes and the aggrieved Presbytery against the Synod of Philadelphia were triumphantly sustained. This was gall and wormwood to the defeated party. Again they met, and, encouraged by their previous experiment, summoned a Convention to meet in Philadelphia, a few days previous to the meeting of the Assembly in 1837. They had gone too far to recede, and felt the necessity of prompt action in order to maintain the position they had so boldly taken."*

When it is remembered that one hundred and nine of the wisest, most prominent, most learned, and most godly men in the church, who were among Mr. Barnes' judges, signed a Protest, in which they condemned his doctrines; when it is considered, also, that these were native-born, pronounced and original Presbyterians, whilst those who sustained the Appeal and the Complaint were, for the most part, imported from other denominations, and that after a few years some of them returned to the connections whence they had come; and when, in addition, it is remembered that the acquittal was the result of a party vote, the "triumphant" elements of the result are not so obvious. To

---

* Vol. ii. p. 492.

speak of that result as being "gall and wormwood" to such men as Drs. Miller, Hoge, Phillips, and McElroy, is certainly to use a style of party intensity rather than that of sedate narrative. In what sense a defeated minority "had gone too far to recede," is not so obvious, for they had simply failed in vindicating what is now on all hands conceded to be the doctrine and order of the church of their fathers. No doubt, like Israel in captivity, they were sad; but that "gall and wormwood" is the proper metaphor for the feelings of godly, learned, and earnest men, when mourning over the perils of the truth and the distractions of a once peaceful church, would be difficult to prove. The Convention was not called by the meeting of the minority at Pittsburg, but they left it discretionary with the Committee above named.

When his duties at Pittsburg were ended, Dr. Junkin returned to Easton, to the arduous toils of the College enterprise, to which he added, during this year, an important literary undertaking.

CHAPTER XXVIII.

Results of the Barnes Trial—His Plea characterized—Its Influence upon Theological Opinion—Upon Students and Ministers—New Theology has made no Progress since—Its Effect upon the New School Body—It was an Original Cause of the Reunion, and of the Advanced Efficiency of the Church—Work of the Committee of Correspondence—Circular Letter—The Address—Delegation to Princeton—Conference—J. W. Alexander—Purpose to found a New Seminary—Robert Lenox, Esq.—Union Seminary founded—Its Origin and Aims—Call of a Convention—It meets—Its Doings—Memorial and Testimony—Dr. Breckenridge its Author—Assembly of 1837—Old School Majority—Its Men—Its Debates—Its Doings—Sketches of its Prominent Speakers—Abrogation of Plan of Union—Various Proposals for Division—All rejected—Incidents of Debate—Final Measures.

THE results of Dr. Junkin's arduous and self-denying labors in the Barnes trials can never be fully estimated; and yet a biography of him would be incomplete, and fail to do justice to his memory, if no indication of those results should be attempted. His argument, as presented to the Presbytery, to the Synod, and ultimately to the General Assembly, has been pronounced by many of the most astute and scholarly minds of his generation one of the most full, well-ordered, and demonstrative that had ever been constructed upon the points involved. Dr. Ely, in his "Contrast," had done a good work, in presenting the antagonisms of Hopkinsianism to the Calvinism of our Standards; and Dr. Joshua L. Wilson had drawn from Dr. Beecher very important concessions in the direction of orthodoxy; concessions that greatly crippled and trammelled divines of his own school in their subsequent war upon old Calvinism. But Dr. Junkin's argument set the two systems side by side in such distinct detail, and threw upon each such a flood of Scripture light and perspicuous logic, as enabled all minds of ordinary power of discrimination to see the contrast between them. Possessing, as he did, extraordinary powers of analysis and synthesis; keen in detecting the most plausible sophisms; looking to particulars and details with a microscopic exactness, yet grasping them all in their relations as components of a system with wondrous constructive skill, he was successful in setting forth the system of doctrine contained in our Standards with a boldness of relief, a distinctness of outline, and a symmetry of proportion which the logical mind contemplates with delight. With similar skill and power he arrayed the opposing errors, pointed out their relations, and showed their dangerous tendencies. We know that some who came to the Assembly of 1836 strongly biassed in favor of the New Theology, lived to become thorough advocates of the Old, and to ascribe the change in part to his argument. And would it be claiming too much to express the belief, that the extraordinary explicitness and ardor with which the majority of that Assembly declared their loyalty to the Standards of the church may have been attributable, in a measure, to the clearness and force with which those Standards were defended? It is true, some writers have ascribed those expressions of fealty to less worthy motives, and supposed that they were dictated by party policy; but we ought always to impute the best motives. Certain it is, that the abettors of the New Divinity acknowledged the force of Dr. Junkin's plea for orthodoxy confessing it to be the clearest argument then produced on his side of the question.

Besides the influence which it had upon the minds of those who heard it, it was read by many thousands of the best minds of the country, and as the students of theology were strongly interested in the discussions of that period, it was much consulted by them, and accomplished great good in assisting them to form clear and discriminating views. It aroused many of the ministers of our church to a fuller investigation of the points in controversy, and proved a valuable contribution to Polemic and Practical Theology. A perusal of his argument, it is thought, will do much to convince the mind of any candid reader, that the great truths which it defends, are of the utmost *practical* importance, and that belief in them must form the basis of all true and thorough piety.

It is now also *matter of history*, that *ever since the conflict* at Pittsburg, in the Barnes trial, the tide of the New Theology, which at one time threatened to overflow the Presbyterian Churches, has been *ebbing*. As we have seen, the New School majority of that Assembly, in their answer to the Protest of the orthodox, *committed* themselves, in the most explicit terms, to a "cordial and *ex animo*" adoption of the Confession of our church, "on the points of doctrine in question, according to the obvious and most prevalent interpretation." That pledge was the result either of honest conviction, or of the force of circumstances, or of both. And from the hour in which it was recorded, that pledge has operated with a centripetal force, drawing the great body of the New School in the direction of the "Standards, pure and simple." This proclivity in a right direction was accelerated by the disruption of 1838, and the necessities growing out of their claim to be the true constitutional church. In order to maintain that claim, adherence to the doctrine and order of the Standards became a logical and legal necessity, especially after the Lawsuit was instituted. And, as there can be no doubt that a large proportion of that party were really sound in doctrine, and were found in its ranks from sympathy and the force of circumstances, the pledge and the necessities above mentioned gave to that portion a power over the whole body, to draw it in the direction of sound Presbyterianism.

Now, to the prosecution of Mr. Barnes, and the thoroughness with which it was conducted, is to be attributed, in a large degree, the rousing of the Old School to a sense of the danger of the church, and the necessity of reform; and it was that prosecution, and the incidents inseparable from it, which called forth the pledge, and brought about the state of things which operated so happily, in causing the New School ranks to *oblique to the right*, until, in the march of thirty years, the columns of the two hosts were found advancing in parallel lines. Indeed, so inevitable was this tendency, under the forces just indicated, that, in less than fourteen years after the disruption, our New School brethren were found battling with the same breezes of Congregational voluntaryism to which we had attributed the raising of the waves of trouble previous to that disruption. Nor did this virtuous conflict cease, until many of the *men* and many of the *methods* which had troubled us, were eliminated from the other Branch, leaving them a homogeneous, effective, and thoroughly Presbyterian body. If "all things work together (co-operate) for good to them that love God," if He causes "the wrath of man to praise Him, and restraineth the remainder of wrath," and if He

"From seeming evil still educes good,"

may we not, after all, have reason to bless the great Head of the Church, that He has graciously overruled the storms of the past, so as to effect greater *purity*, and secure more perfect and abiding *peace*, to our Zion? It seems scarcely possible, for the candid and sagacious philosopher of history, to avoid the conclusion, that the Great Controller of events, who is "Head over all things to the Church," did employ the very process, which it has been our painful duty to sketch upon these pages, for the grand purpose of *removing* evils, and averting dangers, which good men were slow to believe existed, and of bringing about a more blessed condition of the great Presbyterian Church in this land. There was doubtless much of human frailty and passion exhibited on both sides, in the progress of the struggle, whilst there was also much of Christian zeal, and meekness, magnanimity, faithfulness, and heroism. Intellectual ability of the highest order was exhibited, and whilst it was sad to behold brethren arrayed against each other in stern conflict, the very earnestness which they displayed was proof of the depth of their convictions, and of the high estimate they placed upon the great principles of religion for which they contended.

Again: Can it be reasonably supposed that, if the prosecution of Mr. Barnes had not been conducted with ability, Christian meekness, and firmness, the Presbyterian Church would have been, at this day, the large, sound, homogeneous, and effective body which she is? Had the Plan of Union been maintained; had the Domestic missions of the church been consigned to the voluntary Society which aspired to control them; had the New Theology, through that irresponsible but efficient agency, been shed, like the leaves of autumn, over her congregations; had she been content to remain an auxiliary to the American Board of Foreign Missions; had she surrendered, to a Society beyond her surveillance and control, the education of her ministers; had she yielded the right of examination, and compelled her Presbyteries to admit all intrants who came with clear credentials; and had she completed the system of disorganization and dependence, by declaring her Standards so plastic and so elastic as to admit of any construction, and her government and discipline, however excellent, was never to be enforced to the exclusion of error; would she have been the church which we this day behold and venerate?

The storm seems terrible, but it clears the skies, exhausts the clouds, purifies the air, and brings out the sun in fuller splendor.

In addition to the benefits resulting from Dr. Junkin's agency in conducting the doctrinal struggle to an issue, the influence it had in bringing the entire body of the Old School into line at the alarming crisis now reached is worthy of mention. Many good and sound men were reluctant to believe that the errors charged upon Mr. Barnes were so wide-spread, or that there could be found so many in the church willing to tolerate them. Proof, such as the acquittal of Mr. Barnes and the circumstances attending it, was needed, to convince these excellent brethren of the real state of things. And although some of them were slow to adopt decisive measures, they no longer acted with the innovating party. In all his reasonings and pleadings upon the doctrinal issues, Dr. Junkin kept his eye upon the other phases of the great controversy. "Unity in the truth, in order to evangelical efficiency," was his great aim. He often uttered the sentiment, that it was the great mission of the church to send the gospel to all the world. This he believed she could do efficiently only by being herself a Missionary society. He believed that the new and "other gospel" of the semi-Pelagian system, was not *worth* sending to the heathen, or preaching at home, and that its introduction into the Presbyterian Church had occasioned all the divisions and distractions which prevented her from accomplishing her mission, at home and abroad; hence he was earnestly anxious to eliminate error as a means of restoring peace and unity, and of fitting the church for her great work. At this he aimed, and the just and candid verdict of posterity will aver that he did not labor in vain! If he had done nothing else for his generation, and the church of his choice, he did not live for naught.

The Committee of Correspondence, appointed by the minority of the Assembly of 1836, entered with promptness upon the delicate and important duties assigned them, and performed them with much wisdom and ability. Shortly after the adjournment of the Assembly they prepared a letter, caused it to be lithographed, and sent it to prominent office-bearers in all parts of the church. In this letter they proposed certain questions, in regard to the present state and future prospects of the church, and requested explicit answers, with a view to collect facts and opinions. They set forth the recent history of the struggle, and quoted the declaration of leading New School men in the last Assembly, as indicating revolutionary designs. They also presented a critical and just exposition of the errors which they believed had been proven against Mr. Barnes in the trial, "so faithfully and laboriously conducted by Dr. Junkin," bore testimony to the Christian spirit with which it was conducted, and appealed to their brethren to do for the preservation of the church of their fathers, whatever a good conscience might in the sight of God demand.

Some have, at different times, and especially in late years, attempted to deny that the schism of 1838 was really the result of doctrinal diversity. But that it was so, is proven by the whole history of the controversy, and especially by the testimony of this able document of the Committee of Correspondence. Their chief aim, in this circular, was to point out the serious and fundamental errors which were spreading, and which the votes of the last General Assembly had declared should be tolerated in the Presbyterian Church. And, in their seventh inquiry, they indicated the source whence chiefly they supposed these errors to flow,—connection with the churches and voluntary societies of the Congregationalists.

Of course this circular called forth from the other party strong expressions of indignation. It was denounced as a secret conspiracy to divide the church, and by other opprobrious names. But the men whose names were appended to it, were of too high character to be very successfully charged with such designs. They were pure, grave, godly, wise, dispassionate, and intelligent men,—men who occupied the highest social and official positions in the church, and who commanded respect throughout the nation. Their circular accomplished its purpose, and was blessed of God as the means of calling forth the strength of the church to the rescue of the truth.

The Committee, after obtaining a vast amount of information in reply to this circular, published, in a pamphlet of forty-one pages, "An Address to the Ministers, Elders, and Members of the Presbyterian Church." In this they set forth the necessity of *purity of faith* as an element indispensable to the *efficiency* of the church; the necessity of a *sincere* and *honest* adoption of the Confession, in order to doctrinal purity; and the danger of subscription "for substance of doctrine."

They reviewed the case of Mr. Barnes, and the decisions of the Assembly therein, and upon the questions of Missions and Education. and dwelt with particular force upon the repudiation of the treaty which the previous Assembly had solemnly authorized with the Western Foreign Missionary Society. From the whole survey they came to the conclusion expressed in the following paragraph:

"Fathers, brethren, and fellow-Christians, whatever else is dark, this is clear,—*We cannot continue in the same body* We are not agreed, and it is vain to attempt to walk together. That those, whom we regard as the authors of our present distractions, will retrace their steps, is not to be expected; and that those who have hitherto rallied around the Standards of our church, will continue to do so, is both to be expected and desired. In some way or other, therefore, these men must be separated from us."

Thus was foreshadowed a result, which was realized

within the next two years. But this Committee did not indicate the process.

It was deemed of great importance that all the orthodox should be brought to hearty co-operation in the same processes of reform. Hitherto their opponents were a unit in action, while some of the best men of the Old School party hesitated to go with the majority in the *measures* which that majority deemed right and wise. Sometimes, indeed, as in the Barnes trial, thoroughly orthodox men voted with the New School, although they acknowledged, as we have shown, by their own signatures, that fundamental errors had been proven. The position occupied by the Princeton Professors, who justly had great influence with their former pupils, was of an intermediate character, and many went with them. It was deemed of great importance to induce them to take a stand with the majority of their brethren. It was known that they as fully deplored the action of the Assembly of 1836 as the Old School minority of that body; but they faltered with regard to *methods* of averting the evils deplored.

With the hope of removing their scruples, "a company of gentlemen were designated, by a large and respectable number of the Old School, to proceed in a noiseless and unobserved manner to wait upon the Professors at their homes, to reason and remonstrate with them on the subject of their position, and to induce them, if possible, to concur with their brethren in the public action of the church. These gentlemen assembled at Princeton in the autumn of 1836, and met the Professors in Dr. Hodge's study, whither they had been invited to repair. At this conference the three Professors of the Seminary attended, and the Rev. James W. Alexander was also present. The following members of the Old School deputation were in attendance: Rev. Drs. James Blythe, of Indiana; C. C. Cuyler, of Philadelphia; George Junkin, of Easton; W. W. Phillips, of New York; and Rev. Isaac V. Brown, of New Jersey."*

This conference did not result in any decisive action or promise of action at the time; but there is reason to believe that its influence tended to secure the ultimate co-operation of Princeton with the rest of the Old School party. Dr. James W. Alexander, then comparatively a young man, is represented by Mr. Brown as having made some remarks at this interview "in a very unassuming and respectful manner" which seemed to produce a deep impression, and a tendency in a right direction. There was evidently *some* approximation towards less divided counsels.

Mr. Brown mentions in his book, "The Old School Vindicated," a fact illustrative both of the strong apprehensions of men's minds at that period, and of the critical condition in which our oldest Seminary was placed, by what many considered a lack of decision on the part of its Professors:

"In a neighboring city lived a rich, intelligent, and very devoted elder of the Old School body, of Scotch education and type of religion. His zeal for the church and her doctrines was strong. In common with others, he was apprehensive that the church, through the indefatigable and unscrupulous action of the New School, and the unhappy defection of Princeton, would, in a short time, be entirely under New School control. . . . He was consequently very solicitous that this delegation to Princeton should ascertain whether the theological gentlemen at Princeton, who had opposed the Act and Testimony, were determined to persist in their course. Unless some favorable indications should be given, he, and others like-minded, had resolved to abandon Princeton to the control of the adversaries, and immediately establish another Seminary on a basis entirely out of their reach. For this purpose the money was already in bank; a beautiful site, with appropriate grounds and edifices, was selected; the

---

* Brown's Historical Vindication, p. 175.

principal officers for the institution were designated from among the most prominent in our church, and everything was ready for action. But the delegates did not, on the whole, consider the condition of the Seminary at Princeton, exposed as it was, sufficiently desperate to warrant so great a sacrifice, and so decisive a change, at that time; and the friends in New York cordially acquiesced."*

Of course (although Mr. Brown does not say so) nothing of this was known at the time to the gentlemen at Princeton. No doubt pains were taken to avoid anything that would look like an *in terrorem*. The Elder alluded to was Robert Lenox, Esq., the father of James Lenox, Esq., than whom no more faithful ruling elder, wise counsellor, liberal benefactor, or eminent philanthropist has been vouchsafed to our church by a kind Providence. Although the Committee of Conference left Princeton somewhat discouraged, yet subsequent events afforded evidence that their visit had not been in vain. The Presbytery of New Brunswick, to which the Professors belonged, and which had hitherto maintained an attitude of non-co-operation with the Old School majority, shortly afterwards took more decisive conservative ground; and the venerable Dr. Alexander, who represented that Presbytery, in part, in the next General Assembly, was forward and decisive in proposing and securing the adoption of measures which caused the triumph of truth and order.

About the same time that this delegation of gentlemen visited Princeton, another event occurred which was part of the programme of the party of innovation, and which gave evidence that they were not satisfied with the theology taught at the Seminary at Princeton. This was nothing less than the establishment of another Theological Seminary, within two hours' ride of Princeton, viz., in the City of New York. Mr. Gillett says it was projected a year

* The Old School Vindicated, p. 176.

before (1835), founded in January, 1836, and went into operation December 5, 1836.* The same writer informs us that one of the considerations which led to this project was, to have a Seminary *beyond the control of the General Assembly*. His language is:

"It was felt, moreover, that, sustained by the patronage and confidence of the pastors and churches of New York, and those that sympathized with them throughout the church, the proposed institution might be competently endowed, ably officered, and well sustained. It would at least, in the hands of directors *independent of the Assembly*, remain under the control of men who would promote its interests without reference to an accidental majority in the Assembly."†

This movement was, no doubt, the result of the counsels of men of a higher tone of Christian honor than some of their brethren,—men whose sense of propriety shrunk from the proposal that had been suggested at Pittsburg, to seize upon Princeton and revolutionize its teachings. Such men as Drs. Erskine Mason, and Henry White,‡ and Thomas H. Skinner, and Ichabod S. Spencer, and the laymen of high-toned principle who were associated with them, however zealous they might be for their opinions, would not consent to pervert an institution and its funds from the purposes to which they had been devoted. They wished for an institution in which the modified Calvinism, which some of them favored, should be taught without the restraints which the Old School seemed determined to impose; but they were too honorable and fair-minded to repeat the history of Harvard, even in the slightest measure, and seize upon an institution consecrated to other ends.

The founding of this Seminary, however, was a *confession*

---

* History, vol. ii. pp. 501, 502.

† Gillett's History, vol. ii. p. 501.

‡ Drs. Mason and White were sound Calvinists.

that the New School Theology *did* differ from that taught at Princeton, to *such an extent* as to justify the cost of money and men which would be necessary to establish another school in the vicinity of that institution of the church. This was rather a contradiction of the loyal declarations made in the answer to the protest in the Barnes case. The fact that the Union Seminary was projected in 1835, and not put in operation until the close of the following year, renders it probable that the delay was occasioned by a waiting upon the developing of events.

The Committee of Correspondence, whose labors have been mentioned above, invited the members of the Assembly of 1837 to convene for consultation a week before its meeting. The call for this conference was issued on the 12th of January. It stated that the result of their extensive correspondence had produced the conviction, that a very general desire prevailed among the conservative portion of the church to have the agitating contentions ended, "by removing the causes in which they originated." And they recommended that the day upon which the Convention was to assemble in Philadelphia—the second Thursday of May—should be observed as a day of fasting, humiliation, and prayer throughout the churches. The call was published in all the conservative papers, and the opposite party had full warning of the earnest efforts that were to be made.

Meanwhile there was a very general expression of opinion that something decisive must be done. The *Princeton Review* raised its voice in warning against the "imminent dangers of the church." Dr. Miller, Dr. McFarland, Dr. John Breckenridge, at that time a Professor in Princeton Seminary, and others, known hitherto to be men of mild counsels, wrote effective appeals to the ministers, elders, and people of the church, and every indication pointed to a unity of counsels not previously attained. The Old

School, who had hitherto been excelled in ecclesiastical tactics, who had, indeed, seemed to shrink from even the most obviously necessary means for concentrating their forces, now began to imitate the example of their opponents, so far as to arouse the interest of their friends, and gather their forces to the conflict. The consequence was that the delegations from Old School Presbyteries were fuller, the eldership came up in force, and pains seem to have been taken to send as Commissioners men of power, influence, and distinction. This was the case, indeed, on both sides, and the result was that rarely has there been assembled in our country, either in a civil or ecclesiastical body, such a number of men eminent for talent, wisdom, experience, and social position and influence as the General Assembly of 1837. "The parties into which the Assembly was divided," says Mr. Gillett, "were ably represented. On one side were the Rev. Drs. Green, Elliott, A. Alexander, Junkin, Baxter, Cuyler, Graham, and Witherspoon, and Messrs. R. J. Breckenridge, Plumer, Murray, and others. On the other side were Drs. Beman, Porter, of Catskill, McAuley, Peters, and Cleland, and Rev. Messrs. Duffield, Gilbert, Cleveland, Dickinson, and Judge Jessup."

The Convention met on the 11th of May. Rev. James Blythe, D.D., was temporary Chairman, and Rev. Thomas D. Baird temporary Clerk. The entire day was devoted to humiliation and prayer. Next day they organized fully by appointing Dr. George A. Baxter, of Va., President, Dr. C. C. Cuyler, Vice-President, Rev. T. D. Baird, Recording Clerk, and Rev. H. S. Pratt, Reader. The Convention first brought before it all the facts relating to the condition of the church, by calling the roll, and asking every member to state what fell within his own knowledge. This array of facts left the most skeptical of the doubting brethren without excuse for longer denying the existence of the disorders of which the Old School had for years complained.

A Committee was appointed to prepare, from the facts thus elicited and their own knowledge of the history and state of these troubles, a Testimony and Memorial, to be laid before the Assembly. Dr. Robert J. Breckenridge was Chairman of the Committee, and Dr. Potts, Dr. Smyth, of Charleston, Judge Ewing, and Hon. David Fullerton, members. The paper was such as might have been expected from the pen of that vigorous thinker who was at the head of the Committee. It was an earnest, solemn, calm, logical, and determined document, lucidly arraying the facts of the great struggle, pointing out the evils under which the church had been groaning, vindicating the measures which the Old School party had hitherto adopted, and insisting that the evils complained of must be remedied without further delay. Like the Memorial of the Pittsburg Convention, it enumerated the errors in doctrine against which it bore testimony, and protested against permitting the church any longer to be held in bonds by the Voluntary Societies. "We contend especially, and above all, for the TRUTH, as it is made known to us for the salvation of men. We contend for nothing else, except as the result or the support of this inestimable treasure. It is because this is subverted that we grieve; it is because our Standards teach it that we bewail their perversion; it is because our church order and discipline preserve, defend, and diffuse it that we weep over their impending ruin."

The Memorial asked for the abrogation of the Plan of Union, the discountenancing of the Voluntary Societies, the separation from the church of all inferior courts not Presbyterially organized, the enforcement of the duty of examining intrants, the due discipline of errorists, and of courts that tolerate them, and the adoption of appropriate measures, so "that such of these bodies as are believed to consist chiefly of unsound or disorderly members may be separated from the church."*

This Memorial was signed by the officers of the Convention, and presented to the Assembly in its name.

The Assembly met in the Central, but on Monday removed to the Seventh Church.

The Old School had, at the opening, a majority of thirty-one, as was indicated by the election of Dr. David Elliott, Moderator, over the Rev. Baxter Dickinson. This majority was increased by subsequent arrivals. The Memorial was presented on the second day of the sessions, and referred of course to the Committee of Overtures, who, next day, reported it to the Assembly, and it was again referred to a Committee, consisting of Drs. Archibald Alexander, Plumer, Green, Baxter, and Leland, with Elders Walter Lowrie and James Lenox.†

The doctrinal testimony was first reported to the house, and, after a long discussion and no little parliamentary manœuvring, temporarily postponed. This was the great issue upon which hung all other parts of the contest; and the New School leaders sought to render the testimony absurd and useless, by moving many additions to it of matters about which there was no dispute—the process, in secular legislation, called "putting on riders."

The other points of the Memorial were reported from time to time, discussed, and adopted. Resolutions proposing to continue fraternal correspondence with the Congregational churches, and to abrogate the Plan of Union, were introduced. Upon the latter proposal warm discussion ensued. The writer of this memoir heard this debate, and the others which took place in that General Assembly, and he was impressed with the ability and

---

* Baird's Hist., p. 522.

† Ibid., p. 523.

earnestness displayed upon both sides. Men of power were there, and their powers were called forth, in highest exertion, by the vastness and vitality of the issues involved, and by that stimulus which is furnished by a great occasion, and the collision of giant with giant, in a grand intellectual struggle. Beman was there, with his unfailing flow of plausible *ore rotundo* oratory and metaphor, forcible, if sometimes mixed. McAuley was there, with his earnest manner, ready command of language, and somewhat invective style. Peters was there, with his small stature, smooth tone, and quiet manner, his deep-gray eye that twinkled shrewdness from beneath its socket, his imperturbable self-possession, and keen readiness to seize upon the weak point of an adversary's argument. Dickinson was there, with his taller form, his anxious expression, his somewhat positive and blunt eloquence, and his deep devotion to the interests of his party. Duffield was there, earnest, watchful, and eloquent. Cleveland was there, with his fine form, fair complexion, bold and forward mien, prompt and outspoken address, and impressive eloquence. Judge Jessup was there, with his noble countenance, that indicated honesty of conviction, his earnest manner, astute powers of reasoning, and forceful, rugged eloquence. These, with others scarce less notable, were present. On the other side was the venerable Alexander, slight of stature, quick in movement, with a keen gray eye that read the soul, with quiet, unobtrusive mien, and habitual reticence, except when duty bade him speak; but when he spoke, with his slender, clear voice and style of translucent simplicity, all listened, for his lips dropped wisdom, and all *knew* the man to be sincere. There, too, was Cuyler, tall, slightly stooped, gray-headed, with an expression of benevolent gentleness on his countenance, the love of truth in his heart, and with lips ever prepared to defend it in a style gentle, perspicuous, and firm. Elliott, sedate, judicious, dignified, and prompt, occupied the chair. Plumer was there, with his commanding stature and presence, his raven locks, his dark, expressive eye, his peculiar eloquence, which swelled to the storm, then sank to the gentle murmur of the billow, and again came rushing on like the gale-driven surf. With less rigid and consecutive logic than some of his peers, his wit alternating with awful solemnity of thought and manner, combined with fine powers of illustration, made him one of the most effective debaters of that great occasion. There was Baxter, portly, pleasant, solemn, yet genial, with high powers of analysis, a manner of speech that commanded attention, and a personal bearing that won respect. The patriarch Green was there: large, stately, venerable, clear-headed, earnest-hearted, erudite, logical, terse and curt in his statements, he possessed great weight in the counsels of the Assembly. William Latta was there, of medium stature, venerable in years and in wisdom, not ready in *extempore* debate, but the author of one of the most impressive arguments delivered upon the doctrinal testimony in that Assembly. Robert J. Breckenridge was there: the Kentucky gentleman, of rather more than medium height, slender, well knit, and dignified in bodily stature, with a face handsome, expressive, and promptly conforming to the dominant emotions, an eye that could melt with tenderness, or kindle with scorn, or grow bland with frankness and conciliation, with a mind that grasped a subject with vigor, perspicuity, and comprehensiveness, with a power of verbal criticism that always commanded the right word, and often the intensest epithets, and an elocution terse, incisive, commanding, and sometimes almost vehement, he was often heard, and always *heard* when he spoke. Breckenridge was a great debater, direct and logical, smiting his adversary point-blank, terrible in retort, and skilful in fending the shafts of an opponent. If there were defects in his parliamentary qualifications, they lay in his impatience with slower minds among his friends, when they could not follow him in advance of their convictions, and in a certain impetuosity that gave the impression that he aimed to *rout* his adversaries rather than to convince and win them. The subject of this memoir was there: of medium stature, but powerful in bone and muscle, with a keen black eye, which, in repose, or when under the influence of the gentler affections, looked lovingly forth, but which beamed brilliantly in obedience to emotional impulse, a face of the classic mould of manly comeliness, a manner reserved, reticent, almost abstracted, with a ready perception of all the phases of the theme of his thoughts, discriminating, perspicuous, logical, and comprehensive in his grasp of a subject, always ready with the right word, with unusual quickness to detect a sophistry, and wondrous skill in pulling it to pieces and exposing its useless fragments, his arguments were always forceful, often overwhelming. His voice was defective, particularly to the ear of strangers, being slender and almost shrill in its higher tones. But his elocution was distinct, his manner collected and often ardent, and his "faculty of being heard," as Dr. R. J. Breckenridge would phrase it, unsurpassed. Indeed, Dr. Junkin, with all his defects of voice, could be heard farther and more distinctly than most men of his day. His custom, in a deliberative body, was not to speak often, and not at all unless there seemed to be a real need. He took a more active part in the debates of this Assembly than was his wont, because his brethren asked it. Perfectly at home, and recently practiced in doctrinal debate, he was expected to bear his part in such discussions. And as he was recognized as one of the ablest expounders of the Constitution, it was not unusual to hear the younger members, and those less skilled in debate, whispering, "Dr. Junkin ought to speak on that constitutional question,'' or expressions of similar kind. Forceful and often brilliant in his illustrations, he lacked skill in the witticism of debate, and he rarely attempted retort.

There were other men of mark in that Assembly, whose characteristics are remembered after the lapse of thirty-four years; but our space will not permit an attempt to sketch them. Among the elders on the Old School side, were such men as James Lenox, the philanthropist, ex-Senator Walter Lowrie, Judge Nathaniel Ewing, and the Hon. Samuel C. Anderson, of Virginia. Mr. Lenox, although a man of fine mind, scholarly, well read, and a safe counsellor, rarely, if ever, attempted public speech. Mr. Lowrie spoke seldom, but always sensibly and to the purpose. Mr. Ewing was a pleasant speaker, and an ingenious debater, and was somewhat prominent. Mr. Anderson was a fine speaker, and upon the question of the elimination of the Congregational Synods, delivered a very powerful argument, which had much influence in producing the result.

After protracted debate, the resolution to abrogate the Plan of Union "as unnatural and unconstitutional," and productive of abnormal results, was passed by a vote of 143 ayes to 110 nays.

After this was done, various measures were proposed for the remedy of existing evils; but each met with persistent opposition from the New School members, and in the course of discussion, such practical objections to them were discovered as led to their abandonment. One of the first of these was moved by Dr. Plumer, to the effect, "that such inferior judicatories as are charged by common fame with irregularities" be cited to the bar of the next Assembly, —that a Committee of investigation and arrangement be appointed to ascertain the facts and digest a plan of procedure, this Committee to report "as soon as practicable,"

—and that the judicatories accused should not vote in their own case, or sit pending the process.

The proposed discipline of non-orderly judicatories was resolved upon; but the vote was by a diminished majority, many considering it impracticable.

The next suggestion was to attempt an amicable division of the church. This was made by Dr. R. J. Breckenridge, in consequence of a proposition submitted to him by Dr. Peters.* This was adopted, and a Committee of each party was appointed,—Drs. Breckenridge, Alexander, Cuyler, Witherspoon, and Judge Ewing on one side, and Drs. McAuley, Beman, Dickinson, and Judge Jessup on the other. The Committee and the subject referred to them were commended to God, by the Assembly, in prayer led by Dr. Baxter.†

On a subsequent day (May 30) this Committee reported, through Dr. Alexander, that they could not agree upon all the details. Their minutes showed that in regard to funds, corporate succession, seminaries, and the records they came to terms. They agreed that the Old School should retain the name, and the other be called the American Presbyterian Church; but they failed to agree in regard to an immediate division, as to the power of the Assembly to do it, and as to breaking off the ecclesiastical succession; the New School insisting that neither body should be the lineal successor of the existing body. Thus this measure failed, and the Old School thought the other side were aiming to secure delay. The Committee was discharged and the subject tabled.

As all hope of an amicable separation seemed ended, the majority were forced to choose between decisive action or continued strife, with the possibility of being either forced to succumb to their opponents, or of being by them

---

* Gillett, vol. ii. p. 508. † Baird's Hist., p. 525.

cut off. Indeed, they had proof of the existence of a plan, on the part of the New School, quite as decisive as that which the Old School adopted, provided the former had been in the majority, or could gain a majority next year.*

It is believed to have been Dr. Baxter, who, in conversation with Mr. Plumer, Dr. Junkin, Mr. Anderson, and some others, suggested that the abrogation of the Plan of Union as unconstitutional carried down with it and out of the church all those abnormal judicatories that had grown up under the operation of that Plan. The Convention being called together during the negotiations for voluntary separation, this suggestion was laid before it, and it was resolved to apply the principle. When the efforts for amicable separation failed, therefore, Dr. Plumer moved

> "That by the operation of the abrogation of the Plan of Union of 1801, the Synod of the Western Reserve is, and is hereby declared to be, no longer a part of the Presbyterian Church in the United States of America."

Dr. Baxter advocated the resolution in an able and earnest speech, in which he cited cases from the civil courts, in which the principle was affirmed that what was unconstitutional was void *ab initio.*

Judge Jessup replied to him, denying the constitutional power of the Assembly to "cut off" a Synod. He thus gave the key-note, which has been followed by his party ever since, that an act declaratory of the *status* of a body making an unconstitutional claim to be Presbyterian, is a "cutting off" of the body; whereas the Assembly claimed that the Synod (so called) *never had* a constitutional connection with the Presbyterian Church, and never was entitled to representation in the Assembly.

Dr. McAuley made a pathetic speech, portraying the awful consequences of the proposed action, which, he said,

---

* Baird's Hist., p. 527.

would be dissolving Synods and Presbyteries, deposing ministers, dissolving churches, and spreading confusion.

Dr. Plumer replied, denying that any such results would follow; that, as the vast majority of the churches were Congregational, and the ministers only nominally Presbyterian, this separation from the Assembly would not affect the standing of ministers or the organization of churches.

Mr. Cleveland followed, affirming his desire for peace, but his determination to resist the proposed action; and, after a speech occupying parts of an evening and morning session, he moved to postpone the resolution under debate, in order to take up the question of separation in a constitutional way.

Dr. Junkin opposed postponement, and advocated the resolution. The overwhelming majority of the churches in the Synod of the Western Reserve, he declared, were not Presbyterian. He pointed to the fact that, on the floor of the Assembly, there were fourteen men who represented but two Presbyterian churches, and that by this process a body of Congregational churches actually held the balance of power in the General Assembly, and governed the Presbyterian Church, whilst they themselves not only did not submit to the constitution and laws of that church, but maintained a constant protest against Presbyterianism. Their very existence, in the attitude which they held, was a protest against Presbyterian government, whilst they claimed the right to exercise that government over others. He was proceeding to recite the various disorders and doctrinal errors which were known to exist in the Synod, when he was interrupted by the Rev. Mr. Seward, of the Western Reserve, who proposed to testify in favor of the Synod.

He was asked, "Did you assent to the constitutional questions prescribed for ministers at your ordination?" He declined answering the question. Dr. Beman interposed, to relieve Mr. Seward's embarrassment, with the remark, "Mr. Seward has been interrupted by questions."

The Moderator said, "Mr. Seward requested that he might be questioned."

Mr. Seward said, "I do adopt the Book."

"Did you do so at your ordination?" To which Mr. S. gave no reply.

Mr. Brown, an elder from the Presbytery of Lorain, said, "We have been greatly misrepresented. There are thirty Presbyterian churches in our Synod."

Dr. Cuyler. "There are one hundred and thirty-nine churches in the Synod."

Mr. Brown. "The Confessions used in these churches are abstracts of the Presbyterian Confession. My Presbytery consists of twelve churches. I do not know of more than one that is strictly Presbyterian."

Mr. H. Kingsbury, an elder from Cleveland church, said, "I have a copy of a certificate given me by the Rev. S. C. Aikin, and which I have carried for two years, to show that I am an Elder. I got it because I was once a committee-man, and sat in the Assembly, where my seat was challenged."

Mr. Breckenridge. "Is he a ruling elder according to the Book?"

Mr. K. "I will answer no questions. I am not on trial."

Mr. Breckenridge. "I am credibly informed that he never was an elder, and that there is no Board of Elders in his church. I now ask Mr. Kingsbury if he ever adopted the Book."

Mr. Kingsbury. "I answer no questions."

Dr. Peters afterwards stated that Mr. Kingsbury had authorized him to explain; that he had declined answering because he was not on trial; but that he was ordained an elder two and a half years before.

Mr. Breckenridge. "Will Mr. Kingsbury now say that he ever adopted the Constitution of the Presbyterian Church?"

Mr. Kingsbury. "I answer no questions."

Mr. B. "That's enough."*

The discussion was continued by Dr. Peters, Judge Jessup, Hon. S. C. Anderson, and Judge Ewing, extending through several sessions, after which Mr. Cleveland's motion to postpone was lost, and the resolution carried by a vote of 132 to 105.

"The Rubicon was now crossed," says Mr. Gillett; "the decisive principle had been adopted; and all that remained was simply a matter of detail. The majority were sure of their ground. They proceeded to perfect their work with coolness and deliberation. On Friday a resolution was passed 'affirming that the organization and operations of the so-called American Home Missionary Society, and American Education Society, and its branches of whatever name, are exceedingly injurious to the peace and purity of the Presbyterian Church. We recommend, therefore, that they cease to operate within any of our churches.'"† This was carried, 124 to 86.

The Assembly also declared the Synods of Utica, Geneva, and Genesee to be subject to the same rule as had been applied to the Synod of the Western Reserve, and that they were not a portion of the Presbyterian Church. Vigorous resistance to these acts was of course made by the minority, and a protracted debate preceded the vote, which stood 115 to 88.

In connection with these disowning acts, the Assembly assigned, as reasons for them, the original unconstitutionality of the Plan of Union, the abnormal evils it had wrought, "the gross disorders which are ascertained to have prevailed in those Synods—it being clear to us, that

* Baird's Hist., pp. 529, 530.

† History, vol. ii. p. 513.

even the Plan of Union itself was never consistently carried into effect, by those professing to act under it," and the manifest impropriety of a people helping to administer over others, a government to which they themselves refused to submit.

The Assembly further declared, that "by these resolutions they had no intention to affect, in any way, the ministerial standing of any members of either of said Synods, nor to disturb the pastoral relation in any church, nor to interfere with the duties or relations of private Christians in their respective congregations."

The Assembly also made provision for such Presbyteries, ministers, and churches, in the bounds of those Synods, as were truly Presbyterian in doctrine and order, to adhere to the church. Presbyteries were directed to make application to the next General Assembly, ministers and churches to the Presbyteries most convenient to the several locations of the applicants.*

The Elective Affinity Presbytery (Third) of Philadelphia was also dissolved, and its ministers, licentiates, and churches directed to go to the Presbyteries within whose limits they were located. This was done on the motion of Dr. R. J. Breckenridge.

The testimony against doctrinal error was also adopted; a Board of Foreign Missions was instituted, in pursuance of the treaty with the Western Foreign Missionary Society;† and, in short, the entire system of reform, proposed by the memorialists, was adopted. Against all these measures of the Assembly Protests were presented, admitted to record, and answered, all of which can be seen by the curious in the Minutes and in Baird's Assembly's Digest.‡

---

* Minutes, 1837, p. 440.

† Dr. Junkin was a member of the original Board of Foreign Missions.

‡ Dr. Junkin was author of the Answer to the Protest against the Abrogation of the "Plan of Union."

In view of the important and extraordinary measures adopted by this Assembly, it was deemed necessary to explain to the churches the grounds of this action, and a Committee was appointed to prepare a letter addressed to the churches of Christ Jesus throughout the earth. Dr. R. J. Breckenridge was Chairman of this Committee, and doubtless the author of the letter which was adopted.

This document is a noble specimen of apologetic writing, using that adjective in its ancient sense. It is marked by a sedate dignity of tone, an elevation of style, a spirituality of temper, a lucidness of narrative, and a clearness and thoroughness of explanation, which make it admirably adapted to its object. It carries with it the conviction, at least to all unprejudiced minds, that the writer and his brethren who adopted the paper, sincerely and sorrowfully felt that, in God's providence, a necessity had been laid upon them to do what they had done, and that whilst the acts were painful to their hearts as Christians, they were *right*, and had been done in the fear of God. We have not space to quote much from this document, and will only insert one paragraph, which contains a description of the misrepresentations which they sought to correct. This is done, because the subject of this memoir, in common with the writer of the circular letter, and a few others of the Old School leaders, was made an especial target for such shafts. Addressing believers throughout the earth, it says:

"You have heard the motives of the friends of truth reproached; their name cast out as evil; their zeal for maintaining the purity of the gospel represented as a mere struggle for power; and all their attempts to detect and censure heresy held up to public view as the efforts of restless and ambitious men to gain the pre-eminence for themselves. Amidst these ineffectual attempts to banish error and restore order, vital piety has languished; mutual confidence has disappeared; the reviving and converting influences of the Holy Ghost have been withheld ; and our time and strength have been painfully occupied with strife and debate, instead of being wholly given to the spread of the gospel and the conversion of the world."

As was to be expected, the defeated party, and those who sympathized with them, made loud, acrimonious, widely-spread, and persistent outcry against these measures of the General Assembly. The terms unconstitutional, unchristian, arbitrary, tyrannical, and other epithets tending to bring them into reproach, were lavishly applied to them. The organs of the innovating party, and even portions of the secular press, were liberal of their censures. The acts of the Assembly were characterized in such a way as to set them before the public in the strongest light of reprobation, as they appeared to the more ardent New School brethren. The changes were rung upon "excision," the "exscinding acts," the enormity of excluding from the church four Synods, and so large a number of Presbyteries, ministers, churches, and communicants, without citation, trial, or conviction ; and although the acts of Assembly made very full and specific declarations to the contrary, this exclusion was spoken of, much as if the ministers had been deposed, the church courts dissolved, and the church-members excommunicated.

Nor was it unreasonable to expect such representations to be made by men smarting under defeat, and who really and sincerely thought that the Assembly had exerted powers not clearly granted in the constitution,—men who looked upon matters from an entirely different standpoint, and with wholly different feelings and convictions, from those of the Old School. And it is due to the truth of history to say, that many who were not personally, or by reason of denominational connection, involved in the controversy, men, too, of sound judgment and of acknowledged fairness, differed in opinion about the constitutionality of these measures. And whilst it is due to the majority (O. S.) to admit, that they acted under a high consciousness and a profound conviction of the necessity, the constitutionality, and the righteousness of their acts, and also that their measures were adopted with a calmness and solemnity that could not have been exhibited in such stormy times by men of ordinary mould, it is due to the other side to attribute to them similar motives and a like sincerity, where there was no proof at the time, and none furnished by subsequent events, of a contrary state of things. Of the great mass of real Presbyterians then in the New School body, nothing impeaching their sincerity can be said. But of those who had put on the Presbyterian name without adopting the principles of our church, and who, after the division of the church, returned to Congregationalism, or continued to perplex the New School Church with continued controversy, so charitable a judgment can hardly be expressed by a candid historian.

For another year the church was agitated by the discussion of these grave issues; and both parties looked forward to the next Assembly with the intensest solicitude. On both sides the discussions were warm, able, and earnest; and it would be expecting too much from partially sanctified human nature to suppose, that in all cases the utmost proprieties of Christian controversy were observed.

The history of the great ecclesiastical struggle which resulted in the division of the Presbyterian Church has been narrated, with a fulness and detail that might seem unnecessary in the biography of a single actor in those scenes. But it seemed to the writer impossible to delineate the part borne in those great events by Dr. Junkin, so as to do simple justice to his memory, without narrating the whole. Things must be seen in their relations in order to be fairly understood. Conduct, in any given set of circumstances, cannot be rightly described nor justly estimated if the circumstances are unknown. And as the same events here narrated have been professedly recorded by others,—with what measure of accuracy and fairness the public will have to judge,—the writer of this book felt it to be his duty to present the facts as collated from the documents and records of the church.

Dr. Junkin was not a member of the General Assembly of 1838; and whilst it may be that he was consulted in regard to some of its measures, he was not so identified with its acts as to make them a part of his personal history to any appreciable extent. It is not, therefore, the design of the present writer to carry forward the history of the church, in its minute details, beyond the period now reached. That was the great crisis; the actual secession that took place the next year was but the result of what had been already done.

CHAPTER XXIX.

Struggles of Lafayette College—Dr. Junkin invited to a Pastorate in Cincinnati—Declines—Work on Justification—College Printing-Press—Prof. Cunningham—The Educator—The Normal School—The Faculty—Standard of Scholarship in the College high—Disruption of 1838—Results in Inferior Courts—Dr. Junkin in the Synod of New Jersey—Who is responsible for Religious Controversy?—The Results of the Great Struggle recapitulated—The Reunion, how brought about—Dr. Junkin's Agency.

IT was deemed most conducive to a lucid arrangement of the narrative, to complete the history of the ecclesiastical events, in which Dr. Junkin was more prominently concerned, without interrupting it by other incidents. It will be necessary to bring up his more private history to the same period.

Whilst Dr. Junkin was lending his strength and influence to the great interests of the church, as narrated in the previous chapters, his toils and solicitudes in the College enterprise were by no means abated; and serious embarrassments sometimes arose. The want of any endowment occasioned ever-recurring pecuniary pressure. The Board of Trustees had to incur some debt in order to provide the necessary buildings; and part of this debt was owing to the President for money advanced, and as they were unable to refund, he sometimes was almost constrained to abandon the enterprise for want of means to carry it forward. Buoyant in spirit and hopeful, as he was, he at times was almost in despair of success.

On the 27th of August, 1835, he wrote to his old and attached friend, the Rev. Robert Steel, of Abington:

"Our state is critical. Money I must have in a few weeks, or down this institution must go. I have written to the brethren in Philadelphia, stating the case, and asking co-operation as the only alternative. Ten thousand would enable us to go on decently. . . . Now, here, I think, is a noble oppoitunity to do good to our church. Our Board are willing to mortgage the College property to any good Presbyterians for the sum named, and that will clear us of all debt, and leave some two thousand dollars to buy books and other necessary appliances. Thus Lafayette may be secured forever to the interest of our church. Will not the friends of this cause do something? I have tendered to our Board the alternative of stopping finally, at the end of the present year (Sept. 23), or of paying me my debt,—about $3400. They will pay part in a few days, but this will not suffice; there are other debts that must be met; and we must have books, etc.

"Now, I am the more anxious to have this matter issued, as the Lord has thrown open a door of honorable retreat, by an invitation from the First Presbyterian Church of Cincinnati, in which Dr. Wilson cordially joins, to become co-pastor with him. To leave this enterprise would blast the fondest desires of my heart; but I cannot endure it thus. To go on is impossible in the present state of things; and I have thrown the responsibility upon a few brethren in the city; and this I had done before I knew of the offer from the West. My friends here say that if I go the College must fall, or pass into different hands, and those, probably, our enemies.

"Now, my dear brother, I wish you would go on Monday and attend the meeting at Dr. Green's,* and have some talk about it; and if encouraged, I will go down again."

Relief was obtained to some extent; but not in such measure as would have induced a man of less perseverance than Dr. Junkin to continue the struggle.

The invitation from the First Church of Cincinnati and its venerable Pastor was very urgent. The correspondence,

* Ministers' Prayer-Meeting.

still on file, indicates a very strong desire to obtain Dr. Junkin's services; but his heart was set upon educating men for the Ministry, and he gave a respectful negative to the call.

At the request of his friends, Dr. R. J. Breckenridge and Rev. A. B. Cross,—the Editors of the Baltimore *Religious and Literary Magazine,*—Dr. Junkin contributed a series of articles to that monthly on "The Moral Government of God." These constituted the basis of his Treatise on Justification, the first edition of which he published in 1839. Of this treatise the *Princeton Review* remarked, that its title was too modest, and was a misnomer, for that, instead of being simply a Treatise upon Justification, it was really a compact and complete system of Theology. It does not become the present writer to speak of its merits; but he will say this much, that he knows of no book in which the Calvinistic theology is stated so succinctly, yet so fully, lucidly, and suggestively, as in this small volume. The arrangement is philosophical, one part following the other accordantly with the laws of mind, "so that every preceding vehicle, with its treasure, has a certain aptitude to draw after it the one precisely adapted to it, and which will secure a similar sequence." In this, as in all his works, Dr. Junkin's method of expounding Scripture is the inductive,—collating all the passages where a term is used, and thus making Scripture the interpreter of Scripture. He demonstrates in this book that the doctrines of the Bible, embraced in the great question of justification, contain the essence of all morality, and form the *substratum* of all sound social, civil, and political government; that there are not two systems of morals, one for the Christian and one for the citizen, but one system only, and that covering the entire existence of the man in all his relations and all his duties; hence the name first given to the Essays, —"The Moral Government of God." In this volume the metaphysics of theology is so popularized and simplified, that no unsophisticated reader would suppose there is any metaphysics in the book; proving that sound, even profound, philosophy is nothing more than common sense. The objections to the distinctive doctrines of grace are answered with very satisfactory conclusiveness, and on this and other accounts theological students and private Christians have found it one of the most convenient and reliable hand-books.

He added to the work a chapter upon Sanctification; but, later in life, he prepared a separate treatise upon that subject. It so happened that several young men were in the College who had learned the art of printing; and with a view to give them employment, and at the same time increase the means of disseminating educational knowledge, and promote both common-school and collegiate education, Dr. Junkin purchased a printing-press and complete set of types. His book upon Justification (1st edition) was printed on the College press, the work being done by students; and he commenced a periodical called "THE EDUCATOR," which was under his editorial control, assisted by the Professors of the College, and other contributors. The book on Justification was published under the imprimatur of a Philadelphia publishing house, although all the printing and press-work were done in the College by students.

The immediate occasion of the establishment of a printing-press in connection with the College, was the desire of the President to engraft upon the usual college system a branch for the especial training of teachers for Academies and common schools. It has already been mentioned, that Dr. Junkin felt and manifested a lively interest in the system of general education then being inaugurated in Pennsylvania, and that he bore an efficient part in promoting it. From 1836 to 1840 there was much discussion of teaching, and its modes and appliances. The great want, universally felt, was that of competent teachers, who could be induced to make teaching a profession. The impossibility of retaining the services of competent teachers with the low compensation usually paid; the defects of school-houses and school apparatus; indeed, the entire subject of education, were extensively discussed, both on the rostrum and through the press. In these discussions, Dr. Junkin, in Pennsylvania, and his younger brother, in New Jersey, bore some part. But there was no medium of communication with the public, through which such discussions could be regularly and effectively carried on; and Dr. Junkin had for some time been pondering the propriety of attempting to supply this want by the establishment of an educational journal.

His determination to attempt it was rendered definitive by the arrival of a Scotch gentleman of mature scholarship, who desired to prosecute in this country the business which he had pursued in his own,—that of an educator. This gentleman, Professor William Cunningham, was a licensed preacher of the gospel, but had consecrated his powers to the important work of improving the modes of education.

About the time of his arrival in this country, the Chair of Languages in Lafayette College was vacant, and it was tendered to Mr. Cunningham. As it was his great aim to be a teacher of teachers, he was unwilling to accept such a Professorship as that offered, except with the ultimate expectation of being placed in connection with a Normal School for the training of teachers. Upon the subject of elevating the standard of common-school education, and improving the attainments and skill of teachers, Mr. Cunningham was an enthusiast. He had visited some of the most improved institutions of the Old World, and made himself familiar with the theories and the practice of teaching, and was seeking for an opportunity to make his knowledge available. In Dr. Junkin he met a brother enthusiast in his favorite field, and, for the sake of securing the services of so valuable an auxiliary, the President of the College determined to make Lafayette, if possible, a fountain whence streams should flow to refresh and fertilize the field of common-school education as well as that of other professions.

To accomplish this it was not difficult to get the necessary action on the part of the Board of Trustees. And when this was attained, two other means to the desired end were to be provided,—a Periodical to reach the public mind with healthy light upon the subject of education, and a *model school* in which teachers could be *trained* in the arts of teaching and pedagogics, whilst they were acquiring the requisite knowledge in the College classes. But the College had no funds to be used for such a purpose; and, with the hope of ultimate reimbursement for the model school, Dr. Junkin, with his private means, erected, upon the College grounds, the stone edifice still standing, the first story to be used as a Laboratory and chemical and philosophical Lecture-room, the upper story to be devoted to the purposes of a Normal School. This was the first institution of the kind in the Commonwealth, and, so far as known to the writer, the first in the country. During the erection and furnishing of the Normal School, Professor Cunningham occupied, with marked ability and efficiency, the Chair of Languages; the arrangement being that he should assume the superintendence of the normal institution when it was ready for pupils.

Meanwhile the press was bought, and "THE EDUCATOR" issued, in a bi-monthly folio, and it was filled with most valuable matter, not only upon the subject of education, but of general science and art. Mr. Cunningham was associated with Dr. Junkin in the editorship, and contributed very valuable matter for its columns, but the burden of details, and much of the editorial, rested upon Dr. Junkin. Nor did he, with these additional labors, abate anything of his toils in the regular routine or the extra demands of the College.

It was in the autumn of 1837, that Professor Cunningham came to Lafayette. Professor Kuhn had resigned and gone to Georgia, and Mr. Cunningham was elected in his place. The College was still growing in numbers and in public favor. The Legislature of the State was induced to extend aid to it and some others, on condition of their making certain provisions for the education of teachers; and there seemed, at one time, a fair prospect that the profession of teaching would be elevated to the position to which it is entitled beside the other learned professions, by the system proposed by Dr. Junkin, of connecting the training of teachers with the *curriculum* of Colleges. The partial failure of the scheme will be accounted for hereafter.

At the time of Prof. Cunningham's accession, the Faculty of the College consisted of the President; the Vice-President (Mr. C.) and Professor of Ancient Languages; Washington McCartney, Esq., Professor of Mathematics; Traill Green, M.D., Professor of Chemistry and Natural Philosophy; the Rev. Frederick Schmidt, Professor of Modern Languages; Hon. James M. Porter, Professor of Law; and the writer of these pages, Professor of the Belles-Lettres; all, except Mr. Cunningham, having occupied their places for some time previous. The President was Professor of Logic, Mental and Moral Science, Political Economy, and the Evidences of Christianity. Mr. McCartney had held the same position in Jefferson College,—and is the author of a valuable book on exact science. Dr. Green was a physician, then young, but of eminent scientific attainments; and he is still, after the lapse of thirty-five years, connected with the institution. Mr. Schmidt was a German, and a man of ripe scholarship and fine mind. Col. Porter was a man of marked ability, and was an eminent practitioner at the Bar. The Professor of Belles-

Lettres was Pastor of a neighboring congregation; and gave his services gratuitously, for the sake of helping on with the College enterprise.

Already had Lafayette College sent forth sons who have made their mark in the country and in the world, in the various learned Professions and in other lines of life; and had either the justice of the Legislature or the liberality of private individuals supplied the pecuniary means, that Institution would have much earlier assumed the position which she now occupies. As it was, the number of her students increased, her classes grew larger, and it was acknowledged that her *Alumni* compared very favorably in scholarship and mental maturity with those of other institutions. On one occasion, when the writer of this memoir was at Princeton, the venerable Dr. Alexander said to him, "Tell your brother that I congratulate him, and the members of his Faculty, upon the fine character and high scholarship of the students who have come from Lafayette to our Seminary." This, from a man who rarely paid compliments and was the very impersonation of sincerity, was no inconsiderable praise.

The disruption of the Presbyterian Church took place in May, 1838. Of that Assembly Dr. Junkin was not a member; and it is not necessary, upon these pages, to detail at large the incidents of that unpleasant scene. The Assembly met in the Seventh Presbyterian Church, the same one in which they had held the sessions of the previous year. The edifice of that church, sometimes called "The Tabernacle," stood near the centre of the square which is bounded on the north and south by Market and Chestnut Streets, and east and west by Fourth and Fifth Streets. It was reached by a narrow avenue called Ranstead Court, extending west from Fourth Street, to the church, and no farther. There was attached to the church at that time a small cemetery, densely filled with graves, and covered with tomb-stones. The edifice itself, the tomb-stones, and the bodies of the dead which they covered, have all disappeared; and the locality, so interesting in the history of the Presbyterian Church, would scarcely be recognized by the actors in the scenes which marked the Assemblies of 1834, 1837, and 1838.

The General Assembly of 1838 met in that place on the 17th of May, at 11 o'clock, and was opened with a sermon by the Rev. Dr. David Elliott, from Isaiah lx. 1, "Arise, shine," etc. After the sermon, the Moderator constituted the Assembly with prayer, and directed the Clerk to read the roll. The Rev. Wm. Patton, a commissioner from the Third Presbytery of New York, rose and asked leave to offer certain resolutions.

The Moderator declared the request to be out of order *at that time*, as the first business was the report of the Clerks on the roll. In narrating this decision of the Moderator, Mr. Gillett omits the important words "at this time" with what follows.

Dr. Patton appealed from this decision. The Moderator declared the appeal, for the reason already stated, to be out of order at that time; as there was no constituted Assembly to which the appeal could be made, it not being known who, of the crowded congregation, were members and who not members of the General Assembly. Dr. Patton stated that the resolutions related to the formation of the rolls, and began to read them; but, being called to order, took his seat.

The Clerks then reported the roll, and also the names of sundry commissioners whose credentials were incomplete. After this was done, the Moderator stated that the commissioners whose names had thus been reported were members of the Assembly; and that if there were any commissioners present, from Presbyteries in connection with the Assembly, whose names had not been enrolled, then was the time for presenting their commissions.

Dr. Erskine Mason rose, as he said, to offer a resolution "to complete the roll," by adding the names of certain commissioners who, he said, had presented their commissions to the Clerks, and had been by them refused. The Moderator inquired if they were from Presbyteries belonging to the Assembly at the close of the sessions of last year. Dr. Mason replied that they were from Presbyteries belonging to the Synods of Utica, Geneva, Genesee, and the Western Reserve. The Moderator stated that the resolution was out of order at that time.* Dr. Mason appealed from the decision of the Moderator; which appeal, also, the Moderator declared to be out of order, and repeated the call for commissioners in connection with the Assembly.

The Rev. Miles P. Squier, a member of the Presbytery of Geneva, then rose, and stated that he had a commission from the Presbytery of Geneva, which he had presented to the Clerks, who refused to receive it, and that he now offered it to the Assembly, and claimed his right to his seat. The Moderator inquired if that Presbytery belonged to the Synod of Geneva. Mr. Squier replied that it did. The Moderator then said, "Then we do not know you, sir," and declared the application out of order.

Mr. Cleveland then rose, and began to read a paper, the purport of which was not heard, when the Moderator called him to order. Mr. Cleveland, however, persisted in the reading, notwithstanding the repeated call to order. During the reading the Rev. Joshua Moore, from the Presbytery of Huntingdon, presented a commission, and was enrolled, and took his seat.

It was then moved to appoint a Committee of elections, to which informal commissioners might be referred. But

---

* See Digest, book iv. § 108.

the reading by Mr. Cleveland still continuing, and the Moderator having in vain again called to order, and taken his seat, and the residue of the Assembly remaining silent, the business was suspended during the short but painful scene of confusion and disorder which ensued. After which, the actors therein having left the house, the Assembly resumed its business.*

The account given of this same transaction, by Mr. Gillett, the New School historian, is as follows. After narrating the declaration of the Moderator to Mr. Squier, "We do not know you, sir," he says:

"Upon this Mr. John P. Cleveland, of the Presbytery of Detroit, rose, and, amid much interruption and many calls to order, proceeded to read a paper which he held in his hand. The contents of it were, substantially, that whereas the rights of certain commissioners have been violated, in their being refused their seats as members of the General Assembly, and the Moderator has refused to do his duty, it therefore becomes necessary to organize this General Assembly at this time, and in this place, in the most prompt manner, and with the least interruption practicable. To this they had been advised by counsel learned in the law, as a measure necessary to retain their rights in the Presbyterian Church.

"He then moved that Dr. Beman, Moderator of a previous Assembly,† take the chair till another Moderator should be chosen. The motion was carried by 'a very loud *aye*.' Dr. Beman took his station in the aisle of the church, and a motion was made that E. Mason and E. W. Gilbert be the clerks, which was agreed to. Dr. S. Fisher was, in like manner, elected Moderator. The questions were moved and taken both affirmatively and negatively, with but few negative voices. It was then moved that the Assembly, as thus constituted, adjourn to the First Presbyterian Church. This motion was carried.

"The members of the body then withdrew from the house. It was announced, in a loud voice, at the doors,

* Minutes, 1838, pp. 3-7.

† 1831.

and in the body of the house, that the Assembly had adjourned to the First Presbyterian (Mr. Barnes') Church."

Such, as described in a history published by authority of the New School Committee of Publication, was the tumultuous and unprecedented process by which these brethren sought to constitute themselves the General Assembly of the Presbyterian Church in the United States. The noise and confusion were such, that it was difficult for those not in the counsels of the actors therein fully to know what was going on. It might be interesting to put on record here, as descriptive of the scene, the testimony of some of the witnesses, given under oath, upon the trial in *Nisi Prius.* That of the venerable Samuel Miller, D.D., Professor in Princeton Seminary, will, however, be sufficient. After describing his presence and position in the church edifice, and stating that he was not a commissioner, he says:

"Mr. Cleveland rose, and held a paper in his hand, which he seemed to be attempting to read. There were cries of order. He began in a loud voice, but seemed to experience a great deal of difficulty in proceeding. The contents of the paper, so far as I heard them, were, that they had been advised by counsel learned in the law, that at that time and place they must organize a new body, and that they would proceed, in as few words, in as short a time, and with as little discourtesy as possible, to do so; and he moved that Dr. Beman take the chair. That is the amount of what I heard. Then there was a great deal of tumult, and disorder, and calls to order. What Mr. Cleveland said appeared to be by no means distinctly uttered. With the exception of a few calls to order, all the tumult was in that part of the house where Mr. Cleveland was. I heard no vocal utterance in other parts of the house, excepting the calls to order. The nays were not called for on either of Mr. Cleveland's motions. After moving, without reversing the question, that Dr. Beman should take the chair, he made, I think, a similar motion, also without reversing it, that Dr. Mason and Mr. Gilbert should be clerks. After these resolutions had passed, that is, after the ayes, which came principally from that part of the house, had been called for, Dr. Beman immediately stepped out into the aisle, and appeared to place himself in the situation of a presiding officer. The whole body of those engaged in these proceedings moved down the aisle, near the door opposite to the pulpit. I afterwards heard a confused murmur, but no distinct, articulate sounds; what words were spoken, or with what result, I am wholly unable to testify from my own knowledge. . . . The great body of the Old School occupied the part of the church where I stood. . . . I think I was standing in the midst of that body. I heard no vote from this part of the house. So far as I could see and hear, not a single man of the Old School, in the whole house, voted. I heard no negative votes on any of the motions. When the vote 'aye' was given, there was a character about it that convinced me that a number in the gallery had voted. These were sharp, shrill cries, which I could not believe came from considerate, dignified, and serious men. I took it for granted that they came from the gallery and from the boys about. This, however, was my own inference. There was a certain character about the ayes that I had been altogether unaccustomed to."

Rev. I. V. Brown, testifying to the same point, says:

"I think there were voices from the gallery, and voices that clearly manifested that they did not belong to members of the Assembly. They were shrill and squeaking, more like female voices, or, if not so, came from minor youth."

Several of the witnesses testify, that many of those who joined in the movement with Mr. Cleveland and Dr. Beman, were standing on the seats, and some on the backs of the pews; that the galleries responded, and that the whole process was one of indescribable confusion.

It was the Rev. Mr. Edward Beecher, of Jackson Seminary, according to the testimony of Samuel P. Wilson and Jerome Twitchell, who returned to the door, after the mass of the New School had retired, and repeated the announcement that the General Assembly had adjourned to the First Church; the same being proclaimed by another and more elderly person at another door.* And it is a noteworthy fact, as the testimony shows, that the most active and forward men in this odd ecclesiastical *coup de main* were men of New England origin, of Congregational prepossessions, and some of whom afterwards left the New School Body and returned whence they had come.

The persons who thus withdrew repaired to Mr. Barnes' church, and entered upon their mission as a separate branch of the Presbyterian Church.

The General Assembly, after the withdrawal, proceeded with its business, and from that time forth its counsels were marked by great harmony, and its enterprises prosecuted with an energy previously unknown.

The year intervening between the General Assembly of 1837 and that of 1838, was of course a year of preparation, especially on the part of the New School party. Conventions had ceased to be, in their estimation, such disorderly and unconstitutional gatherings, and they held no less than five during the year: one in Mr. Barnes' church, immediately after the adjournment of the Assembly of 1837; another, soon after, at New York; a third at Albany, N. Y., on the 17th of August; a fourth at Ann Arbor, Michigan, at the close of the same month; and a fifth in Mr. Barnes' church, Philadelphia, on the Monday evening (May 14) previous to the meeting of the Assembly of 1838.

At these, and especially at the latter, the programme which was carried out on the morning of the 17th was definitely settled upon, and the *dramatis personæ* selected. The Old School also held a convention, at the same time,

* Miller's Report of Church Case, pp. 173, 175, 177, 181.

in Ranstead Court. The former sent a deputation to the latter, proposing "to open a friendly correspondence, for the purpose of ascertaining if some constitutional terms of pacification might not be agreed upon." But as, in their communication, they assumed that the disowning acts were unconstitutional, and the Old School refused to admit that they were so, no understanding was reached. The results have been mentioned above.

The General Assembly was, of course, placed under the necessity of taking such measures as were called for by this new state of things, and they proceeded to do it with great calmness, deliberation, and wisdom. They first placed upon record, after calling the roll, the names of those commissioners who, having been enrolled, had gone off, and directed that they be reported to their several Presbyteries. They then appointed a Committee to report measures for the pacification of the church, the adjustment of all questions that might arise, and changes that might be required by the dismemberment.

This Committee, of which Dr. R. J. Breckenridge was the chairman, reported a voluminous paper, marked by great forecast and practical wisdom, prescribing methods for the details of separation, such as would secure adherence to the church of all really Presbyterian and congenial elements, and facilitate the withdrawal of such as could not be amicably and constitutionally retained. A long and well-considered pastoral letter was also proposed, and addressed to the churches, reciting the events that had occurred, and exhorting to the exercise of Christian wisdom and charity in the trying circumstances in which the church was now placed.

The carrying out of the acts of the Assembly, in the several Synods and Presbyteries, was attended with some practical difficulties, in those Synods especially in which there was an admixture of the two parties. In the Synod of New Jersey, of which Dr. Junkin was a member, there was some embarrassment in the enforcing of the Assembly's behests. A part of that Synod was New School, and yet the New Theology had not spread to such an extent as it had in other quarters. Many of the men who were decidedly with the New School in feeling and action, were considered sound and valuable men; and the "middle men" of the Synod, pretty numerous as they were, seem to have clung to the hope that, by treating the New School Presbyteries with forbearance, they might be induced to remain with the General Assembly. In this hope the decided Old School men did not share. They knew that conciliation would be thrown away, and that a failure to carry out the directions of the General Assembly would only lead to injurious complications, without any countervailing benefit. The Presbyteries of Montrose, Newark, and a few churches and pastors in other Presbyteries, expected and intended to go out; but they came to the Synod, were enrolled, and awaited the process of "excision." Their policy, as was supposed, was to *get put out*, and, if possible, in a way to secure to themselves the popular sympathy. A large portion of the Synod wished to avoid this process, and let them *go out* at their own convenience. Dr. Junkin was in favor of simple straightforward obedience to the directions of the Assembly; and when a set of resolutions of a delaying and, as he considered, a temporizing character were proposed, he opposed them earnestly. He considered them as nullifying the acts of the Assembly, and jeoparding the very existence of the Synod; and when they were passed, he withdrew from the body and went home.

The friends of these resolutions discovered, when too late, that Dr. Junkin was right in his prognostications; that, so far from being conciliated by these measures, the New School members both voted against them, and presented a protest against them, in which they entered into an argument to prove that the General Assembly to which this Synod adhered was not a "valid Assembly," nor the Synod itself, thus adhering to said Assembly, a "valid" Synod. The writer of this book had gone with the majority of the Synod (a small one) in adopting the conciliatory minute, differing from his brother upon this question; but was afterwards convinced that obedience to the supreme judicatory would have been the wiser course. It was a time of great perplexity and of much excitement, and good men did not know which policy was the best.

The results of the disruption of the church have been in part stated in a former chapter. A few additional effects of it may now, with propriety, be indicated, as illustrating the wonderful kindness of the Head of the Church in overruling present evils so as to make them productive of greater good, and as vindicating the course pursued in these agitations by the subject of this memoir, and those great and good men with whom he acted.

Doctrinal and ecclesiastical controversy, if not evil in itself, is apt to evolve serious evils by reason of the infirmities of the men who engage in it. Controversy is a necessary condition of the mission of the church of God in this world. That mission is essentially aggressive. The church, in the present state, is militant. Conquest is her aim,—the conquest of a world that is in a state of rebellion against God and His Christ. And until the last rebel is subdued, the controversy between light and darkness, holiness and sin, God and Satan, the church and her foes, must go on. In this warfare it is sadly, eminently true, as predicted by the Great Captain, that "a man's foes shall be they of his own household." It has been the misfortune and the sin of the Christian brotherhood that they will often "fall out by the way." Disputes arise about drill, and discipline, the weapons and the material of the warfare, and the best modes of using them; and hence the ranks are often thrown into disorder, and instead of battling with the common foe, they get into contention with one another.

The great instrument of conquest is "the sword of the Spirit, which is the word of God,"—TRUTH. No other weapon will avail to gain a single valuable victory. "Sanctify them through thy truth: thy *word* is *truth*." And just in proportion as *truth* is perverted or *amalgamated* with error, is the temper of the sword of the Spirit impaired, and its edge blunted. Knowing this, the Spirit of inspiration has commanded his ministers to "earnestly contend for the faith which was once delivered to the saints."* And if some of them are not contented with the faith thus once delivered, and think they can improve it, and make the effort, *upon them rests the responsibility of inaugurating controversy.*

Controversy between professed believers is an almost unmitigated evil; but the blame of it rests upon the errorist, not upon the defender of the faith. And yet the world is apt to reproach the defender of the faith, who resists the propagation of error, as the author of all the disturbance occasioned by religious controversy. It has not unfrequently occurred, in the history of the church, that the faithful men who stand for truth and purity, are traduced for their very faithfulness, whilst the errorists, whom they opposed, are the objects of public sympathy whilst they live, and the subjects of eulogy, and almost of apotheosis, when they die.

In the controversies that resulted in the sundering of the Presbyterian Church in 1838, there was no doubt much on both sides that was to be deplored. Ministers and elders are men of like passions with others, and it would not have

---

* Jude 3.

been reasonable to expect, nor would it now be historical truth to record, that there were no unhappy exhibitions of human temper and conduct in the progress of the conflict. There was much more than it is deemed necessary to record. The rules of manly and Christian contest were not always observed. Those who strove for the mastery did not always strive lawfully; and sometimes there were departures from magnanimity and fair dealing, which, no doubt, the men themselves lived to deplore. But in view of all that was wrong and humiliating, facts, already developed in the results of the struggle, warrant the belief that greater good, to both branches of the church, and now to the whole church reunited, has been brought out of these agitations, than probably would have been reached without them.

The opinion has already been expressed, and the facts adduced to support it, that doctrinal error, in the Presbyterian Church, had reached its *aphelion* at the termination of the Barnes trial; and that ever since, either by the force of conviction or the force of circumstances, there has been a gradual return towards the truth, until now, with a few eccentric exceptions, the church and her ministry move in the normal orbit. The Assembly that restored Mr. Barnes to the exercise of his ministry felt constrained, either by conviction or policy,—we decide not which,—to make a most explicit declaration of loyalty to the Standards. And even if we surmise that, with some of the leaders, it was a matter of policy, it would be uncharitable to suppose that this motive could pervade the whole body of the majority. The strong presumption is that the larger number of the New School brethren joined in that declaration sincerely, and felt bound, as candid men, to make it good in their future preaching and practice. And even the leaders would be restrained from language and conduct inconsistent with the declaration; for a contrary course would have shaken the confidence of their followers in their integrity. In truth, even those men felt that the declarations in which they had joined, held them to a more respectful treatment of the Confession and the Form of Government than they had been accustomed to render.

And after the disruption, and the formation of the "Constitutional" General Assembly, and particularly after the suit at Law was commenced, all the external circumstances of the New School body operated in a direction favorable to the Standards. A body claiming, *par excellence*, to be the "Constitutional General Assembly" of the Presbyterian Church, would feel especially called upon to treat the Constitution with respect, and to avoid all appearance of violating its provisions. A body claiming the control of the property of the Presbyterian Church, as the Assembly in legal succession, must be careful to respect the doctrine and order which the world knew that church had always maintained. And although it was not in all cases done, yet the necessities of their position created a tendency in a right direction. And when it is remembered, that the great mass of them were sound, good men, who had been led into the attitude which they occupied by the accident of position, the force of an amiable, if misplaced, sympathy, and by the shrewd management of adroit and able leaders, the return to "the old paths" will appear to have been inevitable. Besides, these circumstances which trammelled the energies of those who were desirous of revolutionizing the church, at the same time strengthened the hands of the large portion of the body which was really Presbyterian, and gave them the ascendency.

It is also undoubtedly true, that the agitating discussions of the doctrinal questions roused men's minds to fresh inquiry, stimulated thought and research, and led to a more thorough comparison of the system of doctrines laid down in the Standards with the Bible, and all this promoted the spread of sound principles, and the triumph of truth.

The discussion of constitutional questions of church order also led to a more thorough understanding and a higher appreciation of our admirable system of government. And when, at last, the force of that system was exhibited in the measures of reform, and a demonstration was made of the recuperative energy of Presbyterianism, the confidence of the sons of the church in her system of government was increased, whilst those who had taunted her with the charge of imbecility were forced to recall their sneers.

There can be no reasonable doubt, that what the storm does for the atmosphere the great struggle for truth and order did for the Presbyterian Church,—restored purity, health, and vigor. By that struggle, a tendency to doctrinal error, laxity in discipline, and extravagance in measures, was certainly arrested. And ever since the culminating moment both branches have been waxing stronger in the Lord. If there was "dead orthodoxy" in the Old School, the Spirit of God made use of the agitation to quicken it to life. If there was a disposition in the New School to charge the church's inefficiency upon her orthodoxy, and to adopt some modifications of sound doctrine, with a view to make truth more palatable to the carnal mind, in order to facilitate conversions, the danger and inexpediency of the experiment were exposed; and from the moment of the culmination of the struggle there was a palpable abandonment of the specious schemes, and a gradual return to that truth which only is the instrument of salvation.

It is on record that the New School branch, on all proper occasions, began to testify in favor of the Standards and the Constitution; and whilst they claimed a certain latitude of interpretation, and showed a disposition to tolerate sporadic cases of error, which the Old School did not, still there was a steady return towards the point of original divergence. It is on record, and in stereotype, that Dr. Beecher and Mr. Barnes modified their publications, so as to make them less objectionable to the orthodox. In regard to the latter it was plead in his behalf, at his trial before the General Assembly, that he had made these alterations; and although these changes did not meet the wishes of the Old School, still they made his publications less objectionable. And it is worthy of remark that, after the reunion, that distinguished writer considerately withdrew such of his doctrinal books as were published by the "Committee of Publication," so as to disembarrass the united Board of Publication in the readjustment of their catalogue.*

The WHOLE RESULT is that the two branches, whilst apart, probably made more effective aggressive progress than they would have done had they remained united,—certainly more than they would if they had continued together in a state of internal war. Sound Presbyterianism was revived, both as regards doctrine and order. A glorious Foreign Missionary enterprise was begun by the Old School. The New School, in the progress of events, were relieved of many disturbing and enfeebling elements by the sloughing off, or the assimilation, of Congregational material. By this process they became more thoroughly Presbyterian, and at the same time more homogeneous and effective as an ecclesiastical organization. And when the great Head of the Church had, by means of these

---

* Since the above was written, the following notice of the tenth edition of the NOTES ON ROMANS appeared in the *Presbyterian* of April 15, 1871:

"This book created at its first appearance an immense excitement, and helped forward the division of the Presbyterian Church. Its reappearance will not make a ripple on the surface. Mr. Barnes made a number of changes in the fifth edition, and rewrote some pages, withdrawing many words and phrases which had given offence. He left standing, however, many erroneous interpretations, and some which no change but entire abandonment would cure."

agitations, purged both branches, so as to fit them for bearing *more* and *better* fruit, He prepared the way, in His wondrous providence, for reingrafting both into the same old stock, to the praise of the glory of His grace. UNITY and PEACE in the TRUTH is the grand result!

And this was the END set forth by GEORGE JUNKIN, in his first letter to Mr. Barnes, proposing an amicable trial of the doctrinal issue. "The OBJECT is PEACE through union in the TRUTH!" Let the fair and candid philosopher of history decide, in view of all the recorded events, whether that "OBJECT" HAS BEEN GAINED. And whilst his biographer asks nothing for the subject of this memoir, except that *justice* which a consideration of his self-denying, faithful, and arduous services in the cause of truth and order demands, he cannot doubt that his memory will long live in the hearts of those who love the purity and peace of Zion.

"What hath God wrought!" A glorious UNION in the truth, upon the simple basis of our Standards, has been reached;—one of the most wonderful events in the history of the Church of Christ. Is the history of this union to be written, and the *causes* which rendered it *necessary* ignored? *Can* that history be fairly, truthfully written, whilst the *causes* which produced that homogeneousness in doctrine and order, which rendered a reunion possible and desirable, lie unnoticed and unexplained? Are *events* of any value upon the pages of history, if the agents and causes by which they were accomplished are either unmentioned or misrepresented?

Whilst, then, all the glory of the present happy condition of the Presbyterian Church in America is ascribed to the great Head of the Church, it would be wrong to withhold from the faithful and self-sacrificing men, who were instruments in working out these results, that grateful consideration to which their toils entitle them.

CHAPTER XXX.

College Labors—Lectures on the Prophecies—Discouragements in College Enterprise—Prof. Cunningham returns to Europe—Dr. Junkin elected President of Miami University—Accepts—Aids in obtaining a Successor at Lafayette—Departure from Easton—Enters upon Duty at Oxford—Peculiarities of the Position—Opposition—Inaugural Address and Ceremonies—Dr. Johns—Sectarian Jealousies and other Embarrassments—A Newspaper War—Progress.

AFTER the termination of the agitations in the Presbyterian Church, by the disruption of 1838, the labors of Dr. Junkin were chiefly bestowed upon the College, upon his editorial engagements, and upon some literary undertakings, to be mentioned in their proper place. He abated not his toils in preaching Christ. Not only in the regular service kept up in the College Hall, but in the pulpit of Dr. Gray, pastor of the Presbyterian Church of Easton, in other pulpits in that city, in the pulpit of Greenwich, N. J. (his brother's), and in many others, he was a frequent and a welcome visitor. For a considerable period he supplied the first-mentioned church, during the illness of its pastor, and he was ever ready to lend assistance to his brethren, and all these services were gratuitously rendered.

It was during the year 1839-40 that the course of lectures on the prophecies, afterwards published, were first delivered from the pulpit. The Rev. Dr. B. C. Wolff, of the German Reformed Church of Easton, being engaged in an effort to endow a literary institution connected with his own church, was much absent from home, and he invited Dr. Junkin to occupy his pulpit statedly during his absence. The lectures on the prophecies were delivered on the afternoons of Sabbaths in that church, the students of the College attending with the congregation. The large edifice was usually crowded; and the discourses produced a profound sensation. They were subsequently delivered at Miami University, and published, by request, in an octavo volume. The request for their publication came from the people, who had first heard them at Easton, and who desired to see them placed in a more enduring form. Books upon the prophecies, with scarce an exception, rarely go to a second edition. The very nature of the subjects treated in them unfits them for the mass of readers, and confines their circulation to the ranks of the learned and the curious. The edition of "Junkin on the Prophecies" was large, but was soon exhausted, and it is now out of print. But if those who possess the book will take the pains to examine its interpretations of the prophecies of Daniel and of John, they will be surprised at the accuracy with which events that have since transpired—some of them since the author's death—were indicated. With great modesty, yet with much confidence, he had fixed the dates of the downfall of the temporal power of the Papacy, and of the powers that upheld it, as he supposed them to be foretold; and EVENTS have literally VINDICATED his correctness.

Passages of the truest and most thrilling eloquence are found in these lectures; and, as a gentleman of high literary culture once remarked to the present writer, "There is no book known to me that contains, in such small compass, so perspicuous a diorama of universal history." It is also rich in thought, and a mine of suggestive ideas.

The College, notwithstanding its lack of endowment, increased in the number of its students, in its general efficiency, and in reputation. The Normal School for a time was successful, but did not ultimately realize the expectations of its founders. This was attributable chiefly to three causes:—First, the locality; being upon a lofty eminence overlooking the city of Easton, and difficult of access for such scholars as usually make up a common school. Second, the want of an endowment, by which gratuitous tuition could be offered to candidates for the office of teacher, such persons usually belonging to the impecunious classes. And third, the popular mind had not yet been educated up to that point which would encourage candidates for the profession of teacher to duly prepare themselves for it. Well-qualified teachers were not so much in demand as cheap teachers; and it is a law of production that supply will not go in advance of demand. The truth was, that Dr. Junkin and Prof. Cunningham were many years in advance of their times; and they did not possess the pecuniary ability to sustain the institution until public sentiment might overtake them. The Normal School edifice was completed in the summer of 1838, and the institution inaugurated as soon as it was ready. The publication of "*The Educator*" had been commenced shortly before. Both were continued until the summer of 1840, when Prof. Cunningham, becoming discouraged by the backward state of public sentiment in America upon the subject of education, resigned his position, and returned to Scotland. Dr. Junkin continued the effort to establish a Normal Institute in connection with the College until the time of his translation to the Presidency of Miami University. The period of that translation was now approaching.

The Miami University, at Oxford, Butler County, Ohio, had been established about 1823, in pursuance of a gift by the United States to the State of Ohio of a township of land in the fertile valley of the Miami, for the purpose of founding a literary institution. The venerable Dr. Robert H. Bishop, a native of Scotland, and a man of mature erudition, was inaugurated its first President, July 9, 1824. But, by reason of age and infirmity, he had resigned the situation in 1840; and the Board of Trustees had elected Dr. Junkin to the office in the winter of 1841. This tender was wholly unsought by him, and the question of accepting it occasioned him great perplexity. His *heart* was in Lafayette. There his toils, and tears, and prayers, and sacrifices had consecrated in his affections the entire institution, and even the locality itself. His fondest hopes were centred in its success. The very idea of abandoning it was painful in the extreme. For eight years he had struggled, amid appalling discouragements, to secure its establishment. A part of his private fortune was locked up in its edifices and appliances; and the institution had now attained such a position as to command public respect and confidence.

But the invitation from Miami University came to him at a time when, in addition to the difficulties of building up a college without adequate endowment, and without effective co-operation, embarrassments from an unexpected quarter had arisen. It would not be profitable to go into the details of a college difficulty, in which the general reader would feel little interest, and nothing more will be narrated than what is necessary to account for the fact, that a man of Dr. Junkin's energy and persistence should leave a field of labor to which he was so fondly devoted, in which he had been so successful, and which seemed to promise so hopefully for the future.

The gentlemen composing the Board of Trustees of the College were resident in different places, some at a distance from Easton, in Philadelphia, and other places. But in that town there were so many of the trustees resident as to constitute usually a majority of all in attendance at any one time. Of these, none had ever enjoyed the advantages of a college education, and few of them had any practical knowledge of the working of such an institution. Indeed, there were but a few of them that took any decided interest in the College. These were energetic friends of the institution, so far as personal influence was concerned, although none had made any large pecuniary advances. In a body of men such as composed this Board, it could not be expected that proper ideas of college discipline would prevail; and it so happened, that a student, a near relative of two or three members of the Board who had previously been very active and efficient friends of the College, became a subject of discipline by the Faculty. He had gotten into a personal encounter with another student in the refectory, and had used a knife, slightly wounding his antagonist. The matter was investigated by the Faculty, and the offender was temporarily suspended from College privileges, until he should make suitable expressions of regret for his conduct. This, it was understood, he was inclined to do, under the advice of an older brother, also a student, and judicious and thoughtful beyond his years. But parties outside of the College interposed, and the result was, that the influential relatives of the censured student, instead of advising him to submit to the mild sentence of the College authorities, counselled a contrary course, and a serious spirit of opposition to the Faculty was awakened in these prominent members of the Board.

This feeling of resentment was carried so far, by the friends of the recusant student, that pupils on their way to Lafayette were dissuaded from coming, by their influence, and persuaded to go elsewhere. By the same influence, such a construction was put upon a law of the State, by which an annual sum had been appropriated to the use of the College, that this appropriation was withheld from the current expenses of the Institution, to which it had previously been given. These, and other efforts of a hostile character, added to the previous pecuniary difficulties with which he had been struggling, so discouraged the President, that he came reluctantly to the conclusion, that it was his duty to resign to other hands the enterprise which he had sustained through so many years of toil and trial. It is due to the President to say, in this connection, that whilst in the Faculty he advised the mildest sentence, at all consistent with discipline, yet, when the decision of the Faculty was made, he sustained and carried it out with his accustomed quiet firmness.

But although he had made up his mind to tear himself away from his "lovely Lafayette," his interest in her flagged not for a moment. It was his wish that, if possible before he left, a successor should be obtained. Several names were suggested to the Board of Trustees, and, among others, those of the Rev. Dr. James W. Alexander, at that time connected with the College of New Jersey, and the Rev. John W. Yeomans, then of Trenton, N. J. It was agreed that Dr. Junkin should repair first to Princeton, to see Dr. Alexander, and, if he was found not available, then to Trenton, to confer with Mr. Yeomans. This he did; and the writer well remembers, that upon a bleak and stormy winter day, his indefatigable brother stopped at the Manse of Greenwich, on his way to Princeton, in his own private conveyance, over impracticable roads, upon this disinterested mission for the College.

Dr. Alexander peremptorily declined, from considerations of health and other reasons, to entertain the proposal to become head of the College; and from Princeton Dr. Junkin repaired to Trenton, where he labored to show to Mr. Yeomans that Lafayette College offered a fine field of usefulness for a gentleman of culture and energy. His mission to Trenton was more successful; for although Mr. Yeomans gave no pledge of acceptance, he consented to take the matter into consideration.

The result was, that Mr. (afterwards Dr.) Yeomans was chosen President of the College, made a visit of inquiry and observation to Easton, and ultimately became President; so that there was no embarrassing hiatus between the departure of Dr. Junkin and the arrival of his successor.

Meanwhile, and indeed previous to his going to Princeton and Trenton, Dr. Junkin had visited Miami University, with a view to decide the question of accepting its Presidency, and the visit resulted in an affirmative decision.

It was the 30th of March, 1841, when, with his family, he departed from Easton for his future field of labor in the Valley of Miami. At that time there was no railroad connection between Easton and Philadelphia, and a recent storm and high waters had made the ordinary connection, by stage-coaches, impracticable. Both the Delaware and the Lehigh were swollen beyond their banks, and on a Monday morning a small fleet of "Durham boats" was about to depart for Philadelphia, one of which had been comfortably fitted up for the accommodation of Dr. Junkin's family, and perhaps a few others that availed themselves of that novel mode of transportation. The boats were to depart at an early hour, in order to reach the city with daylight. His farewell discourse had been delivered the preceding Sabbath to tearful crowds;* but, anxious to

---

* We find, among Dr. Junkin's papers, in the handwriting of the late Rev. John Gray, D.D., the following Ode, written by the gifted wife of the latter, Mrs. Gray, and sung by the choir of the Presbyterian Church, Easton, at the close of Dr. Junkin's farewell sermon. The latter knew nothing of it until they began to sing:

PARTING HYMN.

1. Brother, go, the Master calls thee
   Other duties to fulfil;
Well we know, whate'er befalls thee,
   'Tis thy joy to do *His* will.

take a last look of the man and the family that had won such a deep place in their affections, a large concourse of the citizens, male and female, old and young, thronged the north bank of the Lehigh,* where the boat lay, to greet with a sorrowful farewell the man whose departure from their midst was felt to be a public loss. The morning had been cloudy and threatened rain; but that did not deter the people from thronging to the shore. After a few words of farewell, addressed by a gentleman present to Dr. Junkin and his

---

Hark! He calls thee;
Go, obey thy Master's will!

2. Shall we from this sacred altar,
Hear no more thy warning voice,
Making sternest sinners falter,
Bidding feeblest saints rejoice?
Shall we never
Hear again thy warning voice?

3. O! may all that thou hast taught us,
Sink each melting heart within;
How the gracious Saviour sought us,
Rescued us from death and sin!
May thy lessons
Sink each melting heart within!

4. Go! may Jesus guide thy going,
May He be where'er thou art;
May His love, forever flowing,
Cheer, refresh, and warm thy heart!
May His presence
Never from thy soul depart!

5. And where no farewell is spoken,
Where no tear the cheek shall stain,
Where we give no parting token,
There shall Christians meet again!
Yes, in heaven,
Saviour, let us meet again!

* The Delaware was so swollen that the high dam of the Lehigh was submerged.

family after they were seated in the boat, the Doctor responded in a short speech marked by much feeling, and bade farewell. The boat pushed off, and was soon carried by the rapid current out of sight, whilst the silent and, in not a few cases, the sobbing crowd, waved adieu. Just then the sun broke brightly through the clouds, and a pleasant day was vouchsafed to the voyagers. This demonstration of the popular feeling was entirely *impromptu*. There was no pre-arrangement, no concert. Everybody seemed surprised to see everybody there; and none were more taken by surprise than the travellers themselves. It was a spontaneous throb of the popular heart; and, as the people withdrew to their homes in silent sadness, all seemed to feel that they had lost a friend.

Dr. Junkin entered upon his duties as President of Miami University on the 12th of April, 1841, and the 11th of August following was appointed for his formal inauguration. Upon his suggestion, Prof. James C. Moffat, who had occupied the Chair of Languages in Lafayette College, was elected to the Professorship of Latin in the University; to which was soon after added the Professorship of History. Mr. Moffat accompanied Dr. Junkin to Oxford, where he remained some ten years. He was then called first to Princeton College, and afterwards (1861) elected to a chair in the Theological Seminary at that place. He is one of the ripest scholars of our country.

The University is a State institution; that is, it is under the control of the Legislature of the State of Ohio, so far as that the Legislature appoints the trustees who manage it. When the University was at first organized, a Presbyterian clergyman was appointed president, and most of the professors were of the same denomination. Indeed, at that time, no other religious society in the West could supply men of the requisite scholarship in sufficient numbers to man the colleges, and the Presbyterians were the people who exerted the broadest influence in the West, especially in the matter of education. In this remark it is designed to include all the several bodies that adopted the Presbyterian Form of Government.

But, about the time Dr. Bishop resigned, and Dr. Junkin was chosen President, other denominations of Christians had risen to importance in the Commonwealth of Ohio, both in point of numbers, and social and political influence; and some degree of jealousy had begun to manifest itself among them, that the Presbyterians should control the two State Universities, at Oxford and at Athens. Besides this, the Presbyterians were now divided into Old and New School, and, whilst the former predominated in the region of which Miami University was the literary centre, the latter possessed very considerable influence.

It was not to be expected, that the fact that the new President of the University had been prominent in the recent ecclesiastical conflict would be forgotten, nor that his appointment should meet their cordial approval. Nor was it to be supposed, that the sects which stand arrayed against the Calvinistic creed would relish the advent of a Calvinist so pronounced as Dr. Junkin was known to be. Whilst, therefore, he was welcomed by most of the Old School Presbyterians, by the Associate Reformed, the Associate and the Reformed Presbyterians, by the Episcopalians, and by considerate and unimpassioned men of all parties who desired to see the University well conducted, irrespective of sectarian prejudices, there were some who accepted the new régime with less cordiality.

The former President remained a member of the faculty, being appointed to a chair that did not require much toil; and probably some of his friends and former pupils would have preferred to have had him retained at the head of the institution; and, no doubt, the presence of his venerable predecessor in the faculty, demanded of the new head of the institution peculiar watchfulness, in order to treat him with due consideration. In this, it is conceded, he was successful; and yet there was sometimes evidence that, in regard to this matter, he was narrowly watched.

Dr. Junkin was distinctly given to understand by the Committee which informed him of his election, that one consideration, among others, which led the Board to select him as President, was their desire to have a firmer and more healthful *discipline* inaugurated in the College than had for some time been maintained; that his reputation as a skilful and firm disciplinarian had no little weight in determining their choice, and he would be expected to restore discipline *at all hazards*.

All persons familiar with college government, and especially as administered over American youth, will readily understand what a delicate and difficult task was imposed upon the new President by this requirement. A stranger, coming from a remote part of the land, the successor of a kindly and lenient officer, whose very leniency made him beloved by youth, and entering upon his duties in the face of no small amount of prejudice, from causes already indicated, the work before Dr. Junkin was peculiarly difficult, and required unusual caution, tact, wisdom, and firmness. But he met these difficulties with a calmness, a courage, and a disposition that were equal to the exigency. The struggle was ardent on the part of the opponents of order,—almost fierce; but order ultimately triumphed. Several students were expelled within the first months of his administration, others were more quietly sent home, and order, discipline, and study were restored. This result could not, of course, be reached without displeasing, not only the families and friends of the subjects of discipline, but also their sympathizers in the College. No heart felt keener sorrow at the necessity that was laid upon the faculty than that of the President. Nor was he insensible to the animadversions made upon the conduct of the college government; but he endured it all with quiet patience, and quailed not for one moment before the storm of opposition.

An incident that gave Dr. Junkin's friends, and kindred at a distance, great distress for a while, will illustrate the spirit that animated some of the unruly elements over which he presided. One morning, during the first year of his presidency, there appeared in the *United States Gazette*, a leading daily paper of Philadelphia, a letter, dated Oxford, Ohio, and addressed to the Hon. Joseph R. Chandler, editor of the *Gazette*, stating that the writer was sorry to inform him that the Rev. Dr. Junkin, President of Miami University, had died, after a short illness, that day, at his residence in Oxford, and expressing regret at the loss the public had sustained. The letter was duly signed, and seemed to bear evidence of genuineness. On account of the fact that Mr. Chandler was known to be very cautious in publishing information from unknown correspondents, no one suspected that it was a wicked and cruel canard, perpetrated, probably, by some mischievous and heartless student.

At that day there were no telegraphs, and no rapid railroad mails; and before the truth could be known, Dr. Junkin's kindred and friends had mourned him as dead for a week,—some of them longer. The newspapers spread the tidings, accompanied, in many cases, by eulogies of the supposed departed. Prayers were offered in the churches for the bereaved family; and in two cases, at least, funeral sermons were prepared by eminent clergymen, who had been his life-long and intimate friends. But before any sermon was delivered, it is believed, the truth of the story was doubted, and in due time its falsehood was ascertained.

It was a most cruel and distressing infliction of sorrow upon the friends of Dr. Junkin; and yet it accomplished an object which the writer of the letter did not contemplate. It called forth so general and hearty an expression of love and veneration for his memory as few men have lived to read of themselves. It evoked a premature record of his posthumous fame, which was of such a character as did the living man and his friends no injury.

The Rev. Dr. T. L. Cuyler informed the writer that a short time after the reported death of Dr. Junkin, he (Mr. Cuyler), whilst travelling in Europe, met a gentleman in a boat on one of the beautiful little lakes of the North of England. A mutual introduction having disclosed the fact that Mr. Cuyler was from America, his fellow-voyager became sad, and remarked, "Meeting a gentleman from America recalls the very sad tidings that have just reached me through the public journals." "May I ask to what you allude?" "It is the death of a very dear and highly-esteemed friend, with whom I was intimately associated whilst I resided in the United States, —the Rev. Dr. Junkin." "I am happy to assure you," said Mr. Cuyler, "that your friend still lives, and was well when I left America. The report of his death was a foolish and wicked canard." Mr. Cuyler added that he had rarely witnessed so rapid a transition from sorrow to joy as this stranger exhibited; the whole scene proving the deep affection and regard which he entertained for Dr. Junkin, whom he had mourned as dead. The stranger was Professor Wm. Cunningham.

On the day appointed for his inauguration (August 11), the ceremonies pertaining thereto were performed in the presence of a vast concourse of people. Prayer was offered by the Rev. J. C. Barnes; an address was delivered by the Rev. Dr. H. V. D. Johns, of Cincinnati, of the Protestant Episcopal Church; the keys of the University were delivered, the charge given, and the oath of office administered by Col. John Johnston. The President then pronounced his inaugural address, the theme of which was, "THE ORIGIN, UNITY, AND POWER OF MORAL LAW."

Dr. Johns' address was an able one, upon the subject of "Obedience to duly constituted authority a primary obligation of American citizenship." He urged in eloquent diction the duty and necessity of such obedience, pointed out the dangers which threatened our free institutions from the rapid increase of lawlessness; traced that increase to its sources, in the laxity of family, school, and college government, and earnestly called upon all friends of liberty and law to rally to the effort of arresting the evil by staunching its source.

Dr. Junkin's address was a vigorous and unique evolution of his subject, and an application of its principles to the interests of government among men, of college government, and of regulated liberty. All moral law originates in the will of God,—that will, when known, becomes the rule of moral action,—it is *one* and *uniform* in its requirements, not multifarious nor variant, and when obeyed as a rule of life, the energy of its operation transcends all other created power.

It would be impracticable to transfer to these pages any considerable part of this, or of any others of his very numerous public addresses. If we should attempt selections, we would scarcely have completed the transcription before we would feel that we ought to have chosen others. To give the reader some idea of the sprightliness which his genius imparted even to dry subjects, we take, almost at random, a short extract or two from this inaugural address. After demonstrating that God is the ORIGIN of moral law, and his WILL, made known, the RULE, he proceeds to show that the UNITY of moral law consists, not in the fact that it is alike clearly made known to all men, but in the fact that actual compliance with the will of God secures happiness; failure to comply, imposes misery:

"Upright action—action according to the will of God, and because it is the will of God—is uniformly connected with enjoyment and life; and the contrary leads to death and woe. This is the essential nature of moral law. It holds out rewards and punishments, and without these, it would not be law at all; it would be mere advice. Here is the fundamental principle of all morality. Here is the original conception, without which no man has any definite notion of duty or of sin, of law or of government. Here is the central point of the moral universe, where stands Jehovah's throne, and whence radiate all the forces which sustain and regulate the movements of created intelligences.

"Such is the grand principle of unity in morals. It is of little concern what external things constitute the test of obedience to man or angel,—whether it be one or one thousand acts,—whether the moral agent have laid upon him one or one thousand requisitions,—whether a man's knowledge of his Maker's will be limited to a few things or extended to many things,—whether the moral agent be a man or an angel,—whether Lazarus or Gabriel,—the question submitted is, whether he will comply with *that* will of God which is made known to *him*. The extent of his knowledge may and must affect the *degree* of his reward or his punishment, as the case may be; but the *character* of his account and final destiny is determined simply by his obedience to the will of God or his refusal to obey. This *one principle* pervades all intelligent creatures of which we have any knowledge. In the regions of celestial light, obedience to the will of God secures, increases, and perpetuates the felicities of the blessed. In the world of woe, disobedience to the will of God aggravates, increases, and perpetuates the wretchedness of the lost. . . . Here is the one all-pervading principle of moral law, the grandeur of whose simplicity thrills the bosoms of angelic hosts, while it prostrates in profound reverence the consciences of men on earth, and flashes upon the realms of darkness and of death that terrific thunderbolt of Heaven's vengeance,—'YE KNEW THE WILL OF GOD, BUT DID IT NOT!'"

After discoursing of the POWER of moral law, he thus asserts the *amplitude of its range:*

"This I have said is co-extensive with the moral universe. There is not a rational intelligence in heaven, earth, or hell beyond its reach. . . . It covers our world. It places the autocrat and the beggar alike under its commanding requisitions. . . . It repudiates the idea that there is one code of morals for the rich and another for the poor; one for the private citizen and another for the public functionary; one for the farmer, another for the artisan, another for the merchant, and still another for the professional man. On the contrary, this mighty principle of morality —THE WILL OF GOD MUST BE OBEYED—ascends the throne and the presidential chair; it pervades the halls of legislation, and demands that laws and their executors be in subordination to the will of God. The husband and the wife, the parent and the child, the master and the servant, the living, the dying, and the dead, all are equally amenable to the will of God. It descends with the miner to the bowels of the mountains; it ascends with the aeronaut above the clouds; its power is felt in the peaceful cottage, by the tempest-tossed mariner at the mast-head; it rules in the civic procession, and the storm of battle is subject to its control. The Greenlander, in his snow-built hut, bows to the will of God; the European, in his marble mansion, bows to the will of God; the African, on his parched sands, bows to the will of God. Lo! the amplitude of its range!—it girdles the globe, and binds it to the footstool of its Maker's throne!"

Another brief extract is added, not only because it contains a strong statement of a great truth, but because it discloses what those who knew its author believed to be the *very soul* of his own actions, and the power that sustained him through a life of trial and of toil:

"Let us advert for a moment to the *energy of its operation.* This is seen first in the easy resolution of doubtful questions in morality. We have only to inquire what is the will of God in this? *That settled*, the path of duty is plain, and then

"We have the spirit of *unbending integrity.* He, in whose soul this principle is settled, knows nothing but the will of God, and this can never lead him astray into the wayward paths of folly and of crime; and thus

"We have the spirit of *true heroism.* The energy of this divine rule lifts him above the fear of all created things. The fear of God is the all-absorbing affection of his soul, and he knows no other fear. Obstacles apparently insurmountable may stand before him, and obstruct his path of duty, but onward he presses in the face of them all. Tell him 'there's a lion in the way, you'll be devoured;' be there a hundred lions in the way, that is the way which by the will of God I am bound to go. He'll take care of the lions. 'But if you hold on to these principles of yours you will suffer loss of goods, and be reproached, and scourged, and burned.' Let them confiscate my goods, and reproach, and scourge, and burn me, if God give them power; I am not accountable for these consequences; I am responsible only for this,—THAT I OBEY THE WILL OF GOD."

Into the performance of the duties of his office in the University, Dr. Junkin threw all the energies of his earnest nature. Few men of his generation, more thoroughly met the requirement of the Scripture maxim, "Whatsoever thy hand findeth to do, do it with thy *might.*" He had a difficult and delicate task to perform, and one that called for a peculiar phase of self-denial. But he shrunk not from doing it faithfully.

It would have been much more pleasant to flesh and blood, and much more in accord with the aspirations of a natural ambition, to have adapted the administration of the Institution, and the standard of its scholarship, to the popular but unhealthy public sentiment that prevailed at that time in the West, and thus to have attracted *great numbers* to the college classes. A lax, accommodating discipline, and a low standard of scholarship, would have done this; for neither rigid rules nor hard study are apt to be popular with American youth. A short cut through college, and early entrance upon active life, were demanded by the utilitarian sentiment of the times, and parental stinginess too often backed the claim. To weed out the disorderly and the indolent students, and thus to reduce instead of increase the College rolls, was not a pleasant process; but it was the one prescribed by the Board of Trustees, and it was in accord with the President's habits and high sense of right. Even when the whole pecuniary responsibility of a College had rested upon him, and he was dependent upon tuition fees for paying the salaries of professors, he maintained the discipline and the high standard of scholarship; and, as he had accepted of the Presidency of the University when he knew that a similar administration would be expected of him, he was not the man to sacrifice the prospective and permanent interests of the Institution to a desire for temporary popularity, and the retention or attraction of numbers. The consequence was that the number of students decreased for a time. This fact was made the basis of newspaper attacks, in which the President himself was assailed, and the control of the denomination to which he belonged over the instructions of the Institution was complained of. This newspaper war about the University was quite voluminous, and sometimes personal and acrimonious. Most of the papers containing it, papers published in Cincinnati, Dayton, Rossville, Xenia, Maysville, Ky., and other places, are in possession of the writer; but, as it was one of those local and many-sided controversies in which the writers sometimes exhibited a temper and used a style that the same men would probably deplore when the heat of the conflict was over, and as the storm appeared to spend itself by its own violence, it does not seem to be demanded by any great interest, past or present, that the details of it should here be given. It has been alluded to only as an incident of a trying character in the life of Dr. Junkin, and in the further mention of it no reflections shall be made upon the actors in those scenes, most of whom have gone from the conflicts of earth.

To record the fact that Dr. Junkin was President of Miami University for a number of years, and to make no mention of the commotion excited by his election and administration, would be to ignore very important links in the chain of his history. Whilst to enter into the details of a newspaper controversy, of which he and the Institution over which he presided were the subjects, would be to revive issues that are past or dead, and open wounds which time's soft hand has closed, and would demand a record which might grieve the living and needlessly reflect upon some who are dead.

Suffice it to say that the new President had scarcely been inaugurated when his qualifications for the place began to be assailed, and a general onslaught was made upon the Board for calling him, and upon his person and administration. The charge of unfitness for the place was not based upon any defect either of talents, scholarship, moral integrity, aptness to teach, or other attributes usually required in the principal of a college. Indeed, the objections urged would not prove him unfit to be at the head of *a* University, but only of *that* University in particular. It was a *State* institution. Every citizen had an equal right in it. No one Christian sect ought to have a dominant control over its instructions. It ought to be kept entirely free from sectarianism; and, as Dr. Junkin was so pronounced a Calvinist, it was supposed that he was unfit for the place, because it would be impossible for such a man to abstain from inculcating his own peculiar views. Some of the professors, too, had been appointed, it was alleged, by his recommendation, and it was presumed that they were men of like cast with himself. In addition to all, he was a rigid disciplinarian, a man of reserved and abstracted manner, and personally objectionable to one branch of his own denomination (the New School), who, although not numerous in that part of Ohio, were a considerable body in the State. The Church of God (Campbellites) disliked his opinions; the Universalists thought him too sectarian and pronounced upon the subject of future punishment; and whilst the Methodists were very moderate in their animadversions, their organ was still of opinion that students of their church could hardly have fair play under a professor of mental and moral science, who, in his theological writings, was so strongly against the Arminian system.

This last-named denomination had grown strong in the West, and had begun to bestow more attention upon education than in the earlier periods of their history. About the time of Dr. Junkin's advent to Miami, they had taken order upon the subject in their Conference, and had adopted a very able report. This report alluded to the fact, that the State Universities of the West were too much under Presbyterian control, but took no very decided ground. In the controversy which we are now describing, the *Western Christian Advocate*, the Cincinnati organ of that church, very moderately and in good temper, but still decidedly, bore a part. It pointed to the fact, that both the Ohio Universities, and the State College of Indiana, at Bloomington, were under Presbyterian control, and complained of this as an inequality. In their paper published on the 20th of January, 1843, in reply to an article from the pen of Dr. Macdill, of the Associate Reformed Church, the editors say:

"When we spoke of the *control*, which Methodists claimed in the Ohio Universities, we neither said, meant, nor hinted at any other or different control than such as is now used by the Presbyterians. . . . As far as we have yet seen, we have no counter-information to rebut the charge that the President of Miami University interferes with the religious creed and privileges of Methodist students; if, however, we have been misinformed, we will gladly correct the mistake, whenever we have adequate rebutting testimony. We still say that Miami University is no place for Methodist students who desire to enjoy their religious privileges.* . . . We still advise them, if only for the sake of peace, to go elsewhere."

In another part of the same article they say, in regard to Indiana University:

"Mr. Wylie refused to have a Methodist professor in Indiana State College. . . . It is just like some of the former acts of the Trustees of Miami University. To refuse the appointment in consequence of the name *Wesleyan*, argues much more narrow sectarianism than what appears on the part of those who desired that name. . . . We still affirm that the Methodists of Ohio *will* have something to do with the State Universities."

There were some grounds for the claim of our Methodist brethren to have a share in one or other of the Universities of the State. No candid mind can blame them for the wish, nor for the efforts which they made, with ultimate success, to obtain control; but they were certainly unjust to Dr. Junkin, in charging him with interfering, in his official capacity, with the rights of Methodist students. No doubt, in his many ministrations of the gospel in the churches of Oxford, Cincinnati, and other places where he preached, he would occasionally state his distinctive views of gospel truth; but he never obtruded these views upon the students.

But there were various dissatisfied parties, not of the Methodist denomination, who took advantage of these allegations, and raised a clamor. Of these, some had ecclesiastical recollections of an unpleasant kind; others were disobliged at the time the new President was elected; others

* After the publication of the above, a certificate was voluntarily given, signed, it is believed, by all of the Methodist students in the College, correcting this statement very explicitly.

did not approve of the change in the discipline; and others, still, differed in opinion with him upon questions of public polity which agitated the country at that time. Some assailed the institution and its head from one stand-point, and some from another. He had many strong and able defenders, too, who no doubt said sharp things, which provoked acrimonious retort; and it can with truth be said, that rarely has a public man passed through such a fiery and stormy ordeal. He took no personal part in the controversy, until a formal accusation had been made before the Board of Trustees, when he published a statement over his own signature in his own defence. The Board of Trustees, in response to the formal accusation, which came from some of the *Alumni*, passed the following:

"*Resolved*, That after as careful an investigation of this subject as it is in their power at present to make, the Board are of opinion, that there is no evidence yet presented on which to ground any serious charge of incompetency or unfitness in the President of this institution to fill this office."

It was after this that Dr. Junkin published the defence above alluded to, which was towards the close of his administration, and not long before his recall to Lafayette College.

Previous to this date, however, other incidents in his history occurred, which no doubt imparted intensity to the spirit and the exertions of his opponents. These we go back to narrate; but, before doing this, the writer will offer a remark or two in regard to the most unprecedented treatment which President Junkin received whilst in Ohio. It was a persecution conducted with intense vehemence, on the part of a few, whilst it was magnanimously resisted by many others, upon whom Dr. Junkin had no claims, except those which a just man, misunderstood and misrepresented, has upon the adherents of righteousness and fair dealing.

Whilst it really was a PERSECUTION, so conducted as to mar the comfort and usefulness of its object, and to greatly wound the hearts of his family, it can be accounted for, and that truthfully, as the writer supposes, without assuming that *all*, or even *many*, of those who joined in it, directly or remotely, were actuated by a persecuting or a malignant spirit. No doubt a few were prompted by feelings of personal resentment, especially the subjects of discipline and their friends. But it is probable, that much of the opposition proceeded from motives such as were natural for the parties to feel, and which, *in them*, were not blameworthy.

This may seem to be a strange admission to be made by one who had absolute confidence in the purity, the integrity, the piety, the learning, the intellectual power, the aptness to teach, and the governing ability of Dr. Junkin. Pre-eminent as he was in all these, he was *not qualified*, in the writer's judgment, to be the President of Miami University, *at the time* he was called to that office. The reasons for this opinion are—

(*a*.) It was a State college, under control of the civil government of Ohio, and, of course, all the Christian sects felt that they had equal rights to its privileges. This feeling had found public utterance before his accession, and continued to grow afterwards.

(*b*.) In such a state of things, no man of pronounced opinions, synthetical habits of thought and speech, and incapable of disguising his sentiments, could have met the growing demand of the public for absolute *neutrality* in doctrinal opinion. No matter what he might be, Calvinist, Arminian, Pelagian, Socinian, or Infidel, the jealousy which was rife at the time would have *suspected* him of obtruding his views, and would have charged him with so doing.

(*c.*) Dr. Junkin was wholly disqualified for a position which demanded *temporizing;* and whilst it is believed that, in the class-room and in his preachings to the students, he was very careful to abstain from disputed points, yet in his ministrations and labors outside of the College, he did not disguise his convictions of truth; and it was very natural for those who heard him, in pulpits near to or distant from the University, to *suspect* that he would carry his opinions into the College.

(*d.*) Dr. Junkin brought with him to Ohio a reputation of being a very thorough Calvinist of the Old School. He had taken part in a great and recent ecclesiastical struggle. The bitterness of that conflict was hardly allayed. He was known, too, to be decidedly conservative upon other questions of exciting interest; and it was very natural that all men of opposite opinions should be reluctant to have such a man in so important a position. Hence men, who greatly differed among themselves in many points, made common cause against him. Had he been a man of inferior intellectual power, less pronounced opinions, and more negative character and disposition, he doubtless would have been less obnoxious.

(*e.*) His long habit of trusting his good name in the hands of his Master, and his distaste for, and, indeed, lack of skill in, self-vindication, made him comparatively helpless in such a war as was waged upon his administration; and for such a position as the presidency of a State college the man is disqualified who has no aptitude either to employ the arts for gaining popularity, or for adroit defence when assailed. In these Dr. Junkin had no experience or skill. His character was too transparent, his temper too frank, his manner too abstracted, his disposition too unsuspicious, and his conduct too undisguised, to qualify him for a post in which everybody was to be pleased, and men of all opinions conciliated. *He was not fit for the place,* especially *at that time,* when prejudice was rife, and when the cauldron of conflicting opinions was already boiling.

All this can be said without abating our high estimate of his character and abilities, and without assuming that *all* those who doubted his qualifications for the position acted insincerely or with malice. The difficulty lay in the *times,* and in the essential viciousness of a system of college education controlled by civil authority, and in which the jealousy and the conflict of sects demand the emasculation of education by the repression of all distinctive morality and religious truth.

This singular conflict which we have described, did not interfere with the regular operations of the University. The Faculty was united, able, and industrious. Good order, as a general thing, was preserved among the students. The agitation had rather increased than diminished public confidence in the faculty and its chief. A distinguished gentleman from Xenia, who had been in attendance at the Commencement in August, 1844, the last one at which Dr. Junkin presided, wrote for the *Torchlight* of that town an account of the College, from which the following extracts are made:

"The Annual Commencement of this noble State institution came off on Wednesday and Thursday, the 7th and 8th inst. Having been present through all the exercises, permit me, Mr. Editor, to express the high gratification which I experienced. . . . The graduating class . . . acquitted themselves with much credit, both to themselves and their teachers. As I have no connection whatever with the University, nor any interest in it, except that which belongs to the whole community, I feel an entire freedom in expressing my opinions, unrestrained either by fear or favor. And my deliberate conviction is that the Institution, if suffered to prosecute its operations free from the restless and revolutionizing spirit of our day, will prove a rich blessing to our State and country.

"The University has been industriously represented as having 'fallen from its high estate,' and as having all its energies utterly prostrated. It may be true that it does not flourish to the extent (in point of numbers) that all right-hearted men could wish. But it might be a curious problem how much of this alleged prostration has been owing to *these very representations*, so industriously circulated through the whole community. Nothing is more fully attested by experience and observation than this,—that the best of men may be prostrated, and the energies of the best institutions paralyzed, by the untiring efforts of restless demagogues wielding the all-powerful weapon of the spirit of party. From personal observation, attentive, and, as far as I know myself, unbiassed, I am convinced that the present professors of the Miami University are men well acquainted with their business, and having the welfare of their pupils and of the Institution sincerely at heart. There is one thing especially worthy of notice, which should give this University a strong hold upon the affections of a Christian people, viz., that, while nothing properly sectarian has a place, the philosophy of the Bible stands forth in bold relief. Through all the exercises of the late Commencement we were constantly reminded that this is a Christian institution, and that we are a Christian people, who claim an open Bible as our dearest treasure.

'*Fiat justitia, ruat cœlum.*' "

But whilst this writer, and many who felt with him, were satisfied with the state of things in the College, and could thus speak of its President and Faculty, others took an opposite view of things, and, with a disregard of the amenities both of style and of matter, such as too often marks bitter political conflicts, they assailed the Faculty and those who wrote in their defence.

The storm seemed to have spent its fury in the summer of 1844, and a reaction began; and it is likely that Dr. Junkin and his friends would have been sustained by the public, and been left to their work in peace; but other events were maturing which entirely changed his future life. These, with other matters not yet written, will occupy another chapter.

CHAPTER XXXI.

Labors to elevate the Standard of Scholarship—Baccalaureates—Decision of Character—Pulpit Labors—Anti-Slavery Controversy—Speech in the Synod of Cincinnati—Introductory Letter—John McDonough—Dr. Junkin's Plan of Emancipation the same with that of President Lincoln —Opinions of Conservatives—Probabilities—Opinions of Reviewers—Assembly of 1844—Dr. Junkin, Moderator—Questions before the Body —*Quorum*—Ordinations—Slavery—Free Church of Scotland Commissioners—Reception—Dr. Junkin's Speech—Action of the General Assembly.

DURING Dr. Junkin's administration of Miami University, he not only was diligent in performing the duties pertaining to his offices as President and Professor, but he employed his pen in endeavoring to increase public interest in the subject of education, and especially to superinduce a higher standard of scholarship in American Colleges. There had arisen a strong prejudice, in many quarters, against the ancient College *curriculum*, especially against the study of the ancient languages; and there seemed to be a growing demand for what was assumed to be a more *utilitarian* course of study. The popular conception of a College education seemed to be to prepare young men for practical life, in the shortest time, and by the easiest and most direct course possible. Study, as a means of mental training and development, was not by such persons appreciated. The impartation of thoughts and information—not teaching men to *think* for themselves—was the too popular notion of education. Against this mistaken theory Dr. Junkin set himself, and did what he could to correct it. In his Baccalaureate address in 1843, he embodied an argument against it, and aimed to explain to the popular mind "The Bearings of College Education upon the Welfare of the whole Community." This he did in so simple, illustrative, and convincing a manner that none who heard him, or who read the address, could fail to see that every interest of the community, every profession, occupation, and business among the people, and all other departments of education were benefited by thorough College education. He unfolded its influence upon science, the arts, commerce, civilization, political economy, government, liberty, and religion; and demonstrated that all depended upon the reign of enlightened mind; and that they *had* prospered, and would prosper, in the direct ratio of the progress of that intellectual and moral culture which right College education only could secure.

After a discussion of his theme, marked by lucid logic, telling facts, and ardent eloquence, he applied the principles evolved to the institution over which he presided. He said:

"What, then, is our policy? Raise the standard high! HIGHER! STILL HIGHER! If you want the noblest youths of our land to rally round your College, this is your true policy. Make them believe the truth—not that the top of your pyramid is lost in the clouds, but that it towers to heaven, and yet it may be reached. This is our duty. We owe it to our State and to our country. We owe it to our country's Great Benefactor. God and Washington have committed to us these ten talents; and woe to us if we bury them in the earth,—if we invert the pyramid, and send the youth of the land downward, to seek its glorious summit in the grossness of a base materialistic utilitarianism!

"Let us turn an adder's ear to the siren song of a temporary expediency. Let us not listen to the whinings of sectarian jealousy. . . . . Let us not cut down our mountain to the mole-hill dimensions which some may have prescribed to professional qualifications. Let us not go into the market with our roll of parchments, and enter into an inglorious competition from the lowest bidder! We have defended our position. . . .

"Such, gentlemen of the Board, is the understanding in this institution,—such the views of this Faculty.

"Such, young gentlemen of the Senior Class, we well know to be your views and feelings. You now leave us, to carry them out, we fondly hope and trust, through long, laborious, respectable, and happy professional lives. . . .

"And now, my dear young friends, time has brought us to the sundering-point. When, and where, and how we shall meet again is known only to Him who sees the end from the beginning. The changes of this world appear to us, who see so small a portion of the Creator's universal plan, utter confusion; as do the movements of the planetary orbs to the illiterate; but to Omniscience all is order, harmony, beauty. . . .

"Look forward to the vast field before you. Look beyond to the rewards of faithful devotion to the cause of truth. Look upward to the Star of Bethlehem, so often pointed out to you from these high places, and it will be a light to your feet.

"Short, but most happy, has been the period of my intercourse with you. Should we all prove faithful to ourselves and our friends, to our country and our God, we shall shortly meet in that bright world, where language is all living, science all light, happiness unspeakable and eternal. Amen. So let it be!"

It was Dr. Junkin's custom always to select a definite subject for his Baccalaureate addresses. His reason for this is stated in the exordium of his Baccalaureate of 1842:

"That our annual high-day may not be characterized, in one of its exercises, by a mere series of stereotyped remarks, it is my purpose always to select a *subject.* The relations which *terminate*, and those which *begin*, at Commencement, are almost perfectly the same on all occasions; hence some of the matter proper to be uttered must necessarily be repetitions. There is no necessity, however, to limit a Baccalaureate address to these items of inevitable identity. The larger portion of it may, with great propriety, vary perpetually; and thus abate the satiety which otherwise would result to those attending every year."

That year he discussed the topic, "The Bearings of Christianity upon Republican Government." In 1844 his subject was "Decision of Character." In his introduction he said, after announcing his subject:

"The honorable Board will perceive at once that novelty, and the hope of profiting by its charms, had nothing to do with this selection. The subject is trite and hackneyed. Since the masterly essay of the late John Foster, none but the novice would select this topic in the hope of gaining admiration by originality."

After an able and a far more unique and original discussion of the subject than his modest introduction would lead us to expect, he summed up all in six practical rules for the formation of a character of decision, which rules he commended, in an eloquent and tender appeal, to the students of the University:

"1. If accuracy of knowledge is so radically important toward forming correct judgments, thence results the maxim, '*Whatever is worth doing at all is worth doing well.*'

"2. *Let knowledge be perfect.* This regards the *parts* and the *degree* of every part. Let no man, who aims at independent thinking and true decision, sit down contented, in a vain flattering belief that he understands a given subject.

"3. *Choose your particular field of scientific investigation,—your profession; and confine your main exertions to that field.* No man possesses a *universal genius,*—the phrase embodies a contradiction. *Genius* is a *particular* adaptation, and cannot be *universal.*

"4. *Let deliberation be repressed, until investigation has completed her work.*

"5. *Let the intensity of desire never outstrip the tardier movements of investigation, deliberation, and judgment.*

"6. *Let desire always wear the habiliments of virtue.*

Never cherish for a moment a desire to accomplish a wrong thing. Success, in such a case, can only be temporary; for right will ultimately triumph. . . . . Under this rule you avoid the most fearful of all opposition to a decided purpose,—the stern rebuke of a condemning conscience. Even in the most resolute and hardened villains, their determined purpose is but feebly executed; the nerve of resolution being shivered by the appalling voice of conscience. Whereas, with all the force of her approval, the desire of doing right becomes overpowering, and binds forever a free spirit to its cherished purpose.

> " 'What stronger breastplate than a heart untainted?
> Thrice is he armed who hath his quarrel just;
> And he but naked, though locked up in steel,
> Whose conscience with injustice is corrupted!'

"This is the man who stands erect amid the ruins of a crashing world."

From Dr. Junkin's published addresses scores of such passages might be selected. But space forbids. So much is transferred merely as specimens of his modes of thought and utterance. The perorations of his baccalaureates were filled with tenderness, especially toward the young men who were about to take their departure.

Whilst Dr. Junkin resided at Oxford, he was of course a member of the Presbytery of that name, and of the Synod of Cincinnati. As a Presbyter, he was always at his post, if not providentially hindered, and bore his part in the deliberations of the church courts. He never felt like a minister without charge, for he considered himself *ex officio* the pastor of the University, and not only lectured and preached in the College Hall, but performed pastoral duty in visiting the students. He also, for a time, preached part of the Sabbath at a church four or five miles from Oxford.

It has already been stated, that shortly after going to Miami, he repeated, in the College Hall, to the students, and such of the citizens as attended, his lectures on the Prophecies, and he prepared them for publication at the request of many who heard them at Easton.

We come now to narrate an episode in the life of Dr. Junkin which has been very much misapprehended and misrepresented, and which no doubt had an important influence in intensifying a part of the opposition to him in the West.

It is well known that about the time of his advent to Miami the Abolition excitement was at its height. For nearly ten years it had agitated the country, North and South, East and West. The anti-slavery men of the country had become divided in their counsels, in such a way as to separate them into several classes. The Garrison school of abolitionists had advanced much further, in their aggressive doctrines and measures, than many others, equally hostile to slavery, were willing to go. There was another school equally opposed to it, but who were less violent in their language, more moderate in their counsels, and more considerate in their measures; but both schools had adopted the principle that slavery was *malum in se*—a sin in itself; and of course, with such a premise assumed, the inference was unavoidable, that it ought instantly to cease and be abolished. The Garrison school had, as a general thing, broken away from the Holy Scriptures as a guide, because they seemed to tolerate slavery in certain circumstances.

But there was a large class of anti-slavery men who were Christians, believers in the Bible, and who were unwilling, like the infidel abolitionists, to reject the Word of God because it seemed to give countenance to the evil which they detested. These, like the others, assumed that slavery was *per se* a sin, and like them held that, as a sin, it should immediately be given up. The necessary consequences of this assumption were the corollaries:—First. That no slaveholder ought to be a member of the church of Christ.

Second. That the church should not only testify against slavery, but exclude all slaveholders from her communion. And, although they rarely asserted it, another necessary corollary was, that the non-slaveholding part of the church ought to separate themselves from the slaveholding part.

Against these doctrines, of course, almost the entire South was arrayed, and a large portion of the North also, and the agitation of the public mind upon the subject had been increasing from year to year. It was no new cause of disturbance in church and state. At the very foundation of the national government this great acknowledged evil met our fathers, and embarrassed the framers of our Constitution. And all down through our history, the existence of slavery in one part of our land, after it had been abolished in others, had proved an ever-recurring source of difficulty in national legislation. Frequently it had threatened the dissolution of the Union, and called for repeated compromises. These only served to postpone, for a time, the threatening dangers, without removing them.

The Presbyterian Church had also, at an early period of her history, recognized slavery as a moral and social evil, and borne decided testimony against it; which testimony she reiterated from time to time, and *never withdrew it.*

The anti-slavery sentiment, at one time, was an *American* sentiment. It pervaded both North and South. Several States, that had been slaveholding States, had abolished it, by a gradual process,—as Pennsylvania, New Jersey, and New York. Kentucky had taken up the subject of abolition, and discussed it in her legislature, with strong tendencies to emancipation, before Garrison's *Liberator* made its appearance. Similar movements had been made in Virginia. That great, good, and eloquent statesman and patriot, James McDowell, afterwards Governor of Virginia, as early as 1831–2, introduced resolutions looking to emancipation, into the Virginia Legislature.

But when aggressive, and especially when abusive, abolition commenced its career, and interference with Southern slavery by Northern agency was threatened, the power of Southern emancipationists was soon paralyzed, and the very men who were opposed to the system, and had begun these movements, were forced not only to relinquish their efforts, but to stand in defence of what they deemed the safety of their section. It was the aggressive abolition movement that arrested these efforts, and consolidated the South in opposition to what they deemed unjustifiable interference with their domestic affairs.

The overwhelming majority at the North was also opposed to the abolition agitation. No political party of the larger national organizations had ever identified itself with aggressive abolition. The profound conviction of the great mass of Northern citizens was, that slavery ought to be left to the control and management of the States within which it existed. There our fathers had left it when they framed the Constitution, and for a long time no considerable body of men had proposed to interfere with it.

Love for the Union had always been a dominant sentiment—almost a passion—in the American bosom. Anything that endangered the Union was repelled with impatience; and, as the aggressive abolitionists had sometimes uttered sentiments which were considered hostile to the Union, strong indignation was felt and often expressed against them on that account; and this indignation occasionally took such possession of masses of the people as to lead to unjustifiable means of opposition, and to mob violence. The burning of Pennsylvania Hall, and other demonstrations of the kind, were as foolish as they were wicked; for persecution always gives ultimate strength to the persecuted principles and the party which upholds them.

In the church courts, too, the wisest policy was not always pursued. The right of petition and memorial was sometimes infringed, or, at least, the petitions upon the subject of slavery were not treated with the same respect that those upon other subjects received. Discussion in the church courts was discouraged, sometimes prevented by the motion to lay on the table; and a most decided reluctance was for a long time shown to tolerate the agitation of this exciting topic.

The writer of these pages was always of opinion, that this was a mistaken policy on the part of conservative men. Discussion is a safety-valve through which it is often wise to "let off" the steam-like enthusiasm of extravagant reformers. If such enthusiasm is repressed, especially when it is the offspring of conscientious convictions, it is sure to find vent somewhere and somehow, either by a secret escape-pipe, or by the crashing explosion.

In the National Legislature a similar policy was adopted, with similar results, viz., the intensifying of the repudiated abolition sentiment, and the gradual strengthening of the party.

Good men trembled for the result. Violent and imprudent things were done in both sections of the country, and to many it began to appear probable, that if the abolitionists could not be met and defeated upon their own ground, and with their own weapons,—facts and arguments,—a division of the Church and of the National Union would be the ultimate result.

To this conclusion Dr. Junkin seemed at last to have been brought, in September, 1843. In the Synod of Cincinnati, the subject of abolition had frequently been presented, but the policy above described appears to have been usually pursued. Dr. Junkin himself had objected to the agitation of the subject in his Presbytery; and when a paper was offered to the Synod by his venerable colleague and predecessor, Dr. Bishop, embodying a deliverance of abolition opinions, he voted to lay it on the table. This led to some banter and challenging on the part of the abolition members, which roused a spirit of defiance in the minds of their opponents, and resulted in a motion to take the paper up for discussion. Against this motion Dr. Junkin voted, but was in a minority of four. He then entered upon the discussion; and, on the 19th and 20th of September, delivered his celebrated speech, which was so extensively read, so violently attacked, and so generally misrepresented to and by many who had never heard or read it.

A portion of this speech was published in a pamphlet of eighty octavo pages, and aroused, of course, the very determined opposition of those who had so zealously taken different ground. The intensity of their hostility to the man seemed proportionate to the difficulty which they found in answering his argument. The speech has been represented, or, rather, misrepresented, as being a *pro-slavery* argument, and its author a pro-slavery man, but no candid reader can so characterize it. The part of it which was published was entitled:

"THE INTEGRITY OF OUR NATIONAL UNION *versus* ABOLITIONISM. AN ARGUMENT FROM THE BIBLE, IN PROOF OF THE POSITION, THAT BELIEVING MASTERS OUGHT TO BE TOLERATED IN, NOT EXCOMMUNICATED FROM, THE CHURCH OF GOD."

To the pamphlet is prefixed a letter, addressed to the gentlemen at whose request the speech was published. An extract from this letter will explain the character of its argument and the object of its publication:

"To the REV. JOSHUA L. WILSON, D.D., REV. J. C. BARNES, GENERAL ROBT. B. MILLIKIN, and C. K. SMITH, ESQ.

"GENTLEMEN,—You were among the first of my friends to solicit the publication of that part, at least, of my argument before the Synod of Cincinnati, which went to show from the language of the Bible, that slavery is tolerated therein, and not made a ground of excommunication from the Church.

"The copy is now at your service. You will find it not so full as when spoken. Eight hours were occupied in the delivery of the whole, and the last three parts were compressed into half that space of time. . . . But, having conceived my plan, I adhered to it throughout, giving my principal attention to the Scriptural argument. I have long believed that if this nation is to be saved from a deluge of suicidal blood, it will be through the conservative power of the Word of God. . . .

"Truth requires the public to know my general plan, lest they should suppose I had not met the whole subject. The plan of the whole speech contained four general heads, beside the prefatory remarks against introducing the matter into ecclesiastical bodies at all:

"I. The Scriptural argument, which only you have here.

"II. An aggressive movement into the abolition camp,—in which I carry the war into their country. Here I sustained four propositions:—1. The abolition movement occasions the riveting of the chains of temporal bondage more tightly upon the colored race. 2. It tends to increase the intellectual bondage and the spiritual enthralment of that unhappy race. 3. It is a treasonable movement against the Constitution of the United States. 4. It aims at and tends to the dissolution of the Union; and there is reason to believe that English abolitionists, and the British government, are co-operating with American abolitionists to divide our republic.

"III. The question of slavery, as viewed by the eye of political philosophy, and of moral and municipal law.

"IV. The divine plan of restoring man universally to his freedom,—first in *fact*, then in *form*,—and the application of it in the noble scheme of African colonization. This topic I did not fully discuss; nor the great question why God *permitted* the introduction of slavery into this republic, and what were his designs concerning it. In regard to African colonization, I hastily referred to the success in Liberia as evidence of its practicability; and especially since the noble, philanthropic, and eminently successful experiment of John McDonough, of New Orleans, has demonstrated the easy practicability of universal emancipation and real freedom. Whether ever this plan shall be filled up is a contingency.*

"Very respectfully, your humble servant,

"GEORGE JUNKIN."

As great pains were taken by the aggressive, immediate abolitionists to make and spread the impression that Dr. Junkin was a pro-slavery man, his biographer deems it a duty to correct this impression; and perhaps no better method could be adopted than to make such extracts from this speech as will exhibit his true position. He always esteemed slavery an abnormal condition of society, and a great social evil. He believed and taught, that the true spirit of Christianity was opposed to it, and tended to its removal. He was an early and a zealous friend of a judicious scheme of emancipation. Long before the name of Abraham Lincoln was heard of, beyond his immediate neighborhood, George Junkin had publicly recommended and advocated the plan for compensated emancipation, which Mr. Lincoln proposed after he came to the Presidency. As early as 1835 Dr. Junkin publicly advocated the consecration of the entire proceeds of the public lands

---

* The Mr. McDonough mentioned in the above letter, was a wealthy gentleman of New Orleans, who fitted his servants for freedom by a gradual process of education and instruction in the arts of useful industry, and *then* freed them. Two of his servants, whom he designed for professional life, he sent to Dr. Junkin's care at Lafayette College, to be educated. One of these has long been a useful teacher in Liberia. It is a suggestive fact, that when black men were excluded from most, if not all, of the Colleges in the land, Dr. Junkin, whom his opponents tried to brand as a *pro-slavery* man, received them. Not only the two mentioned, but others received instruction under him; one of them, the son of an African king or chief. No man was more practically and truly a philanthropist; and he longed and labored for the *real* freedom and elevation of all men, irrespective of color.

to the grand scheme of compensated emancipation and colonization. His scheme was substantially the same with that proposed by our late murdered President. Like Mr. Lincoln, Dr. Junkin perceived the immense hardship, if not the injustice, of any sudden breaking up of the system of labor which had prevailed for more than a century and a half in the Southern country. He was not ignorant of the history of the introduction of the African race into this land as slaves. He knew, as every well-read man knows, that the African slave-trade, by which this injured race had been introduced into our country, had been carried on chiefly by *English* and *New England capital, men*, and *ships*, and not by the people of the South; that the Southern people had originally been merely the *purchasers* of "the stolen chattels," whilst, in many cases, the ancestors of the very men who were now clamoring for the destruction of that species of property had been the *sellers* of it. A sense of public justice and equity led his mind, as it did that of Mr. Lincoln, to desire that slavery might be removed gradually, and upon a plan that would work the least possible amount of injury to the slave, to his master, and to the republic. He foresaw, what has since happened, that a violent abolition of the evil would cost an ocean of blood and treasure, and superinduce a state of things which would imperil, if it did not destroy, our beautiful and beneficent system of government. He foresaw that the abolition movement, if persisted in, would lead, as it has done, to an attempt to sunder the American Union; which attempt, from whichever section it came, would involve the country in all the horrors of civil war. He knew that, if such an attempt should prove successful, it would inaugurate, as in Europe, the wars of many generations; and that, if unsuccessful, it would still leave the sections exasperated against each other, with no real bond of union except the sword. He, as a far-seeing statesman, knew that a forced Union would greatly endanger our free institutions by familiarizing our people with military coercion. And he knew—or thought he knew—that the inevitable results of a military emancipation on the soil would be the arraying of race against race, in mutual and enduring prejudices, if not in a war of extermination. Hence his warm heart and active brain were early employed in devising a scheme for removing this terrible evil, in a way and by a process that would avoid these calamities. His scheme was compensated emancipation and colonization,—the separation of the races,—the very scheme to which President Lincoln stands committed in one of his ablest state papers.

With such views, it became the duty of every good citizen to discourage the aggressive abolition agitation. Dr. Junkin, and thousands of the best minds and hearts of the land, desired to avoid exasperating the sections of the country against each other; hoping that, by delay, the South might discover that slavery was not only wrong, but also a politico-economical blunder; and that a peaceable solution of the great and alarming problem might be reached.

As a student of history and of the Bible, he had learned that grand and valuable results in God's providence, are always reached by slow and gradual processes. In the case of one of the greatest emancipation enterprises ever accomplished,—one which was achieved, too, by preternatural Divine interposition,—the process was gradual. For centuries God had permitted his covenant people to dwell in "the house of bondage;" and when the hour of emancipation came, the instruments of deliverance were required first to *reason* with Pharaoh, and *ask* him to let the people go; nor did force interpose until argument and terror had exhausted their resources. Even after the exodus, it required forty years of careful training, under immediate divine supervision, to fit that nation of slaves for freedom.

It can readily be conceived that a conservative mind, imbued with such views, would shrink from all rash attempts at sudden and violent abolition, even of an acknowledged evil; and that, when driven into discussion, he would resist doctrines which he believed tended to injure both his church and his country, whilst they did not promise any real benefit to the slave himself.

Whether Dr. Junkin and the conservative men of the country were right or not, has not yet been demonstrated by events; and it is possible that such a demonstration can never now be made. *Their* plan has not been tried, and now never can be. Slavery is gone, so far as the system in its former condition is concerned. The sword has *cut* the Gordian knot which reason had failed to *untie;* but it remains to be proven, whether the fragments of the cord can ever be so united or so used as to benefit permanently the emancipated race. Every good man will hope and pray and labor, that the best results may be attained; but the intelligent statesman must sorrowfully feel, that the tremendous problem of the African in America is, as yet, far from solution.

Had the zealots of the North and the "fire-eaters" of the South not prevented the experiments which the conservatives were disposed to make, it might have been that, a century hence, happier results for both races would have been secured than will now be attained in that time. But that can never now be known. One thing is already manifest,—that the war, under which slavery went down, has cost the belligerents a much larger amount of money than would have sufficed to carry out the scheme of compensated emancipation, which Dr. Junkin suggested as early as 1835, and which President Lincoln recommended nearly thirty years afterwards—and the *blood* might have been saved.

But we must let Dr. Junkin define his own position in regard to this great issue, upon which he has been so much misrepresented. When the crisis came, and it was necessary for him to decide whether he would remain under the banner that had been raised by the slaveholding States, or under the flag that his father had aided in consecrating to freedom, he hesitated not one moment, but, as we shall see, left all, and stood for union and liberty. In the introduction of his speech, he says:

"MR. MODERATOR,—Ever since modern abolitionism developed its true character it has been my policy to avoid all public discussion of the subject. The anger and bitterness and distraction and alienation among brethren, which have so generally attended its agitation, early convinced me that prudence for peace's sake required the exclusion of this exciting controversy from our church courts; and this policy has actuated the brethren generally with whom I have been called to act in my former field of labor. When it pleased God to locate me in a new field, I thought I saw additional reasons confirming the wisdom of this course. It was early impressed upon my mind that this brand had already kindled a fire which had well-nigh consumed Miami University. To such a ruinous degree did the fire burn within her bosom, that the Trustees took up the subject, and passed strong resolutions condemnatory of this wildfire, and commendatory of a more prudent course.* Hence I felt called upon to discourage a class of disputations that resulted in evil, and only evil. The consequence is peace and kindly feeling between young men from all the States. Hence my opposition in Presbytery and in Synod to all attempts (and they have not been few) to agitate and agitate and agitate this subject. . . . .

"Sir, we have been *bantered* into a discussion of this subject. We have been told that we are afraid of the light; afraid to meet the argument; that it would soon be seen, upon the vote to take up, who were afraid of the truth. Sir, 'let not him that girdeth on his harness boast himself as he that putteth it off.' It may appear hereafter who will shrink before the sword of the Spirit."

---

* See Annual Catalogue of 1840, the year before Dr. J.'s advent.

He then describes the effect that this insinuation of cowardice had upon the members of the Synod, especially the young men, and adds:

"Thus the fire passed from bosom to bosom, and *thus* the present speaker was left in a lean minority of four against taking up the slavery resolutions. He had been threshing his wheat by the wine-presses, to hide it from the Midianites, and, being often urged to go forth to battle in this war, he had declined. Nevertheless, he had put a fleece of wool upon the floor to obtain a sign from the Lord. And now that there seems to be no longer any evasion, he takes it to be the Master's will that he should discuss this subject; and, being forewarned by others than these last signs, he has not come up to this Synod wholly unprepared. Nor is it my purpose to skim over the surface of things. If we *must* discuss, let us do it thoroughly. . . . Shallow furrows make short corn; and shallow discussion yields a light harvest of knowledge. Let us take time to dig deep for the golden treasure in the mine of the Holy Scriptures.

"Notwithstanding all this, Mr. Moderator, I was opposed to entering upon this subject here, because——"

And he proceeded to specify and elaborate a number of reasons, which cannot be here inserted at length. A syllabus, however, will help to understand the real position which he occupied upon this subject:

"I. Ecclesiastical courts in a Free State have no jurisdiction of any kind over slavery.

"II. The discussion will most probably degenerate into a mere debate or hot controversy, in which something else than blood will be shed. Can any brother who considers the excitability of the public mind doubt it? Is it reasonable to expect that slavery, abolitionism, and colonization will be discussed here with that coolness and subdued temper, which their importance demands and Christian courtesy requires? Does any man expect it? For myself, I have passed through some stormy scenes, and have learned by experience that the more boisterous the elements become, the more perfectly all my faculties are at command. Brethren must not infer, from my repugnance to this discussion, that individually I fear the heavings of the billows and the violence of the blast. He who commands me into these troubled waters, will keep me in safety. . . . Let us follow peace with all men as much as lieth in us.

"III. I object to entering upon the abolition controversy, in an ecclesiastical court, because its advocates are organized into a political party.

"There is a sense in which the adage, 'Religion has nothing to do with politics,' is true; when by politics is meant party wrangling and defamation. But there is also a sense in which the proverb is corruptly false, when by it men mean that the obligations of religion ought to have no governing influence upon political conduct, that, for their acts in affairs of government, men are not accountable to God, but only to the people or to party.

"All true Presbyterians believe that the civil government has no power over religious matters; and that officers of the church, as such, have no kind of control in civil affairs. Even protection for person and property, in religious privileges, we ask not as religious men, but as civil citizens. As members of the *civil Commonwealth* we have a right to hold property, and to assemble for a lawful purpose; and the law protects us, not because we are religious persons, but civil citizens. . . . I therefore contend, peremptorily, that this Synod has no right to intermeddle with political partyism. . . . And that the Abolition party is organized as a political party, . . . with its candidates for office, nominated and in the field, from the Presidency of the Union down, no one disputes. Let officers of God's church pause a little upon the margin of this crater, before we take the leap of Empedocles; let us calculate consequences before we take the fearful plunge.

"IV. This controversy places the peace party, as we may call ourselves in the premises, in a *false position.* It lays us open to the illogical and unjust, yet plausible, inference that we are advocates of slavery. The brethren, who urge this controversy upon us, are everywhere known as abolitionists, anti-slavery men; men who labor to do away slavery from the land and from the world,—this is their boast. They wish to be called 'the Liberty party.'

Liberty, what things have been done in thy sacred name! The popular mind is often charmed and governed by a word, and the moment the anti-slavery men of this school meet with any opposition, the cry of *pro-slavery* is raised. Here is the anti-slavery party. But *anti* means *against;* if, then, they are *against* slavery, whoever opposes them must be *for* or in *favor* of slavery: *for* and *against*, *pro* and *anti*, —there it is, clear to a demonstration. All who oppose the political abolitionists are in favor of slavery. Such is the logic that actually governs many a mind. Many good, honest-hearted people do not know how to escape from it. They never perceive that there are different kinds of opposition; that men may be opposed to a thing in one respect, yet not in another. Paul was a sound, clear-headed, warm-hearted preacher of the Gospel; but Peter was opposed to Paul on a certain occasion; therefore Peter was a muddy-headed and heterodox preacher. This is the argument by which opposers of ultra abolitionism are proved to be pro-slavery men. Even learned divines and erudite editors are caught in this cobweb. . . . . We are not willing that honest-hearted people, by a little false reasoning, should be led to suppose that we are in favor of slavery. We are, in truth, opposed to slavery, and are doing as much in our respective positions to abate its evils as our brethren are. We differ from them as to the *manner* of doing away with these evils; whilst we suppose we are much more efficient in the matter of meliorating the condition of the colored race. No disclaimer will avail. We tell the world—we tell our Christian brethren—our objections to slavery. We point to Liberia, the land of the free colored man, as proof of our success. But all in vain,—you are opposed to the political anti-slavery party, and, therefore, you must be *pro-slavery* men.

"Such is the false position in which the shape of the question puts us; and our brethren *know* and rejoice in it. They make the charge, and hold us to it, unless we prove our innocence. All advantages are fair in war!"

Having thus stated his objections to the intermeddling of the church courts in this matter, he proposed to take up the question, "What does the Bible teach upon this subject?" And having explained the true process of exegetical analysis, by which the real meaning of the Scriptures was to be ascertained, and the synthetical process, by which the results of such analysis were to be imparted by a teacher, he indicated his purpose to pursue this mode in his argument, and then said:

"The opposite method I will not pursue; it is, alas! not uncommon even on this subject, viz., first to determine what the truth is,—what the Bible ought to teach on a given point, and then come to it in order to *make* it teach accordingly. Human reason sets itself to work, and comes to the conclusion that such a doctrine is true, and then proceeds to examine the Bible for proof of its truth; and, of course, what a man's reason assures him *ought* to be in the Bible, the same reason, with the aid of a little torturing engine called criticism, can easily discover in it. According to this method, one affirms, 'It is contrary to reason that three persons should exist in one Godhead.' He then proceeds to examine the Bible, not, you will observe, to ascertain what it actually does teach in regard to the mode of the Divine existence, but to interpret the Bible language so as to make it teach his own preconceived doctrine. Another says, 'If the horrible doctrine of eternal punishment were taught in the Bible, I would kick it out of my house;' and yet another, 'If I thought the Bible tolerated slavery, I would turn infidel and trample it under my feet.' Now, all these belong to the same school of interpreters. They all form their opinions of what the sacred volume *ought* to say, and go to it to ascertain whether it will dare to teach differently from their particular notions of truth.

"But is not all this folly? . . . Let us not come to God to tell Him what He ought to say in his word; but let us draw near with holy reverence upon our spirits to learn what He hath said."

It would be impracticable to attempt, upon these pages, even a syllabus of the argument of Dr. Junkin on this occasion. It was admitted by all, but those whom he opposed, to be conclusive; and even some of the maturest scholars among the anti-slavery men have conceded that, if the Bible be the rule of morals, Dr. Junkin has demonstrated, by a full and fair exegesis of all the passages which bear upon the subject, that the assumption that the relation of master and slave is *of itself* and necessarily a sin, cannot be maintained. Dr. Junkin did not argue that the relation was a desirable one, or a normal condition of society; but that it might exist without the master being a transgressor in such a sense, as that he ought to be excommunicated from the church of Christ, and that, therefore, the church had no authority, from the Scripture, to make slaveholding a term of communion. He was unwilling to admit a principle which, if applied, would have excommunicated Abraham, the father of the faithful, and Isaac, and Jacob, and Moses, and David, and Cornelius the Centurion, and Philemon, Paul's friend, and vast numbers of the primitive Christians. He was unwilling, in opposition to what he really believed to be the teaching of the Bible, to admit a postulate in morals that tended immediately to the sundering of the unity of the church, and to the dissolution of the Union of his country. He plead for patience and forbearance. He deprecated measures which, he foresaw, would deluge his country in blood; and he endeavored to show that the Gospel of Peace, if left to its normal action, would inevitably remove slavery, and all like evils, from our world, but that it forbids the use of the sword for the accomplishment of its peaceful and beneficent ends. We give in his own words the conclusion of this part of his argument. It seemed, no doubt, to his opponents like the tones of unmeaning alarm. We now know that, although not *inspired* prophecy, it was the deduction, by reason, from the well-known laws of cause and effect, of the result which might have been expected. It is now in part history,—history written in terrible lines of blood:

"But let us return to the conclusion furnished by the Scripture argument. Slavery is tolerated in the Bible. It is not made a term of communion, by the King of Zion.

Consequently the officers of his church have no power to make it one. Here is the doctrine for which we contend; and by this we hope to save this fair land from being deluged in the blood of its inhabitants, and this free nation from the chains of servitude to European despots.

"Should the opposite doctrine prevail; should the holding of slaves be made a crime, by the officers of the churches of the non-slaveholding States; should they break communion with their Southern brethren, and denounce them as guilty of damning sin, as kidnappers and man-stealers worthy of the penitentiary, as has been done in this Synod, at this time; should this doctrine and this practice prevail throughout the Northern States, can any man be so blind as not to see that a dissolution of the Union, a civil and perhaps a servile war, must be the consequence? Such a war as the world has never witnessed,—a war of uncompromising extermination, that will lay waste this vast territory. All the elements are here—the physical, the intellectual, the moral elements—for a strife, different in the horribleness of its character from anything the world has ever witnessed. Let the spirits of these men be once aroused, let their feelings be chafed up to the fighting-point, let the irritation be kept up until the North and the South come to blows, on the question of slavery, their 'contentions will be as the bars of a castle,' broken only with the last pulsations of a nation's heart.

"On the contrary, let the opposite doctrine prevail, and the practices which necessarily flow from it; let the North feel for their Southern brethren, who are afflicted with slavery; let the churches of the North deal kindly and truly with those of the South; let them continue to recognize and treat them as Christian brethren, and entreat them, and urge them to 'give unto their servants that which is just and equal,' to treat them as Christian brethren; let them aid them in the splendid scheme of colonization; let them seek union, and peace, and love, and they will not seek in vain. Thus the integrity of the nation will be maintained. The happiness of the colored race will be promoted, in the highest degree, in the land of their fathers.* God will be

* It is an impressive fact that, after the war ended, by the destruction of slavery, large numbers of the blacks are emigrating to Africa. Since

glorified, in the triumphant success of free, republican America."

Of course the delivery of this argument, and the publication of part of it, aroused an intense opposition to its author, from the abolition ranks. The speech was reviewed with great acrimony, as was to be expected; attempts were made to answer it, with what success men would decide very differently, and a great clamor was raised against the man, as an advocate of slavery. No candid hearer or reader of the speech can infer from it that this charge was just.

On the other hand, this argument was received, by the conservative part of the country, as the most conclusive, able, and temperate that had been presented. It was very extensively noticed, and other editions, besides the one originally published, were produced and exhausted. We cannot transfer to these pages the various opinions of the public press in regard to this speech. A brief one from the *Protestant and Herald*, then edited by Dr. Hill, will be a sufficient specimen of the approbatory notices. After giving the title, in the usual way, that paper said:

"We have read no document of the present age with more interest and satisfaction than this. Our only regret is, that the author has not given us the whole speech, of which we had heard so much at the time of its delivery. The abolitionists of the Synod of Cincinnati had made many strenuous efforts to commit that body to an approval of their efforts. The Synod from time to time laid the subject on the table, refusing to discuss it; which action led the former party to suppose that the majority of Synod were afraid of discussion, and that it was the lack of moral courage which prevented them from avowing themselves as abolitionists. At the late meeting the anti-abolition party, after much provocation, determined to take up the subject,

---

this chapter was begun, official notice has been given of seven hundred and fifty asking to go from a single district in North Carolina.

and give it a fair, full, and impartial investigation. In the discussion, Dr. Junkin took a very prominent part, and was requested, by some of the ablest members of the Synod, to write out his speech for publication. In his pamphlet before us, he has given to the public the first part only, which contains the scriptural argument, leaving it doubtful whether the whole will appear or not. . . . The main argument of the discourse is taken up in establishing the position that the Bible TOLERATES, but does not *sanction*, the relation between master and slave. He does this by examining first the Old Testament, from which he establishes the following propositions. [Here the reviewer inserts the six propositions.]

"He next examines the New Testament, from which he establishes the following propositions:

"I. There is not, in the New Testament, a sentence which expressly forbids the relation of master and slave.

"II. There is not, in the New Testament, a sentence which, by a fair and just interpretation, gives ground for the logical inference that the simple holding of a slave, or slaves, is inconsistent with a Christian profession and Christian character.

"These general propositions he sustains by five subordinate ones:—1. That the Greek word *doulos*, usually translated servant, properly and commonly means a person held to service for life,—a slave. 2. Paul advises servants to abide quietly in their condition. This he could not do, if the relation of master and servant were in itself a sin. 3. The New Testament recognizes *some* masters as good men,—true and faithful believers. Therefore the relation of master and slave may exist consistently with Christian character and profession. 4. The New Testament recognizes the existence of slavery. 5. The New Testament prescribes the duties of servants to their masters, and of masters to their servants,—enjoining to the former, obedience; to the latter, kind treatment.

"From the whole he deduces two inferences, viz.:

"I. According to the Bible a man may stand in the relation of a master, and hold slaves, and yet be a Christian—a fair, reputable, and consistent professor of the religion of the Bible.

"II. There is no power on earth, no authority in the

church, to make the holding or the not holding of a slave a term of communion, or condition of admission to the privileges of the church.

"Each of these propositions is sustained with great learning and eloquence, and we venture to predict that the abolitionists will rue the day when they forced this champion into the field. They may abuse him; they may call him the advocate of slavery, and many other hard names; but *answer his argument* they will not. We give his closing remarks as a specimen of the whole."*

Of course those who took the opposite side from Dr. Junkin put a very different estimate upon the merits of the speech. And it is not the prerogative of his biographer to decide between the friendly and hostile opinions that were expressed. Nor is it his province to determine, whether it was wise and expedient for the author of the speech, in his circumstances, to throw himself into the breach and do battle for what he thought to be right. Of one set of facts the writer hereof *is* certain, viz., that Dr. Junkin thought it to be right,—to be his *duty;* that he sincerely believed the positions he maintained; that he honestly supposed that he was laboring in the interests of truth, peace, and brotherly kindness among Christians, the safety and union of his country, and the ultimate welfare of the African race; and that if he erred in judgment, he erred in common with very many of the mightiest minds and the purest patriots of his generation. If his name and his fame are to be reproached, on account of this well-meant effort to arrest a tide of opinion which he believed tended to the ruin of his church and his country, they will be reproached along with the names of Webster, Clay, Frelinghuysen, Southard, Cass, Judge MacLean, Woodbury, Douglas, Lincoln, and scores of other illustrious Northern statesmen, and along with the names of Alexander, Miller, Hodge, Green,

* Protestant and Herald, Dec. 28, 1843.

McElroy, Phillips, Cuyler, Maclean, Wilson, Murray, Boardman, Knox, Milnor, Potter, Nott, Finley, Proudfit, and hundreds of the brightest lights of the church of all denominations.

But whilst honesty of purpose, conscientiousness of conviction, and pure patriotic motive are claimed for the subject of this memoir, the same is accorded to those who differed in opinion with him in that ardent controversy. Good and sincere Christian men were arrayed upon both sides. And if it shall ever be ascertained this side of the judgment bar, which of the contending parties was nearest the truth, and which mode of removing the acknowledged evils of slavery, if fairly tried, would have accomplished that object with the least injury to all parties, in the way most analogous to the modes of the Divine procedure, and with the largest measure of good to the whole African race and to the human family, that question CANNOT YET be determined. The great problem is *in process* of solution; but the social philosopher who would undertake to pronounce it already solved, would only prove himself capable of jumping at conclusions without facts to sustain them, or reasons to justify his inferences. Every patriot, North and South, ought to rejoice, and the great mass of the people, in both sections, do rejoice, that slavery has been removed; but the wisest patriots rejoice with trembling, and are bending their efforts to lift up the emancipated race, and fit them for the freedom so suddenly thrust upon them. If elevated by Christianity and education, they will become civilized and free; if not, they will relapse into barbarism. And, so long as he lived, no American was more solicitous to promote the welfare of the colored people than Dr. Junkin.

The General Assembly of the Presbyterian Church met in Louisville, Kentucky, in 1844. Dr. Junkin was elected Moderator. His younger brothers, Colonel Benjamin Junkin, an elder, and the writer of this book, were also members, as also a nephew. It is not necessary to say, that a man so familiar with the constitution and the rules of order presided with dignity and tact. That Assembly was memorable for several interesting subjects which were before the body, viz., the questions of the right of ruling elders to lay on hands in the ordination of ministers; the question of the *quorum* of a Presbytery; and the action of the Assembly in regard to the then recent exodus of the Free Church of Scotland from the Establishment. "The Elder questions," as they were technically called, were brought up by the Rev. Dr. R. J. Breckenridge, on complaint against the action of the Synod of Philadelphia. Dr. Breckenridge, and those who acted with him, held that ordination was not a charm, nor a sacrament, nor a rite peculiar to the teaching ministry, but a *governmental act*,—that the ceremony of laying on of hands was merely a symbolical act, denoting consent to a transfer of authority to perform certain functions,—that in the ceremony there was no efficacy *opus operatum*, such as the clergy only could exert; and that all the men constituting the Presbytery who could vote to grant ordination, or to refuse it, had a right to join in the ceremony by which the vote was carried out, in actual ordination.

They held that scriptural ordination was performed "by the laying on of the hands of the Presbytery," and that, as a Presbytery is composed of teaching and ruling Presbyters, the Presbytery does not properly lay on hands if half of its members are thrust aside and forbidden to join in the ceremony.

Along with this view, they also held that, by the definition of a *quorum* (Form of Government, chapter x., sec. vii.), the presence of one or more ruling elders was necessary to constitute a Presbytery. In this view many concurred, who did not agree with Dr. Breckenridge in his views of ordination.

In opposition to the above opinions, it was urged, that a Presbytery might vote many acts to be done which none but the ministers could properly do. The ruling elders might vote that certain sermons might be preached, but that did not prove that elders should preach them. They might vote that Baptism and the Lord's Supper should be administered, but they could not assume the function of dispensing these ordinances. It was urged, also, that a church officer could not confer upon another a function which he was incompetent to perform himself; and that immemorial usage had confined the imposition of hands to the bishops or teaching Presbyters.

In favor of the position, that the presence of one or more ruling elders is necessary to constitute a quorum of Presbytery, it was alleged, that the definition of a *quorum* in the book specifically mentions the elders; that if the framers of the constitution had meant that three ministers, without any elder, could form a quorum, they would have said so; that the words "as many elders as may be present" could not mean "without any elders;" that, in every description of a Presbytery, two constituent elements were mentioned; and that to admit that a valid Presbytery could be constituted with only one of those elements, was to stultify the Book, change our representative system into a simple hierarchy, and discourage the attendance of the ruling elders in the church courts.

In opposition to this view, it was urged that the office of ruling elder was included in that of minister; that the language of the *quorum* clause was designedly left indefinite; that usage and expediency had sanctioned this interpretation of it, and that to adopt another construction might seriously embarrass the transaction of Presbyterial business, in places where it might be difficult to secure the attendance of ruling elders.

These questions had been before the preceding Assembly

(1843), and decided adversely to the views entertained by Dr. Breckenridge and many others; and it was on this account he sought a reconsideration of them. The present writer was a member of both Assemblies, and agreed with Dr. B. on the *quorum* question, and was the author of the protest presented in 1843, against the decision on that subject. Dr. Breckenridge was not permitted to be heard before the Assembly, being ruled out upon a technicality. The questions were decided against his views.

Dr. Junkin, being Moderator, took no part in the discussion, but it was well known that he was with the majority upon both questions, whilst his brothers took the opposite view of the quorum question, and joined in a protest against the decision.

Memorials upon the question of slavery were presented to this Assembly from the Presbyteries of Chillicothe, Beaver, and others, and a motion was made to treat them with disrespect. One member moved that they be put under the table; another, that they be not received. The present writer resisted such imprudent action, because he thought it tended to exasperate, and was an infringement of the right of petition, a right dear to all freemen. The petitions were decorous in language, and he urged that it was a wiser and a more Christian course to receive them with respect, and refer them, in the usual way, to the appropriate committee. This course was taken; and the writer was gratified to learn, after it was over, that his brother, the Moderator, approved of his action in the premises. Thus, in the great emporium city of a slave State, slavery memorials were treated with parliamentary courtesy.

But the most interesting incident, in the history of the Assembly over which Dr. Junkin presided, was the reception of the Commissioners on behalf of the Free Church of Scotland, the Rev. Messrs. Lewis and Chalmers, and the action of the General Assembly in regard to that body, which had recently renounced the Establishment, and asserted their independence of the civil government. The gentlemen named had been commissioned by the General Assembly of the Free Church to visit the churches of the United States, and make known to them, as they might have opportunity, the causes of their self-denying and heroic exodus from the church established by law, and their assumption of a separate and independent ecclesiastical *status*.

They were present at Louisville, and, at an appointed time, were presented to the General Assembly, in the presence of a vast concourse of people. They delivered to Dr. Junkin, as Moderator, a *fac-simile* copy of the Act of Separation and Deed of Demission, by which the General Assembly of the Free Church of Scotland explained and vindicated the important step they had taken in renouncing connection with the civil government of Great Britain, relinquishing their church property, their houses of worship, their manses and glebes, and the pecuniary support hitherto derived from the State. In this memorable document they set forth the reasons for this movement; declaring their readiness to submit to any privations rather than compromise the rights of Christ's crown and covenant by permitting the civil authorities, or careless or ungodly patrons, to intrude into the sacred office as pastors, in opposition to the convictions and the will of the Presbyteries, men of improper qualifications.

Messrs. Lewis and Chalmers, in earnest and eloquent addresses, narrated the history of the exodus, and set forth the reasons therefor. It was a theme well calculated to warm the heart and kindle the enthusiasm of such a man as the Moderator. The Church of Scotland was the church of his ancestors. Covenanter blood coursed warmly through his veins. He gloried in the history of the church of North Britain,—in her trials,—her faithfulness,—her martyrs,—her glorious struggle for the truth of God, and for spiritual freedom. He had always been an uncompromising opponent of the union of the spouse of Christ with Cæsar, and of the support of the church by law and by forced taxation. He had watched with intense interest the progress of the struggle of the friends of purity and freedom against patronage and the crown and the temporizing clergy, ever since the Auchterarder case attracted public attention; and no heart more truly exulted in the triumph of right principles, and the demonstration of the recuperative power of Presbyterianism, than did his. When he rose, therefore, upon the Moderator's dais to respond to the address of the Scotch delegation, his eye sparkled with that peculiar brilliance which all, who heard him often, recognized as the harbinger of glowing thoughts and deep feeling. His whole countenance was radiant with emotion and the grand associations which crowded upon his mind. He began with a low, distinct, deliberate enunciation that was heard over the vast assemblage, and advanced, through a speech which none who heard it will ever entirely forget, rising in fervor, in feeling, and in tone, until a thrilling climax was reached. He welcomed, in behalf of the Assembly, the Commissioners of the Free Church; welcomed them to the hearts, the homes, the churches, and the fellowship of American Presbyterians; welcomed them as the representatives of a great body of believers, whose recent struggles and sacrifices had proved them worthy of a glorious ancestry, and as representatives of great principles, which, long recognized on this side the water, had at last, in despite of mighty repressing influences, nobly asserted themselves in the land of the Covenanters. He congratulated the Commissioners upon being the representatives of such men and of such principles. He gave a rapid, but glowing, glance at the history of past religious struggles in the land from which they came. He spoke of Knox, and Henderson, and Renwick, and Argyle, and many of the Scottish worthies and martyrs, who had battled and suffered for the rights of Christ's crown and covenant. He rapidly traced the progress of free opinion as it struggled up against the weight of the crown and the crosier. He recapitulated the incidents of the recent conflict which ended in the disruption, and hailed that movement as an august triumph of the principle of religious liberty. He then recurred to the signing of the national league and covenant, described the sublime scene of its ratification by the masses with hands uplifted to heaven, whilst tears of enthusiasm rolled over their unblanching cheeks. He compared to this the recent gathering of the General Assembly of the Church of Scotland, and the exodus of the friends of freedom, their imposing procession through the streets of Edinburgh with the illustrious Chalmers at their head. He then alluded to the signing of the solemn document (the Act of Separation) a copy of which he held in his hand—said its signers were worthy followers of those who had battled for Christ's crown and covenant beneath "the banner of the blue,"—declared that, in his judgment, the men of the exodus, who had made such sacrifices and renounced such temporal advantages for the sake of religious liberty, had taken a step far in advance of their worthy ancestors, and when they signed and unfurled the declaration which sundered their connection with the civil power,—when they FLUNG forth this glorious banner inscribed with some of Scotland's most illustrious names, they raised a standard around which would play the brightest beams of the Sun of Righteousness, and which would never be lowered until the principles of truth should triumph, and the whole church and the whole world be free!

As he pronounced the word "flung," he threw forth the document in front of him, retaining in his hand the baton upon which it was rolled up, in such a manner that the scroll instantly unfurled, and displayed to the Assembly and the audience its entire length, with its engrossed declaration and its long list of distinguished names. The effect was electric. It was done at the moment when his voice had reached its most impassioned tone. The vast assemblage was thrilled. Few eyes were dry. Rarely has a finer impression been produced by a public address.

There are members of that Assembly still living, and many others, who will remember the scene here so imperfectly described. It was deeply engraven upon the mind and the memory of the writer of these pages; and although, after the lapse of twenty-seven years, he does not pretend to give the precise words of the Moderator of the Assembly, he thinks those that were present will recognize the meagre syllabus as substantially correct so far as it goes, and that all will concede that the description is rather underdrawn than exaggerated. Its *impromptu* and *spontaneous* character made the address and its manner all the more effective. The writer, who occupied the same room with his brother during the sessions of the Assembly, knows that he had made no preparation for the occasion, unless such as might be made in a rapid walk from his lodgings to the church.

The General Assembly adopted a paper warmly approving of the conduct of the Free Church in renouncing the Establishment; deeply sympathizing with them in the sacrifices they had made; bidding them God-speed in the maintenance of their new position, and the grand principles which led to it; urging the ministers and churches under the care of the General Assembly to aid their Scotch brethren with material means, and inviting the

Free Church to a correspondence by an interchange of delegates.

After the Assembly was dissolved, Dr. Junkin returned to Oxford, where he continued his labors in the University, passing through some scenes of external trial that have been already narrated.

CHAPTER XXXII.

Dr. Yeomans President of Lafayette College—His Administration—Resigns—Dr. Junkin recalled—Causes thereof—Mode of it—Faculty at that Time—Return—Assembly of 1845—His Opening Sermon—Doings of that Body in which he shared—Deliverance on Slavery—On Romish Baptism—Newspaper Discussion on that Subject—Marriage Question—Charge to Mr. Knox—Second Church, Easton—Opposition to it—Troubles arising therefrom in the College—Student Drowned—Dr. Junkin elected President of Washington College—Sketch of its History—Visits Lexington—Domestic Affliction—Accepts the Call to Washington College—Résumé of Lafayette—Her distinguished Alumni—Farewell Scenes.

NOT long after Dr. Junkin was translated to Miami University, the Rev. John W. Yeomans was inaugurated President of Lafayette College. He had been pastor at Williamstown, Mass., and, more recently, pastor of the First Presbyterian Church, Trenton, New Jersey, where he had succeeded the late Rev. Dr. James W. Alexander. Mr. Yeomans, soon after his accession to Lafayette, received the honorary degree of Doctor of Divinity, and we shall speak of him by that title. He had, upon invitation of the Brainerd Society of Lafayette College, delivered an address before them during Dr. Junkin's presidency. This address drew attention to him as a man of mind and scholarship. It was marked by that vigor of thought and lucidness for which its author was remarkable.

When, therefore, Dr. Junkin had made up his mind to resign the presidency, Dr. Yeomans was among those early spoken of as his successor; and, as we have seen, Dr. Junkin made him a visit, and prepared the way for his election.

He was duly chosen and inaugurated, and entered upon his duties with zeal and ability. The writer of these pages continued for some time to be a member of the Faculty of instruction in the College, occupying the Chair of Belles-Lettres, and was thus so associated with Dr. Yeomans as to have good opportunities of forming an estimate of his talents, scholarship, and capabilities. And it is his deliberate judgment that he was eminently qualified, in most respects, for such a position. He had brain, was a thinker of very superior order, a ripe and accurate scholar, a terse, lucid, and forcible writer, a master of great pulpit power, understood the philosophy of education, and was excelled by very few as a clear, skilful, and practically effective teacher. It was a mystery to many that he did not succeed better as the head of a college, for he possessed so many of the qualifications for such an office.

His want of success was not attributable entirely, perhaps not chiefly, to himself; and yet there were two or three traits of disposition that barred his full success. He wore a cold and reserved exterior, a phlegmatic manner which made the impression that he lacked *heart.* But this was not so; for often, when drawn out in an unbending mood, he was a very genial and interesting companion. Still it was true that his development was intellectual rather than affectional, and whilst in the pulpit or in other public speech, he could rouse and play with or allay any passion of the human mind, he himself would at the same time seem to be passionless. This habitude disqualified him from finding his way to the hearts of young men, and when trouble arose, either within the college, in the administration of discipline, or from without, he had not ardent friends to rally to his support. Encountering many of the same difficulties which met his predecessor, arising out of deficient endowment of the institution, he probably lacked his patience in enduring them.

And questions of policy arising between him and the Board of Trustees, he, towards the close of his administration, found nearly the same parties arrayed against him whose want of cordial co-operation had discouraged the former President. This he might have disregarded if he had been sustained by warm-hearted loyalty among the students. But whilst they could not but admire his great abilities and qualifications as an instructor, his reserved manner had kept him from their hearts, and he had not fully their moral support. After a laborious and faithful occupancy of the place for some three years and a half, he resigned it, and left Easton.

It is but simple justice to Dr. Yeomans' memory to say, that he rendered very valuable service to Lafayette College. He kept the standard of scholarship at the full elevation at which he found it, and introduced some beneficial changes. He encouraged and required thorough study, and the literary morale of the institution did not suffer in his hands.

Upon his resignation, there seemed to be a spontaneous turning of all minds to Dr. Junkin as the man best suited to fill the post of President in the college he had founded. Without any apparent concert, his name was in every mouth; nor is it known to this day from whom the suggestion first came. The students, the citizens of Easton and vicinity, neighboring ministers, and gentlemen of prominence, in the Board of Trustees and out of it, all began to ask, "Would Dr. Junkin return?" His brother, the present writer, lived a few miles from Easton, in New Jersey. He had resigned the chair he held in the College some years before, on account of the increase of his pastoral duties, and took no part in the councils of the Institution. He was surprised with the inquiry, "Do you think it possible your brother would return to Easton?" and still more surprised to learn that before he heard it, or had thought it probable such a wish should prevail, it was generally spoken of in the community.

The Board of Trustees, feeling a weight of responsibility for the success of the Institution, moved, too, by this generally prevailing sentiment of the community and of the students, and no doubt prompted by their experience of Dr. Junkin's former administration, and by confidence in his qualifications, elected him President, and invited his return. It was unsought and unexpected by him or any of his kindred, and the announcement took him by surprise.

The vote for his recall was unanimous in the Board. The nomination was made by one of the members, and seconded by another, from neither of whom such a movement could have been expected. But both of these gentlemen not only took the lead in the re-election of Dr. Junkin, and joined in the official request for his acceptance, but they wrote private letters assuring him of a cordial reception and co-operation.

Some of the students, who had entered the lower classes whilst Dr. Junkin was President, were still in the College, and longed for his return; and, indeed, there had been kept up a sort of traditional feeling of regard for him, which was participated by many who did not personally know him. Besides this, he had been invited, in 1842, to deliver the annual address before the Literary Societies of the College. He had accepted the invitation, and pronounced a very effective and eloquent discourse on "The Spirit of Protestant Colonization of North America." The students passed resolutions expressive of their desire that he would yield to the request of the Board of Trustees and resume the Presidency. Citizens of Easton, and clergymen of the vicinage, wrote letters of encouragement; and at last, after examining with care into the state of affairs, his brother joined in the request.

He was no longer expected to assume the pecuniary responsibility of the Institution. He was guaranteed a fixed salary, and the Board undertook, as they had done during the administration of Dr. Yeomans, the management of the funds of the College. The result of all was, that he returned to Easton, in October, 1844, and resumed his labors in the still favorite field of his former toils.

At the time of his resumption of the Presidency, the Faculty of the College consisted of Rev. Charles W. Nassau, Professor of Languages; Washington McCartney, Esq., Professor of Mathematics and Natural Philosophy; David Yeomans, Esq., Professor of Chemistry and Rector of the Normal School, and Hon. J. M. Porter, Professor of Law. In 1846, Professor McCartney resigned, and Professor James H. Coffin was elected.

After his entrance upon his official duties at Easton, the life of Dr. Junkin was, for some years, little diversified by incidents out of the ordinary routine. He performed his duties with his accustomed zeal and energy, and the Institution over which he presided continued to grow in reputation and usefulness. As formerly, he was ever ready to lend a helping hand to his brethren in the pastoral office; and, in fact, preached the gospel as often and as earnestly as if he had been a pastor, and was as constant in attendance upon the church courts.

In May, 1845, he went to Cincinnati as a Commissioner to the General Assembly, from the Presbytery of Newton. He opened the Assembly with a sermon from John viii. 32, "The truth shall make you free," and presided until another Moderator was chosen. The sermon, delivered upon this occasion, was published, at the request of many members of the General Assembly, during the sessions of that body, making an octavo pamphlet of twenty-eight pages.

This discourse made a strong impression at the time, and may have had some influence upon the deliverances of the

Assembly that year, upon the question of human freedom. It evolves the author's theory of the process by which true liberty is to be obtained and perpetuated among a race once fallen. The first sentences disclose the author's views of genuine piety:

"In the absence of practical holiness, there can be no sufficient evidence of true piety. Speculative orthodoxy, deep and pungent conviction, emotions of joy even to ecstasy, high-toned and fiery zeal, may all have existed, and most of them may co-exist, and yet the heart not be right with God. It is easy to say, Lord, Lord; to avow our belief in the doctrines of religion, to love in tongue, to attach ourselves to some division of the great Christian army; . . . but to fight the good fight of faith, to evince the truth and reality of our love by actions, to embody the doctrines of religion in a life of holiness, and show to all men that we are freed from the bonds of corruption; this is a different matter. Yet this is indispensable as an evidence of discipleship."

He discussed the subject, "Truth and Freedom," under three heads:—I. Man's estate of slavery to sin; II. His restoration to freedom; III. The means of his restoration.

I. He very briefly pointed out the causes and the nature of man's bondage to sin:—1. Sin entered through the door of the understanding. The leading faculty, judgment, first failed by reason of false perceptions. The mind cannot determine in favor of evil *as such*. Nothing can become a prevalent motive to action, but that which *appears* good. Our first mother, "being *deceived*, was in the transgression." Hence—2. Ignorance of God, of ourselves, and of our relations to Him, produces and belongs to our moral degradation. 3. The pride of free will is the strongest link in the chain of human bondage. . . . Scorning subordination to the will of his Maker, man threw himself upon his own sovereignty, and plunged into the abyss of woe. 4. This leads to a total debasement of the affections, which rivets his manacles. 5. This produces utter indisposition and incapacity of this slave of sin to break off his chains and restore himself to true freedom.

II. Under this head he stated and answered the question, What is true freedom? And, after a careful and thorough analysis, he declared it to be voluntary and cheerful action in obedience to the rule of right,—*pleasing* to do *right*,—doing the will of God from the heart. And he proves that freedom in doing wrong is the opposite of this,—is slavery.

III. He pointed out the means of restoration,—THE TRUTH.

True knowledge of God, law, duty, connected with a true and heart-swaying knowledge of the WAY in which a creature, once fallen, can be brought to a state of cheerful obedience to the rule of right—this is found in the grand remedial law,—the Gospel,—which contains all the elements of freedom; and which, when made effectual upon the heart by the Spirit of freedom,—*i.e.* the Holy Ghost,—makes the man free with the glorious liberty of a child of God. He shows that the soul which truly believes in the vicarious obedience and death of the Son of God, will, by the power of that faith, be made to love God and his law,—to *love* the *right*,—and to do it freely, cheerfully; and when a man pleases to do right, he can *safely do as he pleases*,—he is free. He draws a contrast between the *free-will* scheme and the *free-grace* scheme; and shows that the latter only can produce true liberty, whilst the former leads away from God and the right, and into deeper bondage. He traced the history of these two antagonistic systems, and exhibited their workings in human society, and their past influence upon the morals and the liberties of mankind; and having exhibited the *facts*, he explained their philosophy. In doing this, he demonstrated that spiritual freedom, as produced by the grand TRUTH of the Gospel, in its natural outgrowth, produced personal, social, and political freedom. After designating other elements of social liberty, embodied in the remedial law,—the free-grace system,—he points to one distinguishing element, as follows:

"But the principal point of special adaptation in the free-grace system to be the precursor and promoter of a free system of government, is found in its federative or representative principle. We have only to transfer this prominent feature of our theology into government, ecclesiastical and civil, and religious and political liberty are both secured. That this transfer should be made first into the social body called the church, when framing her form of government, is exceedingly natural; and such was the fact. The churches, in the very first age, organized their government on this principle. They built up an *imperium in imperio*,—an ecclesiastical government within the civil,—an extended plan, which gave the people the choice of their own immediate spiritual rulers, and the right of being represented in all the courts of the church by their own chosen officers. Thus sprang up in the Christian church a representative government, limited, in its action, to matters purely religious, and interfering not at all with the civil affairs of the empire; but always seeking the peace of the world and the glory of God. The light of this spiritual rule continued to shine upon the path of the Roman monarchy, Pagan and Christian, until, finding itself in peril of sinking under accumulated difficulties, the monarchy threw out its arms for help and grasped the Church. From this coalition resulted the hybrid monster of the Papal despotism. Upon its development, and before its cruel tyranny, the true church—Christ's own holy spouse, the republic ecclesiastical—retired into the fastnesses of the Alps, the Grisons, the Apennines, the Pyrenees, the mountains of Bohemia, the hills of Caledonia, the wilds of America. In this last wilderness retreat, after centuries of iron oppression and compression, the grand representative principle, which the true church had preserved, found room to expand itself in the ecclesiastical and to pass over into the civil government. The result is, a vast, free, republican empire, founded upon the broad basis of federal representation! How interesting the *fact!* How beautiful the philosophy! The truth shall make you free!

"Fathers and brethren beloved, you,—and thereby I mean the General Assembly of the Presbyterian Church,—and in this I mean no offence to other denominations who (I rejoice to know) hold the same doctrines,—you have a fearful responsibility in reference to the truth. To your hands hath the Captain of Salvation committed the Protestant banner. Yours be the honor of rallying round the flag of the covenants, during the conflicts of the present times, and during that fearful war of opinion to which all Christendom looks forward with such trembling solicitude. Yours, I confidently believe, is the glorious destiny of bearing it onward, over hill, and dale, and valley, and moor, and mountain, until beneath its ample folds and heavenly sway, all the nations shall rejoice in the freedom of THE TRUTH!"

Dr. Junkin's fellow-student, and life-long friend, Dr. John Knox, was a delegate to the General Assembly this year from the Reformed Protestant Dutch Church, and they had much pleasant, fraternal intercourse. Dr. N. L. Rice, Dr. John T. Edgar, Dr. James H. Thornwell, Dr. J. C. Lord, Dr. Krebs, Dr. McGill, Dr. Jos. T. Smith, and others distinguished for ability, learning, and practical wisdom, were members of the Assembly. Among the ruling Elders were Judges Grier and Leavitt, and Hon. Walter Lowrie. According to an immemorial usage, Dr. Junkin, as the retiring Moderator, was Chairman of the Committee on Bills and Overtures. A number of important subjects came before that committee, and were reported to the house.

Among these Overtures was one from the Presbytery of Ohio, asking for a decision of the question, "Is Baptism by the Church of Rome valid?" It was proposed to answer the question in the negative. This led to a long and animated debate, continuing through parts of six sessions. It was finally decided to answer the question in the negative, 173 voting for that deliverance, 8 against it, and 6 *non liquet*. A committee, of which Dr. Junkin was one, was appointed to prepare a paper explanatory of the grounds of this action. This committee prepared a paper which was adopted by the Assembly. This decision led to a subsequent discussion of the question through the press, in which Dr. Junkin took a somewhat prominent part. The *Princeton Review* disapproved of the decision of the Assembly, and published some able arguments in opposition to it. Dr. Junkin, Dr. R. J. Breckenridge, and others defended the action of the Assembly. In that decision the church has ever since acquiesced.

As chairman of the Committee on Bills and Overtures, Dr. Junkin reported Overture No. 3, being a collection of petitions and memorials upon the subject of slavery. The committee recommended that the petitions from Chillicothe and Donegal Presbyteries be read before the Assembly, and that a special committee of seven be appointed, to which all papers on the whole subject be referred. This was done. The petitions were read, and a committee appointed, consisting of Messrs. Rice, Lord, McGill, N. H. Hall, Lacy, Leavitt, and Dunlap.

This committee, on the fifth day of the sessions, made a report, which gave rise to considerable discussion, and which was adopted by the very decisive vote of 168 yeas to 13 nays, and three *non liquet*.

This deliverance of the General Assembly* has been, perhaps, more misunderstood and misrepresented by the churches and parties holding to extreme abolition views than any other act of our chief judicatory. But it is thought that a candid perusal of that able paper will show that,

---

* See Minutes, 1845, pp. 16, 17, 18; also Baird's Digest, p. 811.

whilst the Assembly refused to take steps in advance of the authority of Scripture, and to adopt measures divisive of the church and the country, there is no approval of the evils of domestic slavery, and no withdrawal or denial of the previous testimony of the church upon that subject. So, indeed, the Assembly of the following year explicitly declared.*

After the Assembly dissolved, Dr. Junkin returned to his home and to his duties in the College, and was not much engaged in other public affairs for some time, if we except the discussion already alluded to upon the validity of Romish baptism. His communications upon this question were published in the PRESBYTERIAN.

In the church courts Dr. Junkin was always a welcome member, and, although he did not often speak, his counsels were listened to with profound respect. He was called upon not unfrequently to preach upon special subjects, and to take part in ordination and installation services. On such occasions he was always rich, instructive, and suggestive. One of them will be remembered with interest by the members of the Presbytery of Newton who still survive. It was the ordination of the Rev. J. H. Mason Knox (now Dr. Knox), and his installation over the church of German Valley, New Jersey. Dr. Junkin delivered the charge to the pastor. Mr. Knox was the son of the fellow-student and beloved friend of Dr. Junkin, Dr. John Knox, of New York, and the grandson of his revered theological preceptor, Dr. John M. Mason. Dr. Knox was present, and had preached the sermon upon the occasion.

When Dr. Junkin arose to deliver the charge, the memories of the past, and the tender associations of three generations, seemed to crowd upon his heart; and his voice trembled with emotion as he uttered the first sentences of his address:

---

* Minutes, 1846, p. 207.

"My dear young brother," said he, "this day, with gratitude and joy of heart, we behold another proof of the faithfulness of a covenant-keeping God. A hundred generations have passed since He recorded the sweet promise, 'My Spirit that is upon thee, and my words which I have put in thy mouth, shall not depart out of thy mouth, nor out of the mouth of thy seed, nor out of the mouth of thy seed's seed, saith the Lord, from henceforth and forever.' 'The children of thy servants shall continue, and their seed shall be established before thee.' (Isa. lix. 21; Ps. cii. 28.) A thousand proofs of its verity have been witnessed in the past; and we this day see another added to the already long list. Here stands the son, the grandson, the great-grandson* of those whom God enabled to be faithful to their covenant engagements that they might become the living and honored witnesses of his own covenant faithfulness. The son of my early friend, the companion of my youth, with whom, oh, how often! I have taken sweet counsel, and gone to the house of God, stands before me. The grandson of my venerated, almost adored, theological teacher stands forth this day appointed and commissioned, by the authority of Jesus Christ, to preach the glorious Gospel of the blessed God. And by the same authority, it has become my duty to address to this son of a godly, a ministerial ancestry, the word of solemn exhortation. Can it be otherwise, then, but that my mind should teem with visions of the past? How can I exclude from my thoughts the image of the venerated dead? Can thirty years break down the laws of association, and erase the deepest impressions of the memory? Can time annihilate the strong and tender bonds of Christian love?

"But, if possible, would it be expedient? If I could command away these memories,—what the profit? May not their entertainment and presentation to you, sir, and to this auditory, be the very best accomplishment of my present function? Paul enjoins, 'Be ye followers of me, even as I also am of Christ.' And we may learn many useful lessons from the example of those who have gone before us, even when they were not infallible.

---

* The father of Dr. John M. Mason was Dr. John Mason, an eminent minister of Christ.

"Now, among all the dead, and all the living, of whom I have obtained knowledge, personally or by reading, none comes so near my *beau ideal* of the great Apostle to the Gentiles as John M. Mason, of New York; unless it be John Calvin, of Geneva, whom the former used to denominate the Paul of the Reformation. For mere physical properties,—for all that is addressed to the eye and to the ear,—for dignity of mien, for impressive influence of presence and of manner, for loftiness of style and tone, for the thunder-storm of eloquence, deep, awful, and resistless, the American excelled both the European and the Asiatic; for both these labored under physical disadvantages which never impaired the power nor impeded the progress of the other."

This introduction to the charge is quoted for the double purpose of giving the reader some insight of the author's *heart*, and as a specimen of the ardor of his manner upon interesting occasions.

The whole address is richly instructive in the varied duties of the pastoral office, abounding both in the philosophy and the scriptural lessons of the subject, and in practical illustrations drawn from the example of Dr. Mason and other eminent ministers.

Ten years before this, he had thrilled a vast congregation of the same Presbytery by a charge given, upon a similar occasion, to his own brother, when ordained pastor of the First Church of Greenwich, New Jersey.

The population of Easton was increasing during these years, and many persons in the place, and others in the Presbytery, within whose bounds it then was, were of opinion that Presbyterianism ought to enlarge its borders in that town. The First Presbyterian Church, then under the pastoral care of the late Rev. John Gray, D.D., was full to overflowing. The edifice had been enlarged several times, but still many who desired it could not obtain seats.

With a view to meet the demand for increased means of grace, Dr. Junkin commenced a series of lectures on experimental piety in a Baptist church located in a part of the town remote from the Presbyterian church. This exercise was held in the afternoon of the Sabbath, so as not to interfere with the worship in the other churches, whose services were conducted morning and night. Before engaging in this work, he had made a request, in writing, addressed to the Session of the Presbyterian Church, for their consent to the undertaking and co-operation in it.

The Session gave consent to his preaching, but in such terms as indicated that the proposal was distasteful to them. The lectures were commenced, were well attended, and were maintained so long as Dr. Junkin remained in Easton. Many were edified, some were converted to God, and the result was what Dr. Junkin had frankly informed the Session was the intention at the time he asked permission to begin the service,—a movement for the organization of a second Presbyterian church. Notice of their purpose to apply to the Presbytery for an organization was duly given to the authorities of the First Church by those who favored the enterprise, and in process of time the application was made.

To the surprise of many, the movement was strenuously resisted by the Session of the First Church, and by some of its prominent members who were not in official station; whilst others of that congregation favored the movement. After a very full investigation of the whole matter, the Presbytery resolved, with a great degree of unanimity, to grant the request of the applicants; and a committee was accordingly appointed to carry the order of Presbytery into effect. Shortly afterwards the Second Presbyterian Church was duly organized, and went into operation. Dr. Junkin, and other members of the Presbytery, continued to supply the new church until it obtained a pastor.

But this result was not reached without a most unexpected amount of opposition, and a warm conflict in the Presbytery. This could not have been foreseen, for the necessity for church extension in that place was almost universally admitted. The *animus* of the opposition it is not easy to conceive, but it was powerful, persistent, and lasted three years beyond the period at which Dr. Junkin was translated to Virginia. The Rev. Dr. John Skinner was the pastor of the church during this time. At last, after a struggle of four years or more against the difficulties in its way, the church applied to Presbytery to dissolve its organization, assigning as the reason the opposition above alluded to. Accordingly, at the meeting of the Presbytery in April, 1851, the church was dissolved. Most of the material of which it was composed sought and obtained organization as a Reformed Protestant Dutch Church, which is still in existence,—a highly respectable congregation.

Into the merits of the controversy concerning the subject of a second church in Easton, it is not the intention of the biographer to enter, and it is mentioned chiefly because of the influence it had in ultimately leading Dr. Junkin to yield to a call to another field of labor. It is probable, that if he could have anticipated the nature and intensity of the opposition to a second church he would have refused, from prudential considerations, to join in the movement. But that opposition did not fully develop itself until he was so far committed to the movement that he could not recede with honor and a good conscience. He was profoundly convinced that the welfare of souls and the glory of Christ demanded the enterprise. And whilst some may doubt the wisdom of his participation in the movement after he found that the authorities of the First Church were against it, especially in view of the fact that this opposition included Trustees of the College, who had hitherto exerted a controlling influence in the Board; yet none who knew the man will for a moment doubt the purity and disinterestedness of his motives.

The *personnel* of this opposition, with the exception of the pastor of the First Church, was identical with that which, in 1840, had wrought annoy, and, including him, was identical with the agency which had removed Dr. Yeomans from the College. As might have been apprehended, at the first opportunity the bad feeling which had been excited showed itself, in the Board of Trustees of the College, to the embarrassment of the President and the Faculty in the administration of its affairs. A rule, which had been adopted in 1840 by the Board, to cover the case of discipline already mentioned, and which Dr. Junkin was assured was abrogated before he was recalled to the Presidency, was revived. This was a rule granting to a student an appeal to the Board of Trustees against the decisions of the Faculty in certain cases: which would give to the portion of the Board living near to the College practical control over its discipline,—a result inevitably destructive of the paternal authority of a faculty and of the discipline of a college. This and other matters gave opportunity for the inauguration of one of those struggles, alas! too common in the history of American colleges, which marred the comfort and usefulness of the President and the Faculty of the College.

The details of it would have little interest for the general reader; and, as all the men prominent in these scenes have gone to their final account, we dismiss the subject with only the mention which is necessary to vindicate the memory of the chief sufferer. This can be done by a statement of *general facts*, which all persons familiar with the constitution and workings of Boards of Trustees of colleges will understand. 1. A portion of the members of the Board lived in Easton, and they, of course, would feel a lively interest in the College, and would be apt to have their *feelings* interested in case of any trouble. 2. Of these a small majority, and they active and influential men, took part against the President and against the Faculty, who, with one exception, were with him. 3. When the distant members of the Board, who were unaffected by local interests and feelings, were present, the majority was the other way, and the course of the President was sustained. 4. But it was difficult, except at the Annual Meetings, to obtain a full attendance, so that local details fell under the control of those resident in Easton. 5. The great mass of the citizens of Easton, outside of a single church, and many within it also, were with the President and the Faculty in judgment and feeling. 6. The students also, with a single exception, adhered loyally to their President. 7. His brethren of the Presbytery, with two or three exceptions, approved of his course. 8. At the time he ultimately left, the College was in a highly prosperous condition, so far as numbers and morale were concerned; the classes being larger than usual, and the last class that graduated under his administration being the largest that had ever left the Institution; and immediately after his departure, the attendance of students was reduced to a mere handful.

It might excite surprise, that in such a condition of things, a man of Dr. Junkin's vigor and firmness would become in any degree discouraged. But the men who had grown lukewarm or hostile, although few in numbers, had been among the most demonstrative friends of the College, were persons of social position, controlled some wealth, possessed much adroitness and pertinacity, and held on to their places, and the College was like a house divided against itself.

Still, though perplexed, the President was not cast down, but continued to labor for the welfare of his favorite Institution.

On the 10th of June, 1847, an event occurred which threw a deep gloom over the College and the community, and deeply moved Dr. Junkin's tenderest sensibilities.

The only son of his beloved friend and fellow-student, Dr. Robert Steel, of Abington, was in attendance as a student in the College, in his second college year. He was a youth of much promise, peculiarly correct, kind, and courteous, and much beloved by his teachers and fellow-students. On the day above mentioned he had gone into the Delaware to bathe, and was drowned. So soon as the tidings of the sad event reached the President's ears, he hastened to the river, and, with characteristic energy, made every exertion for the recovery of the body. His heart was deeply affected, and when others, after nightfall, abandoned the search as useless, he, with some of the students, continued it; nor did he relax his diligence until all that remained of his beloved pupil was restored to the anguished hearts of the stricken parents.

In the summer of 1848 the Trustees of Washington College, at Lexington, Virginia, elected Dr. Junkin to the Presidency of that Institution, to fill the vacancy occasioned by the resignation of the Rev. Henry Ruffner, D.D.

Washington College had grown out of a Classical School or Academy founded by the Rev. William Graham, assisted and encouraged by other Presbyterian ministers and the people of their charges.

That part of Virginia (the Valley) had been settled chiefly by Scotch, or, rather, Scotch-Irish, people, who adhered to the Presbyterian faith and forms.

Mr. Graham was the boy, mentioned in a previous chapter, who was a fellow-refugee with Dr. Junkin's father, in the block-house, on the banks of the Paxtunk. He was a man of devout piety, considerable learning, and an earnest worker. As the School began to flourish about the time of the commencement of the struggle which resulted in the independence of America, it was called "Liberty Hall." It was eminently useful in training men for the ministry, and for other professions, and was justly beloved by the people of that part of Virginia.

During the Revolutionary struggle, the prince of patriots, George Washington, himself an Episcopalian, had seen men and their patriotism tried in the crucible of war; and he had found that the cause of his country had no more reliable friends than the Scotch-Irish Presbyterians of "West Augusta." When, therefore, the Legislature of Virginia had made repeated efforts to induce him to accept some pecuniary expression of their love and veneration, he persisted in refusing, until at last he consented to *give direction* to the bestowment of a gift of stock in the James River Canal, but not to receive it himself. The Legislature consented, and Washington directed that the gift should be bestowed upon "Liberty Hall," near Lexington.

This was done, and, the stock having been commuted, the chief part of the endowment of the Hall was derived from this source. The Trustees accepted the benefaction, obtained a college charter, changed the name to Washington College, and inaugurated a Faculty. Funds from other quarters were received, a beautiful site was selected, handsome buildings were erected, and the Institution has been a source of great benefit to Virginia and the country, numbering among its Alumni some of our most eminent men.

Dr. Junkin made a visit to Lexington to examine for himself the character and prospects of this new field. After his return, and under the urgency of his brother and other friends, he came slowly and reluctantly to the conviction, that the hand of God was again beckoning him away from his "Lovely Lafayette." The College to which he was called had what was then deemed a respectable endowment. A majority of the Board of Trustees were Presbyterians, and in full accord with his own views. It was surrounded by a homogeneous population, and there was every prospect of a peaceful prosecution of his favorite work.

Besides this, his friends, in Pennsylvania and New Jersey, felt that he had endured enough of the toils and sacrifices incident to the founding of a college, and that he ought to accept of a place where some at least of these would not be required. And it seemed to them, that such a man ought no longer to be held to a labor which some, from whom he had a right to expect better things, had been endeavoring to make the task of Sisyphus. He accepted the appointment.

There was another consideration, which may have had influence in inclining Dr. Junkin to seek a field of labor in a milder climate. His second son, Joseph, had, for some years, been in imperfect health. He was a young man of fine scholarship, a graduate of Lafayette College. He had been laboring as a classical and mathematical teacher at Edge Hill School, Princeton, N. J., where, indeed, he had sustained the burden of the Institution, on account of the almost constant absence of the principal. Under his arduous labors his health declined, and pulmonary disease manifested itself, and, before the removal to Virginia was decided upon, it had been determined that the invalid should seek a Southern clime.

Dr. Junkin had now been connected with Lafayette College for about thirteen years. It was sixteen years since he first entered upon his duties, and he had been three years and a half at Miami. When he came, there was not a foot of land, a stone, or a dollar belonging to the Institution. When he left it, it was in such condition as to promise that, if properly managed, it might reach the eminence which it has since attained. Perhaps no College in the land had, at the age of sixteen years, given so large a number of scholarly, valuable men to the Church and to the country. To name but a few, Lafayette already numbered among her Alumni such men as the Rev. David Coulter, of Missouri; Rev. James B. Ramsey, D.D., of Virginia; Rev. W. H. Green, D.D., of Princeton; Rev. Ninian Bannatyne, of Washington; Hon. William A. Porter, of Philadelphia; Rev. John M. Lowrie, D.D., of Fort Wayne; Rev. Wm. D. Howard, D.D., of Pittsburg; Rev. Thomas C. Porter, D.D., of Easton; Rev. Charles Elliott, D.D., of Chicago Seminary; Rev. Isadore Loewenthal, the erudite and gifted Israelite, who gave the Bible in their own language to the people of Afghanistan; Rev. Robert Watts, D.D., of Belfast, and others worthy to be named in such a catalogue. Besides these, many other eminent men obtained part of their education and mental development, under Dr. Junkin and Dr. Yeomans, in this Institution.

The last Commencement of Lafayette College, at which Dr. Junkin presided, was a day memorable in his history and that of the Institution. Not having, as on former occasions, the use of the Presbyterian church, the Commencement exercises were held in the spacious assembly-room of the Odd-Fellows' Hall. A large audience was present,—many from a distance. The Board of Trustees was more full than usual, although that part of the local Board, which had not been in accord with the Faculty, did not appear until near the close of the public exercises. When the President of the Board came in, and made an announcement in regard to the opening of the next College term, he was received with a very general and decided demonstration of disapprobation by the audience and by the students, which was very improper, and which none deplored more than Dr. Junkin himself. But it was a spontaneous outburst of pent-up feeling, which he could not have anticipated, and could not instantly repress, although he immediately made the attempt.

When the exercises closed, and the parting moment had come, the members of the Senior class approached their beloved President to bid him a final farewell. They could not speak,—tears rolled down those manly, youthful cheeks. They grasped his hand, one after another, in silent adieu. The undergraduates pressed forward and did the same, until every student present, numbering about one hundred and twenty, had taken his hand and bade a silent, tearful farewell. It was a spontaneous movement, without preconcert or arrangement. The young men wept, the President wept, the audience was in tears, whilst no sound was heard except the quiet tread of those noble young men as they advanced to the dais, pressed their President's hand, and retired.

The writer of this page was present at that scene, of course not an unmoved spectator. Beside him, on the stage, sat the Rev. Dr. John M. Krebs, of New York. This eminent minister was deeply moved by what he saw, and exclaimed, in a voice choked with emotion, "This is the proudest day in George Junkin's history! The tears and silent eloquence of these young men present a vindication and a eulogy that need no addition!"

Another eye-witness of this impressive scene, the Rev. Dr. J. H. Mason Knox, thus alludes to it in his eloquent memorial discourse, delivered shortly after Dr. Junkin's death:

"It was no small trial for Dr. JUNKIN a second time to give up the care of an institution in which he had spent so many of the best years of his life, for which he had toiled assiduously and sacrificed so much, and in which, moreover, he had been so eminently successful as an educator, and had established his fame in this regard in all the land. The parting was a most thrilling scene. I can see him now as he stood upon the Commencement-stage, in September, 1848, and apostrophized 'Lovely Lafayette,' bidding her, in any time of need, to 'send down the Valley for her friend, whose devotion to her interests could never grow less until his heart should cease to beat.' The students rushed from their seats to his side, and each young man, as he bade his honored, beloved President farewell, was bathed in tears; and the Rev. Dr. Krebs gave utterance to the feeling, which was welling up in every heart, in the exclamation, 'GEORGE JUNKIN, this is the most glorious day of your life!'

"It may not be amiss," Dr. Knox continues, "to say further, that Lafayette did not recover for many years from the staggering blow she received from this second resignation of her Father and Founder,—not, indeed, till the name of GEORGE JUNKIN again appeared in her list of instructors."

Whilst this last remark of Dr. Knox is literally true, it is not claimed that the revival of the College was promoted so much by Dr. Junkin's direct agency, as by the fact, that its authorities and its very efficient President, Dr. Cattell, were known to be in accord with him; and that his faith, prayers, and known zeal for it may have aided to secure public confidence and the blessing of God. His professorship was *Emeritus* in the department of Political Economy. We shall see that after his return from Virginia he took a lively interest in Lafayette.

Alluding to the above scene, Dr. Sprague says, in his biographical sketch in *The Memorial Volume:*

"His parting with his classes at Lafayette, on Commencement-day, was a scene of the most tender interest; and the estimation in which he was there held was sufficiently indicated by the fact that twenty-six of those who had been his students there, appeared at Washington College to resume their studies under his direction."*

These were chiefly of the higher undergraduate classes, and among them were such men as Robert Watts, D.D., the successor of Dr. Cooke in the Chair of Theology in Belfast; Rev. R. M. Wallace, of Altoona; Rev. A. W. Sproull,

---

* Memorial, p. 145.

of Chester, Pa.; Rev. John Armstrong, of Iowa; Rev. A. M. Lowry, of Port Carbon; Rev. E. D. Finney, of Maryland, and others.

When it is remembered that, at that time, Lexington could only be reached by one hundred and twelve miles of staging from Winchester, the estimate of his instructions formed by these young men will seem enhanced.

A few days before his departure from Easton, the following paper was presented to him, expressive of the sentiments of the citizens:

"At a numerous meeting of citizens of Easton and its vicinity, assembled at the Odd-Fellows' Hall, in pursuance of public notice; on motion of Mr. John J. Burke, Hon. John Cooper, M.D., was called to the chair, and Dr. Charles Innes appointed secretary.

"The object of the meeting being stated, the Rev. John Vanderveer moved that a committee of *seven* be appointed to draft resolutions, whereupon Messrs. T. M. Cann, John J. Burke, Daniel Lachenaur, M.D., R. S. Chidsey, John Eyerman, George Field, and Philip Mixell were chosen.

"The committee retired, and, after a short deliberation, submitted the following preamble and resolutions, which were unanimously adopted:

"'*Whereas*, The Rev. George Junkin, D.D., the *founder* and firm supporter of Lafayette College, has resigned the Presidency of the same; a station, the duties of which, in the language of the Board of Trustees announcing the fact, "he has ably performed for *sixteen* years, with the exception of a short absence;" and

"'*Whereas*, During all this period, he has most ably and zealously advocated, and sustained in our midst, the interests of education, morality, and religion; therefore,

"'*Resolved*, That we receive with deep and heartfelt regret the announcement of his removal from a sphere in which he has been so pre-eminently useful, and that we regard his departure as the withdrawal of one of our purest and brightest luminaries.

"'*Resolved*, That, though we recognize the fact that the labors of the Christian philosopher, wherever put forth, enure to the benefit of the world in general, yet we cannot but lament the departure of one who has been, and is still, so deeply cherished by those with whom he trod the classic ground, and who is beloved, by every true philanthropist, for his unwavering integrity, his fearless and indefatigable efforts for the promotion of *truth;* and we feel assured that the community, which has secured his services, has obtained a most valuable acquisition.

" '*Resolved,* That the thanks of this meeting, together with a copy of these resolutions, be given to the Rev. George Junkin, D.D., for his eminent services, and that these proceedings be published in the papers of our Borough, *The Presbyterian,* of Philadelphia, and the *Watchman of the South.*'

" JOHN COOPER, *Chairman.*

" CHARLES INNES, *Secretary.*"

CHAPTER XXXIII.

Award in Dr. Junkin's Favor—Departure for Virginia—Farewell—Washington College—Enters on Duty—Inaugural Address—No Change in his Instructions—Faculty—Route—The Invalid goes South—Dies—His Character—Dr. Junkin's Preachings—Bensalem—Baccalaureates—Influence on General Education—Family Statistics—Major Jackson—Heavy Afflictions—Mrs. Junkin's Death—Her Character—Consolation—Mrs. Jackson's Death—Prof. Fishburn's Death—The elder Daughter married—The colored Boy taken—Blessed are they that mourn—Educational Correspondence—Fraternal Fellowship—New Brunswick Speech—LL.D.—Temperance Labors in Virginia—Agricultural—Public Troubles—Labors and Sacrifices for Peace and Union—John Brown Raid—Resistance to Secession—Letter to Governor Curtin—Letter of Eli K. Price—Correspondence on Public Affairs—Virginia Secedes—The Flags raised, taken down, burned—Commotion in the College—Resigns—Exodus from Virginia.

SOME delay in his departure for the future scene of his labors was occasioned, by the difficulty of obtaining a settlement of Dr. Junkin's claims upon the Board of Trustees of the College. A disposition to deny those claims, in part, was shown by two or three, but at last a Rule of reference was obtained by him, and the choice of the arbitrators left to the Board itself or its representatives; and there was awarded to him, after a thorough investigation of the accounts, a little more than he had claimed. This matter adjusted, he and his household took another affectionate leave of their numerous friends in Easton, and set forth for the Valley of Virginia, to make another home among strangers, and to enter upon a new field of labor.

Washington College, Virginia, although a well-appointed institution, and usually manned by an able Faculty, had never attracted to its halls the numbers which its reputation and appliances for education merited. It was difficult to account for the fact; yet some reasons were palpable. The University of Virginia, located at Charlottesville, just over the Blue Ridge from Lexington, was the favorite resort of the sons of that ancient Commonwealth. The optional character of its curriculum—*i.e.* the plan of allowing the student or his parent to select which of the studies, taught in the institution, he would pursue—had peculiar attractions for some. Hampden Sidney College also divided the Presbyterian patronage of Virginia. The Virginia Military Institute, in the same town with Washington College, was also a rival, and had attractions for youth in its military appointments, and, being sustained in part by State bounty, was less expensive; whilst many of the sons of Virginia still resorted to the older colleges of the North and East.

Dr. Junkin did not find so much difficulty in inaugurating suitable discipline in Washington College as he had at Miami University. The morale of the institution was better; and he had comparatively little change to make in the *régime* of the institution.

He entered upon his duties as President of Washington College in October, 1848, but was not formally inaugurated until the next Commencement, the latter part of June, 1849, when he delivered his inaugural address. He was not long in identifying himself with the new community in which his lot had been cast, and with the interests of the grand old Commonwealth of which he had become a citizen, so far, at least, as its real advantage was concerned. Whilst he had in the North resisted aggressive abolition as tending to break up the peace of the country, divide the Union, and deluge the land in blood, he never was of opinion that slavery was a normal condition of society, or of any advantage to the moral or material interests of the country in which it exists. Whilst he was not willing, as we have seen, to adopt the principle that in every case the holding of a slave is a sin *per se*, and whilst he resisted with all his power the proposal to excommunicate from the church men who gave evidence of piety, though they held servants in bondage, he never held that slavery was a blessing, but rather a curse. His residence in a slave State did not abate this conviction. He considered it a great evil in its moral, religious, and economical aspects. As a system of labor, he saw that it paralyzed the impulses of industry, and retarded improvement. He looked upon it as a wrong to the servant, but as a greater curse to the master.

Had the field been open for fair, calm, and instructive discussion of this great social problem, it cannot be reasonably doubted that Dr. Junkin would have aimed to bring the lights of science, economics, and religion to bear upon it. But the abolition excitement had rendered that field a field of fire. Men's passions were roused, and discussion would have placed the interests with which he was identified in peril, without any reasonable prospect of countervailing good.

True, he did not change his lectures upon moral philosophy and political economy so as to adapt them to the latitude in which he now labored; the manuscript notes of his lectures show, that he did not fail to teach the same systems of moral philosophy and political economy as formerly; but to have assailed slavery upon the soil where it existed, and in the style of the abolitionists, would have been to do what he believed to be wrong, what the ultra abolitionists themselves never did, and what would at once have banished him from his field of labor. It cannot be reasonably doubted, by any who knew Dr. Junkin and the breadth and thoroughness of his teachings, that the thirteen years of his labors in Virginia have told, and will yet tell, beneficently upon the minds that were brought under his influence; and that the principles which he inculcated have had, and will continue to have, in the several communities in which these minds are found, a happy tendency in the reorganization of Southern society, and adapting it to the new state of things which has been forced upon it.

At the time Dr. Junkin became President of the College, its Faculty consisted of the Rev. Philo C. Calhoun, Professor of Greek, George E. Dabney, Latin, Rev. Dr. George D. Armstrong, Natural Philosophy, and Major D. H. Hill, afterwards Major-General Hill of the Confederate Army, Professor of Mathematics.

The route and the mode of travel by which the family reached Lexington illustrate the changes which have taken place in the country since 1848. They went by steamboat from Baltimore to Fredericksburg, by rail to Gordonsville, and thence in stage-coaches to Lexington.

A few weeks after the family arrived at Lexington it became manifest, that, unless the efficacy of a milder climate would produce a change, Joseph, the second son, whose loss of health has been already mentioned, must sink into an early grave. It was determined that he should proceed to Florida, in the hope of recovering his health. The older son, John M. Junkin, had recently settled at Trenton, New Jersey, as a physician, and it was deemed best for him to accompany his invalid brother to the South, so that every possible attention might be secured. The medical brother came on to Lexington, and, after a tender parting from the anxious and affectionate home circle, the two set out upon that long journey from which but one of them was to return. In due time they arrived at Marianna, Florida, where they obtained comfortable quarters for the winter. The tidings that reached the home circle at Lexington from the absent one, who was now the object of concentrated solicitude, varied almost weekly, sometimes awakening hope, and again bidding it expire. But as the months rolled on, the expectation of ever seeing his face in the flesh became feebler; and on the 3d of April, 1849, this noble youth laid his pilgrim mantle by, and found a grave in a land of strangers, in the sands of Florida. He died in the twenty-sixth year of his age. His was a peculiarly lovely character; amiable, discreet, affectionate, intelligent, scholarly, pious. Although he had been deterred from making a profession of religion by a self-distrust, superinduced by the very high standard which he had formed of the requisites to a Christian profession, none who knew him, much less any who knew him intimately, doubted that he was a true Christian.

The decease of this lovely and beloved son and brother, was a heavy stroke upon the family at home, and it was an event which was mourned by a very wide circle of kindred and friends. But they sorrowed not as they who have no hope.

That part of Dr. Junkin's life which he spent in Virginia was not marked by many incidents of the kind to impart interest to narrative. Its tenor was even. The regular routine of college duties, and the constant preachings of the gospel, in which, of course, he still abounded, whilst they make up the chief part of a man's usefulness, do not furnish the staple of attractive biography. From prudential considerations, he, of course, made as few changes in the college routine and curriculum as possible, but aimed, by an energetic practical administration, to make the scholarship of the College high and thorough; and in all his efforts he had able and effective assistance from the other professors.

Wherever he went he must needs preach the gospel, and he soon established a regular religious service in the College Chapel, at such an hour as not to interfere with the attendance of the students upon the morning service of the churches. Besides this, he soon took charge of a small congregation called Bensalem, four miles from Lexington, which he continued to serve, much to their edification, for about ten years. The people of this little flock became much attached to him, and he to them, and pleasant fruits of his ministry were there gathered. He also preached frequently in the church of Lexington and in others in the region round about, far and near, and, as in the former fields of his labors, was always welcomed to the pulpits of his brethren, both by pastors and people.

He still aimed, in his baccalaureate discourses, to advance the interests of general education, as connected with, and dependent upon, a high standard of college education. As examples, his first baccalaureate was "An Apology for College Education;" in which he illustrated and enforced its bearing upon schools of every inferior grade. In the next, he presented a kindred subject, "The College Curriculum;" and, in 1851, a strong plea in behalf of the proposition, that "The Colleges of Virginia have a right to a part of the Literary Fund." In his next, he unfolded some of the causes of the failure of a college course, in many cases, to produce the desired results, tracing the failure, in most instances, to the evil of "premature entrance," which was his theme. Thus, from year to year, he produced a series of educational papers, exceedingly suggestive and valuable in themselves, and well calculated to lead their readers and hearers to a higher and broader appreciation of the great work of education, in its philosophy, its *materia* and practical details.

In conventions which were held with the object of advancing the general interests of education, he bore an active part, and was always vigilant and untiring in personal efforts to that end. His correspondence shows that he exerted an extensive influence with his pen, by conferring with other men in different parts of the State and of the country, and he neglected no opportunity of advancing the cause of education and religion.

Thus several years of his life were passed in the quiet and happy discharge of the duties of his position. The society of Lexington was very congenial to his tastes and to those of his family. It was a highly intelligent community, and the general sentiment was decidedly favorable to religion. The Presbyterian Church was the largest and the most influential in the place, and the prominent men of the community threw the weight of their influence in favor of religion and good morals. Indeed, many of the leading men were professing Christians, and some of them office-bearers in the churches. That excellent minister, the Rev. William S. White, D.D., was pastor of the Presbyterian church of Lexington, during most of the time of Dr. Junkin's sojourn in that place, and with him he had much pleasant fraternal intercourse.

At the time Dr. Junkin removed to Lexington, his oldest son, John Miller, was located at Trenton, as a physician; his third son, and namesake, had just completed his law studies in the city of Philadelphia, where he opened an office, and has ever since remained in successful practice. His fourth son, Ebenezer Dickey, having graduated at Lafayette, was engaged as a classical teacher in Fredericksburg, Virginia, and his fifth, William Finney, remained for a few months teaching in New Jersey. Afterwards, the latter repaired to Lexington, where he took his first degree in the arts, in the class which graduated at Washington College in 1851. In the autumn of that same year, he and his brother, E. D. Junkin, who, meanwhile, had been teaching at Mount Holly, N. J., with Dr. Samuel Miller, entered the Theological Seminary at Princeton, in which they remained until they graduated in 1854.

On the 4th of August, 1853, the second daughter of Dr. Junkin, Eleanor, was united in marriage to a young man named Thomas J. Jackson, a native of Virginia, and a professor in the Virginia Military Institute. He was a graduate of West Point,—had served with some distinction in the war with Mexico,—had been several times brevetted for gallant and meritorious conduct,—and had retired from the army with the brevet rank of major, by which title he was usually addressed. He was an unobtrusive—almost diffident—young man, of good mind, exemplary morals, devout piety, and remarkably conscientious upon all questions of duty. The young people continued to be members of Dr. Junkin's family until the tender tie that bound them was sundered by the hand of death, a little more than a year after their marriage.

But before this sad event another heavy affliction fell upon the stricken household. On the 23d of February, 1854, the wife and the mother "was not, for God took her." On the 11th of the next month there appeared in the PRESBYTERIAN, of Philadelphia, an obituary notice from the same hand that traces these lines, and it is, in part, transferred to these pages as a just tribute to the memory of one well known and dearly loved:

"The departure from this to a higher life of this gifted and lovely Christian woman, is an event of its kind of more than ordinary interest, and demands more than a transient notice.

"'Precious in the sight of the Lord is the death of his saints,' and it ought to be precious in the estimation of all that love the Lord. Precious, considered as an accession to the ranks of the saints in glory; precious, as a proof of God's faithfulness; precious, as an illustration of the efficiency of the grace of Christ in giving the victory over pain, and fear, and death, and the grave; precious, as an earnest of a like triumph of all who possess 'like precious faith;' precious, as a means of converting those who have not this faith. Such was the death of Mrs. Junkin. She lived a life that was sure to end in such a death; and no believer can be indifferent to a scene so demonstrative of

42*

the power of godliness, so radiant with the presence of Jesus."

After a brief account of her birth, parentage, education, conversion, and marriage, the notice proceeds:

"Soon after her marriage, in 1819, Mrs. Junkin accompanied her husband to the field of labor to which he had been previously called at Milton, Pennsylvania. There she passed about eleven years of her life, devoted to the happiness of her family, the service of her Lord, and the interests of Zion. Universally admired and beloved in tha community, perhaps no lady ever withdrew from it whose departure was more generally and sincerely lamented; and many hearts, in that first field of her usefulness, will swell with sorrow when the tidings of her death shall be announced.

"After her husband was summoned from pastoral life to the field of Christian education, her position made her more widely known, and wherever known her character inspired the warmest regard. In her native city, in Germantown, in Easton, at Oxford, and in the Valley of Virginia, in which she ended her pilgrimage, she was beloved and venerated by all who made her acquaintance.

"Hers was a most symmetrical Christian character. In it were blended, in finest harmony, all the elements most desirable in a Christian lady. Without the splendor that dazzles, or the masculine vigor that annihilates the peculiarities of her sex, her mind was above mediocrity, and was well stored by wise and apposite reading, whilst her sweet and gentle temper, her unsullied delicacy, her perennial Christian cheerfulness, her sincerity, her wit sprightly but never barbed, her affability and considerateness, her benevolence, her warm and loyal friendship, and, above all, her delicate and steady reverence for the *right*, eminently fitted her for the sphere of life to which she was called, and which she so happily adorned.

"She was indeed a 'helpmeet' for the Christian pastor, and for the presiding officer of a literary institution; and many a fond parishioner, and many a grateful student, will cherish to their latest day the remembrance of her counsels and her kindness. To her counsels and to the gentle eloquence of her lovely Christian example did the writer of these lines owe more, whilst a student, than to any other human instrumentality. And he is not alone.

"Mrs. Junkin's was a life of unceasing Christian industry, cheerful, unostentatious, yet effective. In her family, in the church, and in the field of Christian education, her toils and sacrifices were constant, and a goodly number of valuable ministers owe their introduction to the sacred office in a greater or less degree to her industry and her means.

"As a daughter, a wife, a mother, a sister, a friend, who that knew her needs to be told what she was? Her life was a self-denying yet happy 'patient continuance in well doing,' and, as might have been expected, her end was peace,—more than peace,—it was triumph.

"Throughout a protracted and painful illness, every Christian grace, demanded in her circumstances, seemed to be in lovely, placid exercise. After conscientiously acquiescing in every effort of medical skill for her relief, when told by her dearest one that 'hope had fled, that the Lord was coming,' she calmly and sweetly replied, 'Well, his will be done. How soon? To-day?' 'Yes,' said the anguished husband, 'in a few hours.' 'Thank the Lord; the struggle will not be long. He that shall come will come, and shall not tarry.'

"This opened a scene which is seldom witnessed, even in

'The chamber where the good man meets his fate,
So privileged beyond the common walk
Of virtuous life, quite on the verge of heaven.'

"But, however desirable to describe it for the praise of the glory of God's grace, there is not space for detail. A sentence or two must suffice.

"When asked, 'Have you any word of advice for us?' she replied, 'I'm so exhausted I cannot say much. "The Lord will provide:" trust Him. I put my trust in Him long ago. He'll not forsake me. He has given sweet promises; *I just took Him at his word*. . . . Well, let Him—let Him come! He'll do all that's right. He'll take me to Himself. I have no fears,—no fears at all.' When subsequently asked, 'Is Jesus with you?' 'Yes; He is precious. I put my trust in Him alone,—alone.'

"Her two younger sons are just about closing their course in the seminary at Princeton; and when asked if it would not have gratified her to have lived to hear them preach the gospel, she touchingly replied,—alluding to her difficulty of hearing,—'But I *could* not have heard them!' When asked for a message for them, she said to them and all her children, 'Live near to Christ, and be kind to one another;' and subsequently added, 'Don't banish me,—*talk* cheerfully of me,—*think* cheerfully of me. I'll be with you oftener than you think. I'll watch over you: "Are they not all ministering spirits, sent forth to minister to them who shall be heirs of salvation?"' Laying her hand upon the head of her youngest child, who, a fortnight before, had completed the family ingathering by uniting with the church, she said, 'It is such a comfort, Julia, that you were brought in before I was called.'

"After sending messages to her absent dear ones,—giving a parting kiss to her children,—she sought her husband's hand, gazed intently upon him, and faltered, 'Darling husband, we have lived long and happily together, and we'll not be long apart.' She gave him a parting kiss, and passed to the better land.

"'She died as sets the morning star, which goes
Not down behind the darkened west, nor hides
Obscured amid the tempests of the sky,
But melts away into the light of heaven!'"

Rarely, if ever, did the hand of death sunder a marriage tie of greater tenderness, or one that had been productive of a larger amount of real felicity. For nearly thirty-five years it had held them together in a life of unbroken harmony, unfaltering confidence, and deep affection. Those who lived in the closest intimacy with them never knew of the slightest ripple in the sweet and smooth current of their affection; and it is believed there never was one. Of course the stroke was, upon the survivor, a very heavy one. He mourned her deeply, and with a tenderness truly affecting; but such was his perfect faith in the blessedness of her change, and such his unshaken confidence in the wisdom and goodness of a covenant-keeping God, that his sorrow was not like the sorrow of other men. There was a brightness—almost an exultation—in it which nothing could impart except that faith which is "the evidence of things not seen." Indeed, for years he seemed to feel that she was more constantly present with him than she had been whilst in the body; and this feeling never left him until consciousness seemed suppressed in his own dying struggle. Nor do we know that it then forsook him. Her miniature was always placed upon his study-table, so that at any moment he could turn an affectionate glance upon it; and memories of her seemed to mingle with all his thoughts, and even with his severer studies, without in the slightest measure interrupting them. In speaking of her to his children, or writing of her to them, or to his brother, he usually spoke of her as "sweet mother;" and it was affecting to witness the tenderness with which this man of strong intellect and mighty will cherished the memory of this best of wives. He sometimes in his letters expressed the fear that this sentiment was verging towards the idolatrous.

A few extracts from his correspondence with his elder daughter, who spent the winter of 1855 in Philadelphia, and his son, Rev. E. D. Junkin, will give some insight of his inner life in this season of affliction. Less than a year after Mrs. Junkin's death, he wrote as follows:

"LEXINGTON, Jan. 8, '55.

. . . . "Yes, indeed! I remember the Christmas glee of last year, and your sweet mother's happy face. It has rarely been two successive hours from before my eyes since last February 23d, whilst I am awake. Ah! how I see her everywhere! . . . And when I turn toward the unpressed and unruffled pillow at my side. Every night I have a quarrel with God for taking her away. I say, 'Why? oh, why? Could she not have done immense good for many years to come?' But the Lord answers me, 'I gave her to you for thirty-five years. Was that not enough? Who else has been so blessed? Who ever folded in his arms for so long a time one of my sweet, precious ones, so ready for the heavenly fold?' And thus, dear M., I am stricken dumb, and find not one word to say against it. And yet, when the next night comes, the same battle has to be fought over, and He gives the same victory. Thus He is drawing me up!

"Oh, yes! Your sweet mother and sweet E.* are sitting in the glorious, holy society above. Oh that I were fitted, as they were and are, for the happy home! She said, 'I'll know dear Joseph!' Yes, she knows him well; and she has not forgotten us,—'I'll be often with you when you don't know it.' This, too, is doubtless realized. My spirit has often, I believe, sweet intercourse with theirs; and sometimes a fragment of the joy is left in the confused relics of dreamy consciousness.

"Well, my dear child, I can hardly say I passed a sorrowful Christmas; or that any other day is so. It can hardly be called *sorrow*. I dare not call it joy; but it is a mingled state of emotion higher and holier than either, or both. I seem to myself to have a more constant apprehension of your sweet mother's presence than when she used to sit at the window or flit about the house. In all positions I see her,—blooming in youth, and more sweet in her last years,—or emaciated, and breathless, and cold, —all sights are lovely, *because* I obey her dying breath,— 'Think of me as a happy spirit in heaven.' That's the end of it all. And we'll soon see it so, if we prove faithful and submissive. . . . You give very good advice about health. Yes, *her* advices have far more influence over me than when she too was in the flesh. I do take extreme care of myself for her sake and her children's. . . .

"Major J.† is well, and growing heavenward faster than I ever knew any person to do. He seems only to think of E. and heaven." . . .

To his son, Rev. E. D. Junkin, he wrote, January 8, 1858:

"I have no better wish for you than that you find as

---

* Mrs. Jackson.

† The late Lieutenant-General Jackson, who was still an inmate of Dr. Junkin's family.

good a wife as I had, and live as happily and as long,—or so long as God pleases. It is wonderful the proportion of my thoughts that are devoted to your dear mother. She is still a more constant companion with me than when she sat in this very room. When I look at the miniature, morning and evening, the question, When shall I see her sweet face? almost idolatrously precedes the question, When shall I see my Lord face to face? I often pray to be delivered from this kind of idolatry. . . . As to praying for you,—that duty is as regular as eating my own meals. I doubt not, our prayers mingle as they rise."

Afflictions seldom come singly. Eight months after the decease of the mother, the daughter, Mrs. Jackson, was also taken. Eleanor Junkin had been married, as has been stated, to Major T. J. Jackson, on the 4th day of August, 1853, and on the 23d of October, 1854, a little more than one year thereafter, she went to the better land. Her babe and she were laid in the same grave. It was a terrible blow to the father, the brothers and sisters, and especially to the gallant and the godly young husband, who loved her with a most intense affection, of which her beautiful and symmetrical character and personal loveliness were worthy. He continued an inmate of Dr. Junkin's family for several years thereafter, and to him, and to them all, the sore affliction seemed to be greatly sanctified.

During a visit made to Lexington in the winter of 1856, the writer of these pages became more thoroughly acquainted with this young man, who, a few years afterwards, was so famous for military prowess and strategy, the almost idol of the Southern Confederacy. No one could, at that time, have perceived, in the modest, almost diffident, young professor of the Virginia Military Institute, the elements of high command and soldierly genius which were subsequently developed in the world-renowned "Stonewall" Jackson. He appeared to be a plain, unassuming

Virginia gentleman, possessed of sound judgment, good common sense, high-toned honor, deep Christian humility, and remarkable conscientiousness. Many sweet and pleasant hours did we spend in private Christian fellowship. The impression was left upon the writer's mind, that he was indeed "a devout soldier," but he never suspected that beneath that quiet, almost bashful, exterior there slumbered the genius and the energies of a great captain.

The relations and the intercourse between Dr. Junkin and this son-in-law, both before and after the death of Mrs. Jackson, were those of a fond father and an affectionate son. In his letters to the present writer, the former usually spoke of Major Jackson as "my dear young son." And few can appreciate the anguish it cost those hearts to be torn asunder by the public calamities which shortly after ensued.

Other changes occurred in Dr. Junkin's family from year to year, by which a part of it was taking deeper root in the Southern country. His younger son, William F., became the pastor of a church in the vicinity of the celebrated "Natural Bridge," in the Valley of Virginia, and married a Virginia lady in 1855. His fourth son, E. D. Junkin, settled as pastor in North Carolina, and, in 1858, married the daughter of a minister of the gospel in the neighborhood of his field of labor. In 1856, his younger daughter was married to Junius M. Fishburn, Professor of Latin in Washington College. But this happy union proved of short duration. In a year and seven months after their marriage, Professor Fishburn was summoned away by death. He died on the 26th of March, 1858, much lamented by all who knew him. He was an accomplished scholar, an amiable man, and a devoted Christian; and his death made a profound impression upon the students and the community. Previous to this affliction the elder daughter, Margaret, was married (in 1857) to Col. John T. L. Preston, of Lexington, a Professor in the Virginia Military Institute, and a gentleman of high social position. Mrs. Preston, both before and since her marriage, has not been unknown to fame as a graceful and effective writer, in the departments both of poetry and prose. She is the author of three volumes which have commanded high eulogy, and of many fugitive pieces.

By these extensions of the family affinities a mysterious Providence was preparing the way for severer trials, as yet in the womb of the future, which, in a few years, were to test the faith and lacerate the affections of the subject of this memoir, and of his household. Before the trials incident to the breaking out of the civil war befell him, his heart was to be again sorely wounded by a shaft from the hand of death: another lovely object of his affections, upon whom he had bestowed an almost idolatrous love, was smitten down. His sprightly and beloved little grandson, George Junkin Fishburn, the child of the deceased professor, was taken from them on the 15th of August, 1859, at the age of two years and two months. In his loneliness, after the death of Mrs. Junkin, this child seemed to have come into Dr. Junkin's inmost heart. He had been his almost inseparable companion, and perhaps no other trial of his life more deeply affected him. Ever after this loss he seemed fearful of permitting his affections to cling to any earthly object. These and other afflictions had a manifest mellowing influence upon his heart and upon the tone of his piety; and thenceforth his "conversation was in heaven" to a marked degree.

A few extracts from letters written during these years to Mrs. P., and others of his children, will indicate his habitudes of thought and feeling:

. . . . "In permitting this trial, God has wise ends, which you may not now be able to see, but may hereafter. 'He will make it plain.' All things shall work together for good. There is no sweeter and more practical doctrine in the Book than this of the Divine sovereignty. My habit has been to study all the facts before me, get all the light I can, pray for direction, then decide according to the dictates of conscience, and follow up the decision with all my might, assured that it is the Lord's will. And even when it turns out badly, I don't murmur against God,—scarcely against myself: I take it as a chastisement.

"This method has been censured in Cromwell; but I never could see a reason, good and sufficient, for the censure. If I can find an error in judgment, or from wrong feeling, that has led me into trouble, I submit, without repining, to all its inconveniences,—confess my sin before God, obtain absolution, and begin anew. There is no safer method than entire submission of our own will to that of God. 'Commit thy way unto the Lord, and He will bring it to pass:' 'He will never leave thee:' 'I just took Him at his word,' and 'He'll never forsake me.'"

In a letter to his son, Rev. E. D. Junkin, he says:

"M. and hers are well. G. is a fine boy; but I cannot love him as I did G. J. F. No! no! nor will I ever love a creature of God *so* again, till I go to the place where love and bliss immortal reign."

Among the correspondence of Dr. Junkin we find many letters from other educators, presidents, and professors of colleges, and gentlemen interested in the great subject of education, asking for his views upon various topics connected therewith. These letters attest that his reputation as an educator was wide-spread, and that his opinions were sought under the conviction that they were of value. One (from the University of Michigan) asks his opinion upon the great question of the co-education of the sexes, and the admission of females to the college classes. Another asks his opinion in regard to the value and importance of the Greek and Latin classics as instruments of mental culture. Others seek for hints in regard to the best process for organizing new colleges. Others ask—and this catalogue is quite numerous—for his opinion of the effect of *secret fraternities* among students and the alumni of colleges, upon their discipline and efficiency, and upon the standard of scholarship. To all these, it appears from the indorsements, he returned prompt answers; but, as no copies were retained, we have no means, except from a general knowledge of his opinions, of ascertaining the character of the replies given.

His letters to his children, and to his brother, afford abundant proof of the kindly feelings which he cherished towards his ministerial brethren in Virginia, and of the measure in which he prized and enjoyed their fellowship. Letters received from these brethren abound with proofs that his regards were reciprocated; but we cannot afford space for extracts. A single specimen must suffice. On the 17th of February, 1853, in a letter to his son, then in the Princeton Seminary, he replies to inquiries made by the latter, in regard to the state of morals and religion in Washington College, and gives statistics, some quite encouraging, some less so, and adds:

"One circumstance which greatly encourages us is the fact that the pious and sedate students have, beyond dispute, the pre-eminence in scholarship; and our mark is high. My fond hope is, that from twelve to twenty of those now here will find their way up to the high and solemn office.

"The cry for help rings through our mountains and valleys, and we tremble in apprehension of an increase of our need by the calling away of two of our most valued and beloved brethren, Dr. McFarland and Brother Morrison. The former has been down all winter, and it is feared he may not rise until the trump of judgment awakes his glad dust from its long slumber. The latter has had a bad hemorrhage within a week, and great fears are entertained, and little hopes, as to the result.

"Pray ye the Lord of the harvest. But, alas! those in the office cannot get bread. Oh that He, whose are the silver and the gold, would put into the hearts of his own people to devise just things!"

With the brethren named in this extract he had much pleasant intercourse. He often assisted the latter, the Rev. James Morrison, at communion and other services; and their correspondence discloses a very cordial brotherly affection. Neither of these excellent ministers was taken at that time; and after Mr. Morrison was laid aside from labor, Dr. Junkin supplied his church (New Providence) for a time, and his son, Rev. E. D. Junkin, was afterwards called to the pastorate, in which he still continues. Dr. McFarland lives (1871), but Mr. Morrison went to his rest a few months ago.

In 1856 Dr. Junkin was invited, by the literary societies of Rutgers College, New Jersey, to deliver before them the annual address. This duty he performed, much to the satisfaction of the societies, the authorities of the College, and a large and appreciative audience, as was indicated by repeated and enthusiastic applause during the delivery of the discourse, and by approbatory notices after it was published by request of the societies. This was the more remarkable, because his subject embraced topics of great delicacy and difficulty, and such as five years later involved the country in the horrors of civil war.

The authorities of Rutgers College conferred upon him, at that time, the honorary degree of LL.D.

During these years Dr. Junkin did not relax his efforts in the cause of temperance, but labored to promote the principle and practice of total abstinence. He was urged to this not only by the many cases of intemperance in the community in which he dwelt, but more especially by the fact that the demon had invaded the College and compelled the discipline and, in some cases, the expulsion of students who, but for this destroyer, might have been ornaments of the institution and a comfort to their parents. Of course his efforts awoke some opposition, but the moral tone of Lexington society repressed the exhibition of the rougher style of opposition, and confined it chiefly to parties who either were engaged in the traffic or were themselves fond of the dangerous indulgence.

It ought to be mentioned, as part of Dr. Junkin's Virginia life and labors, that he could not abstain from his favorite pastime—agriculture. During his entire life he was fond of "tilling the ground." In his first pastorate, and whilst presiding over the three colleges which claimed his labors, he found time for this employment. He purchased a small farm near Lexington, to which he added by purchase from time to time, until, at the date of his exodus from Virginia, it contained two hundred and sixty acres. This he caused to be cultivated under his personal supervision, and with improved modes and implements of husbandry. Its productiveness was steadily increasing; and had he remained, he would have demonstrated the capabilities of the lands of the Valley to the great encouragement and improvement of the agriculture of the region. As it was, his influence in this direction was beneficial.

Thus did years pass usefully and pleasantly until the time approached in which, by God's mysterious permission, the madness and folly of men brought upon our beloved country the dire calamities of civil war. To avert these evils Dr. Junkin did what he could. Always conservative,—cherishing a profound veneration for the Constitution of his country, and convinced that that instrument contained ample provisions for securing all the rights of all sections of the nation,—he had always labored, both North and South, to inculcate the doctrines of the Constitution, and to inspire his countrymen with love for its principles. When the imprudence of violent and extreme men had at last involved his country in the storms of political strife, and threatened to precipitate a war of sections, he redoubled his efforts to allay the storm and arrest the thunderbolts.

With the great mass of the men by whom he was immediately surrounded, he was happily in accord upon most of the questions at issue. He was an intense lover of the Union; so was Virginia, and especially the people of the Valley. The country in which he lived gave a fraction more than ten to one of a Union majority at the election for members of the Convention which ultimately proposed the secession movement. In that Convention, when it first met, there was a large majority of men utterly opposed to secession. But the people of Virginia were almost unanimous in their opposition to aggressive abolition, and so was Dr. Junkin. They and he held that the subject of slavery ought to be left where the fathers had left it in the Constitution, a question, not between the national Government and any of the States, but between State and State. He held that the Constitution required of each State the rendition of fugitives from criminal justice and from labor, upon legal demand sustained by proof; but that the claim for such rendition lay against the authorities of the State in which the fugitive was found, not, in the first instance, against the Government of the United States; and he held that the latter had no jurisdiction over such questions, unless brought before the courts of the United States by due process of appeal. He of course held that all legislation in contravention of this doctrine was unconstitutional. These views, upon proper occasion, he advocated.

There was a society of the citizens of Lexington for mutual improvement, called "The Franklin Society." It embraced men of the highest intelligence and social position. Among Dr. Junkin's papers is found an official invitation, in pursuance of a formal vote, asking him to attend at his convenience and take part in its discussions. In 1859, at the time when public troubles were topics of discussion, his voice was earnestly raised in behalf of conservative principles and measures, and especially in behalf of the American Union. At the meetings of this society, and upon other suitable occasions, he pointed out the danger of rash counsels and of extreme views, sought to reassure his Southern fellow-citizens in regard to the designs of the great majority of the Northern people, and gave freely and fully his interpretation of the Constitution, which was, that this great charter of our country's safety was alike opposed to secession on the one hand, and to the invasion by the national Government of rights properly belonging to the States on the other. He neglected no opportunity of allaying needless agitation, and of striving to avert the impending dangers. He deprecated, as utterly useless and mischievous, the whole agitation connected with the assertion and denial of the right to carry slaves into the Territories of the United States. He considered the Southern claim an abstraction of no practical value, and resistance to the claim equally futile as a practical question, for he knew that there was no Territory into which slavery could be profitably carried, and that, therefore, it was worse than folly for the one party to assert a right which they never could use, and for the other party to dread an evil that never could, in the nature of things, become a reality.

After the John Brown raid, his correspondence shows, that he labored to allay the sectional excitement which it produced, by assuring those among whom he dwelt, that it was the mad effort of a disordered enthusiast, which they ought not to ascribe to the whole North; and by decided remonstrance against that morbid sentiment which, in a few Northern minds and presses, seemed inclined to justify invasion, riot, and murder, because they were professedly done in the anti-slavery cause.

When the dreadful crisis which he had long apprehended, and which, seventeen years before, he had predicted, seemed just at hand, he put forth every exertion which his circumstances permitted to avert the calamity of civil war. Not satisfied with the positions assumed by either of the larger parties into which the country was divided in 1860, he voted for Hon. John Bell, of Tennessee, and Hon. Edward Everett, of Massachusetts, for President and Vice-President, and that ticket received the vote of the electoral college of Virginia.

After Mr. Lincoln was elected, although he had not been his choice, he advocated acquiescence in the decision of the country, and deprecated any and every other course. And he was anxious, that every just pretext for refusing acquiescence on the part of the South should be removed by the Northern States; and, in his correspondence with influential Northern men, he urged the repeal of all unconstitutional and unfriendly legislation which was found upon the statute-books of some of the Northern States.

Among other efforts of this kind, he addressed a letter to the Hon. A. G. Curtin, who had just been elected by the Republican Party Governor of Pennsylvania. Mr. Curtin, when a youth, had pursued his studies under Mr. Kirkpatrick, at the Milton Academy, and had been a frequent hearer of Mr. Junkin, then the pastor at that place. The letter was entitled,—

"A VOICE FROM A PENNSYLVANIAN IN THE HEART OF VIRGINIA."

After some kindly allusions to their former acquaintance, and to the satisfaction he felt in seeing so many of the former pupils of the academy which he had helped to found rising to eminence, and a tribute to the Hon. Andrew Gregg, the grandfather of Mr. Curtin, after whom he had been called, who had been the personal and political friend of Mr. Junkin's father, he expressed the hope and belief, that "the family blood had not degenerated in the third generation," and that the Governor would "not turn a deaf ear to the voice of a son of Pennsylvania sounding out from the heart of Virginia." He then proceeds:

"I feel constrained to address to you, to my beloved friends who still survive, and to all to whom these presents may come in my own, my beloved, my native Pennsylvania, an earnest and solemn appeal in regard to the perils of the times.

"And first let me state my conviction, fully matured and perfectly settled, that, of all the products of human wisdom within the sphere of political philosophy, the Constitution of the United States is the most profound, the most transcendent. Indeed, sir, it having been for a quarter of a century my duty annually to expound this instrument to the senior classes in college, every time I repeat the lesson, new evidences of its amazing wisdom reveal themselves to my admiring mind. Such a system of checks and balances is found in no other human production. . . . There it stands, in its sublime grandeur, the Temple of Liberty, in which the nations may bow and worship that God whose truth hath made them free! Now, who will win a disgraceful immortality, who will damn himself to eternal infamy, by applying the brand to this glorious structure? Who? Shall Pennsylvania apply the hellish torch, or fan the flame, and bury beneath the gray ashes of this temple the hopes of freedom for the world? Shall the Keystone become a splitting wedge, to rive rather than to sustain its arched vault, and leave this glorious structure like Dagon's temple? —a ruined monument of man's folly and inability to govern himself,—the jeer of despots all over the earth. Forbid it, proud old Commonwealth! Forbid it, ye spirits that bled at Brandywine, at Paoli, at Germantown!

"Then bear with me, sir, whilst I point warningly to the first infraction of the Constitution, . . . a brand that has long lain smouldering within the temple, and has recently been fanned to flame by the breath of fanaticism and faction."

He then quotes and expounds Art. iv. sec. 2 of the Constitution in regard to the rendition of fugitives from justice and from labor, and constructs a strong argument in favor of the faithful and sacred observance of the covenant of the Constitution by each and all of the States; and then makes a most earnest appeal to Governor Curtin, and the people of his native State, to prove faithful in this crisis of their country's history to her Constitution in all its stipulations, and not only to meet its requirements, but to wipe from the statute-books of the State any enactments which may seem to conflict with the national charter.

He then exposes the unlawfulness of secession, and quotes from President Jackson the language, "Secession does not break a league, but destroys the unity of a nation. To say that any State may, at pleasure, secede from the Union, is to say that the United States is not a nation." And, having shown that secession by force is treason, he shows, that any other refusal to abide by the stipulations and the authority of the Constitution, is equally a blow at the national unity. And having spoken eloquently of the mission of our great model Republic in guiding the nations of the earth in their efforts after regulated liberty, he beseeches the Governor and his fellow-citizens of Pennsylvania, by all the glorious memories of the past, and all the inspiring hopes of the future, to be loyal to the Constitution.

The doctrines of this letter are precisely the same which the new President, Mr. Lincoln, laid down in his inaugural address, three months later, and which he pledged himself to carry out. And the writer of these lines never doubted, that Mr. Lincoln would have redeemed his pledge, had extreme measures not been resorted to by the Cotton States.

This letter to Governor Curtin was dated "Lexington, December 11th, 1860." It was published in the Philadelphia *North American* of the 18th of that month. It attracted much attention, and elicited from some of the best minds of the country decided expressions of approval.

On the very day of its publication, the Hon. Eli K. Price, an eminent Jurist of Philadelphia, addressed a note to Dr. Junkin, of which the following are extracts:

"PHILADELPHIA, Dec. 18, 1860.

"DEAR SIR,—I have read in this morning's *North American* your sound and eloquent letter to Mr. Curtin, and sincerely thank you for it. It sets forth most clearly what is our plain duty, and it is directed to the right person, the Governor-elect, and ought to shape one feature of his inaugural address. From him the legislature will more willingly take this policy than from any other man in the State; and the power is now wholly with the Republicans of this State.

"I write to you to say that you are right, notwithstanding C. G. (Charles Gibbons), and notwithstanding Story's opinion in Prigg's case, and right as since decided by the Supreme Court of the United States. This I pointed out, under my initials, in the next paper after C. G.'s of the 8th December."

Then follow some citations of authorities in corroboration of the views expressed by Dr. Junkin, and the note ends:

"Pray write again to the Governor-elect before his inaugural.

"With thanks, I am, etc.,

"ELI K. PRICE."

As Mr. Price was a man of eminent legal learning, and was also in sympathy with the Republican party, his commendation of this "Voice of a Pennsylvanian from the heart of Virginia," ought to be deemed valuable, especially as it was a spontaneous utterance.

After South Carolina had passed her ordinance of secession, and State after State began to move in the same direction, a convention was called in Virginia to decide the question of her future relations to the American Union.

To this Convention was chosen a very decided majority of avowed Union men. In the Valley the majorities were very large. Rockbridge, in which Dr. Junkin lived, voted for Union men by more than ten to one. His great gratification at this result is indicated by a paragraph which we extract from a letter to his son, the pastor of New Providence church, dated February 6, 1861:

"What a tremendous defeat the secessionists have met in Rockbridge! A little more than ten to one,—and in Old Virginia they will be in a decided minority. *Nil desperandum*,—the heavens do rule. We are wicked enough to deserve destruction; but the Lord is long-suffering. The Brownsburg vote fills me with gratitude to God and the noble congregation of New Providence. The people claim to say something in regard to their own destiny."

In the deliberations of the Convention, Dr. Junkin was intensely interested. There are on his files letters from members of the Convention breathing an intense spirit of Union, and showing that, in his correspondence with the writers, he had used all his influence and power of argument to encourage them to resist the secession movement. These letters show, that their writers had great respect for the opinions of Dr. Junkin upon the questions then agitating the public mind. They also disclose some parts of the more secret history of secession in Virginia. There were powerful influences exerted by parties outside of that Commonwealth, to goad and drag her into that infatuated movement—influences which were not suspected at the time by the people remote from Richmond. One writer from that city says:

"We have great difficulties to contend with here. All the metropolitan press is against us, and the greatest money power is active against us. The negro-traders have an immense capital, and I have no doubt use it freely in buying up votes and presses, and paying agents to get up county secession meetings."

But it were needless to attempt, in such a work as this, the details of the process by which that noble old Commonwealth was, contrary to the repeated vote of her people, and the better judgment of many of her best citizens, dragged into the list of seceded States. The Union majority in her Convention, under influences above alluded to, and under the combined force of sectional prejudice, the violence of ultra men, and the dread of being suspected of disloyalty to the Southern cause, gradually dwindled, until the secession party gained the ascendency, and the fatal step was taken which made her fair fields the theatre of

"The bloodiest picture of the book of time."

Against this dire result the subject of this memoir exerted all the influence he could put forth; but it proved in vain; and events hastened on which constrained him, either to sacrifice his conscientious convictions and self-respect by succumbing to the popular tide, to jeopard his personal safety, or to withdraw from the State and from the field of labor in which he had spent so many peaceful, useful, happy years. He decided to depart.

No one can estimate the sacrifice made by Dr. Junkin in executing this decision without knowing the man, and what he was forced to leave behind. He had been happy and useful in that field of labor for nearly thirteen years. The society of Lexington was highly intelligent and genial. The roots of his family tree, as we have seen, had struck deep and spread wide in Virginia soil. Three of his children, with their interesting families, were left behind him, —his two sons, being pastors of important churches, and married into Southern families, and his daughter, the wife of a Professor in the Virginia Military Institute. In the same institution, too, was Jackson, still dear as a son. At Lexington cemetery he had "purchased his cave of Machpelah, and buried his dead out of his sight. There he had made the sacred deposit, first, of one who had sojourned by his side for almost thirty-five years; then of his second daughter, Mrs. Jackson; then of a noble and beloved son-in-law; then of the lovely boy who soon followed his father to the grave; and there he had reserved a burial-plot for himself." In Lexington, —beautiful, picturesque, and healthful,—near to the ashes of his dead, and surrounded by so many surviving dear ones, he had hoped to spend the evening of his days.

There, too, were his farm, his library, and other property. His salary was ample and satisfactory; and he was surrounded by all the appliances which might smooth and comfort his later years.

But he left it all, in his seventy-first year, for love of his country, her Constitution and her flag, and returned to his native Pennsylvania. It was a crushing trial, and a heavy sacrifice; and all the more so to a heart like his. Of all the refugees from the insurgent section, perhaps none were more distinguished, and none adhered to principle at greater cost.

We will give the story in his own *naïve* style, as published in the *Presbyterian Standard*, a paper ably edited by the Rev. Alfred Nevin, D.D., in Philadelphia. It was copied into nearly all the newspapers in the North, and was printed also in his book entitled "Political Fallacies:"

"EXODUS OF DR. JUNKIN.

"MR. EDITOR,—The following is no Parthian arrow, but a simple history, designed to correct misapprehension and let my friends in Virginia and Pennsylvania know the truth in reference to MY EXODUS from the former to the latter.

"In the month of February last, I took up the Constitution of the United States for exposition to the Senior Class in Washington College, Virginia, of which I was then president, using Sheppard's excellent little work as a text-book. This was an anticipation of some two months, in accordance with the desires of the class and my own convictions of duty, in reference to the dangerous misconstructions of that highest production of human genius. I wished, by a fair and honest exposition, to convince my young friends that UNION preceded *Independence*, and even the *Articles of Confederation*—much more the present *Constitution;* that neither the Continental Congress nor the Articles of Confederation created and constituted a *Government:* they had neither supreme, legislative, judicial, nor executive powers. The Congress was simply a grand Committee of the States, exercising many powers of sovereignty, but by no means all that belong to national sovereignty. In these lectures I dealt largely with the archives published by United States authority, reading from them to sustain my positions, and especially from the minutes of the Convention that formed the Constitution, passing through the entire volume, and demonstrating the fact of *union* as the leading principle—the polar star recognized by these wise men of the west, from the very first meeting in this city in September, 1774, and again in May, 1775. I showed that they felt themselves a unit—they recorded themselves a unit: as the United Colonies they appointed and commissioned George Washington as Commander-in-chief, in whose commission the phrase 'United Colonies' occurs three several times. My object, in these extended preparatory discussions, was to rivet the conviction in the minds of these dear young men, that UNION was always the master-thought in the minds of American patriots; that UNION was the basis of all their actions; that without UNION there could be no *freedom*, no *national government*, no *independence.* From this position, it follows irrefragably, that there never existed a State sovereignty; the supreme power is in the States UNITED: no State ever declared itself an independent nation—none was ever recognized by any power on earth as an independent sovereignty; the doctrine of State rights, or State sovereignty, outside of the limits of State constitutions and the lines of demarcation fixed in the United States Constitution, is necessarily subversive of the national government, as General Jackson proved in his proclamation to the people of South Carolina, and from this follows the doctrine which he affirmed, that 'disunion by armed force is treason.' The pseudo right of secession is a national wrong. . . .

"But in the progress of these discussions I observed a growing restiveness among the students, heard myself called a 'Pennsylvania Abolitionist,' and saw written on the column opposite my recitation-room door 'Lincoln Junkin.'

"About the close of March, a Palmetto flag was placed on the centre building of the college, surmounting the wooden statue of Washington. . . . In this process, led on by a Georgia student, the copper lightning-rod was bent, and subsequently broken off. For a student to go out on the roof has always been an offence, punished by demerit. This flag I ordered the servants to take down and bring to me. I was asked what I would do with it, and replied, 'Burn it after evening prayer.' But whilst I was at dinner, they procured a ladder, climbed into the window of my lecture-room, and took the flag away.

"About a week after, it was again erected. I immediately ordered the servants to take it down, and at an hour when all except the Freshmen were at their recitations; these stood about as spectators, and asked what I was going to do with it. I answered, 'I'll show you.' I ordered the servants to hold the butt of the flag-pole firmly, and throw the top over from the chapel roof, which is a story lower than the centre building. When the flag came within reach, I stepped up and took some matches out of my pocket, set it on fire, and, when it blazed up, told the servants to throw the pole out from the building, and whilst it flamed up, I said, '*So perish all efforts to dissolve this glorious Union!*'*

---

* "It is worthy of special notice here, that the young men who were chiefly active in the erecting of these flags perished on July 21, 1861, in the first battle of Bull Run. Two of them were killed by one cannon-shot, and a third (and he the leader) perished from excessive over-exertion in carrying his wounded companion three miles to the railroad car. This companion breathed his last just as they were lifting him on the car. And thus, to a melancholy and fearful extent, has the malediction prophetic been accomplished. I am to this day—Dec. 9, 1862—but very imperfectly informed on the subject, by reason of the rebellion cutting off all intercourse between me and my two sons and daughter in Rockbridge; but, from all I have heard, I am painfully impressed with the belief that more than fifty per cent. of all those misguided youth who were active in rebelling against me have paid the forfeit of their folly by the sacrifice of their lives. This is cause of unfeigned sorrow; for a very large proportion of them were youth of remarkable promise for talents, diligence in study, purity of moral and religious character; who, but for these bloody fallacies, would have lived long and adorned the higher walks of professional life.

"On the 15th of April, my lecture-room door was much injured by attempts to break it open with a strong iron bar. The library door they succeeded in forcing open. The object was to procure the jointed ladder, which the servants had put behind the amphitheatre for safe keeping. (A door opens between the library-room and my lecture-room.) On the morning of the 17th, I saw a disunion flag surmounting the statue of Washington and the lightning-rod. After prayer I detained the members of the Faculty, and waved my hand to the students to retire. I stated to my colleagues that this thing must be stopped, etc. One of them said he had just received a petition on the subject, signed by most of the students. I asked him to read it. The substance (I have not a copy) of it was, that the flag which they had erected might be permitted to remain. I stated to the Faculty that it had been placed there in violation of law, and in contemptuous resistance to my express order, and, of course, if they would grant the prayer of the petition, my course of duty was clear and plain—I could not be coerced, but would instantly secede; and left them to deliberate, and let me know their decision.

"At eleven o'clock, the usual hour, the Junior class came into my room. I asked whether the flag was on the top of the College, and received an affirmative answer. 'Then, gentlemen,' said I, 'I am under the necessity of assuring you that I cannot submit to this kind of coercion,' and dismissed them. One rushed toward the door, shouting, 'Thank God for that! thank God for that!'* and yelled his utmost, in which he was joined by a few others.

"At twelve o'clock, when the Seniors came in, I read to them the substance of what I had said to the Juniors, and which, meanwhile, to be sure of the identical words, I had written down as follows:

"'Is the flag still on the top of the College?'

"Answer, 'Yes.'

"'Well, then, gentlemen, as you put it there in express opposition to my order, I am under the necessity of telling you that I have never been ridden over rough-shod in that style, and I never will be; therefore, I never will hear a

* "Killed at Bull Run, as I learned shortly after from a Richmond paper.

recitation or deliver a lecture under a rebel flag. The class is dismissed.

"'April 17, 1861.'

"They rose and withdrew in the most gentlemanly and respectful manner, with every appearance of sincere regret.

"In the evening of the same day, I received from my colleagues a paper, of which the following is a copy, viz.:

"'W. COLLEGE, April 17, 1861.

"'*Action of the Faculty in relation to the Flag on the College Buildings.*

"'*Whereas,* The students, in reference to the tidings that the Virginia Convention are about to adopt an ordinance of secession, have hoisted a Southern flag upon the college building, and have made a respectful request of the Faculty that they would permit it to remain; and *whereas,* the Faculty have assurance that this act has not taken place in any *desire to violate* college laws, or offer indignity to any member of the Faculty—an assurance given by the students themselves to a member of the Faculty, and confirmed by the fact that they promptly took down, at the request of the Faculty, a similar flag, erected on a former occasion; and *whereas,* Dr. Junkin regards this act as a wilful violation of law and a personal indignity, and requires the Faculty to have it removed at once, on penalty of his resignation—an alternative which the Faculty think that Dr. Junkin has no right to impose, and which we cannot allow to influence our action in the premises, although we are fully determined to sustain the president, or any individual member of our body, in the maintenance of discipline; and *whereas,* the sole object of the Faculty is to allay excitement, and insure good order and attention to study in college, in this time of civil disturbance, believing, as we do, that these ends will be best promoted by not requiring the *immediate* removal of the flag; therefore,

"'*Resolved,* That the flag be permitted to remain, at the discretion of the Faculty.

"'Copied from the minutes, and communicated to Dr. Junkin by order of the Faculty.

"'J. L. CAMPBELL, *Clerk.*'

"There is but one point in which there is positive inaccuracy in the above. It is in regard to the flag said to have been taken down at the request of the Faculty.

"The flag there referred to was not 'a similar flag' (as I was afterward informed, for I never saw it, and knew not of its erection until after it was taken down); it was a *red flag*, and it was not erected on the centre building, but on the building in which my lecture-room was. It was therefore entirely different in its significance. And it was not taken down at the request of the Faculty, for the Faculty, as such, knew nothing about it; it was taken down at the remonstrance, as I understood, of Professor White, for which interposition I felt thankful.* After what had already transpired, neither I, nor the public, could be at any loss to know what was meant by erecting a *red* flag, not on the centre building over the statue of Washington, as had been the others, but over my lecture-room.

"On the next day, I called a meeting of the Trustees at 2½ P.M., the earliest hour practicable, on account of the meeting of the Presbytery of Lexington, and of the Superior Court. In urging the Trustees individually to attend, I assured them it would take but a few minutes, for my resignation would be peremptory and absolute, and leave no room for discussion. I mention this circumstance, in order to counteract the gross misrepresentations which I have been told have found their way into some of the Richmond papers, but especially the *Dispatch*.

"The Trustees met accordingly, and the Board was opened with prayer, as usual, and my resignation was presented, as follows:

---

* "The lovely youth who took down this red flag from over my lecture-room, perished at the second battle of Bull Run, on the 28th of August, 1862, aged about eighteen years. He was an ardent Union man—a devoted student, pure-minded as the blood of sprinkling ever cleanses sinners here below. A nobler boy never took seat before me in class, during the thirty-one years of my presidency in colleges. But this accursed rebellion crushes into its ranks the hoary head and the beardless boy, and drags them on to the slaughter. His brother, a former graduate, lost an arm in the same fight, and two others of my dearly beloved young friends, graduates of two years' standing, the pride of their parents, and ornaments to society, fell likewise on the same bloody field. Oh, ye conspirators against our glorious Union and the peace of the world, look at the slaughter you have brought about, and think of the dread tribunal of Eternal Justice!

" 'WASHINGTON COLLEGE, April 18, A.D. 1861.

" '*To the Board of Trustees of Washington College.*

" 'GENTLEMEN,—I hereby resign the office to which you called me more than twelve years ago.

" 'Very respectfully,

" 'Your humble servant,

" 'GEO. JUNKIN, President.'

"Dr. McFarland took the chair, made a few kind remarks; others were made—especially by Lawyer Davidson, who was quite complimentary; the vote was passed, I shook hands with all the members, many of whom, as well as myself, were overpowered with tender emotions.

"Thus, within twenty hours from the time I was informed that my colleagues had determined to permit the secession flag to wave over the head of Washington, my connection with the College which he had so nobly endowed ceased forever.

"With pleasure I append the following, which shows truly, that no personal ill feeling has ever existed toward me on the part of my late colleagues, as I doubt not they are perfectly aware, that my mind is equally free from every emotion inconsistent with our literary and Christian relations. These difficulties have sprung from the false political maxims of Calhounism, which break down all the barriers of moral truth, and are rushing human society into the vortex of anarchy, and which must end in iron-handed despotism.

" 'WASHINGTON COLLEGE, April 18, 1861.

" '*Rev. Geo. Junkin, D.D.*

" 'DEAR SIR,—Although we, your recent colleagues, as members of the Faculty of Washington College, felt it to be our duty, under peculiar circumstances, to pursue a line of policy which you did not approve, and in consequence of which you have felt constrained to resign your connection with the Institution, we wish to say, that we were actuated by no feelings of disrespect to you personally, or disregard of the high position you have filled in the College for so many years. And we desire now to express our high regard for your manly virtues as a Christian minister, and as a gentleman of distinguished talents and learning; and to assure you of our entire confidence in your integrity, of our sincere friendly regards for yourself and family, and our earnest prayer, that the twilight of your life may be its brightest and happiest period.

"With much esteem, we are, very sincerely,

"Your friends,

"'J. L. CAMPBELL,
"'A. L. NELSON,
"'JAMES J. WHITE,
"'C. J. HARRIS.'

"Next day after these transactions I set to work in winding up my business, selling my property, paying my debts, etc., and, as the ways of public conveyance were then blocked, I purchased a carriage, drove my own horses three hundred and fifty miles to Oxford, Chester County, and came in on the cars from that place yesterday morning.

"'The Lord shall keep thy soul; he shall
Preserve thee from all ill:
Henceforth thy going out and in
God keep forever will.'

"GEO. JUNKIN.

"PHILADELPHIA, May 18, 1861."

No discourtesy, much less violence, was offered to Dr. Junkin, after his resignation and previous to his exodus; but he foresaw, that it would be impracticable for him to reside in a Southern community with his intense sentiment of loyalty to the Union.

"I saw plainly," said he, in his introduction to the "Political Fallacies," "that if I remained, absolute silence, or a voice in favor of secession, must be the price of my personal safety. This price was too great for me to pay. It would bankrupt my self-respect and pollute my conscience. The only alternative was flight. So, leaving all, . . . I crossed the Potomac at Williamsport, after dark, on the 9th of May, 1861, having driven the last thirty-five miles from Winchester without stopping to feed my horses."

The haste indicated by this drive from Winchester, was not prompted by any dread of molestation from the Southern troops; for Dr. Junkin had with him a "pass" from

Governor Letcher of Virginia, but found no occasion to exhibit it on the journey; and although Harper's Ferry had been taken, and troops were in motion throughout Virginia, there was as yet no exasperation of feeling, and had been no bloodshed. Dr. Junkin was accompanied in this hegira by his younger daughter, the widow of Professor Fishburn, and also by his niece, the daughter of the author of this book, who happened to be on a visit to Lexington at the time the civil war broke out. No incidents other than the usual toil and perils of travel occurred. His route was *via* Hagerstown, Chambersburg, Carlisle, and Harrisburg, past the place of his birth, and through the scenes familiar to his boyhood. The refugees halted a short time in Chambersburg, where they met kind friends. On the 13th of May he stopped at the house in which he had been born nearly seventy-one years before; and, as stated in his own narrative, proceeded to Oxford, where some relatives reside, and thence to his son's residence in Philadelphia. There he found a home, of the pleasantness of which he was fond to speak to his intimate friends, and in which he was cherished with veneration and affection until the moment of his departure to his home in the heavens.

CHAPTER XXXIV.

Residence in Philadelphia—Abundant Labors—In the Camp—Among Soldiers—Colporteur—Sabbath Question—"Sabbatismos"—Benevolent Institutions—Preaching—Private Studies—Treatise on Sanctification—Treatise on Tabernacle—Commentary on "Hebrews"—Death—Estimate of Character—Intellect and Work—Piety—Prayerfulness—General Assembly of 1861—Spring Resolutions—"Political Fallacies."

ALTHOUGH constrained to abandon the field of labor in which he had spent so many happy and useful years, Dr. Junkin could not, did not, rest. With him life was labor, and labor was necessary to a happy life. Probably no years of his earthly pilgrimage were more diligently and usefully occupied, than those which intervened between his exodus from Virginia and the period of his death. No man of his generation more fully observed the Scripture injunction that forms the motto of the title-page of this volume,—"Be not slothful in business, fervent in spirit, serving the Lord."

The reader of this book must have observed that, in speaking of the man whose life and labors it commemorates, the writer has stated facts, and has rarely indulged in epithets; and he feels it to be a privilege to permit others to *characterize* the man whom he so tenderly loved. Perhaps no language which the author could employ would so concisely, yet truthfully, portray the labors of the last years of Dr. Junkin, as the following extracts from the sermon already quoted. Dr. Knox says:

"Dr. Junkin was in his seventy-first year when he returned to Philadelphia. His residence, thenceforth, till his days on earth were ended, was in the family of his son, in which he received the honor, the veneration, the love, the attention which such a father might expect at the hands of such a son. The Lord will remember, and richly recompense him and his for their devotion to his venerable servant. Freed thus from worldly cares, his eye not having grown dim, nor his natural force abated, Dr. Junkin was enabled to fill up his remaining years with deeds of mercy and kindness. In the last seven years of his life he preached about *seven hundred* times. His activity during this period was simply amazing—almost past belief. While the civil contest raged, his zeal in the behalf of the soldiers in the field and the hospitals led him to unwearied efforts for their material, and especially their spiritual, benefit. As a Colporteur of the Board of Publication, he visited encampments whenever they were within his reach, and distributed tracts and books, and preached the Word of Life. At Fort Delaware and Point Lookout he spent whole days, and even weeks, among the Southern prisoners; and after the decisive battle of Gettysburg, he was among the earliest on that field of blood, seeking to relieve distress, and to direct the wounded and dying to Jesus, the all-sufficient Friend and Saviour of Men. These labors of love were rendered at large cost. Many of those who were associated in them with Dr. Junkin found them too much for their strength; but the deprivations and exposures they involved he endured without any apparent personal damage.

"I need not do more than mention his efforts during the recent agitation in this community of the Sabbath question. He did his utmost to maintain the quiet observance of God's holy day. In ecclesiastical assemblies and in public meetings his voice was heard pleading the strict interpretation of the Divine Commandment. Throughout large portions of the State, as well as in the city, he preached the doctrine of Sabbath-sanctification, by a holy resting on that day from all secular employments and recreations. He visited the Legislature of the State, and besought its members to lay no profane hand on the Divine Institution. The newspaper press fairly teemed with the articles of 'Theophilus,' which were afterwards reproduced in the volume 'Sabbatismos,' and by the untiring energies of its venerable author, sent far and wide to influence the public mind against consenting to any lowering of the standard of legislation in the matter of the first day of the week.

"He also officiated with great punctuality and with deep interest in two of the institutions of benevolence in the city. In one of them the inmates had arranged his desk in anticipation of his service on the very day of his death. They were to hear his voice on earth no more.

"These employments and engagements would seem to have been quite enough for one of such advanced years, but they were not enough for Dr. Junkin. As he had been all his life, so during this last period he was a diligent student, and especially of the Word of God. His Bible, in the languages in which it was originally written, was ever open before him, and was the subject of his most earnest and prayerful investigation. During these last years he wrote and published a treatise on Sanctification, a treatise on the Ancient Tabernacle of the Hebrews, explaining the evangelical meaning of all its parts, and other smaller works. And he has left behind him, every line written since his seventy-fifth year was completed, a Commentary on the Epistle of Paul to the Hebrews, in seven hundred and fifty pages of large quarto manuscript, in not one word of which can be detected the slightest tremulousness or other sign of failing age.

"Nor have I yet exhausted the catalogue of the things he did during the time of his so-called retirement from public life. There was not a subject of current interest in Church or State on which he did not express himself, and always with vigor and clearness, in the public press. The end of this life of work was, however, at hand. The Master whom he served so long and well saw that the time had come for him to rest. Dr. Junkin throughout his life feared the pains of death. Of this he often spoke and wrote to those most familiar with him. God was most gracious to him in this regard. He was taken ill on Monday, on Tuesday was so much relieved that there was little apprehension concerning him, and on Wednesday, with no apparent aggravation of his symptoms, so suddenly, that there was scarcely time to intimate to him that he was dying, and for him to murmur the words, 'Saviour,'

'Heaven,' he fell asleep, and was with Christ, which is far better. So closed his grand, his heroic life. 'He walked with God, and was not, for God took him.'

"This sketch of the life of Dr. Junkin, though exceedingly incomplete, shows him to have been a great and a good man. In the well-chosen words of Dr. Breed, 'The mind of Dr. Junkin well harmonized with the material home in which it lodged—massive, compact, and strong. To say that he was a man of talents—of talents of a very high order—is to say the truth; but only a part of the truth. He was a man of genius—with all the force, fire, and originality of true genius.' I would not represent him a universal scholar, for this were to say that he was superficial, which is precisely what he was not. His knowledge, however, was very extensive. A most diligent and patient student during his *entire life*, he did not fail to make important attainments in nearly every branch of science. But his chosen subjects of study were Theology, and the philosophies most closely allied to this science of sciences. On these great subjects he was a profoundly learned man. To use again the language of Dr. Breed, 'It has not been our lot to come into intimate contact with another man who had possessed himself of, and thoroughly thought out and mastered, so many of the leading topics of educational, mental, and moral science, and political economy, and of theology. These topics, stripped of irrelevant surroundings, were laid away, like specimens in a museum, upon the shelves of a capacious and wonderfully faithful memory; and there always were within reach, to be summoned forth at will for use, whether in conversation, debate, or literary composition.' Nor was his learning a dry accumulation of knowledge. It was only the fuel which supplied the flame of his genius. In this lay the secret of Dr. Junkin's power in the pulpit, in the arena of debate, and in the lecture-room. He was denied the voice of an orator, or his fame in this respect would have been well-nigh unsurpassed. Notwithstanding this great disadvantage, the vigor of his thought, the fulness of his knowledge, his burning words, his touching pathos, and his brilliant imagery, and the *blood-earnestness* with which he spoke, often overcame all obstacles, and held his hearers spell-bound. In debate his pre-eminence was confessed. I have heard that the late

Rev. Dr. Samuel Miller pronounced him the most irresistible man in public discussion whom he had known. The same thing is true of him as he appeared before his classes. He had a magnetic power over his students. He not only instructed them, but transferred to them the enthusiasm of his own nature, and moulded their minds into form and fashion like to his own. Of this the most valuable evidence has been given since Dr. Junkin's death, by men of eminence in Church and State, who sat at his feet during their educational career.

"And how can I tell of *his heart*, that generous, noble *heart*, which, alas! for those who loved and cherished him—for every cause of humanity—for the Church of Christ—*beats no more?* A man of greater magnanimity, of truer, deeper, tenderer affections, I do not believe *ever lived.* Here I dare not trust myself. I have been overwhelmed by the outflow of the greatness of his love. How much more others! and I cannot safely attempt to speak of that which I know is incapable of expression.

"But, after all, Dr. Junkin's greatness was in his goodness. He was an humble follower of the Lord Jesus Christ. Like his Master, he was among his fellow-men as one that served. Great things he never sought for himself. He was desirous only of knowing what the Lord would have him to do, and to do it heartily, as to the Lord, and not unto man; 'knowing that of the Lord he should receive the reward of the inheritance.' His humility was wonderful. I do not think I ever saw it equalled; I am sure I never saw it surpassed. He asked nothing for himself, and received whatever was given to him, not as of reward, but as of pure, unmerited grace. He confessed himself to be an unprofitable servant. I need hardly say he was a man of prayer. He dwelt in the secret place of the Most High. He loved his closet. He knew *well* the path, and trod it constantly, to the Holy of Holies. And in all places where prayer was made he delighted to be. The noontide hour found him as often, probably more often, in the prayer-meeting than any other person. From the ministers' meeting for prayer he was never absent. During the week appointed in the beginning of the year to supplicate for the conversion of the world. he was always to be seen and heard in the services, and if the interest excited led to the continuance of them, he continued to attend. Too many appointments of this kind could not be made for him. His necessary food he would forego rather than be away. He was a man of God—full of faith and of the Holy Ghost—and gave himself continually to prayer and the ministry of the Word.

"The services of such a man, protracted through so long a life, eternity alone can tell! Nearly five thousand times he preached the gospel in the regular ministrations of the sanctuary. His other ministrations were also very numerous. Who can measure the influence which he has exerted through these labors? Probably as many as a thousand young men passed through the whole or a part of their college life under his guidance and instruction. There are students of his in nearly every State of our Union, and in nearly every position of honor and usefulness. In Japan, in China, in India, in the Islands of the sea, there are missionaries of Christ, in whose hearts the name of Dr. Junkin wakens a thrill of grateful love, as that of the man to whom, under God, they are indebted for whatever they have been enabled to do for the coming of the Kingdom of Christ in all the world.

"Time fails me, and ability fails me, to tell of his heroic services in the behalf of the pure faith of the gospel, of his patriotic zeal, of his abundant labors in the cause of temperance, and every other work of reform,—performed with a spirit as brave as was that of Luther or Knox,—of his publications, by which so many have been enlightened and instructed, and by which he, being dead, shall continue to speak to the generations to come."

A brief detail of facts will vindicate the compact, yet eloquent, general statements contained in the foregoing extract, and illustrate Dr. Knox's words, "His activity during this period was simply amazing—almost past belief."

Shortly after the arrival of Dr. Junkin in Philadelphia, the General Assembly of 1861 convened in that city. The streets resounded with the rattle of drums, the tramp of soldiery, and the noise of military preparation. The North was rushing to the defence of the border and the capital, against the threatened invasion of the Confederate forces.

The deliberations of the Assembly were literally drowned at times by martial sounds, and, of course, the members of that body shared in the enthusiasm and excitement of the hour.

Dr. Junkin was not a member of this Assembly, but he felt an intense interest in the extended discussions occasioned by the celebrated "Spring Resolutions," and was much engaged in conversing with members of the body upon the questions involved in that now historical paper. It need scarcely be said that he was in favor of the resolutions; and after the Assembly adjourned, and the discussion of the action of the Assembly, in regard to the state of the country, passed into the public press, he employed his vigorous pen in defending that action. This he did, both in the columns of the newspapers and in a volume which he began to write shortly after his exodus, and which he published some months afterwards. This volume is entitled "POLITICAL FALLACIES: AN EXAMINATION OF THE FALSE ASSUMPTIONS, AND REFUTATION OF THE SOPHISTICAL REASONINGS, WHICH HAVE BROUGHT ON THIS CIVIL WAR." The book was widely read, and did much good in refuting the Calhoun doctrines of secession, and unfolding the true principles of our Constitution. He demonstrates historically, and by an inspection of the Constitution itself, that such a thing as *national* sovereignty belonging to a State of this Union is a mischievous absurdity. The book contains the same doctrines in regard to our Union which he had always taught, and in which many of his fellow-citizens of Virginia had agreed with him, before the frenzy of sectional jealousy had become so rife. The volume is a mine of political wisdom, stated in such simple style, and with such apposite illustration, as to make it comprehensible by the masses.

And yet the book has its defects. Written as it was under the excitement incident to the civil war, *currente calamo*, and with a feeling of intense indignation against doctrines which he believed to be the cause of the carnage and horror which were desolating his country, there is a tone of impetuosity in some passages which, whilst it suited the times, would seem discordant in a period of profound peace. Nor does he always distinguish with his accustomed acumen between rights which may justly be claimed by the States, and those which were unjustly assumed by the secessionists, and which never were *rights*, but *wrongs*.

In his zeal against the foolish claim of absolute national sovereignty by a State of the Union, he, in a few instances, seems to ignore the fact, that over certain things the Constitution guarantees to the States supreme control—*i.e.* sovereignty; but not such a supreme control as would permit resistance to the National Government or secession from the Union. And yet it is well known by those who knew Dr. Junkin's opinions, that he was a thorough Jeffersonian in the interpretation of the Constitution of the United States, and was profoundly convinced, that the centrifugal forces of our system are as important to union and liberty as the centripetal. He dreaded consolidation only less than secession.

His defence of the Spring Resolutions in this book, and his answer to the animadversions of the *Biblical Repertory* upon them, were not satisfactory to all his readers. Granting his assumption, that those resolutions did *not decide* for the members of the Presbyterian Church in the Southern States the question of civil allegiance, and his argument is conclusive. But that is the very thing in dispute. Dr. Hodge, and many with him, verily thought the Assembly *did* decide that political question, which an ecclesiastical court had no right, by our Standards, to do. If their interpretation of Dr. Spring's paper is correct (and many think it is), then there was no such inconsistency as Dr. Junkin charged upon Dr. Hodge, in expressing a willingness to vote for such a paper in the Synod of New Jersey, but not in the General Assembly; for nobody in New Jersey denied the authority of the United States as a government *de facto* over New Jersey, whilst many denied it in the Southern country. It might be right to enjoin Christian citizens to be loyal to an acknowledged government which is able to protect them; whilst it might not be right to extend the same injunction to Christians living in an insurrectionary district where a government *de facto* exists so strong as to banish every other flag but its own. It might be inexpedient for our General Assembly to decide that the Christians in China ought to adhere to and support the ancient dynasty, even if they lived in the districts in which the Chinese rebellion had excluded the flag of the empire. Such a decision might destroy practically the catholicity of the church of Christ, and estop, in many portions of the world, her missionary work. Upon these questions good and patriotic men may differ in opinion. But, whether right or wrong upon this question, the "Political Fallacies" has been acknowledged by the public to be a very valuable contribution to our ethico-political literature, replete with important truths and patriotic fervor.

CHAPTER XXXV.

Visits to Native Place—To Harrisburg—To Susquehanna—Preachings—Newport—Old Ironsides—Dr. Hopkins—Assembly of 1862—Omnipotence of General Assembly—Labors in Canal Street—Patriotic Labors --Doctrines of the "Political Fallacies"—Secession and Consolidation —Prisoners his former Pupils—Gettysburg—Prof. Stoever's Letter—Death of "Stonewall" Jackson—His Creed and Course—Colonel Preston —The Two Commissions—Canal Street—Meeting of the Brothers—The Widows—The Magdalen—Temperance and Sabbath Labors—Sabbatismos—Hebrews—Opinions on Public Affairs—On Church Union —Last Labors—Illness—Death—Funeral.

DURING the years immediately succeeding his return to Pennsylvania, Dr. Junkin made many visits to different parts of our country; all of which he seemed greatly to enjoy, and in all of which he was greeted with that warm welcome which was due to a man whose labors and sacrifices in the cause of God and his country had been so remarkable.

One of these visits he has described with some minuteness in his Reminiscences, having dropped the chronological order for the purpose:

"Having for some months cherished a fond desire to visit the place of my birth, the Rev. Mr. Kopp, the Lutheran minister at New Kingston, Cumberland County, whose church building stands on the north side of the street, on the old Junkin farm, just south of the 'Widow Junkin's tent,' was so kind as to make arrangements for me to preach there on the 71st anniversary of my birth. I arrived at his hospitable house on October 31st. Next day, November 1st, being the end of the 71st and the beginning of the 72d year of my sojourn in this beautiful though sin-stricken world, Mr. Kopp accompanied me to the old stone house in which I was born, now occupied by

Mr. Joseph Kanaga, son of the Joseph to whom my father sold it."

He then proceeds to describe his survey of the house, the farm, the vicinity, and the various objects associated with his childhood's memories. The description is too minute to interest the general reader, but it gives an insight of the *heart-workings* of this man of strong mind and glowing affections, which perhaps nothing else that he has written could so effectively do. He seems to have gazed upon everything on the dear domain, with an eye and a memory that repeopled it with the loved and lost. Even "the slate rock on which I fell, when about five years old, receiving the wound that left this small cicatrix upon my brow," was noticed. The changes in the features of the locality are marked. "But seven of the old apple-trees planted in his childhood remain." "Two of the old walnut-trees in the meadows only survive." "I noticed the stump of the locust which my sister Eleanor had planted near the window of her chamber in 1804. . . . The garden which these hands often turned over, is still rich, but now rough, and all the trees of my acquaintance gone. The old weeping-willow, at the northeast corner, passed away—all gone." He and his friend walked to several of the neighboring farms familiar to his childhood, but rarely met any of the acquaintances of his youth:

"I went on toward the old school-house where first I learned to read; but there was no school-house there, not a fragment, not a stone. . . . I wished to tread alone the very path my feet had trodden sixty-three years ago, but the grove was gone; all, except the land, was changed. I could not find the trace. . . . Arrived at the venerated ground, a thousand thoughts rushed upon me. This is the very spot on which I was taught my earliest lessons; here, every Saturday, without fail, we answered the questions, 'What is the chief end of man?' etc. Here I talked with my old masters, Jamieson, Henderson, Caruthers, and the rest. On this very spot I hit the ball against the gable ; just there I often struck the lever which sent the ball aloft in 'sky-ball;' down yonder we played 'cat and ball;' just here I had the only pugilistic contest of my life—politics the cause—in my eighth year; over these fields, then covered with forest, we played 'fox-hunt;' but where are all the Walkers, and the Irvines, and the Andersons, and the Junkins, and all the rest? Where? . . . Filled with such thoughts, I wended my way back, as nearly upon the old school-path as I could steer, to the old homestead, thence returned to Mr. Kopp's, and went with him to the church at 7 o'clock P.M., and preached from Matt. xi. 28–30. House full, and close and solemn attention. I pleaded for the conversion of some souls, as a memorial of my birthday. I doubt not that the Spirit of God was there, and the fruit will appear in eternity,—COMFORT. . . . After sermon went to Mr. Kanaga's and slept in Sister Eleanor's room,—a very happy night, both sleeping and waking. Where will I be at the end of seventy-one years more? And then, how many of my childhood's and youth's companions will I find in that happy home? Oh, my God, seal the truths I have uttered this night upon the hearts of the children and grandchildren of my early friends!

"On Saturday afternoon, Mr. Dinsmore, pastor elect of Silver Spring Church, conveyed me to Mr. B. Bryson's. Here I found children and grandchildren of my early friends. Next day I preached at Silver Spring, from John xiv. 27, in the very house where first I had heard the gospel from the lips of Mr. Waugh and Mr. Linn. Went into the graveyard and found many old friends, and gazed upon the spot where lies the dust of my grandparents, my uncles and aunts, my dear sister Elizabeth and her child, and two of my infant brothers.

"Went from church to Hogestown, the guest of Mrs. S., formerly Margery L. There found poor 'Jack' L., one of my most intimate schoolfellows, a thoughtless boy, and still, and all through life, thoughtless on the subject of salvation. Had a long talk with him and others in his sister's room, then a long, serious, and tender talk with him alone, on the subject of his life, death, and future destiny. We both wept. He is waiting till God changes his heart,—substantial antinomianism. Closed our interview with solemn and tender prayer. He came out to hear me at night. My text, 'Cut it down: why cumbereth it the ground?' Upon the whole, I left him, hoping against hope, that my poor old schoolmate will be brought in before he dies. The Lord grant it for Jesus' sake. House crowded at the service to-night."

He then describes a short visit to Harrisburg, and to his oldest son, a surgeon in the Union army, and then at Camp Cameron, and concludes the sketch of his visit as follows:

"Thus have I been preserved and carried mercifully through one of the most delightful visits which I ever enjoyed. My happiness was of course of that sombre tinge which leaves the deepest impression; and fondly do I hope that God will make it, to many, a blessing even more valuable than it has been to myself."

A few weeks after his return from his native place, he made a visit to the field of his former ministerial labors on the Susquehanna. The last days of November, and the first two weeks of December, were thus occupied. From the 28th of November to the 1st of December, he preached six times in Danville, and assisted at the dispensation of the Lord's Supper. Thence, he visited Milton, Turbot, White-Deer Valley, the fields of his former labor, taking sweet counsel with such of his former parishioners and friends as survived, and preaching the Word in those places. He preached eight times in these congregations, and visited many of his former friends, receiving everywhere a warm and affectionate welcome. Among others whom he found surviving, and with whom he held sweet Christian fellowship, none stood higher in his regards than the venerable woman who, almost forty years before, had kept angel-like vigils beside that bed of sickness which, in a former chapter, we have described,—the mother of ex-

Governor Pollock. "It was truly affecting," said the Governor, in making mention of the visit, "to see those aged people sitting closely side by side, for hours at a time, conversing quietly, and sometimes tearfully, about the past, the present, and the eternal future, weeping together over the memory of the departed yet dear ones whom they had both known and loved, talking of the scenes and the persons of the past and of their common hopes in regard to that heavenly home to which most of their loved ones had gone, and to which they both expected soon to follow."

In churches of Philadelphia he often officiated, and in Pottsville, Port Carbon, and other places. It is surprising to learn, from his register, the frequency with which he preached the Word during this winter. On the 16th and the 23d of February, we find this record in the register: "16th. Silent, by order of Dr. Darrach. 23d. Ditto." On May 11th, 1862, he preached in Dr. Swift's church, Alleghany, and in Dr. Howard's, in Pittsburg; next Sabbath in the First Church, Columbus, the next in the Methodist church of that city, the next in the First Presbyterian Church, Oxford, Ohio, where he had formerly resided, and the same day in the chapel of Miami University. On the 5th of June, he made a patriotic address in the court-house at Madison, Indiana; and on the 8th he preached twice in Indianapolis; on the 14th, one sermon and an address in Valparaiso; and on the next day, Sabbath, preached three times for the Rev. Dr. Logan, then the pastor of the church in that place. The next day he made a speech in the same city upon national affairs. On the next Lord's day, we find him in Mercer, Pennsylvania, where he preached twice. The same amount of labor was performed at New Wilmington on the next Sabbath. Three days after, he preached in the Methodist church, Mercer; two days thereafter (July 4th), in the court-house in that town, he made a speech to a large assembly, among whom were three surviving members of the company of "Mercer Blues," which his brother John had led to the Northwestern frontier in 1812. On this day half a century before, he had delivered to that same company his first public speech, at the time they volunteered for the war.

This brief summary is given as a specimen of the manner in which this minister of Christ labored, week after week, to the end of his life.

In April, 1862, he made a visit to his brother, then resident at Newport, R. I., as chaplain of the United States Naval Academy, which Institution had been removed to that city from Annapolis shortly after the breaking out of hostilities. Dr. Junkin enjoyed this visit very much. The pure, bracing sea-air of Newport invigorated him, and the historical associations of that ancient city interested him very much. Whilst there, he officiated often, at his brother's request, and with much acceptance to the officers and cadets of the Academy, in the religious services of the Institution, both on ship and shore. He was much gratified with the opportunity of causing "the gospel's joyful sound" to echo through the wooden walls of "Old Ironsides" (the frigate Constitution, then the school-ship), which had so often trembled beneath the cannon's roar, when the gallant Stewart and Hull trod her decks, and guided her to conquest amid the storm of battle. He preached, also, in the First and Second Baptist Churches, and in the First Congregational Church twice, then and still under the pastoral care of the lovely and accomplished Dr. Thayer, and once the pastoral charge of the celebrated Dr. Samuel Hopkins, whose peculiar views it had been the lot of Dr. Junkin to controvert in earlier life.

Returning from this visit, he called at New York to renew fellowship with his life-long and beloved friends, Dr. McElroy, who was still, as he had been for more than thirty years, the eloquent and able preacher and model pastor in the Scotch Presbyterian Church in that city, Dr. Phillips, the excellent and beloved pastor of the First Church, and Dr. Knox, the judicious and venerated pastor of the Collegiate Dutch Church.

He had meanwhile become a member of the Mother Presbytery of Philadelphia, and that body chose him one of her commissioners to the General Assembly of 1862, which that year met in Columbus. His younger brother was also in attendance upon the Assembly, and they were both invited guests of that earnest patriot and efficient supporter of the Union, David Tod, then Governor of Ohio. His Excellency entertained them with a large hospitality, and took a deep interest in those discussions and acts of the Assembly relating to public affairs, and in which Dr. George Junkin bore so prominent a part. In this Assembly Dr. Junkin spoke oftener than had been his wont, and he seemed always to be listened to with that respect and interest, which his talents and his peculiar relations to the past and the present of his church and his country naturally inspired.

The patriotic zeal which had exhibited itself in the Assembly of the previous year seemed to have become intensified in this; and Dr. Junkin stood full abreast of his fellow-members in his readiness to do anything which an ecclesiastical court might lawfully do, in encouraging the civil authorities in maintaining the government and preserving the Union. At this Assembly, and in connection with questions relating to civil and ecclesiastical affairs in Kentucky and Missouri, issues arose, which, four years later, culminated in the exciting scenes and the doubtful doings of the Assembly at St. Louis, in regard to those that have been called the "Declaration and Testimony men."

Into these issues and the details of their results it is not necessary, in a biography of Dr. Junkin, to enter. All that pertains necessarily to his history is the statement, that he was with the majority of the Assembly in their patriotic deliverances, spoke earnestly and eloquently in favor of the paper introduced by Dr. Breckinridge, but at the same time deprecated and deplored all personal animosities growing out of the diversities of opinion concerning them, and was also steadfastly opposed to some of the principles asserted and the measures adopted by the Assemblies of 1865 and 1866, in relation to these troubles. Whilst he went further than some of his brethren deemed ecclesiastically lawful in deliverances favorable to the Union and to the suppression of armed resistance to the government, and whilst he disapproved of the course and the language of the "Declaration and Testimony men," yet he deprecated and resisted with his influence and his pen the measures adopted by the Assembly in regard to them. He saw no necessity for resorting to expedients of doubtful constitutionality, much less to expedients flagrantly unconstitutional, in order to reach with rapid and severe discipline these recusant brethren. He deplored the assumption by the General Assembly of powers not granted to that body in the constitution, powers which he verily believed were dangerous to the liberties of God's people, and destructive of the beautiful and well-balanced Presbyterianism which our fathers had deduced from the Bible. He felt that the assumption by the Assembly of the powers of a court of original jurisdiction, in cases of discipline, was unconstitutional, and tended to the utter destruction of our system of appeals from a lower to a higher court. He abhorred the doctrine of the "omnipotence of the General Assembly," and in a series of vigorous articles, published in the *North-Western Presbyterian*, a paper ably edited at Chicago by the Rev. E. Erskine, D.D., and the Rev. D. McKinney, D.D., he showed the unconstitutionality and the dangerous tendency of this dogma, and besought his brethren to beware, lest, in their excited zeal for a good end, they should adopt doctrines and measures which were revolutionary and destructive. In his Presbytery also, and in his Synod, he raised his voice against this sacrifice of great and essential general principles to temporory expedients. Admitting the maxim, *inter arma leges silent*, as sometimes applicable and necessary in temporal governments, he claimed that it is never necessary in governments ecclesiastical.

It is believed that his views of this matter are the views which prevail with the great mass of Presbyterians, especially since the reunion. The Old School branch, before the reunion, had substantially receded from and repudiated positions taken in 1865 and 1866, and the New School branch stand committed, by all their deliverances, in all their separate history, against the high church doctrines of the "omnipotence of the General Assembly,"—the right of the Assembly to assume original jurisdiction in cases of discipline, and the possession by the higher courts of all the powers of the inferior judicatories. This would be a consolidation of power more puissant than the Popedom, and more dangerous to the liberties of God's people. Against it Dr. Junkin left his latest, almost his dying, testimony; for, in some of the last letters traced by his pen, he charges his brother to resist it everywhere, and all the time.

The summer of 1862 found the writer of these pages, by orders from the chief of his department, chaplain of the line-of-battle ship North Carolina, then the "receiving-ship" at New York. He had, in addition to his official duties, the supplying of the pulpit of the Canal Street Presbyterian Church, being invited thereto by its Session. In the autumn of that year he was ordered to the steam frigate Colorado, then put in commission at Kittery Navy-Yard, in the State of Maine, and ordered on blockade duty. At his suggestion, Dr. George Junkin was invited to take charge of the pulpit of Canal Street when the younger brother went to sea. He consented, and preached in Canal Street on the 8th of October. But previous engagements prevented him from entering fully upon this charge until the month of November. Meanwhile he made another visit to the West Branch of the Susquehanna, preaching and making addresses with great frequency. Williamsport, Muncy, and his favorite charge, White-Deer Valley, shared in these labors. In November he went to New York, and began his work in Canal Street; he made his home with his brother's family, at 79 Sands Street, Brooklyn, and continued to labor with his accustomed assiduity until the battle of Gettysburg was fought, when he hastened to that scene of carnage, and toiled in arduous attendance upon the sick and wounded, and in constant preachings and ministrations in the general and smaller hospitals. He labored about ten months in Canal Street, and with great acceptance and usefulness. His memory is cherished anong that people with much reverence and affection.

Whilst located in Brooklyn, and, indeed, from the commencement of hostilities between the insurgents and the United States Government, Dr. Junkin was as zealous for maintaining the government and preserving the Union as he had been in efforts to prevent the appeal to arms. He omitted no opportunity and no exertion, compatible with his profession as a minister of the gospel, to encourage his fellow-citizens to maintain the Constitution and the Union.

Approving, as he did, the declaration of Congress, in regard to the objects of the war, viz., to maintain the authority of the government, and preserve the Union and the Constitution, he lent all his influence and employed his voice and his pen in helping forward the good work. His patriotism partook of the vigor of his mind and the intensity of his ardent affections. He had made sacrifices for the cause of the Union such as few other men were called to make, and he seemed willing to add the sacrifice of time, toil, substance, and all he had, rather than witness the disruption of his country.

He was repeatedly called upon to deliver addresses in vindication of the cause of the country, and generally responded to such calls, sometimes travelling long distances to do it.* These speeches were marked by his usual vigor of thought and fervor of manner; but, whilst he advocated the energetic defence of the government, he at the same time aimed to abate the exasperation of sectional hate. He did not believe that bitter hatred to the *persons* of the secessionists was a necessary or proper element of success in a war for the Union; and, like Mr. Lincoln and the Congress, at the beginning of the war, he did not contemplate or advocate anything beyond the preservation of the Union, and the restoration of the *statum quo ante bellum.*

Early in the war, he prepared and published, through the house of Charles Scribner, of New York, a volume of 332 pages *duodecimo*, "Political Fallacies," already noticed.

There is not space for quoting, upon these pages, any part of his admirable argument, and, as the book was widely circulated, it is the less necessary. We can only say that, in the judgment of at least his Northern readers,

---

* As a specimen of these invitations, take the following telegram, dated

"BRIDGEPORT, CONN., April 4th, 1863.

"To REV. DR. GEO. JUNKIN, 79 Sands Street, Brooklyn.

"Come, if possible, to Bridgeport to-night—a short speech—and you can return before Sunday. Take the New York and New Haven cars.

"F. W. SMITH, JR."

He acceded to this invitation, as well as to similar ones from Somerville, Oxford, and other places.

he demonstrated the "fallacies" of the secession doctrine —showed, historically and by an inspection of the Constitution itself, and from the recorded interpretations of its framers, that no colony or State of this Union ever possessed an independent national sovereignty; that the functions of absolute political sovereignty had never been allowed to, or claimed and exercised by, any State; that national sovereignty, when it passed from the British crown at the Revolution, had passed to, and been exercised by, not the several States, but "the United States of America in Congress assembled." He proved that the United States was a NATION, not a congeries of independent communities, transiently confederated; that the right of a State to come into the Union and to go out at its own option, never had been conceded and had no place in our Federal Constitution, and that the disintegrating doctrine of secession, as taught by the Calhoun school, was as inconsistent with every acknowledged principle of common law and national structure, as it was with the fundamental law of our country as written in the Constitution. Admitting a modified sovereignty over its own internal police as the inherent and guaranteed right of every State, and deprecating the assumption by the national government of any powers not constitutionally belonging to it, he showed that the right to withdraw at option from the national Union never pertained to State sovereignty, and that the assertion of such a right was as preposterous as it was suicidal. He also demonstrated, that our admirable Constitution contained within itself a perfect system of checks and balances, by which, when normally worked, all the ends of a grand, free, and effective nationality could be attained, whilst, at the same time, the rights and interests of the smallest States, and the privilege of local self-government, could be secured. He demonstrated, that consolidation on the one hand, and the disintegration inevitably resulting from secession on the other, would be alike destructive of our beautiful and massive continental system; that the State governments, working in their proper orbits, strengthened the nation, and that the national government, operating within the sphere prescribed in the Constitution, would prove mighty and beneficent for all national purposes, whilst it was the only guarantee against foreign invasion and wrong, and domestic strife of State with State.

There is reason to believe that this book was instrumental of great good, in placing before many of the influential men of the country a distinct, lucid, and forceful exhibition of the great issues of the war, so that thousands could more clearly understand what we were contending for.

As was intimated by Dr. Knox, in his memorial discourse, Dr. Junkin was one of the most prompt, faithful, and laborious of those ministers of Jesus who hastened to the fields of battle to assist in attending upon the wounded, the dying, and the dead. Many have expressed their astonishment at the fact, that a man of his years could endure the exposure, and perform the amount of labor, through which he actually passed. In these toils he not unfrequently was called to minister to his former pupils, whom he found among the wounded and the prisoners from the Confederate armies. They invariably met him with affection, and received his attentions with gratitude. He was often moved to tears in witnessing the sufferings of Southern soldiers; and whilst he strongly reprobated the cause in which they suffered, he commiserated their woes and did what he could to alleviate them. And even when he did not come in personal contact with them, he received letters from prisoners who knew him personally, asking for relief and counsel. And he always extended aid, to the limit of his means and opportunities. On his files are letters from Confederate prisoners, written from Fort Delaware, from Johnston's Island, from David's Island, from

Rhode Island Hospital, and other points, some of them his former pupils, others only acquaintances, asking, some for books, some for other aid, some seeking his intercession for their release, others thanking him for favors previously extended to them in their distress.

Did our space permit, it would be interesting to insert some of these letters. One of them is from a former pupil, who was at the Theological Seminary when the war began, and left his books to take up arms. It is dated after the surrender, and in it he entreats Dr. Junkin to intercede with the proper authorities to procure his early release from the condition of a prisoner of war, that he might return and resume his studies in order to enter upon his Master's work. The writer of the letter deplores the time already lost from the work to which he had devoted his life, and appears to long for an opportunity to redeem the time. Of course, as the young man had taken the oath of allegiance to the United States Government, Dr. Junkin did not hesitate to exert all the influence he could for his prompt release.

In a letter addressed to George Junkin, Esq., by Martin L. Stoever, LL.D., Professor in Pennsylvania College, and dated Gettysburg, December 28th, 1868, one of those scenes, between Dr. Junkin and the Confederate prisoners, which illustrate their mutual feelings, is graphically described. We shall have occasion to quote other passages of this letter, but cite the following in this connection. Prof. S. was a native of Germantown, and, when a youth, had met Dr. Junkin when he was Principal of the Institution there. Thirty years after separating at Germantown, they met in Arch Street, and the Professor was surprised to be promptly recognized and cordially greeted. He then proceeds:

"I did not see him again until we met in Gettysburg, after the memorable battle which proved the turning-point in the history of the war. He was frequently at my house during the period he labored so faithfully in the service of Christian humanity. I was often struck with his power of endurance, the earnest and indefatigable efforts he put forth to relieve human suffering, and to minister to the spiritual welfare of the wounded and dying. We were often together in the hospital during the week and on the Lord's day, and I know how earnest and faithful he was in the good work, how his heart yearned to bring souls to Christ, to prepare the dying for the great change which so soon awaited them.

"His manner, too, was peculiarly happy, especially when he came in contact with his erring brethren from the South. He seldom failed in conciliating them, and awakening their personal interest, always without the compromise of his loyalty or patriotism. His connection with 'Stonewall Jackson,' and a golden-headed cane which he carried, the gift of that General, were often made the occasion of introducing the subject of religion when he entered the tents of the prisoners. One Sabbath afternoon, when he consented to preach on the grounds of the consolidated hospital, I found perhaps a dozen of his former pupils in Washington College, whom I persuaded to attend the services in the chapel. Dr. J. delivered a very pungent discourse; the services were of a very solemn character. After they were concluded, these college young men all remained to take their old preceptor by the hand. Among the number was a Confederate chaplain; and it was most touching to see the aged man of God throw his arms around the young man's neck and weep, exclaiming, 'I never thought *you* would be engaged in this work!'

"As they gathered around him, apparently most glad to meet him again, he took from his pocket the old class-book, and commenced to call the roll, and rehearsed the history of each member, showing how all had suffered more or less in consequence of their resistance to the best government which God had ever given to men."

Whilst Dr. Junkin was serving the Canal Street Church, and his brother was at sea, their correspondence was kept up, and an extract from a letter which passed between them may disclose something of their peculiar trials, and shed light upon the spirit by which they were animated in that dark period. Two months before the battle of Gettysburg, that of the three terrible days at Chancellorville had been fought, in which General Jackson was mortally wounded. The following are extracts from a letter written by the younger to the elder brother in reference to that event:

"U. S. S. FRIGATE COLORADO, May 18th, 1863,
"OFF MOBILE BAY, NEAR FORT MORGAN.

"MY DEAR BROTHER,—For the last half-hour there has been the severest struggle in my breast between two conflicting emotions—my *love of country* and my love for your *noble, dear, godly,* but *misguided,* and now *dead,* son, General Jackson. I knew not fully how much I loved him, despite his zeal in a bad cause, until I heard, a few moments ago, of his death. My judgment and my conscience cannot but approve of this dispensation of Divine Providence, whilst my *heart* cannot but mourn, and mine eyes cannot but weep, for the loss of one so justly dear (except for the one great error) to us all. I have never for a day forgotten your emphatic prediction, uttered in a mournful tone, more than two years ago, 'Jackson will perish in this war.' And now that sad apprehension is *history.*

"Eight days ago, viz., on the 10th inst., I learned, from some prisoners taken in a prize, that Jackson had been wounded, and his arm amputated near the shoulder. I feared the worst; for I knew that his constitution must have been pretty well run down with toil and exposure. This morning, about three o'clock, Lieutenant-Commander Jouett sent in nine prisoners, whom he had taken from under the guns of Fort Morgan, having boarded a large schooner loaded with cotton and burned her within three hundred yards of the fort. The captain of this schooner, who is quite an intelligent man, was standing on the quarter-deck of our ship this morning at half-past five, when I approached him, and, after some other inquiries, I asked him if he had heard how General Jackson was getting. 'He's dead, sir,' was his reply. 'Dead, sir?' 'Yes; he only lived about a week.' I confess I was shocked, stunned; for I had heard that after the amputation he was doing well. I was completely *unmanned,* and had no heart for the congratulations that I heard around me, concerning the capture of several vessels last night and this morning. I sought my state-room, to weep there. Is it wrong, is it treason, to mourn for a good and great, though a mistaken, man? I cannot feel it to be so. I loved him dearly—but now—he is with *dear*, *dear* ELLIE and the rest! O God! thou doest righteously. Yea! is there not *mercy* in this sad end of him we could not but love? Oh, give us grace to acquiesce in these terrible mysteries of thy providence! God comfort *thee*, my brother; I know He will. . . .

"I now have more confidence in the ultimate success of our cause. So long as such men as Thomas J. Jackson and Thomas Cobb were against us, I was puzzled to know why the God, whose I believe them to be, should permit them to be on the wrong side. But now they have both fallen; I *feel* that God is taking them away *from the evil to come;* and if our rulers will only yield to the wishes of the people and make the Constitution of the United States the basis of adjustment and the aim of the war, God will soon give us the victory. The moral effect of the loss of Jackson will be greater to them than the loss of 20,000 men.

"I am glad, too, that since it was God's will he should die, he should fall by the hands of those whom he was helping to destroy our country, instead of by our own bullets. It seems that eight of them fell by the fire of their own troops as he and his staff were returning from a reconnoissance. Three were killed at once, and Jackson and four others wounded. My informant could not give me any of the names of his staff that were shot.

"God comfort and pity his poor bereaved widow! I believe she got to him, and was with him when he died. I try to pray for her—for she is desolate indeed.

"I do not know that I described to you the parting scene between General Jackson and myself. It was at the base of that huge precipice, the Maryland Heights, at Harper's Ferry. We had been conferring for two hours; I striving to show him that the rebellion was inexcusable. The time arrived that we must part. None were present but my poor boy, the General, myself, and our God. He held his magnificent field-horse by the bridle-rein. His left hand was gauntlet-gloved. He grasped mine with his right. I said, 'Farewell, General; may we meet under happier circumstances; if not in this troubled world, may we meet in'— My voice failed me,—tears were upon the cheeks of both, —he raised his gloved hand, pointed upward, and finished my sentence with the words—'in heaven!' And so, without another word, we parted; he mounted and rode away, and if we ever meet it will be 'in heaven!' God comfort us and all that mourn his loss, and give us all grace to secure *that meeting!*

"Oh, my heart is sometimes broken—sometimes, alas! *bitter*, when I think of these desolations, caused by the ambition and fanaticism of bad men! . . .

"Please, as you have opportunity, assure our friends of my sincere condolence in this last sorrow. We hear that Hooker's defeat was terrible, and that but for an error of Lee, in ordering the recovery of a fortified hill, Jackson and Longstreet would have environed our whole army. My dear wife will give you all details of personal news. Pray much for me. *I want to be holy*, for our Lord is coming, either personally or by terrible judgments.

"Love to all with you and at Philadelphia.

"Your sympathizing brother,

"D. X. JUNKIN.

"REV. DR. G. JUNKIN."

As much curiosity has existed in regard to the man whose death is alluded to in the foregoing letter, it may be acceptable, by way of showing his spirit, to insert one from himself, addressed to his father-in-law, after the latter's exodus from Virginia, but before any blood had been shed:

"HARPER'S FERRY, May 22d, 1861.

"MY DEAR DOCTOR,—Since we parted, I have frequently thought of you, and was much gratified at the reception of your letter. Say to Uncle D. X. that Major Preston has in charge the carrying out of his request respecting G. He volunteered to see G. on the subject, or I would have attended to it in person. Should it appear that G. is willing to be discharged, I will write to the Governor at once. At present, Major P. is at Martinsburg, as an officer for taking the vote on the ordinance of secession, but he will return as soon as his duties shall have been discharged.

"It is more than gratifying, in these times, to see our General Assembly convening at the appointed place and time, under the banner of the Prince of Peace. May the blessing of GOD rest upon them and their efforts, is my earnest prayer.

"I feel unusually concerned about our Foreign Missionaries, but my consolation is, that '*all things work together for good to them that love God.*' We know that the church is safe. Give my love to J., George, John, Uncle D. X., and their families.

"Affectionately yours,

"T. J. JACKSON."

The original of this letter is in possession of Dr. Sprague, the biographer, having been given to him at his request.

It is evident, from this letter, that such men as Jackson did not contemplate at that time the severance of the Presbyterian Church. The vote of Virginia upon the Ordinance of Secession had not as yet been ascertained, and the troops under Jackson were professedly defending the soil of Virginia against a threatened invasion; and up to this time he had hopes that an adjustment of the public troubles might be reached. His solicitude about our Foreign Missionaries rose from the fear that amid the agitations of the country they might be left to suffer for want of funds to support them.

The course of General Jackson, and of thousands of others, illustrates the danger of a single important error of opinion. The parting scene alluded to in the first of the foregoing letters, was at the close of a protracted conversation between the General and the writer, in which the latter sought to convince him that the attitude assumed by the Southern States was a great blunder,—a rebellion without a cause; that Mr. Lincoln sincerely designed to administer the government in a constitutional way; that whilst he would discourage the extension of slavery into the Territories, he would not interfere with it, or any other domestic institution of the South, in the States; that if the Southern States would remain in the Union they and the conservative party of the North had a clear and decided working majority in both houses of Congress, and that if the South would stand by the Union and the Constitution they would find all their rights secured; but that the attempt to disrupt the nation would bring inevitable disaster, and, even if successful, would result in the destruction of the very interests they aimed to secure; whilst the sundering of the Union would inaugurate the wars of a hundred generations in America, and repeat the bloody history of Europe.

The doctrine with which General Jackson replied to all this reasoning was simple, comprehensive, plausible, yet fallacious and disastrous. It was:

> "As a Christian man, my *first* allegiance is due to my State, the State of Virginia; and every other State has a primal claim to the fealty of her citizens, and may justly control their allegiance. If Virginia adheres to the United States, I adhere; her determination must control mine."

This is the substance of his creed upon the question of allegiance. It was in vain we argued with him that this doctrine was false, disintegrating, destructive of all possible nationality; that under our glorious Constitution, which secured all necessary rights to every State, strong or weak, and guaranteed the advantages resulting from distributed powers and local legislation, such a doctrine was as useless as it was dangerous: he still adhered to the opinion. It had been early inculcated, and had strengthened with his strength. With him it was a *conscientious* conviction, and with almost the entire population of the South. And with such a conviction, it is not matter of wonder, that those who held it would go into the war *honestly* and from a *sense* of duty. Like Paul when he persecuted the church, they verily thought they OUGHT to obey each the behests of the State to which they owed allegiance. Their sin lay in a *false faith.* And this proves that *belief* is never a matter of indifference. An erroneous belief does *always,* in honest minds, lead to error in practice. It is only the hypocritical who fail to carry out in action their convictions. With a man like Thomas J. Jackson there could be no such hesitancy; his career was dictated by conscientious principle. We of the North think the *principle* is wrong, dangerous, disastrous. The men of the South may have been just as honest in thinking it right and safe.

Before Virginia made the fatal decision to adopt the Ordinance of Secession, there were no more earnest Union men in the country than Jackson and Preston; but the moment their State seceded they felt it to be *duty* to go with her. We think they were wrong, but they were conscientiously wrong.

And this view of the case shows the absurdity of expecting evangelical repentance for political sins, and of making political opinion a test of piety. A Scotchman may conscientiously believe that monarchy is the best government, and may feel it to be his duty to be *loyal,* even to a bad king; an American may claim the right of resisting the authority of that same king, and may do it *conscientiously.* May they not both be Christian men?

On the 6th of May, 1864, Dr. Junkin, by invitation, delivered a sermon at Altoona, Pa., upon the occasion of the installation of a former pupil, the Rev. Robert M. Wallace, as pastor of the church in that place. It was a discourse which had been delivered several times before, but the members of the Presbytery of Huntingdon then present expressed a wish to have it printed. It was accordingly published in a neat pamphlet of 48 pages. It is entitled THE TWO COMMISSIONS—THE APOSTOLICAL AND EVANGELICAL, and is one of the most compact, lucid, and conclusive arguments extant against the arrogant claims of the prelatical doctrine of apostolical succession. Every young preacher who desires to possess a brief and satisfactory statement of the true idea and authority of the Christian ministry, and the constitution of the church, ought to obtain it.

In June, 1864, he was again invited to resume labor in the Canal Street Church, N. Y.; but as he was employed ministering to the soldiers and prisoners at Fort Delaware, he declined the invitation. An extract or two from the letter to his brother, declining the proposal, will throw light upon this period of his life:

"I have concluded to say nay to the Canal Street people. Tell Brother Lowrey* my heart is with them, and I should delight to serve them did not Providence seem to call me elsewhere. I have just returned from Fort Delaware, where I have been preaching and distributing the books of our Board. There are at Fort Delaware 9000 prisoners, and I see by this morning's paper that 450 more will reach there to-day; and there are 1500 soldiers, and some hundreds of mechanics, etc., making, perhaps, 11,000. Now, there I can have an audience of 2000 hearers almost any hour, and they are anxious hearers. The privates (prisoners) are the most hopeful. They press and pack close up, and stand for more than an hour, listening, and weeping often. I find many old acquaintances. Dr. McFarland's second son is here in the officers' barracks. Dr. Handy, in the eleventh month of his prisonership, is doing a blessed work. My books the poor fellows almost tear, pulling them from one another. Oh, they are very hungry! sorrow makes them ready to hear the gospel. Many are sick. . . A regiment from Steubenville, O., went down the same day with me. Captain Boals says he knows the mayor of that city, our brother, M. O. J. . . . I never had such a field of labor; tell the people of Canal Street I can't refuse to work at the Fort; they must excuse me."

---

* Elder of Canal Street Church.

In this manner did Dr. Junkin labor on until the surrender of General Lee brought the terrible struggle to a close. When the last of the prisoners were permitted to return to their homes, he felt at liberty to turn to other work, but seemed not to think for one hour of putting off his harness; and for one so willing to toil, employment is always ready.

In July, 1865, he went to meet his surviving brothers at the old family homestead, Hope Mills, in Mercer County. There the five surviving brothers enjoyed a reunion after years of separation. William lived in the homestead, Benjamin in the vicinity, Matthew came from Steubenville, and the younger brother from Chicago, where he then resided as pastor of the North Presbyterian Church of that city. The meeting actually took place at Pulaski, on account of the detention of one of the brothers. Two years thereafter they again met at Steubenville, and enjoyed a sweet season of fraternal fellowship, and parted, never all to meet again in this life. Before another year two of them were not—for God had taken them.

In 1865, his work on Sanctification was written and issued by the Presbyterian Board of Publication. It is a book of 268 pages, and is a lucid and thorough discussion of the subject indicated by its title, explaining the doctrine, the means, the agency, and the process of sanctification, and exhibiting its connection with the other parts of the scheme of salvation. Perhaps no book that he has written is likely to be more useful than this short but admirable treatise.

About the same time, he published a brief treatise on the subject of Baptism. This was elicited by circumstances which occurred previous to his taking his pen; but, although written with a special object, the tractate is worthy of its author and is of permanent value.

In addition to this, he shortly afterward prepared a work

of 168 pages, entitled "THE TABERNACLE; OR, THE GOSPEL ACCORDING TO MOSES," which was issued in 1865, by the Board of Publication. In this he evolves, with admirable clearness, the lessons of the Mosaic ritual, and points out the "better things to come," of which that ritual was an instructive "shadow." It is a volume that ought to be in every Christian's, at least in every minister's, library.

There are, in Philadelphia, two charitable institutions of an interesting character, humble in their pretension, but beneficent in their design and influence,—the Asylum for Aged and Indigent Widows, and the Magdalen Asylum, for the rescue and reformation of fallen women. In both of them there is provision for religious worship; but, for special reasons. the preaching and devotional services are held on a week-day. Dr. Junkin was requested, in 1864, to undertake the work of ministering in both of these institutions. The appointment came from the Board of Trustees of the General Assembly, in pursuance of a clause in the will of Elias Boudinot, LL.D. He consented, and continued to perform the duties of this humble mission until the hand of death was laid upon him. Perhaps no work of his life furnished a lovelier illustration of his perfectly unambitious and Christ-like consecration to the business of saving souls than this. To behold this man of mighty intellect and commanding pulpit power, gliding weekly to these homes of the aged, the feeble, and the fallen, and preaching to the inmates in tender, earnest words, adapted to their several conditions, the unsearchable riches of Christ, and to witness the fact that he executed this humble mission with as much punctuality, solemnity, and faithfulness as if it had been the gravest undertaking of his life, was proof that he was largely possessed of the spirit of Him who was "meek and lowly of heart." This Christ-like portion of his labors was all the lovelier when contrasted with other synchronous toils. For whilst he was thus instructing and comforting the weak, the world-worn, and the straying, he was grappling with giant strength two of the mightiest enemies of religion, liberty, and social order—Intemperance and the Anti-Sabbath spirit of the age. Intemperance was rife, and the abettors of the liquor-traffic rampant, at the close of the war. Efforts were being put forth by the friends of temperance to check the tide of evil, and Dr. Junkin threw himself into the enterprise with all the fervor and energies of his younger years. In speeches, in conventions, through the press, and by personal visits to the Legislature, he sought to help forward the good cause.

About the same time, the enemies of the Lord's day were seeking to have the laws for the protection of citizens in the enjoyment of that holy day repealed. The daily press was extensively enlisted by this demoralizing interest, and a powerful effort was inaugurated to prostrate the day of rest. Against this Dr. Junkin lifted up a standard. He wrote for the press, he travelled, he lectured, he corresponded, he rallied others to the rescue, he wrote a volume in defence of the Sabbath, he repaired to the Legislature, and by argument and personal influence, strove to protect the memorial day from desecration. It was amazing the amount of work he bestowed upon this matter in addition to his other labors.

In a letter to the author, resident then in Chicago, dated Philadelphia, March 7th, 1866, he says:

"I have been very busy with my book on the Hebrews; have written three hundred and sixty pages of large letter sheet, and have got to Chapter vi. 20. But for two months this has been arrested by the Sabbath war. The conspiracy of the Romanists, the infidel Germans, Jews, Unitarians, Universalists, Deists of all forms, and the rum and lager men, is very formidable in numbers; and having —— for their leader, and we having no daily press open to us, the battle has to be fought at great disadvantage. We are now certain of defeating them this time. But they have taken a new tack, have a bill up in the House to authorize a vote at the next general election, 'Sabbath Cars' or 'No Sabbath Cars.' Thus the law of God is to be submitted to a popular vote! If this succeeds, we cannot buy votes as they can. The liquor and the money we might get, but conscience forbids bribery. We have a sure majority in the Senate.

"Our ninth week of the union prayer-meeting is in progress. This takes one to two hours every day. I miss none. But my time is chiefly thrown upon the Sabbath question. I am preparing a book of some 175 pages. It will be ready in three weeks, D. V."

The book here alluded to is his "Sabbatismos," a volume of 215 pages, containing a succinct, yet original and powerful argument for the Holy Day, which was published soon after the date of the above letter. He not only published this volume, and wrote copiously for the weekly press in behalf of the Sabbath, but he traversed many portions of the State, delivering sermons and lectures upon the subject, and was instrumental in awaking the people to a consideration of the importance of this great safeguard of religion and liberty. It would astonish the reader to examine his register of preaching, and reckon the number of places visited, and of discourses delivered. How he endured the physical toil is marvellous!

Meanwhile, the subject of this memoir was far from indifferent to the political condition of his country, for whose union and government he had sacrificed and toiled so much. Concerning public affairs he was intensely solicitous. With the murdered President, he thought that the seceded States had never been out of the Union. Like him, he was unwilling to acknowledge that secession had been a success; but held, with him, that when the insurrection was suppressed, the State governments, which had been temporarily whelmed beneath its surges, would rise and resume, under proper guarantees, their normal positions in the Union.

He approved of Mr. Lincoln's theory of restoration, and, with that good and sagacious magistrate, was of opinion, that the Constitution itself contained enough recuperative energy, if rightly applied, to restore the health of the nation. With every civist who understands the principles of free government, he held that crime was to be punished by *adjudication*, not by *legislation*. He judged that it would have been safer, juster, wiser, and more in accordance with the rights of man and regulated liberty, to have arraigned and consigned to exemplary penalties a few of the leaders of the revolt, rather than, by a system of punitive and vindictive legislation, to vex and oppress the masses; and he was especially opposed to those measures which punished the innocent with the guilty, making no distinction between the intensest secessionist and the Union man. He held that no man ought to be punished before fair trial and just conviction; and most earnestly deprecated every expedient which seemed to dispense with the judiciary branch of the Government, or to trench upon its sacred functions. Not only acquiescing but rejoicing in the downfall of slavery, yet he doubted the wisdom and humanity of entrusting to the emancipated the control of the government of the States in which they are found, until after a season of education and probation. He at one time was seriously apprehensive, that the judiciary branch of the Government would be prostrated before the legislative, and rejoiced greatly when that danger seemed to pass. He doubted the wisdom of settling great principles of constitutional law, at a time when the waves, which had been lashed into wild commotion by the storms of civil war, were still unquieted. He venerated the Constitution of his country as the grandest effort of human wisdom and patriotism, and trembled to see that stately bark straining every timber upon a stormy sea, whilst unskilled hands were tampering with her planks. Many an utterance of solicitude could be quoted from his correspondence of these later years,—all fraught with statesmanly sagacity, warm with patriotism, and ennobled with that Christ-like magnanimity which pities the erring and esteems it *base* to insult or oppress the fallen.

In regard to the progress of affairs in the Presbyterian Church he was also deeply solicitous. His mind and his habits were essentially conservative. With a heart glowing with affection, yet he always kept his feelings subject to his judgment. When the movement toward a union of the two branches of the Presbyterian Church was proposed, first at Newark in a voluntary assemblage, afterward at St. Louis in the General Assembly, he apprehended evil, and discouraged the movement. He feared that a reflex wave from "the battle of the warrior" was about to submerge much that was valuable in the church. He feared that the cry of "UNION" which was raised, was a mere echo of that which was started by the voice of patriotic enthusiasm. He knew that there was no analogy between the union of the nation and the union of the church, yet he feared that the civil sentiment had begotten the ecclesiastical, and that there was a disposition to compromise *truth* in an enthusiastic zeal for *unity*. He had witnessed, nearly forty years before, the turmoil produced by the effort to make those walk together who were not "agreed." For thirty years he had seen the happy results, in both branches of the church, of separate organization and action, and he feared that a premature attempt to unite in one organization men who yet entertained diversity of doctrinal opinions, would result in one of two evils, either of which he deemed a terrible price to pay for visible unity, viz., a compromise of essential truth and the estoppel of discipline at the start, or a renewal of the strife which had formerly diverted the energies of the church from her appropriate work, and which had been allayed only by separation.

With these views, he could not favor the proposed union. He resisted with all his power and influence the propositions which were subsequently embodied in the Albany basis of reunion, and advised their rejection. He still feared that latitude of interpretation in matters essential might be claimed, and he knew that if claimed and yielded, corruption of doctrine would result, and if resisted, strife.*

Since the union has been consummated, it is devoutly to be desired that his apprehensions may prove groundless. If such shall be the result, and the spirits of the departed are permitted to know the condition of the church militant, none will rejoice over that result more than the glorified spirit of GEORGE JUNKIN.

He did not live to witness the reunion, as his death occurred the day before the meeting of the General Assembly of 1868.

Thus did this man of thought, of heart, of prayer, of wondrous work, labor on until his Lord sent suddenly for him. The very week before he was taken, he had finished and put in complete order for the press, a work which he had been often urged to undertake,—a Commentary on the Epistle to the Hebrews. This portion of God's word had been a favorite theme of study with him, and a subject of frequent pulpit exegesis during all his life. Probably no man of his generation had bestowed upon it more thought and investigation. The work is very thorough and complete. He had been negotiating with a publisher, and the manuscript was in his hands, but no definite arrangement had been effected. He had continued to preach until a few days before his decease. On the 29th of April he had preached with his usual power and tenderness, in West Spruce Street, from that favorite Psalm, cxvi. 1–9. He officiated regularly in the Widows' and

---

* See Appendix.

the Magdalen Asylums. His last recorded text of discourse to the widows was John xiv. 1, "Let not your heart be troubled: ye believe in God, believe also in me. In my Father's house are many mansions." A few days preceding his death he preached at the Magdalen Asylum, his last public official duty. It was fitting, that one so much like Jesus, for he was the purest man the writer ever knew, should make the last offer of the gospel which he announced on earth to the fallen, bidding them look up and hope, trusting in that blood which cleanseth from all sin.

On the day of his departure, and just about the time the spirit was leaving the body, the congregation of aged widows, in the asylum, had made their customary preparation for divine service, expecting their venerated and beloved pastor. The seats were arranged, the little stand and Bible set out, the widows gathered, but he came not! A number of them attended his funeral, and one of them said, alluding to the arrangements they had made, "He never disappointed us before!"

Dr. Junkin had sometimes expressed to his brother, and other intimate friends, the apprehension that he would shrink with timidity unbecoming a Christian from the approach of death. With all his indomitable courage, he confessed to a dread of the pains of death. But the illness which terminated his life was so sudden, painful, and rapid in doing its work, that this apprehension did not appear to be realized. On Monday morning, May 18th, he arose as usual, dressed himself, and, entering his daughter's room, adjacent to his own, remarked that he felt a severe pain in his breast, and asked her to prepare a remedy, which was done. But the application gave no relief. Medical aid was summoned; the disease proved to be *angina pectoris*. That day he seemed to suffer intensely, but made no complaint, except the utterance, "You do not know how dreadfully I suffer." Still, neither he nor his children, who attended upon him, seemed to apprehend a fatal issue.

On Tuesday, the 19th, he seemed easier, and less lively, probably the effect of anodynes. And the same condition continued till the afternoon of the 20th. His son, who was a Commissioner to the General Assembly, had purposed to set out for Albany, so little was a serious result apprehended. Up to the time that he was seized with this complaint, his health was good, "his natural strength seemed scarce abated," and the apprehension that death was so near did not appear to have occurred to him. Toward evening his extremities became somewhat cold, and, whilst his daughter was fetching appliances for producing warmth, he grew suddenly worse, attempted to speak, but effected no utterance of a connected sentence. The only words that the eager ear of his son could distinctly catch, were the words, "Christ," "The Church," "Heaven;" and "he was not, for God took him!" It was scarcely a struggle, and all was rest. The Angel of the Covenant was better to him than he had ventured to hope. He literally fell with his harness on, in the fulness of his strength, trusting, loving, working to the last. So many of his cherished ones were already in the house of many mansions, that it would seem more like home to him than any place on earth. He was a pilgrim and a sojourner here. There he is AT HOME!

The funeral was attended, on Saturday, May 23d, from his son's residence, in Spruce Street. A large number of clergymen and other citizens, Dr. Cattell, President of Lafayette College, several members of the Board of Trustees of that Institution, and many sympathizing friends, were in attendance, notwithstanding the inclemency of the day.

The services were directed by the Rev. Wm. P. Breed, D.D., pastor of the family, who delivered an eloquent address commemorative of Dr. Junkin's life, characteristics, and labors. Dr. J. H. M. Knox and Rev. John Chambers also made earnest and touching addresses, and the Rev. Dr. James Clark, long a co-presbyter and friend of the deceased, offered, impressively, the concluding prayer.

His mortal remains rest beneath the grand old forest trees which shadow the graves in the beautiful Woodland Cemetery, on the banks of the Schuylkill, there to await the resurrection of the just.

A simple monumental head- and foot-stone, of massive marble, marks the lovely spot, bearing the inscription:

THE REV. GEORGE JUNKIN, D.D., LL.D.
BORN November 1st, 1790.
DIED May 20th, 1868.
"Well done, good and faithful servant."

CHAPTER XXXVI.

Testimonials—Of Rev. Charles Elliott, D.D.—Of Rev. T. H. Newton—Incidents—Characteristics—Of Martin L. Stoever, LL.D.—Of David Elliott, D.D.—Of Rev. R. M. Wallace—Of Mr. Fishburn—Action of General Assembly—Of Board of Publication—Testimony of his Brother.

IN response to a request, inserted in two or three of our religious newspapers, that any of the friends, acquaintances, or pupils of Dr. George Junkin, who had letters or other documents that might be useful in the preparation of his biography, would transmit them for such use, and that any who could furnish incidents illustrative of his life and character would favor the writer with them, many replies were made, and a large amount of valuable material furnished. Some of this has been interwoven in the narrative contained in preceding chapters. It is proposed in this to insert a few of the many testimonials which have been voluntarily sent; and it is only regretted that the limits of the volume forbid the use of them all.

One of his pupils, the Rev. Dr. Charles Elliott, Professor of Biblical Literature in the Seminary of the North-West, wrote as follows:

"PRESBYTERIAN THEOLOGICAL SEMINARY OF THE NORTH-WEST,
"CHICAGO, ILL., January 3d, 1870.

"REV. D. X. JUNKIN, D.D.

"REV. AND DEAR SIR,—You kindly asked me to communicate to you some reminiscences of your departed brother. Were I to relate all that I remember of him, it would greatly exceed the brief limits which a sense of propriety dictates to me to observe, and probably reiterate what you have already received from others more capable than myself of estimating his exalted character.

"Your brother, Rev. Geo. Junkin, D.D., LL.D., was a remarkable man. There was nothing negative in his character; everything was decidedly positive. He was endowed with a vigorous, discriminating mind, which rendered his conceptions of truth clear; and possessed of a strong and intense moral nature, which gave him great depth of conviction and energy of will.

"He was a man of great sincerity and transparency of character. It was not necessary to study him; the whole man shone out. Everything about him was eminently self-revealing. He was neither a simulator nor a dissimulator; but sincerity embodied. He had one aim,—the glory of God,—and his whole life was moulded by that aim. Utterly unselfish, he was always ready to sacrifice himself and all that he had for the cause of Christ and the good of mankind.

"As an educator of youth, he possessed many excellent qualifications. Among these the foremost was his positive and upright character. Next was his fresh and original method of communicating knowledge. He would frequently strike rich veins of thought, which would require much labor and time to explore and work out.

"As a preacher, in some respects, he had few equals. He was exegetical, argumentative, and hortatory in the same discourse. He had great power over both the reason and the feelings. I have seen whole audiences enchained by the power of his logic, and moved to tears by his tender appeals. In argument he struck with the hammer of Thor; and in his appeals he glowed and spoke with the love of a seraph.

"To him, under God, I am chiefly indebted for what I am. His memory is fragrant to me: I will cherish it until my latest breath. Had I the privilege of placing an inscription on his tomb, it should read:

To

My Dear Friend,

who, during many days of toil and darkness, held the lamp of human love so high that its radiance shed a glory on those days, and made them the noontime of my life.

"Yours very fraternally,

"CHARLES ELLIOTT."

The Rev. Thomas H. Newton, also a graduate of Lafayette College, some time Seamen's Chaplain in the Island of St. Thomas, and, whilst there, an interesting correspondent of *The Presbyterian*, subsequently a faithful but afflicted missionary in the West, sent a long communication, the whole of which, but for our limited space, we would insert. We give some extracts:

"CARLINVILLE, ILL., Dec. 9th, 1868.

"To REV. D. X. JUNKIN, D.D.

"DEAR FRIEND,—My soul looks out of, and works through, a body so enfeebled by protracted illness that it is out of my power to write all I would like to say concerning your late distinguished brother. But if a few notes can be of any service to you, ... I shall be exceeding glad, for he was held in highest estimation. I entered Lafayette College during the Presidency of Dr. Yeomans, and only became acquainted with your brother after his return from Oxford. I was soon attracted to him,—I could scarce tell why; but subsequent years, with their experiences, taught me that my *extempore* impressions were well founded."

After alluding to some irregularities of the students formerly witnessed, Mr. Newton proceeds:

"But such things were never attempted under Dr. Junkin's administration. He was never nicknamed, and never intentionally disobeyed, so far as I know, and had wonderful influence in restraining evil. To illustrate this point, take a well-remembered incident. A charcoal-dealer from New Jersey had, on one occasion, discharged, for the use of the College, a load of coal, and, being belated, left his wain or wagon in a part of the College campus until morning. After he had gone to his lodgings, some of the students—fledgeling lawyers, and embryo divines or doctors—proceeded to disintegrate the wain, and take it piecemeal to the third story of the College edifice, and there reconstruct it in the large hall. At early dawn, next day, they were chuckling over the astonishment of the teamster, when, coming with his horses, he found that his wagon had been spirited away without making any *tracks* by which it might be traced. But their triumph was short. The tidings of the practical joke had reached the President's ears. He made no demonstration until we met him in prayer-hall. He rose to lead the worship; but with a countenance awful as the storm-cloud. He surveyed the congregation a few moments in silence; his breath and eye made the culprits cower, and subdued all into solemnity. After this searching pause, he said, 'I understand some of you have been acting like *fools*. You have put a poor man to a great deal of trouble, and caused him to lose much time that was precious to him. You have disgraced yourselves and the College; and I shall expect you, immediately after prayers, to undo what you have done, so far as you can; and never to repeat such an act, or you will escape with far different consequences to yourselves.' It was amusing to see how the parties to the mischief rushed to the aid of the injured coal-man, whose wain was soon again dismembered, borne to *terra firma*, and reconstructed, so that he went on his way rejoicing. . . .

"One of the characteristics of Dr. Junkin which always impressed me was the simple and firm nature of his belief. I had been a professor of religion for some years, and had seen men of eminent piety, but there was something about Dr. Junkin that evidently 'exceeded.' His belief was not something stretching simply beyond, a projection into the penumbra of the future, and not adapted to contact with mortal and temporal affairs. His religion was a system more than a philosophy, but containing a philosophy, and reaching to God as well as embracing man. His acts were regulated by a delicate and lofty conscientiousness, and founded on great principles. He acted as if he felt that all belonged to God. He would descend to no act for the sake of having offered to him the incense of adulation. He sought nothing as a favor which he felt entitled to as a right, nor would he purchase any elevation at the price of promised recompense in kind. And it is proper to add that he urged the same upon his students. . . . He walked in a constant light, which beamed all around him as a halo from heaven, as it really was.

"I may be permitted to say, that I am indebted to no person, living or dead, so much as to Dr. Junkin, for a confirmation of my faith and the elements of right character. He referred everything to divine laws and fixed principles, beginning with our being, never leaving us, inseparable from us. He was in moral philosophy profound and exact, simple and comprehensive, ever identifying it with Christianity itself. In this department I never met his equal. Nor is it disrespectful to the teachers under whom I subsequently sat, to say that they added nothing to my attainments—his instructions were exhaustive. I have always thought that the church lost much by not placing him in one of our theological seats, some of which have been occupied by far inferior men. . . .

"Upon his students he ever enjoined usefulness instead of self-seeking. An incident in my own history will illustrate this. When about to leave the Seminary, I was trying to decide the question of accepting an invitation to labor in a destitute field in the 'Pines' of N. J. I asked the counsel of a professor, who advised me to 'go a year and prepare for a better place.' Doubting the propriety of making that humble field a stepping-stone, I wrote for advice to my old master, then at Lexington, Va. I received a prompt reply, which I regret was lost when I fled from the Rebels of Missouri. I remember these words, characteristic of their author, which have proved the key-note of my life: 'You had better be the Oberlin of the Pines than the —— of ——.'*

"My means were limited, and when I came to graduate I had so many liabilities that I was constrained to forego taking a diploma until my arrearages could be paid. I dreaded the *dénouement* which I knew was inevitable on an approaching day. I kept silence, and nursed my sorrow, but in cheerfulness. However, when that day came, I took advantage of an accidental meeting with the President, just at the head of the long stairs which climb the Bushkill Bluff on which the College stands. 'Can I detain you a moment, Doctor?' 'Yes, sir.' 'Then I beg to say that the state of my funds is such that, for the present, I cannot take my diploma: I must ask the Trustees to bear with me till I can liquidate my indebtedness.' 'Your bills are all paid, sir; you can go on and graduate.' 'Paid, sir! To whom, then,

* We omit the names of the eminent pastor and church, for obvious reasons.

must I feel obliged for this opportune kindness, that I may thank him?' 'Thank your Saviour, sir,' said he, and started on with his peculiar abruptness. And I *did* thank my Saviour with tearful eyes, and have thanked Him ever since; more for such an instructor, however, than for relief from my embarrassments. I never knew how he had found out my difficulties: I had no claim upon him; it was his spontaneous kindness."

Mr. Newton then recites some incidents illustrative of Dr. Junkin's penetration, parliamentary tact in the General Assembly, and his power in rebuking ambition in his brethren; but we have not space for them. Mr. Newton further says:

"He never forgot his students. They were his adopted children. He followed each one to the ends of the earth, if he went there, noticing everything they did, if open to observation. 'I was much interested in your letters from the West Indies,' said he to me, on my return thence. 'I am glad you are back;' and away he posted to join in the deliberations of the General Assembly. It was his brusque fashion, born of his intense thoughtfulness and devotion to the business in hand. It was his *style*,—as unavoidable in his manners as in his writings and his discourses. He arises to his theme like the king of day, throwing light on it at once, and burning on and upward with an irresistible power, and to a splendid zenith. And he recedes from the noon of his argument to its close, scattering light along his path till it needs no more, and drops it easily into the bosom of grateful shades, leaving it where it is natural to rest. He never is diverted from his main point in quest of ornaments, but his inspiration draws them to him, just as orderly as the genius of night belts the sky with constellations.

"Everything finds its place in his well-ordered mind. He was unconsciously poet and syllogist. If his premises glowed with the blooms of his rhetoric, his argument was so prominently held up that no wreaths and posies could hide it. He taught logic,—was able to teach it,—it was inseparable from the constitution of his mind. Every proposition inevitably resolved itself, in his mind, into major, minor, and conclusion. Hence it was hard to deceive him, as he with magic adroitness laid all sophistry bare. . . . In logical power he was, in my judgment, the peer of Calvin, though (and it is no disparagement) inferior to him in classic grace. In depth of emotion he was scarce inferior to Luther. He was not behind Knox in intrepidity. In zeal for truth and devotion to God, he came behind none of these; whilst his heart, full of the fellowship of Jesus, ever yearned for the good of society and overflowed with love to man. His modesty sometimes bade him stop where a Knox or a Luther would have called for an advance.

"His love to God and to man was an overflowing spring, welling over in his instructions to his pupils and flowing into his writings. Even his kingly *logic* could never break fellowship with sentiment. . . . But the strong man has run his race; yet his strength will never die, for his *spirit* has passed into institutions that can never perish.

"Deeply to my regret, all my letters from Dr. Junkin were lost during the rebellion, and I have but one, his last. It is characteristic of much that I have ascribed to him in what I have said. It shows the grand elevation of his piety, his patience under terrible trials, his magnanimity; and in the simple account he gives of his present employments, we see how he 'endured hardness as a good soldier.'

"Though then seventy-four years old, he for the first time in his life had been to the sea-shore, in quest of health! What a contrast with the kid-gloved and perfumed little effeminates, redolent with musk or balm of a thousand flowers, that sometimes fill our pulpits as *divines*, and who are yearly *habitués* of Saratoga and Newport, or the heroes of the more 'ambitious trip to Europe'! And his rest, so needful and so grateful, was induced only by his toil in the self-denying duties of preacher among the prisoners of war. And he modestly proposes to add to these labors the function of a colporteur. 'I may have to distribute the tracts and books myself,' he quietly suggests.

"'Digging can't degrade me. I am Gurowski,' said that famous count. A noble sentiment, beautifully illustrated in these humble labors of your brother.

"Once more: this letter reveals a characteristic of Dr.

Junkin peculiarly lovely and honorable, his love of domestic life. I had observed it long ago, and remember that in all his moral teachings he set forth the FAMILY as of prime importance. And his teachings were embodied in the realities of his own home. To him the family was a joy forever. He looked on it as the source of all good human influences. Hence in the family he forgot his severer duties, his heart was unlocked, his soul flowed out in innocent simplicity, its graver greatness melted and mingled with the gentler impulses of domestic affection. Here he filled his duty, as in the professor's chair, the pulpit, or the arena of debate. He was president, professor, preacher, moderator, disputant, friend, brother, father, with equal facility and completeness. He felt that God had called him alike to each office, and he discharged the duty with holy fidelity.

"We open this letter, then, and find without surprise the naïve description it contains of his happiness in his present domestic relations. He was happy with his grandchildren as he had been with his own, suffused with delight in the family of his son, whose no small praise may be that he seeks to conform to his father's model. 'How happy I am,' exclaims he, in this letter, 'and how grateful I ought to be!' Adding, with illustrious modesty, 'Excuse the egotism of an old man.' And happy are we for thee, thou aged and wayworn servant of God! Glad that thy sun is setting amid things so long beautiful to thy own conceptions, and that thy heart sings thereat,—glad that it shall rise again, and beam upon thee, amid thy sainted dear ones, and in the presence of thy God, in one perpetual noontide of delight!"

From the letter of M. L. Stoever, LL.D., Professor in Pennsylvania College (Lutheran), an extract has already been inserted upon a previous page. The following is the first part of the same:

"GEORGE JUNKIN, ESQ.

"I am gratified to learn that a memoir of your worthy father is to be prepared. Such a volume will be interesting to his numerous friends, and a valuable history of the times in which he lived. He was identified with so many interests, and exercised so decided an influence in every sphere in which he moved, that his biography will necessarily be rich in incidents, and full of instruction.

"Dr. Junkin was, in many respects, a most remarkable man, and wherever he labored he left the indelible impress of his character. When a boy of eight or ten years old I met him first. He was at that time principal of the 'Manual Labor Academy,' in my native place, and frequently visited my mother's home. His appearance, his manner, his characteristic speeches, his earnestness, and kindness of heart, are just as fresh and vivid before me as the scenes of yesterday. I followed him with affectionate interest to Easton, and thence to other points of influence and usefulness which he occupied, but never had any correspondence with him, and supposed that I had been entirely forgotten. My surprise was, therefore, very great, more than twenty years after our separation in Germantown, on casually meeting him on Arch Street, to receive from him the cordial recognition, the warm grasp of the hand, the friendly salutation by my Christian name. To hear him recount occurrences of the past, and to recall familiar faces, seemed a most wonderful exercise of memory. I did not see him again till we met at Gettysburg after the memorable battle."

From the pastor of the First Presbyterian Church, Altoona, the following was received:

"ALTOONA, PA., May 31st, 1870.

"REV. D. X. JUNKIN, D.D.

"MY DEAR SIR,—Understanding that you are preparing for the press a biography of your deceased brother, the late Dr. George Junkin, and believing that anything relative to that venerated and excellent man must possess more or less interest to those who know him best, I send you the following, which you are at liberty to use in any manner you think proper:

"In the year 1848, Dr. Junkin was called from the presidency of Lafayette College, Easton, Pa., to that of Washington College, Lexington, Va. This was regarded as a sad blow to the former college, as Dr. J. was not only its founder but its greatest benefactor. Indeed, so essential did his official connection seem to the prosperity of the college, that many began to suppose, when that connection was once severed, the institution would go down, and that, consequently, there was very little encouragement for students to remain there. Accordingly, influenced partly by this feeling, but *mainly*, I think, by a devoted attachment to the retiring President, many of the more advanced students determined to follow him to Virginia, in order that they might still enjoy the privilege of sitting, as learners, at his feet, and of graduating under him.

"The names of my classmates who went with me, if I remember rightly, are as follows, viz.:—Samuel Campbell, E. D. Finney, John M. Godown, G. K. Marriner, S. K. Raymond, Robert Watts, John Armstrong, A. M. Lowry, G. A. Mitchell, A. W. Sproull, W. Redfield Sharpe.

"Indeed, I think I may say, without the least color of exaggeration, that I never knew a man who possessed the faculty of attaching students to himself more strongly than Dr. Junkin. And this was owing to the fact that he was not only the student's friend, but, also, to the possession of consummate ability, and entire disinterestedness in his aims and purposes, qualities which never fail to excite confidence, as well as to awaken admiration, on the part of others. Taking him all in all, Dr. Junkin was certainly a very remarkable man, and few have ever lived to better purpose than he. To many of us, who knew him only to love him, his memory is precious; and we cherish the fond hope of seeing his venerable form again in heaven, and of uniting with him in celebrating the rich grace of that adorable Saviour whom he loved so well.

"Very truly and respectfully yours,

"R. M. Wallace."

The venerable Dr. David Elliott, of Alleghany, in a letter already quoted in part, says:

"Of the time of my first acquaintance with Dr. Junkin my recollection is not exact. We were members together of the General Assemblies of 1830, 1835, 1837, and 1844. Of this last he was Moderator, and discharged the duties with promptness and ability. In the discussions of 1835 and 1837, on the great questions then at issue, he took an active part, although not as often on the floor as some others. He was a man of quick and strong perceptions, whose mind took a vigorous grasp of any subject presented to it, especially if it was one which was debatable. His convictions in relation to the various questions brought into controversy during his public life, were very decided, and he never left any one in doubt as to what his opinions were. Hence, when called upon to defend his opinions, or to oppose views which he deemed erroneous, he did it 'with his might.' And, however others might differ with him, they could not fail to recognize and approve the depth and sincerity of his convictions. Being endowed with a vigorous mind and warm affections, when he entered the field of controversy, the ardor which he evinced made the impression, upon those who did not know him, that he was under the influence of excited temper. The peculiarity of his voice doubtless tended to make this impression, it being of a sharp and penetrating character. He himself was aware of this. I once heard him, in the midst of an earnest speech in the General Assembly, when his voice had reached its highest tone, stop and admonish his hearers not to attribute the fault of his voice to his temper, assuring them that he was in perfect good humor, but only earnest in his advocacy of truth in opposition to that which he believed to be error. . . .

"Persons who have read Dr. Junkin's publications, need not be told that he was a man of vigorous and brilliant intellect. This his opponents can testify. If there was a weak point in their argument, or a defect in their logic, he was quick to detect and powerful to expose it. . . . But his work for Christ on earth is done, and he has gone to occupy 'a place' in one of those mansions which his Saviour has prepared for him."

One of his pupils, a graduate of Washington College, and a gentleman of high standing in Virginia, in a letter of condolence to a member of Dr. Junkin's family, says:

"It will prove an abiding consolation to you to know, that the long life which has just ended, has been marked with everything that can assure a believer of the religion which he professed, that he will reign glorious among the master-spirits of heaven, with a crown brighter than most of them, radiant with stars that indicate the souls saved by his instrumentality. A man of his decided character could not lead the life and do the work he did, without running counter to the prejudices and passions of many of his fellows; but no such man has ever deserved or obtained a fuller share of the respect of all honest men, for the boldness and candor which always marked his conduct, while those who knew him best loved him for all the qualities in man that are worthy to be loved.

"There is no one man whose influence on my mind and habits of thought has been so much felt, and to whom I owe so much. I never heard a public address by a student under his tuition, the most striking parts of which were not traceable to the impression of the ideas and modes of utterance of Dr. Junkin. But I need not be writing to you how highly I estimated his powers of mind, and how greatly I admired the goodness and tenderness of his heart."

A number of public bodies adopted resolutions expressive of their estimation of Dr. Junkin, and of sympathy with his surviving family. The General Assembly met in Albany the next day after his death, and the following paper indicates their action:

"GENERAL ASSEMBLY OF THE PRESBYTERIAN CHURCH IN THE UNITED STATES OF AMERICA, met at ALBANY, NEW YORK, May 27th, 1868.

"To George Junkin, Esq., of Philadelphia, Pa., representing the family of the late Rev. George Junkin, D.D., LL.D., the following minute is respectfully communicated, adopted unanimously by this body in a standing vote:

"'This General Assembly, having heard, since our sessions began, that the Rev. Dr. George Junkin has departed from this life, record with sadness our sense of loss in his death, and our memory of the long and signal service he has rendered the church as a teacher, an author, a defender of the faith, and an exemplary patriot, in times of trial and perplexity, when the foundations of order in the state and in the church were overturned.

"'The Stated Clerk is hereby directed to communicate this minute to the family of the deceased.'

"ALEXANDER T. MCGILL, *Stated Clerk.*"

The following minute was adopted by the Presbyterian Board of Publication at its annual meeting, on Tuesday, June 23d, 1868:

"*Whereas*, The Rev. George Junkin, D.D., for many years a member of this Board, departed this life on the 24th ult., at the venerable age of nearly seventy-eight years;

"*Resolved*, That the Board hereby records its sorrow at the sudden departure of this learned, able, and eminent servant of God, who, by his long and faithful services in the pulpit and in various literary institutions; by his able and intrepid defence of the truth whenever he saw it exposed to peril; his valuable contributions to our theological literature; the purity and piety of his life; and his frank, sincere, and genial character, had endeared himself greatly to the Presbyterian Church he loved so well, and to those who were associated with him as members of this Board, the interests of which lay near his heart.

"*Resolved*, That the Corresponding Secretary communicate a copy of this minute to the family of Dr. Junkin, and to *The Presbyterian.*

"A true copy.

"WILLIAM E. SCHENCK, *Corresponding Secretary.*"

The Trustees of Lafayette College adopted the paper which follows:

"The Trustees of Lafayette College have heard with deep sorrow of the death of the Rev. George Junkin, D.D., LL.D., and order the following minute to be entered upon their records, expressive of their sense of the great loss which the Institution has suffered by his removal from earth to heaven.

"Dr. Junkin became President of our College upon its organization, in 1832, and continued to administer its affairs, and to give instruction in Mental and Moral Philosophy, till 1841, when he assumed the Presidency of Miami University at Oxford, Ohio. In 1844 he was recalled to the Presidency and Professorship, and remained at Easton until 1848, when he removed to Virginia to become President of Washington College, at Lexington, in that State. In 1864 the Trustees appointed him Emeritus Professor of Political Philosophy, in which position he died, full of years and honors, in May, 1868.

"To this eminent man of God belongs the praise of having been the father and founder of our College. Its existence, continuance, and usefulness, under God, are due to the devoted piety, great learning, rare aptness to teach, indomitable perseverance, unsparing self-denials and sacrifices, unfaltering faith, and labors beyond measure, which characterized his administration of its affairs; and its present enlarged prosperity, we receive as the answer to his unceasing prayers for the College he loved as his life. With profound gratitude and ardent love we cherish his memory as the earliest and most efficient benefactor of our College, who almost literally gave himself for it; holding back nothing of his great talents, or acquisitions, or property, or toil, or power with God, that it might be a blessing to the church and the world. His earthly reward was to send forth from its halls, men whose distinction in various walks of life—but especially in the ministry of the gospel—has shown the thoroughness of their training, and given to Lafayette College a name among the literary institutions of the land, in which we have a just pride, and which we cannot be too careful to maintain. We bless God for him, for what he was, for what he did; and we give thanks that, in the Divine Goodness, he was permitted to live to see the College, which is built upon him, Jesus Christ Himself being the chief corner-stone, rising to the goodly proportions which now greet our eyes. 'Having served his generation, by the will of God he fell on sleep.'"

We refrain from further quotations, gratifying as it would be to put them on record, as spontaneous tributes to the character and the life-work of their venerated subject.

There was a characteristic of the man whose life is commemorated upon these pages, which ought to be mentioned with emphasis. The statement of it may worthily close this narrative. He was a man of THE MOST PERFECT PURITY of mind and habit: pure in heart, life, and language. The writer can testify, after an intimacy of fifty years, that Dr. Junkin was the purest man he ever knew. Never, in the course of all his life, and in the most familiar and free intercourse which brothers could hold, did the lips, the looks, or the conduct of George Junkin betray the remotest approach to the domain of moral impurity. No word of doubtful modesty, no *double-entendre,* no trifling sallies of wit or jest, ever gave proof of the presence in his mind of any thought inconsistent with the most unsullied modesty. In this he was the most remarkable man known to the writer of this book,—in this the most like JESUS.

BLESSED ARE THE PURE IN HEART, FOR THEY SHALL SEE GOD.

END OF THE MEMOIR.

APPENDIX.

AS explanatory of the position occupied by Dr. Junkin upon the question of reunion, we append the following paper found in his handwriting, which he presented in his Presbytery, and advocated, as the writer is informed, with an eloquence and a power of argument worthy of his best days. But the union spirit prevailed:

"*Whereas*, The General Assembly of 1867 commended to the careful consideration of the churches and Presbyteries the Report on Reunion of the Old and New School branches (Min., p. 362):

"*Therefore*, As a partial expression of our opinions, be it

"*Resolved*—I. That the Terms of said Report, so far as known to us, are not satisfactory:

"1. In that the right and duty of a Presbytery to examine each and every intrant from another Presbytery or body is surrendered: which right we consider inherent and indispensable to the preservation of the church's purity.

"2. In that, by the eighth term, any book is to be rejected from our Catalogue against which three members, on either side of the Committee, object. Thus, our Digest, Hodge on Ephesians, Hodge on Atonement, in short, any book, may be stricken off by any three, on either side, of this Committee.

"3. In that other property, stereotype plates, vested funds, of Seminaries, of the Boards, etc., are exposed to imminent peril.

"4. And principally, in that the doctrinal basis, as we understand, reported by the Joint Committee, is too vague and indefinite. The Standards are to be received honestly and sincerely, but with such explanations and interpretations as each subscriber may choose to put upon them; that is, each man's own notion is our basis of union.

"5. In that Congregational churches are to continue in full standing, with right of representation in Presbytery and Synod, thus controlling, it may readily be, our highest court, by electing Commissioners thereto.

"*Resolved*—II. That, in our opinion, the cultivation of friendly Christian intercourse and ministerial interchanges between the two bodies—that is, the 'keeping of the unity of the spirit in the bond of peace'—is greatly more important and conducive to the practical efficiency of both than any mere external, visible, organic union.

"*Ordered*, That the Stated Clerk be directed to deliver an attested copy of this paper to the Moderator of the next General Assembly."

Extract from Minutes of the Pittsburg Convention, page 17.

"It may be proper simply to present an outline of the system:

"Thus—1. The doctrine of Adam's federal headship, or representative character, is denied.

"2. The doctrine of original sin is denied.

"3. The doctrine of the imputation of Adam's sin to his posterity is denied. The rejection of these necessarily leads to—

"4. A denial of Christ's federal headship, or representative character.

"5. A denial of the imputation of his righteousness to the believer, as the essential procuring cause of his justification.

"6. A rejection of the true, proper, vicarious nature of the atonement of Christ." . . .

Page 18. "But these errors do not terminate in simple negation. Another system is substituted in room of the gospel thus rejected. It is the system of human perfectibility:

"Thus—1. The doctrine of human ability is held, involving the principle, and gratuitously assuming it as true, that man's moral obligations are measured and bounded by his present ability to meet all the requirements of God's law.

"2. Accordingly, the necessity of the agency, the omnipotent agency of the Spirit of God in the conversion of the soul, is denied, and conversion is affirmed to be the work of the creature. Man regenerates his own soul. The Spirit's agency is that of mere moral suasion. Regeneration is simply an act of the mind, the first in the series of holy acts. Faith is an act of the mind, and nothing but an act of the mind."

This memorial was signed by seventy-two ministers and thirty-six elders; among the former, we notice Charles C. Beatty and George Marshall. It was referred to a Committee, of which Dr. Elliott was Chairman.

BRIEF MEMOIRS.

It was the original intention of the author, to insert, in an Appendix to the Life of Dr. Junkin, brief sketches of the lives of several of his contemporaries who were either life-long friends, or who were associated with him in some of his more important efforts for the good of Zion and the world. For this purpose the writer collected material for such notices of Drs. McElroy, Phillips, Knox, McKinney, Elliott, and others. But the biography itself has swelled to such dimensions as to render the execution of his plan impracticable; and he can only find space for a tribute to the memory of two of those of whom he proposed to write. To this necessity he more cheerfully yields because, in the "memorial volume," he has been anticipated in regard to some of these distinguished brethren, and because some of them still survive.

The beloved brethren whose lives are briefly sketched in the following pages are selected as subjects of memoir—1. Because no other writer has paid a permanent tribute to their memory; 2. Because their names are fragrant with godly graces and holy works; and 3. Because, when the writer was a student and in his early ministry, these men of God took him by the hand and "showed him no little kindness;" and he seeks expression for gratitude, a sentiment that, in his heart, never dies.

THE REV. WILLIAM LATTA McCALLA

Was born on the 25th of November, 1788, in Jessamine County, Kentucky. His father was Dr. Andrew McCalla, of Bucks County, Pennsylvania, who, with his father, Captain Wm. McCalla, participated in the War of Independence. Dr. McCalla was a surgeon in the service. At the close of the war Dr. McCalla removed to Kentucky, and settled at Lexington, then the principal town in the State. The paternal relatives of the subject of this memoir were all Presbyterians, among whom were the Rev. Wm. Latta of the Revolutionary era, and his five sons, all of them eminent ministers of the gospel. The maternal ancestry were of the excellent but exiled Huguenots; a descent of which Mr. McCalla was justly proud—in the religious sense.

In 1813 Mr. McCalla was married to Miss Martha A., daughter of General Samuel Finley, of Chillicothe, who still lives. In 1811 he began the study of theology, under the direction of the Presbytery of West Lexington; and he was licensed to preach by the Presbytery of Chillicothe, into whose bounds he had removed after his marriage.

He spent the early years of his ministry in Ohio and Kentucky; but the details of his labors, and the several fields which he occupied, the writer has not been able to ascertain. It is well known that from the first he was a man of mark as regards vigor of mind, dignity of presence, impressiveness of style, and the eloquence of solemn, earnest simplicity. At the close of the War of 1812–1815 General Jackson was made commandant of the Southern Department of the United States army, and soon thereafter Mr. McCalla was appointed chaplain under him; and he proved himself a faithful, eloquent, and effective preacher in this field of labor.

He was settled as pastor of the church of Augusta, Kentucky, in 1819, where he labored for some years.

Whilst Mr. McCalla was one of the simplest, most lucid, earnest, discriminating, powerful, and affectionate preachers of the gospel, in its didactic and hortatory forms, to whom the writer has ever listened, he excelled in the polemic defence of its precious truths. He was a great controversialist. That great orator, Henry Clay, of Kentucky, pronounced him the best debater of his times. The rife and rabid heresies that early sprang up in the West, called for a man of Mr. McCalla's power to stand in the breach and defend the truth, and he was ever ready to do it.

Shortly after his settlement in Augusta, having expounded the account of our Lord's baptism in Matt. iii., he was replied to by a Mr. Vaughn, of the Baptist Church; and this led to some discussion, in which public opinion did not accord the victory to Mr. V. Worsted in this encounter, the Baptists made arrangements to have the celebrated champion of immersion, Alexander Campbell, brought on to debate with Mr. McCalla. After some six months' correspondence, the debate was held, and lasted for seven days. Mr. Campbell and his friends, as usual, claimed the victory, but the great mass of hearers accorded it to Mr. McCalla.

In the year 1824 Mr. McCalla was a Commissioner to the General Assembly, which met in Philadelphia, and whilst there made a decided impression, both upon the Assembly and the community, by his fine appearance, his terse and vigorous elocution, his attractiveness as a preacher, and his power as a debater.

He still wore the costume of the chaplains of the army; and his tall and perfectly erect form, his fine proportions, his well-formed head, dark-gray eye, jet-black hair combed back from his brow, and his grave and handsome features made a strong impression upon every beholder.

After the rising of the Assembly he engaged in a debate with the notorious Abner Kneeland, who had been holding his infidel meetings, and challenging everybody to dispute with him, in Philadelphia. So crushing was the defeat of this unbeliever by Mr. McCalla, that Kneeland was forced by public sentiment to leave the city.

This and his fine pulpit powers drew general attention to Mr. McCalla, and the Eighth Presbyterian Church (the Scots Church), in Spruce Street near Third, which happened then to be vacant, extended a call to him, and he shortly afterwards commenced pastoral labors in that congregation. This church was originally in connection with the Associate Reformed body, and was the one in which Mrs. Junkin had been brought up, and in which her father was a leading ruling elder. It had been served by such men as Dr. James Gray and Dr. Robert McCartee, but was much run down at the time Mr. McCalla assumed charge. Under his ministry it soon revived, and became a strong congregation. His pastorate there was very successful. The writer of this sketch, when a licentiate, sometimes preached for him, and the house was crowded both below and in the galleries. Mr. Henry McKeen informs us, that soon after Mr. McCalla's advent he united with the church along with forty-seven others; and large accessions were frequent during his ministry. He had round him in the eldership such men as Joseph P. Engles, Alexander Symington, and Henry McKeen.

Mr. McCalla soon took a prominent part in the general affairs of the church in Philadelphia. When Mr. Barnes was called to the First Church, in 1829, Mr. McCalla was one of those who, with the venerable Dr. Green, opposed his reception and induction, on the ground of doctrinal errors contained in the sermon called "The Way of Salvation." And throughout the entire controversy beginning with that event, Mr. McCalla was a prominent and efficient actor. The part he bore in that protracted struggle, which ended with the disruption of 1838, has been mentioned in the body of this work, and need not be repeated. In the Presbytery, the Synod, and the General Assembly, he was a man of great power in debate. In 1830 he published "A CORRECT NARRATIVE" of these proceedings, in a pamphlet of forty pages, in reply to an erroneous statement previously published.

As a debater he was calm, wary, far-seeing, logical, and especially illustrative. His power in pointing an argument with an illustrative anecdote, and in making it sting with sarcasm, was wonderful; but he never used the latter except in retort. Rarely was he the aggressor in this sort of weapon; but woe to the adversary that threw stones at him; he hurled them back with tenfold momentum. There was a calmness in his manner, a smoothness in his tones, and an imperturbability of temper which made him all the more formidable as an antagonist. When his adversary would be boiling, McCalla would be cool as an evening zephyr. It was this characteristic that drew from the venerable Dr. Miller, on one occasion, after listening to a speech from Mr. McCalla in the General Assembly, the remark, "Mr. McCalla's speech was as *smooth as oil*, but verily, Mr. Moderator, it was the *oil of vitriol.*" But this characteristic was observable only when some unfairness or lack of Christian magnanimity was shown by his opponents. It cannot be denied that this occasional severity in debate roused a feeling of personal opposition to him with some of his brethren of the New School, whilst it was also regretted by some of those who acted with him. Keenly sensitive to censure, when he thought it undeserved, and that it had been incurred when he was in the discharge of his duty, he was sometimes chafed by it. And it cannot be denied that, on some occasions, his brethren who acted with him, and who rejoiced in the power with which he defended their cause, failed to sustain him as they might have justly done against the charges of undue zeal and severity brought by his antagonists.

In 1831 Mr. McCalla, by invitation of some ministers of New Jersey, consented to meet a Rev. Wm. Lane, an Arian Baptist, in a debate upon the subject of the Deity of Christ. The debate was held in Milford, New Jersey, and the Arian proved a pigmy in the hands of a giant.

After serving the Scots Church with great acceptance for ten years, he was induced by some of his brethren to go out as a lecturer against Romanism. In the years 1833–4 the lovely and gifted Dr. John Breckenridge had engaged in a controversy with the Rev. John Hughes, a Catholic priest, then of Philadelphia, afterwards Archbishop of New York. The controversy was long continued in the newspapers, and subsequently renewed in an oral form in a debating-society of the young men of Philadelphia. Some of the Catholic young men had brought in Mr. Hughes, and some of the Protestants invited Mr. Breckenridge. The latter being constrained to go to the West on public duty before the debate closed, Mr. McCalla was asked to take his place. This he did ; and so effectually did he overwhelm the arguments of the adroit priest, that many who were zealous for the arrest of papal encroachments joined in urging Mr. McCalla to go forth as a champion of the Protestant cause. A fund was raised; he accepted the mission, and labored effectively for a time in the United States and Canada; but the zeal of those who sent him forth did not last, or at least was not effective in supplying necessary pecuniary aid, and he had to leave this field.

He took the pastoral charge of the Fourth Presbyterian

Church, Philadelphia, where he labored for some time with great acceptance and usefulness. A large portion of the Scots Church congregation, as a surviving officer of it informs the writer, left it and went to the Fourth Church, from their attachment to Mr. McCalla's person and ministry. The dates of his installation and of his resignation we could not ascertain.

Some time about 1842 he inaugurated a service for the French people, who, in considerable numbers, were scattered about Philadelphia as sheep without a shepherd. He gathered a congregation of them, preached to them in their own language, and even collected and published for their use a small collection of psalms and hymns in French. But he found too much indifference among the churches to sustain the enterprise.

In 1840–41 he performed an extensive tour of observation and missionary labor in Texas, and, after his return, published a book descriptive of his journey and his observations. The volume is fraught with stirring incident and pithy sentiment, and breathes throughout a spirit of piety.

He was for two terms, about this period of his life, minister of the church of Bedford, Pennsylvania, at which place his widow still resides. But whether his tour in Texas was performed before, after, or during his ministry at Bedford, the writer of this memoir has not been able to ascertain.

In 1850 he became the pastor of the Union Presbyterian Church, Philadelphia, where he continued to labor until May, 1854, when he resigned his pastoral charge, with a view of entering another field of labor at St. Louis, Missouri.

At the time of his retiring from the pastorate of this church, the congregation, in a minute assenting, at his urgent request, to the dissolution of the pastoral relation, expressed themselves as follows:

"*Resolved*, That we express our regret that circumstances have been such as to lead our beloved pastor to this view of his duty; therefore,

"*Resolved*, That our confidence in him is unabated, as a sound and able divine, and as a faithful and laborious minister of Jesus Christ. His labors among us have awakened feelings of most sincere affection and respect, and we cannot part with him without offering grateful testimony to his usefulness among us, and we do most earnestly pray that, wherever he may go, the great Head of the Church may accompany him."

In dissolving the pastoral relation at his request, the Presbytery of Philadelphia, with which he had now been connected for thirty years, adopted a minute declaring that they "notice with pleasure the feeling of mutual regard between the pastor and the people, and express their deep interest in Mr. McCalla as a minister of Christ, with whom they have been long acquainted, and who has, on several occasions, and with distinguished ability, done substantial and lasting service to the blessed cause to which he has consecrated his life. Presbytery do also express their sincere affection for Mr. McCalla, on account of his many private and social virtues, and do assure him of their best wishes and earnest prayers for his usefulness and success in the field of his future labors."

It was whilst pastor of this church that he held the celebrated debate with the infidel, Joseph Barker.

Of his labors and their results in St. Louis, we have not been able to obtain specific information. But, from what we know of his ability, his devout godliness, his eloquence and zeal, we cannot doubt that there, as in other fields, the Lord gave him many seals of his ministry. One incident, illustrative of the zeal and the unquailing courage of the man, has come to our knowledge.

The lawless and daring character of the boatmen and other habitués of the wharves of St. Louis, especially when idle and intoxicated, is proverbial. Mr. McCalla thought they formed a class of as unhappy outcasts as ancient or modern society could show, and one for whose souls no one seemed to care. The sight of them melted his heart, and he resolved to make an effort in their behalf, and on the next Sabbath to inaugurate his missionary enterprise. Some of his pious friends agreed to accompany him, while others strongly dissuaded him. Finally all drew back, but he persisted. Even the police of the district warned him that his life would be in danger, and that they would not be able to protect him. He told them he asked no such protection. Accordingly, he went to the wharves (or levee, as it is called), quite unarmed, and, mounting an empty box, in the presence of a few loiterers, began, in his clear, sonorous voice, to sing the appropriate hymn:

"I'm not ashamed to own my Lord,
Nor to defend His cause."

The first tones of his voice brought out, from the dens of the vicinity, many of the class of whom he had been warned, gathering in a disorderly manner around him. And now began an exhibition upon which angels doubtless looked with interest. This faithful servant of Christ preached the precious gospel in this very seat of Satan. The result justified his expectations. Some threatened, others applauded, but finally order reigned, and he poured tenderly and faithfully into their ears the long-delayed news of salvation. When he was about to retire, a sturdy and formidable "bully" came up to him, laid his hand on Mr. McCalla's arm, thanked him for coming, invited him to come again, and pledged protection.

His last years were spent in affectionate and self-denying labors among the slaves of the South, to whom, as well as to their educated and refined masters, he was an acceptable preacher. Here, as everywhere, he was faithful to his Master, to the truth, and to souls; and we cannot doubt that he is now surrounded, in the land of glory, by many, both of the lowly and the high-born, the poor and the polished, who, in the various fields of his labor, were won to Christ, and who now call him blessed.

Mr. McCalla died at the house of Mrs. Ogden, in Madison County, Louisiana, on the 12th of October, 1859, having nearly completed his seventy-first year. The disease which cut him down was congestive chills, peculiar to that climate. His family were absent in Missouri on a visit at the time of his death.

Mr. McCalla, though a man of wondrous work, was a constant and systematic student. He was extensively read in all useful knowledge, and had marvellous command of his knowledge for useful ends. He was master of Hebrew, Greek, Latin, and Syriac, and was able to use with ease French, Spanish, and German. He was mighty in the Scriptures, and in most departments of the lore necessary to their illustration. As a preacher of the gospel, he had few equals in his generation. He was, in the judgment of the writer, one of the most perfect verbal critics in *extempore* speech. The *right* word—the only word of the language that perfectly fitted the place—was always at command. His style was clear, simple, vigorous, flowing, his form tall, erect, commanding, his manner solemn, earnest, impressive, and often very tender and affectionate. He possessed an exhaustless fund of apposite anecdote, which always *told*. And his deep, reverential, and tender piety, which none who knew the man could help but feel, gave unction to his utterances. He was a great preacher.

As a debater he was unexcelled. We will not add to what has been written on this subject, except to say, that while remarkable in strength of argument, force of illustration, and power of exposing the weak points of an adversary, no man excelled him in the terrors of retort. In this he was never ill natured, but always to be dreaded. His wit was genuine, keen, and abundant, perhaps to a fault, and sometimes irresistible in the grotesqueness of its gravity. He rarely smiled, even when others were convulsed. To give a single specimen. When a distinguished preacher had delivered before the Synod a great sermon on *literalism* and the premillennial advent, and the question of publishing it by the Synod was under discussion, Mr. McCalla rose, and, with the imperturbable solemnity of manner which never left him, said, "Mr. Moderator, if we are to be held to the *literal interpretation* of Scripture, that woman to whom the preacher alluded, 'who sitteth upon seven mountains,' must have *vast sitting capacity*." It was all he said; but it ended the discussion in a storm of merriment.

Mr. McCalla was a *great* man. To quote the language of Dr. James Clark, uttered but an hour before this line was traced: "Ordinarily, and when not excited by any special impulse, he was *great;* but when *roused*, he was a *giant* in intellectual strength." And the conviction that God's precious truth was in danger was enough to rouse, at any time, all the Hercules within him. And yet this man of mighty power was gentle as a woman, and tender as Mercy's self in all the duties and the intercourse of private and pastoral life. Like most men of pronounced opinions and uncompromising integrity, he was often misunderstood and often misrepresented; and it is perhaps true that he was sometimes too unyielding where the principles involved were not essential; but even then he was conscientious. He did a great work for Christ and his church, and we are sure that his reward, through grace, is proportionately great.

REV. ROBERT STEEL, D.D.

THIS excellent and beloved minister of Christ was a native of Ireland. He was descended from that vigorous, godly, and liberty-loving race, the Scotch-Irish; a race that for more than two centuries has constituted a very important portion of the population of that island, and which has given to America a large number of her most valuable citizens. He was born of highly respectable and pious parents, near the city of Londonderry; a city memorable in the history of the struggle for Protestant supremacy and the liberties of the British empire. The year of his birth was 1794; but the day we have not been able to ascertain.

Mr. Steel pursued his English and, to some extent, his classical studies in his native land. His first classical teacher was a Mr. Culbertson, who was a graduate of the University of Glasgow, and a student of theology, who had opened a school not very distant from the residence of Mr. Steel's parents. It was the wish of his parents that he might be led to enter the ministry, and with this view they sent him to study under Mr. Culbertson.

The following record occurs in a journal kept at the time, and found among his papers, and indicates that his mind had already been turned toward the holy office:

"I distinctly remember that, before reaching Mr. Culbertson's residence, I was impressed with the importance of the step I was about to take; as I was aware that my parents hoped that I might be led to preach the gospel. I paused, and went behind a hawthorn hedge, and prayed to God to guide me, and enable me so to study and so to act that I might be counted worthy to be put into the ministry."

An elder brother, the late John Steel, Esq., had emigrated to America some years before this, and was in a prosperous mercantile business in Philadelphia. Mr. John Steel was a man of great moral excellence, probity, and generosity of character. He sent a pressing invitation to Robert to come to America and pursue his studies in this country. The invitation, with the consent of his parents, was accepted; and in 1811, in his seventeenth year, the younger brother came to Philadelphia, became a member of his brother's family, and continued under his care until his education was completed.

After arriving in America, Mr. Steel spent one year in "Gray and Wylie's Academy," then kept in Locust Street. In 1812 he entered the college at Princeton, and remained in that institution until he graduated, which was probably in 1815; for he entered the Seminary of Dr. Mason, in New York, to prosecute his theological studies, in 1816.

There he and Dr. Junkin became acquainted; and a friendship was formed which endured through life. Their correspondence was frequent and voluminous, as letters still on file attest. And, as has been mentioned in the body of this work, Mr. Steel had more agency than any other individual in bringing Dr. Junkin into the field of his chief life-work,—education.

Mr. Steel was licensed to preach the gospel in April, 1818, by the Presbytery of New York, and whilst still attending upon the instructions of Dr. Mason, was for some time employed by the Young Men's Missionary Society of that city. This engagement appears to have continued for a season after he left the Seminary. When it ceased, he came to Philadelphia, and labored for a time in a city mission.

He was then for a short time employed by a female Missionary Society to labor in Moyamensing, in which service he continued until called to Abington. In this ancient congregation, which in earlier times had enjoyed the labors of such men as the Treats and the Tennents, Mr. Steel was ordained and installed in November, 1819, by the Presbytery of Philadelphia.

This was his first and his only pastoral charge. There he labored faithfully and successfully for about forty-three years, until 1862, when his Master came, released him from his earthly cares and labors, and took him to a higher service above.

During all these years of constant toil in the vineyard, Mr. Steel was seldom or never interrupted by bodily sickness. He possessed a remarkably vigorous constitution, and could endure an amazing amount of labor.

A little below the medium height, robustly built, closely and firmly knit, of florid complexion and sanguine temperament, he was the very embodiment of vigorous activity. Possessed of a strong and well-balanced mind, great warmth and geniality of affection, and a cheerfulness of heart that seemed rarely interrupted, he was a most agreeable companion and loving pastor. His manner in the pulpit, the prayer-meeting, and the family visit was ardent, earnest, tender, often tearful. His mind was not marked by any extraordinary vigor, grasp, or originality, but he was a clear, sound, effective thinker; and as his great and life-long aim was to "know nothing among his people save Jesus Christ and him crucified," he was better than a great preacher—he was an earnest, instructive, effective, useful one. And the fact that he served an intelligent people for forty-three years, and that he interested them as much in his last years as in his first, is a eulogy that can be pronounced over few.

During part of his ministry he added to his pastoral toils the superintendence of a seminary for the instruction of youth. His first school was a classical and mercantile school for boys and young men. Afterward he superintended the Abington Female Seminary for some years; and in both he and his family, and the teachers under his control, contributed largely to the interests of higher education. By this instrumentality he was the means of bringing into the ministry some very valuable men. The Rev. Alfred Ryors, D.D., President of Indiana University, the Rev. George D. Stewart, and the Rev. Joseph Stevens, may be named among the number.

In the agitations that resulted in the disruption of the Presbyterian Church, Dr. Steel occupied a peculiar position. Thoroughly sound in doctrine, decidedly opposed to the New Theology, and never faltering when anything was to be done which he could do for the interests of orthodoxy, his kindly and genial disposition, and friendliness of manner, retained the affection of the New School brethren longer than did the Old School men who lived in the city. When the first troubles connected with Mr. Barnes arose, his distance from the city, and his gentleness of disposition, kept him in more pleasant relations with the New School brethren than were the city pastors. And when the second trial of Mr. Barnes was about to be commenced, he was in a position to be of essential service to the cause, and to his old friend and fellow-student, Dr. Junkin.

Accordingly, it was through his agency that Dr. J. tabled the charges, not being able to be present himself, on account of his imperious engagements at the College. A few extracts from the correspondence of Dr. J. and Mr. Steel, will throw some additional light upon the motives of the one, and the agency of the other.

In a letter, dated Lafayette College, March 9th, 1835, after some business statements relative to College affairs, Dr. Junkin adds:

"Ought not Brother Barnes to be tried on his Notes on Romans? I have been reading them. He is sadly astray. There will be no difficulty in showing that he denies the doctrines of Adam's federal headship, of Christ's federal headship, of the covenants of works and of grace, of imputation of Adam's sin, and of Christ's righteousness. He makes justification, just as Dewy did, a mere act of pardon, and that a *sovereign* act, like the Priestleyans. Christ's obedience to the law, for his people, he never brings into view at all. Man's inability he seems to deny. He sets up the doctrine of the Confession, states it distinctly, and goes on to refute it.

"Now, as Mr. Alexander Henry often told me, this is the tender, the turning point. For myself, I feel that he who takes from me the righteousness of Jesus strips me of my hope; he who robs me of all *covenant* security sweeps away my consolations.

"Will the church bear such sacrilege? Ought the Presbyterian Church to tolerate it? Is there no man who will throw himself into the breach, and bring up the doctrinal question on its naked merits? Has not God opened a door here, by which the *real Old School* and the Orthodox Moderates must both enter the citadel together, bound, under the oath of God, to defend it or to perish in its ruins? 'Who is on the Lord's side? Who?'

"I declare, my dear brother, the question is a solemn one to me. I feel that I have *some* of the talents necessary for such a work; I am conscious that I lack others. But, all things considered, the question with me is not of *abstract duty*, but of *prudence*. Were I simply a pastor, there would be no question except this, 'Will no one else do it?' But how would it affect Lafayette? This question I ought seriously to consider. If you will say you will prosecute, you will put an end to my troubles on the whole matter. Will you? If not, how do you think my doing so would affect the College? Brothers Gray and Candee have given their opinion that it would not prove injurious.

"My own hope is, that a prosecution would lead to a *settlement* of great principles, and thus to *peace*. I think it would *unite* all real Presbyterians. . . . Let me have your opinion.

"Your brother,

"GEO. JUNKIN."

To this Mr. Steele replied as follows:

"ABINGTON, March 11th, 1835.

"DEAR BROTHER,—The great importance of your letter would make me desire more leisure and consideration to answer it. But, as J. is to go to Easton in the morning, I will give you briefly my views. That it is the duty of some one to come forward and take the constitutional steps in this matter I cannot doubt for a moment, from your representation of the dangerous errors contained in the book. . . . If I possessed one-half of the qualifications which you do to conduct such a prosecution, I would feel it a privilege as well as a duty to go forth in the strength of the Lord to the conflict. As to injury to Lafayette, I am almost sure it can have no effect. But I doubt whether, even if it were otherwise, you should hesitate for a moment. Go on, then, dear brother; you will have the countenance and the prayers of hundreds, and, above all, the approval of the Master. I think if you cannot get it issued before the Assembly, it might be well not to commence until after the Assembly.

"Yours truly,

"R. STEEL."

Again, in a letter dated

"PHILADELPHIA, March 20th, 1835.

"DEAR BROTHER,—The Second (Affinity) Presbytery have just determined to hold their regular stated meeting on next Monday morning at 9 o'clock. Whether this was done to get over your business, I know not. But this I know, that if so they will be disappointed. By the leave of Providence, I will be here on Monday, and present the charges and your letter, and then ask for the ten days, to give you an opportunity to come down. I must close, but will write to Brother Gray from Abington to-night. Of course I cannot be at David's* ordination. May the Lord be with him and the Presbytery.

"Yours affectionately,

"R. STEEL."

Again:

"PHILADELPHIA, March 23d, 1835.

"DEAR BROTHER,—As I feared and expected, they have given your business the go-by for the present. The general cry was, 'We cannot entertain charges when the accuser is not present.' I plead for a day to be named, that you might be present; but they refused, and finally adjourned, to meet at the call of the Moderator. He promised to let me know when that will be; but I fear that the whole will be shifted off until after the Assembly.

"I will send you a sketch of the debate, so soon as I can write it out. I think a good impression was made. They tried to make out that your charges were the result of a *caucus*, but I exposed the fallacy of that. But I must close.

"Yours affectionately,

"R. STEEL."

A week later he writes to his friend, the late Dr. John Gray, of Easton:

"I suppose you heard, from Dr. Junkin, the result of the first meeting on his business. The Presbytery is to meet again on Thursday morning, April 2d, at 9 o'clock. I understand the Stated Clerk was requested to inform Dr. J. of this fact. But, lest it should not be done, I deemed it

---

* David X. Junkin, at whose ordination he had been invited to assist.

best to ask you to let him know, as he will be expected by the Presbytery. Although that body, I fear, will not permit him to prosecute, yet, as a powerful sensation was produced in many minds by their refusal to entertain the matter, they may drop all opposition, and let the trial go on immediately. Let the doctor be prepared, at any rate. I hope you will come with him. It will never do to let him appear alone among the new light brethren. Come with him to our house on Wednesday. . . . I do not think I can venture down again alone."

In a letter to Dr. Junkin, dated the 24th of March, he gave a graphic sketch of the scenes in the Presbytery, alluded to in his letter of the night before, but the report is too voluminous to insert here. Dr. Ely's speech, Mr. Barnes', Mr. Dodge's, and Mr. Steel's own remarks, are sketched in brief, and the various expedients by which, as he supposed, they sought to avoid the issue.

In this whole matter, it was shown that, with all his kindness of heart and geniality of manner, when he supposed God's precious truth was endangered, Dr. Steel was firm, zealous, and persistent in the discharge of duty. When Mrs. Junkin departed this life, Dr. Steel addressed to his life-long friend a letter of condolence, of the tenderest character, which called forth a response in which his afflicted friend poured forth all his heart. These letters are beautiful specimens of affecting Christian sympathy, but we have not space to insert them. These men of God have renewed, we cannot doubt, in the higher life, that close friendship which, for so many years, sweetened their cares in this.

INDEX.

THE END.

www.ingramcontent.com/pod-product-compliance
Lightning Source LLC
LaVergne TN
LVHW021104110826
845150LV00001B/169

* 9 7 8 1 4 2 5 5 6 5 4 9 7 *